IOM Editorial Team

World Migration 2003 / Managing Migration – Challenges and Responses for People on the Move **is produced by IOM's Migration Policy and Research Programme (MPRP) and Media and Public Information Department (MPI)**

Contributing Authors

Chapter 1: Thomas Lothar Weiss (IOM Geneva), *textbox 1.1.* Irena Omelaniuk (IOM Geneva), *textbox 1.2.* Thomas Lothar Weiss, *textbox 1.3.* Thomas Lothar Weiss, *textbox 1.4.* Richard Perruchoud (IOM Geneva), *textbox 1.5.* Christopher Lom (IOM Geneva) and Thomas Lothar Weiss; **Chapter 2:** Catherine Withol de Wenden (Centre d'Etudes des Relations Internationales Paris) and Thomas Lothar Weiss, *textbox 2.1.* Neil Clowes (IOM Geneva) and Thomas Lothar Weiss, *textbox 2.2.* Christopher Lom and Thomas Lothar Weiss; **Thematic Section Introduction:** Migration Policy and Research Programme (IOM Geneva) and Thomas Lothar Weiss, *textbox T.1.* Migration Management Services (IOM Geneva); **Chapter 3:** Marco Gramegna and Charles Harns (IOM Geneva), *textbox 3.1.* Niurka Pineiro (IOM Geneva), *textbox 3.2.* Richard Danziger (IOM Jakarta); **Chapter 4:** Barbara John (Commissioner for Migration and Integration Berlin), *textbox 4.1.* Migration Management Services; *textbox 4.2.* Thomas Lothar Weiss; **Chapter 5:** and all textboxes: Danielle Grondin, Jacqueline Weekers, Mary Haour-Knipe, Akram Eltom and Julia Stuckey (all IOM Geneva); **Chapter 6:** Michèle Klein-Solomon (IOM Geneva) and Office of the United Nations High Commissioner for Refugees; **Chapter 7:** Shyla Vohra (IOM Geneva), *textbox 7.1.* Diego Beltrand and Liliana Arias (both IOM Bogota), *textbox 7.2.* Christopher Lom; **Chapter 8:** Erica Usher (IOM Geneva), *textbox 8.1.* Agustín Escobar Latapi (Centro de Investigaciones y Estudios Superiores en Antropología Social de Occidente Guadalajara) and Amanda Klekowski von Koppenfels (IOM Brussels), *textbox 8.2.* Pär Liljert (IOM Lusaka) and Thomas Lothar Weiss, *textbox 8.3.* Michèle Buteau (IOM Geneva); **Chapter 9:** Demetri Papademetriou (Migration Policy Institute Washington D.C.), *textbox 9.1.* Rodolfo Casillas (Latin American Faculty of Social Science Mexico City); **Chapter 10:** Lelio Mármora (IOM Buenos Aires), *textbox 10.1.* Lelio Mármora, *textbox 10.2.* Diego Beltrand, *textbox 10.3.* Juan Artola (IOM Santo Domingo); **Chapter 11:** Manolo Abella (International Labour Organization Geneva) and Florian Alburo (University of the Philippines Quezon City), *textbox 11.1.* Biao Xiang and Jian Zhao (both IOM Geneva), *textbox 11.2.* Aiko Kikkawa (IOM Geneva), *textbox 11.3.* June Lee (IOM Geneva), *textbox 11.4.* Frank Laczko (IOM Geneva); **Chapter 12:** John Oucho (University of Botswana Gaborone), Jörg Kühnel (IOM Geneva) and Thomas Lothar Weiss, *textbox 12.1.* Thomas Lothar Weiss, *textbox 12.2.* Thomas Lothar Weiss, *textbox 12.3.* Jean-Pierre Cassarino (IOM Rabat), *textbox 12.4.* Marta Lorenzo (IOM Tunis), Samia Chouba (Ministère des Affaires Sociales et de la Solidarité Tunis) and Ali Jaouani (Office des Tunisiens à l'Etranger Tunis), *textbox 12.5.* Jean-Philippe Chauzy (IOM Geneva), *textbox 12.6.* Lauren Engle (IOM Washington D.C.); **Chapter 13:** Rainer Münz (Humboldt Universität Berlin) and Frank Laczko, *textbox 13.1.* Jill Helke (IOM Geneva), Mary Sheehan (IOM Tbilissi), Nilim Baruah (IOM Yerevan) and Joost Van der Aalst (IOM Baku), *textbox 13.2.* Redouane Saadi (IOM Geneva), *textbox 13.3.* Andrej Gjonej (IOM Rome), *textbox 13.4.* Thomas Lothar Weiss, *textbox 13.5.* Rainer Münz; **Chapter 14:** Sandra Pratt (European Union Commission Brussels), *textbox 14.1.* Jörg Kühnel, *textbox 14.2.* Thomas Lothar Weiss, *textbox 14.3.* Thomas Lothar Weiss; **Chapter 15:** Irena Omelaniuk, *textbox 15.1.* Philippe Boncour (IOM Geneva), *textbox 15.2.* Migration Policy and Research Programme; **Chapter 16:** Hania Zlotnik (United Nations Population Division New York); **Chapter 17:** Migration Policy and Research Programme.

Acknowledgements

The editorial team wishes to thank all contributing authors and is especially grateful to **Brunson McKinley,** *IOM Director General, for his vision and encouragement to produce this book.*

The editorial team wishes to thank the following persons for their kind assistance and support:

Maureen Achieng, Eugenio Ambrosi, Carmen Andreu, Kerstin Bartsch, Igor Bosc, Anne-Marie Buschmann-Petit, Michèle Buteau, Cecilia D'Angelo, Françoise Droulez, Heather Fabrikant, Claudine Favrat, Erin Foster, Nicoletta Giordano, Aiko Kikkawa, June Lee, Nena Marco, Heikki Mattila, Zoran Milovič, Pierre Nicolas, José-Angel Oropeza, Angela Pedersen, Richard Perruchoud, Camille Pillon, Ilse Pinto-Dobernig, Damian Popolo, Kakoli Ray, Jillyanne Redpath, Marta Roig, Caroline San Miguel, Jörg Stüwe, Teodora Suter, Yorio Tanimura, Elisa Tsakiri, Michael Tschanz, Mariko Tomiyama, Michel Tonneau, Shyla Vohra, Lotten Wendelin.

Several organizations generously shared their data and other research materials:

Asian Development Bank; Australia Department of Immigration and Multicultural and Indigenous Affairs; Caritas Diocesana di Roma; Sri Lanka Centre for Women's Research; Citizenship and Immigration Canada; Council of Europe; Statistical Office of the European Commission-EUROSTAT; European Commission Directorate General for Employment and Social Affairs; Global IDP Project; Global March against Child Labour New Delhi; International Labour Organization; International Monetary Fund; Japan Institute of Labour; Japan Ministry of Justice; Migration Policy Institute Washington D.C.; New Zealand Immigration Service; New Zealand Statistics; Office of the Commissioner for Migration and Integration Berlin; Organization for Economic Cooperation and Development; Population Reference Bureau Washington D.C.; Scalabrini Migration Centre Manila; South Korea Ministry of Justice; South Korea National Police Agency; Thailand Department of Employment; United Kingdom Home Office; United Nations Educational, Scientific and Cultural Organization; United Nations High Commissioner for Refugees; United Nations Cartographic Section; United Nations Population Division; United Nations Statistics Division; United States Census Bureau; United States Department of Justice; United States Department of State; United States Immigration and Naturalization Service; World Bank; Zentralstelle für Arbeitsvermittlung Bonn.

Table of Contents

List of Graphs and Tables	p. VI
List of Maps	p. VII
Foreword by the Director General	p. VIII

GENERAL SECTION: **AN OVERVIEW OF INTERNATIONAL MIGRATION**

Chapter 1. – Approaches to and Diversity of International Migration p. 4

TEXTBOX 1.1. Feminization of migration
TEXTBOX 1.2. Basic notions of migration
TEXTBOX 1.3. Inventory of migration theories
TEXTBOX 1.4. Respecting the rights of migrants
TEXTBOX 1.5. The International Organization for Migration in brief

Chapter 2. – Update on International Migration Trends p. 25

TEXTBOX 2.1. Migration and security after September 11, 2001
TEXTBOX 2.2. Update of IOM activities and service areas

THEMATIC SECTION: **MANAGING MIGRATION – CHALLENGES AND RESPONSES FOR PEOPLE ON THE MOVE**

Introduction
Why and How to Manage Migration? p. 52

TEXTBOX T.1. IOM's concept of migration management

MIGRATION MANAGEMENT AT WORK - SELECTED POLICY ISSUES

Chapter 3. – Ways to Curb the Growing Complexities of Irregular Migration p. 58

TEXTBOX 3.1. A migrant's story - The human tragedy of trafficking in migrants from the Dominican Republic to Argentina
TEXTBOX 3.2. Irregular migration in Indonesia

Chapter 4. – The Challenge of Integrating Migrants into Host Societies – A Case Study from Berlin p. 71

TEXTBOX 4.1. The relationship between integration, development and migration
TEXTBOX 4.2. The integration of migrants – an issue of concern to IOM stakeholders

Chapter 5. – Health - An Essential Aspect of Migration Management p. 85

TEXTBOX 5.1. Migration and health at IOM
TEXTBOX 5.2. Components of migration health assessments
TEXTBOX 5.3. Health hazards related to trafficking in women and girls
TEXTBOX 5.4. Promoting the mental health of migrants – a perspective from IOM
TEXTBOX 5.5. IOM's work to address migration and HIV/AIDS

Chapter 6. – The Link between Asylum and Migration p. 97

Chapter 7. – Internally Displaced Persons - An Issue of Migration Management? p. 111

TEXTBOX 7.1. Internally displaced persons in Colombia
TEXTBOX 7.2. The plight of the internally displaced persons of Afghanistan

Chapter 8. – Managing Migration at the Regional Level - Strategies for Regional Consultation p. 123

TEXTBOX 8.1. The Puebla Process – A case study of regional consultative process development
TEXTBOX 8.2. The Migration Dialogue for Southern Africa
TEXTBOX 8.3. Emergence of common principles in international migration management through RCPs

IV

*MIGRATION MANAGEMENT AT WORK – **SELECTED GEOGRAPHIC REGIONS***

Chapter 9. – Migration Management in the Traditional Countries of Immigration   p. 142
▨ **TEXTBOX 9.1.** The migration agenda between Mexico and the United States

Chapter 10. – Mutually Agreed Migration Policies in Latin America   p. 173
▨ **TEXTBOX 10.1.** Migration realities in Hispaniola
▨ **TEXTBOX 10.2.** Focus on Argentina – The effects of the economic crisis on migration
▨ **TEXTBOX 10.3.** Managing migration in Colombia

Chapter 11. – Driving Forces of Labour Migration in Asia   p. 195
▨ **TEXTBOX 11.1.** Changes in contemporary Chinese migration
▨ **TEXTBOX 11.2.** Demography and migration in Japan
▨ **TEXTBOX 11.3.** Focus on smuggling and trafficking in South Korea
▨ **TEXTBOX 11.4.** Migration patterns in the Gulf States

Chapter 12. – Linkages between Brain Drain, Labour Migration and Remittances in Africa   p. 215
▨ **TEXTBOX 12.1.** Migration – A reflection of socio-economic dynamics on Africa
▨ **TEXTBOX 12.2.** Filling the labour market gaps in the United Kingdom with help from Africa
▨ **TEXTBOX 12.3.** Dealing with migration issues in Morocco
▨ **TEXTBOX 12.4.** The migration context in Tunisia
▨ **TEXTBOX 12.5.** A migrant's story – Happy to be back in the Democratic Republic of the Congo
▨ **TEXTBOX 12.6.** A migrant's story – "You are a big girl now" - from Sudan to the United States

Chapter 13. – International Labour Migration and Demographic Change in Europe   p. 239
▨ **TEXTBOX 13.1.** Migration dynamics in the South Caucasus
▨ **TEXTBOX 13.2.** Migration dynamics in the Western Mediterranean
▨ **TEXTBOX 13.3.** A migrant's story – A new start through a regular labour migration programme from Albania to Italy
▨ **TEXTBOX 13.4.** Irregular migration into Europe
▨ **TEXTBOX 13.5.** Dispositions of a planned German immigration law

Chapter 14. – Towards a Common Immigration Policy for the European Union   p. 259
▨ **TEXTBOX 14.1.** Migration dispositions in the Cotonou Agreement
▨ **TEXTBOX 14.2.** Immigration at the 2002 European Union Summit in Seville
▨ **TEXTBOX 14.3.** Free movement in Europe - the Schengen Agreement

Chapter 15. – Elements of a more Global Approach to Migration Management   p. 271
▨ **TEXTBOX 15.1.** Migration for Development in Africa – An IOM programme
▨ **TEXTBOX 15.2.** The Berne Initiative - A global consultative process for inter-state cooperation on migration management

STATISTICS SECTION

Chapter 16. – Statistics and the Management of International Migration – A Perspective from the United Nations   p. 293
Chapter 17. – A Selection of International Migration Statistics   p. 303

ANNEXES

General Bibliography   p. 319
Acronyms and Abbreviations   p. 349
Alphabetical Index   p. 353
Photo Credits   p. 371
Maps   p. 373

v

List of graphs and tables

GRAPH 1.1.	World Population – Non-Migrants and Migrants (Stock Figures), 1965-2050	p. 5
TABLE 2.1.	Inflows of Non-Nationals into Selected OECD Countries, 1990-2000	p. 28
TABLE 2.2.	World Population and Migrant Stocks by Continent, 2000	p. 29
TABLE 4.1.	The Foreign-Born Population in Berlin, 2001	p. 76
TABLE 4.2.	The Commissioner for Migration and Integration in Berlin and its Main Stakeholders and Interlocutors	p. 76
GRAPH 5.1.	Number of Immigration Health Assessments by IOM, 1990-2001	p. 89
GRAPH 5.2.	IOM Immigration Health Assessments per Country of Destination, 2001	p. 89
GRAPH 5.3.	IOM Immigration Health Assessments per Region of Origin, 2001	p. 89
TABLE 8.1.	Participation in Major Regional Consultative Processes	p. 137
TABLE 8.2.	Major Regional Groupings with a Migration Focus or Interest	p. 138
TABLE 9.1.	Immigrant Admissions in TCIs	p. 156
TABLE 9.2.	Foreign Born Population in TCIs, 1995 and 2000	p. 157
TABLE 9.3.	TCIs – Inflows of Permanent and Long-Term Settlers by Region of Origin, 1998 and 2000	p. 158
TABLE 9.4.	Immigrant Classes – United States	p. 159
TABLE 9.5.	Immigrant Classes – Canada	p. 160
TABLE 9.6.	Immigrant Classes – Australia	p. 161
TABLE 9.7.	Immigrant Classes – New Zealand	p. 162
TABLE 9.8.	TCIs – Family Programme Descriptions	p. 163
TABLE 9.9.	Preference System – United States (first introduced in 1952)	p. 164
TABLE 9.10.	Canada - Former versus New Point System (Bill C-11)	p. 165
TABLE 9.11.	Working Temporarily in the United States - Selected Sectors	p. 166
TABLE 9.12.	Working Temporarily in Canada – Selected Sectors	p. 167
TABLE 9.13.	Working and Training Temporarily in Australia - Selected Sectors	p. 168
TABLE 9.14.	Working and Training Temporarily in New Zealand - Selected Sectors	p. 169
TABLE 9.15.	Student Visas, Permits and Admissions in TCIs, 2000	p. 170
TABLE 9.16.	Australian Points Test in 2002 (first introduced in 1989)	p. 171
TABLE 9.17.	New Zealand Points System-2002 (first introduced in 1991)	p. 172
TABLE 10.1.	Bilateral Migration Agreements in Latin America (1948-2000)	p. 178
TABLE 11.1.	Estimated Annual Emigration of Labour from Asian Countries	p. 196
TABLE 11.2.	Intra-Asian Labour Migration – Estimated Number of Non-National Asian Workers in Selected Countries, circa 2000	p. 199
TEXTBOX 11.2. TABLE 1.	Foreigners Entering Japan for the Purposes of Employment, 1997-2001 (flow figures)	p. 201
TEXTBOX 11.2. TABLE 2.	Trainee Entries to Japan, 1997-2001 (flow figures)	p. 201
TEXTBOX 11.3. TABLE 1.	Number of Persons Smuggled to South Korea, 1994-2001	p. 203
TEXTBOX 11.3. TABLE 2.	Entertainer Visa Holders in South Korea, 1995-2000	p. 203
TABLE 11.3.	Employment of Asian Migrant Labour in the 1990s and Possible "Pull" Indicators	p. 204
TEXTBOX 11.4. TABLE 1.	Expatriate Population as Percentage of Total Population in the GCC States, 1975-1999 (estimates)	p. 207
TABLE 11.4.	Major Countries of Emigration in Asia and Possible "Push" Indicators	p. 208
TABLE 11.5.	Immigration to the Asia – Pacific Region of the Highly-Skilled, 2000	p. 210
TABLE 11.6.	United States H-1B Visas Issued to Asians, 1990-1997	p. 211
TABLE 11.7.	Skill Mix or Occupational Classification – Flow Data for Selected Labour-Sending Countries in Asia	p. 212
TABLE 12.1.	The African Diaspora in Selected Countries of Europe and North America (stock data)	p. 219
TEXTBOX 12.3. TABLE 1.	Morocco – Migrant Remittances and Balance of Trade Deficit, 1996-2001	p. 224
TEXTBOX 12.3. TABLE 2.	Geographical Origin of Moroccan Migrant Remittances, 2000	p. 225
TABLE 12.2.	Annual Remittances to Selected African Countries (in million US$)	p. 226
TABLE 12.3.	Volatility of Annual Remittances from 1980 to 1999 (in million US$)	p. 227
TABLE 12.4.	Financial Inflows – ODA, FDI, and Remittances (averages of the years 1980-1999)	p. 228
TABLE 13.1.	Net Migration Flows in Western Europe, 1960-2000	p. 240
TABLE 13.2.	Labour Force Participation and Projected Population Decline, 2000-2050, in Selected European countries, Age Group 15-64 years	p. 246
GRAPH 13.3.	Relative Population Decline in Selected European Countries, 2000-2050, Age Group 65+, as % of Population	p. 243
GRAPH 13.4.	Relative Population Decline in Selected European Countries, 2000-2050, Age Group 15 - 64 years, as % of Population	p. 244
TABLE 13.5.	Labour Migration Schemes in Selected European Countries	p. 249-250
TABLE 17.1.	Number of Countries Providing Statistics on Long-Term Emigrants and Immigrants, 1971-2000	p. 303
TABLE 17.2.	The World's Foreign-Born Population from 1965 to 2000	p. 304
TABLE 17.3.	World Population and Migrant Stocks by Continent, 2000	p. 304
TABLE 17.4.	Top 10 Countries of Immigration, 1970-1995	p. 305
TABLE 17.5.	Top 10 Countries of Emigration, 1970-1995	p. 305
TABLE 17.6.	Top 15 Countries with the Largest International Migrant Stock, 2000	p. 305
TABLE 17.7.	Top 15 Countries with Highest Percentage of Migrants in Total Population, 2000	p. 306
TABLE 17.8.	Top 10 Emigration Countries with High Ratios of Female to Male Migrants, 1990	p. 306
TABLE 17.9.	Top 10 Emigration Countries with Low Ratios of Female to Male Migrants, 1990	p. 307
GRAPH 17.10.	Foreign Labour Force in Selected OECD Countries, 1999	p. 307
TABLE 17.11.	Migrants in Labour Importing Countries in Asia, 2000	p. 308
TABLE 17.12.	Foreign Students in Higher Education in Selected Countries by Continent of Origin, various years	p. 309
TABLE 17.13.	Top 5 Countries of Origin of Foreign Students in Selected OECD Countries, 1998	p. 310
TABLE 17.14.	Top 20 Receiving Countries of Migrant Remittances, 2000	p. 311
TABLE 17.15.	Migrants Remittances from various World Regions, 1988-1999	p. 311
TABLE 17.16.	The World's Refugees by Region of Asylum, 1999-2001	p. 312
TABLE 17.17.	Top 10 Refugee Sending Countries, 1999-2001	p. 312
TABLE 17.18.	Top 10 Refugee Host Countries, 1999-2001	p. 313
TABLE 17.19.	IDP Estimates by Country	p. 314
TABLE 17.20.	Overview of Estimated Annual Flows of Irregular Migrants	p. 314
TABLE 17.21.	Fees Paid to Smugglers for Travel Assistance to Selected Destination Countries	p. 315

List of maps

MAP 1 IOM Member and Observer States, December 2002 p. 374
MAP 2 Net Migration: Total Numbers, 1995-2000 p. 375
MAP 3 Net Migration: Migration Ratios, 1995-2000 p. 376
MAP 4 Migrant Stocks: per cent of Total Population, 2000 p. 377
MAP 5 Origin of Asylum Seekers in Industrialized Countries, 1997-2001 p. 378
MAP 6 Refugee Population by Country or Territory of Asylum, 2001 p. 379
MAP 7 Refugee Outflows by Country or Territory of Origin, 1997-2001 p. 380
MAP 8 Internally Displaced Persons p. 381
MAP 9 Regional Consultative Processes on Migration (RCPs) [1/2] p. 382
MAP 10 Regional Consultative Processes on Migration (RCPs) [2/2] p. 383
MAP 11 Regional Economic Groupings in Africa p. 384
MAP 12 Remittances to Selected African Countries p. 385
MAP 13 Africa: Highly Qualified Citizens with Overseas Education p. 386
MAP 14 Political Map: Traditional Countries of Immigration p. 387
MAP 15 Latin America: Regional Integration Areas that include Migration Issues p. 388
MAP 16 Political Map: Islands of the Caribbean p. 389
MAP 17 Colombia: Locations of IOM Operations p. 390
MAP 18 Afghanistan: Locations of IOM Operations p. 391
MAP 19 Political Map: Asia p. 392
MAP 20 Gulf Cooperation Council: Total Population and Proportions of National and Non-National Population, 2000 p. 393
MAP 21 Political Map: Europe p. 394
MAP 22 European Union: Asylum Seekers, 2001 p. 395
MAP 23 European Union: Migrant Stocks (totals and percentages), 2000 p. 396

Foreword
by the Director General of the International Organization for Migration

It is hard to pick up a newspaper or to switch on the TV or radio these days without finding a reference to migration issues. This is not surprising since one in every thirty five people is a migrant. The current global estimate of international migrants is 175 million, i.e., some three per cent of the world population, and the number is increasing.

Migration has become the concern of all in some form or another, and I mean concern rather than simply interest, because the understanding of migration, and how to take advantage of it, live with it and manage it has not kept pace with the growth of the phenomenon and the complexity of its linkages with other issues.

Understanding of migration by both policy makers and the general public can make the difference between migration having a more positive or negative impact on a region, country or society. Precise and reliable information on international migration trends and the accurate analysis of key migration issues are indispensable to the formulation of effective migration management policies. They can be used to curb such negative aspects of migration as irregular migration, including smuggling and trafficking, and to support regular migration schemes and proven integration policies that can help to maximize the positive outcomes of migration. Such material can also be used to help counter racism and xenophobia, which tend to be fostered by misconceptions. Guided by these convictions and the need to contribute to an enhanced understanding of international migration, IOM has produced its second World Migration Report to provide a wide spectrum of experience and information on the phenomenon.

Encouraged by the success of the first edition of the IOM World Migration Report published in 2000, we have decided to make this publication a regular feature. In response to comments on the first edition, and with a view to increasing the relevance to migration practitioners, this Report offers a thematic focus - which will vary with each subsequent edition - and includes a general section providing an overview of international migration principles and recent trends as well as a statistics section.

Most of the more than fifty contributing authors are IOM staff members from missions worldwide, colleagues who deal with the day-to-day realities of migration, its causes, consequences, and its human, social and political aspects. Selected migration experts from academia and practice outside of IOM complete the list of contributing authors.

The Report approaches migration management and the migration process in a comprehensive manner, encouraging policy makers to do the same, and seeks to demonstrate that migration, when properly managed, is positive for both individuals and societies. Moreover, the Report illustrates the complex linkages of migration with economic, social, cultural, labour, trade, health and security policy areas. It also highlights rights and obligations of migrants and states. It addresses the sensitive issues of national security, identity, social change and cultural adaptation and emphasizes the importance of regional and international cooperation and partnerships.

The issues raised in this Report represent important challenges to migration policy makers. In response to these challenges, policy choices made now will serve to determine whether migration is managed to maximize its benefits or will remain a source of concern and potentially of tension between states. In an increasingly globalized world where movement of people is a fact of life, the ultimate goal is not to obstruct or prevent mobility but to better manage it for the benefit of all.

We hope that the 2003 edition of the World Migration Report will shed more light on the challenges and responses for people on the move, and will contribute toward enhancing migration management approaches that uphold the principle that "humane and orderly migration benefits migrants and society".

Brunson McKinley

x

GENERAL SECTION

2

AN OVERVIEW OF INTERNATIONAL MIGRATION

3

CHAPTER 1

Approaches to and Diversity of International Migration

The world migration landscape has undergone sweeping changes in the past decade or so. The enduring impact of globalization has brought significant consequences for the socio-economic phenomenon of migration. At the same time, migration is helping to transform contemporary economic and social relations. With its place now firmly established on national and international agendas, policy-makers around the world are challenged to better understand the nature and scope of migration, so as to better manage it for the benefit, growth, security and stability of their societies.

Diversification of migration flows and stocks is the new watchword for the current dynamics. The number of countries and nationalities concerned and directly involved in human mobility is rising steadily. None of the roughly 190 sovereign states in the international system is now beyond the reach of migration circuits. Indeed, they are all either countries of origin, transit or destination for migrants, and increasingly are all three simultaneously. Migration circuits span the globe like a spider's web, with complex ramifications and countless intersections. The current world map of migration is therefore multipolar.

Migration is being shaped by multiple pull and push factors – primary among them are economic development and its disparities, population trends, the existence of migratory networks, access to information, the ease of travel today, armed conflicts, environmental deterioration and human rights violations. Changes in these factors may be gradual or abrupt and bring corresponding changes in migratory behaviour. Mobility is being hastened by the entry and integration of local communities and national economies into global relations. As such, migration represents a significant variable in the evolution of societies and economies. This evolutionary process is being amplified by globalization, which is marked by the broadening, deepening and acceleration of global interconnection in all aspects of life (Held *et al.*, 1999). Like other flows, whether financial or commercial, flows of ideas or information, the rising tide of people crossing frontiers is among the most reliable indicators of the intensity of globalization.

In traditional societies, most people spent their entire existence in their village or town of origin. Today, migration has become a routine process for persons wishing to improve their material living conditions and find greater security. Migration follows a variety of routes: from the village to the city; from one region to another; from one country to another; or from one continent to another. Non-migrants are themselves also affected by migration since they are members of the same family, friends or descendants of migrants or members of local communities that receive migrants.

Migration movements were long confined to relatively straightforward and linear relations between closely linked poles – a sending country automatically had its receiving country, based on age-old ties that were mostly cultural, emotional, economic or historical in nature; however, these special relations are today rapidly giving way to an unprecedented widening of the migration landscape. This broadening is moving hand-in-hand with the evolution of the types of migration. The classical, long-term migration model will dominate less and less in the future as other types of migration – including short-term and circulatory migration – come to the fore.

One thing is beyond doubt: migration is gradually eroding the traditional boundaries between languages, cultures, ethnic groups and nation-states. A transnational flow par excellence, it therefore defies cultural traditions, national identities and political institutions, contributing in the long run to curtailing nation-state autonomy and to shaping a global society. No longer simply the result of identifiable push and pull factors, human mobility is developing a life of its own.

The Scale of Migration

At the start of the twenty-first century, one out of every 35 persons worldwide is an international migrant. The Population Division of the United Nations estimates the total number of international migrants at approximately 175 million (United Nations, 2002). This number includes refugees and displaced persons, but does not capture irregular migrants who escape official accounting.

Based on the world population of 6.057 billion in 2000, migrants represent some 2.9 per cent. This percentage has changed in recent decades and has been rising steadily over the past 15 years. Although representing a relatively small percentage of the world's population, if all international migrants lived in the same place, it would be the world's fifth biggest country.

There were some 75 million international migrants in 1965. Ten years later, in 1975, the number was 84 million, then 105 million in 1985. International migration rose less rapidly between 1965 and 1975 (1.16 per cent per annum) than the world population (2.04 per cent per annum). This situation has been changing since the 1980s, as the rate of world population growth began to decline

(1.7 per cent per annum) and international migration increased significantly (2.59 per cent per annum).

While the number of migrants more than doubled between 1965 and 2000 (from 75 to 175 million), the world's population also grew twofold over the same period (1960-1999), from 3 to 6 billion people. Demographers project an increase in the world population to approximately 9 billion by 2050, to include some 230 million migrants. **Graph 1.1.** illustrates the above figures.

GRAPH 1.1.

World Population – Non-Migrants and Migrants (Stock Figures), 1965-2050

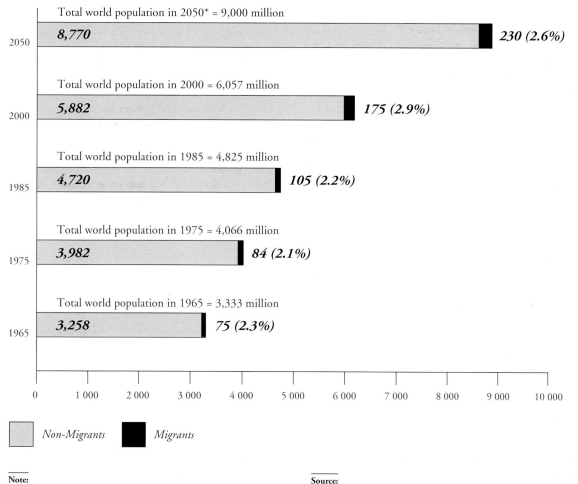

Note:
* Figures for 2050 are extrapolations.

Source:
United Nations Population Division (2002), IOM (2000), MPRP calculations.

The annual flow of migrants is now somewhere between 5 and 10 million people (Simon, 2001), including undocumented migrants. If we take the upper limit as a basis, it represents roughly one-tenth of the annual growth in world population. Of this number, according to estimates published by the US Justice Department in 1998, between 700,000 and 2 million women and children were estimated to be trafficking victims (IOM, 2001).

The scale of migration varies significantly between world regions. South-North international migration flows are but one aspect of the reality and there are appreciable South-South intercontinental or intra-continental migration flows: in 1965, the western industrialized countries absorbed only 36.5 per cent of international migrants as compared to 43.4 per cent in 1990 and 40 per cent in 2000. Migration streams among developing countries are generally inter-regional (Zlotnik, 1998). In other words, most migrants are from the South and are received by countries in the South.

Migration is difficult to quantify at the national and international level because of its inherent changeability, the large numbers of undocumented migrants and the lack of established governmental systems in most countries for collection of migration-related data. Migrants' mobility means that they can often be elusive and the migration process reversible or renewable. However, it is generally agreed that the number of movements has increased significantly over the past 10 years, particularly through the emergence of "new" groups of migrants, such as women migrating individually and highly qualified migrants.

Women now move around far more independently and no longer in relation to their family position or under a man's authority. This reflects women's growing participation in all aspects of modern life. Roughly 48 per cent of all migrants are women (IOM, 2000). In some regions, this proportion is even higher. Yet the feminization of migration is not a positive development in all instances. While, as with men, women often choose to migrate because of poverty and the lack of professional prospects, women migrants are more exposed to forced labour and sexual exploitation than men and are also more likely to accept precarious working conditions and poorly paid work. **Textbox 1.1.** outlines various aspects of the feminization of migration.

Highly educated and qualified persons are also migrating more. This movement of skills affects both developing and developed countries. More and more persons are pursuing the attraction of the most dynamic economic and cultural metropolises of the global economy. As for other types of migrants, the absolute number or even the proportion of highly skilled migrants is extremely difficult to estimate. In the African context, the World Bank estimates that about 70,000 African professionals and university graduates leave their country of origin each year to work in Europe or North America (Weiss, 2001a). This exodus is delaying economic, industrial and agricultural development considerably by, among others, hampering technology transfer possibilities. Brain drain results when these highly skilled migrants do not re-enter the home economy.

Yet European countries also suffer from this phenomenon, especially in high technology, natural sciences and engineering. Many European scientists are being lured away by better working conditions and salaries offered by the private sector or universities, mainly in the United States or Canada.

The last quarter of the twentieth century constituted "an era of migration" and demonstrated that no continent is beyond the reach of global migration streams (Castles and Miller, 1996). However, most of the world's inhabitants remain where they are as they have no resources, networks, opportunities or quite simply any personal benefits to be derived from mobility. Lack of any desire and motivation to leave home, family and friends is a powerful "non-migration" factor (Martin and Widgren, 2002). Many field studies demonstrate that most people do not wish to emigrate to a foreign country, and that given the choice, many migrants would much prefer to be "circular" rather than permanent migrants (Sassen, 2002). After all, remaining in one's country of birth is the norm and migration to settle elsewhere the exception.

TEXTBOX 1.1.

Feminization of Migration

More women are migrating independently to be employed abroad

Not a new phenomenon, female migration has been the focus of growing attention among the world's migration policy makers. Almost half of the estimated 175 million migrants worldwide are currently women. While many migrate as spouses or family members, more women are migrating independently of family, often to work abroad as principal breadwinners.

Population movements can be highly gender-specific, with women and men migrating for different reasons along different routes and with different results. But most migration-related policies and regulations have not adjusted to this – at either the country of origin or country of destination end of the migration spectrum. Policies are frequently non-existent or neglect the gendered nature of migration, with unforeseen consequences for women.

With limited legal migration opportunities in some parts of the world, such as Europe or North America, many women have resorted to irregular forms of migration, involving migrant smugglers and traffickers, that are particularly prone to gender-specific forms of abuse and exploitation. Once they are clandestine, and in the hands of these unscrupulous agents, women are more prone to abuse and exploitation than men for biological, cultural, ethnic, religious and other reasons.

Moreover, many female migrants are more vulnerable to human rights abuses since they work in gender-segregated and unregulated sectors of the economy, such as domestic work, entertainment and the sex industry, unprotected by labour legislation or policy. Many women are in unskilled jobs with limited prospects for upward mobility; they earn low wages, work long hours, and have little or no job security or rights to social benefits. They are frequently unaware of their rights and obligations, and hesitate to lodge formal complaints against employers or others, preferring to suffer harassment and violence. This is a familiar scenario for many female migrants, such as Asians in the Middle East, Moroccans and other Africans in southern Europe, Latin Americans in the United States.

Despite these difficulties and constraints, migration can empower and help to emancipate migrant women. It offers new opportunities and financial independence abroad as well as status within their family and home community. In Asia, for example, women now make up the majority of expatriates working abroad: in 1986, female migrants represented 33 per cent of all Sri Lankan migrant workers overseas, increasing to 65 per cent by 1999. In the Philippines, women accounted for 70 per cent of

migrant workers abroad in 2000, most living without their families and providing for those who stayed behind.

Female migrant workers are major contributors to their home country's foreign revenue through remittances. In Sri Lanka, they contributed over 62 per cent of the more than US\$ 1 billion total private remittances in 1999, accounting for 50 per cent of the trade balance and 145 per cent of gross foreign loans and grants (CENWOR, 2001). In the Philippines, they contributed considerably to the US\$ 6.2 billion total remittances in 2001. At another level, Moroccan women in Italy have forged effective informal trade links between their home and host countries. Women migrants are becoming agents of economic change.

But origin and destination countries still need to define clear measures to promote and protect the human rights and dignity of female migrants, and maximize the benefits they can bring. These measures should allow migrant women to choose their employer; ensure proper monitoring and regulation of recruitment agency practices; and provide advice on employers with a history of abusive and discriminatory behaviour. Many women migrant workers maltreated by their employers do not complain because they are frightened of losing their jobs. Some who complain do not proceed with prosecution.

Policies in countries of destination play an important role in determining the position of migrant women in the host societies. Most policies are still primarily oriented towards immigration and border control, and while not necessarily hostile to women, can inadvertently discriminate against them. For example, they can perpetuate gender-discriminatory practices in countries of origin by selecting immigrants on the basis of skills and education that women may not have access to in their home country. Preferences for certain nationalities can also compound discrimination against women who already have a reduced role in their home cultures. Canada is one host country that now subjects all new immigration policy to a "gender-based analysis" to ensure more balanced selection.

More and more IOM activities are also being tailored to the needs of migrant women: information campaigns aid decision-making among women migrants; language and cultural orientation training prepares them for work abroad; protection, assistance and return/reintegration into their home communities in dignity support those who have suffered abuse; and advocacy and capacity-building ensures the appropriate regulatory framework for all these activities. But IOM's most pioneering work is in the area of counter trafficking, where it provides training to police, judiciary, health workers and others, direct assistance with the aid of NGOs, and psycho-social trauma therapy and health support to the victims.

Much remains to be done to understand the impact of female migration on both countries of origin and destination, on the families left behind, and on their own empowerment both at home and abroad. For IOM, which bases much of its work on the belief that effective migration management is principally a question of good governance, this is a key issue that needs to be examined as carefully as the socio-economic causes and effects of migration *per se.*

Source:
Women Migrant Workers of Sri Lanka, www.cenwor.lk/migworkers.html, CENWOR, Colombo, 2001.

Terminology Issues

How should we define *"migration"* and, by extension, *"migrant"*? Providing a commonly accepted definition is not easy (see also **chapter 16**). As they result from distinct political, social, economic and cultural contexts, definitions of migration are highly varied in nature. This makes comparisons difficult not only because statistical criteria differ, but because these differences reflect real variations in migration's social and economic significance, depending on the particular contexts (Castles, 2000).

For the sake of uniformity, the United Nations has proposed that migrant be defined for statistical purposes as a person who enters a country other than that of which he/she is a citizen for at least 12 months, after having been absent for one year or longer (United Nations, 1998). As in the case of seasonal workers who migrate for the duration of an agricultural or tourist season, the duration criterion can nevertheless be flexible.

Depending on the country, migration data relates either to migrant populations (e.g., in the United Kingdom[1]), or to foreign populations (e.g., in France). The various national data-gathering systems are also linked to each country's history and its laws on acquiring nationality, etc. Definitions often vary from one state to another (*Le Monde,* 2002).

1) The British citizen returning home after spending more than one year in another country will be considered an immigrant (Petit, 2000).

In addition to problems in recording movements, some countries of emigration do become countries of immigration over time, and vice versa.

The Geographical Aspect

Migration is the movement of a person or group of persons from one geographical unit to another across an administrative or political border, wishing to settle definitely or temporarily in a place other than their place of origin.

As regards the geographical space in which the migration takes place, it is useful to distinguish between the *place of origin,* or *place of departure* and the *place of destination,* or *place of arrival.* Migration often does not occur directly between these two places, but involves one, or several places of transit.

A distinction may be drawn between *internal migration* and *international migration.* Internal migration is movement within the same country, from one administrative unit, such as a region, province or municipality, to another. In contrast, *international migration* involves the crossing of one or several international borders, resulting in a change in the legal status of the individual concerned. International migration also covers movements of refugees, displaced persons and other persons forced to leave their country.

A hard and fast distinction between *internal migration* and *international migration* can nevertheless be misleading: *international migration* can involve very short distances and culturally very similar populations, *internal migration* can cover vast distances and bring markedly different populations into contact.

In some rare instances, borders themselves can "migrate". For example, the break-up of the Soviet Union transformed several million internal migrants into international migrants. The Russians in Estonia or Tajikistan who left their region of origin as internal migrants in the USSR have become foreigners in the new independent States. The break-up of Czechoslovakia or the Yugoslav Federation are other examples.

International migration becomes *immigration* or *emigration,* depending on how the place of destination or place of origin is considered. There are two aspects to *migration flows,* or the sum total of people moving from one place to another: reference is made to *outflow* or *emigration,* and conversely, to *inflow* or *immigration.*

The Human Aspect

Any person who leaves his or her country with the intention to reside in another is called an *emigrant* or *émigré.* In the new country, that person will be considered as an *immigrant* or any other similar designation determined under national laws as every state frames its own immigration laws. The term *migrant* is more neutral than those of *emigrant* or *immigrant* as it disregards the direction of the movement (Petit, 2000).

Other definitions put the emphasis on the voluntary nature of the movement. Under this approach, the term *migrant* designates a person who, voluntarily and for personal reasons, moves from his/her place of origin to a particular destination with the intention to establish residence without being compelled to do so. This definition covers persons moving regularly as well as irregularly, that is, without being in possession of legitimate papers (passport with a visa, work permit, residence permit, etc.). Those travelling on vacation, a business trip, for medical treatment or on pilgrimage are not generally considered as migrants, even though their movement is voluntary, as they do not intend to establish a habitual residence in the place of destination.

Finally, migration may be *temporary* or *permanent* depending on the duration of absence from the place of origin and the duration of stay in the place of destination.

Textbox 1.2. presents basic notions of migration.

TEXTBOX 1.2.

Basic Notions of Migration

The following definitions are not technical or legal in nature for most of the terms but are intended to provide succint, readily-understandable and widely applicable explanations for some of the most commonly used migration terms. A particular case of migration may fit several definitions; a migrant may embody characteristics that reflect more than one of the meanings given. A wide range of international sources was consulted to produce these definitions.

Various Types and Practices of Migration

Return migration – the movement of a person returning to his/her country of origin or of habitual residence after spending at least one year in another country. This return may or may not be voluntary, or result from an expulsion order. *Return migration* includes voluntary repatriation.

Forced migration – the non-voluntary movement of a person wishing to escape an armed conflict or a situation of violence and/or the violation of his/her rights, or a natural or man-made disaster. This term applies to refugee movements, movements caused by trafficking and forced exchanges of populations among states.

Irregular migration – the movement of a person to a new place of residence or transit using irregular or illegal means, as the case may be, without valid documents or carrying forged documents. This term also covers trafficking in migrants.

Orderly migration – the movement of a person from his/her usual place of residence to a new place of residence, in keeping with the laws and regulations governing exit of the country of origin and travel, transit and entry into the host country.

Smuggling of migrants – this term describes the pro-curement, in order to obtain, directly or indirectly, a finan-cial or other material benefit, of the illegal entry of a per-son into a state of which he/she is not a national or a per-manent resident. Illegal entry means the crossing of borders without complying with the necessary requirements for legal entry into the receiving state.

Total migration / Net migration – the sum of the entries or arrivals of immigrants, and of exits, or departures of emigrants, yields the total volume of migration, and is termed *total migration,* as distinct from *net migration,* or the migration balance, resulting from the difference between arrivals and departures. This balance is called net immi-gration when arrivals exceed departures, and net emigration in the opposite case.

Trafficking in persons – this term describes the recruit-ment, transportation, transfer, harbouring or receipt of persons, by means of the threat or use of force or other forms of coercion, of abduction, of fraud, of deception, of the abuse of power or of a position of vulnerability or of the giving or receiving of payments or benefits to achieve the consent of a person having control over another person, for the purpose of exploitation. Exploitation includes, at the minimum, the exploitation of the prosti-tution of others or other forms of sexual exploitation, forced labour or services, slavery or practices similar to slavery, servitude or the removal of organs.

Re-emigration – the movement of a person who, after returning to his/her country of departure for some years, again leaves for another stay or another destination.

Categories of Persons Involved in Migration

Asylum seeker – a person who has crossed an international border and has not yet received a decision on his/her claim for refugee status. This term could refer to someone who has not yet submited an application for refugee status or someone who is waiting for an answer. Until the claim is examined fairly, the *asylum seeker* is entitled not to be returned according to the principle of non-refoulement. Not every *asylum seeker* will ultimately be recognized as a refugee.

Economic migrant – a person leaving his/her habitual place of residence to settle outside his/her country of origin in order to improve his/her quality of life. This term is also used to refer to persons attempting to enter a country without legal permission and/or by using asylum procedures without bona fide cause. It also applies to persons settling outside their country of origin for the duration of an agricultural or tourist season, appropriately called seasonal workers.

Irregular migrant (or undocumented or clandestine) – a person without legal status in a transit or host country owing to illegal entry or the expiry of his/her visa. The term is applied to non-nationals who have infringed the transit or host country's rules of admission; persons attempting to obtain asylum without due cause; and any other person not authorized to remain in the host country.

Displaced person / Internally displaced person – a person forced to leave his/her habitual residence spontaneously in order to flee an armed conflict, situations of widespread violence or systematic human rights violations, or to escape natural or man-made disasters or their effects. This term also covers persons displaced within the borders of their country of origin (i.e., *internally displaced persons*), who are not covered by the 1951 Convention as they did not cross an internationally recognized border.

Refugee – pursuant to the 1951 Convention relating to the Status of Refugees, a *refugee* is a person who, owing to well-founded fear of being persecuted for reasons of race, religion, nationality, membership of a particular social group or political opinion, is outside the country of his/her nationality and is unable, or owing to such fear, unwilling to

avail himself/herself of the protection of that country. In 1969, the Organization of African Unity (now the African Union) adopted a broadened definition to include any person who is forced to leave his/her habitual residence on account of aggression, external occupation, foreign domination or events seriously disrupting public order in a part or the entirety of his/her country of origin or his/her country of nationality. In adopting the Cartagena Declaration in 1984, the governments of Latin America also consider as refugees persons fleeing their country because their life, security or their freedom are threatened by widespread violence, foreign aggression, internal conflicts and large-scale human rights violations or any other circumstances seriously disrupting public order.

Frontier worker – this expression refers to a migrant worker who retains his/her habitual residence in a neighbouring state to which he/she normally returns every day or at least once a week.

Migrant worker – a person engaging in a remunerated activity in a country of which he/she is not a national, excluding asylum seekers and refugees. A *migrant worker* establishes his/her residence in the host country for the duration of his/her work. This term is applied to irregular migrant workers, as well as to staff of multinational companies whose duties require them to move from one country to another. The 1990 International Convention on the Protection of the Rights of All Migrant Workers and Members of Their Families defines other more specific categories such as "seafarers", "project-tied workers" and "itinerant workers" (Article 2).

Seasonal worker – a migrant worker whose work depends on seasonal conditions and is performed only during part of the year.

Sources:
- Council of Europe. *The integration of immigrants: Migration and integration – basic concepts and definitions,* www.social.coe.int/en/cohesion/action/publi/migrants/concepts.htm
- IOM (unpublished working draft), *IOM Migration Terminology – Concepts and Definitions.*
- *Le Monde* (2000). "Le grand dossier : L'immigration en Europe", 9 and 10 June, Paris.
- Perruchoud, R. (1992). "Persons falling under the mandate of the International Organization for Migration (IOM) and to whom the Organization may provide migration services", *International Journal of Refugee Law,* vol.4, no.2, Oxford University Press.
- UNHCR. *Refugee Protection and Migration Control: Perspectives from UNHCR and IOM,* Global Consultations on International Protection

- UNHCR and Inter-Parliamentary Union (2001). *Refugee Protection – Guide to International Refugee Law.* Handbook for Parliamentarians, no.2.
- United Nations (1958). Multilingual Demographic Dictionary - French Volume, Department of Economic and Social Affairs.
- United Nations (1998). *UN Guiding Principles on Internal Displacement.*
- United Nations (1998). *Recommendations on Statistics of International Migration,* Department of Economic and Social Affairs, Statistics Division.
- United Nations (2000). Protocols additional to the United Nations Convention against Transnational Organized Crime, 55th Session of the General Assembly, November, A/55/383.
- United Nations (2000). *The Rights of Migrant Workers,* Human Rights Fact Sheet no.24, Geneva.
- Van Krieken, P.J. (Ed.), (2001). *The Migration Acquis Handbook,* T.M.C. Asser Press, The Hague.

Which Typology for Migration?

Like definitions of migration, the typologies proposed for categorizing the phenomenon are extremely broad in scope. These typologies aim at making it easier to analyse and understand the complex realities of migration.

At the end of the eighteenth century, Kant drew a distinction between a "right to hospitality" (*Gastrecht*) and a "right to visit" (*Besuchsrecht*) in his opuscule entitled *Perpetual Peace*[2]. According to Kant, a stranger cannot claim the right to be permanently admitted, but may claim the simple right to visit based on the notion of hospitality, which means the right not to be treated as an enemy when he/she arrives in another land.

Since then, many migration scientists and professionals have addressed the issue of an integrated migration typology. The result is a range of approaches: mainly geographical, demographic, sociological, political, legal or even multidisciplinary in nature.

Dumont (1995) proposes an interesting synthesis in terms of completeness: it is possible to construct complex, multipolar and complementary migration systems by associating a spatial typology of five types (one-way journeys, return journeys, frequent two-way journeys, re-emigration, indeterminate, i.e., nomadism or vagrancy) with another, broken down in terms of four types of borders (cross-border, international, regional, intercontinental).

A social and cultural typology is composed of different models, arranged according to a series of migrant characteristics: gender, marital status, age, professional qualification (like the brain drain), ethnic background (such as *Aussiedler*[3]) or religious persuasion (such as the exodus of Jews or of "Old Believers"[4]).

A typology distinguishing between forced and voluntary migration is simple on the surface only. For example, labour markets may not be sufficiently structured to meet the needs of local people in a post-crisis situation when everything must be rebuilt, especially for more qualified persons. In such a case, is the person who migrates in search of a new job forced to do so or is it a voluntary decision? (McKinley *et al.,* 2001).

The various reasons for migration can also form the basis for a different typology. Migration caused by economics (migration for commercial or technical reasons, migration triggered by environmental factors or by economic imbalances or breakdowns), demography (family migration, migration of young people and retirees, "replacement migration"[5]), politics (refugee movements, colonial or inherited migration within "migration pairs"[6], repatriations, forced exchanges of populations) – all these reasons combine to produce composite types of migration.

The legal typology is also important for migration as it directly affects migrants' daily life. A regular situation implies access to a host country's labour market, eligibility for social and medical assistance, and certain civic rights such as the right to vote in local elections. By contrast, a migrant in an irregular situation may be subject to detention, expulsion, deportation, prosecution or even human rights violations. Legal measures vary from one country to the next based on other variables regulating *inter alia* access to nationality and the naturalization policy in the host country; determination of refugee or family reunion status; or even rules on labour access.

Nevertheless, it is relatively easy to draw a basic typological distinction between established emigrant populations, often long-standing (i.e., *stocks*) and those entering and

---

2) Emmanuel Kant (1795). *Perpetual Peace: A Philosophical Sketch.*
3) German term designating the descendants of German settlers in Eastern and Central Europe entitled to "return" to Germany under certain conditions.
4) This community split off from the Russian Orthodox Church in the seventeenth century. To escape the Bolshevik revolution, the "Old Believers" fled to Siberia and then to China's Manchuria province.
5) Taken from the title of a UN study published in March 2000: "Replacement Migration: Is it a solution to declining and ageing populations?", ESA/P/WP.160.
6) Dumont (1995) defines a "migration pair" as made up of two countries with regular migration exchanges which constitute a significant part of their international migration over a meaningful time span, mainly because of their proximity or their particular history.

11

leaving at a given point in time (*flows*). In practical terms, however, the aforementioned problems of data collection need to be reckoned with.

Far from being artificially constructed around relatively abstract criteria, the best typology will offer explanation and be adapted to the context under examination. For globalization, the most relevant typology would distinguish between the forms, factors and aims of mobility (Withol de Wenden, 2001). Therefore, we should not be constrained by overly restrictive and often abstract models when attempting to translate a reality as changeable as migration. Ultimately, there are as many types of migration as there are migrants.

Migration Theories

Since the world of academia has been attempting to explain migration in scientific terms, an abundance of theories, explanatory models and systems, conceptual and analytical frameworks or empirical approaches have come to light. Regrettably, more often than not, these approaches are created independently of each other.

As they focus mainly on the causes of migration, most of these theories[7] have failed to consider other dimensions and factors. These theories advance *ex-post* explanations rather than providing empirical tools for guiding research and policy, and proposing verifiable and quantifiable assumptions. Moreover, many theories were not designed to explain migration *per se,* but rather to elucidate a specific facet of human behaviour; they were later extrapolated or adapted to migration.

When it comes to obtaining a theoretical grasp of migration, the broad spectrum of variables further amplifies the age-old dilemma of the social sciences that has dogged attempts to explain human behaviour. Migration is hard to define or measure since it is extremely wide-ranging and multiform and defies theoretical conceptualization (Arango, 2000). Modern science can draw on a much more varied range of conceptual frameworks, which indicates the unquestioned progress made over the past two decades. However, these frameworks contribute relatively little to understanding migration and its mechanisms.

7) The terms "theories", "models" and "conceptual frameworks" are being used interchangeably here to refer to all the outcomes of the scientific thought referred to in the preceding paragraph.

There is consequently no general theory for explaining migration as a whole. **Textbox 1.3.** provides an update on the best-known migration theories. They should be assessed based on their usefulness in guiding theory and practice as well as their capacity to provide cogent assumptions for empirical testing. They are justified in that they promote a better understanding of the various facets, dimensions and specific, albeit sectoral processes of migration.

TEXTBOX 1.3.

Inventory of Contemporary Migration Theories

The theories listed here rest on variables such as the behaviour of persons or households, or economic, societal and political influences. Rather than being exclusive of one another, they should be seen as complementary in their approach. The diversity of these approaches neatly illustrates how theoretical thinking has evolved over the past half-century or so.

The theory of *development in a dual economy*

Conceived by W.A. Lewis in 1954, the "growth with unlimited labour supply" model was the precursor to models explaining migration, though not a *sui generis* migration theory. Labour migration plays a key role in the economic development process. The modern sector of developing country economies can only expand with the labour supply from the traditional agricultural sector, in which productivity is limited. Labour migrates from the traditional sector to the better paid jobs created by the modern sector. As labour supply is unlimited, wages remain low in this sector, making it possible to sustain large-scale production and generate profits. By exploiting the growth opportunities arising from demand in the modern sector, migration creates a leverage effect that benefits both the modern and traditional economic sectors, which receive and produce labour respectively.

The *neo-classical* theory

In the 1960s, Lewis' theory was deepened and adapted to migration by Ranis, Fei and Todaro among others. Inspired by the neo-classical economy, the neo-classical theory of migration combines a macroscopic approach focussed on the structural determinants of migration, and a microscopic approach based on the study of individual behaviour. At macroscopic level, migration results from the uneven geographical distribution of capital and labour. This reflects disparities in wages and standards of living, and migration is therefore generated by supply push and demand pull. Migrants will go where jobs, wages and other economic factors are most advantageous. The gradual disappearance of wage differences will eventually lead to the cessation of labour movements, and the disappearance of migration and the original disparities. The microscopic approach to the neo-classical theory postulated by Todaro and Borjas in the 1960s and 1970s examines the reasons prompting individuals to respond to structural disparities among countries by migrating. Migration therefore flows from an individual decision taken by rational players anxious to improve their standard of living by migrating to places that offer higher wages. It is a voluntary decision taken in full awareness of the facts after a comparative analysis of the costs and benefits of migration. Migrants will therefore choose the destination where expected net benefits will be the greatest.

The *dependency* theory

The predominance of the neo-classical theory was challenged during the 1970s by a school of thought situated at the other end of the ideological spectrum. The contributions of the neo-Marxist dependency theory to the study of migration, by Singer in particular, focussed primarily on the rural exodus to the big cities. This exodus is viewed as a conflictual social process that can create and reinforce inequalities between rural and urban areas, chiefly through brain drain. The underlying message is the existence of unequal relations between an industrialized centre and an agricultural periphery. Countries at the centre are developed through exploitation of the countries on the periphery, in which developmental momentum is hindered by asymmetric dependency relations. In this light, migration would be a corollary of the centre's domination of the periphery.

The *dual labour market* theory

Elaborated at the end of the 1970s by Piore among others, this theory links immigration to meeting the structural needs of modern industrial economies. It therefore places the emphasis on migration motives in the host countries.

The permanent demand for immigrant labour is the direct outcome of a number of features characterizing industrialized societies and underlying their segmented labour market.

There are four operative factors. Advanced economies display a dichotomy favouring unstable employment through the coexistence of a capital-intensive primary sector and a labour-intensive secondary sector. These two sectors operate like watertight compartments and lead to the emergence of a dual labour market. The lack of upward mobility makes it difficult to motivate local workers and convince them to accept jobs in the secondary sector. The risk of inflation precludes any mechanism for wage increases, thereby stabilizing the system. Prompted by the opportunity to transfer funds to their countries of origin, immigrants from low-wage countries are inclined to accept jobs in the secondary sector because wages in that sector are still higher than in their home countries. Lastly, the structural demand of the secondary sector for unskilled labour can no longer be met by women and young people who had hitherto occupied these jobs. Women have now moved from occasional to permanent employment. Moreover, the declining birth rate has reduced the number of young people available for jobs at the bottom of the scale.

The *world-system* theory

Dating back to the 1980s and the work of Sassen and Portes, this theory postulates that international migration is a consequence of globalization and market penetration. The penetration of all countries by modern capitalism has created mobile labour that can move about in search of better opportunities. This process is favoured by neo-colonial regimes, multinational corporations, and the growth of foreign direct investment. It destabilizes huge swathes of population in emerging countries, especially those uprooted as a result of agrarian reforms and the progressive disappearance of the farming class. The result is a sharp growth in rural-urban drift, which in turn swells the ranks of the relatively unproductive and traditional tertiary sector. Many migrants are consequently attracted by jobs in more developed countries where many economic sectors depend on cheap and abundant labour to remain competitive. Migration therefore acts as a gigantic mechanism that regulates worldwide labour supply and demand and allows for interaction based on migration flows. Movements between former colonies and former colonial powers are one example.

The theory of the *new economy of professional migration*

This theory was developed by Stark in the 1990s based on the neoclassical tradition and emphasizes the role of the migrant's household or family in the process leading to migration. It focusses specifically on the causes of migration in countries of origin.

While migration is always triggered by rational choice, it is in essence a family strategy. The main focus is on diversifying sources of income rather than maximizing income at any price. The theory therefore considers the conditions on various markets and not just labour markets. It ascribes less importance to the wage disparities defended by neo-classical theorists because migration is no longer necessarily triggered by these differences, which are not considered indispensable. The new economy theory also underscores the role of financial remittances and the complex interdependence between migration and the specific socio-cultural context in which it takes place. The theory helps us to understand why community members that could be apt candidates for migration, especially poorer people, are often less inclined to migrate than people with financial resources who are more attracted by the prospect of migration. Thus people who could lose their income are more likely to minimize the risks since they generally have less money available to spend on travel.

The *migration networks* theory

In the 1990s, the old sociological notion of "networks" began to be considered in formulating a new approach to explaining migration. Massey defines a migration network as a composite of interpersonal relations in which migrants interact with their family, friends or compatriots who stayed behind in their country of origin. The links cover the exchange of information, financial assistance, help in finding a job and other forms of assistance. These interactions make migration easier by reducing the costs and inherent risks. The network paves the way for establishing and perpetrating migration channels, given their multiplier effect. As they are cumulative in nature, migration networks tend to become denser and more ramified, thereby offering the migrant a vast choice of destinations and activities. Some informal networks enable migrants to finance their travel, to find a job or even accommodation. Others are more sophisticated and use recruiters hired by companies or, in extreme cases, criminal networks of professional traffickers who act as smugglers. Hence they help migrants to cross borders illegally. Depending on the difficulty and duration of the trip, traffickers may even demand tens of thousands of dollars for services. Migrants who use these networks must frequently repay a debt based on the salary they receive in the host country. These migrants may also be subjected to pressures, violence and intimidation. Trafficking in migrants has proved to be the most degrading form of migration for human dignity and also the most dangerous for the safety of victims, especially in cases of sexual exploitation.

Sources:
- Arango, J. (2000). "Explaining migration: a critical view", *International Social Science Journal,* no.165, September, UNESCO, Paris.
- Brettell, C.B. and J. Hollifield (Eds.), (2000). *Migration Theory: Talking across Disciplines,* Routledge, New York.
- Cohen, R. (Eds.), (1996). *Theories of Migration,* The International Library of Studies on Migration, vol.1, Elgar Reference Collection.
- IOM (2000). *World Migration Report 2000,* IOM and UN, Geneva.
- Massey, D., J. Arango et al. (1998). *Worlds in Motion. Understanding International Migration at the End of the Millenium,* Clarendon Press, Oxford.

While they cover a broad range of situations and ideological approaches, the theories discussed above are not sufficient to explain all the ramifications of migration. Their principal shortcoming is that they only discuss the reasons behind migration and look much less at the phenomenon's interconnections with cultural, health, security, social, or trade policy areas, to name just a few. These theories also concentrate largely on explaining migration for work purposes, whether by unskilled labour or qualified persons, often overlooking the other types of migration.

Despite the high absolute number of international migrants, they ultimately represent only a small percentage of the world's population. What are the underlying reasons in this age of globalization? Current models offer no satisfactory answers. Migration theories should therefore not only examine mobility, but also immobility. The study of centrifugal forces should be matched by an examination of centripetal forces. The classical pull-push duo should incorporate the notions of "retention" and "refoulement" (Arango, 2001). Recently, researchers have been paying more attention to issues of family structures, family ties, social systems, social structures in general and the emergence of transnational societies in particular. The cultural dimension of migration, including its cost in terms of integration, is occupying an increasingly prominent place in modern research.

The political sciences add yet another dimension to identifying the causes of limited mobility. The immigration policies advocated by countries of origin and of destination directly impact the flows and types of migration. Therefore, any immigration theory that overlooks migration policy in favour of migration's economic determinants may be addressing only some of the complex issues thrown up by attempts to build migration models.

Despite the significance of irregular flows, migration movements are generally controlled and regulated by state laws and regulations, including border controls; the obligation to hold a work permit; penalties for illegal entry; and selection criteria for legally admitted persons. All these elements influence the potential migrant's decision to take the risk of leaving his country and the price to be paid.

Lastly, migration is largely impervious to theoretical reasoning and to formal models in particular because of its broad diversity of expressions, forms, types, players, motivations and cultural and socio-economic contexts (Davis, 1988). Theoretical approaches to migration would be more coherent if they were applied more regularly from a multi-disciplinary perspective to produce a holistic view of this complex subject.

The Causes of Migration

The most obvious cause of migration is the disparity in income levels, employment possibilities and social well-being between the countryside and the city, between one region and another, and between one country and another. In addition, there are demographic differences in terms of fertility, mortality, age groups and labour supply growth (Castles, 2000). Forced migration, as identified previously, results from a host of other factors including conflict, violations of human rights, and man-made and natural disasters.

In the future, demographic pressures will continue to exert a major influence on labour migration, more particularly for unskilled labour. The world population is growing by some 83 million per annum, of which 82 million are born in developing countries. Demographic pressure is affecting income levels in the countries of origin, thus favouring migration. High population growth goes hand-in-hand with emigration (World Bank, 2002: 82).

Yet there is no cut-and-dry relationship between poverty, demography and emigration. While economic and demo-graphic disparities between North and South remain important causes of international migration, these flows are not simply as mechanical as communicating vessels. Therefore the poorest countries or the worst-off populations do not necessarily supply most of the potential emigrants. The simple explanation is that a person must have enough money to reach the country of destination within the global migration system. In spite of globalization, the poorest people very often lack direct access to information that would enlighten them about opportunities elsewhere. There are no social mutual help networks, indispensable to finding a job and adapting to a new environment (Castles, 2000). Yet even the poorest may be forced to leave their homes if overtaken by a disaster that completely destroys the livelihood of local people. Such migration usually takes place under deplorable sanitary, medical or nutritional conditions. Castles (2000) underlines that migration flows are simultaneously a consequence and a cause of development.

However, field observations of the causes of out-migration show that migration flows have a temporal and spatial dimension and that they depend considerably on policies implemented in other fields (Sassen, 2002). Migration streams are generally neither mass invasions nor spontaneous movements from poverty toward wealth. For example, Sassen affirms that Europe's recent history shows that few people leave poor regions for richer ones in the absence of controls, even where the travel distances are reasonable and conditions vary considerably from one country to another.

Distinctions between immigrant and settled person, economic migrant and refugee, foreign worker and travelling businessman, student and highly-skilled professional, are more blurred today than ten years ago. Individual motives and ambitions that influence migration are intertwined with external factors and pressures. This means that highly qualified citizens of poor countries may be simultaneously attracted by greater professional recognition and a higher salary, but also motivated by the chance to contribute to the development of their country of origin through remittances and the transfer of skills. Asylum seekers may be both fleeing persecution as well as poverty in their country origin. All this demonstrates that migration has numerous and varied causes and that even in one individual, the motives may be mixed and multiple.

For many people, mobility has become a full-time way of life involving constant travelling back and forth. The motto of this new breed of migrant is leaving in order to be better

15

off at home afterwards. Although economic motives are among the most important drivers of migration, other motives must not be underestimated. For countless men and women, migration is a window on the world that enables them to secure financial and personal independence (Tacoli and Okali, 2001). Specific social or ethnic communities sometimes value mobility. Hence, in south-eastern Nigeria for example, young males who do not become involved in migration are viewed socially in a very poor light (Weiss, 1998).

Diversity and Complexity of Migration

For some years now, migration streams have become more diversified and complex. Receiving countries on all continents are encountering highly disparate population movements: students, women, migrants for family reunion purposes, highly qualified professionals, returning migrants, temporary workers, victims of trafficking, refugees, and undocumented persons (often emerging from one of the aforementioned categories). Migration is made even more complex through the various forms of settlement in the host country, i.e., temporary or definitive, seasonal or periodic, legal or clandestine.

New migration networks are appearing almost every day. Most often, these networks circumvent government control of flows and draw on a wide range of transnational channels. These channels can be economic, cultural, sociological, political, ethnic, religious or even criminal in nature. At the same time, more and more people have been involved in organizing migration for some years now. The emergence of a veritable migration industry is noteworthy. Accordingly, migrants are both assisted and often exploited by a disparate body of agents, traffickers, smugglers and recruitment agencies.

Tougher rules and regulations in a steadily increasing number of host countries have considerably inflated the financial cost of migration to migrants. Repeated attempts must be made to get through, and routes are becoming longer. Migrants must therefore often make stopovers in different transit countries before managing to settle in a country which is not always the one originally envisaged (Simon, 2001).

Over time, opportunities and constraints change flow directions: former host countries are becoming sending countries and former sending countries host countries; other countries become countries of transit, transfer points not only for neighbourhood migration but also for migration to settle in third countries. A growing number of countries are now simultaneously generating and receiving migrants.

Nowadays, geographical distance is becoming relative through technological advances that are benefiting more and more people. Travel time is diminishing and travel costs are more accessible to a greater number of people. Information is being exchanged by mobile telephones or the Internet. The news is readily available in newspapers, radio broadcasts and television programmes via satellite. There are more channels for cultural dissemination through audio or video cassettes. Economic exchanges are becoming more diversified with the appearance of an ever-growing number of individual operators. Images of western "El Dorados" can now reach just about everyone, attracting migrants from the poorest countries. These images of the consumer society in host countries are publicized worldwide through mass media and are also often carried through returning migrants, representing a powerful force for migration. This increase in media coverage and the associated desires it fosters are entirely beyond the control of official migration policies (Simon, 2001).

Hence, the "global village" is simultaneously restricting and opening up geographical space (Weiss, 2001b). While more and more people have the desire and means to go to other places than ever before, paradoxically, enhanced border controls are making it more and more difficult for them to do so, whether for purposes of migration or even routine tourist travel.

As mentioned above, most migration takes place within regional settings on one continent rather than between two continents. Most migrants and refugees remain within their region of origin, such as the former Soviet Union, sub-Saharan Africa, Asia, Europe or the Middle East. Asian labour migration statistics for the period 1975 to 1994 for instance, show that a mere 10 percent of Asian migrants left Asia - except for Chinese migrants (IOM, 2000). It is also estimated that most migrant trafficking occurs in one and the same region. Often only secondary movements bring the victims of trafficking to other continents: for example, the countless Thai women who become displaced within Thailand, usually concentrated in Bangkok, before being sent to the United States.

On balance, more people today are attempting to leave their land of birth to seek asylum elsewhere and requesting international protection under the 1951 Convention relating to the Status of Refugees. Most asylum seekers try to find refuge in a country in their region of origin. About 180,000 people filed asylum requests in industrialized countries in 1980, this figure nearly tripled in the space of a decade (572,000 in 1989) to reach 614,000 in 2001 (UNHCR, 2001a). The cumulative number of refugees has also grown: there were an estimated 8.8 million refugees in 1980; this figure peaked at 17.2 million in 1990 and subsequently fell to stabilize at around 11.62 million in 1999, 12.06 million in 2000, and 12.02 million in 2001 (UNHCR, 2000, 2001b, 2002).

Although employment growth has been mainly concentrated in northern hemisphere countries over the past 20 years, most labour migration takes place within countries in the South, for example: the roughly 300,000 Nicaraguan nationals migrating to Costa Rica (IOM, 2001); hundreds of thousands of Malians or people from Burkina Faso in Senegal, Côte d'Ivoire and in other West African countries, Bolivians and Peruvians in Argentina; as well as migrant workers from China, Indonesia, Thailand and Malaysia in South-East Asia.

Labour migration has important side-effects for countries of origin. Many labour migrants send remittances back home. Globally, these remittances represent a major source of hard currency (especially for the least developed countries) and make often substantial contributions to gross domestic product (GDP). In 2000, remittances sent by the diaspora to El Salvador, Eritrea, Jamaica, Jordan, Nicaragua and Yemen, enabled these countries to augment their respective GDP by more than 10 per cent (United Nations, 2002). These resources allow foreign goods to be imported and national production to be strengthened. At micro-economic level, remittances reinforce household revenues and are frequently used to purchase consumer goods or services.

Migration is now a multinational process and can no longer be managed bilaterally or unilaterally. Hence, migrants transiting through countries in Latin America on their way to the United States are a matter of regional concern and no longer exclusively the concern of one or two countries, i.e., the country of origin and country of final destination. Regular and irregular Latin American migrants usually pass through Mexico before reaching the United States. Growing numbers of Sri Lankans, Afghans, Iranians or Iraqis are transiting through the countries of the former Soviet Union (especially the countries in the Southern Caucasus or the Baltic States) on their way to the European Union (EU). More and more migrants from Sub-Saharan Africa are travelling through the Maghreb or the Middle East to reach Europe. This increase is mirrored in many IOM surveys as well as asylum figures (IOM, 2000; UNHCR, 2002). Indeed, for about a decade now, Afghanistan, the Democratic Republic of the Congo, Iran, Iraq, Somalia, Sri Lanka and Turkey have figured regularly amongst the largest suppliers of asylum candidates to have filed an application in an EU country. Regional cooperation is proving increasingly useful and necessary when dealing with migration originating in other regions.

Yet many migration flows are still bilateral, such as that between Mexico and the United States, or between Turkey or Poland and Germany. Although these flows are often not permanent, they reflect the migrants' strong connections to the two countries and are thus a prime example of transnationalism, which is one of the most significant contemporary migration-related trends. More and more individuals are maintaining links to two or more countries, not least of which through their work, families, residences, financial support and investment.

Virtually no receiving country anticipates the arrival of foreigners wishing to settle and become permanent residents. Immigration is often discouraged by stringent laws and relatively strict border controls. In fact, only five countries officially receive migrants as permanent residents. These traditional countries of immigration (Australia, Canada, Israel, New Zealand and the United States) officially accept between 1.2 and 1.3 million migrants each year. In 2000, the United States topped the list with 849,000 immigrants, followed by Canada with 227,000, Australia with 94,000, Israel with 65,000, while New Zealand took 44,000. These figures nevertheless represent only a part of annual migration flows to those countries. There are in fact substantial irregular migration streams to those destinations.

Return migration is yet another aspect of the diversity of international migration. Many descendants of migrants who have been resident in their new host country for one or two generations are indeed taking the opportunity to return to the land of their ancestors. Thus, the precarious economic situation in Zimbabwe is prompting many persons of British origin to return to the United Kingdom. Some South Africans of Australian or British origins are doing the same. The Argentine crisis has triggered return flows to Italy or Spain. Many Americans of Irish origin have taken advantage of Ireland's new economic dynamism to return to that country.

Right to Leave Versus Right of Entry

Migration flows and the accompanying cultural differences and diverse human beings they bring are not as well received by societies as flows of capital and goods. As the nation-state historically has been and continues to be responsible for the security and well-being of its citizens, migration is often perceived as a threat to national sovereignty and identity, and thus many states tend to restrict it. Countless persons wishing to migrate temporarily or definitively consequently find themselves in an ambiguous situation. They can now leave their country but are not authorized to enter another.

While the right to leave is enshrined in Article 13(2) of the Universal Declaration of Human Rights adopted in 1948 by the United Nations[8], there is no corresponding right of entry. With the progressive realization of the right to leave, today we face the opposite situation to that denounced by Voltaire in the eighteenth century: "As men go to excess in everything when they can, this inequality has been exaggerated. It has been maintained in many countries that it was not permissible for a citizen to leave the country where chance has caused him to be born; the sense of this law is visibly: This land is so bad and so badly governed, that we forbid any individual to leave it, for fear that everyone will leave it. Do better: make all your subjects want to live in your country, and foreigners to come to it"[9].

Far from being a precursor of globalization, the eighteenth century was characterized by less freedom of movement than today. As the economic counterpart to political absolutism, mercantile theory and practice in Voltaire's day were guided by an equation in which the number of their subjects determined the economic and military strength of monarchies. The mercantile monarchs were therefore in the habit of limiting their subject's movements. Restrictions on freedom of movement were only gradually lifted during the nineteenth century. Applied to the present day, Voltaire's observation can be translated to mean what Hirschmann has called "voting with one's feet"[10].

Voltaire and, to some extent, Hirschmann's principles are at odds with the modern reality of mobility. As the number of totalitarian states has decreased, preoccupation with limitations on a right to leave have diminished. Indeed, the most significant political development of the end of the twentieth century was the fall of the Soviet Union and its "iron curtain", restricting the emigration of its citizens. A shift in focus has occurred in many countries from the prohibition to leave towards a restriction of entry; states continue to guard the prerogative to restrict freedom to enter.

This leads to a paradox of globalization. While stimulating reduced barriers to circulation of services, consumer goods and information, official liberalization has not extended to human mobility, especially of people from poor countries. In contrast to authorized opportunities for migration, irregular or clandestine migration is increasing[11]. The phenomenon is both a response to this limitation and a symptom of the international community's inability to come to grips with the demands and disparities of today's global economy.

While the right to leave continues to be limited in a very small number of countries, it is also being facilitated by many developing countries, which enable their citizens to leave without providing proof of the right of entry into another country. Developing countries are counting on remittances and other positive spin-offs from their diaspora.

The Future of Migration

Since the end of the Cold War, migration has not only been high on the national political agendas, but has also been taking an increasingly prominent role in the international media, in public debate, and on the international policy agenda. It is pivotal in determining how individuals respond to the opportunities offered and the constraints imposed by the world around them and how policy-makers seek to manage the behaviour of individuals.

Migration will be a major topic in the twenty-first century and will therefore pose certain challenges in the future.

8) "Everyone has the right to leave any country, including his own, and to return to his country."
9) Voltaire (1764). "Equality", *The Philosophical Dictionary*. (English Translation by H.I. Woolf, New York, Knopf, 1924).
10) Albert O. Hirschmann (1970) *Exit, Voice and Loyalty: Responses to Decline in Firms, Organisations and States,* Harvard University Press (cited by Withol de Wenden, 2001).
11) Or as Simon (2001) puts it: "It is not possible to place an entire segment of humanity under house arrest".

Migration Policy and Management

Migration is an eminently political topic. Over the past decade, the politicization of migration has been evidenced by a series of developments: the fear in Western countries of an influx of masses of migrants from countries of the former Soviet bloc and in European Union countries of an invasion by citizens from new member countries with each enlargement of the Union; the questioning of the role of migrants in the economic and social upheavals triggered by the financial crisis in South-East Asia; restrictive policies and anti-immigration backlash in the wake of the terrorist attacks of September 11, 2001; renewed outbreaks of xenophobia in several African countries that blame domestic crises on migrants; and the exploitation of migration issues by some politicians to gain electoral mileage. All these examples illustrate the close links between economic, political and social issues on the one hand, and mobility on the other. More than ever therefore, migration is a ready target with psychological, economic, and public relations connotations.

IOM programmes and policies promote regular migration

Yet most attempts by nation-states and the international community to regulate migration have been sporadic and dominated by *ad hoc* considerations. Too often, these attempts are framed as a reaction to isolated and highly publicized events, such as humanitarian crises or personal tragedies. It is as necessary as ever to forge an international strategy to align migration with the political, economic and social objectives laid out by national and international decision makers. If it is to succeed in the long run, this strategy must lead to enhanced migration management that takes account of the interests of all states, i.e., those of origin, transit and destination, and the situation of migrants themselves. Such migration management should be designed to make migration more orderly and more productive, providing a national and multilateral framework that addresses the interests of all the stakeholders.

The implementation of migration management mechanisms is a daunting challenge to states. Unlike other flows, migration flows are an aggregation of individual choices that almost always fall outside the scope of a collective strategy and organizational control. Therefore, the state is no longer necessarily the prime agent for their materialization. On the contrary, it is exposed to migration fluctuations and forced to formulate migration policies; in doing this, it has to contend with the effects of a dynamic social process that is impinging on several of its sovereign powers as well as underlying civic relations (Badie and Smouts, 1999).

This fact is all the more interesting given the growing role of supranational entities or agreements, such as the European Union, the North American Free Trade Association (NAFTA) or the World Trade Organization (WTO). Hence, many tools for controlling populations and territories, as well as migration – illustrating the dynamic relationship between the two – are now jointly exercised by or in the hands of non-state institutions. Evidence of this trend can be seen in the privatized transnational regimes governing cross-border trade and the growing ascendancy of the world financial markets over national economic policies (Sassen, 2002).

While the new special regimes governing the movement of service providers under NAFTA or the WTO General Agreement on Trade in Services (GATS)[12] do not address migration directly, they do provide a framework for and encourage the migration of temporary workers. In fact, they are both aimed at managing certain aspects of mobility under the supervision of supranational entities. Sassen (2002) views this as the incipient privatization of certain aspects of mobile and cross-border work regulations. In this way, NAFTA and the GATS are to some extent approving the privatization of what is manageable and profitable, i.e., high value-added, flexible and financially profitable migration (migration of highly qualified personnel to work temporarily in high-technology sectors, subject to effective regulation based on a liberal concept of trade and investment).

19

12) In January 1995, following the Uruguay Round negotiations, the WTO succeeded the GATT (General Agreement on Tariffs and Trade), which had existed since 1947, as the organization overseeing the multilateral trading system. This system is comprised of rules and agreements, including the GATS, which is the first set of multilateral rules with the force of law covering international trade in services, including the movement of natural persons as service providers.

Migration management policies, however, need to encompass all facets and forms of migration. They cannot ignore the migration of low skilled and unskilled workers, refugees, dependent families, disadvantaged persons, etc. Their effectiveness and responsiveness to the needs of the international community and economy depend directly on this.

The Economic and Socio-Cultural Sphere and the Reception of Migrants

Human history has demonstrated that international migration plays a positive role in societies and helps to forge economic, social and cultural links between peoples and states. If it is to continue to play this role, international migration should be orderly and humane; this way it will reduce the risks of exploitation by traffickers and other criminal profiteers and conflicts with host populations can be avoided. To benefit everyone, international migration should also be tied in with sustainable development strategies in order to create a fairer world.

This migration-development link naturally involves better understanding between migrants' countries of destination and origin: the former need workers in order to address the consequences of profound demographic changes in their societies; the countries of origin depend considerably on transfers of funds, including remittances, and skills as well as return migration. This combination will underpin and cement their own development efforts. A major challenge for improving migration management will be for countries of origin and of destination to identify common or complementary ground that supports economic development objectives.

It is vital to understand that all forms of migration bring about socio-cultural change. Attempts to suppress or ignore such change may lead to outbursts of violence and conflict between local and migrant populations.

The traditional countries of immigration have demonstrated their capacity to manage migration. It has become an integral part of the founding myth of the nation. In contrast, countries in which nation building has focussed on a uniform identity or culture, or a social welfare system, are finding it extremely difficult to assimilate immigration. These countries have reacted to immigration with restrictive legislation on naturalization and citizenship and are less inclined to integrate migrants.

According to Dumont, the issue of immigration confronts every society with an opening/closing dialectic: a self-doubting society fears for its future and is afraid immigration could alter its frames of reference; conversely, a strong, balanced society with well-anchored identity traits knows that it can be enriched by immigration. In any society, therefore, the challenge is to develop a positive and coherent policy approach, which can bring about a centripetal process if everyone can identify with a set of shared values while respecting the differences and to avoid unsuitable policies and/or poor relations between immigrants and the host society, which can unleash centrifugal forces to widen the rift (Dumont, 2001).

Participation of all stakeholders[13] in the migration debate in order to inform decision-making is a crucial element. Communities and societies that are able to develop participatory approaches to migration management are more likely to achieve positive results. Globalization is leading us toward the formation of increasingly diverse societies and of multicultural citizenries. Migration holds enormous potential for altering the fundamental relationship between societies and territories. By adding to the ethnic and cultural diversity of nation-states, migration can change the sense of national identity, without necessarily weakening it. Quite the contrary, strong national identities can be forged in the midst of diversity if identified values are shared by all. The multifaceted cross-fertilization engendered by migration movements implies an evolution in national identities, as well as changes in scales and frames of reference. If we are to preserve "coexistence" in this new context, we must embrace the tradition of human rights and all that we have learned from the tragedies of history concerning hospitality to our fellow human beings (Bernard, 2002).

One of the most significant migration trends of the late twentieth century, the emergence of transnational communities is yet another challenge to the nation-state. Thanks to modern transport and communication resources, migrants and their descendants can maintain close links with their country of origin or with other groups in the diaspora. The very principle whereby a state must necessarily be built on a homogenous national community is therefore becoming increasingly anachronistic. In any case, transnationalism leads to an institutional expression of multiple belonging: the country of origin becomes a source of identity; the country of residence a source of rights; and

13) These include migrant communities, members of the host society, employers, governments, non-governmental organizations, intergovernmental organizations.

the emerging transnational space a source of political action combining the two or more countries (Kastoryano, 2001).

New Legal Reference Points for Migration

Lastly, yet another transformation of international relations is affecting the prospects for the effective management of migration. States are increasingly turning to international legal tools to help regulate discreet aspects of international migration.

The increasing popularity of human rights regimes is transforming certain "forgotten" players into subjects of international law, namely migrant workers, refugees, and women (Sassen, 2002).

Indeed, migrants – as all human beings – are entitled to enjoy fundamental human rights. In a society where mobility is the rule there can be no "humane" future for migration without this recognition (Farine, 2002).

While there is no comprehensive legal framework governing international migration, five major legal instruments covering various aspects of international migration illustrate some possibilities[14]: the Convention relating to the Status of Refugees (1951); the Protocol relating to the Status of Refugees (1967); the International Convention on the Protection of the Rights of All Migrant Workers and Members of Their Families (1990); the Protocol to Prevent, Suppress, and Punish Trafficking in Persons, Especially Women and Children, supplementing the United Nations Convention against Transnational Organized Crime (2000); and the Protocol against the Smuggling of Migrants by Land, Sea and Air, supplementing the United Nations Convention against Transnational Organized Crime (2000).

While the instruments on the status of refugees entered into force soon after their respective adoption, the 1990 Migrant Worker's Convention will enter into vigour in 2003. Requiring 40 ratifications, the two 2000 Trafficking and Smuggling Protocols have not yet taken effect.

The International Convention on the Protection of the Rights of All Migrant Workers and Members of their Families was adopted by the United Nations General Assembly in 1990, after a decade of negotiations and drafting. Its ratification by Timor Leste in December 2002 brings the number of ratifications to the minimum required for the Convention to enter into force[15] (see **textbox 1.4.**).

TEXTBOX 1.4.

Respecting the Rights of Migrants

Given the contrasting and paradoxical picture involved, tackling the issue of migrant rights in a few short lines is nothing short of attempting the impossible. Indeed, two contradictory reactions are revealed: growing concern on one hand, and discreet sidelining on the other.

Stranded Cambodian migrant fishermen awaiting IOM return assistance

Concern regarding migrant's rights is evident on several levels. At the regulatory level, many instruments set forth standards to protect the rights of migrants, and the 2003 entry into force and implementation of the United Nations Convention of 18 December 1990 on the Protection of the Rights of All Migrants Workers and Members of their Families holds out much hope. Once the Convention takes effect, its impact will be measured primarily in terms of the number of states party[16] and their migration status – whether country of origin or of employment. At the regulatory level, remarkable progress has also been made in the fight against trafficking. The recent past has brought a flowering of

---

14) For a comprehensive discussion of the international legal regime relevant to migration, see: IOM (2002). *International Legal Norms and Migration: An Analysis.* International Dialogue on Migration Series, vol.3.

15) The Convention enters into force on the first day of the month following a period of three months after the date of the deposit of the twentieth instrument of ratification or accession.

16) The following 20 States had ratified the Convention as of 10 December 2002: Azerbaijan, Belize, Bolivia, Bosnia-Herzegovina, Cape Verde, Colombia, Ecuador, Egypt, Ghana, Guinea, Mexico, Morocco, Philippines, Senegal, Seychelles, Sri Lanka, Tajikistan, Timor Leste, Uganda and Uruguay.

declarations of intent, political commitments and other non-regulatory texts, chiefly in regional consultation processes, but also in the final document of the Durban World Conference Against Racism. There are countless other examples.

The number of actors involved in protecting migrants' rights has burgeoned; the institution of the United Nations Special Rapporteur on Human Rights of Migrants is one prominent illustration. There is also an increasingly dynamic and growing number of non-governmental organizations caring directly for victims of abuse or preferring to gauge and assess state behaviour. Lastly, the media are not remiss in keeping the public abreast of the problems or abuses facing migrants. Moreover, the number and seriousness of the abuses could lead us to conclude somewhat hesitantly that migrants' rights are not being adequately protected.

The discreet sidelining of the issue of migrants' rights appears to stem from two closely related imperatives: national sovereignty and the fight against terrorism. The sudden arrival of migrants in irregular situations, whether by land or sea, is often perceived as a breach of security, leading the states concerned to step up controls and tighten entry formalities in order to show both nationals and potential irregular immigrants that they are in charge of the situation and will brook no abuse. Naturally, statements on security and associated tough measures are not lost on the electorate.

The fight against terrorism, particularly since the events of 11 September 2001, is undoubtedly impacting on support for migrants' rights. Given suspicions about the exogenous origin of terrorism, migrants and foreigners in general could well become saddled with a presumption of guilt that could sometimes be aggravated by the migrant's specific origin. The upsurge in intolerance, xenophobia, rampant or declared racism and discrimination are finding their "justification" – too facile and specious – in the need to root out the causes or agents of terrorism.

Will the coming years bring a renewal of concern or even further sidelining? Which way will the balance shift? The challenge to states will be to ensure the observance of migrants' rights while addressing legitimate security and national sovereignty concerns. A different approach is needed to strike this balance than that followed for decades, which consisted of juxtaposing seemingly antinomic concepts rather than seeking convergences. The emphasis by the 1990 Convention on the need for international cooperation on migration is encouraging.

This new approach must begin with a new awareness of the key ingredients of good migration management and the need to incorporate them into a coherent national, regional or international migration policy. Respect for the rights of all migrants is an essential component of good migration management, as is the fight against terrorism or border control. Denying this, whether consciously or otherwise, should remain the dubious preserve of those given to political short-sightedness.

IOM and the rights of migrants

"Underlying IOM's work since its inception has clearly been the recognition that, in the final analysis, all that it does is on behalf of individual human beings in need of international migration assistance, and toward whom the international community recognizes a responsibility. The disturbing rise in xenophobia and the tendency to target the foreigner as the scapegoat for any number of societal ills is in fundamental contradiction with the aims of such an organization. Increasingly, then, IOM sees the need to use means and occasions available to stimulate awareness of the contributions migrants can and do make, the difficulties they often face, and the rights to which they are entitled as human beings. IOM also sees the need to help clarify with migrants their lawful obligations to the States offering them admission" (IOM Strategic Planning: Toward the Twenty-First Century" MC/1842 §27).

The dignity and self-respect of migrants are fundamental concepts within all activities of IOM. They are stated in its Constitution, thus forging a link between the Organization and human rights. Strictly speaking, however, IOM does not have a legal protection mandate. Yet, the fact remains that many of its activities contribute to protecting basic human rights. In other words, the actual assistance rendered to migrants constitutes a form of protection, especially where it protects the life and physical well-being of persons at risk. For example, by providing safe transportation and related assistance, IOM contributes to the full realization of the right to leave any country and to return to one's country of nationality. IOM's special resettlement or emigration programmes in situations of internal strife may contribute to implementation of the right of all people to seek asylum. IOM's focus on trafficking in women is surely assisting to protect the fundamental human right not to be held in slavery or servitude. These are only a few examples of how IOM *de facto* protects individuals as a consequence of the assistance that it renders.

While the principle of non-discrimination against migrants concerning economic and social rights is central to the Convention, it also highlights the need for intergovernmental cooperation on migration. The fostering of healthy, equitable, dignified and legal conditions for international migration is a special part of the Convention, which will have a lasting impact on dialogue and cooperation among states (Perruchoud, 2002).

In the long run, only the establishment of an international migration management framework will make migration – and indeed mobility – safe, fair and constructive, failing which the principal beneficiaries risk being those who are more opportunistic and the smuggling rings. The free movement of people appears to be a reasonable approach to migration, without restrictions other than those addressing criminal activity, public security and economic conditions. The founding principle of the International Organization for Migration underlines this; IOM is committed to the principle that humane and orderly migration benefits migrants and society.

To echo the words of the United Nations Special Rapporteur on Human Rights of Migrants, to be able to meet the challenges raised by international migration and give priority to orderly and humane migration, "the regularization and creation of a migration management framework should ensure that migrants' human rights are respected" (IOM, 2002).

As a reflection of trends toward decentralization, migration will be a substantial element in the future shaping of the international order. The international community must understand all the challenges and issues inherent to migration, transforming this dynamic process into a positive and lasting heritage for the benefit of future generations.

TEXTBOX 1.5.

The International Organization for Migration in Brief

With half a century of worldwide migration experience, the International Organization for Migration (IOM) is recognized as the leading international, intergovernmental and humanitarian organization dealing with migration. Committed to the principle that humane and orderly migration benefits migrants and society, IOM meets the operational challenges of migration in arranging the movement of migrants and refugees to new homes and providing other migration assistance to governments and its partners in the international community.

IOM believes that international migration presents an opportunity for cooperation and development and acts with its partners in the international community to: encourage social and economic development through migration; uphold the dignity and well-being of migrants; assist in meeting the operational challenges of migration and advance understanding of migration issues.

Mr. Brunson McKinley of the United States has been IOM's Director-General since October 1998. The Deputy Director-General, Ms. Ndioro Ndiaye of Senegal, took up office in September 1999.

Established initially as the Intergovernmental Committee for European Migration (ICEM) to help solve the post-war problems of migrants, refugees and displaced persons in Europe and to assist in their orderly transatlantic migration, IOM's activities have expanded and now include a wide variety of migration management issues. It adopted its current name in 1989 to reflect its progressively global outreach and diverse programme activities.

At the request of its member countries, and in accordance with its Constitution, IOM launched a process in 2001 in order to establish a global forum for policy dialogue within the Organization, focussed on managing international migration and other related policy issues.

As of December 2002, IOM counts 98 Member States and 33 observer States, with more than 50 organizations holding observer status. Since it was set up, IOM has assisted over 12 million refugees and migrants to settle in over 125 countries. The Organization currently employs over 3,344 staff worldwide, working in some 165 offices in more than 80 countries.

The administrative budget funds core staff and office structure at its headquarters in Geneva, as well as in the field. For 2002, this budget amounts to Swiss Francs 35.7 million raised through annual contributions of IOM Member States. IOM's 2002 operational budget totals US$ 420.6 million and covers the implementation of IOM operations worldwide. It is made up of voluntary contributions from bilateral and multilateral donors.

With offices and operations on every continent, IOM helps migrants, governments and civil society through a large variety of field-based operations and programmes:

- Rapid humanitarian responses to sudden migration flows;
- Post-emergency return and reintegration programmes;
- Demobilization and peace-building programmes;
- Assistance to migrants on their way to new homes and lives;
- Development and management of labour migration programmes;
- Recruitment of highly qualified nationals for return to their countries of origin;
- Aid to migrants in distress;
- Assisted voluntary return for irregular migrants;
- Training and capacity-building for governments, NGOs and others;
- Measures to counter trafficking in persons;
- Mass information and education on migration;
- Medical and public health programmes for migrants;
- Programmes for the effective integration of migrants in destination countries and for the enhancement of country of origin development.

IOM has been represented at the UN General Assembly as an observer since 1992. In that same year, a resolution of the General Assembly made the Organization a standing invitee to the Inter-Agency Standing Committee (IASC). This relationship with the UN led to the signing of a Cooperation Agreement in 1996. Other agreements exist with individual UN agencies, such as UNAIDS, UNDP, UNFPA, UNHCR and WHO.

CHAPTER 2

Update on International Migration Trends

The two years from mid-2000 to mid-2002[1] witnessed a variety of new developments that have impacted world-wide international migration, influenced migration management policies and raised doubts about the effectiveness of migration control measures.

The year 2000 saw discussions on new forms of mobility and replacement migration in the light of labour shortages and the expected ageing of the European and Japanese populations by 2020. A United Nations report, *Replacement Migration: Is it a solution to Declining and Ageing Populations?*, put forward three scenarios: the first to address labour shortages; the second to increase the proportion of the active versus the inactive population; and the third to restore balance to the age pyramid. Depending on the scenario chosen, the number of new arrivals would range between 17 and 700 million. The report underlines the absurdity of any policy aimed at using immigration to offset population ageing. It tends to demonstrate that immigration could be a realistic solution to the decline in the overall population, or even in the active population in the countries concerned (Weil, 2001).

Let us first consider Europe. In Germany, a new immigration law (*Zuwanderungsgesetz*) was drawn up in 2001 and signed by the President of the Republic in June 2002, significantly modifying previous policy and sparking an acrimonious debate among the country's various political forces. The law proposed allocating point-based permits based on the Canadian and Australian models to address sectoral skilled labour shortages. However, just two weeks before it was due to come into force, Germany's supreme court blocked this landmark law in mid-December 2002 on the grounds that it had passed through parliament unconstitutionnally.

In the United Kingdom, the influx of asylum seekers continued in 2001-2002, via the Eurotunnel, with flows fed by the Red Cross Centre at Sangatte (Pas de Calais), until its closure in December 2002.

Generally speaking, migration flows to Europe are continuing subject to border control policies and the international networks trying to circumvent these policies. Migrant profiles are also becoming more diversified. Consequently, European migration policies originating from border closures 25 years ago need to be reviewed. Over the past two years, legislative elections in several European countries have shown that some far-right political parties have found fertile ground in local people's misgivings towards immigration and its many associated ill-defined fears. Thus, parties advocating "zero immigration" have garnered more than 10 per cent of the votes cast in half a dozen European Union (EU) countries.

The other major immigration regions are North America, Oceania-Pacific and some countries in Africa or Asia (South Africa, Côte d'Ivoire, Senegal, Republic of Korea, Thailand). While these countries are also origin countries, they are mainly countries of destination and are finding it difficult to prevent unwanted population movements. Despite deportations of irregular migrants by some of these countries and the reinforcement of controls and fences along borders, such as those between the United States and Mexico or between South Africa and Mozambique, migration is continuing. Often, development policies in countries of origin have only a limited effect in controlling mobility.

The desire to be mobile and to alternate stays between regions of origin and destination without ever opting for definitive establishment or return is shaping new migration trends with considerably different actors and profiles.

This global challenge has generated a widening gap between national migration management policies caused by over sensitiveness in years of crisis (dominated by restriction, dissuasion and repression) and new migration trends. Furthermore, no modern discussion of migration can be divorced from human rights, the development of countries of origin, the question of social cohesion and the future of the welfare state in host societies.

While the impact of September 11, 2001 ~~~~~~~~ negligible impact on migration manageme~~~~~ flows and stocks of aliens are fuelling d~~~~~ around internal and external security iss~~~~ in the United States, but also in oth~~~~ countries.

25

1) Period covering the time lapse since the publication of the last
   World Migration Report.

TEXTBOX 2.1.

Migration and Security after September 11, 2001

The events of September 11, 2001, have reminded us how mobile the world has become in recent years. Millions of migrants cross borders, continents and oceans every year to settle far away from their homelands. Does unlimited geographic mobility accelerated by globalization represent a security threat to states and societies and play into the hands of international terrorism?

Azeri border official checks a passport

International terrorism is a test *in extremis,* revealing the degree to which national immigration policies continue to be relevant in an increasingly border-less world. Just as trade, capital and services are moving quickly and freely around the world in ever-complex globalized networks, terrorist activities have acquired supra-national dynamics beyond the reach of many national law enforcement agencies.

Border and regular immigration control measures are only of limited value. Effective controls and effective information sharing are likely to pick up people already identified as terrorists and placed on watch lists as well as forged travel documentation. However, terrorists can easily resort to clandestine entry methods and are likely to use forged papers. Entry point controls therefore need to be part of a wider effort, which should include border surveillance, intelligence gathering and internal security measures. The focus of most measures implemented since September 11 has been on better intelligence and information sharing within and among affected states.

As September 11 demonstrated, terrorists frequently operate outside the purview of immigration enforcement, often with residence status and even citizenship. One option for states is a clearer regulatory basis for rescinding status, including citizenship, and extraditing persons found to be associated with terrorism, when prosecuted.

While immigration policy cannot prevent terrorism, IOM believes it can be an important vehicle for more efficient law enforcement and intelligence. Immigration authorities can contribute to national and international intelligence through direct encounters with illegal immigrants and through partner networks with transnational law enforcement and immigration agencies.

Appropriate systems and mechanisms for sharing information among authorities and states need to be installed. But migration policy, legislation and practice should be careful to protect people's right to be internationally mobile, as well as the integrity of regular migration regimes.

In the wake of the September 11 events, most states have tightened their immigration systems. The focus is mainly on control through enhanced information and identification systems, information sharing and inter-agency/inter-state cooperation. New strategies are being tested including biometric profiling, such as iris scanners and finger printing. All major immigrant-receiving states are examining ways of increasing data exchange among themselves, and with carriers and other states.

But most observers agree that immigration control can only be a "needle in a haystack" measure to control terrorism. Therefore, workable control mechanisms and improved migration management are urgently needed, especially for regular migratory flows.

Strengthening cooperative links between countries of origin, transit and destination on matters relating to both immigration and transnational crimes would make it easier for countries to monitor and document migrant flows and help identify criminals, individuals or networks.

Without effective data sharing systems, information collected by specific carriers or individual governments will be of limited value in what is inherently a global issue. Privacy and civil rights issues must be safeguarded while security is promoted through information sharing. These activities can still be regulated by a data protection authority for example. Issues of systems and format compatibility will need to be addressed before too many non-compatible systems proliferate. Acceptable interfaces will have to be found between legislation which points in different directions such as the US Freedom of Information Act, the EU Privacy Directive, and the European Convention on Human Rights.

This exchange of information among immigration authorities and greater cooperation between justice and the police of all countries will curb irregular immigration and favour legal migration.

To assist states in this endeavour, IOM initiated a policy dialogue during its governing body session in November 2001. For the first time, more than 130 Member and Observer States were able to discuss the cornerstones and requirements of a migration management policy that would encompass all of the basic aspects, ranging from security to migrants' rights.

Regional consultative processes, as well as the Bern Initiative launched in 2001, propose a framework to facilitate inter-state cooperation in managing international migration.

It is also necessary to create legal migration channels, which encourage mobility and help to manage it. Labour migration programmes can regulate labour markets in countries of origin and destination efficiently. Examples of successful programmes include Germany's "Green Card" programme or the IOM-managed labour migration pilot project between Albania and Italy.

Information and awareness campaigns to inform potential migrants about the pitfalls of irregular migration are also an important instrument in migration management.

Finally, public awareness must be raised in order to counter misconceptions that undermine successful migrant integration. Host governments should create more targeted and tailor-made integration activities for migrants, based on the mutual respect of cultures and traditions. Negative perceptions can lead to the marginalization and social exclusion of migrants, creating a divisive environment and undermining socio-economic stability in host societies. This life of exclusion is a fertile recruitment ground for terrorism.

Cooperation among countries, international technical cooperation, labour migration programmes, and better integration measures for migrants – these activities will help to reduce inherent security risks and work towards detecting and, ultimately, curbing transnational crime and terrorism.

If countries commit to better migration management, migration will remain a positive and constructive force and will address the security concerns raised by the events of September 11. IOM has a key role to play.

Source:
IOM News, March 2002

The persistence of irregular migration and trafficking of vulnerable individuals at the mercy of unscrupulous agents or employers, remains a permanent challenge for border control policies. Although bilateral and multilateral agreements have been adopted over the past two years to curb irregular migration, its scale often leaves states helpless in the face of human distress.

Economic and political, social or cultural development continues to create disparities between countries that encourage heavy migration flows. Media-generated desire for the West, salary levels and imported consumer goods fuel migration dreams. This then translates into irregular entries into a world that is often sealed off by entry and residence visas.

An embryonic trend only fifteen years ago, widespread possession of passports and lower travel costs have been accompanied by a growth in smuggling and trafficking networks, for whom the closing of borders has become a resource. Smugglers and traffickers are now well established in many countries of origin (Eastern and South-Eastern Europe, South-East Asia, Maghreb), and often derive greater profits from this new activity than from their traditional activities. As with other organized crime activities, migrant trafficking has become highly lucrative in a few years.

Globalization of Migration - Recent Trends

Although most of the world's population remains sedentary, the globalization of migration flows continues to produce extraordinary diversification. The number of origin, transit or destination countries and regions is increasing constantly, gradually diminishing the importance of colonial or historical links and altering the bilateral nature of the flows.

New networks are creating circuits that no longer have any traditional ties with the countries of destination: Iranians in Sweden, Romanians in Germany, Vietnamese in Canada and Australia, Senegalese in the United States,

Bangladeshi or Brazilians in Japan. Trends indicate that the globalization of migration flows will continue, given the persistence of development gaps and the growing sophistication of clandestine immigration networks. As border security is tightened, the smuggling networks refine ever more elaborate ways of thwarting controls.

The real extent of global migration remains unknown (see **chapter 1**) since records of the various forms of mobility in the least developed countries and war-torn regions are often haphazard and random. Figures vary, sometimes significantly, even on migration flows among industrialized countries (*The Economist,* 2002).

The most reliable data come from the Organization for Economic Cooperation and Development (OECD), but only concern the organization's Member States, recorded regular flows and some estimates of irregular migration.

During the 1990s, the influx of non-nationals into OECD countries followed a "cycle", which peaked in 1992-1993 and then declined following the application of more restrictive measures. Flows started to accelerate again in 1997. The OECD has grouped some of its Member States by the relative trends observed over a decade (OECD, 2002).

- An ongoing increase for most of the period, despite sporadic shifts that do not alter the overall trend: Australia, Belgium, France, Ireland, Italy, Japan, Luxembourg, Norway, United Kingdom, United States.

- A significant decline after 1993 and a renewed rise to levels seen in the early 1990s: Canada, Denmark, Finland, Netherlands, Portugal, Sweden and Switzerland.

- A downward trend during the period: Germany, New Zealand.

In absolute terms, however, the seven leading OECD countries of immigration in 2000 (in descending order) remained: the United States, Germany, Japan, Australia, Canada, Italy, and the United Kingdom (OECD, 2002). **Table 2.1.** shows the entries of non-nationals in certain OECD countries during the period 1990-2000.

TABLE 2.1.

Inflows of Non-Nationals into Selected OECD Countries, 1990-2000

	Inflows in 2000 (Thousands)	Average 1995 - 1999 (Thousands)	Average 1990-1994 (Thousands)
Australia**	316.2	222.1	240.6
Permanent inflows	92.3	99.3	86.8
Temporary inflows	224	122.8	153.8
Austria*	66	-	65.8
Belgium*	-	53.7	52.6
Canada**[1]	313.4	269.4	269.5
Permanent inflows	227.2	235.5	203.8
Temporary inflows[2]	86.2	63.9	65.7
Czech Republic*	-	-	9.9
Denmark*	-	16.1	23.9
Finland*	9.1	9.5	7.9
France**	119	103.9	99.5
Germany*	648.8	946.3	678.2
Greece*	-	-	38.2
Hungary*	-	20.9	13.1
Ireland**	24.1	13.1	20.2
Italy**	271.5	-	189.5
Japan*	345.8	244.2	251.5
Korea*	-	137.1	173.9
Luxembourg*	10.8	9.5	10.1
Netherlands*	-	80.9	76.2
New Zealand**	38.8	29.1	46.4
Norway*	27.8	17.8	22.9
Portugal*	-	9.7	5.8
Sweden*	33.8	53.2	33.8
Switzerland*	87.4	103.8	79.2
United Kingdom**	260	136.8	194
United States**			
Permanent inflows	849.9	1,209.30	748.4
Permanent (non legalisation)	849.4	769.8	745.9
Temporary inflows[3]	1,534.80	-	1,008.30

* Inflow of data based on population registers.
** Inflow of data based on residence permits and on other sources.

Notes:
1) Fiscal years (July to June of the given year) (Statistics Canada).
2) Inflows of foreign workers entering Canada to work temporarily (excluding seasonal workers) provided by initial entry.
3) Excluding visitors, transit migrants, foreign government officials and students. Accompanying dependents are included.

Source:
OECD (2002)

28

According to the latest figures published by the United Nations, Europe is the continent sheltering the largest numbers of international migrants, followed by Asia, North America and Africa (United Nations, 2002). But as regards the percentage of migrants vis-à-vis total population, Oceania-Pacific precedes North America, Europe and Africa. **Table 2.2.** provides an overview of the number and percentage of international migrants.

TABLE 2.2.

World Population and Migrant Stocks by Continent, 2000

	Total Population (Millions)	Migrant Stocks (Millions)	Per cent of population (%)
Asia	3672.3	49.7	1.4
Africa	793.6	16.2	2.1
Europe	727.3	56.1	7.7
Latin America / Caribbean	518.8	5.9	1.1
Northern America	313.1	40.8	13.0
Oceania	30.5	5.8	19.1
Global*	**6056.7**	**174.7**	**2.9**

Note :

*does not add up due to rounding

Source :

United Nations (2002)

Generally, since the end of the 1990s, migration from Asia has been increasing, notably to Japan, Australia, Canada, Italy, and France. These flows are mainly made up of Chinese and Filipinos. There is also a steady migration flow from Russia and the Ukraine to Western Europe, Poland and southern Europe. Permanent migrants in search of work have contributed most to these flows. These migrants include many highly qualified professionals and students.

The number of asylum requests filed worldwide increased slightly between 2000 and 2001 from 570,000 to some 614,000. The six countries recording the highest number of requests for asylum in 2001 were: the United Kingdom (88,300), Germany (88,290), the United States (86,170), France (47,290), Canada (42,750) and the Netherlands (32,580) (UNHCR, 2001b).

Other countries receiving a significant number of asylum requests are Austria, Belgium, Spain, Sweden, Switzerland, the countries of Central and Eastern Europe, Turkey, and even South Africa. The newcomers are usually citizens from Afghanistan, China, Colombia, Iran, Iraq, the Democratic Republic of the Congo (DRC), Russia, Sierra Leone, Somalia, Sri Lanka or the former Yugoslavia.

Applicants who are refused asylum often remain in the host country and become part of the population of irregular immigrants who can "neither be regularized nor deported", though some do return home once the conflict is over.

Totaling 12,029,000 in 2001, the number of refugees showed a slight decrease compared to 2000 (UNHCR, 2001b). In 2001, the largest concentrations of refugees were located in Asia (47.9 percent), Africa (27.3 percent), and in Europe (18.5 percent).

For the past twenty years, Asia and the Pacific region have been involved in migration processes which host countries are finding difficult to control: rural exodus; birth of a "migration industry" spearheaded by organized networks; feminization of migration; migration of contract workers, skilled workers, students, refugees and asylum seekers to different destinations (North America, Europe, Oceania-Pacific and the Middle East).

Africa is also experiencing steadily increasing migration streams linked to brain drain. There are two streams: the movement of skilled professionals within the continent, very often to South Africa; as well as brain drain movements, in which many Africans leave the continent to settle elsewhere.

Other regions in the world are similarly affected by this widespread mobility. Causes of migration abound in Latin America, the Caribbean or the Middle East, where emigrants include graduates, victims of political crises, farmers ruined by natural disasters, or ethnic and religious minorities subject to persecution.

Significant differences have been observed over the past two years between the new and the old flows. First, the "migration pairs", a legacy of colonial history and of privileged relations between country of origin and country of destination (Algeria/France, Turkey/Germany, Commonwealth countries/United Kingdom), have lost their importance. There are now increasingly diversified flows from origin countries to destination countries having no apparent link with the newcomers.

In addition, new forms of migration are emerging that are quite different from the mass migration of "birds of passage" (Piore, 1979), e.g., male manual workers who leave intending to return. Finally and most importantly, the "pull" or attraction factor of migration is today as strong as the "push" or repulsion factor. Migratory pressure is not just created by a combination of poverty and demographic pressure, which is actually declining in several countries of origin. Popular images of migration are also at work as the visible trappings of western comfort can be seen on television or in local markets (household appliances, electronic gadgetry and other consumer goods).

It is rarely the poorest people who leave for foreign countries, but rather the middle classes, qualified professionals or single women, attracted less by specific countries than by the economic and cultural metropolises. The poorest people, and particularly asylum seekers or displaced persons, will perhaps much sooner head for other developing countries than for Europe and North America. These developing countries are themselves origin and destination countries for such forced displacements. But everywhere, the existence of transnational networks is a necessary condition for mobility. They either emerge before the closing of borders or thrive on legal and illegal border closings. Globalization is generating migrant populations of varied backgrounds. These people wish to improve their living conditions, not only economically but also socially, culturally, politically or spiritually. Travel-oriented economies foreshadow this mobility: Romanians migrating to Western Europe to "do a season" (e.g., selling newspapers in the streets), profiting from intra-European freedom of movement; Chinese from well-defined regions who maintain or create sending and receiving networks; or students moving between the two shores of the Mediterranean. Europe is sometimes no more than a temporary destination, a staging post for onward migration to preferred countries, such as the United States or Canada.

Migration Policies - Control or *Laisser-Faire ?*

The trend towards circumventing the obstacles to entering or remaining in the host country illegally was analysed in the early 1990s by Aristide Zolberg (1992). Methods of clandestine entry are now supplanting official policies.

Over the past quarter of a century the debate has often centred on two issues; the wisdom of border closures and their effectiveness in dissuading new arrivals; and the conviction that the era of mass migration of earlier years had ended. Yet this has not been the case. On the one hand, repressive strategies have only had a limited impact on mobility and the desire to penetrate the "fortresses" or areas of attraction in Europe, Japan, North America or South Africa; on the other hand, the principle of border closing has been undermined by the variety of forms of mobility - sometimes under the mantle of human rights (e.g., political asylum), constitutional principles (the right to live as a family) or humanitarian concerns (the protection of refugees). The notion that countries cannot indefinitely prevent the movement of people is now becoming widely accepted and the first timid calls for a right to migrate are now beginning to be heard from some experts and human rights circles.

Public migration policy faces several dilemmas: government approaches (border control) versus market forces (free trade); freedom of movement (deriving from private law and international public law) versus freedom of establishment (which falls under the law of states and the exercise of their sovereignty to safeguard internal security and ensure successful integration).

In countries of destination, several yardsticks exist to measure the political costs and benefits of migration management versus a *laisser-faire* policy: offsetting the effects of population ageing, meeting labour shortages, facilitating relations with countries of origin, contributing towards national cohesion, helping to preserve the benefits of the welfare state. Although theoretically not exclusive of one another, these factors are often contradictory. In addition, there is pressure from public opinion keen on "controlling the control". In most destination countries the result is "navigation by sight" and short-term migration, which depends more on political agendas than on any long-term vision of countries' shared interests.

In countries of origin, the pressures are just as contradictory: they seek easier conditions of entry and more diversified visa regulations to facilitate flows and alleviate unemployment and sometimes even social confrontation, and yet are reluctant to close their own borders in order to control clandestine departures.

Because of the allegedly harmful economic, social, political and demographic consequences of immigration, about 40 per cent of all states implement policies aimed at reducing immigration. This trend can be observed in developed as well as in developing countries. Twenty-five years ago, only 6 per cent of all states practiced such policies (IOM, 2002).

The advantages of migration management for origin, transit and destination countries, as well as for the migrants themselves would clearly appear to outweigh the case for no migration management. However, only very few of the world's regions apply or attempt to implement migration management and even then, with rather limited success.

Therefore, the globalization of migration is only superficially affected by flow control and integration policies practiced by host countries. Together with its associated transnational networks, globalized migration represents one of the greatest challenges nation-states have to contend with.

**

The following sub-sections provide a brief overview of recent migration trends in the world's major regions.

The thematic section in the second part of this book explores contemporary trends and issues in more depth. The text below includes a number of references to the chapters and textboxes from the thematic section as they relate to the regions or countries under review and describe some current migration management policies.

**

The Americas

Some of the main origin and destination countries in world migration are to be found on the American continent. Every year, between 300,000 and 400,000 Mexicans cross the 3,200 km border separating their country from the United States, often putting their lives at risk. Indeed, between 1998 and 2001, more than 1,500 migrants lost their lives trying to cross the desert regions separating the two countries. Each year, Canada and the United States rank among the countries receiving most regular as well as irregular migrants.

The American continent, and the United States in particular, was considerably affected by the events of September 11, 2001. The following results can be observed: stronger security measures at domestic and international airports in the United States; the battle against clandestine entry and stays (tightening of visa-issuing procedures, border controls, selection of migrants and refugees in countries of origin); and the revamping of the US immigration services (INS/PRM[2]).

As stated by the Director General of IOM at the end of December, 2001[3]: "Many things have changed since September 11 even though at the same time a number of situations have remained the same". We must not confuse migration and terrorism because curtailing mobility would have a negligible impact on crime. After all, mobility is an essential source of dynamism for countries such as the United States and Canada (Weiss, 2001).

North America

The United States and Canada have opted for a policy of recruitment through immigration based on skill requirements and decided annually by entry quotas or targets. This policy makes the labour market more competitive, but does not overlook humanitarian considerations.

With 850,000 legal permanent entries per year and 1,535,000 entries with temporary visas, the United Sates is the foremost destination country for migrants in absolute terms. Since the end of the 1990s, Congress has authorized the issue of a greater number of temporary visas for highly qualified migrants who are expected to return home after several years. This is not considered as migration for permanent establishment.

In 2001, Congress took the decision to admit a larger number of unskilled migrants, Mexicans in particular. Today, the United States is host to approximately 8 million irregular immigrants, 54 per cent of whom are Mexicans. Moreover, the prospect of a policy of blanket regularization is not universally supported. During the last massive regularization operation in 1996, 3 million persons were granted regular status (Miller, 2002).

Currently, most immigrants entering the United States are from Latin America and Asia. The Bush Administration's opening up to Mexican immigration appears to be related to the growing importance of the Hispanic vote in the United States.

Just before September 11, 2001, Mexicans had greater scope to apply for legal employment in the United States. But terrorism put an end to the "immigration honeymoon" between Mexico and the United States, in which NAFTA might have become the framework for regional

31

2) Immigration and Naturalization Service / Bureau of Population, Refugees and Migration.
3) In a public statement marking the International Day of the Migrant.

integration modelled on the European Union. Indeed, a proposal for the regularization of undocumented Mexicans had already been tabled by trade unions.

Since September 11, the United States has been stepping up security and control along its borders with Mexico and Canada. The admission of refugees into the United States has slowed down considerably; the issue of visas has been tightened and anti-terrorism measures have been reinforced. However, overall immigration policy has not been changed by stricter control over various types of entry visas and the new security measures adopted, particularly at airports, even if they have temporarily frozen the American-Mexican 2001 immigration initiative launched by Presidents Bush and Fox. **Textbox 9.1.** illustrates the immigration agenda between Mexico and the United States since September 11. In terms of contact between the host communities and immigrant communities, migrants have sometimes been the targets of serious physical violence[4].

In fiscal year 2002 (October 2001 to October 2002), the Bush Administration had decided to admit 70,000 refugees but only 14,000 had effectively entered by June 2002. This figure represents the lowest level of refugee arrivals since 1987. By way of comparison, during the fiscal year 2001, the country admitted 47,000 refugees[5]. There are three reasons for this slowdown: the increasing difficulty facing INS-PRM staff during inspection tours to some countries considered dangerous for American citizens; the tightening of security measures; and the verification procedures of case files of admission candidates.

In recent years, Canada has witnessed rapid growth in its foreign-born population. Like the United States, Canada is attempting to attract highly qualified migrants for permanent employment through a "point system". The temporary immigration programme is based on labour market tests. In 2000, Canada recorded more than 227,000 permanent arrivals. Student migration is considered a source of qualified immigration since the country is also losing its own nationals and some of its high-level professionals to the United States.

Regional integration in North America has now been included in several agreements. Apart from selecting the most sought-after migrants in any particular sector, the objective is to limit population movements between the

United States and Mexico by controlling the regions of origin and retaining populations within them. It is still difficult to say whether the NAFTA agreement has reduced or increased migration. The text contains no reference to migration movements. Many analysts believe that the agreement has had little effect, but that it has amplified the informal economy and the presence of maquiladoras – American companies established along the Mexican border to stem the flow of potential migrants (Canales, 2000).

In short, the migration management policies of the United States and Canada are aimed at maximizing the contribution of immigration to the economy. They rely on long-term strategies in framing and implementing their migration policies. Chapter 9 is devoted to a comparative analysis of migration policies in the traditional countries of immigration, including Canada and the United States.

Latin America

In recent years, Latin America has witnessed mobility beyond the control of the countries of destination, and a change in the nature of migration trends. The difficulty in managing migration flows is a potential source of friction among states in the region, owing to the highly volatile political and economic situation and substantial increase in intra-regional flows.

Several major migration patterns can be identified:

• Migration to the United States and Canada, notably from Mexico and other Central American countries and the Caribbean.

• Migration within Central America (Nicaraguans to Costa Rica, Salvadorians to Guatemala, Guatemalans to Mexico).

• Migration within the Andean region (Colombians to Venezuela, Ecuadoreans and Peruvians to Argentina).

• Migration flows in the Southern Cone (Argentina, Brazil, Chile and Uruguay). Long open to immigration, Argentina has regularized irregular migrants from Bolivia, Peru and Paraguay under bilateral agreements. Brazil, another major country of destination, has a migrant population of almost 1 million from Argentina, Uruguay, Chile and Paraguay, while some 50 per cent of the foreigners in Paraguay are Brazilians (Santillo, 2002).

4) "Bush condemns 'revenge attacks'", *BBC News,* 18 September 2001; "Arab-Americans concerned about treatment", *CNN.com*, 25 October 2001.
5) *International Herald Tribune,* 8 and 9 June 2002.

- Guerrilla warfare and ensuing refugee movements (Mexico, Guatemala, Colombia), return migration (*nikkeijins* from Brazil resettling in Japan where they benefit from ethnic preference and special programmes sponsored by the Japanese government, and Chileans returning to Chile), and internal migration flows within Brazil add to the multiplicity of migration typologies.

Regional integration has now been enshrined in various international treaties (Andean Pact, Central American Common Market, Mercosur), but continued mobility is being fuelled by the diversity of these countries. **Chapter 10** is devoted to migration policies and regional consultation processes in Latin America.

The most interesting recent phenomenon has been the reversal of traditional migration streams, with a drop in European and Asian migration to Argentina, Venezuela and Brazil and an increase in cross-border Latin American migration to Venezuela, Costa Rica, Paraguay and Mexico.

Migration in Argentina, a destination country turned origin country, has been strongly impacted by the economic crisis prevailing since late 2001. Indeed, many Argentines are trying to escape the non-payment of salaries and the freezing of their bank accounts. A large number of Bolivians, Paraguayans and Peruvians who arrived in Argentina in the 1990s and occupied vacant positions in the building and service industries are now returning home to escape rampant unemployment. **Textbox 10.2.** examines the impact of the Argentine crisis on immigration.

Brazil was long considered exclusively a country of destination but now faces an increasingly precarious employment situation, particularly in the informal labour market where jobs are often taken by Bolivians. Thus, Brazil is currently witnessing the emigration of its own nationals: about 300,000 Brazilians work in Paraguay, where they have been dubbed Brasiguays. More highly skilled migrants set their sights on the United States.

The second most heavily populated country in the region, Colombia, is another major country of emigration. Economic recession and persistent violence have provoked not only the displacement of several hundred thousand people within the country itself but also heavy migration flows to Ecuador, the United States, Canada, Australia, Spain and even Costa Rica. However, the number one des-

tination is Venezuela, where at least 2 million Colombians live. For more information on migration in Colombia, see **textbox 7.1.** and **textbox 10.3.**

The Peruvian Government estimates that about 2.2 million of its nationals live abroad, 75 per cent as irregular migrants. Some 250,000 to 300,000 people leave Peru each year[6]. The principal countries of destination for these labour migrants are Argentina, Bolivia, Chile and, outside of the region, Italy, Spain and the United States.

The Caribbean

Made up of fifteen independent countries and several overseas dependencies and territories, the Caribbean is recording some of the highest emigration rates in the world. Some 80 per cent of the 37 million inhabitants in the region are nationals of the three largest islands, namely Cuba, Jamaica, and Hispaniola, the latter being divided into the Dominican Republic and Haiti. Each of these countries sends large numbers of migrants to the United States and Canada.

In 2001, 900,000 Cubans were living in the United States, i.e., one tenth of the population born on the island. They are to be found predominantly in Florida, a state that has become an important Latin American business and financial centre.

With a community that is 700,000-strong and concentrated largely in New York City, the Dominican diaspora constitutes the second largest Caribbean group in the United States. Dominicans make up the biggest foreign community in New York. As elsewhere in the Caribbean, migrant trafficking is increasing in the Dominican Republic. This phenomenon is illustrated in **textbox 3.1.**

While Jamaican migrants to the United States only occupy the third place, emigration from that island is one of the oldest migration flows in the region. In fact the recruitment of Jamaican farm workers in the United States dates back to the 1940s. Until the 1990s, some 10,000-12,000 Jamaicans would migrate every year, either to Florida to work in the cane fields, or to the East Coast to pick apples. Today, about 411,000 Jamaicans live in the United States (Martin and Widgren, 2002). Jamaicans also migrate to the United Kingdom.

33

6) *IOM News,* 16 July 2002.

More than half of the 335,000 Haitians in the United States arrived during the 1990s in a bid to escape difficult economic conditions, often transiting through the Bahamas. The largest Haitian diaspora is to be found in the Dominican Republic, which hosts about 500,000 nationals from its close neighbour. **Textbox 10.1.** examines the specific migration context in Hispaniola.

Puerto Rican nationals were accorded American citizenship in 1917 and enjoy unrestricted entry into the United States. At the end of the 1990s, 2.7 million of the 6.5 million Puerto Ricans were living in the United States, mainly in New York and Chicago. Their migratory movements are largely dictated by economic conditions. As the discrepancies in revenue between the two countries gradually diminished and social security services improved in Puerto Rico during the 1980s and 1990s, net migration from Puerto Rico fell to almost zero (Martin and Widgren, 2002).

Caribbean member countries of the Commonwealth maintain migration links not only with the United States and Canada, but also with the United Kingdom. Accordingly, many citizens of Dominica, Barbados, Grenada or the Bahamas migrate to the former colonial power. Other Caribbean overseas dependencies and territories enjoy privileged migration relations with their respective European counterparts: thus persons from Guadaloupe and Martinique migrate to France, while nationals of the Netherlands Antilles (Aruba, Bonaire, Curacao, etc.) migrate to the Netherlands.

Asia

Asia defies attempts to synthesize recent migration typologies and policies, due to its diversity and vastness, stretching from the eastern Mediterranean to the western shores of the Pacific. More than 60 per cent of the world's population lives in Asia and there are major migration flows from this continent to Europe and North America. Yet, the most distinctive feature is the high number of intra-regional migration flows. Asia also has the highest level of rural-urban mobility (migration from the countryside to the cities). Tens of millions of Chinese fall into this category (see also **textbox 11.1.**)

Asia is made up of both highly developed countries, exerting an enormous "pull" effect on migrants, and some of the world's poorest countries. In these countries, recourse to migration is a form of survival, a means of escape or the result of forced departure. Consider the case of Afghans in Iran, Pakistan, Turkey and the Commonwealth of Independent States (CIS). Some countries receive massive inflows of refugees from neighbouring countries; Iran and Pakistan are the world's leading asylum countries, providing shelter to a cumulative total of 4 million refugees in 2001. Worldwide, Afghanistan is the country with the largest numbers of refugees (3.8 million) and internally displaced persons (1.2 million). **Textbox 7.2.** examines the plight of the internally displaced persons in Afghanistan.

Thailand and Malaysia are both origin and destination countries. These countries have experienced chain migration, whereby some migrants leave in search of better jobs, and are replaced by others seeking employment. They accommodate a large diversity of types of migrants: contract workers, highly skilled migrants, students, asylum seekers, persons displaced by natural disasters, returning migrants (particularly to India and Japan), irregular migrants, women and children who are victims of trafficking. **Chapter 11** is dedicated to labour migration mechanisms in Asia.

The Middle East

For the past twenty years the Middle East has been a highly attractive destination for labour migrants. Records show that 25 per cent of the workers in Saudi Arabia are foreigners, 65 per cent in Kuwait, 67 per cent in the United Arab Emirates and as much as 70 per cent in Qatar. Most of these migrants come from South Asia (Bangladesh, Sri Lanka), South-East Asia (Philippines, Thailand) or Africa (Egypt, Sudan). They were attracted by the oil boom and their occupations range from building and construction, maintenance, to repairs and domestic work.

Yet most host countries in the Gulf are taking a second look at labour immigration given the rapid increase in the local population and their preference for nationals in the allocation of skilled jobs. However, the "re-nationalization" policy has not really borne fruit. Many nationals from Gulf countries are not keen on working in the private sector and employers prefer migrant workers as they are considerably more flexible in terms of working hours and wages. **Textbox 11.4.** illustrates present migration dynamics in the Gulf countries.

Israel is a traditional country of immigration with a structured migration policy. Between 1989 and 2000, the country received over 1 million migrants mainly from the former USSR, thereby increasing the population to around 6 million. Jewish migration to Israel continues to play a major role, as illustrated by the case of Argentine Jews in the wake of the economic and financial crisis since the end of 2001. There are some 200,000 Jews in Argentina. At the end of May 2002, more than 2,200 had left for Israel, which finances their transportation, provides an integration allowance and assists them in acquiring Israeli citizenship[7].

In recent years, Turkey has been severely affected by transit and refugee migration. While Turkey is a country of origin for migrants to Europe, more recently it has become a transit country on the way to a second destination. According to various sources, some 200,000 persons in irregular situations transit through Turkey each year[8]. They come from Afghanistan, Bangladesh, Bosnia-Herzegovina, the Democratic Republic of the Congo, Egypt, Ghana, Iran, Iraq, Morocco and Kosovo, and are either economic migrants re-routed after failed attempts to enter Europe's Schengen area, or migrants seeking refuge in a foreign country. Nevertheless, Turkey applies geographical asylum legislation which accepts only European refugees. There are also more and more eastern European immigrants looking for work in Turkey, often entering illegally or ending up in irregular situations.

In its fight against irregular migration, Turkey made significant headway in summer 2002 with the implementation of a joint programme of action with the EU and the introduction of penalties for trafficking in migrants. Irregular immigration is viewed with concern by Brussels, it turns Turkey's candidacy for admission to the EU into a somewhat sensitive issue.

South, South-East and East Asia

Over the last decade, various patterns of migration have emerged in this region. They include:

- continued Chinse emigration adding to a diaspora of some 30 to 50 million people (Guerassimov, 2002) (see also **textbox 11.1.**);

- the emergence of a skilled workforce in India, giving rise to strong demand for Indian workers within and outside Asia;

- a decline in fertility rates and the appearance of demographic disparities, creating a need for migrants in Japan and South Korea in particular;

- the impact of the economic recession on countries with export economies, such as Singapore and the Philippines;

- the appearance of transit migration patterns, for example in Indonesia, which has become a preferred transit point to Australia (see also **textbox 3.2.**);

- a general increase in irregular migration, including migration of Chinese labourers and trafficking in women and children, especially from the Philippines, Thailand and Myanmar.

Asia has witnessed a feminization of migration flows from the Philippines, Indonesia and Sri Lanka (partially due to the demand in the domestic services sector) and countries of origin are increasingly dependent on migrant remittances.

The Philippines is the largest exporter of manpower in Asia, followed by Bangladesh and Indonesia. About 7 million of 85 million Filipinos live and work overseas. Their remittances contribute considerably to the Philippine economy. There are Filipino workers throughout South-East Asia, especially in Malaysia, but also in the Gulf countries, Europe, Australia and North America. Actively supporting these labour migration flows, migration management has clearly become one of the priorities of the Philippine Government (IOM, 2002a).

Like countries in Europe, many Asian countries are now facing a demographic transition (declining fertility and mortality), particularly in Thailand, Singapore, South Korea and Japan, as well as a migration-based transition (from labour-surplus to labour-shortage).

Apart from China (with a total diaspora of 30-50 million) and India (20 million), the main flows of migrants are from Indonesia and the Philippines (7 million) mainly to Malaysia, Singapore and the Gulf; from the Indo-Chinese Peninsula (Cambodia, Laos, Vietnam, Myanmar) to Thailand; and from eastern Malaysia to Brunei.

35

---

7) "Argentinische Juden fliehen nach Israel", *Neue Zürcher Zeitung*, 9 June 2002.

8) "Près de 200 000 personnes en situation irrégulière transitent chaque année par la Turquie" , *Le Monde*, 2 August 2002.

The two largest diasporas – Chinese and Indian – are exhibiting complex forms of migration characterized by circular mobility of some family members travelling frequently between the host country and their region of origin; an increasing number of dual residence cases; and final return home for retirement. In addition to international migration from these two countries, there is also massive internal migration: in India, for example, a large percentage of the Kerala population migrates towards the large northern cities; in China, there is also significant migration to the cities from regions of origin such as Fujian, Guandong, and Zhejiang.

Significant human trafficking also exists both within and outside Asia. This was illustrated by the tragedy at Dover in June 2000, where 58 clandestine Chinese migrants suffocated to death while locked in a fruit and vegetable transport lorry.

The precarious situation of newcomers in Asian countries has been compounded by the tardy implementation of immigration policies. Previously, these countries saw themselves merely as countries requiring temporary labour and sometimes entertained the myth of ethnic homogeneity, as in Japan.

Migration in Asia will continue to increase for a number of reasons: the varying levels of development; demographic disparities; and structural labour shortages in Japan and South Korea – **textboxes 11.2.** and **11.3.** are devoted to the specific migration context in these two countries. New issues that will need to be addressed include the integration of newcomers and the issue of depopulation. In addition, significant political, economic and social transformations are already occurring in countries of origin. Other factors will also influence migration, such as recession and the eventual implementation of more restrictive immigration policies in host countries.

In the summer of 2002, for example, Malaysia deported hundreds of thousands of irregular migrants back to Indonesia and the Philippines. Immigrants and their families made up some 10 per cent of Malaysia's 22 million inhabitants and after a surge in crime, Malaysia gave them four months to leave the country. One consequence of these repatriations has been a slowdown in the Malaysian economy, which depends heavily on immigrant labour.

Oceania – Pacific

With a population of barely 31 million, Oceania-Pacific is the least populated of the world's major regions. Two-thirds of this population live in Australia and New Zealand. These two major countries of immigration annually receive many tens of thousands of new arrivals under their respective governments' immigration programmes. The programmes are discussed in **chapter 9**, which focusses on the traditional countries of immigration. In addition, the Trans-Tasman Travel Agreement also permits the free movement of persons between these two countries.

Despite its remote geographical location, Australia constantly faces new waves of asylum seekers. In August 2001, the "Tampa" incident made the headlines of the world press. Following the sinking of an Indonesian boat attempting to carry irregular migrants to Australia, 434 persons were recovered by the Norwegian vessel "Tampa". Most of these people were of Afghan and Iraqi origin. Australia put in place arrangements to transfer them to the Pacific island of Nauru to determine their status.

Australia's regular immigration patterns include skilled migrants, business migrants, family migration as well as a humanitarian stream. Policy concerning skilled immigrants is regularly revised based on economic conditions. It includes a points system, annual quotas sponsored by employers and granting of residence permits to foreign students, to attract qualified permanent residents. New Zealanders are not subject to quotas. Immigrants come mainly from Oceania-Pacific, Asia and Europe, but also Africa and the Americas. In addition, Australia accepts highly qualified temporary residents (mainly researchers and other beneficiaries of exchange agreements).

Since the 1990s, some anti-immigration movements have from time to time gained ground in both Australia and New Zealand. Their arguments are based on fear of an alleged Asiatic invasion and the apparent unwillingness of Asians to integrate. The leader of the New Zealand First Party and former Deputy Prime Minister, Winston Peters, would like to see the New Zealand government slash the annual immigration quota from 55,000 to 10,000[9].

The Pacific islands, with the exception of Nauru, have not experienced major migration movements. However, an

9) "NZ nationalist slammed for demand to slash immigration", *The Associated Press,* 19 June 2002.

environmental problem could propel them to the centre stage of world migration in the decades ahead. Climate change and global warming may eventually lead to rising sea levels which could submerge some of these islands, leading to the forced displacement of local people.

Africa[10]

Over the years and successive generations of migrants, migration trends in the various regions of Africa have developed along the following major patterns:

- in North Africa, the flow of regular labour migration is directed towards the EU, as is the transit migration from sub-Saharan Africa;

- in West Africa, regular and irregular labour migration is largely determined by the agricultural seasons;

- in Southern Africa, contract labour migration is a major feature of the mining industry and commercial agriculture;

- in Central and Eastern Africa and – since the onset of civil wars in Liberia and Sierra Leone – West Africa, massive flows of refugees and displaced persons have occurred.

These features, however, are not stable. They evolve with the economic, social and political changes prevailing in the continent, illustrating the intrinsically changeable nature of migration. To some extent, all the different types of migration flows can be observed throughout Africa. The economic and social mechanisms underlying African migration are explained in **textbox 12.1.**

In the African context, the linkages between brain drain, labour migration and remittances to countries of origin have acquired special importance from the development standpoint. These linkages are analysed in detail in **chapter 12.**

North Africa

Due to geographical proximity, the largest flows of northern African migrants toward EU countries are made up by people from Algeria, Morocco, Tunisia, and to a lesser degree, Egypt. Egyptians have also traditionally been one of the largest groups of migrant workers in the Persian Gulf States. Remittances from the northern African diaspora make a significant contribution to GDP in countries of origin. **Textboxes 12.3.** and **12.4.** examine the specific case of Morocco and Tunisia.

Established migration channels have often existed for several decades. The historical relations between the Maghreb and France lay behind the recruitment of North African workers in Germany, the Netherlands, Italy and Belgium in the 1960s and 1970s, during the economic boom in Europe. This pattern has continued until today.

As the only country in the region with a positive migration balance, Libya counts a very large community of migrants from sub-Saharan African countries, in particular from Nigeria, Ghana, Chad and other Sahel countries. There are an estimated 1 million migrants from these countries, compared to a population of 5 million Libyans. These migrants were invited to Libya in the 1990s to take up positions that Libyans were reluctant to fill, especially in the informal and construction sectors.

The major roads through the Sahel and the Sahara have become migration highways used by African workers attracted by the oil wealth and labour shortages in Libya. Although this country has experienced outbursts of xenophobia, Libya continues to be the beacon destination in North Africa. Crowds killed over a hundred migrants in attacks against sub-Saharan migrants in 2000. Thousands of others took flight and returned to their countries of origin[11].

For several years now, the Maghreb countries, particularly Morocco and Algeria, have become transit countries, enduring the pressure of ever-growing migration flows from sub-Saharan Africa. On their way to the EU, thousands of West African irregular migrants transit through the Maghreb trying to reach the shores of Europe. These long and dangerous trips often end in tragic shipwrecks on the high seas, in the Straits of Gibraltar, or en route to the Canary Islands.

37

---

10) The content of this section has been adapted from the article by Weiss, T.L. (2001), published in: *La Géographie – Revue de la Société de Géographie de France,* Paris.

11) "Libya: Tens killed and hundred[s] injured in latest violence events", *ArabicNews.com,* 30 September 2000; "Ghanaians flee Libyan attacks", *BBC News,* 9 October 2000; "Another 255 Sudanese flee from Libya", *ArabicNews.com,* 12 October 2000.

West Africa

In West Africa, people and merchandise have traditionally enjoyed freedom of movement unrestrained by borders. The establishment of the Economic Community of West African States (ECOWAS) and its protocols on freedom of movement and freedom of establishment of persons have perpetuated migration dynamics in the region.

Besides Nigeria, most countries in the region share a common feature: a small, low-income population with a high growth rate. Migration mainly involves the movement of temporary workers from the land-locked countries (Burkina Faso, Mali, Niger) to the more prosperous coastal countries (Côte d'Ivoire, Ghana, Nigeria, Senegal). These flows originated from colonial policy in West Africa. The scale and direction of migration flows were prompted by the greater demand for labour caused by the establishment of an export-oriented agricultural economy and the emerging mining industry in coastal countries. In the immediate post-independence period, industrial development was promoted in several urban centres and fuelled rural-urban migration even further. Today, the trend is beginning to wane because of overcrowded cities and lack of professional prospects and there is return migration to rural areas.

The Côte d'Ivoire is among the largest host countries in sub-Saharan Africa. The plantation economy attracted sizeable numbers of migrant workers from neighbouring countries such as Mali and Burkina Faso. Thus, almost 30 percent of the resident population was born in a foreign country. In 2000, a wave of anti-foreigner violence in the Côte d'Ivoire tarnished the country's image, which was largely based on hospitality toward migrants[12]. This was repeated in September 2002 following a failed coup attempt.

Triggered by civil strife and political unrest particularly in Liberia, Sierra Leone, Chad, Togo, Mauritania and Guinea-Bissau, refugee movements are also a component of West Africa migration. The largest concentrations of refugee populations are found in Guinea and the Côte d'Ivoire. West Africa sustains the main flow of migrants transiting the Maghreb countries on their way to the EU. For generations, nationals from the Sahel countries have been migrating to France, benefitting from migration networks guaranteeing them support and assistance.

The migration of traders, particularly female traders, is also typical. These migrant traders profit from exchange rate differentials to determine their sourcing and sales strategies. The Nigerian, Ghanaian and Senegalese populations in particular are renowned for their business acumen and take advantage of merchant networks throughout the region.

Another regional migration phenomenon is migrant trafficking. This includes Nigerian women who feed the prostitution market in Europe and in Asia and children sold as slaves in the region or in Central Africa. It is estimated that several tens of thousands of child slaves currently work on West African plantations (ILO, 2002a, b).

Central Africa

Traditionally, migration in Central Africa has been limited by the dense vegetation and lack of roads in most countries of the region, which restricts mobility and opportunities for trade. The relatively scattered population distribution has also been a constraint. Traditionally, historical migration patterns in this region had various origins: religious factors; tribal expansion; the quest for food for survival; and spontaneous movements across artificial political borders inherited from the colonial era, which split up socio-economic entities and separated peoples.

Labour migration also plays an important role in Central Africa, albeit to a lesser extent than in West or Southern Africa. Up to the 1990s, skilled and unskilled foreign workers found employment in the mining industry in the former Zaire, as well as on the agricultural plantations of Cameroon or Equatorial Guinea. In both cases, expansion was financed by foreign capital.

Nowadays, the oil windfall and the lumber industry have transformed Gabon into a country of destination. It currently hosts the largest number of migrant workers in Central Africa. These workers come from the sub-region as well as from overseas. The discovery of oil deposits in Equatorial Guinea in the mid-1990s led to the creation of another centre of attraction.

But movements triggered by conflicts most characterize the region. More than anywhere else in Africa, the central region demonstrates the close links between migration and ethnic conflicts. The civil war and massacres in Rwanda

12) "Burkinabé immigrants flee persecution in Ivory Coast",
 Agence France Presse, 15 January 2001;
 "Many flee from Ivory Coast Attacks", *Associated Press,* 19 January 2001.

and Burundi displaced three million people. Civil strife in the Republic of the Congo uprooted countless Congolese. The conflict in DRC and its regional extension toward the Great Lakes generated massive flows of refugees and displaced persons within borders. Even though the DRC has also lost a good many of its highly qualified professionals through emigration, **textbox 12.5.** shows that they can return. At the same time, the DRC is host to Angolan refugees fleeing the civil war that has been ravaging their country for over 25 years now.

The breakdown of government authority in Central Africa has helped foster a climate of permanent instability in the region, making these forced population movements unlikely to end anytime soon.

East Africa

Like Central Africa, East Africa is one of the principal centres of refugee movements. Massive displacements of persons both within and outside borders have been caused by conflicts and civil wars, as well as environmental disasters in the Horn of Africa, first and foremost the persistent drought. The countries most affected are Eritrea, Ethiopia, Uganda, Somalia and the Sudan. **Textbox 12.6.** tells the story of a Sudanese girl who was relocated to a third country thanks to an IOM programme. Tanzania is one of the leading host countries for persons displaced by conflicts raging in Eastern Kasai, in Kivu (DRC), and in Rwanda and Burundi.

The predominance of refugees in East Africa does not preclude other types of migration. In the past, various factors have impacted migration in the region: the arrival of slave hunters and Arab and Asian traders due to the proximity of the ancient trade routes; barter; the development of export agriculture; the growth of the mining industry; the restrictions placed on the free movement of people after independence; and, finally, sporadic outbreaks of fighting between countries (e.g. Uganda and Tanzania; Ethiopia and Somalia; and Ethiopia and Eritrea).

The exodus of qualified professionals is also an important regional pattern. While Kenya was one of the main destinations for qualified Ugandan workers only a few years ago, the latter country is today feeding the brain drain to South Africa and overseas. Nevertheless, the situation in Uganda seems to be changing gradually with the return of many qualified Ugandan expatriates. Political stability and the

establishment of a dynamic private sector are among the reasons for this development.

The free movement of people enshrined in the COMESA Agreement (Common Market of Eastern and Southern Africa) may well increase in scope, as could similar arrangements governing the East African Community. The development of channels for the irregular migration of Ethiopian and Somali women to the Gulf States – either as labourers or to enter prostitution networks – is a recent phenomenon that could escalate further.

Southern Africa

By virtue of its strong economic position on the continent, Southern Africa traditionally experiences widespread migration movements because of major work opportunities in its mining, manufacturing and agriculture industries. The enclaves of industrial development in the region (South Africa, as well as Zimbabwe, Botswana and Zambia) have always been a powerful attraction for the abundant labour in overpopulated bordering regions (Malawi, Mozambique, Lesotho, Swaziland). These countries have been a source of labour migration flows for almost a century, based mainly on income disparities and the persistence of poverty.

Certain characteristics and mechanisms which typified labour migration in colonial southern Africa can be seen today in countries that have been economically and politically liberalized, alongside large-scale irregular migration streams. The nature of labour migration changed after the implementation of structural adjustment policies in most countries in the region, and as a result of the end of apartheid in South Africa (Weiss, 1999). Regulated during the colonial era, the migration of unskilled labourers has been gradually replaced by two distinct migratory flows: massive irregular migration and the migration of skilled workers. Income disparities among countries of the South African Development Community (SADC) have triggered brain drain, mainly to South Africa, Namibia and Botswana.

There are several reasons behind the recent threat to regional labour migration: growing xenophobia in certain countries; the lack of political will to reach an understanding on the regulation of flows among SADC member countries (see **textbox 8.2.**); and the recession, which forced many migrant miners to leave the South African mining industry. The return of thousands of miners to Lesotho from South Africa is one such example.

39

A further characteristic of regional migration is the flow of refugees and displaced persons within national borders. Until it was settled, the conflict in Mozambique generated large-scale population displacements and led to the creation of refugee camps in Zimbabwe, Malawi, Tanzania and South Africa. Ongoing strife in Angola has triggered one of the largest population displacements within the borders of any one country, as well as refugee streams to Zambia, Namibia and the DRC. Zambia is also sheltering numerous refugees who are victims of the conflict in the DRC and the Great Lakes region.

As the part of the world worst affected by HIV/AIDS, Southern Africa represents a particular challenge in relation to the linkage between migration and AIDS (see **chapter 5**). Infection rates could be as high as 40 per cent, especially in Botswana, Zambia and Zimbabwe.

TEXTBOX 2.2.

Update of IOM Activities and Service Areas

In 2001 and 2002, IOM programmes spanned the globe. Asia, and in particular Afghanistan, figured prominently in IOM's work. Even before the events of September 11, 2001, IOM was active in Afghanistan, managing camps for internally displaced persons in the north and west of the country. Since then it has set up programmes including an internal transport network to help displaced persons and refugees return to their homes; a programme to encourage qualified members of the Afghan diaspora to return; and transitional community development initiatives to stabilize returning populations and help rebuild the shattered economy.

Elsewhere in Asia, IOM continued to help a total of over 150,000 East Timorese refugees to return from West Timor in the run-up to the territory's independence in May 2002, in addition to implementing a variety of development programmes. In the Indian state of Gujarat, IOM's early response to the January 2001 earthquake translated into further projects with the Indian authorities and local NGOs to support migrant salt workers and their families affected by the disaster.

In recent years, IOM has been increasingly recognized as a key player in the post-conflict phase of the transition from emergency relief to long-term development. Programmes in areas such as returns, migrant's health, reintegration of refugees and displaced persons, registration for elections, community improvement projects, and grass roots governance have placed IOM on the global map of humanitarian assistance. The international community increasingly relies on IOM to bridge the relief to development gap.

IOM works to return and reintegrate demobilized soldiers into civilian life in post-conflict situations. Recent programmes have included initiatives in the Republic of Congo and East Timor. In the spring of 2002, IOM launched two similar programmes in Sierra Leone and Bosnia Herzegovina.

In March 2002, the IOM office in the Former Yugoslav Republic of Macedonia launched a programme funded by USAID/OTI to promote confidence building among diverse groups of Macedonian citizens. With a US$ 7 million grant from OTI, IOM is funding projects to support NGOs, the media, and local institutions that promote multiethnic cooperation.

IOM assists migrants, refugees, internally displaced persons, and other persons in need by providing a full range of migration assistance services. The objective is to foster orderly migration flows throughout the world by working with governments, the UN and other international organizations and NGOs.

IOM has defined several service areas that form the backbone of the Organization's expertise.

Movements: resettlement, repatriation and transportation assistance for migrants constitute the core IOM activities. Aspiring to provide the most efficient and humane movement service for migrants, governments and other implementing partners, IOM organizes safe and reliable transfer of individual migrants for resettlement, work, studies or any other purpose of orderly migration. Regular movement services include selection, processing, language training, orientation activities, medical examinations and various activities to facilitate integration. One of the most prominent movement programmes implemented by IOM on behalf of the United States Government since the early 1950s is the US Refugee Programme (USRP). In the last 45 years, IOM has assisted close to 5 million persons to start new lives in 24 countries of resettlement.

Labour Migration: IOM's activities are geared to assisting regulated and properly managed labour movements and programmes to support governments and migrants in the selection, recruitment, cultural orientation, training, travel, reception, integration and return of labour migrants.

Movements

Counter-trafficking

Labour migration

Assisted voluntary returns

41

Technical cooperation

German forced labour compensation programme

Mass information

Migration health

IOM carries out its activities in both countries of origin and countries of destination.

Technical Cooperation and Capacity-Building: governments are faced with a complex set of challenges when managing migration, particularly when it comes to irregular migration. They find themselves involved as origin, transit or destination countries of migration flows. IOM's technical cooperation on migration helps governments to develop the necessary legislation, administrative structures, knowledge, and the human resources to better manage migration and facilitates cooperation between countries.

Assisted Voluntary Returns: many migrants wish to return, at some point, to their country of origin. Others may have to return from a country of intended residence after being denied permission to stay by the authorities. Migrants should be able to return in safety and dignity; and their return should contribute to the social and economic development of their country of origin. IOM's assisted return activities include voluntary return programmes for individuals, and also migration diplomacy, with IOM acting as an independent and neutral broker and facilitator. Major voluntary return programmes for unsuccessful asylum seekers and other migrants in need have been put in place by IOM in countries such as: Belgium, Germany, Hungary, the Netherlands, Portugal, Switzerland and the United Kingdom. The IOM Constitution precludes any involvement in forced return (Art.1(d)).

Migration Health and Medical Services: movements of people involve important aspects of public health. Migrants and mobile populations may carry health characteristics of their place of origin to new destinations. Migration itself gives rise to vulnerability to certain medical and mental health problems. IOM has over time gathered considerable experience from medical screening of millions of migrants assisted by the Organization. Based on this experience, the IOM provides appropriate treatment and preventive health services to migrants, promotes and assists in the standardisation of immigration, travel and international health legislation/guidelines. IOM Medical Services offer support to training and education of staff involved in migration health care. The linkage between migration and HIV/AIDS is of particular concern to IOM. Emphasis is placed on research and programme development and implementation, with IOM working closely with UNAIDS.

Counter Trafficking: an increasing number of migrants are trafficked and/or smuggled worldwide every year generating large amounts of money for organised criminal networks. These networks misinform would-be migrants by exploiting their ignorance, often exposing them to physical harm and danger, economic despair, forced labour and vulnerability in destination countries. IOM contributes to the prevention of migrant trafficking and smuggling by providing factual information on the dangers of irregular migration. IOM also provides assistance to victims of trafficking by offering protection, counselling and voluntary return and reintegration. IOM's work in the fight against trafficking and smuggling also involves research, compilation of data, dissemination/exchange of information and experience, and assistance to governments to enhance their capacity to combat this phenomenon.

Mass Information: migrants as well as governments need to make migration-related decisions on the basis of accurate, reliable and timely information. Many people cross borders in an irregular fashion and make unjustified claims for asylum or residence because they are not aware of the actual situation and regulations, or requirements for regular migration. In countries of destination, IOM counters xenophobia and other forms of discrimination by giving the public unbiased and accurate information on migration issues. Based on thorough research, IOM develops efficient public information campaigns targeted and adapted to specific audiences, such as women and children who may be potential victims of traffickers.

Other global activities

Migration Policy and Research Programme: in response to requests from Member States, IOM launched the "Migration Policy and Research Programme" (MPRP) in March 2001. MPRP is designed to increase global understanding of migration issues and strengthen the capacity of governments to manage migration more effectively, to promote the positive aspects of migration and reduce irregular migration, particularly trafficking and exploitation of migrants, while promoting the protection of migrants' rights.

Compensation Programmes for Victims of Nazi Persecution: IOM was designated by the German Government to be a partner organization of the Federal Foundation handling claims and paying compensation to former forced and slave labourers under the Nazi regime. IOM is in charge of claims covering the so-called "rest of the world" category. This category comprises non-Jewish victims living anywhere in the world except in nine countries in Central and Eastern Europe, which are covered by other partner organizations. As of August 2002, more than 328,000 potential claimants had submitted their claims to IOM. Of these, 68,000 are deemed to be eligible under the German Foundation Act; over 22,000 have received compensation under the programme. In December 2000, IOM was also designated as an implementing organization of the Holocaust Victims Assets Programme, a claims programme designed to compensate victims of Nazi persecution arising out of litigation against Swiss banks.

Regional Consultative Processes: With increasing migration pressures, there is a greater need for effective migration management to ensure orderly migration. Thus, IOM has been fostering regional consultative processes for a number of years. These processes bring together government representatives, civil society and international organizations at a regional level to discuss migration-related issues in a cooperative spirit. These regional processes emphasise information exchange, confidence-building and technical cooperation. In February 2002, IOM took part in a regional conference on people smuggling and trafficking in Bali. Co-hosted by Indonesia and Australia, the two-day conference brought together 30 Ministers, IOM's Director General Brunson McKinley and high-level delegates from Asia Pacific and Middle East countries. The Bali Conference was the most significant gathering in Asia to address the subject of smuggling and trafficking since the 1999 Bangkok Symposium. IOM has convened similar processes in Africa (the Migration Dialogue for West Africa, the Migration Dialogue for Southern Africa).

Europe

During the 1990s, Europe became a continent of immigration. It took some time for states and a large part of public opinion to recognize this. Resenting the massive influx of people from poor countries, some countries still feel the need to preserve national identity. The European continent is now a destination for all categories of migrants the world over, as well as for refugees and asylum seekers.

The Commonwealth of Independent States (CIS)

Since 1989, the CIS has been witnessing major population movements. The former republics in the south have now become nation-states, leading to the departure of large numbers of Russians and Ukrainians. Apart from the repatriation of migrants from Armenia, Azerbaijan and Georgia, five million Russians returned to their native regions, the vast majority (75 per cent) from Central Asia and the Caucasus. Other migrants have returned to the Ukraine, Belarus or the Baltic States. Others have left for Germany (*Aussiedler*) or Israel (Jews).

The whole region has been affected by a variety of factors impacting migration patterns: ethnic conflict; civil strife (Chechnya); movements of refugees (for example between Afghanistan and bordering countries and between Armenia and Azerbaijan); labour migration in the form of chain migration from East to West (CIS nationals moving to Russia and from there to Europe); and the exodus of qualified professionals (especially Armenians, Russians and Ukrainians).

However, compared with the early 1990s, recorded migration flows have generally dropped in the CIS countries, because of stricter border controls. A recent IOM report outlines the most important current migration trends as follows (2002c):

• Russia remains by far the most important migration partner of countries in Eastern Europe and Central Asia, followed by Ukraine, Kazakhstan and Belarus;

• Kazakhstan has the largest flow of migrants and also accommodates the largest number of migrants from Central Asia;

• Populations in the Caucasus, the Republic of Moldova and Tajikistan, are continuing to leave their countries. **Textbox 13.1.** sums up the specific migration context in Caucasus countries;

• Resettlers from Russia, Ukraine and Belarus continue to be the main players in regular migration flows. Between 1998 and 2000, some 787,000 persons returned home from former Soviet Republics;

• More than 60 per cent of all the migrants are of working age. However, there are far more retirees and women among the emigrants than in previous years, which suggests that repatriation movements are ongoing.

A major migration problem in the Russian Federation is the growth of trafficking in women for sexual exploitation. A recent IOM study revealed that trafficking in Russian women has become a thriving industry in the space of a few years. This industry is currently among the main sources of revenue for organized crime in Russia.

43

IOM has drawn up an inventory of some forty countries of destination for victims. In 1997 alone, the US State Department estimates that over 100,000 women were victims of trafficking from the former Soviet Union (IOM, 2002b).

Although the whole region is affected by new forms of mobility, there has been no large-scale migration to the West for two reasons: the volume of intra-regional movements, and the buffer zone represented by countries in Central and Eastern Europe. With respect to transit migration, countries in Central Asia, the Russian Federation and the Caucasus have become major transit points for migrants from other regions, for example, South and East Asia.

The countries of Central and Eastern Europe (CEE)

Most of the EU candidate countries are found in Central and Eastern Europe[13]. Membership negotiations centre on these countries' ability to comply with EU obligations and to apply the so-called "acquis", a body of EU rules and regulations which includes provisions and instruments on migration (van Krieken, 2001).

Migrants from Poland constitute the largest component of migration flows from CEE countries to the EU. Ethnic migration has also been significant as some 700,000 *Aussiedler* [14] from the former USSR, Romania and Poland have arrived in Germany in recent years. In Germany this group now numbers 2 million people who have acquired German nationality by virtue of ancestral rights. Similarly, 300,000 Bulgarians of Turkish origin have returned to Turkey since 1989, while Finland has seen the return of ethnic Finns from the former USSR and the Baltic States. Migration to neighbouring countries (Romanians to Hungary, Czechs to Slovakia, Ukrainians to Poland or Bulgaria) is more significant than global migration in this region.

On January 1, 2002, Romania became associated with the Schengen area, prompting the migration of numerous people to the EU, many of them ethnic Roma. These migrants are often exploited by criminal networks involved in organized begging. The handicapped are frequently the main actors and victims in this human traffic. Freedom of movement in the Schengen area makes it impossible to estimate the number of people involved with any accuracy[15] (see also **textbox 14.3.**).

Officially there are 2.6 Roma in Europe; however, their leaders estimate the population at more than 6 million. The largest minorities are in Central and Eastern Europe, particularly in Romania (2,000,000), Bulgaria (800,000), Hungary (600,000), Slovakia (500,000), but also in Spain.

CEE countries represent a major crossroad for irregular migration. For example, about 40,000-50,000 irregular migrants pass through Bosnia-Herzegovina each year. Originating mainly from Turkey, Iran or China, they enter by land from Serbia or Montenegro[16] and attempt to reach the EU. The Balkans is also a major origin and transit region for the trafficking in women, though it is impossible to determine the exact number of women involved. IOM assistance programmes for victims of human trafficking in the Balkans, however, offer an insight into the scale of these flows. In 2000 and 2001, the IOM offices in the Balkans extended assistance to some 1,200 trafficking victims.

Migration policies stressing orderly migration do however exist in Central and Eastern Europe. Examples of efficient migration management policies include a successful labour migration programme between Albania and Italy (**textbox 13.3.**).

The European Union

Almost 19 million of the 370 million people residing in the fifteen EU countries are non-nationals, representing 5.1 per cent of the total population. Some 6 million are nationals of other EU Member States; the others are from non-Member States. These include roughly 3.5 million nationals from candidate countries (2.7 million Turks, 450,000 Poles and 160,000 Romanians); approximately 2 million citizens of the former Yugoslavia; and 500,000 citizens from other European countries, such as Russia and Albania (OECD, 2000; Eurostat, 2000).

13) These countries are Bulgaria, Estonia, Hungary, Latvia, Lithuania, Poland, Czech Republic, Romania, Slovakia, and Slovenia. There are three other candidate countries, namely Cyprus, Malta and Turkey.
14) These are "foreign Germans", i.e., former colonies of Germans who - in some cases over three centuries ago - settled to the east of Germany's eastern borders, mainly in Russia, Ukraine, Poland and the Baltic States.
15) *Le Monde*, 13 July 2002.
16) *IOM Notes for the Press*, 24 April 2002.

Some 2.3 million nationals from North African countries (1.2 million Moroccans, 700,000 Algerians, and 300,000 Tunisians) are resident in the EU, mostly in France (90 per cent of the Algerians and 70 per cent of the Tunisians). Moroccan nationals are distributed throughout several EU countries, primarily France, Spain, Italy, Germany. **Textbox 13.2.** analyses migration dynamics in the Western Mediterranean, which links the Maghreb countries to south-west Europe. One million sub-Saharan Africans are distributed between the United Kingdom (27 per cent), France (23 per cent), Germany (12 per cent) and Portugal (9 per cent).

Asians have settled mainly in the United Kingdom, including 25,000 Indians and 185,000 Pakistanis. An estimated 170,000 Chinese live in the EU and 400,000 Latin American nationals have settled mainly in Spain and Portugal. Finally, records indicate that there are over 400,000 North Americans and 100,000 nationals from Oceania-Pacific living in the European Union.

An extremely large mobile population must be added to these figures - tourists, students, traders, business people, asylum seekers and irregular migrants. While the number of Europeans resident in an EU country other than their own has not increased significantly over the past two decades, the number of nationals from third countries increased from 2.3 per cent in 1985 to 3.5 per cent in 2000 (OECD, 2000).

These foreign populations are unevenly distributed among European countries (Eurostat, 2000; OECD, 2000; Withol de Wenden, 2001; United Nations, 2002). With 7.3 million resident foreigners and 9 per cent of the population foreign, Germany is by far Europe's leading country of immigration. It is followed by France with 6.2 million foreigners, representing 10.6 per cent of the population. Next on the list are the United Kingdom (4 million foreigners or 6.8 per cent of the total population); Switzerland[17] (1.8 million foreigners or 25 per cent of the total population); Italy (1.6 million foreigners representing 2.8 per cent of the total population); Spain (1.2 million foreigners representing 3.2 per cent of the total population). Austria, Belgium, Denmark, Finland, Greece, Ireland, Luxembourg, the Netherlands, Portugal and Sweden each host less than a million foreigners. Former countries of emigration such as Italy and Spain have now become countries of immigration. To some extent each country has its "own foreigners" as a result of colonial heritage, privileged and often bilateral links or geographic proximity to the countries concerned.

Certain nationalities can therefore be found in large numbers in a single host country, e.g., 97 per cent of Algerians in Europe live in France, as do 75 per cent of Tunisians and Portuguese, and 50 per cent of Moroccans. Germany for its part hosts 68 per cent of all Polish immigrants in Europe, 80 per cent of Greeks, 72 per cent of Turks and 68 per cent of former Yugoslavs. The United Kingdom receives most immigrants from Ireland and the Commonwealth. Other migrant populations are spread through various European countries. They include Turks, with the largest numbers in Europe (more than 2 million), followed by Moroccans (1.5 million), Yugoslavs (1 million) and Italians (600,000), not including those who have acquired the nationality of their host country. Sixty per cent of foreigners who have settled in Europe have been resident for over 10 years; in most European countries, this 60 per cent comes from only 4 countries of origin (Turkey, Morocco, Italy and the former Yugoslavia).

Finally, the features of intra-European mobility are still relatively unknown; the largest number of intra-European migrants are located in Luxembourg, followed by Ireland, Belgium, Portugal, Sweden, Spain and Greece. In Western Europe, on the other hand, the number of foreigners from third countries has increased over the past 20 years with some nationalities gaining in importance: migrants in Germany from Central and Eastern Europe; Moroccans and Senegalese in France; former Yugoslavs in the Netherlands or in Switzerland. Also new nationalities are entering the migration landscape, including Afghans, Iraqis, Vietnamese, Iranians, Sri Lankans and Chinese, suggesting changes in the origin and nature of migration flows. The scale and characteristics of irregular migration in Schengen countries are illustrated in **textbox 13.4.**

Shifting migration paradigms in Europe

Europe has difficulty in seeing itself as a continent of migration. Many EU states are concerned about their national identities and obsessed by the notion of migration risk, which they perceive as a challenge. During the 1970s, most European countries believed that the era of mass international migration had ended. This was borne out by the suspension of the flows of foreign labour in 1973 and 1974 during the oil crisis; the mooting of the topic of a new international division of labour; and repatriation policies in Germany, France and the Netherlands, which only had a minimal impact.

17) Switzerland is not a member country of the European Union.

In addition to ongoing traditional streams (mainly family migration as the main avenue of legal entry), more diversified sources emerged: an influx of asylum seekers; greater labour immigration; the feminization of migration; and intra-European mobility.

Current migration policy in Europe is caught between European and individual national approaches to integration. This in turn has led to a lack of synchronization between the major migration trends to Europe and the implementation of a strong security-based European area for immigration and asylum (De Lobkovicz, 2002). **Chapter 14** reviews and analyses EU migration policy. As migration evolves with globalization, immigration policy frameworks begin to encompass more and more actors (European institutions, states, as well as employers and non-governmental organizations), the Union is pressing ahead with its policy of community-wide decisions, based mainly on border controls. Europe is adapting as best it can to emerging migratory flows given the plethora of transnational networks, the demand for labour and predicted population ageing and decline.

Under pressure from public opinion to take a firm stand on border controls, European countries must also meet labour requirements in order to take account of demographic trends and to comply with international undertakings on human rights, commitment to dialogue and co-development with the countries of origin; see also **textbox 14.1.** on the Cotonou Agreement between the EU and countries in Africa, the Caribbean and the Pacific (ACP). Many EU countries opt for compromise rather than any radical questioning of their migration policies. Chapter 13 is dedicated to new migration policies in some European countries facing population decline.

In concluding the Spanish presidency of the European Union for the first half of 2002, the Seville Summit made virtually no decisive progress on the thorny issue of immigration, despite the electoral successes of far right parties in several European countries. The subject finally gave rise to disagreement on UK and Spanish proposals for sanctions to be applied to countries outside the Union which fail to curb irregular immigration. France and Sweden opposed the proposal. Finally, it was decided that the Union would cooperate with third countries to combat irregular immigration, though without withholding development aid from recalcitrant countries. The development of a common corps of border guards proposed by the EU Commission is not currently being discussed. Subsequent negotiations on asylum and immigration policy have been referred to the ministries of justice and home affairs in member countries together with a clear timetable. **Textbox 14.2.** provides further details on the conclusions of the Seville Summit.

THEMATIC SECTION

MANAGING MIGRATION CHALLENGES AND RESPONSES FOR PEOPLE ON THE MOVE

51

INTRODUCTION

Why and How to Manage Migration?

In the traditional viewpoint, migrants move across borders and barriers in search of a better life both pushed by lack of opportunities at home and pulled by the hope of economic gain and freedom abroad; in the process, they often risk their savings, health and even their lives. This analysis is still relevant today.

Increasingly, however, a new supplemental or alternative view is emerging - that migration has a life of its own. In a world characterized by vastly improved transport facilities and global networks for the production and exchange of goods, services and information, the world's population is increasingly mobile. International movement of people is now a firmly established feature of modern life. In an increasingly integrated international labour market and economy, migration has now become an integral part of the phenomenon commonly referred to as globalization.

As international migration increases in scale, its economic, social, cultural and political impact also increases in tandem with policy implications in these areas in most of the world's states. As a result, new responses are needed to achieve and maintain the orderly movement of people in a global society that is increasingly committed to mobility.

Migration can be a constructive economic and social force, bringing about a dynamic labour force, economy and community, and rich cultural diversity. For countries with ageing populations and economic difficulties, the benefits of migration are particularly notable. Immigrants are willing to move to areas with possible labour shortages. Migrants often bring skills that may be scarce in many destination countries: highly-qualified engineers or medical doctors, but also labourers in agriculture, construction or other lower skilled fields. Also, taxes paid by immigrants often exceed the costs of social, health and welfare benefits to which they have access.

But migration can also have negative consequences and associations: trafficking and smuggling, irregular migration, security, and xenophobia and racism. The positive aspects of migration can be obscured by these and other potential negative manifestations. In recent years, xenophobia has found a political platform in many anti-immigration political

parties worldwide. In addition, the security implications of migration have gained considerable attention since September 11, 2001.

As societies become more and more affected by migration, the central challenge is how to manage migration to maximize its positive effects and minimize potentially negative results. States are increasingly looking to **migration management** to reap the potential gains of migration without incurring too many of its potential costs.

Historically, governments have reacted to changing migratory trends and pressures in an ad hoc way, responding to the "issue of the day", often without considering the broader implications. For instance, although effective, greater controls have often had the secondary effect of pushing more people into the hands of smugglers. This in turn has led to exploitation and trafficking, and to growing insecurity because of links to organized crime, violence and corruption. In another example, a focus on asylum management to the exclusion of a more comprehensive approach to migration has resulted in distortion of the asylum system in many countries and its misuse for migration-related purposes.

More and more governments recognize that a uni-dimensional approach to migration creates problems. There is a growing awareness that contemporary migration can no longer be treated in isolation but must be managed more comprehensively. While irregular and other abusive forms of migration must be prevented and curtailed, most migration, if properly managed, can be positive for individuals and societies and is indeed necessary in today's global world. However, migration cannot be managed in isolation; like other aspects of globalization, migration is more manageable when countries work together.

The Migration Process

Migration is a dynamic process. Every migration process includes different stages: the impetus for migration (i.e., root causes - the push and pull factors, forced or voluntary); the movement from origin to destination; entry into another country (either by regular or irregular means, and either facilitated - legally or illegally - or spontaneous); settlement and/or return; integration and/or reintegration; and ultimately, in some cases, the acquisition of nationality.

A number of offshoot relationships occur, including the potential contribution that a diaspora can make to the growth and economic development of their countries of origin as well as cross-cutting themes such as protection, health or security.

The stages of the migration process are interlinked, involving a variety of actors, partnerships and policy considerations at different levels and to varying degrees. Participants in the contemporary migration process include such diverse public and private individuals and institutions as employers, family members, community organizations, government migration managers, international organizations, NGOs, smugglers, traffickers and other criminal elements. The migration process includes complex relationships between the migrant, the country of destination and the country of origin as regards rights and obligations. In addition, migration has broader linkages to policy in the economic, social, environment, trade, labour, health, cultural and security domains. In this regard "it will be important to recognize those areas where, and under what conditions, migration can contribute to economic, cultural and social development as well as those areas where it does not"[1].

Ideally, law and policy makers should take potential migration implications into account when making decisions in major policy areas; further, the interplay of the factors outlined above should be considered in migration-related decisions. Cooperation and information-sharing among the various actors are therefore central to achieving a migration strategy that is comprehensive and coherent – a key theme underpinning the concept of migration management. Rather than addressing migration in a reactive way, migration policies and approaches need to be proactive in order to be effective and sustainable over time.

At the same time, migration management partnerships and international cooperation might benefit from some basic shared understandings, including the following: properly managed migration should benefit migrants and societies; legal migration should be encouraged and irregular migration discouraged; all migrants should be entitled to protection of their fundamental human rights.

1) See: IOM (1995). *IOM Strategic Planning: Toward the Twenty-First Century*, MC/1842, 9 May, para.11.

TEXTBOX T.1.

IOM's Concept of Migration Management

In general, migration management is an overarching term referring to the range of measures needed to effectively address migration issues at national, regional and global levels. It encompasses policy, legislation and administration of migration issues, and contributes to good governance.

IOM's concept of migration management relates to the shaping of clear and comprehensive policies, laws and administrative arrangements to ensure that population movements occur to the mutual benefit of migrants, society and governments.

Mutual benefits can be achieved through policies, laws and administrations that balance the rights and obligations of migrants with social interests and government responsibilities. Given the transnational nature of migration, this endeavour naturally has national, regional and global ramifications, and thus requires close cooperation among all players. Since migration is also inextricably linked to other major policy issues such as trade, development, security, environment, health and economics, these issues should be taken into account in management efforts.

IOM headquarters in Geneva

Unregulated migration can often have financial and political costs for the and government, at any point on the i.e., for the country of origin, tra Comprehensive, transparent and coh migration will help minimize those " the integrity of migration as a natural

53

A Comprehensive and Cooperative Migration Management Approach

The challenges of effective migration management include finding and maintaining a balance among measures addressing various migration-related issues, without improving one sphere to the detriment of another. Identifying the essential components of a national migration policy is one important step in developing a strategy to manage migratory flows. Beyond that, policy should aim at taking into account the impact of single components on the others and, as far as possible, integrating them into a comprehensive unit.

Any discussion on the elements of a managed migration approach would need to take into consideration a comprehensive set of issues, including the following:

- opportunities for legal migration (including labour migration programmes to alleviate demographic pressures, open up labour markets and to facilitate financial remittances to needy countries of origin);
- effective border management (for border security, protection against crime, combating of irregular migration and especially trafficking and smuggling, and maintaining the integrity of the asylum system);
- understanding the link between migration and health;
- integration and participation of migrants in the host society;
- facilitation and promotion of voluntary return of persons unable or unwilling to remain in host countries (including sustainable reintegration of returnees);
- recognition and respect of the rights of migrants and refugees;
- building bridges between diasporas and home countries so they can contribute to development efforts; and
- programmes to address "root causes" of migration (including targeting of international trade, investment and development aid to facilitate development in countries of origin).

It is not easy to adopt a comprehensive approach to migration management given its multidimensional nature. On the contrary, a number of necessary preconditions are required, which must be progressively developed through cooperation and coordination at national and international levels. Any discussion of methods to ensure effective application of the key elements of migration management should consider:

Increased Coordination among Government Agencies Concerned

Work towards a systematic approach to migration management begins at national level. Without rationalization **within** a state, there will be little progress **among** states. Often, migration-related issues are managed with relatively little or even no coordination among concerned government agencies within the same government. Typically, ministries of the interior or justice deal with entry control issues; ministries of foreign affairs handle humanitarian issues; ministries of social affairs are responsible for integration, etc. A comprehensive approach would consider the implications and impact of certain policies vis-à-vis others, requiring coordination and partnerships among all relevant government agencies.

International Cooperation

Given the international nature of migration, national migration strategies developed in isolation are unlikely to yield effective results. Thus, a sine qua non condition for effective international migration management is inter-state cooperation. This tendency is clearly highlighted by the growing number of regional consultative processes on migration emerging in all of the world's regions. These cooperative mechanisms focus on sharing of information, discussions and strategizing with a view to enhancing migration by adopting common approaches and even harmonized migration policies in some cases.

Inclusion of all Actors Involved in the Policy-Making Process

A comprehensive approach should consider migration issues from all perspectives, with relevant government and non-government partners. Migration's interrelationship with other cross-cutting issues should be recognized. Therefore, a comprehensive approach to migration should include a wide range of stakeholders who need to become involved – including governments, international organizations, NGOs, employers, community organizations, migrants, etc.

Access to Migration-Related Information

It is important that all actors involved in the migration process have access to consistent and unambiguous information on roles, rights, procedures and expectations. For example, migrants should be made aware of legal migration opportunities in order to limit the incidence of migrant trafficking and smuggling. To reduce the incidence of xenophobia and discrimination in host societies, migrants should understand and comply with local laws, and migrant-hosting societies should be made aware of the positive contributions migrants can make to their communities, thereby enhancing social cohesion.

Statistics Standards Regarding Migration

The availability of meaningful data on migration stocks and flows is a key element of effective migration management. At present, much of the statistical and documentary information required for sound decision-making is not available or does not reach policy makers. In addition, information is not shared among governments, partly because information provision and requirements vary from country to country. Reliable data is essential for monitoring flows and understanding trends as a basis for policy and programme development and cooperation. For the first time, the statistics section at the end of this volume attempts to collect and present such data in a comprehensive way.

What to expect from the 2003 World Migration Report

The phenomenon of international migration brings into play many sensitive issues connected with national security and identity, social change and cultural adaptation, and resource allocation and management. These issues and their linkages represent important challenges to migration policy makers. Policy choices made now will help determine whether migration will be managed in the future to maximize its benefits, or whether it will increasingly be a source of concern, potential social destabilization and friction among states. The ultimate key is not to prevent mobility but to better manage it.

Based on these premises, the thematic section of the World Migration Report approaches migration management from the two complementary angles of general policy issues and specific geographic application.

Authored by a number of international experts in the field of migration, representing the International Organization for Migration but also a variety of other actors involved in tackling, managing and reflecting upon the phenomenon, the different chapters and textboxes analyse migration management strategies at work. The thematic section does not claim to cover all facets of migration, but focusses on a few priority areas. The contributions usefully combine operational practice and experience with academic reflection in order to give credibility to any position taken in the Report.

In its **first part,** the thematic section considers major **generic policy issues of migration** management. These include approaches to reducing the incidence of irregular migration, such as border management; migration and health; integration of migrants in host societies; regional consultative processes; the management of the phenomenon of internally displaced persons; and the link between migration and asylum.

The **second part** explores various **aspects of migration management in different parts of the world.** It examines successes and failures of certain migration management approaches before presenting some key elements that have proven their efficiency and efficacy, and that could contribute to the establishment of a more systematic, global approach to the phenomenon. Emphasis is placed on issues that are of particular interest to governments and migrants in the different regions under discussion, for example: orderly migration programmes in countries built on immigration (Australia, Canada, New Zealand, and the United States); consensual migration policies in Latin America; labour migration mechanisms in Asia; cross-linkages between brain drain, labour migration and remittances in Africa; demographic changes and the development of a common immigration policy in Europe.

MIGRATION MANAGEMENT AT WORK

SELECTED POLICY ISSUES

57

CHAPTER 3

Ways to Curb the Growing Complexities of Irregular Migration

Migration has rarely been more prominent in national and international discussions than in the past year or two. At some point, migration themes all converge on the issue of irregular migration[1] and shed light on ongoing efforts on how best to address this phenomenon.

This chapter will not attempt to recount the many discussion points or changes in policy or practice planned or implemented. It will rather draw upon them to illustrate the contention that edges between regular and irregular migration have not always been clear, and that increased clarity in policy and practice is needed if irregular migration, and its pernicious subset of trafficking, is to be curtailed. Further, the chapter makes the case that the overall migration project of the past two years, if only *de facto* in nature, has been to create just such clarity: to draw lines of distinction between regular and irregular migration that have practical effect – that, in sum, make migration more manageable.

Characteristics of Irregular Migration[2]

It can be helpful to think of irregular migration as a broad category that includes various kinds of movements, including some that, while possibly in conflict with migration laws or regulations when they occur, are nonetheless deemed to be acceptable and justifiable by the receiving state, such as:

• persons later judged to be *bona fide* refugees who were compelled to migrate to a country of safe haven and who, in the process, contravene migration laws and regulations;

• persons who are logistically compelled to cross the nearest safe border without proper clearance while fleeing massive disruptions such as war and natural disaster; some may prove to be *bona fide* refugees at a later time, others may not; and,

• depending on the legislation and policy of a receiving country, a person who is being exploitatively trafficked into or through a country. For example Italy, Belgium,

The Netherlands and the United States of America have recently enacted special protective legislation for trafficked women, including women who entered or remained in their countries irregularly. In certain circumstances these trafficking victims will be considered legitimate within the country, even if they have violated entry or residence laws.

The definition of irregular migration has an even more complex dimension: while persons are often categorized as irregular due to the manner in which they entered or remained in a country of destination or transit, some migrants may be irregular in their countries of origin as well. For example, some countries restrict outward travel by certain segments of their citizenry to external destinations. Some Asian countries prohibit the emigration of women of a certain age to become domestic workers abroad. Others may prohibit labour migrants from leaving without completing certain registration procedures. Migrants who contravene these requirements may be considered irregular in their origin countries, whether or not they are considered irregular in the transit or destination countries.

Scale of Irregular Migration

There are inadequate data on the number of irregular migrants; precise figures on irregular migrants are as elusive as the routes and mechanisms for irregular migration itself. Commonly used data and assumptions include the following points[3].

• Irregular immigrants account for one-third to one-half of new entrants into developed countries, which is an increase of 20 per cent over the past ten years.

• According to high-end estimates, the United States may now be host to as many as twelve million irregular migrants. For perspective, this figure equals the total

---

1) In view of consistency in using terminology, throughout this text "irregular migration" incorporates the various appellations of this specific type of migration, including "clandestine migration", "illegal migration", "undocumented migration". See also **chapter 1** on migration terminology.

2) Much of the following discussion is drawn by Ghosh (1998) and OECD (2000).

3) Figures and assumptions in the following discussion are drawn from a number of sources, including: National Foreign Intelligence Board (2001), United Kingdom Home Department (2002) and United States Immigration and Naturalization Service.

IOM information campaign in Peru

number of migrants processed at Ellis Island in the first sixty years of its operation – through the early 1950s. Up to 4,000 migrants successfully enter the United States every day in an irregular fashion and up to 1.5 million aliens are arrested on the United States-Mexico border annually (many repeatedly).

• Within the European Union, irregular immigration was estimated to be approximately 500,000 persons per year in 1999, a nine-fold increase over a period of six years (National Foreign Intelligence Board, 2001)[4]. Asylum-seekers totalled nearly 400,000 in 2000. With approval rates declining, many rejected asylum seekers go underground, while others opt for an irregular entry route outside the asylum system from the start. Approximately one million irregular migrants applied for amnesties or regularization during the last five years – a reasonable reference point for assessing the scale of the phenomenon. Another indicator is the number of persons detected trying to evade border control, which in the United Kingdom alone has risen from 3,300 in 1990 to over 47,000 in 2000.

• Despite the significant numbers of incoming migrants in Europe and North America, it is the less developed countries in Asia and Sub-Saharan Africa that host the greatest number of migrants, and whose resources and governance systems are most challenged in the process.

Clear global migration and irregular migration are increasing and attempts at irregular migration are increasing exponentially. Immigration now accounts for approximately 65 percent of population growth in the OECD countries – up from approximately 45 percent during the mid-1990s, and still on the rise (National Foreign Intelligence Board, 2001). Strong supply lines, surging demand, limited regular migration schemes and inconsistent approaches and capacities for control and enforcement – all these factors mean there is fertile ground for criminal enterprises to step in and facilitate the movements. While irregular migration can and does occur without the aid of facilitators, smuggling and trafficking are major criminal enterprises that fuel and facilitate the irregular movement of persons, often with strong elements of exploitation and abuse.

Migrant Smuggling[5]

Migrant smuggling is now a ten billion US$ a year growth industry[6], serving approximately half of the irregular migrants worldwide. The United Kingdom estimates that over 75 percent of its illegal entrants used the services of smugglers[7]. Well-tuned to market economics and with operational flexibility insufficiently constrained by legal mechanisms, these smuggling groups offer a range of services to the various consumers. An organized illegal trip from Morocco to Spain is possible for as little as US$ 500, while more elaborate passages and border crossing from Asia to the United States may cost above US$ 50,000[8]. As conditions for operations change, so do the routes and prices. Following the crackdown on the United States-Mexico border after September 11, 2001, demand for smuggling apparently decreased with the recognition that interdiction was more likely. In response, smugglers are reported to have slashed prices by half, down to US$ 600 for a trip across the border and into Phoenix, Arizona[9].

The implications of smuggling operations extend beyond the numbers of migrants served and the resultant imbalance in immigration planning scenarios. Given the vast amounts of money involved, such operations erode normal governance and present real challenges and threats to national sovereignty. Efforts at more representational and democratic governance in developing countries and countries in transition are undercut by the presence of such networks, as they entwine themselves with official government structures and representatives, or push these into marginal positions. From the public perspective and operational realities, this process undermines government ability to control their borders and their interior management functions. An increasingly common outcome is the call to limit or stop migration through stronger measures, as attempts to reasonably manage the process appear continually unsuccessful.

4) Additional figures on irregular migration into Europe can be found in **textbox 13.4**.
5) Reference is made here to the definition of smuggling as included in the Protocol Against the Smuggling of Migrants by Land, Sea and Air, which supplements the United Nations Convention Against Transnational Organized Crime, adopted in November 2000 (see also **chapter 1**).
6) United States Department of State (2001).
7) United Kingdom Home Department (2002).
8) Further details on smuggling fares can be found in the **chapter 17**.
9) National Public Radio (2002). *Strangers at the Gates*. All Things Considered, Special Report, 30 January.

Trafficking in Persons[10]

IOM information campaigns in Romania

Due to the interplay of various issues and disparate definitions it is difficult to establish estimates of human trafficking. Issues such as the lack of registration and control systems, the illegal and clandestine nature of these movements and the low rate of denunciation by victims complicate and cloud quantitative data.

Rough estimates suggest some 700,000 persons, especially women and children, are trafficked each year across international borders[11], and approximately 120,000 trafficked into the EU yearly, mostly through the Balkans[12]. Some observers estimate that the numbers may be significantly higher. According to the Swedish NGO, Kvinna Till Kvinna, an "estimated 500,000 women from over the world are trafficked each year into Western Europe alone. A large proportion of these come from the former Soviet Union countries"[13].

The defining variable of trafficking in persons is the violation of the migrant's human rights. Trafficking affects mainly, but not exclusively, women and children. They are most frequently trafficked for sexual abuse or/and labour exploitation, though they sometimes end up falling into begging, delinquency, adoptions, false marriages or trade of human organs. Victims of trafficking are exposed to physical and psychological violence and abuse, denied labour rights, are illegal before the law and are often found in a forced and unwanted relationship of dependency with their traffickers. This dependency normally results from the financial debt incurred vis-à-vis the trafficker to pay for migration and placement services.

Trafficked migrants are prompted to migrate for the same reasons as many other migrants: the possibility to improve their living and working conditions; to escape from poverty;

lack of opportunities; violation of human rights; violence and civil strife; persecution; discrimination and ecological disasters. However, in the context of migration management, trafficking in persons is mainly, but not exclusively, caused by the lack of appropriate employment opportunities in the countries of origin.

Trafficking is different from smuggling, although abuse and violence can occur in both circumstances. Trafficking, however, amplifies many of the problems linked with irregular migration overall. Like other forms of irregular migration, it poses great challenges to states, governments, institutions and individuals. These challenges arise equally in countries of origin, transit and destination. States involved are often in a conflict situation due to lack of border control, unequal treatment of irregular migrants, and migrants' exploitation in countries of destination. This can be further aggravated when trafficking victims are detained in the country of destination or transit. Pointing the finger at countries of transit for allowing irregular migrants to transit can also cause diplomatic tensions. Clearly, cohesive or complementary migration legislation, regulation and operational procedures in regions affected by irregular migration can help defuse such situations[14].

10) As defined in the Protocol to Prevent, Suppress and Punish Trafficking in Persons which supplements the UN Convention Against Transnational Organized Crime, adopted in November 2000 (see also **chapter 1**).
11) United States Department of State (2001).
12) UNICEF *et al.* (2002).
13) Kvinnaforum (1999). *Crossing Borders against Trafficking in Women and Girls. A Resource Book for Working against Trafficking in the Baltic Sea.* Stockholm – quoted by UNICEF *et al.* (2002).
14) The Council of the European Union has adopted in 2002 a Framework Decision for the adoption and approximation of anti-trafficking legislation among EU Member and candidate States.

TEXTBOX 3.1.

A Migrant's Story – The Human Tragedy of Trafficking in Migrants from the Dominican Republic to Argentina

Like thousands of young girls before her, Alex believed in someone who promised to introduce her to "a person" who could help her find a job.

Back home after one year in hell Alex wipes away a tear and recalls, "She was my neighbour, I trusted her. She said this was a good lady who would help me."

Alex was introduced to a Dominican woman living in Argentina who immediately promised her a job as a domestic in her own home. Young, naïve and extremely poor, Alex accepted her offer. She paid 2,500 Dominican Pesos (US$ 145) for a passport and visa and a few days later was on a plane, with another 17 year-old girl, bound for Buenos Aires.

"The same day we arrived the lady told us things were bad and that she had no money. She took us to an apartment and left us there. There were other girls living there and many men coming in and out. We had no idea what kind of place this was." She soon realized the house was used for prostitution. Finally, hunger and fear got the best of her.

"The woman told me I owed her US$ 2,500 for the airfare and that I could not leave until I had paid her back. I was forced to have sex with nine to 12 men each day. When I asked her for something to eat, she said, 'ask the customers for tips and buy your own food'. I cried myself to sleep every night."

Three months later, the girl who had travelled with Alex managed to escape. This prompted the trafficker to increase surveillance on the rest of the girls. The woman threatened the girls by saying she would sell them to a man who owned a nightclub on the outskirts of the city. "I could not see a way out. I was so scared. I had no money, not even to call home. I had no passport, because it had been taken away. Many times I thought about committing suicide. Oh God how I prayed for a way out."

Alex's prayers were answered when a woman who visited the apartment saw her mental and physical health deteriorating and promised to help her. "The first thing this woman did for me was call my sister and arrange for her to call me at a time when the trafficker would not be in the apartment.

When I was on the phone with my sister, the trafficker's daughter arrived, grabbed the phone out of my hand and beat me."

Again the lady came to her rescue and arranged for her to escape and run to the police. After speaking with the police and testifying against the trafficker, Alex was referred to a lawyer who contacted the IOM office in Buenos Aires. Immediately, travel documents were arranged and Alex returned home two weeks after escaping from her captor.

But what's next for a 17 year old girl with a tainted reputation and a third grade education?

As Alex recounts her story, she avoids eye contact. "I'm suffering from depression, I can't seem to stop crying. I'm running a fever and have had a headache for the past week. I need to see a doctor." One of IOM's partners in the Dominican Republic is COIN, *Centro de Orientación e Investigación Integral,* a local NGO that provides health care and counselling for victims of trafficking.

Francisca Ferreira runs the education and information department of COIN. She has seen hundreds of girls return home in the same situation - penniless, physically ill and mentally broken. "Our young people are seeing a world on the Internet and on television filled with things they want. It's normal to want a better life. This pushes the boys into the drug trade and the girls into prostitution. Hundreds of persons have come to our office asking for help in tracing lost relatives. Once, we traced a young girl to a jail in Mexico. Not only was she duped with a bogus job offer in Mexico, she was obliged to carry drugs for the traffickers."

As part of an awareness raising information campaign being carried out by IOM, COIN and the State Secretariat for Women, trained workers visit communities with a high rate of emigration to warn potential victims of the risks of irregular migration. Television and radio spots are also spreading the message. The programme also distributes small booklets with instructions and contact details for Dominican embassies throughout the world, as well as photo booklets recounting the experiences of girls who managed to break free from their captives.

Juan Artola, Chief of the IOM Mission in the Dominican Republic says, "In the past few years Argentina had become the new destination for trafficked Dominican women. In February 2002 we began receiving information confirming the dramatic situation of some 5,000 Dominican women currently in Argentina. This coincided with the economic crisis in that country, so many migrants are desperate to return home." Artola adds, "We have to determine what exploitation mechanisms are in place so that we can counteract accordingly. Legislation must be prepared to enable the authorities to find the criminals, arrest them and bring them to justice."

Following discussion of the problem in newspapers and television, the Ministry of Foreign Affairs initiated an investigation and is seeking support for the return of the victims.

IOM is also working with the Dominican Inter-institutional Committee for the Protection of Migrant Women (CIPROM by its Spanish acronym), which gathers five public institutions and 12 local NGOs and has put trafficking as the main point in its agenda.

IOM, the Government, NGOs and the United Nations Population Fund (UNFPA), all agree that the fight against trafficking of Dominican women has just begun. According to Artola, "We may not be able to nip this in the bud right away, but we must be ready to provide return and reintegration assistance to all of the women anxious to return home."

Gina Gallardo of the State Secretariat for Women is adamant about fighting and beating the traffickers. "We must pressure the authorities to visit the travel agencies involved in this illegal traffic. These people need to know they will not be allowed to act with impunity. The law needs to be modified to include sanctions for the trafficking of women for sexual exploitation."

In the first six months of 2002, IOM and the Dominican Government assisted 44 women to return from Argentina. IOM estimates that as many as 1,000 may need urgent assistance to return home. At the same time, it is estimated that there are over 60,000 Dominican women living in Spain, Italy, France, the Netherlands, Austria, Germany and Switzerland.

One of the most serious internal problems for a society plagued by trafficking is that these migration flows are often organized by international criminal organizations. The presence of crime syndicates explains the increase of criminal activities of all types, including sexual exploitation of women and children, forced prostitution, drug abuse and an overall feeling of insecurity for the local population.

Trafficking is also an abuse and violation of national legislation and international covenants. With respect to migration legislation, a trafficking victim is also a migrant who has not respected the migration laws of the host country either by entering without necessary documents and through non-controlled entry situations or by overstaying in the host country beyond the legal timeframe. Obviously, these are matters of national concern and control by national authorities. Irregular migrants violate labour laws by working without the required permission of national labour authorities.

Corruption among government officials is one of the ways the trafficking system maintains itself. Officials receive money from the traffickers in order to tolerate or ignore their illicit activities. This may occur at all levels of a given society in developed and developing countries.

Patterns of trafficking in persons vary according to the regions, and change rapidly in relation to market demands and obstacles traffickers may face. Despite the fact that the countries of the European Union and the United States of America continue to be preferred targets for traffickers and victims, movements within the same region, such as in South East Asia (Cambodia, Vietnam, Myanmar and Thailand) or in South Asia (Nepal, Bangladesh and India) or among countries in West Africa, have become increasingly significant. Also, trafficking between countries in different continents is increasing: IOM has assisted women from Peru and Colombia, who had been trafficked to Korea, Thailand and Japan, as well as women from Moldova and Romania trafficked to Cambodia.

Recent Management Trends

Both enforcement and facilitation strategies have taken on new energy in the past year or two. Certainly in the aftermath of September 11, 2001, enforcement actions for pre-clearance abroad, controls at the border, and internal measures, have been particularly strengthened.

Off-Shore Approaches

At the pre-clearance stages, airlines and airport authorities are being held to stricter criteria in passenger screening, some of which attends to travel authorization within the framework of heightened general security. Additionally, efforts to reduce irregular flows before they reach the destination border are being strengthened, though most of these efforts were initiated well before September 11.

Some EU countries are strengthening the presence of Airline Liaison Officers and Immigration Officers abroad, the latter in a manner similar to the US INS Global Reach Programme. Visa regimes are under review with higher standards being implemented to qualify for non-visa status. Various other mechanisms for pre-screening passengers prior to allowing travel are under study, and the inclusion of biometric identification data in various parts of the travel identity and clearance system is being seriously considered.

Border Management Approaches

At border points in many countries, but particularly in North America, intensified procedures are evident, at times backed up with more technology. The United States now requires its border agents to personally question every would-be entrant, or each vehicle, rather than sampling approximately 5 percent of travellers as before September 11.

In Europe, various kinds of scanners and new technology to detect concealed persons attempting to cross borders illegally are being deployed. In response to the mobile and multi-faceted nature of immigration fraud, in what is termed intelligence-led control, the United Kingdom is strengthening mobile immigration intelligence units that are quickly deployed to areas of need, and equipped to assist in diverse ways. The challenge at border points remains one of facilitating and speeding the entry and exit of legitimate travellers, who comprise the great majority of the traffic, while considerably restricting opportunities for illegal entry.

In-Country Management Approaches

For in-country management, there are moves toward greater cooperation among migration authorities and local police, better sharing of needed data, and changes in visa extension and case adjudication procedures. Again looking at the United States in this regard, it seems clear that the Immigration and Naturalization Service (INS), even with staff and budget increases, is overstretched in trying to track and in some way respond to up to several million irregular migrants and hundreds of thousands of active deportation orders. However, in some instances, local police authorities are discouraged by local ordinances to get involved in migration matters. As such, the nearly 1 million state and local law enforcement staff in the United States are only marginally engaged in migration management.

In a security-first atmosphere, however, some of these constraints may be breaking down. The INS is now adding thousands of names of persons with deportation orders or other immigration violations to a database that will be available to local law enforcement, enabling at least the identification of these persons when apprehended for local offences, and the quicker engagement of the INS on follow-up matters. The United States reports over 300,000 outstanding deportation orders on migrants who have disappeared, presumably gone underground in the US society. The United States will also take further steps to speed up and simplify the process of appealing cases in the immigration court system, which is confronted with over 270,000 cases per year (United States Department of Justice, 2002), and is considering steps to significantly reduce the length of validity of most entry visas and the ability to upgrade visa status while in the country.

On all fronts, increased and well-structured methods of cooperation between intelligence and migration services are being planned or implemented. This includes actions among the agencies of a country, as well as bilateral and multilateral actions across these portfolios. The cross-seconding of staff and establishment or strengthening of inter-agency working groups is an increasingly common approach.

The impact of irregular migration on compliance with some international covenants, particularly the abuse by irregular migrants of the covenants on asylum and refugees (1951 Convention) has also inspired responses from interior management agencies. It is generally acknowledged that the asylum system is being misused and abused by irregular migrants having no legitimate claim to protection.

The different procedures for application and approval established by different destination countries encourages this abuse, as do extended timelines in processing asylum claims and differing levels of benefits to asylum seekers and successful claimants (see also **chapter 6**).

The work of the European Union following the Dublin Convention to rationalize across the EU the processes and the responsibilities of the Members for addressing asylum claims, and to establish a Community-wide fingerprinting system for asylum applicants, is in response to the problems of abuse of the protection system. Additionally, the efforts to build the capacity of transit countries to be safe countries of first asylum are steps in this direction. Coupled with these particular initiatives, or perhaps spawning them, is the growing awareness that protection systems should work as a component within a migration management perspective, rather than as separate conceptual and operational features. As such, where safe first asylum capacity is being built, it is sensible to do so within the context of the overall migration management system. The desired results include full protection to the truly vulnerable, a significant decrease in the abuse of the protection system by other migrants, and an enhanced capacity to manage the majority of the caseload who are irregular migrants not meriting special protection.

Other EU-Specific Responses

EU Members are considering the establishment of a Europe-wide corps of border guards and a European entry visa to tackle the problem of irregular immigration (see **textbox 14.2.**). The guards could cover the land and sea borders while the visa system would be linked into a computerized database for easy access by all member states. In the medium term, the European Commission is recommending changes to the visa system operated by individual EU members. This would involve a joint office for the issuing of visas and a database of all visas issued that would be available to all member states. Overall, EU member states have begun to accept that they must have similar attitudes

and laws regarding irregular immigrants, if they are to be successful in tackling the problem. A series of measures has been agreed upon, including, as earlier mentioned, the finger printing of all asylum applicants to preclude their pursuing an application in another member state if their application has already been denied or is in process elsewhere. Also, minimum standards for the reception and hosting of asylum seekers are being discussed to ensure one country does not appear more attractive than another.

Other measures being considered or initiated include establishing regular and closer contact and co-operation with the countries from which the irregular immigrants originate, and better assisting these countries in building their capacity to manage and minimize irregular outward migration, while strengthening legal migration options[15].

TEXTBOX 3.2.

Irregular Migration in Indonesia

In 2001 the most significant issue concerning irregular migration in Indonesia was that of the migrants interdicted in transit to Australia. Although this situation has received much widespread publicity, Indonesia faces other major migration challenges most notably the return and reintegration of over one million IDPs and a durable solution to the problem of East Timorese refugees.

During 2001, the Indonesian authorities interdicted some 2,800 irregular migrants, most of whom were of Afghan and Iraqi origin and attempting to reach Australia. Under an arrangement entitled the Regional Cooperation Model (RCM), IOM worked with the Governments of Indonesia and Australia to address this problem. The numbers of irregular migrants transiting through Indonesia had been rapidly growing since 1998 and every indication was that this trend was set to continue.

Despite attempts to stem the flows through activities carried out under the RCM, including humane detention practices in Indonesia, asylum referrals to UNHCR, voluntary return, information sharing, irregular migrants continued to arrive and transit Indonesia. This posed not only a problem for the Government of Indonesia, which was then facing other migration challenges, but also became the subject of intense discussion with the Government of Australia.

---

15) In this regard, the European Commission programme "Cooperation with Third Countries in the Area of Migration" (budget line B7-667, follow up to High Level Working Group initiatives) with Government of Sri Lanka and the International Organization for Migration is a notable example.
The single programme integrates capacity-building with Sri Lanka for improving enforcement functions, enhancing regular labour migration options, and expanding the ability of Sri Lanka to accept voluntary returnees.

In September 2001, Australia started implementing firm measures intercepting irregular migrants before reaching Australia. This coupled with other external factors, such as the political changes in Afghanistan, has led to a marked decrease in the use of Indonesia by people smugglers as a transit point toward Australia. At this stage it is difficult to assess future trends in irregular migration through Indonesia, but there is every indication to believe that levels will not reach those attained previously. Indonesian law enforcement agencies have arrested several alleged smugglers and legislation targeting people smuggling is currently being drafted.

A major development arising out of the problem of people smuggling affecting Indonesia and the region was the Bali Ministerial Conference on People Smuggling, Trafficking in Persons and Related Transnational Crime, held in February 2002. Co-hosted by the Governments of Indonesia and Australia, 37 countries from across Asia participated, along with UNHCR and IOM. The Conference demonstrated a clear political will to tackle the problem of irregular migration and an immediate outcome was the creation of two ad hoc working groups chaired by Thailand and New Zealand.

East Timorese refugees return to the remote Oecussi enclave

One working group will focus on International and Regional Cooperation, the other on Policy, Legislative Framework and law Enforcement Issues. Specific areas of action will include information and intelligence sharing; law enforcement; border control, visa systems, and fraud detection; public awareness; effective returns; and identification of irregular migrants. IOM is working closely with both Working Group Chairs in developing plans of action. Results will be reported back to Bali participants at a follow-up conference in 2003.

The Management of Illegal Employment

Enhancing the responsibility and culpability of employers who hire irregular migrants is another area of attention for internal management. It is perhaps at this point in the migration policy and practice chain that the problems are most resistant to change. While security-related concerns have dominated the agenda following September 11, 2001, economic hardship as well as the attraction of the western consumption society remain the most common motive for both regular and irregular movements. These movements are encouraged by push factors in regions of meagre economic opportunity, as well as by pull factors on the other side.

Economic disparities between countries of origin and countries of destination are indeed enormous: Mexican migrants earned nine times as much in the United States as in their last job in Mexico; Polish construction workers earned over three times as much in Germany as in Poland; Indonesian labourers in Malaysia earned nearly eight times as much as in Indonesia; Mozambican labourers flock into South Africa to work in industry, agriculture and the informal sector, earning many times more than at home. Both the availability of jobs at better wages and employers willing to hire irregular workers are significant pull factors.

Quote from a Mexican irregular migrant apprehended in the Arizona desert:

"Because of this bearded guy, what's his name, Bin Laden, it is harder now. There are more reinforcements now because America is afraid of terrorists. But we won't stop trying to cross until we get paid better in Mexico. We will keep trying one hundred, two hundred times - regardless of what happens to us."

Source:
National Public Radio (2002). *Strangers at the Gates,* 30 January.

An example from Europe

The changes proposed in the United Kingdom illustrate a the greater focus on illegal employment as a facilitation of irregular migration. In the United Kingdom, the current practice toward employer sanctions is detailed in Section 8 of the Asylum and Immigration Act of 1996, which makes it an offence for employers knowingly or negligently to employ people who have no permission to work. The maximum penalty that can be imposed on an employer is £5,000 for each illegal employee. Employers can establish a defence by proving that they were shown one of a number of documents entitling them to work and that they believed this to be genuine, and the documents currently specified are wide-ranging. As the figures indicate, these measures have not proved to be an effective deterrent. The number of people prosecuted successfully under this Section of the Act since 1997 are (United Kingdom Home Department, 2002): 0 in 1997; 1 in 1998; 9 in 1998; 23 in 2000 (provisional).

New and stronger measures proposed under a broad United Kingdom immigration reform package include:

• greater emphasis on managed migration schemes integrated with wider employment policies to ensure that labour market demands can be met through legal sources and that those wishing to work in the United Kingdom have legal routes available to them;

• increasing the possible prison sentence for those who facilitate the illegal entry of people to the United Kingdom or harbour them, including employers, to a potential fourteen year prison term (equivalent to that of drug related offences, and significantly higher than the EU's proposed eight year maximum), and applying the United Kingdom's Proceeds of Crime Bill to maximise the chance that those who profit from this crime will also face the prospect of losing those profits; this also includes reducing the scope for fraud by limiting the range of identification acceptable as evidence of Section 8 compliance;

• improving the enforcement capacity and capability of the Immigration Service, to make tackling illegal working a higher priority and developing joint Immigration Service and police teams with specialist skills to target illegal working; this includes mounting joint operations to tackle illegal working and other workplace offences;

• using existing Crime Bills to remove the profits of those who exploit illegal working for their own advantage; and making it clear that the new penalties for facilitating people smuggling will apply to all those who facilitate the illegal entry of migrants and assist in hiding these migrants;

• producing and promoting guidance to support Section 8 compliance; and providing support, possibly through an improved telephone helpline;

• developing industry codes of practice; and working closely with the Office of Government Commerce to address this issue in the public sector; and,

• establishing a high-level steering group consisting of representatives of business and the trades unions to consider these issues and develop innovative solutions.

An example from Africa

Africa provides another example of the management of illegal employment with particular emphasis laid on the preservation of the rights of migrant workers.

As the economically strongest country on the African continent, South Africa counts between 3 to 6 million migrants. According to Migration News (2002), most of these migrants are in an irregular situation. According to South Africa's Minister in the Presidency, Essop Pahad[16], "given the role of migrant labour in South Africa and the experience of illegal and abusive labour practices, the Government is working towards a comprehensive and coherent labour migration policy that will ensure standards that and the rights of migrant workers are not undermined" (IOM, 2002).

In the summer of 2002, a new Immigration Act was adopted by Parliament; the law had been under preparation since a White Paper on immigration was published in 1996. Although the new law dropped a proposal for high sanctions on employers who hire illegal workers, it prohibits the employment of illegal foreigners and requires from the employer to make a good faith effort that no illegal foreigner is employed by him or her.

16) In his intervention at IOM's fiftieth anniversary Council session in November 2001.

Forward Perspective

The migrants entering developed countries of destination illegally for employment play an important and even essential role in sustaining these countries' economic vitality. Illegal means are often the only route to the countries' and the migrants' economic goals. The demographic arguments are now well known and are most pronounced in Western Europe and in Japan: in these countries, the old-age dependency ratios, which are already at straining point within the OECD countries, will fall from five-to-one to three-to-one over the next fifteen years. These countries will require immigrants to sustain labour pools, and to support burgeoning public expenditures on care for the retired and elderly (see **chapter 13**).

Within the EU, the issue will be further complicated by the significant reduction in internal border controls within the current and expanded Schengen space, and corollary moves for easier internal and external EU trade regimes. As the Amsterdam Treaty urges the EU to move more of these matters onto a Community platform, national interests (and concomitant anti-immigration sentiments in even the most liberal countries) will push back against the perceived loss of national sovereignty to Community control of migration management. While this tug of war ensues, economic migration pressure – both the need for work from traditional origin countries and the need for workers in the EU – will build up and irregular migration will likely expand despite stronger enforcement measures.

The relief valve of temporary or long-term and targeted labour immigration is likely to be opened further, possibly following the lead of Italy with Albania (see **textbox 13.3.**) and the Maghreb. However useful this approach, it would appear unlikely to provide adequate relief to the fundamental demographic and economic challenges unless implemented on a scale not yet under serious discussion.

The resolution may lie in a combined approach similar to that promoted by the United Kingdom, and including: significant commitment to both temporary and long-term labour immigration; accelerated work and residence privileges for populations from the new EU entry states and those states waiting in the wings; significant investments in training and cultural orientation of migrants pre-departure and in-country - including special programmes to make migrants entering for family reunification economically active sooner.

Reliance on continuing regularization and amnesties, and approaches allowing asylum applicants greater labour and social service rights will be harder policies to accept. They can easily be framed as capitulation measures by anti-immigrant constituencies that feel that migration is in fact unmanaged, and that irregular migrants are being encouraged and rewarded at the taxpayer's expense. As such, a move toward firmer lines of distinction between migrant groups, supported by various enforcement and facilitation initiatives, would seem the most likely course for the EU.

Moving in this direction, the recent European Commission Communication on a Common Policy on Illegal Immigration (European Commission, 2001) calls for increased co-operation with both source and transit countries and practical implementation and efficient enforcement of existing rules aimed at preventing irregular immigration (see also **chapter 14**). It also proposes an Action Plan covering visa policy, information exchange, border management, police cooperation, legislative action and returns policy.

Implications for National and International Investment and Cooperation

Suggestions for Foreign Assistance Investment

• Invest in developing the governance capacity of countries of transit and origin to manage migration flows, both from migration and asylum perspectives. This investment should acknowledge that even when transit countries become countries of safe first asylum, there is not likely to be much difference in terms of resolution for asylum claims for the same caseload that would have reached Western Europe, the United States or Australia. Most migrants will be resolved into a migration, not asylum, status. Governments of transit countries must be able to deal with that caseload in a number of ways: border management, policy and legislative development, case adjudication, management and tracking of internal caseload, assisted and other returns, and regional dialogue and cooperation. Extend technical cooperation activities to include the sharing of effective practices among governments of sending, transit and receiving countries. Awareness raising among public officials as to the particular features of trafficking and smuggling and the necessary protection of victims should also be included.

- Use national and decentralized foreign assistance to build selective labour programmes with key origin countries or specific communities, and link these opportunities with cooperation on matters of enforcement. Include actions to help origin country labour and related ministries better prepare migrants for legitimate labour migration through pre-departure information, skills and language training, and through strengthening of benefits in the origin country to provide temporary legitimacy for labour migrants in such areas as family support and long-term pension schemes. Include support to origin countries for development of better balanced dual citizenship benefits overall, where they apply.

- Target foreign assistance at development strategies in key origin countries to provide economic opportunities in key geographic areas of strong outward migration, and to recapture and better manage remittances and migrant's talent for origin country development.

- Place a strong emphasis on information dissemination at all points on the migration continuum – origin, transit and destination – and on action-oriented research. Information campaigns should actively market and promote viable options for legal movement created or enhanced through the actions earlier described, while actively discouraging counterproductive migration activities and educating about the particularly serious abuses likely from traffickers. Information is an important empowerment tool, diminishing the capacity of traffickers and smugglers to exploit the limited knowledge of potential migrants and counter balancing the false information provided by criminals involved in the facilitation of irregular migration.

Suggestions for National Investment

- Establish strong, widely available economic and cultural integration programmes for migrants in the host country, including family reunification of migrants. Draw a line between those in the country legally, and those of illegal or indeterminate status, including asylum applicants. Reward regular migration substantially and clearly, and provide appropriate assistance to legitimate asylum claimants while implementing strong disincentives for irregular migration and unfounded asylum claims.

- Enhance regular migration options in traditional destination countries to help receiving countries with their population imbalance, i.e., declining and ageing population, and allow foreign manpower to temporarily or permanently migrate within a well-established management system. This system, together with the legitimate enforcement of legislation to combat irregular migration, should decrease the latter.

- Plan with the private sector a phase-out of irregular workers, and a phase-in of regular migrant workers. Strengthen data and identity verification systems in source and destination countries, and on usual transit routes.

- Revise legal and regulatory frameworks to unambiguously define and support clear distinctions between regular and irregular migration, and to protect the truly vulnerable migrants, whether irregular or regular, particularly those with legitimate asylum claims and those who are victims of trafficking.

69

Conclusion

Reducing the complexities of irregular migration is possible but challenging. It will first require a basic reorientation of perspective toward the primacy of national sovereignty in migration matters and a recommitment to the basic compact government has with its citizenry to provide effective and efficient governance. Within these broad but clear boundaries, the national commitment to provide refuge for the vulnerable and welcome for diverse groups of newcomers can be vigorously pursued as national priorities meeting or exceeding current international standards.

Reducing the complexities implies orderly and predictable systems for entry, means of identifying fraud and abuse in the system, and means of managing and supporting the population of migrants legally in the country. It also implies directing foreign assistance at migration management issues at their source, building origin and transit country capacity to co-manage migration, and enhancing national development in origin countries, in part through the very processes of orderly outward migration.

In recent years, governments have become increasingly sensitive to the risks of irregular migration. A positive consequence of this sensitization can be seen in the theme's inclusion in discussions and recommendations related to migration management at regional level. Irregular migration figures prominently on the agendas of most regional consultative processes and has clearly turned into one of the top priorities of migration managers

Sharing information on the phenomenon, including best practices on how to combat it effectively and efficiently is a promising step towards contributing to raising awareness of and, finally, curbing irregular migration.

CHAPTER 4

The Challenge of Integrating Migrants into Host Societies - A Case Study from Berlin

There is broad agreement among international migration managers in governments and organizations that migration rewards a society only when accompanied by successful integration. Without integration, migration may give rise to stresses and strains that can seriously harm social cohesion. Clearly, immigration management and integration represents challenges for all countries affected by migration.

In other words, these challenges apply not only to traditional immigration countries, such as Australia, Canada and the United States of America. Mostly made up of immigrants, the populations of these countries have profited immensely culturally, politically and economically from immigration[1]. The challenges apply equally to certain countries of the European Union, such as Germany, Italy, Spain or Sweden, although the latter might not officially define themselves as immigration countries. In many more contemporary immigration countries, the contributions made by immigrants are often minimized, forgotten or simply under-appreciated because of errors or negligence in the area of integration.

To illustrate their importance, the complementarity of immigration and integration should be analysed from a historical perspective. Indeed, integration is a long-term process in which successes and failures are measured through a comparative analysis spanning several generations. If integration policy is successful, public opinion towards immigration may become more favourable in a few years time than at present.

In this respect, north-western and north European immigration to the United States of America is a useful example. As Germans, Dutch and Scandinavian immigrants arrived in the United States in large numbers, especially at the end of the nineteenth and in the early twentieth centuries, they were generally considered as unwilling to adapt to a new language and to the American way of life. Behavioural norms such as abstinence from drinking in public on Sundays were not easily adhered to by the new arrivals. However, history has demonstrated that these immigrants were both willing to integrate and successful in doing so. Today, the massive influx of north-western and northern Europeans is cited as an excellent example of successful integration because of their unprecedented impact on all facets of American society and the economy.

Immigration, however, is perceived quite differently in the United States of America than in Europe. Though not easily quantified, this difference is nevertheless crucial to the establishment of national policies. The United States receives significant benefits from its immigrants, but at what many Europeans and some Americans view as a cost of constant and sometimes rapid cultural change. Most European nations want to maintain their traditional cultures, while the American tradition is one of change itself (Levine, 2002).

Conceptually, integration policies are often far less popular among migrant groups than among the host population. One reason for this unpopularity is that for a long time after their arrival in the host country, migrants live in uncertainty, permanently facing questions about their own cultural identity and their relationship with local people. How can one retain a sense of one's individuality while being woven into the social fabric of the host society? How can one resist the urge to stay apart in order to maintain one's identity? On the other hand, questions and doubts voiced by members of the local population often point in the opposite direction: why do they live apart from us culturally? Why do they handicap themselves by not learning our language? Why should we change our traditions for them?

"They have to adapt, not us", is a frequent comment heard from local people when faced with an immigration reality. However, concerns arise from both sides. The immigrants' reluctance to assimilate within the majority population is echoed by local people's anguish at seeing their own traditions diluted and threatened by immigration. Although some concerns may vanish with time, they are too often confirmed by reactions stemming from actors in politics and public life. Another problem is that the concept of "integration" is open to interpretations serving different interests. Most local people often expect migrants to adapt to the culture of the host country as soon as possible without defining the standards and norms to which these immigrants should adapt.

1) On migration management in traditional countries of immigration, see **chapter 9.**

71

Recent elections in various EU member countries have shown that immigration issues in receiving countries have a strong bearing on local and national policies. Immigration requires a re-thinking of priorities of the welfare state and provokes numerous fears among local people. In brief, the immigration debate calls imperatively for a direct and honest assessment of the nature, purpose and value of integration.

Considering the continuing nature of immigration, the long-term political stability of immigration countries will depend more and more on sound management of the immigration-integration link. Controlling, to a reasonable extent, immigration flows and achieving visible progress in integrating the newcomers require a sophisticated set of political, administrative and operational instruments and practices at national and local levels. Above all, it demands commitment, understanding and goodwill on the part of both the immigrants and their host societies.

This chapter looks at the meaning, the challenges and the various components of the integration of migrants into host societies. Its arguments are largely rooted in practical experiences and examples of integration policies and measures implemented by the city of Berlin which is one of the European capitals with the highest percentage of foreign-born population. The chapter underlines the importance of tolerance and respect for cultural diversity in the implementation of integration policies. Successful integration measures should be seen as a corollary to migration and an important component of sound migration management.

What does Integration Mean?

In Western European countries facing large-scale immigration, terms such as "assimilation versus reciprocal integration" frequently headline abstract discussions. Assimilation, or one-way integration, whereby newcomers renounce their cultural habits and values in favour of the culture of the receiving society, is normally dismissed by both sides. In theory, a proper integration process is privileged, along the lines that the receiving society adopts some cultural traits of the newcomers while the latter make adjustments in the opposite direction, creating a reciprocal integration process that satisfies both groups. However, abstract theories often raise more questions than they answer.

In many Western European countries, efforts at integration of immigrants, particularly immigrants from Islamic countries of origin, have not been as successful as the integration of European and Asian immigrants. Too many end up in ghettos and subsidized unemployment schemes, only too often generating dependence and resentment, illustrating a classic "downward assimilation" situation. In such situations, the first generation of immigrants aims at integration, works hard and wants to enable its children to be upwardly mobile. Instead, their children behave much like their host-country peers in poor neighbourhoods. But with language and cultural problems to boot, many drop out of school, fall into criminality and never acquire adult social and professional skills (Pfaff, 2002).

A look at real-life situations may help to illustrate the process of integration and assimilation (Wortham, 2001). Let us look at two migration cases that are fairly representative of many countries affected by migration. The following examples come from Berlin, Germany's largest city. In portraying migrants who benefit from family reunification schemes, it shows the two sides of the "integration coin".

Scenario 1

• A young woman from Turkey, whose husband was born in Germany, is permitted to join her husband in Berlin. Upon her arrival, she stays in the same apartment with her Turkish in-laws and hardly has any opportunity to meet Germans or learn the local language. All of her family members and friends speak Turkish; TV and radio programmes are received via satellite from Turkey. She barely leaves the apartment, and when she does, she often has the impression that she is shunned as a foreigner. She would like to get a job, but has no chance as she does not speak German. Local women whom she comes across, dress and behave differently from her. Her first feelings after entering Germany were very positive and a desire of belonging to and identifying with the new country and people. However, after having spent a couple years in Germany, she continues to feel like an unwelcome immigrant, cut off from local society. She has more ties to Turkey – by phone, by TV, by travelling – than with the society she lives in.

Scenario 2

- A young Turkish woman arrives in Germany and easily picks up the new language. She walks around Berlin freely, reads German newspapers, watches German TV and enrols in a vocational training programme to become a secretary. Twice a week she meets with her new German girl friends and joins a women's charity organization. She finds that she often shares the opinions and ideas talked about in the meetings and feels like she is a fully accepted member of German society.

Everyone familiar with the slow step-by-step processes of cultural, behavioural and structural integration will judge the second scenario as being closer to wishful thinking than to reality. Taken wrongly, it can also be seen as implying that radical assimilation is the only appropriate model of migrant behaviour. If rigidly prescribed, it may discourage social exchange, hinder social development and prevent the host society from growing in dynamism and vitality.

Both examples illustrate that an immigrant, or a group of immigrants from the same country of origin, do not generally enter the host society with textbook-like "guidelines on how to become an integral member of the local population".

Additionally, motivation for integration varies widely within different migrant groups and individuals according to their specific ambitions, desires and reasons for leaving. There are numerous causes for emigration such as war, persecution, poverty, underdevelopment, natural disasters, lack of resources, desire to improve living conditions and socio-professional opportunities. Goals and aspirations stemming from emigration can be achieved only if complex and reciprocal patterns of interaction with the native population take place. Sharing the same place of residence is obviously not a sufficient factor to produce integration. Responsibilities are shared by migrants and host societies alike in adapting to the new society and encouraging this society to accept and welcome newcomers.

Migration is about people, and an active and caring integration policy should cater to their needs. Immigration without integration inevitably leads to tensions within societies and attracts high political costs. Economic exclusion of the migrant population not only represents a huge financial burden on society as a whole, but also sheds a negative light on immigration, often accompanied by manifestations of xenophobia and racism.

TEXTBOX 4.1.

The Relationship between Integration, Development and Migration

The relationship between migration, development and integration is not always immediately obvious. The successful integration of migrants is often considered to be of benefit primarily to the individuals concerned and the societies of host countries. The migration process nevertheless operates along a continuum; and countries of origin can also benefit from the successful integration of their nationals in the host country, e.g. through remittances, technology transfer, cultural exchanges and access to new ideas and practices. A stable and supportive host environment for migrants is ultimately also conducive to migrants becoming productive economic forces for their home community.

The effectiveness of integration is enhanced, when the process already begins in the country of origin prior to emigration. Countries of origin and destination should strengthen their co-operation to pave the way for a smoother integration of migrants. To this effect, it may be useful for host countries to support, among others, education schemes in countries of origin, thereby investing both in their own future labour force and potential development of those countries.

This approach to integration is becoming an increasingly critical aspect of effective migration management. It compels countries of origin and destination to cooperate with each other, and to adopt integrated policy approaches that link migration to development cooperation, trade and investment, as well as demographic and social development at the national, regional and international level. It can be most effective at the regional level where countries frequently share common borders and similar migration challenges.

The support of countries of origin in the integration process is important particularly in relation to second and third generations of migrants who often are in search of an original culture. The devastating terrorist attacks of September 11, 2001 seem also to have brought a growing awareness of the importance of integration for social stability, as social alienation and disaffection among minority groups in search of "cultural identity" can increase their susceptibility to recruitment into extremist activities against their own host society. Community education and awareness raising are useful means to promote inter-cultural relations and combat racism, social exclusion and the alienation of ethnic communities from their host society.

73

What does Integration Consist of?

The complex nature of integration means there are no fixed requirements. Rather, the dynamic nature of the interactions implicit in migration necessitates an open approach. However, for both the immigrants and the host society, it is reasonable to argue that certain basic conditions need to be respected in order to make integration happen.

For immigrants, these include:
- command of the language of the host society, in oral and written form;
- access to the educational system and the labour market in the host country;
- possibility of upward mobility through education and job performance;
- equality before the law;
- religious and cultural freedom;
- respect for laws and traditions in host societies.

For the host society, these include:
- tolerance and openness;
- willingness to welcome immigrants;
- understanding the advantages and challenges of multicultural societies;
- access to unbiased information about the advantages of integration, tolerance and intercultural dialogue;
- respect and understanding of the immigrant's condition, traditions and culture;
- respect for migrants' human rights.

This list of fundamentals alone demonstrates how many obstacles must be overcome for integration to occur. Ignorance, lack of knowledge, conflicts or confrontations must be faced and managed on both sides. It is important to underline once more that integration policies are not restricted to the migrant population alone. The host society must be willing to integrate newcomers and allow them to become part of their society which, in turn, will become more diverse and multicultural. In addition, many societies also apply integration concepts and policies towards certain disadvantaged groups, such as the unemployed, the handicapped, the poorly educated and, often, women.

Migrant groups targeted for integration programmes are often stigmatized as being problematic, socially weak and disadvantaged. However, the special socio-economic conditions migrants must cope with require integration measures. Not only does migration deprive people of their language, familiar environment and traditional behavioural patterns, it also reduces their ability to live their own identities as demonstrated in the following examples: often, a person arriving in a host country as a refugee is assigned to a special hostel in a restricted area; a migrant worker has to stick to a given job; a migrating family member has to stay with his or her kin; in short, they all leave behind their own identities and relationships acquired over a long period of time. Integration should not only mitigate the damage caused by these losses, but can – when the process works well – enrich the situation of individuals, groups and societies.

The question begs itself of whether integration policies should be compulsory or voluntary for newcomers. A Dutch pilot case is revealing in this respect. The introduction of the *Wet Inburgering Nieuwkomer* (WIN)[2] in the Netherlands in September 1998, which obliged new immigrants to take part in language and vocational courses, has given rise to debate on whether migrant's participation in integration measures should be voluntary or enforced by sanctions such as reducing welfare payments or limiting residence permits in the case of no-shows. However, the underlying assumption that migrants are not willing to take part voluntarily in integration measures is not based on empirical evidence. What matters to immigrants is whether the training truly improves their access to the labour market and other social facilities. It is equally important to take into account the immigrant's family situation, especially for women. For example, in Berlin, a study has shown that providing childcare for mothers while they attend integration courses makes a big difference in course attendance.

Are there limits to social integration? Opponents of immigration would answer yes, but reality is more complex than that. However, certain situations are not tolerable and can limit the impact of integration measures. Traditional or religiously rooted habits such as circumcision of women, polygamy, or arranged marriages are not acceptable in societies where these are prohibited by law. Claiming tolerance for immigrant groups that continue these traditions is not an option. Tolerance does not necessarily mean giving up values, but rather defending the common core values that a society has agreed upon.

Nevertheless, new problems often occur within host country societies if fundamental beliefs or ideas come into clash. This can be observed in certain non-Muslim countries

2) Literally, the "Integration Law for Newcomers".

with increasing Muslim populations. A recent discussion in Germany revolving around the question of the reconciliation of the freedom of religion with the protection of animals from specific slaughter methods stirred up many questions. Some of the responses may lie within what can be called the "mainstreaming of integration."

Mainstreaming Integration

By nature complex, policies enhancing and fostering integration processes must be comprehensive. It is necessary but not sufficient to focus integrative policies on particular areas such as health, education or discrimination. Poor housing conditions or a concentration of migrants in inner city areas may easily cause poor health conditions or produce below average performance at school. Integration management requires an administrative and political infrastructure that differs from traditional public administration schemes.

To be successful, integration management must straddle different administrative areas. New structures favouring coordination and cooperation must be created since most public institutions and administrations are not equipped to deal with complex issues such as migration and integration management. A central coordinating office managing integration should work in conjunction with all administrative units involved in issues related to integration. The coordinating office has to act not only as a driving force, but also as a monitoring body to ensure that the complexity and challenges of successful integration management are dealt with in clearly defined operational procedures.

In many receiving countries, coordinating offices for integration issues have been operating for some time. They span a wide range of activities, according to their specific mandate and to public administration traditions in the respective countries. In the Netherlands, in 2002, a special Minister in charge of alien policy and integration has been appointed[3]. His office is attached to the Ministry of Justice. In the United Kingdom, a nation state with a strong tradition of central government, the London-based "Commission for Racial Equality" was established in 1976 with branches in six regions. In addition, the "Immigration Research and Statistics Service" (IRSS) works together with the Immigration and Nationality Directorate, and other government departments, on integration issues[4]. Among other things, it has developed concepts for measuring results of integration programmes especially designed for refugees.

The case of Germany is somewhat special since the country has a federal structure. Although it receives more than 50 per cent of all immigrants to European Union member states, Germany is not widely regarded as an immigration country (Bommes *et al.*, 1999). According to Germany's constitution, the Federal Government is the sole authority for migration legislation (Article 73 of the German Fundamental Law[5]). Integration, however, is not mentioned in that Law. Since many functions relevant to successful integration fall under the responsibility of federal states (such as education, housing, social affairs, labour market policies), the sixteen federal states, not the federal government in Berlin, take the initiative in designing integration concepts, establishing administrative structures, and implementing concrete operational programmes.

In addition to the federal states, Germany's civil society plays an equally important role. Churches, trade unions, employers and business associations, sport organizations, neighbourhoods or parental groups are all involved in elaborating and implementing integration programmes. As federal capital and one of the sixteen federal states, the city of Berlin is an interesting example.

The Situation in Berlin

Like many other cities in Germany, Berlin is a city facing economic difficulties and a growing immigrant population. Berlin's present situation as an immigrant destination can in many ways be compared to that of other big European cities. Immigrants and senior citizens are the fastest growing groups in the population. More than 500,000 out of 3.4 million people living in Berlin today do not speak German as their native tongue; twenty years ago, Berlin (West) had 2 million inhabitants and some 250,000 residents of foreign nationality. In 2010, that number will be above 630,000. Berlin is the largest Turkish city outside Turkey, with more than 180,000 people of Turkish origin, 128,000 of them holding a Turkish passport (see **table 4.1.**).

3) In Dutch: *Minister voor Vreemdelingenbeleid en Integratie.*
4) IRSS produces research and statistics on asylum and immigration processes and outcomes, irregular migration, enforcement and return, support and accommodation for asylum seekers, integration and citizenship issues. The results serve to inform ministers, policy makers, parliamant and the wider public about the issues at stake.
5) Article 73 GG, § 3, stipulates that "der Bund hat aussschliessliche Gesetzgebung über: die Freizügigkeit, das Paßwesen, die Ein- und Auswendrung und die Auslieferung."

75

TABLE 4.1.

The Foreign-Born Population in Berlin, 2001

Naturalized German citizens	**100,000**
EU citizens	**68,000**
Including:	
EU labour migrants	32,500
Third country labour migrants:	**217,000**
From:	
Turkey	128,000
Former Yugoslavia	60,000
Poland	29,000
Refugees and asylum seekers	**100,000**
Asylum seekers	9,000
(still in the asylum processing)	
De *facto* refugees	47,000
(not recognized, but return is not	
possible for various reasons)	
War refugees	17,000
(from the Balkans)	
Quota refugees	12,000
(Jewish immigrants from	
Russian- speaking countries)	
Recognized political refugees	15,000
Others	**60,000**
Total foreign-born population	**545,000**
Total population	**3,350,00**

———

Source :
Data compiled by the Office of the Commissioner for Migration and Integration, 2001

Most immigrants are blue-collar workers and poorly qualified for a labour market with high skill demands, a mismatch that can also be found in other European cities. Yet, largely due to Germany's unification, Berlin has lost more of its industrial jobs in a shorter time than other cities. Before 1989, Berlin was heavily subsidized through generous job creation schemes financed by the Federal Government. Shortly after Germany's reunification in 1989, these programmes were downsized, and enterprises had to close their branches or move to areas with a more advantageous cost-benefit ratio. Thus, Berlin has lost more than 300,000 blue-collar jobs in recent years. Immigrants were hardest hit by these changes; immigrant unemployment figures are more than twice as high as those of the native Germans, 36 per cent to 16 per cent. The economic difficulties Berlin is facing impact integration policies considerably as they are indispensable to ensuring social peace and stability.

The City of Berlin - A Test-Case for Integration Measures

A pioneer in the field of immigrant integration, the former Berlin mayor Richard von Weizsäcker seized the initiative in 1981 establishing the "Office of the Commissioner for Foreigners' Affairs"[6], subsequently renamed the "Commissioner for Migration and Integration." The incumbent Commissioner is the longest serving Commissioner for foreigners' affairs in Germany[7]. In fact, all other federal states save two have followed the basic idea and elements of Berlin's institutional structure in establishing their own integration capacities.

Management Structure for Migration and Integration in Berlin

The Senate of Berlin, which is the Federal State Government, played a key role in establishing an administrative structure dealing with integration. Appointing a Special Commissioner and creating a Senate Committee was of strategic importance, as these new structures became the centre of operational and conceptual initiatives revolving around integration (see **table 4.2.**).

TABLE 4.2.

The Commissioner for Migration and Integration in Berlin and its Main Stakeholders and Interlocutors

———

Source:
Office of the Commissioner for Migration and Integration, 2001

6) In German: *Büro des Ausländerbeauftragten.*
7) Editor's note: as the Commissioner for many years, Ms. Barbara John shaped the Office and turned it into a model that has been replicated in other federal states.

In order to steer and control the work of the Commissioner, a Parliamentary Commission on integration was also established. In addition, local governments wishing to be part of the network appointed local commissioners to work within the framework of local governments but exchanging information and ideas with the Commissioner. Senate Departments such as education or housing are required to cooperate with the Commissioner's Office, insofar as their proposals must be submitted to the Commissioner's Office before a decision is made. Although the Commissioner has no right to veto, his suggestions and advice must be taken into consideration when formulating new policy initiatives. The State Parliament provides direct funding for projects implemented by the Commissioner's Office or by different Senate Departments. The Commissioner forwards budget proposals. Her Office administers an annual budget of Euros 6 million and has a staff of 30 people.

Functions of the Commissioner of the Berlin Senate for Migration and Integration

As the key institution with respect to integration/migration in Berlin, the Commissioner's office has the following key functions:

• formulating policies and addressing questions concerning migration and integration issues in Berlin;
• coordinating activities with Government Departments;
• providing information to all residents, campaigning for and publicly promoting integration, tolerance and intercultural dialogue;
• financing "self-help" projects;
• cooperating with partners at the European and national level as well as with countries of origin of migrants living in Berlin.

With the creation of the Commissioner's Office, integration suddenly gained media and public interest in Germany. This interest spread quickly beyond Berlin. The city was suddenly seen as a prototype for integration policy. For the first time in the history of Germany, a Federal State Government made decisions concerning a variety of integration measures, including family reunions, legal status of immigrants and security measures.

Much of the public attention concerned the fact that immigrants and their representatives could communicate directly with a government office which, in turn, would feed the results of these discussions into government decisions and actions. The so-called "guest workers" were no longer treated just as temporary jobholders but as people whose opinions, desires and suggestions were taken seriously by the administration.

What was crucial in its success, however, was that the Office did not focus its activities solely on the migrant population alone, but also directed them towards local people. Regular meetings were held to explain the new integration policy in neighbourhoods with a high percentage of immigrants; public outreach and information campaigns were carried out regularly. For eight years, until the end of the 1980s, Berlin spent Euros 500,000 annually on campaigning for integration, respect for others and social cohesion among its inhabitants. This work led to the people of Berlin recognizing that their city was becoming more ethnically diverse than ever before. Berlin shows what needs to be done for integration. Today schools, districts, labour markets and businesses are different from a generation or so ago; there is no longer cultural, religious or ethnic homogeneity.

The management of multiculturalism is a difficult and challenging experience and Berlin is by no means in a unique situation. Most, if not all large cities in the world are attracting migrants. Jobs, supportive communities of the same ethnic group and broader-minded citizens make big cities an attractive place for migrants. City governments all over Europe are gradually beginning to understand the new role they play on behalf of their nation states: to test integration in areas where the economic and social potential of immigrants are best developed. These cities are also the most likely sites for the social conflicts common in immigrant societies.

Berlin demonstrates that it is important to address local fears and anxieties when dealing with integration. Fears, such as losing one's identity or job because of what is perceived as an influx of too many foreigners must be properly addressed and accompanied by inclusionary politics enabling newcomers to identify with their new environment. Institutionalized integration policies can be the answer by maintaining a sensitive balance between the interests of all parties. Furthermore, innovative integration programmes and administrative structures that combat segregation, intolerance and racism require political and financial support.

Working One's Way into Society

Economic participation is the key to successful integration. Migrants do not only seek jobs per se, they need them to enhance integration potential and their incorporation into the social fabric of the host country. Working opens avenues for contact with other people, enabling the immigrant to communicate in the new language, improve one's vocational qualifications and gain respect from family and friends. If being unemployed is a personal disaster for anybody, it is a tragedy for a migrant, diminishing the individual's potential to integrate considerably. Although unemployment in welfare states does not mean total economic deprivation, it may deprive migrants of a chance to participate in society. Unemployed immigrants run the risk of depending more on family members and reducing their social life and interaction to members of their own ethnic group, thus adding to isolation.

Access to the labour market must be secured by targeted integration management. Unfortunately, opening labour markets for legal immigrants is often seen as a potential threat. "Migrants are taking our jobs" is one of the typical claims heard from people in host societies and extremist anti-immigration political parties.

The "welfare state trap" is another obstacle for labour market incorporation. This is illustrated by the case of a family from Somalia who came to Berlin as refugees:

- after eight years in Germany, a Somali family was given an opportunity to obtain a residence permit if they could prove that family members could make a living. The ceiling to prove financial independence was set at a standard income for a family of four persons. Although the parents did find jobs, residence permits were initially denied by the administration because the income earned was Euros 50 less than the welfare entitlement. As both parents lacked qualifications, their jobs did not enable them to earn more. Consequently, this Somali family was nearly deprived of an opportunity to integrate economically and socially because of the welfare state principle that no family should earn less than what welfare would pay. Ultimately, this case was resolved through a special arrangement. But the root causes of the problem remain unaddressed due to rigid labour laws and welfare entitlement regulations.

Both systems - the legal regulations giving access to the labour market for immigrants as well as the general law for foreigners - require adjustments with respect to the special situation immigrants face in the labour markets of receiving countries. In an ideal situation, the introduction of three conditions would facilitate economic and professional integration:

- delivery of work permits or the permission to be self-employed for all migrants wishing to stay in the long term;
- introduction of new wage schemes in countries with high wage levels opening up labour market participation for poorly qualified migrants through a compensation bonus system paid for by the state;
- provision of systematic vocational training courses, directed also towards second generation migrants, and support mechanisms for migrants intending to become self-employed.

Two concrete examples from Berlin show the importance of integration schemes focussing on economic participation:

- in 1998, a "Consulting Centre for Self-Employment" was established to cater to the needs of immigrants from Turkey. Among immigrants in Berlin, the Turkish population displays the highest interest for self-employment. Currently, there are more than 6,000 Turkish enterprises and businesses in Berlin, employing more than 20,000 people[8]. When young Turkish Berliners were questioned about their professional desires, nearly half of them claimed that they wanted to become self-employed. The establishment of the Centre is a response to this. Government-funded, it provides training in accounting and marketing, advises on business opportunities in Berlin and enhances cooperation between business associations. The Berlin Chamber of Commerce is now considering whether this consulting service should also be provided to other migrant groups such as the Vietnamese.

- "Job Point" is a new initiative promoted by the Berlin Department of Labour, based on a Danish pilot project. It functions as an innovative job agency with branches located close to residential areas where demand and supply are greatest. With the recent establishment of a "job point" in a densely populated inner-city area, the labour department intends to appeal especially to young unemployed migrants. Counselling is provided by Turkish- and Arabic-speaking advisers. The Berlin Turkish-German business association is also present at the "job points" and offers job opportunities to bilingual applicants.

8) *Frankfurter Allgemeine Zeitung*, 5 December 2001.

Education for Social Mobility

Apart from access to the labour market, access to education is one of the core requirements for integration. Education is the springboard to economic and social mobility, in particular for the second generation of migrants. It impacts heavily on one's economic and social development.

Current research in immigration countries suggests that migrant pupils, who attend school in their host country, show higher performance levels than their parents. However, when results are compared with those of local pupils, one realizes that a majority of migrant pupils, though doing far better than their parents, are still behind their peer group. The most striking difference, where immigrant students lag far behind, is in the number of high-school certificates received.

In many cases, the education level of the parent's generation is indicative. To a very large extent, the education of migrant children is determined by that variable. Exposing far below average results for pupils with an immigrant background, the PISA study (Programme for International Student Assessment) published in 2001 by OECD, evaluated and compared competencies in reading, mathematics and natural sciences in the 32 OECD countries. It showed that immigrant pupils in Germany are, on the whole, performing worse than in other countries that have a higher percentage of immigrant pupils (Deutsches PISA-Konsortium, 2001).

School attendance is of utmost importance for immigrant pupils. It is safe to say that migrant children can only integrate at school. The responsibilities are therefore clear. School must provide a sound basis for immigrant children and enable them to acquire the skills they need for social and economic mobility. A migration background – especially when both parents are immigrants – usually impacts on reading and writing abilities. Learning and mastering the language of the new society is the central aim in the formal education of migrant pupils. In addition to educational efforts directed toward children, more systematic language training must also be advocated for adult immigrants. To be successful, efforts in this field should also include the development of appropriate didactic materials addressing the specific needs of pupils and adults.

As an example, since 1998, educational programmes for migrants have been provided in the Netherlands. Aside from teaching the new language, these programmes also provide cultural orientation regarding the principles of the new society and occupational skills training[9]. After successfully completing the training programme, participants are offered jobs or further training. The Dutch example demonstrates that newcomers accept a regulated integration scheme more easily if the objectives are clearly defined and it is implemented to adapt to the needs and special concerns of the participants.

A similar programme was introduced in Berlin in 1999, entitled "Migrant mothers learn German". Since then, 4,000 women who had lived for years in Berlin without mastering the German language, have participated. The courses take place in the same schools their children attend and childcare is provided during the lessons. Family members and husbands disapproved of language training in the evening but now strongly endorse the new programme. Last but not least, being able to communicate in basic German not only convinces mothers to be more supportive of their children's efforts to learn German, but also improves their own job opportunities.

Berlin is in the process of successfully implementing a tailor-made integration programme to address the special needs of students from a migrant background. Launched by a group of students from different ethnic backgrounds at the Technical University in Berlin, the initiative "University-students help students" targets high school pupils. Migrant pupils frequently lack assistance in facing problems linked to knowledge acquisition. Often familiar with these difficulties, university students help them directly and thus enable them to improve their knowledge of various disciplines such as German, biology, English or mathematics. Each semester, more than 200 migrant students participate in this initiative, providing them with a chance to obtain school leaving certificates in order to get into university.

Education is key to integration

9) According to *Wet Inburgering Nieuwkomer:* www.inburgernet.nl.

Taking on Responsibility by Participation

Everyone agrees that "integration is not a one-way street". Migrants do not want to remain voiceless objects of integration measures and are often keen to participate in the local politics of their new home.

Migrant associations are a common way of bringing immigrants together. Built around regional origins, political orientations, professional skills or sports, these associations play an important role in immigrant socialization and acclimatization.

However, all too often, these associations are accused of promoting segregation. Joining an association within the immigrant's group of origin is in most cases a first attempt to break out of isolation upon arrival in the host country. The important issue here is to ensure that migrant associations are both accepted and that they operate in a transparent fashion. The risk that migrant associations will become subversive, as is often advanced by opponents to immigration and integration, can be minimized by allowing them to take an active part in society. The best way to ensure this is to extend cooperation from the civil society as well as local government structures. In addition, financial assistance helps community groups to raise their profile and put forward their case.

Founded in 1989 by Turkish teachers and parents, the "Turkish Parent Association" in Berlin provides consultation for students, parents and school administrators. The Association cooperates with a variety of non-government organizations and government structures and has played an important role in building bridges between local people and Turkish immigrants. Annual funding of Euros 100,000 from the Berlin Senate enables the Association to rent its own premises and employ three full-time staff members.

In Berlin, migrants are also invited to participate closely in public life. Migrant associations are legally entitled to be heard at the Berlin Senate. The Commissioner's Office strongly encourages immigrants to be actively involved in local social activities. Similarly, immigrants are encouraged to take part in public structures such as local committees, councils and advisory bodies. In general, members of minority groups are rarely represented at this level although they are often as qualified as local members. Participation in these public bodies is not only a visible sign of minority integration, but also illustrates a basic democratic sharing of participation and responsibility.

A programme aimed at increasing the inclusion of immigrants is currently being implemented. The Commissioner's Office also keeps a register of skilled people from minority groups interested in becoming actively involved in public life[10].

Assessment of Integration Processes

Integration requires generally scarce resources such as money, time and patience. If measures fail, far more is at stake as immigration can become less credible as a way of improving and enriching society. Immigrants can easily be considered as "intruders", damaging welfare and harmony in their host country. Therefore, the systematic and ongoing monitoring of integration processes should be a standard requirement in implementing any integration project (Ministry of the Interior - The Netherlands, 2000). To be meaningful however, regular monitoring based on well-defined indicators is required. Ideally, the data collected should be comparable and include the following:

• employment;
• migrants' upward mobility;
• school and university achievement;
• membership in advisory boards and consultation structures (i.e., social participation);
• participation (elected and appointed) in local and national politics (i.e., political participation).

However, integration monitoring in no way replaces integration policies; monitoring should indicate if and how specific policies worked. In this way, problems can be detected and corrected and lessons drawn.

In Berlin, meaningful data on the successes and failures of integration measures have been collected for many years. While there has been a clear upward trend in acquiring a secure legal status or German citizenship, unemployment figures among some ethnic groups have increased sharply. There is now a political focus on improving the labour market situation of these groups.

---

10) The Office of Multicultural Affairs in Queensland, Australia, started a pilot project in this field in 1999.

Cooperation - Involving Sending Countries

For a long time, receiving countries considered immigration and integration an exclusively internal issue. This view stemmed from the idea that immigration generates economic and political pressure in societies of destination while playing to the advantage to countries of origin. Such views obviously obstruct integration and cooperation.

Although migrants pay a price when leaving their homes and familiar environment, the countries they leave behind are also affected. Most migrants belong to young and active groups in their countries of origin, so their emigration can have a negative impact on development back home. However, countries of origin also benefit enormously from migrants, especially in terms of remittances or returning citizens who bring back skills and capacities in high demand but short supply (see **chapter 12** and **textbox 15.1.**). Of course, a cost-benefit analysis of migration is difficult to establish because of the many factors to be considered.

Migration can generally yield benefits for the receiving as well as the sending countries if appropriate programmes are implemented to ensure that the migration and integration processes take place in an orderly fashion. In this context, building partnerships between sending and receiving countries represents an interesting and promising method for supervising and steering the process. Such collaboration can ensure that the needs and desires of both parties, as well as those of the migrant, are fully taken into account. The issue here is not so much burden sharing than maximising the mutual interests and benefits for the countries of origin and destination.

Throughout the 1990s, Berlin established successful partnerships with countries of the former Yugoslavia. Relations with Bosnia and the Federal Republic of Yugoslavia (Kosovo and Serbia) revolved around a set of comprehensive policies, combining aid, economic investment, bilateral and multilateral trade. Various programmes, run jointly by the Commissioner's Office and IOM, organized the voluntary return of thousands of war refugees who had sought temporary refuge in Berlin.

The Berlin Senate offered support in rebuilding houses and improving the infrastructure in municipalities where people returned. More than 200 municipalities in the former Yugoslavia received some Euros 2,750,000 between 1998 and 2002 to repair or improve water and sewage systems, rebuild schools and kindergartens, repair and build streets. Besides direct assistance, a variety of measures also benefitted the developing regional economic structures. For instance, after its specialists went to the country to provide training to local counterparts, a Berlin-based carpentry business established a vocational training institute in Bosnia.

The reintegration of refugees and migrants into the labour market of the former Yugoslavia through employment schemes will continue in the years to come with the help of the European Refugee Fund. Under this scheme, local businesses obtain financial incentives if they employ returning citizens. Including local people as recipients of cooperation projects and funds is a crucial part of successful cooperation. To that end, close to Euros 13 million were granted by the European Union for Berlin's support programmes implemented *in situ*.

Another example of a successful partnership is the "Berlin Association for German-Turkish Cooperation". Since 1983, the Berlin Senate has funded the activities of this Association, which aims at exporting specific vocational training modules to Turkey. With the support of the Berlin Chamber of Commerce and the German Federal Ministry for Economic Cooperation, training centres for car mechanics were established in Ankara, Istanbul and Izmir. The scheme is successful largely due to the application of the so-called "dual system", a German vocational system based on a combination of theory and practice in the apprentices' education. The attractiveness of the model explains why it was recommended by the Turkish Education Ministry for country-wide implementation.

TEXTBOX 4.2.

Integration of Migrants – an Issue of Concern to IOM Stakeholders

On the occasion of IOM's fiftieth anniversary Governing body session, which brought together representatives of IOM Member and observer States as well as inter-governmental organizations in November 2001, a panel of international migration experts discussed future challenges in the area of migration management. Respect of the ethnic diversity of receiving societies and integration of migrants were among the topics that received special attention. Extracts of key interventions on the issue are reproduced below[11].

11) IOM (2002). *An international dialogue on migration*, Geneva.

Mr. Antoine Duquesne
Minister of the Interior
Kingdom of Belgium

"[…] Among the interests taken into consideration when drawing up a Community policy, I regularly point to those of third-country nationals who have sometimes been living in the member States of the European Union for a long time. In increasingly diverse societies, the chances of achieving successful integration are predicated on mutual, reciprocal respect. Local populations should welcome the enrichment of cultural differences that the new communities bring with them and the immigrant populations must adapt and not call into question the basic values which form the foundation of our democracies. This is what constitutes reciprocal understanding and it goes by the name of enrichment through tolerance."

***

Mrs. Rosaline Frith
Director General, Integration Branch
Department of Citizenship and Immigration, Canada

"Canada's mosaic now includes most races, religions and cultures and it is expected to become more diverse with time. So how does one celebrate diversity? Promote social inclusion, and live in respect and peace? Not an easy objective, and in Canada our integration policies are intended to help us obtain that goal. The term integration illustrates a two-way process of accommodation between newcomers and Canadians. It encourages newcomers to adapt to Canadian society without requiring them to abandon their cultures or to conform to the values and practices of the dominant group, as long as adherence to their cultures does not contravene Canadian laws.

At the same time, Canadian society and its institutions are expected to change over time to reflect the new Canada, the Canada that is constantly in evolution. Canadian integration policy consciously welcomes all immigrants into the Canadian family and strives to ensure their full participation across the important economic, social, political and cultural dimensions of our country. Integration in Canada is managed in partnership with all jurisdictions, non-governmental associations and the public. It is a continuum beginning with information provided to immigrants overseas, orientation and adaptation services in Canada to the acquisition of citizenship after a relatively short period of time. […]

As long as the public feels that the immigration programme is well managed, the cost of integration is viewed positively. Whatever the type of immigrant, the ultimate Canadian policy objective is full citizenship within an officially bilingual and multicultural policy. Canada encourages newcomers to adopt Canadian citizenship as an official symbolic act of allegiance and attachment, and about 85 per cent of immigrants take the step. Accession to official citizenship is not seen as the end of the journey - it is recognized that integration may require a lifetime. Indeed, research shows that full integration sometimes requires several generations. […]

A stable multi-cultural society depends upon the cultivation of a common sense of belonging among all citizens. This sense of belonging cannot be ethnically based since Canada is such a diverse society. Instead, it must be of a political nature and based on a shared commitment to the political community. The commitment to the political community involves commitment to its continuing existence and well-being and implies that one cares enough for it and does not harm its interests or undermine its integrity. The sense of belonging must be fostered by according equal citizenship to both newcomers and the Canadian-born. This means that all citizens must know that there is a real chance that they can influence the evolution of Canadian society. In a sense, they must feel not only that they belong to Canada but that Canada belongs to them.

As a liberal democracy Canada espouses certain core values to which it expects all its citizens to adhere. Values such as mutual respect, the rule of law, equality and the peaceful resolution of disputes are seen as non-negotiable minimum expectations. In return, Canada guarantees such basic human rights as individual autonomy, freedom of association, freedom of religion, etc. It is clear that Canadian society will not tolerate some behaviours. It will not tolerate the subjugation and abuse of women and children for example. In addition to targeted settlement programmes, Canada depends on its educational system to impart citizenship values to newcomers as well as to the Canadian-born, because if substantive citizenship is our goal, then all Canadians must be integrated in a real sense.

[…] We attempt to create a welcoming attitude towards diversity by teaching the value of diversity in our schools through public campaigns, such as "Canada - we all belong" and through diversity promotion, anti-racism campaigns, etc. Canada remains a cohesive society with low rates of interethnic conflict and low rates of crime.

Our long history of integrating immigrants and our recent history of welcoming immigrants without regard to race or ethnicity has been a successful experiment. Canadians are not complacent. We recognize that our society's stability is ensured only by constant vigilance and sensitivity to the potential fault lines that might divide us. Canada's multi-cultural experiment remains a work in progress."

***

Mr. Ali Kazancigil
Deputy Director General for Social and Human Sciences
UNESCO, Paris

"[…] cross-border population flows lead to increased diversity within receiving societies requiring policies and programmes that inherently promote respect for the rights of migrants. Such programmes and policies need to underscore the benefits of cultural and ethnic diversity in a society that create tolerance and mutual understanding, and maintain a cohesive fabric of shared values within the population. […]

[…] multi-cultural policies [should respond] to the impact of migration. In this field, issues are numerous and very complex and policies are to be developed respecting the migrant's rights and, at the same time, fostering their integration for their own benefit and also for the benefit of the receiving countries.

The successful application of these policies play a key role in the successful management of social cohesion and integration in the context of the increasingly multicultural nature of today's societies. […]

It is also obvious that, in the relationship between international migration and social integration, countries that develop participatory approaches and policies to understanding and regulating the transformations induced by such population movements, are better able to create positive relationships between autochthonous populations and migrant populations. If properly channelled, the input of migrant population into the receiving society and the economy yields positive results.

[…] UNESCO recommends recognizing increasing multiculturalism and dealing with [cultural diversity] through democratic policies, rather than risking marginalization of migrants and ensuing conflict and violence. Indeed, these represent a much greater threat to the unity of a country than a policy of recognition of cultural diversity.

[An example of acting towards the respect of this diversity is provided by] a UNESCO project focussing on international migration integration and citizenship in 16 selected European cities. The *Multicultural Policies and Modes of Citizenship in European Cities* (MPMC) Project is built around the assumption that increased international migration obliges cities to weave together the various communities into a reasonably cohesive society, respectful of cultural and ethnic diversity.

Focussing on so-called "channels of activation and mobilization" in these cities, which are entities through which immigrant and ethnic minority communities are making their interests and concerns known to municipal decision-makers, research has established that the application of the concept of citizenship leads effectively to integration of migrants through participation in local public decision-making and this in due respect of the migrants' human rights[12]".

Integration – an Encounter of Civilisations

Less than two generations ago, the description and analysis of cultural and behavioural differences among civilisations were of interest to only a handful of academics. Today, ethnic groups with different cultural traditions interact everyday in our neighbourhoods, schools and on our streets. Multiculturalism is one of the major consequences of the increase in globalization and international migration flows.

People are becoming more and more aware of differences but also complementarities between cultures and civilisations. People are beginning to understand that "differences are not only real; they are fundamental" (Huntington, 1993). These differences include how people dress and how men relate to their wives and children. Unfortunately, cultural differences can easily be viewed as insurmountable barriers that separate people.

In a society where integration is a daily process, people need to learn to understand that economic success, political stability, friendly neighbourhoods and processes of conflict resolution do not require cultural, ethnic, or religious homogeneity. Society's growing internationalization should be perceived and managed as an opportunity rather than a risk or a burden. Such a learning process requires explanation and time.

12) Results of this study were published by UNESCO in 2001:
    Multicultural Policies and Modes of Citizenship in Europe,
    United Kingdom, Ashgate.

83

Displaying an attitude of "friendliness instead of hostility towards foreigners" is not enough for countries faced with growing ethnic minorities. This attitude is a first step but should and can not be the underlying principle for states and their institutions to base their migration policies on (John, 1997).

Ultimately, state policy governing immigration and integration should be directed towards the migrant's achievement of professional and educational mobility, and equality before the law. States that promote the respect of law and democracy recognize and tolerate ethnic diversity and its inherent wealth. Societies receiving large numbers of immigrants, such as in Western Europe, can only hope that integration will succeed. If it does not, as one American observer stated recently, "the alternative may be demographic and economic collapse together with social and political chaos" (Levine, 2002).

Social cohesion can only be achieved by providing equal opportunities and legal equality to all within a framework set by governments and responsible administrations that respect human rights. Today, people from different cultural backgrounds are living together in often positive relationships more than at any other time. Greater cultural diversity accelerates interest in and the need for commonly agreed upon values among individuals and in society at large.

CHAPTER 5

Health – an Essential Aspect of Migration Management

In today's globalized world, the relationship between migration and health is often ignored partly due to lack of awareness or misinformation. Yet, with more people travelling faster to more destinations, migration health is today a major public health concern, with mounting evidence of a critical relationship between population mobility and emerging infectious diseases (Sattar *et al.,* 1999).

Health issues can trigger, delay, prevent or modify migration; similarly, migration can trigger health problems and concerns. When migrants leave an environment to which they have adapted and move to a new environment they may expose themselves or their host society to new health challenges[1]. Migrants moving from regions with high disease prevalence to areas with lower prevalence, or the other way around, may either introduce new or previously eradicated diseases to the region of destination, or contract diseases unknown to the migrants' region of origin. Moving can also affect mental well-being, as well, as it imposes certain psychological stress[2].

The links and interdependencies between migration and health are not static but evolve with the same complexity characterizing today's migratory flows: individuals fleeing persecution or poverty, persons internally displaced due to conflict or natural disaster, highly skilled professionals migrating through an orderly immigration process. Each typology within the migration process, while defined through specific characteristics, nonetheless shares common factors related to the risk of some health consequences resulting from the migration process.

This chapter focuses on perspectives in managing migration health issues. After considering briefly the international and national regulatory context of migrant health, it looks at selected key migration health issues, and provides recommendations for migration policy makers on how to manage the migration and health nexus to the equal benefit of migrants and their host societies.

1) www.istm.org/news_share/199903/migrant.html.
2) www.istm.org, *op.cit.*

Health Legislation and Regulations

The relationship between migration and health is governed by a number of international and national legal instruments which set out the operational guidelines and structures for bodies concerned with health aspects of migration management. While some instruments apply to people in general, and are not specifically designed to promote the health of mobile populations, it is important to ensure that their application includes mobile populations.

The Right to Health Care – International Instruments

Since its inception in 1919, the International Labour Organization (ILO) recognizes the need to improve working conditions for both national and foreign workers.

Drafted in 1948, the World Health Organization (WHO) Constitution states that the enjoyment of the highest attainable standard of health is one of the fundamental rights of every human being without distinction of race, religion, political belief, economic or social condition. The same year, the United Nations Universal Declaration of Human Rights put forth all elementary human rights, including the right to health.

The International Covenant on Economic Social and Cultural Rights of 1966 recognizes "the highest attainable standard of physical and mental health" for every human being and specifies steps to be taken to achieve this.

In its 1977 Convention on the Legal Status of Migrant Workers, the Council of Europe refers to medical examinations, as well as social and medical assistance for migrant workers.

Several recent major UN conferences have also underlined the linkages between migration and health.

In Chapter 10 of the Programme of Action of the 1994 International Conference on Population and Development (known also as the Cairo Conference, or ICPD), which refers specifically to migration, there are numerous references to health including urging governments to provide migrants and refugees with access to adequate health services.

The 1999 final document proposing key actions for the further implementation of the Programme of Action of the Cairo Conference (ICPD+5) urges governments in both

85

countries of origin and countries of destination, "to provide effective protection for migrants and basic health and social services, including sexual and reproductive health and family-planning". The same document also calls for adequate and sufficient international support to "meet the basic needs of refugee populations, including provision of access to adequate accommodation, education, protection from violence, health services, including reproductive health and family planning, and other basic social services, including clean water, sanitation and nutrition" (A7S-21/5/Add.1).

The international plan of action on ageing adopted by the Second United Nations World Assembly on Ageing in Madrid in 2002 calls for the integration of older migrants with their new communities through "measures to assist older migrants to sustain economic and health security"(doc. A/CONF.197).

Immigration Health Assessment Regulations

Health and medical regulations are among the oldest border entry requirements and predate immigration laws. Traditional countries of immigration (see also **chapter 9**), such as Australia, Canada, New Zealand and the United States, developed health components as part of their regulatory immigration processes early in the twentieth century.

In the early 1900s, third class passengers arriving at Ellis Island in the United States were inspected by doctors to ensure they did not carry any contagious diseases (first and second class passengers usually did not need to undergo this inspection). Doctors had just seconds per person to check for over sixty symptoms - from anemia to goiter, to varicose veins - which might indicate a wide variety of diseases, disabilities and physical conditions. Of primary concern were cholera, favus (scalp and nail fungus), insanity, and mental impairments. In 1907, legislation further barred immigrants suffering from tuberculosis, epilepsy, and the physically disabled[3].

As medical care improved, immigration health practices became less important from the 1960s to the end of the 1980s. However, the resurgence of classical infectious diseases, such as tuberculosis, and the emergence of new diseases, such as HIV/AIDS, has given renewed prominence to migrant health as a pressing government policy concern.

Countries that do not have long-established migration programmes often lack explicitly formulated immigration health policies and practice. This applies especially to countries in Europe (Lohrmann, 1994). Despite population movement across their borders, particularly labour migration, many European countries do not have health related migration laws or regulations or, sometimes, only fragmented ones. This is beginning to change, however. In March 2001, the 43-nation Council of Europe Parliamentary Assembly called for the recognition of the special health needs of migrants and refugees noting that migrants fall outside the specific scope of existing social services in most European countries even though they are considered vulnerable populations. Therefore, it called for the migrant health screening process in Europe to be standardized and for governments to harmonize their legislation and policies in this area[4].

The European Union is also considering accession-related health issues. It recognizes that migration is expected to increase with accession and that this may amplify the concomitant risks for the spread of communicable diseases. The EU encourages the exchange of information and experience among EU countries in view of the fact that health related issues are central to the pre-accession phases[5].

Health issues are beginning to be recognized also in other regions by migration policy makers. Participants of the West African Regional Ministerial Conference on the Participation of Migrants in the Development of their Country of Origin, held in Dakar in October 2000, declared that they were "committed to informing the populations of the West African region and making them more aware of the positive and negative prospects connected with international migration, including public health issues" (Dakar Declaration).

Migrant health has been identified as an issue of concern in other regional consultative processes including the CIS Conference Process as well as in the Plan of Action of the Regional Conference on Migration, known also as the Puebla Process (see also **chapter 8**).

3) Ellis Island History, www.ellisisland.com/inspection.html.
4) www.press.coe.int/cp/2001/181a(2001).htm.
5) www.europa.eu.int/comm/health/ph/key_doc/sec99-713/workpaper_en.pdf.

The legislative base for immigration health assessment is articulated at three different levels:

- WHO's International Health Regulations, adopted in 1971 and currently under revision, ensure "maximum security against the international spread of diseases with a minimum interference with world traffic"[6], and aims at reducing the risk of international dissemination of diseases of global public health importance. These regulations are the only international regulatory health instrument and continue to be used as an international standard[7].

- National quarantine legislation, consisting of legislation and regulations for managing infectious diseases at national level.

- Specific immigration health laws or regulations designed to manage broader health and disease concerns in migrant populations.

Countries, which do include health components in their immigration process, base them primarily on two principles:

- Protection of Public Health: the motive is to prevent the introduction of infectious or communicable disease potentially carried by migrants. Most attention in traditional immigration countries is focused on tuberculosis, vaccine-preventable diseases, parasitic diseases and sexually transmitted infections (STI), such as syphilis or gonorrhea.

- Reduction of Burden on Publicly-Funded Services: the motive is to reduce the costs or demands for health care or social services that may be required by migrants after arrival. Attention is therefore focussed on chronic, high treatment cost diseases and is most often applied in countries that have state-supported national insurance health plans.

6) WHO, International Health Regulations:
www.who.int/emc/ihr/int_regs.html.

7) These regulations have three goals: 1) to detect, reduce and eliminate sources from which infection spreads; 2) to improve sanitation in and around ports and airports; and 3) to prevent the dissemination of vectors. WHO's International Health Regulations are linked to its strategy for Global Health Security, which adopts specific programmes for the prevention and control of known epidemic threats such as influenza, meningococcal disease or cholera. This program also aims at improving preparedness through the strengthening of national infrastructure for disease surveillance and response.

TEXTBOX 5.1.

Migration and Health at IOM

IOM's Migration Health Services Division (MHS) delivers direct health services to individuals and communities and is also deeply involved in providing policy advice to governments. MHS conducts its operations in close cooperation with other IOM core service areas, such as counter-trafficking, movements, assisted voluntary returns, labour migration and technical cooperation.

Returning Kosovars receiving IOM health screening

Facing the increasingly complex challenges of establishing policies, norms, legislative frameworks and best practices to manage migration's health dimensions, MHS has a long history of providing technical migration health services and assistance to migrants and governments.

MHS's scope of activities evolved over time: it does not restrict health to physical aspects, but aims to deal with migrants' "state of complete physical, mental and social well-being and not merely the absence of disease or infirmity"[8].

In the 1950s, IOM's health services concentrated on providing assistance to European migrants displaced as a result of the Second World War. Since then, MHS's geographical area of responsibility has progressively expanded to other regions of the world, now covering most continents. Throughout the 1990s, IOM's growing involvement in humanitarian emergencies, massive population displacement, labour migration and irregular migration, especially trafficking, has translated into a growing diversification of migration health issues and related operational activities.

8) WHO, Health Definition: www.who.int/aboutwho/en/definition.html.

The vast majority of IOM's MHS staff works on established programmes in IOM field missions. At present, MHS has a permanent or intermittent presence in over 25 locations worldwide. MHS staff members are also deployed on temporary duty in areas where there are no permanent MHS structures, as emergency situations require.

MHS has also been active in developing an integrated framework for defining and supporting the study of migration health. Since the 1990 Migration Medicine Conference, jointly sponsored with WHO[9], IOM has been working to further the understanding of health in the context of population mobility. Working closely with Member States, regional bodies and partner organizations, such as UNAIDS and UNHCR, IOM has moved to the forefront of global efforts aimed at addressing migration health issues and establishing best practices.

MHS also promotes the understanding of migration health through collaborative analyses and research done with a variety of partner agencies, migrant organizations and institutions. Through the quarterly publication of the *Migration and Health* newsletter, MHS serves as a forum for information and dissemination of individual and institutional views on matters related to health and migration.

Extensive experience in the delivery and practice of migration health services enabled MHS to establish basic principles in this area. These have led to a series of objectives designed to guide the international community's approach to migration health:

- taking advantage of better and increased access to information technology to capture, store, transmit, retrieve and analyse immigration health information better;

- supporting efforts and initiatives to modernize the approach and rationale underlying resettlement-related migration health assessment so as to improve its relevance and effectiveness;

- exploring the potential role of resettlement-related migration health assessment to improve public health, both in terms of surveillance and increased provision of preventive and treatment services, and assistance to groups at risk;

- increasing awareness of the importance of migration health for all sectors of the health care system through training and education in migration health programmes;

- increasing information on the impact and consequences of migration-associated disease and illness in regions of resettlement, asylum, and return;

- assisting in the modernization, streamlining, and revision of immigration and quarantine legislation to ensure that public health protection is guaranteed with minimal restrictions on international travel.

Applicability of Immigration Health Assessments

Traditional immigration countries require the health of prospective migrants to be assessed before they come to their shores as part of a mandatory migration application process; however, most European countries do not require health assessments for resettled migrants. If health assessments are required, they are performed upon arrival.

The question as to whether migration health assessments for the purpose of protecting public health should be done before arrival or after arrival in host countries has not been sufficiently studied. Although the pre-arrival health assessment appears to be the ideal model to prevent the importation of tuberculosis or other infectious diseases, it can address only well organized and planned migration movements which comprise only a fraction of the global mobile population.

National and international migration legislation and migration health rules and regulations, whose primary purpose have been to prevent the importation of communicable diseases by means of exclusion and of containment no longer respond to today's migration health challenges with the significant increase in global population mobility.

The demographic and personal characteristics of migrants and mobile populations today are very different from those of past decades. Migratory movements take place against an evolving international health background, where patterns of disease and illness are very different from those of only a few decades ago. As a consequence, the traditional focus of border migration health activities, which was often limited to infectious or communicable diseases and focussed on immigrant and refugee populations, has dramatically expanded. More attention needs to be

9) International Migration, Quarterly Review (1992).
   Special Issue: Migration and Health in the 1990s, vol.XXX.

directed to the health needs of increasingly diverse migrant groups, such as the elderly, women, labour migrants, and vulnerable groups. In addition, health effects produced by stress related to the migration process can extend to non-communicable diseases and psychosocial illnesses, which are now important areas of study in the field of migration health.

The Health Dimensions of Regular Migration Flows

One of IOM's major responsibilities in the context of regular migration flows is the migration health assessment, processing and treatment of immigrants and refugees prior to their resettlement in a host country. Globally, IOM is the largest provider of immigration health assessment and evaluation services. Every year, IOM performs some 80,000 health assessments of prospective migrants in Asia, Africa and Eastern Europe before departing for their countries for resettlement (see **graph 5.1.**). In the early 1990's, this figure peaked at 250,000. However, these figures only give a fragmentary idea of annual migration health assessments. Besides IOM, several other organizations and national panel physicians perform migrant health assessments. And, many destination countries do not require health assessments for their prospective migrants.

In 2001, most MHS health assessments took place in Russia (18,828), Ukraine (17,306), Vietnam (9,106) and Kenya (5,475). Most of those migrants traveled to the United States (68 per cent), followed by Canada (19 per cent), Australia (10 per cent) and New Zealand (under 3 per cent) (see **graphs 5.2.** and **5.3.**). Some 47 per cent of all persons that received IOM health assessment in 2001 were refugees. The remainder were economic migrants or migrants moving to join family members.

As already pointed out, the legislative requirements for immigrant health assessments vary from country to country and consequently there is a wide range of assessment requirements. The most common denominator, however, is the need to ensure that the migration process does not endanger the health of the migrants or the host populations. Another major concern of some traditional immigration countries is the assessment of the disease level of the incoming populations and the impact that this level will have on national health or social services. Some countries waive these demands or cost considerations for refugee populations, but they can be applied to immigrants and other voluntary migrants such as students.

GRAPH 5.1.
Number of IOM Immigration Health Assessments, 1990 - 2001[10]

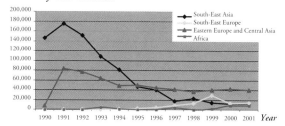

Number of health assessments

GRAPH 5.2.
IOM Immigration Health Assessments per Country of Destination, 2001

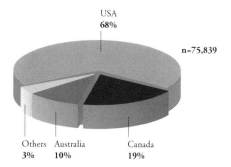

USA **68%**

n=75,839

Others **3%**   Australia **10%**   Canada **19%**

GRAPH 5.3.
IOM Immigration Health Assessments per Region of Origin, 2001

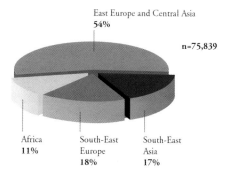

East Europe and Central Asia **54%**

n=75,839

Africa **11%**   South-East Europe **18%**   South-East Asia **17%**

10) The sharp decline in the high numbers of health assessments in South-East Asia in the first half of the nineties was due to the development of the Comprehensive Plan of Action (CPA), which promoted the orderly resettlement of Indo-Chinese refugees under the Orderly Departure Programme. The CPA came to an end in 1996. IOM's services have so far not been requested for Latin American countries.

TEXTBOX 5.2.

Components of Migration Health Assessments

Depending on the situation, the type of migrant and country-specific guidelines, an immigration health assessment may include all or some the following components:

• detailed physical examination;
• clinical or laboratory investigations:
    - serological test
    - radiological screening
      (chest x-ray, usually for tuberculosis)
    - chemical analysis (blood/urine);
• pre-departure treatment and referral;
• HIV counseling and health education;
• referral or consultation with specialist medical staff;
• review of immunization history;
• provision of/arranging for administration of vaccines and/or treatment for some conditions (intestinal and other parasitic infestations, tuberculosis, malaria);
• detailed documentation findings;
• preparation of required immigration health forms and documents;
• transmission of relevant information or documentation to appropriate immigration or public health authorities;
• ensuring fitness for travel;
• provision of medical escorts/special services for travel and relocation;
• analysis and reporting of relevant findings to public health authorities of the receiving countries to facilitate integration into the health system through adequate professional follow-up of identified conditions.

The last point is particularly important for the most vulnerable migrants, such as refugees, who often have mental or physical health conditions related to the conditions suffered during the process of migration (such as torture, loss of family members, rape, malnutrition) and require appropriate health care upon arrival.

IOM strives to ensure that all of the above activities are performed in accordance with medico-ethical, legal and moral considerations, balancing national medical assessment requirements with local customs (i.e. gender and religious issues) and maintaining the confidentiality and security of medical information. In addition, immigration health issues often straddle differences in culture and social practices. The customs and traditions of the migrant as well as of the host population also need to be considered.

While countries of immigration attempt to avoid the introduction of certain health conditions by requesting overseas health assessments for particular categories of migrants, the health assessment process is nonetheless seriously limited. Many immigration countries do not require health assessments for all categories of migrants and travellers, such as long-term visitors.

Non-immigrant visitors can be an important source of tuberculosis morbidity, as demonstrated by a study reporting a higher rate of multi-resistant tuberculosis among the non-immigrant visitors than among refugees and immigrants (Weiss *et al.,* 2001). Consequently, the public health practice of targeting surveillance programmes around the world to refugees and immigrants only should be reviewed.

Against the background of increasing operational challenges, such as operating in emergencies, insufficient equipment and facilities and short timeframes, IOM is tasked with ensuring that immigration health assessments are adequate and meet the national standards of the immigration country, while protecting the health of both the migrants and the local population.

Although the principles and basic structure of migration health assessment programmes are standard, IOM constantly attempts to refine the migration health assessment process in liaison with involved resettlement countries. In doing so, MHS aims at being flexible and attuned to trends in communicable diseases; assessing the impact of introduced diseases on demand from health services; using data on the results of the health assessment process for follow-up care upon resettlement and research and, finally, educating and counselling migrants in order to protect and improve their health.

The Health Dimensions of Irregular Migration Flows

In recent years, irregular migration has dramatically increased, posing serious problems to migration managers (for more details on irregular migration (see **chapter 3**). Irregular migration challenges the basic principles of migration health and thus its health implications deserve special attention.

In many cases, migrants travel between countries with different disease prevalence. For certain infectious diseases such as tuberculosis, haemorrhagic fever, HIV/AIDS and malaria, this signifies a considerable risk to spreading disease through migration. In addition, migrants with limited economic resources are often desperate enough to pursue high-risk behaviour, or ignore health hazards, in order to earn a living.

TEXTBOX 5.3.

Health Hazards Related to Trafficking in Women and Girls

Trafficked women and minors may be exposed to higher risks of HIV transmission and other reproductive and sexual health problems than commercial sex workers due to the nature of their confined and controlled situation and vulnerability to abuse, including violent rape[11].

In addition, trafficked women and minors often have no access to health services and STI treatment due to lack of financial resources, fear of discovery, use of inappropriate health care providers and so on. For instance, almost all trafficked women assisted by IOM Sarajevo (Bosnia and Herzegovina) who agreed to undergo STI testing, had at least one type of STI infection. Other reproductive health risks associated with trafficked women and girls are unwanted pregnancies, unsafe abortions, pelvic inflammatory diseases, infertility and the potential for cervical cancer[12].

Irregular migrants are particularly exposed to contracting or transmitting diseases, to injuries or even death. Health concerns during transportation phase are often directly related to travel conditions such as overcrowded and unsanitary conditions or unseaworthy vessels. Migrants travel hidden in cargo, containers, and closed compartments and sometimes lack access to air, food and water for extended periods of time.

When considering the factors influencing health after arrival in a destination or transit country, irregular migrants are more vulnerable than regular migrants. Many factors put their health at risk, including poverty, powerlessness, discrimination, vulnerability to sexual or labour exploitation, absence of social and legal protection and often lack of access to health care and social services. Their status may not allow them to seek or obtain health care or access preventive health services. Their financial and legal situation affects their ability to pay for health care and forces them to obtain health care through unofficial means, which may

stimulate illicit supplies of drugs, unsafe abortions, especially in the context of trafficking of women or girls, or other dangerous practices. Even if social and health services are available free of charge, migrants with irregular status are often hesitant to use these services out of fear of being reported to immigration or labour officials and deported.

Given its scale, addressing irregular migration is a priority for organizations such as IOM that consider irregular migration as an important social and health challenge. To help alleviate the problem, MHS offers physical and mental health and psychosocial services, in addition to food, accommodation, and environmental hygiene in various locations throughout the world. Voluntary HIV/AIDS or STI testing and health education are offered as well as other reproductive health services, such as pregnancy testing, ante- and post-natal care, access to family planning services and information on referral facilities.

The key message IOM promotes in relation to migrants with irregular status is the right to affordable and accessible health care for all migrant populations, irrespective of their legal status.

Selected Key Migration Health Issues

Mental Health of Migrants

Mental health has long been neglected as a serious medical concern. WHO estimates that the mental health budget of most nations accounts for less than 1 per cent of total health expenditures. Even more telling, one-third of all countries does not have mental health programmes at all. Yet, an estimated 450 million people worldwide suffer from mental health, neurological disorders and/or psychosocial problems. On a global level, major depression is the leading cause of disability. Although mental disorders can affect people in all sectors of society, migrants and refugees are disproportionately affected.

91

11) Javate de Dios, A. (1999). *Macro-economic policies and their impact on sexual exploitation and trafficking of women and girls: issues, responses and challenges.* UNAIDS conference, satellite symposium. Kuala Lumpur, Malaysia: October 22-28.
12) Peroff, N. (in draft, March 2001). *HIV and reproductive health risks to trafficked women in the sex industry,* IOM medical programme for Bosnia and Herzegovina.

The dynamics of migration are complex, and the key driver of migration and population health discrepancies is inequity (IOM, 2002b). Even in the most favourable situations, migration represents a major transition in a person's life. Migrants cross interpersonal, socio-economic, cultural, and geographic boundaries. Leaving behind a familiar environment for an unknown place and a society with different values, perceptions and traditions, strongly challenges the migrant's capacity to cope with change.

In certain cases, migration improves migrants' welfare by allowing for better work opportunities, living conditions and the possibility to reunite with family members. Unfortunately too often migration is triggered by unfavourable situations such as war, famine or human rights violations. Many of the factors that result in a decision to migrate, or to flee a country and become a refugee, are the same factors associated with greater vulnerability to the development of mental health problems (IOM, 2002b).

The extent to which migration poses a potential mental health problem depends on many variables, such as the motives for migrating, the duration of stay in the host community, language and cultural barriers, legal status of the migrant, the migrant's family situation, and the migrant's pre-disposition to psychological problems. Although migration may not necessarily threaten mental health, it creates a specific vulnerability, especially when combined with added risk factors.

Mental health extends beyond a lack of mental disorders and is not a synonym of Western style psychiatric care. According to WHO, a person's mental health is fundamentally interconnected with his or her physical and social functioning (World Health Organization, 2001). As a result, the promotion of mental health must take into account physical as well as social factors.

A particular way of comprehending and dealing with mental health is through the "psycho-social" approach, which implies the existence of a link between social and cultural factors and mental well being. To understand the functioning of the individual affected, he or she must be seen within his or her social context, such as the family, community or culture. A psycho-social approach influences the state of mental health of an individual or a community, by acting on the social factors that surround them. It does not deny or exclude the need for psychological, psychiatric or other direct medical or non-medical interventions to improve the state of mental health.

TEXTBOX 5.4.

Promoting the Mental Health of Migrants – a Perspective from IOM

IOM encounters mental health problems amongst mobile populations on a daily basis. Given growing awareness of the importance of mental health in successful migration, IOM has intensified its mental health services for migrants over the past decade. IOM's activities in this area help internally displaced persons, returnees, refugees, irregular migrants, trafficked populations, demobilized soldiers, irrespective of age or gender. The activities are generally community-based in line with national health plans and focus on a combination of local capacity-building and direct care.

IOM psycho-social counselling programme in Kosovo

For instance, IOM is providing mental health services to irregular migrants in Indonesia and the South Pacific ranging from psychiatric to psychosocial care. Migrants with irregular status have limited access to services and are sometimes kept in detention for undetermined periods of time awaiting the outcome of asylum claims. Insecurity about their fate and inadequate services can affect their mental health, leading to helplessness and hopelessness, and ultimately, profound depression. Acts of self-injury, hunger strikes and fights are commonly observed[13].

13) Steel, Z. and D.M. Silove (2001). "The mental health implications of detaining asylum seekers", *Medical Journal of Australia*, 175: 596-599.

In October 2001, 44 persons of a total of 421 passengers survived a tragic boat incident in the Java Sea off Indonesia. The fishing boat was transporting irregular migrants from Iraq on their way to Australia. The survivors were provided round-the-clock care by the IOM Jakarta medical team. Most survivors suffered severe psychological problems, including depression leading to suicide attempts following the loss of family members or sometimes their entire family.

IOM mental health professionals have also provided care to 1,400 irregular migrants housed on the islands of Manus (Papua New Guinea) and Nauru (Pacific) since September 2001. These camps were set up following a decision by the Australian Government to create offshore migration processing centres to stem the number of irregular migrants arriving at their shores. IOM medical teams have dealt with cases of self-injury, conflict resolution, and the provision of special services to vulnerable groups such as the mentally-ill and unaccompanied minors.

In Cambodia, all basic mental health services and facilities established before 1975 were entirely destroyed by the Khmer Rouge regime. After many years of massive human rights violations, forced displacement, and starvation, IOM began in 1994 assisting Cambodia with the reconstruction of its mental health services within the framework of the country's National Health Plan. IOM trained the first 20 Cambodian psychiatrists and psychiatric nurses follo-wing the Pol Pot regime. As part of the training, over 4,000 patients were treated at outpatient clinics yearly while experienced professionals trained their peers, creating a sustainable long-term solution for the country.

Following the hostilities in Kosovo, IOM assisted in rebuilding local health infrastructures by introducing psycho-social services. Using a community-based and multidisciplinary approach, psycho-social services and training were aimed at responding to the needs of people who had been forced to flee from violence. So far, 76 local psycho-social counsellors have completed their training and are helping hundreds of individuals and families.

While IOM has begun to integrate mental health into its work, much more is required to raise awareness amongst IOM stakeholders and partners about the importance of the mental well being of migrants. Taking care of migrants' mental health contributes to identifying positive and sustainable solutions for their enhanced integration as well as the reconstruction of communities affected by violence. Mental health should be seen as central to all attempts to improve the health of populations.

HIV/AIDS and Migration

The relationship between HIV and population mobility was discussed very early in the course of the AIDS epidemic. In the early 1980s, some of the very first studies of what later became known as AIDS dealt with mobile populations, concentrating on the spread of the new disease along major trucking routes in Uganda. In an interesting mirror reflection from far wealthier regions, early reports in the United States talked about the spread of a mysterious new disease, as gay men with disposable income unknowingly took the new human immunodeficiency virus from one gay community to another against the background of sexual liberation.

Less attention was paid to mobility and mobile populations as resources for AIDS prevention and care tended to go to national citizens (i.e., non-migrants). AIDS prevention efforts turned towards specific groups of people ("risk groups" such as injecting drug users, men having sex with men, and sex workers), as well as to mainstream "general populations". Much of the attention focussed on population mobility concentrated on the fear that migrants entering countries might bring HIV with them. At the same time, many migration specialists were concerned about exposing migrants to racism and stigma by unwarranted association with "AIDS".

Some migrant or mobile populations are at higher risk of HIV infection. In fact, some segments of mobile popu-lations are among the world's most vulnerable groups: would-be labour migrants who slip to the margins of society when they are unable to find employment; refugees and internally displaced people who are victims of physical and social insecurity; and people trafficked for sex work. Migration and HIV/AIDS are linked by the conditions and structure of the migration process, including poverty, exploitation, separation from families and partners, and separation from the socio-cultural norms that guide beha-viour in stable communities.

Risk and spread of the epidemic are also related to travel between countries of higher and of lower HIV prevalence. Some such travellers are tourists while others are migrants returning home permanently or for visits.

93

TEXTBOX 5.5.

IOM's Work to Address Migration and HIV/AIDS

IOM is working closely with UNAIDS and a number of other partners to address population mobility and HIV/AIDS through knowledge-sharing activities such as producing documents and consulting on programme and policy issues. IOM also carries out projects to bring AIDS prevention, access and care to mobile populations throughout the world.

For example, IOM helps with HIV/AIDS prevention, counselling and testing populations along major trucking routes in Ethiopia. This programme offers HIV/AIDS information materials, condoms, voluntary counselling and testing, and treatment of sexually transmitted infections.

In South Africa, IOM is engaged in several HIV/AIDS projects, ranging from organizing a soccer tournament to raise HIV/AIDS awareness amongst migrant workers, to reviewing academic literature and laws concerning migration and HIV in Southern Africa.

In Algeria, IOM works with the Ministry of Health and Population to address HIV/AIDS prevention and care among both migrants returning home for visits from European countries and among migrants transiting Algeria.

In south-eastern Europe, IOM has carried out several projects to assess HIV vulnerability factors among young people in a region affected by massive conflict-related mobility in order to strengthen AIDS prevention capacities and facilitate discussions among health authorities of regional governments.

Such programmes can be effective when migrants have the same access to HIV care and the same degree of protective behaviour as local people in the countries where they live, and when the social conditions that increase migrants' vulnerability to HIV are modified.

Tuberculosis and Migration

Tuberculosis (TB) is one of the most important infectious diseases in the context of migration health. The history and transmission of TB infections are strongly influenced by social and environmental factors, contributing to the greatly disparate rates of disease between populations of different social backgrounds. In addition, unlike sexually transmitted infections, effective preventive measures are limited as TB is an airborne disease.

Although the twentieth century was successful in controlling most infectious diseases, TB has re-emerged as the world's leading curable infectious killer. According to the Center of Disease Control (CDC) in Atlanta, US, "one third of the world's population is infected with the TB bacillus" (CDC, 2001). If untreated, a single infectious person can infect between 10 to 15 other persons per year (Global Drug Facility, 2001).

TB has re-emerged in low prevalence populations, such as in New South Wales, Australia, because of increased immigration from high-prevalence countries (Heath *et al.,* 1998). Some immigration countries report that, while the number of TB cases among their nationals have declined or stabilized over the last 10 years, the number of TB cases among foreign-born people has increased. Between 1995 and 1998, the decrease in TB case rate among US-born people was 3.4 times that of foreign-born persons (Sahly *et al.,* 2001).

In addition, medical literature is consistent concerning the impact of migration on emerging multi-drug resistant tuberculosis (MDR-TB) in receiving countries. Studies from Australia (Yuen et al., 1999), Canada (Hesri *et al.,* 1998) and the Netherlands (Lambregts, 1998) show that MDR-TB occurs in their foreign-born population or is imported.

Sbabaro (2001) states that "MDR-TB represents a failure of physicians, of public health officials and of government". It can thus be argued that current public health systems require attention and improvement.

Managing Migration Health – Some Policy Development Priorities

Attending to the health of mobile populations is an important part of migration and an essential component of migration management. Failure to address the health of migrants during the various phases of migration will hinder successful integration and can hamper effective reconstruction in the case of post-conflict or post-emergency situations.

Regardless of the phase of the migration process, healthy migrants are productive migrants and make important contributions to the communities they settle into. However, the substantial changes in origin and demography of immigrants in many countries mean that immigrant health and disease patterns may vary significantly from the host population.

To facilitate integration, reduce delays in diagnosis and treatment, improve the health of migrants and undertake cost savings, the following measures merit serious consideration:

Building Capacities

Investing in capacity-building in the public health programmes of the countries of origin is a key measure for managing migration and its health consequences. Bridging capacity in public health between countries of origins and destination represents a strategic investment in order to control the spread of infectious diseases such as tuberculosis or HIV/AIDS in mobile populations.

Supporting Public Health Research

Public health research should examine the evidentiary basis of and aim at improving certain migration health laws including, but not limited to, resettlement-related health requirements. In this regard, a broader partnership of concerned stakeholders would not only include public resettlement or public health authorities, but also international organizations, health providers dealing directly with migrants, non-government organizations working with migrants, advocacy groups and leading research institutions.

The ultimate objective should be to ensure that treatment standards, assessment and care for migrants are in line with best practice.

Strengthening of Information and Surveillance Systems

Strengthening existing public health surveillance system within countries and implementing an international surveillance and information exchange system between countries of origin, transit and destination countries represent additional important aspects of efficient migration health management. These systems should be adapted to local conditions and linked to regional, multi-country gatherings such as regional consultative processes in the area of international migration management.

However, ethical standards in data collection and dissemination must be ensured. The confidentiality of migrants must be protected in order to avoid discrimination and stigmatization.

Improving Access to Health Care

Access to health care should be based on pragmatic economic considerations as well as on a rights-based approach encouraging countries to uphold their migrant and human rights commitments in accordance with conventions and international legal instruments.

Although most host countries offer health care to migrants, the level of care may vary according to the migrant's resident status. Governments should provide all migrants with access to the same health care services as their nationals irrespective of immigration or residence status.

In all receiving countries, a culture-sensitive promotion and delivery of curative and preventive care should be implemented, based on knowledge of the migrants' health needs. Health care professionals should be given appropriate inter- and intra-cultural training and should be included in the concept of better health care delivery in order to alleviate cultural and linguistic barriers and to serve as bridges between host and migrant communities.

Finally, vulnerable groups such as refugees, asylum seekers and irregular migrants may refuse access to health care for fear of being denied resettlement, or authorization to stay if they are known to have an infectious disease, placing a risk on public health. In these cases, psycho-social counselling should form part of the health care approach.

Developing Integration and Prevention Strategies

The development of integration and preventive strategies can contribute to decreasing stigmatization and discrimination both within migrant communities and host country societies. In this context, and based on the migrant's right to health, the vulnerability of migrant communities should be reduced by integration policies to overcome their marginalization and improve their working and living conditions which affect their health. Concrete measures should include access to decent housing, water supply, sanitation and education.

95

Conflict prevention should include health aspects of the targeted populations, such as the "Health for Peace" approach pioneered by WHO. In post-conflict scenarios involving internally displaced persons or demobilized ex-combatants, but also in counter-trafficking activities, irregular labour migration and smuggling, migration managers should support humane, orderly and adequate return and reintegration efforts which include the restoration of access to essential health care for migrants.

Conclusion

Attending to the health of mobile populations is an important part of migration and an essential component of migration management. Failure to address the health of migrants during the various phases of the migration process will hinder successful integration and can hamper effective reconstruction in the case of post-conflict or post-emergency situations.

Increasingly migrant health is being recognized as an issue of regional and even global concern as evidenced by its prevalence in regional and international fora. Ongoing efforts are being made to promote better access to health services for migrants and to avoid unnecessary deterioration and marginalization, while avoiding preventable transmission of certain health conditions and the overburdening of health care systems.

The policy development priorities to managing migration health outlined above are increasingly being included in the public policy agendas of new immigration receiving countries and will provide an important foundation from which to manage the complex migration and health nexus. These priorities are summarized as building capacities; supporting public health research; strengthening information and surveillance systems; improving access to health care, and developing integration and prevention strategies.

CHAPTER 6

The Link between Asylum and Migration

Global population mobility is greater today than at any time in modern history and is unlikely to decrease substantially in the near future. While the most visible growth in international migration in recent years has resulted from refugee-producing crises[1], only a small percentage of the 175 million international migrants are refugees or asylum seekers, i.e., persons fleeing persecution and needing international protection[2].

Nonetheless, modern migratory patterns make it increasingly difficult to distinguish between the various groups on the move, and to adopt customized and effective policy responses. Migratory patterns include both persons who are forced to move and others who choose to do so. However, the motivation for movement may be mixed, even in an individual case: "forced migrants" may choose a particular destination country because of family ties or job opportunities; "voluntary migrants" may also feel compelled to move because of dire situations at home, including extreme poverty, population pressure, poor governance, environmental decay, or they may find that conditions in their country of origin have changed and prevent their return home.

At the same time, with demand for legal migration opportunities outstripping supply, many people who are not refugees are seeking to gain access to new countries through the asylum channel in the absence of viable alternatives. Underlying the asylum and migration link is the increasingly apparent reality of a powerful labour supply and demand momentum; in the absence of authorized channels for matching these needs, the situation is leading to the use of asylum mechanisms for migration purposes. Resulting from disparities in wages, job opportunities and demographics between the developed and the developing world, there has been an increased need for the import of labor into the developed world and an excess of labour in the developing world. Thus, both push factors in countries of origin and pull factors in countries of destination fuel voluntary migration to link the global supply of labor to the demand for both highly skilled and unskilled workers (Martin, 2001).

Governmental asylum systems have become a primary – and in many cases the only – official mechanism for regulating the entry and stay of foreigners. Consequently, asylum and migration have become linked both in terms of the means chosen by individuals to move across borders and the measures adopted by states to address the international movement of people.

In the absence of a comprehensive international approach to migration management, migratory flows regulated primarily by control measures alone present three difficult challenges for the institution of asylum: the vexing phenomenon of irregular migration, especially trafficking and smuggling; the economic needs of countries of destination and origin; and the rights of individual migrants and asylum seekers.

The central challenge of the asylum and migration nexus is how to ensure adequate protection for asylum seekers and refugees while managing migration in line with national priorities. These priorities will vary from facilitating migration to address labour market and development needs to combating irregular migration. However, governments can only manage migration and asylum effectively if these issues are addressed in a credible and cooperative manner. This is necessary to restore public confidence in both the institution of asylum and in their government's ability to regain control over the entry and stay of foreigners in their territories.

97

1) For example, in 2001, some 200,000 Afghans fled their war-torn country, 93,000 fled the Former Yugoslav Republic of Macedonia, and some 188,000 refugees from Angola, Sudan, the Democratic Republic of Congo, the Central African Republic, Somalia, Burundi, Liberia, Rwanda and Senegal fled to neighboring countries. At the same time, however, nearly the same number of persons went home. For example, 267,000 African refugees were able to return home including to a range of countries in Africa. See UNHCR Press Release of 18 June 2002, www.unhcr.ch/news; UNHCR 2001 Global Population Statistics, www.unhcr.ch/statistics.

2) UNHCR estimates that at the end of 2001, there w[...] 12 million refugees worldwide. This figure excludes [...] persons. The overall population of concern to UNH[...] certain persons displaced within their own countrie[...] not seeking asylum in another country) was estima[...] persons. In addition, approximately 923,000 perso[...] worldwide in 2001, compared to 1,092,000 in 20[...] op.cit. (on figures, see also **chapter 17**).

This chapter explores contemporary issues of the link between asylum and migration. It begins with a brief overview of the development of the modern institution of asylum and its place in today's migratory context. After highlighting significant state responses to addressing these issues, the chapter concludes with recommendations for better migration management taking due account of the requirements of refugee protection.

Development of the Asylum Regime

A refugee is defined in international law as a person outside his or her country of origin who has a well-founded fear of persecution on account of his or her race, religion, nationality, membership of a particular social group or political opinion[3]. Legal and practical responses to mass movement of refugees in certain parts of the world have contributed to the evolution of broader definitions which additionally consider persons fleeing generalized circumstances of armed conflict, civil strife or other natural or man-made disasters as refugees[4].

Under relevant international standards, a refugee is entitled to protection in a country of asylum against return to the country of feared persecution – the "non-refoulement" obligation[5] – and to be treated without discrimination[6]

3) United Nations Convention relating to the Status of Refugees (hereinafter "1951 Refugee Convention") of 28 July 1951, Article 1, UN Treaty Series no.2545, vol.189, p.137.

4) Article 1 of the OAU Convention Governing the Specific Aspects of Refugee Problems in Africa of 10 September 1969. See UN Treaty Series No. 14691. Paragraph III 3 of the Cartagena Declaration on Refugees of 19-22 November 1984. See Collection of International Instruments and other legal texts concerning refugees and displaced persons (hereinafter "Collection of Int. Instruments"), vol.II, p.206.

5) Article 33 of the 1951 Refugee Convention.

6) The principle of non-discrimination is a common principle to human rights law. The 1951 Refugee Convention contains a general obligation of non-discrimination in Article 3.

7) Under the relevant legal instruments, there is no requirement for an individualized determination of status, and it is generally assumed that once the refugee producing situation has ended, the persons will no longer be refugees and in need of or desiring continued international protection.

8) General Assembly Resolution 428 (V) of 14 December 1950. See Collection of Int. Instruments, vol.I, p.3.

9) Unlike the term refugee, the term migrant is not specifically defined in international instruments and does not have a generally accepted definition, see also **chapter 1**.

10) For details, see **chapter 1** and **textbox 1.4.**, as well as Status of Ratification of the Principal International Human Rights Treaties of 10 July 2002, www.unhchr.ch/pdf/report.pdf.

in terms of access to a host of social benefits and protections in the country of asylum[7]. The Statute of the Office of the United Nations High Commissioner for Refugees (UNHCR) was adopted in 1950, mandating UNHCR to provide international protection for refugees falling within its scope and to seek permanent solutions for the problems of refugees by facilitating their voluntary repatriation, assimilation into new communities, or resettlement[8].

In contrast, while discrete aspects of migratory activity are addressed in international law, there is no comprehensive international regime for addressing broader migratory movements of persons moving to seek temporary or permanent employment or other life opportunities in another country, or to be united with family[9]. In addition, with limited exceptions found primarily in international and domestic labour laws, migrants are not entitled by virtue of their status to international protection beyond that accorded to all persons under international human rights law. For example, the Constitution of the International Organization for Migration (IOM), the only inter-governmental organization whose mandate is exclusively focussed on migration, does not regulate migratory movements *per se.*

The 1990 United Nations International Convention on the Protection of the Rights of All Migrant Workers and Members of their Families sets forth a series of protections to be provided to migrant workers, both regular and irregular, and recommendations for inter-state cooperation in achieving protection of the enumerated rights. While the Convention should soon enter into force, it is primarily countries of origin which have signed up[10] and it appears unlikely that many countries of destination will accede to it as currently formulated. Therefore, its effectiveness as a tool for regulating the movement of persons and for enhancing the treatment of migrant workers is likely to be limited in the near term.

Distinctions in the treatment under international law of refugees and migrants are understandable. For reasons of national identity, security, political independence, tradition, and much more, nation states have been historically vested with the right and responsibility to protect their own citizens and to determine which foreigners may enter and remain in their territories. In discharging this right and responsibility, States have been reticent to accept binding international limitations on their freedom of action in determining the entry and stay of non-nationals.

Legal Norms for the Protection of the Individual

Following the end of the Second World War, and as a direct result of its horrors, international legal norms for the protection of the individual have blossomed. In contrast to the general regulation of relations between states, with states as the subject of legal responsibilities, international human rights law developed to regulate the responsibilities of states towards individuals[11]. The adoption of the 1951 Refugee Convention was an important step by states in accepting limitations on their sovereignty with respect to a narrowly defined category of non-national – the refugee. The failure of the state of origin or nationality to protect parts of its population by in fact persecuting this population created the recognition of the need for other states to assume certain protection responsibilities for the persecuted persons.

Therefore, the entire presumption of the 1951 Refugee Convention regime is a role for action by the international community where the state of origin or nationality fails to protect its citizens or nationals. Consequently, the Convention focusses on two issues: a careful definition of who is a refugee entitled to protection by a state party in whose territory the refugee finds him or herself; and specific obligations states providing protection are required to observe.

A few examples illustrate the disparate and finely tailored obligations states have been willing to accept with respect to refugees as compared to migrants:

Under relevant principles of international law, everyone has the right to seek asylum[12]; refugees have the right not to be sent to a place of persecution[13]; and no one may be sent to a place where he or she would be tortured[14]. However, no one has a right to be granted asylum in any particular state or to enter any state, without permission. States have been willing to accept limitations on their sovereignty with respect to the treatment of refugees within their midst, but have been unwilling to accept such limitations with respect to voluntary migrants or on their sovereign right to determine which non-citizens may enter or remain in their territories. Indeed, even the obligations under international law not to send a refugee to a place where he or she would be persecuted and not to send a person to a place where he or she would be tortured do not require a state to keep the person in its territory. It would be consistent with a state's obligations under international law to send such a person to a third country, willing to accept him or her, provided there are sufficient safeguards in place to preclude the possibility that the person would simply be sent onwards to a place where he or she would be exposed to such risk.

99

11) For example, the adoption of the Universal Declaration of Human Rights by the UN on 10 December 1948 marked the beginning of the development and codification of international law standards and responsibilities to individuals, regardless of the State involved. As a result, no longer could States assert that the treatment of their own nationals was a matter of their own internal affairs and not of consequence to the international community. See Collection of Int. Instruments, vol.I, p.153.

12) Article 14 of the Universal Declaration of Human Rights.

13) Article 33 of the 1951 Refugee Convention.

14) Article 3 of the Convention against Torture and other Cruel, Inhuman or Degrading Treatment or Punishment adopted by United Nations General Assembly Resolution 39/46 of 10 December 1984. See Collection of Int. Instruments, vol.I, p.233.

Historical Underpinnings

Revisiting the historical and political context for the development of the refugee regime is instructive. The mindset of the creators of the international refugee regime in the early 1950s was shaped by the then-recent persecution by Nazi Germany of Jews, gypsies, and various other groups they saw as social misfits, in addition to the Soviet oppression of persons opposing the regime on political or religious grounds. States at the time were keenly aware of the humanitarian imperative of protecting refugees, and were willing to do so even if it meant foregoing certain sovereign freedoms regarding the treatment of foreigners. This humanitarian spirit was not unlimited. By its very terms, the 1951 Refugee Convention was limited to refugees created from events occurring before 1951; moreover, states could opt to adhere to the obligations of the Convention with respect to European refugees only[15].

The International Organization for Migration (originally established as the Intergovernmental Committee for European Migration) was created in 1951 specifically to facilitate the settlement of persons from the displaced persons camps following the Second World War into countries of permanent settlement[16]. Traditional immigration countries and others were willing to extend a generous hand to persons seeking entry and settlement on humanitarian grounds.

At the same time, countries such as Australia, Canada and the United States were seeking to populate their territories and build their economies through the permanent settlement and employment of foreigners. These countries actively promoted immigration based either on uniting families or seeking to encourage the transfer of certain skills and resources needed in the domestic economy, whether temporary or permanent.

Furthermore, in the 1960s and 1970s, Europe, the Persian Gulf states and the Asian economic tigers developed temporary guest worker programmes to meet domestic labor needs. The national development goals of these countries fortuitously coincided with their own – and the world's – humanitarian and political goals of protecting refugees fleeing persecution.

Moreover, the numbers of persons requiring international protection after the Second World War were limited by the fact that many authoritarian regimes of the day prevented or actively discouraged their citizens from leaving. For example, the Iron Curtain seriously constrained the free movement of persons, with a profound impact both on the ability of persons to migrate and the perception of those who were successful in reaching a new destination. As a result, in most industrialized countries, refugees fleeing the persecution of the 1950s through 1970s were welcomed for permanent settlement for economic, political, strategic and humanitarian reasons. In addition, in that particular historical and geopolitical context, it was generally considered obvious which persons were refugees and in need of international protection. For all of these and other reasons, supply of and demand for migrants were largely in equilibrium and refugees benefitted from this general state of affairs.

In 1967, a Protocol was adopted to the 1951 Refugee Convention that expanded both its geographic and temporal application to be both worldwide and ongoing. With respect to refugee situations in Africa and Latin America, regional refugee instruments were adopted: in addition to protecting individual political refugees, these measures specifically addressed massive cross-border flows of individuals arising from civil strife, armed conflict or other man-made or natural disasters.

In summary, therefore, the asylum regime generated after the Second World War in the major industrialized countries was built on the assumption that most refugees were escaping from communist regimes, that there would be fairly limited numbers of such persons, and that their problems in part could be solved through the migration programmes of traditional migration countries. There was ideological convergence between the needs of individual refugees and the policies of the primary refugee-protection states.

---

15) It was only with the adoption of the 1967 Protocol to the 1951 Refugee Convention that protections for refugees were expanded beyond events occurring after 1951 and it was no longer possible for States newly signing on to the refugee protection regime to opt for a Euro-centric refugee protection focus.
Protocol relating to the Status of Refugees of 31 January 1967. See UN Treaty Series, no.8791, vol.606. p.267. At the same time, the evolving body of international human rights law, up to and including recent Protocols, has continued and maintained the essential humanitarian spirit of providing protection against persecution and torture.

16) IOM's name, mandate, presence and membership have evolved since its creation in 1951 to now cover the full range of migration management issues and to include Member States from every continent, see also **textboxes 1.5** and **2.2.**

The Asylum Regime Today

A combination of factors have dramatically altered the political and economic landscape and directly impacted the institution of asylum, including the following: the fall of the Soviet Union and the consequent opening of movement from East to West, the rise of nationalist movements and the outbreak of conflict, and changes in communications and transportation facilitating international travel.

Refugee flows result from serious violations of human rights and armed conflict. However, as identified by UNHCR and IOM, these causes often overlap with or may be provoked or aggravated by factors such as economic marginalization and poverty, environmental degradation, population pressure, and poor governance at both ends of the migration spectrum.

Asylum seekers and refugees may use the same mode of travel as undocumented migrants and resort to, or are exploited by, criminal smugglers and traffickers. At the same time, persons without any valid claim to refugee protection exploit the availability of the asylum channel as a means to gain either temporary or permanent stay abroad.

Refugee Status Determination

With its focus on specifically enumerated grounds of persecution forming the basis for international protection, the

17) While UNHCR has provided States extensive guidance on this question, the 1951 Refugee Convention itself does not require or set forth a standard procedure for individual refugee status determinations. Group or *prima facie* refugee status determinations are fully compatible with the requirements of the Convention. Moreover, while many of the Convention's provisions are of particular relevance in long-term stay situations, the Convention does not require permanent settlement or presume eventual acquisition of the nationality of the host country. Indeed, it is primarily in the western States that national provisions for the treatment of refugees provide for or presume a long-term stay. In contrast to the practice in western States, the focus of the asylum systems in Africa and Latin America, in particular, is not primarily on resettlement or even individual asylum determinations but instead on providing temporary protection to large numbers of persons moving across borders, with the presumption that they will choose to return home once the underlying cause of the forcible movement is resolved. The problem of large-scale, cross border movements of refugees is not addressed separately by the 1951 Refugee Convention. UNHCR's Executive Committee, however, has provided guidance on addressing situations of mass influx. See EXCOM Note on International Protection in Mass Influx, submitted by the High Commissioner 1 September 1995.

1951 Refugee Convention aims at protecting individuals or discretely identifiable groups. To determine which migrants are refugees entitled to protections under international refugee law, states, particularly in the developed world, have set up elaborate administrative systems for examining individual claims to refugee status. Refugee status is primarily determined on a case-by-case basis and the end result is a judgment on whether or not to provide asylum to the individual and his or her family[17].

Many developed country asylum systems include significant procedural protections, such as access to representation by counsel and rights of appeal to higher administrative or judicial authorities. Indeed, in many systems, the administration of the asylum system is characterized by a high degree of litigation. Consequently, it can take months or even years for an individual's claim to be resolved. During this period, depending on the country, claimants are temporarily provided food, shelter, medical care, education for children, legal and other social services. In some countries, asylum seekers are provided authorization to work while they wait for their claims to be determined, are sponsored by private individuals or organizations or otherwise support themselves; in other countries, asylum seekers are detained in prison-like conditions and maintained by the state until their claims are resolved as a way to ensure that they do not evade eventual removal if their claims are unsuccessful.

These procedures and systems can be costly and time consuming. In some countries which have not considered themselves countries of immigration, these procedures have become a principal or sole means for persons to gain admission, regardless of the reasons they have left their country of origin or the situation they would face upon return. Some critics charge that asylum has become a complex legal battlefield in some countries and the "winners" are not necessarily those with the strongest claims to international protection but rather those who are most adept at "playing the system".

Moreover, many countries that once considered themselves exclusively or primarily countries of origin for migrants today are now countries of destination or simultaneously countries of origin, transit and destination. As a result, these countries are beginning to face the same asylum and irregular migration pressures as the traditional destination countries. Many of these countries do not possess the administrative mechanisms or the trained officials to be able to handle these new flows.

An Asylum Crisis?

Since the mid-1980s, the number of asylum claims lodged in developed countries has grown. According to UNHCR figures for the ten-year period 1980-89, 2,200,000 asylum applications were submitted in industrialized countries. For the period 1990–99, more than 6 million asylum applications were filed in these same countries (UNHCR, 2001a)[18].

Most asylum management systems were not equipped to keep pace with the increased number of claims logged and significant backlogs occurred. These backlogs effectively delayed the resolution of individual claims even further and increased the costs of managing the systems. In the meantime, individual asylum seekers developed ties to and stakes in the local community, through, for example, employment, marriage and childbirth. These attachments complicated return prospects for individuals whose asylum cases were eventually turned down.

In recent years, the vast majority of asylum seekers in industrialized countries have been found not to be refugees. For example, in the 16 countries of the Inter-Governmental Consultations on Asylum, Refugee and Migration Policies for Europe, North America and Australia (IGC), in the period from 1992–2001, just 12 per cent of asylum applicants were granted refugee status, while 6 per cent were granted another humanitarian status and allowed to remain, bringing to below 20 per cent the total offered protection on humanitarian grounds. UNHCR figures support the same finding: in the European Union (EU) in 2000, less than 20 per cent of those persons applying for asylum were granted refugee status or received complementary forms of protection (UNHCR, 2001b). Together with those applications which were either withdrawn or administratively closed, therefore, more than 80 per cent of these asylum seekers were found not to be in need of international protection[19]. In addition, the IGC estimates that the approximately 450,000 to 500,000 annual asylum applicants in their countries cost IGC taxpayers approximately US$ 10 billion each year.

However, these costs are partially offset by positive contributions of the asylum applicants through taxes or consumption.

To complicate modern asylum systems in the developed world, most rejected asylum seekers are not sent home or even to a country through which they transited. Between 1995 and 2000 in six IGC states, only 1 out of 5 persons with rejected asylum claims was returned home.

The implications of the lack of return have been widely observed: the failure to promptly return persons determined not to be refugees challenges the entire credibility of the asylum determination system. Because very few rejected cases are returned, many persons apply for asylum not because they are seeking protection from persecution, but simply because this appears to be an effective way of gaining access to the territory of a state they would prefer to live in. Zero immigration policies in many states, including most European countries, have meant that the asylum channel is the only option available to both bona fide refugees and others seeking a migration outcome. Asylum has become a "backdoor" to immigration for many people.

When compared with the scarce financing given annually to support the overwhelming majority of the world's refugees in camps in the developing world, the high costs of maintaining western asylum systems has led some to question the relative allocation of resources. As a point of comparison, the total annual budget for UNHCR is less than US$ 1 billion, which is ten times less than IGC States spend annually on asylum systems (administration of the systems, social benefit costs, etc.), where a majority of the money is not spent directly on the persons in need of protection. With the significant expenditure of resources, and the fact that few persons whose asylum claims have failed are returned, some argue that the current system is little more than a "costly charade". They argue that the current asylum system is "broken" and in need of fundamental repair. In this view, genuine refugees may miss out while only those who can afford the ticket stand to win the asylum lottery.

18) The 1990s have seen major crises such as the Gulf War, the wars in the former Federal Republic of Yugoslavia and various conflicts in Africa (i.e., Angola, Sudan, etc.).

19) However, UNHCR data are more complex than this and illustrate the difficulty of drawing precise conclusions (see UNHCR, 2001b, technical note 17 on page 5). For example, the figures provided reflect administrative decisions, and not always the number of persons involved. In addition, rejections of cases at first instance, and subsequently again at a later stage, may be double-recorded.

Asylum seekers and migrants arrive on the Pacific Island of Nauru

Loss of Control

A particularly disturbing consequence of the rise of smuggling in migrants and the abuse of asylum systems is that states feel they have lost the sovereign right to determine who enters and remains in their territories. This feeling of loss of control has real consequences for the health, safety and stability of society and has led to an increase in public anger and frustration both at government and at the migrant level. Unfortunately outbreaks of xenophobia, discrimination and violence against foreigners in some countries have become commonplace.

In addition, governmental handling of asylum has become a central political issue in some countries. The outcome of the 2001 federal election in Australia is considered to have turned on the government's tough stand in not permitting boatloads of asylum seekers to land in Australia to have their claims adjudicated. The government refused to allow asylum seekers to land and established, and funded, offshore

processing centres in cooperation with the governments of Nauru and Papua-New Guinea and with assistance from IOM and UNHCR. These measures aimed to prevent people smugglers delivering their product – entry to Australia – while ensuring physical protection and access to asylum procedures. The Australian public had been becoming increasingly concerned at the rising number of boat arrivals, as Australia's normal refugee and immigration processes were being undermined. This reflected on the government's capacity to manage its borders and had security implications. While taking this tough stance on unauthorized arrivals, Australia has been able to maintain support for its regular lawful migration program (see **chapter 9**). Both immigration and asylum management issues have also played a significant role in recent elections in Denmark, France, Germany and the Netherlands.

Asylum as Sanctuary vs. Asylum Crisis

In many parts of the developing world, asylum has a wholly different connotation. It involves offering sanctuary primarily to sudden cross-border movements of hundreds of thousands of persons fleeing war, internal conflict, persecution or serious man-made or natural disasters[20]. Camps are established for the care and maintenance of refugee populations pending resolution of the underlying

20) Western Europe experienced this form of refugee crisis with the cross-border outflows of Bosnians and Kosovars in the mid-1990s. The Western response, at the urging of the High Commissioner for Refugees, was similar to that of the developing countries - to offer temporary protection, without individualized status determinations during the height of the crisis.

cause of the cross-border movement. Individual refugee status is not necessarily determined and, even when it is, resettlement is often not considered the preferred solution. In any case, there is no guarantee of eventual resettlement places for those persons determined to be refugees. While the reality may be different, the predominant presumption of asylum in the developing world is that it is a temporary form of refuge. Indeed, many refugee situations are long-standing and protracted. Generations grow up in camps, with makeshift schools, economies, and entire villages created to support the refugee population[21].

In developed countries, as noted above, asylum is often seen as a means to permanent settlement for a comparatively small number of asylum seekers. The numbers of persons crossing borders in emergency situations in the developing world far exceeds by orders of magnitude the number of persons applying for asylum in developed countries. Western government claims of crisis in their asylum systems when a few hundred or even a few thousand individual asylum claims are submitted are met with incredulity by refugee advocates and much of the rest of the world.

Nonetheless, there is a real crisis in terms of the public perception of refugees, asylum seekers and other migrants in some western democracies, and in terms of support for the institution of asylum. Public opinion in some countries increasingly fails to distinguish between asylum seekers and irregular migrants and often views both as common criminals seeking to circumvent immigration laws and cheat public resources. Governments are seen as having lost control over borders and, consequently, national safety and identity is considered under threat. Problems with irregular migration, smuggling and trafficking of persons in some parts of the world, and the security dimensions of refugee problems in other regions, have worsened the situation, leading increasingly to politicization of asylum, and in some instances, to a tendency to criminalize refugees and asylum seekers.

This situation has been further exacerbated by the rise of international terrorism, which has led to greater migration controls and to changes in the asylum policies and practices that often negatively affect *bona fide* asylum seekers and refugees.

Tightening the asylum legislation and practices on account of the fight against terrorism can have the unintended and deleterious effect of reinforcing the erroneous public perception that refugees are responsible for terrorist acts.

Trafficking and Smuggling and the Management of Asylum

Asylum management is further complicated by the rapid rise of human smuggling and trafficking (see also **chapter 3**).

As extreme forms of irregular migration, smuggling and trafficking of persons both challenge government capacities to manage migration and endanger the safety and well being of migrants. Increasingly, asylum seekers and migrants resort to the services of smugglers to facilitate their unauthorized movement across borders.

Recognizing the pervasive nature of these phenomena, in 2000, Protocols to the United Nations Convention against Transnational Organized Crime were concluded on both smuggling and trafficking[22]. These Protocols are a promising development in setting out a multi-faceted and cooperative approach to addressing these issues, including enhanced international law enforcement cooperation as well as technical assistance for governments and protection and assistance for victims of trafficking.

An ever-increasing flow of smuggled and trafficked migrants increase the scope for social destabilization grows and places greater strains on government ability to maintain national security. In a post September 11, 2001, environment, it is vital for governments to know who is in their country and why. Reasons centre around issues such as criminality, organized crime and corruption, particularly where large profits can be made, which tends to further this activity.

Often, persons smuggled into a western democracy are not apprehended. Even if they are apprehended by local law enforcement or border control authorities, the person may lodge an asylum claim simply to defer deportation. The risk of apprehension is not enough to deter persons from employing the services of a smuggler. Without a credible risk of quick return, it is likely that smuggler's

21) Examples for these are the Indochinese boat people as well as huge numbers of people from Angola or Afghanistan.
22) See United Nations Convention against Transnational Organized Crime adopted by the General Assembly on 2 November 2000 as well as the Protocol to Prevent, Suppress and Punish Trafficking in Persons, especially Women and Children and the Protocol against the Smuggling of Migrants by Land, Sea and Air, supplementing the Transnational Crime Convention, www.uncjin.org/documents or www.odccp.org.

services will continue to be used. Many states are adopting enhanced measures to penalize the smugglers; however, it will be difficult for these measures alone to reduce smuggling given the sophistication of the smuggling rings, and the large numbers of middle-men and huge sums of money involved.

The scale of these activities has thwarted efforts by western governments to control the flow of asylum seekers and manage their asylum adjudication systems.

Measures Adopted by States to Manage Asylum

As most rejected asylum seekers are never removed from a country once they enter, many western governments have focussed efforts on managing asylum through preventing and deterring asylum seekers from gaining access to their territories and thereby limiting their ability to lodge claims to asylum. Measures adopted include the imposition of visas for entry, fines and penalties on transportation companies, border controls, employment of pre-inspection or inter-ception officers at airports overseas, and exchange of infor-mation and data about trafficking routes and individuals.

Perhaps the most dramatic measure states adopt to prevent asylum seekers entering their territories is the practice of high seas interception by naval or other sea-borne enfor-cement authorities of migrant shiploads. In the United States case, for example, shiploads of Haitian, Cuban, Chinese and other nationals in the 1990s were intercepted seeking to enter the United States by sea without proper documentation. Those who presented refugee claims were either provided shipboard refugee screening or screened in a third country willing to cooperate with the United States. Only those people whose claims to asylum were deemed credible on a preliminary, more lenient review were allowed to enter the country. If the preliminary threshold was met, they were then admitted to the United States to pursue full asylum claims pursuant to the standards and with the procedural protections applicable to all asylum seekers present in the United States.

In 2001, thousands of persons seeking to enter Australia by sea without proper authorization resulted in entry interdictions and the establishment of processing centers in third countries where refugee status claims are determined by either national authorities or UNHCR for those wishing to apply for asylum. IOM is working with the relevant governments to ensure the care and maintenance of these individuals until their refugee claims are resolved and solutions can be found. To deter further boat arrivals, Australia is seeking commitments from traditional refugee resettlement countries to accept those determined to be refugees, including on the basis of family ties or other connections. Australia announced that it would not accept persons seeking to arrive by sea without proper documen-tation into Australian territory, but that it will uphold its commitments to refugee protection and will ensure that protection is provided to those who genuinely need it.

While some refugee advocates question whether other countries should accept for resettlement refugees seen by many as Australia's asylum responsibility, Australia has secured the commitment of countries such as New Zealand, Sweden and Canada to accept some of the intercepted persons for resettlement. In addition, some are now being resettled in Australia. Of those whose claims to refugee status have been denied, many have requested voluntary return to their countries of origin and are receiving IOM support in facilitating their safe return.

While addressing refugee protection claims outside the domestic asylum procedure, the practice of high seas inter-ception to prevent access to the territory illustrates efforts to "de-link" asylum from migration outcomes. As noted above, one striking feature of the treatment of the movement of persons under international law is that people fleeing persecution have the right to seek asylum and refugees have the right not to be sent to a place of persecution, but there is no corresponding right to be granted asylum or to enter any country. Therefore, in some countries, state policy and practice has evolved towards seeking to separate refugee protection from the migration outcome desired by the individual. In that way, refugee protection obligations are met, but a person would only be able to enter the desired country after receiving governmental permission. While this approach would be problematic in the case of direct flight from a country of persecution, the focus of these efforts is on the phenomenon of "secondary movements". Secondary movements occur when refugees, whether they have been formally identified as such or not (asylum seekers), move in an irregular manner from countries in which they have already found protection, in order to seek asylum or permanent resettlement elsewhere (UNHCR, 1989).

Similarly, some states are proposing to direct their refugee admissions programmes closer to the source of the out-flow. Refugee status would be determined at reception centres in the region of origin. Coupled with this, access

105

to the desired country of destination would be limited for persons other than those applying for refugee consideration at the reception centre in order to deter persons lodging asylum claims to achieve a migration outcome. While most major refugee movements remain within the immediate region owing to geography, this approach focusses on creating disincentives for secondary movements. The notion of providing protection without admission is an innovative and, in the eyes of some, controversial approach to managing migration and asylum.

Another example of de-linking asylum from migration outcomes is the practice of providing temporary protection in the case of mass outflows. By granting blanket protection against return to an entire class of persons during a crisis, as was done in Western Europe in the case of the Kosovo crisis, states have precluded access to individual refugee status determinations until the crisis is resolved and presumably the overwhelming majority of persons could return in safety. Yet when temporary protection ends, return remains a pressing issue for many states. In any event, those persons claiming the ongoing need for international protection would have to have their claims assessed individually, albeit with elements of accelerated procedures being introduced, depending on the circumstances.

In this and other contexts, some states have adopted accelerated procedures for determining "manifestly unfounded" claims, often used in conjunction with presumptions that a particular set of countries are "safe countries of origin", not producing refugees. With this practice, the asylum seeker has the burden of overcoming the presumption that his or her country of origin is safe for him or her. Some states have adopted these measures for asylum seekers who do not reveal their identities or who arrive without proper documentation.

Recently, some states have adopted practices such as "profiling" of groups based on their national, ethnic or religious background, and deciding a priori asylum claims based on these considerations. Since September 11, 2001, some states have instituted policies for the automatic detention of asylum seekers or the application of "exclusion" clauses based on the "profile" of the asylum seeker alone.

States have also adopted measures aimed at determining which state should be responsible for handling a particular refugee status claim, such as the "safe country of transit" designation. In such situations, some states that do not

directly border refugee-producing states seek to return asylum seekers to a "safe" country through which he or she transited to pursue the asylum claim there. This notion has been pursued on both bilateral, such as between the Unites States and Canada, and multi-lateral bases, such as with the Dublin Convention in Europe. The underlying theory is that the first country offering adequate refugee protection to which the asylum seeker flees is the one that should bear responsibility for providing asylum. As many countries bordering refugee-producing countries are developing countries, or already hosting large refugee populations, this practice raises the question of whether there should be some form of burden sharing, either in the form of resettlement places or in terms of financial support. In addition, the labeling of a country as a "safe country of transit" is a matter of judgment, and there are no universally agreed criteria for making the judgment.

In addition to the preventive and other measures discussed, states have employed measures specifically aimed at encouraging potential migrants to alter their behaviour, including information campaigns on the dangers of using smugglers or about the treatment they would receive under the laws and policies of the country of destination. In addition, information campaigns have been devised to advise potential migrants about authorized channels for migration or to seek to persuade the publics in countries of destination of the need for asylum systems and of the benefits of tolerance and integration. For example, in January 2002, IOM and UNHCR jointly developed a public awareness campaign in 14 European Union Member States, funded by the European Community through its European Refugee Fund, to seek to increase public tolerance for refugees, asylum seekers, and other migrants requiring protection[23].

Refugee Protection Concerns Raised by Asylum Management Measures

The overriding issue for ensuring refugee protection in asylum management is that some of the management measures mentioned above do not distinguish clearly between refugees and other migrants. There is a real risk these measures will restrict asylum procedures for genuine refugees. In particular, measures that do not assess the individual circumstances of the person concerned may result in people requiring protection being unable to receive refugee status. Practices which do not provide for a review of the specific individual claim may preclude the "balancing" called for when deciding whether a person is in need of international protection - and the rights to be

23) IOM *Press Briefing Notes*, 22 January 2002.

afforded accordingly - against the risk that the asylum seeker may represent to the host country. In extreme cases, the establishment of "out-posted" immigration control mechanisms without due procedures to ensure adequate treatment of asylum claims, may prevent otherwise *bona fide* asylum seekers from leaving their country of origin, and in effect be tantamount to leaving refugees in orbit or even to the possibility of "refoulement".

Some of the enhanced border control and security-related measures adopted since September 11, 2001, in particular, are blunt tools designed to find a needle in a haystack. The measures target those very few irregular migrants who aim at not only simply finding a better life but at inflicting harm or otherwise engaging in criminal activity. However, the net impact is overly inclusive and not necessarily effective for weeding out persons who may pose a risk to society.

In addition, refugee advocates fear that the example set by the imposition of stringent control measures by the western industrialized countries will negatively influence the willingness of states neighbouring refugee-producing states to accept cross border movements of refugees.

Moreover, some measures may have the deleterious effect of enhancing the attractiveness of smugglers, offering ways of circumventing immigration and border controls. Many refugees and asylum seekers employ smugglers because they may have no other means of reaching safety. And the more states enhance border and access controls, the more likely *bona fide* refugees and asylum seekers will need to utilize the services of smugglers, even with all the attendant risks.

Misuse of the Asylum Channel for Non-Protection Purposes

Is abuse of the asylum system by non-refugees the crux of the problem? There is a strong case to be made that the problem is not asylum abuse per se but the more general phenomenon of irregular migration. Many people who currently misuse the asylum channel for non-protection purposes would seek other means to remain in a desired destination country if the asylum channel were not available: going underground, destroying evidence of identity or citizenship to avoid return, or marriage and family unification fraud. Thus, abuse of the asylum channel may be more properly an expression or a symptom of a broader problem. Abuse of asylum, and public confusion and frustration at asylum seekers, is prevalent primarily because the asylum system is such a convenient or often the only mechanism for many determined migrants.

Irregular migration today is caused by a host of factors but the most important is the fundamental supply and demand dynamic of international labour markets. The world's current demographic realities are compounded by striking wage differentials between the developed and developing world. And these differentials are predicted to become even far more dramatic in the not too distant future (for more details, see UN, 2000 and UN, 2001).

While global trade liberalization has resulted in increasingly mobile international flows of goods and capital, efforts to regulate international labour flows have been limited and have focussed primarily on the high-skill end of the labour market. Progress in trade liberalization with respect to the movement of natural persons as providers of services pursuant to the General Agreement on Trade in Services (IOM, 2002) has not proceeded at the same pace as progress in other areas of liberalization. While the need for multinational companies to have access to highly trained professionals in a mobile manner to provide competitive services is well-recognized, comparatively less official attention has been given to labour market needs at other skill levels. In the absence of authorized channels to regulate the labor supply and demand imperative, individuals manage the flow themselves, and often at great personal peril.

The historical unwillingness of governments to recognize publicly their economic dependency on unauthorized, cheap and unskilled labor diminishes public trust in the effective functioning of government. There are chronic and pervasive labour shortages in many developed countries in certain skill sectors, such as nursing and information technology. In addition, significant underground economies have arisen in many developed countries, particularly in low skill sectors such as domestic, hotel and restaurant services, to fill labour market gaps and to meet the demand for inexpensive labour.

When grey market jobs are filled by irregular migrants, governmental benign neglect erodes the credibility of government migration policies. While the "asylum crisis" may be limited primarily to developed countries, the phenomena of irregular migration, including smuggling and trafficking, certainly are not. Large-scale underground economies pose significant risks both for the individuals and for their host societies. Governments of the host countries are deprived of the opportunity to exercise a fundamental responsibility of sovereignty - to make a judgment about whom to permit to enter and remain in their territories, including critical parameters such as health, security or other legitimate national considerations. In addition, the host societies lose revenue from taxes from these employees as well as other types of social contribution.

From an individual's point of view, while many irregular migrants are responding to the demand for labour in their countries of employment, they are generally not entitled to many of the socio-economic and other legal benefits and security afforded to regular migrants. These migrants are at a significantly higher risk of abuse and exploitation. Often, these migrants have been pressured due to the lack of economic opportunities in their countries of origin to move from their home communities in search of gainful employment and life opportunities only to face lack of protection in their new employment and host countries. They can face considerable alienation and isolation in their host countries, with obvious risks to society as well (see also **chapter 4**).

The Way Forward

The time is ripe for the international community to engage in a comprehensive reflection on the international movement of persons. The refugee protection regime and control measures aimed at addressing address asylum abuse must now constitute part of a broader international migration management approach that ensures refugee protection while addressing other pressing national and international migration priorities. These are not competing but complementary priorities: support for refugee protection depends on effectively functioning migration management systems; and a key component of a fully functioning migration management system is the ability to ensure protection for those who need it. Such an approach needs to take the following factors into account: global population mobility; the integration of the global economy; the political, economic, security and humanitarian needs of states at each point on the migration spectrum; and the protection of individuals, including refugees, asylum seekers and victims of trafficking.

If one state addresses asylum issues in isolation without regard to the impact on other states, the issue will just be shifted elsewhere and the causes will not be addressed or resolved effectively. At its most obvious and practical level, preventing access to asylum in one territory simply shifts the burden to another. Similarly, efforts to address asylum management that disregard related issues such as irregular migration, labour market needs, demographic imbalances, and development needs, can only be partially effective.

A more informed and open debate at national, regional and international levels on migration is essential to provide states and the international community with the understanding and tools they need to manage mixed flows effectively. This debate is now beginning in both refugee protection and migration management circles. Much more is needed, particularly on the basis of solid data about migratory trends and phenomena. Regional and international sharing of information and experience is a critical first step in breaking down barriers to identify possible common ground. Exchanges of this sort enable common language and understanding to be established and the priorities and perspectives of differently situated states and individuals to be assessed.

Refugee Protection Dialogue

On the occasion of the fiftieth anniversary of the 1951 Convention, UNCHR launched a process of "Global Consultations" on International Protection, which brought together representatives of states from all regions of the world, intergovernmental organizations, non-governmental organizations, academics and refugees themselves.

A key event in the Global Consultations process was a Ministerial Meeting of States Parties to the Convention and Protocol held in December 2001 - the first such gathering of States Parties in five decades. The meeting aimed at strengthening commitment to implementing the Convention and Protocol fully and effectively, eliciting recognition of their enduring value and importance, while encouraging additional accessions.

The Global Consultations also paved the way for the "Agenda for Protection", which sets out concrete goals and actions to strengthen protection and will serve as a guide for UNHCR, states, non-government organizations and other protection partners in the years to come. Of particular relevance to the asylum and migration link, goal 2 of the Agenda sets forth a series of objectives and accompanying actions for protecting refugees within broader migration movements[24]: better identification of and proper response to the needs of asylum seekers and refugees, including access to protection within the broader context of migration management; strengthened international efforts to combat smuggling and trafficking; better data collection and research on the link between asylum and migration; reduction of irregular or secondary movements; closer dialogue and cooperation between UNHCR and IOM[25]; information campaigns to ensure potential migrants are aware of the prospects for legal migration and the dangers of human trafficking and smuggling; and return of persons found not to be in need of international protection.

Based on the Global Consultations, UNHCR and IOM established an Action Group on Asylum and Migration Issues (AGAMI). The purpose of AGAMI is to further understanding of the link between asylum and migration; to review substantive policy issues in the management of asylum and migration; to explore ways in which cooperation between IOM and UNHCR can be furthered on these matters; and to increase each organization's capacity to contribute to national efforts to develop migration and asylum policies and programmes.

Migration Dialogue

At international level, the most comprehensive effort to date to address migration and to provide a blueprint for international migration management is found in Chapter 10 of the Programme of Action of the 1994 Cairo International Conference on Population and Development (ICPD), which addresses both regular and irregular migration. Since then, however, a lack of consensus between developed and developing states has precluded the convening of a global conference on migration, as contemplated in the Cairo Programme of Action.

However, much has changed since 1994. Now, there is greater recognition of common and complementary interests between countries of origin, transit and destination on a range of migration management issues. With particular reference to the migration and asylum link, it is understood that these issues cannot be effectively managed in isolation from each other or outside the context of a more comprehensive approach to the movement of persons.

Efforts such as the IOM Council's International Migration Policy Dialogue (IOM, 2002) and the Berne Initiative (see **textbox 15.2.**) are direct responses to the need for more comprehensive investigation into migration dynamics and more debate on migration issues. They both provide encouraging fora for enhancing international understanding and exchange on the full range of migration issues, as well as the search for cooperative approaches. Both initiatives also strive for broad participation from countries of origin, transit and destination as well as of partner intergovernmental and civil society organizations.

In parallel, regional approaches to migration management through mechanisms such as the various regional consultative processes (RCPs) on migration enable the exchange of information on asylum patterns and migration practices in a region (see **chapter 8**). They also foster the development of cooperative measures. For example, the European Union's (EU) efforts to forge common asylum and migration policies acknowledge that migration and asylum issues can no longer be addressed effectively in isolation from each other or by states acting alone. Partnerships with countries of origin, ranging from prevention to return, are now considered essential in achieving the migration management goals of EU countries (see also **textbox 14.1.**). Hopefully EU efforts to standardize and harmonize both substantive and procedural elements of their asylum systems will ensure high standards for refugee protection and diminish incentives for "forum shopping" by individuals and the exploitation of differences in these mechanisms by smugglers.

Each of the RCPs has generated a better understanding and appreciation of the relationship between migration and asylum as well as of the linkages necessary to achieve a balanced and comprehensive approach to migration management.

24) UNHCR Standing Committee of the Executive Committee of the High Commissioner's Programme, *Agenda for Protection,* 26 June 2002, available at www.unhcr.ch.

25) Of particular relevance to the establishment of cooperation in addressing the asylum and migration link, UNHCR invited IOM to present a joint paper (UNHCR and IOM, 2001) and to jointly lead a discussion on this issue during one of the Global Consultations meetings. While the paper presented the distinct perspectives of the two organizations primarily charged by the international community to address respectively the complex issues of asylum and migration, it highlighted significant common ground and a shared commitment to work for the protection of refugees while ensuring effective migration management.

Migration Management Measures

At national level, capacity-building measures to strengthen national migration management are especially important, particularly for states that are in transition or have newly become countries of destination (see also Harns, 2001). Measures may include: development of admission policies supported by adequate laws on foreigners' entry, status and residence coupled with those on asylum; creation of border management and reception centres; legal migration measures within and beyond the region; adequate institutional structures; resources for accommodating or returning irregular migrants; institutionalized and recurrent staff training; adequate technical and physical facilities; formal and informal mechanisms for discussion and planning; and capacity for on-going strategic review and evaluation.

Of particular interest are selected labour migration programmes allowing multiple short-term employment that can lead to long-term or permanent residence, addressing a variety of skill levels and encouraging cooperation between countries of origin and countries of destination, such as linking access to labour opportunities to migrant return agreements. While demand will probably continue to outstrip available legal migration opportunities for the foreseeable future, opening legal channels for migration may help relieve the burden on asylum systems and contribute to re-legitimizing the asylum system.

Measures to facilitate early removal of rejected cases are particularly important in maintaining the integrity of the institution of asylum as well as for an effectively functioning migration management system (UNHCR and IOM, 2001). As noted by UNHCR and IOM in the joint paper for the Global Consultations, a key IOM contribution to the states' efforts to combat irregular migration and to maintain support for asylum is its ability to facilitate voluntary return. Return both helps deter future irregular migration and supports state efforts to establish credible migration management systems. States will find it easier to return unauthorized migrants if the system as a whole is more credible.

Conclusion

Measures to address the root causes and management of migration must now be pursued in parallel with efforts to create international appreciation of the inevitability and need for voluntary migration and migrants and their positive contribution to socio-economic development. Care is needed to guarantee that measures to address forced migration through the institution of asylum and other mechanisms – whether as a result of persecution, human rights abuses, conflict, severe deprivation, or other similar causes – do not assume that all migration is forced and therefore a problem. Not all migrants are victims and not all migration is a problem.

Without elements of force or coercion leading to the requirement for prevention and protection by the international community, migration can be regulated for the benefit of countries of origin and destination, as well as for individual migrants and their communities. The key, therefore, is to work to strengthen the institution of asylum and reduce forced and irregular migration while creating a system that permits and encourages voluntary migration through authorized channels, restoring the element of choice to individuals and governments.

A fully and effectively functioning international migration management system would facilitate voluntary migration to meet the needs of the global economy and mobile populations. At the same time, vulnerable persons would be protected and forced and irregular migration would decrease.

CHAPTER 7

Internally Displaced Persons – An Issue of Migration Management?

"We have often turned into mere firefighters, rushing to tackle one crisis after another, to damp down the flames of one outbreak of uncontrolled migration after another, and in doing so we have often lost sight of the broader picture."
(Tarschys, 1998)

This growing awareness among governments worldwide has led to migration management measures that take the broader context into account. However, even though migration management is increasingly recognised as a useful tool, it has only rarely been applied to forms of forced migration. Forced migration is still largely considered a humanitarian rather than a migration management issue *sui generis*.

One type of forced migration is internal displacement, which has yet to benefit from a managed, strategic approach. To a large extent, fire fighting aptly describes the current international response to internal displacement. Internal displacement has increased in scope and complexity, affecting more and more countries worldwide and becoming the subject of growing international concern. However, measures to address internal displacement are primarily implemented in response to a specific crisis. While international humanitarian actors prioritize immediate assistance and protection requirements, there is a lack of focus on managing the broader picture and developing comprehensive strategies to address the issue.

Displaced due to life or livelihood-threatening circumstances, internally displaced persons (IDPs) have traditionally been relatively neglected by the international community because they remain in their own country. At the same time, national authorities are not able to provide the necessary assistance, or indeed may be the agents of persecution or strife in many IDP circumstances. Known as "the protection gap", this dilemma has only recently started to be addressed by international actors, alongside growing awareness of the plight of IDPs, the increasing incidence of displacement, and the need for management.

As with other forms of forced migration, internal displacement is a multi-faceted phenomenon: causes may be political, military, environmental, or civil; similarly its

effects and the resulting needs of the displaced populations can be just as varied. It is thus necessary to adopt a comprehensive approach in order to address internal displacement effectively, often involving a variety of actors. The internal displacement crisis is growing despite a number of mechanisms set up by the international community to address the issue in recent years. Arguably, therefore, action is still necessary to forge longer-term strategy incorporating current humanitarian responses.

This chapter aims at assessing how, or whether, certain migration management principles can be applied effectively in order to address the growing displacement crisis in an integrated fashion. The following section describes the phenomenon of internal displacement, the international mechanisms for addressing the crisis and the guiding principles which underpin laws pertaining to internal displacement. The chapter will then explore the concept of migration management and the possibility of translating its principles effectively in order to define a policy-oriented management strategy for internal displacement.

Definition and Scope

The definition offered by the Representative of the UN Secretary General on Internally Displaced Persons ("the Representative"), Francis Deng, describes IDPs (1998) as "persons or groups of persons who have been forced or obliged to flee or to leave their homes or places of habitual residence, in particular as a result of or in order to avoid the effects of armed conflict, situations of generalized violence, violations of human rights or natural or human-made disasters, and who have not crossed an internationally recognized State border".

Unlike the definition of refugees, the definition of IDPs is not a legal definition: instead it has been formulated as a tool for describing who falls within the group. Even so, in practice IDPs are such a heterogeneous group that there is often debate over who is an IDP and at what point displacement ends[1]. The International Confederation

1) For example, the Norwegian Refugee Council's Training Modules on Internal Displacement pose the following types of questions for discussion "Does a family living in a permanent structure for several years within a camp setting satisfy the definition of displacement or could they be considered resettled"? In his latest report to the Commission on Human Rights, the Representative of the Secretary General notes that in response to a request by OCHA to explore the question of when internal displacement ends, he plans to call together experts and representatives of international organizations and NGOs to examine the issue and come up with practical guidance (E.CN.4/2002/95 at § 92).

111

of the Red Cross (2000) maintains that "[…] the UN definition does not seem as readily applicable for operational purposes, as it covers a group that is so wide and whose needs are so varied that it exceeds the capacities and expertise of any single organization. Accordingly, several humanitarian organizations depart from this definition when seeking to identify persons falling within the scope of their activities and mandate. Some employ criteria which narrow down the category of persons of concern, for instance by concentrating on those who are victims of persecution. Others seem to go beyond the definition by also including returning refugees or demobilized soldiers".

There has also been debate on the usefulness of categorizing internally displaced persons as a distinct group, rather than addressing vulnerable communities in general. However, as Rudge writes (2002): "the central concern is not to grant internally displaced a privileged status, but to identify who and where they are and then to ensure that their needs are not ignored".

There are two common elements within the definition: forced movement and permanence within national borders. Beyond these shared characteristics, the category is extremely broad. Estimates of the magnitude of internal displacement vary for two reasons: difficulties in establishing the precise number of displaced persons given the flux in conflict situations, and inadequate understanding of who falls within the definition, and for how long[2]. Further, in some situations, lack of humanitarian access to the displaced population means that only rough estimates of the total figure can be made. However, the figure of approximately 25 million displaced due to conflict in 47 countries was given for the end of 2001[3]. The highest figures for IDPs are in Africa with an estimated 13.5 million people forced to flee their homes. Figures have been rising at an alarming rate. One source states that there were approximately 2 million IDPs from 10 countries in 1980 (Loescher, 2000). This rise may be explained by the changing nature of conflict:

current conflicts are largely fought within national borders; mass displacement and targeting of the civilian population are aims rather than the by-product of conflict.

The Special Coordinator of the Network on Internal Displacement (see below) estimates that a further 25 million people have been displaced for reasons other than conflict, such as development projects or environmental degradation (2001). This brings the total IDP figure in the world today to around 50 million. Estimates for this type of displacement vary considerably: the World Bank has estimated that about 10 million people annually enter the cycle of forced displacement due to dam construction and urban/transportation schemes (World Bank, 1994); many other authors claim that about 90 to 100 million people were displaced by development schemes during the period 1986-1993 (McDowell, 1996). The disparity in estimates demonstrates that development-induced displacement and other non-conflict forms of displacement have received scant attention from the international community.

International Mechanisms and the Guiding Principles

The international community has been active in recent years in responding to situations of internal displacement, mainly conflict-induced displacement. Various options were originally presented to the Representative in his work toward establishing an appropriate international framework. These included the creation of a special agency for IDPs, the designation of an existing agency to assume full responsibility for the internally displaced, and collaboration among the various relevant agencies. The model currently being used by the international community is collaboration among agencies: "The scale and the multifaceted nature of displacement crises have led the [Inter-Agency Standing Committee] IASC to recognise that an effective and comprehensive response to the protection and assistance needs of displaced persons necessitates a collaborative approach. Thus, the management model for assistance and protection in situations of internal displacement, rather than a single agency approach, is one that involves government officials, UN agencies, international organisations, and international and local NGOs" (IASC, 1999).

Within the UN system, various units are responsible for IDPs. The Emergency Relief Coordinator (ERC) acts as the focal point at the headquarters level for the inter-

2) In April 2002, a roundtable on "When Displacement Ends" was co-hosted by the Brookings-CUNY Project and ISIM/Georgetown University, and chaired by the RSG for IDPs, Francis Deng, in an effort to determine the criteria for being able to assess when a situation of displacement has come to an end.

3) The Global IDP Database relies on information made available from various public sources. Where lack of humanitarian access to the displaced populations means that only a rough estimate can be obtained, the Global IDP Database has calculated a median figure using the highest and lowest available estimates. www.idpproject.org/global-overview.htm. See also **chapter 17.**

agency coordination of humanitarian assistance to IDPs, and chairs the IASC. Briefly, the responsibilities of the ERC include:

- Global advocacy on assistance and protection requirements;
- Resource mobilization and the identification of gaps in resources for IDPs;
- Promotion of the establishment of a database and global information on IDPs;
- Support to the field on related humanitarian issues, including negotiation of access to IDPs (IASC, 1999).

Additionally, the Office for the Coordination of Humanitarian Affairs (OCHA) has appointed a Special Coordinator on IDPs, who chairs the Senior Inter-Agency Network to Reinforce the Operational Response to IDPs. The Network is made up of the members and standing invitees of the IASC[4]. Upon his recommendation, an IDP Unit has been set up within OCHA to advise and support the ERC in focussing on and coordinating an effective response to the needs of IDPs.

Further, at the request of the Commission on Human Rights, the UN Secretary General appointed a Representative on Internally Displaced Persons in 1992. The Representative was requested by the Commission on Human Rights and the General Assembly to examine existing international law and its applicability to the protection and assistance of IDPs. He was then tasked with preparing an appropriate legal framework in this regard. The Representative presented the Guiding Principles on Internal Displacement to the Commission on Human Rights at its fifty-fourth session in April 1998. Resolution 1998/50 was adopted by the Commission unanimously, taking note of the Principles and requesting the Representative to report back regularly on their dissemination and implementation.

The Principles divide displacement into three phases: protection from arbitrary displacement (pre-displacement); protection and assistance during displacement; and, guarantees for safe return, resettlement and integration (post-displacement). They reflect and are consistent with international human rights and humanitarian law, restating relevant norms in a context of internal displacement,

clarifying grey areas and addressing identified gaps in protection. The instrument containing the Principles is not in itself binding; instead it aims at providing guidance for the various actors involved in internal displacement. However, many of the norms contained are legally binding, as they are restatements of international legal norms found in treaties and conventions. The Guiding Principles consolidate the relevant rights and norms into one document and state them in a way as to be specifically relevant to the internal displacement situation. They thus provide a practical implementation tool and should be closely followed in all programmes benefitting IDPs, and in all attempts to address the issue of displacement.

The Representative uses the Guiding Principles in his dialogue with governments in various parts of the world to provide practical guidance. Intergovernmental and non-governmental actors have undertaken to disseminate and apply them in their work with internally displaced populations. Two examples illustrate this application: in Colombia, national non-government organizations (NGOs) have disseminated the Principles widely, and use them as a benchmark of standards for monitoring and evaluating national policies and legislation (see also **textbox 7.1.**); in Sri Lanka, a consortium of some 50 NGOs have been conducting an outreach programme based on the Guiding Principles among governmental officials, international organizations, other NGOs and displaced communities (E/CN.4/2002/95 at 31). The Principles thus constitute a significant tool in efforts to address internal displacement comprehensively and the resultant protection and assistance needs of affected populations.

TEXTBOX 7.1.

Internally Displaced Persons in Colombia

Dominating the latter half of the twentieth century, the internal armed conflict in Colombia has followed an escalating pattern of human suffering leading to the internal and external displacement of millions of Colombians. Cumulative figures on the numbers of persons uprooted vary greatly between governmental and non-governmental sources. *Consultoría para los Derechos Humanos y el Desplazamiento* (CODHES), a leading NGO working with IDPs estimates that some 2 million Colombians were displaced between 1985 and mid-2001; governmental sources estimate a figure of some

4) The full members of the IASC are OCHA, UNICEF, UNHCR, UNDP, FAO, WFP, WHO. A standing invitation is extended to ICRC, IFRC, IOM, Steering Committee for Humanitarian Response, INTERACTION, ICVA, Representative of the Secretary General, High Commissioner for Human Rights and the World Bank.

Colombian IDPs

614,000 persons for the same period. Notwithstanding this great difference, there is broad consensus on the upward tendency in the rate of displacement, as well as an increase in the number of regions affected. The Social Solidarity Network, the state agency tasked with IDP assistance, reports that the number of municipalities affected by displacement in 2000 increased by 67, reaching 547 in 2001. One thing all sources agree on is the identification of the actors responsible for displacement: self-defence groups (most commonly cited), insurgent groups and, in last place, state forces.

A joint effort has been made in recent years to better understand the patterns of IDP resettlement and the conditions faced by IDPs during this indefinite period of transition, as well as the impact of displacement on individuals, according to ethnicity and gender. One alarming conclusion points to the disproportionate impact of violence and displacement on ethnic minorities. The Social Solidarity Network notes that 24 per cent of displaced Colombians are members of ethnic minorities.

Another growing concern is the concentration of displaced households in deprived neighbourhoods on the outskirts of Colombia's largest cities. The United Nations Thematic Group on Displacement estimates that between 30 and 50 per cent of Colombia's IDP population is located in five major cities. These displaced families not only face inadequate living conditions, but growing violence at the hands of urban militias, often resulting in further displacement, particularly in Medellín and Barrancabermeja.

Government efforts to address the needs of displaced populations have focussed on emergency assistance. However, security conditions have impeded possibilities of return for most IDPs. Many of the displaced think they may never return to their places of origin.

IOM responded to the need for longer-term solutions to IDP needs by complementing existing emergency assistance programmes with post-emergency activities designed to

smoothen and shorten the period of transition faced by IDPs until total social and economic integration.

In Colombia, IOM is working with governmental and non-governmental partners in providing assistance to IDPs, with the aim of building the capacity of key partners to better respond to the challenges posed by displacement in host communities.

A very important part of this work is being carried out by IOM field offices in the departments of Putumayo, Caquetá, Nariño, Valle del Cauca, Santander and Norte Santander. By maintaining a permanent field presence in each region, IOM's programmes are providing hands-on support to the community-led development initiatives. As the programmes aim to respond to the needs of these populations, it is developing activities in a number of inter-connected areas, such as: income generation, health, education, social infrastructure, housing and community organization. At the end of 2001, IOM's Post-Emergency Programme had developed 187 projects in 55 municipalities.

One programme has brought together a group of displaced and local women from Sabalete and San José de Buenaventura in Cauca province. To build a new life, the women needed essential ingredients such as facing life after surviving war and forced displacement, rebuilding broken dreams, the need to feed a family and become self-sufficient.

But starting a new life in a new place without resources was a daunting task. With assistance from IOM and the NGO *Asociación de Mujeres Campesinas e Indígenas de Buenaventura* (AMUCIB), they managed to start a small farm. Initially, the project was a way to raise animals for their survival. But thanks to their hard work, it now provides income and generates employment for other displaced and local women household head.

About 2,500 households and over 200 officials, NGOs and others were interviewed during the initial research and interview phase. The most urgent needs were identified as water and sanitation, clinics, housing, schools, and income-generating projects.

Although IOM assistance programmes for displaced persons and host communities in Colombia are just 2 years old, they are already making a difference in the lives of some 130,000 persons.

Toward a Management Strategy

This chapter does not aim at restating arguments concerning a new agency or a lead agency; the collaborative approach is working well in a number of areas. However, the Representative himself recognizes that the model "has not always proven adequate, especially in the area of protection of physical safety and human rights" and that "the response to specific situations of internal displacement nonetheless remains ad hoc and still largely focussed on assistance" (E/CN.4/2002/95).

Strengthening and improving the inter-agency approach is therefore a task of pressing concern. Steps are starting to be taken: for example, to counter the criticism that much of the international response ignores protection concerns, a new "protection coalition" has been established within the IDP Unit, which aims at identifying critical protection needs in situations of displacement and at improving the quality and efficiency of field protection interventions.

Despite such positive steps to improve the response to addressing internal displacement, it seems uncontentious to state that there is no clear management strategy or vision in place for addressing internal displacement. Factors including resource constraints and different mandates mean international actors largely respond to current situations and divide their labour and responsibility. To a great extent therefore, the international community treats each IDP situation as a specific crisis to respond to, and arguably does not pay enough attention to developing a comprehensive strategy to address the issue as a whole. A more policy-oriented managed approach is needed to ensure that responses are not continually *ad hoc* or responsive but that they are undertaken within the appropriate policy framework. As Rudge writes with respect to European donors (2002), for example, "most officials acknowledged that while they were supporting a range of activities in favour of humanitarian assistance for IDPs, there were many immediate and long-term policy questions that needed addressing and which are not necessarily given due attention on the national level or in terms of European regional coordination. These questions relate to the position of IDPs in the debate over the continuum from relief to development and the appropriate strategies to help IDPs build sustainable lives in the long-term".

In the quest for a policy framework and management strategy, certain migration management principles should be considered in the context of internal displacement. Actors in the migration field, including governments, international organizations and NGOs, have realized in recent years that migration cannot be effectively managed if responses are continually *ad hoc*. There has been recognition that there is a need for coordination, planning and strategy within and between states. The same need is apparent in situations of forced migration, including internal displacement. As Loescher writes (2000): "Humanitarian action alone cannot resolve situations of forced displacement [...] Because forcible movements of people are determined by a number of complex factors, it is also necessary for governments to address not only migration policies and practices but also policies in other areas that influence the movements of people, such as human rights, civil society, trade and development policies, as well as conflict prevention and management".

Relating Migration Management to Internal Displacement

How relevant can the concept of migration management be to the issue of internal displacement? As argued above, a comprehensive strategy could be particularly relevant in responding to internal displacement as responses in this area have often been *ad hoc*, not effectively coordinated, involving a variety of actors, and without a general framework of reference. The tools of migration management may be useful in some aspects of internal displacement; however they have been hitherto developed and applied to "voluntary" migration, i.e., all migration that cannot be considered forced migration. Internal displacement on the other hand is a type of forced migration, where basic characteristics and assumptions may be different, and cannot always be translated by analogy to other forms of migration.

For example, according to some authors, the concept of migration management has developed in recognition of the inevitability of international migration. The rationale is that it is in the best interests of all parties to understand that some degree of migration is inevitable and that it should therefore be addressed in the most effective way possible. "[...] The best that governments can do is to guide and influence flows, implementing policies, which work with the tide rather than against it. They should develop policy measures that are flexible enough to deal with swings in prevailing trends and with sudden lurches into new directions" (Salt, 2000).

However, this rationale is not wholly justified in the case of internal displacement as it should not always have to occur. Internal displacement movement is not undertaken voluntarily and the most important objective in responding is always to minimize the length of displacement and the disruption caused. Return to their homes is often the best solution for internally displaced persons, or settlement to other places if return is not possible. Many wealthy, democratic countries do not experience internal displacement within their borders. Therefore the rationale for migration management, i.e., the inevitability of migration, cannot easily be translated by analogy from international migration to internal displacement. Indeed, underpinning any approach to address internal displacement should be the essential recognition that root causes of displacement need to be tackled in an effort to prevent future situations.

The very nature of the causes of displacement underlines the difficulty in linking this concept to migration management. Internal displacement often occurs because of conflicts which are unpredictable and usually unregulated, often involving non-state actors. Ghosh writes (2000): "Orderliness and manageability are closely interrelated to the predictability of migratory movement. Disorderly and unexpected movements, including, in particular, those that take place in defiance of established rules and systems, are by nature non-predictable and thus more difficult to manage. On the other hand, when a migration system, sustained by a sound information base and robust but flexible rules and practices, is effective enough to anticipate the movements, and handle them in a fair, confident, and timely manner, the risk of non-predictability is considerably diminished". *Prima facie*, therefore, migration management does not seem to be a readily adaptable tool to employ when addressing conflict-induced displacement.

Furthermore, migration management generally involves international cooperation between countries of origin, transit and destination. Indeed, a key instrument for international migration management is the promotion of dialogue and understanding among states. By its very definition, internal displacement occurs within the boundaries of one state. This is not to say that other states need not be concerned by a situation of displacement as internal displacement can turn into refugee movements, affecting neighbouring countries. Further, the entry regulations of third states may indirectly influence the occurrence and magnitude of an IDP situation, as discussed later. Nevertheless, *prima facie*, the concept of inter-state

cooperation which is the key to migration management is largely lacking with respect to internal displacement. Moreover, the state where the displacement occurs is primarily responsible for protecting and assisting the IDPs; there is no "state of nationality" vs. "host state" differential. This also implies that state sovereignty can restrict international coordination.

Therefore, it cannot be assumed that migration management is the key to solving the global internal displacement crisis. A number of basic concepts or assumptions relevant to migration management do not necessarily apply to internal displacement. However, its potential use in preventing, mitigating or eventually helping to resolve a particular situation of displacement, as well as displacement generally, is worth exploring.

Arguably, the international community continues to focus mainly on the "middle" phase of displacement in its efforts, i.e., addressing the immediate and medium-term needs of affected populations. While they must continue, current humanitarian responses focus on the crisis at hand and are therefore ill-equipped to develop comprehensive strategies for the variety of actors involved.

A comprehensive managed approach should: A) be able to assist in developing the conditions needed to prevent displacement; where this is not a realistic goal in the short-term, such an approach will be able to B) anticipate movements and plan ahead to reduce their impact. Where migration is effectively managed, internal displacement (where the needs of the population are not being met) caused by development projects, for example, should either not occur or should be able to be quickly and effectively managed by the state, with the assistance of external actors if required. Realistically, conflict-induced displacement will continue to occur, but the effects may be C) mitigated or more efficiently addressed where a managed framework has been put in place. It will also be easier to end displacement situations through D) return and reintegration or resettlement if clear migration management policies and systems are in place.

Migration management can therefore be used to develop a vision beyond immediate humanitarian needs and to survey the steps needed for long-term planning on this issue. A migration management approach can assist in preventing displacement, especially when root causes are taken into account, and in making return sustainable. Each area where migration management tools may be relevant to internal displacement will be briefly examined.

When can Migration Management be Relevant to Internal Displacement?

A) Developing the Conditions Needed to Prevent Displacement

International migration management recognizes the interplay between economic and development issues, human rights violations and population movements. Even migration characterized as "voluntary" is often the result of poverty, lack of opportunities or the desire to escape a repressive regime or violence (see **chapter 1**). Initially, many destination countries react to migratory flows by tightening border controls considerably. However, today there is growing awareness that controls alone will not tackle the cause of emigration pressures in source countries (nor the pull factors in destination countries such as the demand for labour), and therefore are not enough to manage migration successfully. Increasingly, therefore, migration management recognizes the importance of root causes, and the need to improve conditions in source countries in order to ease emigration pressures. Strategies are increasingly being negotiated which both support the sustainable development of countries of origin and the labour needs of countries of destination – while giving due regard to the rights of migrants (IOM, 2001). For example, IOM has worked with governments to set up and implement labour migration schemes, whereby nationals of developing countries are granted employment in developed countries for a limited time. In this way, the needs of both countries are met in a managed and planned way.

Similarly, any holistic approach to managing internal displacement must recognize the root causes and aim at addressing them. Rhetoric concerning "tackling root causes" is nothing new for international humanitarian actors. There does not seem to be disagreement on the necessity for such an approach, yet rarely can successful examples be cited. Zartman writes: "International aid institutions tend to view 'relief' and 'development' as separate, sequential endeavours. But this dichotomy is artificial. There are historical reasons why the international community has separated relief and development into discrete categories in its response to conflict and post-conflict situations as well as why this separation continues. But the implications for conflict-ridden societies when relief and development are separated into sequential activities are considerable" (1989)[5].

In the context of assisting IDPs in a crisis situation, such implications may include relieving national authorities of their responsibilities or may serve to create inequalities among local people. In Afghanistan for example, IOM found that IDP camps where international aid was being dispensed had a "pull effect" on vulnerable families from urban areas. Only after they were promised food in their local areas did they agree to leave the camps and return home[6] (see also **textbox 7.2.**).

TEXTBOX 7.2.

The Plight of the Internally Displaced Persons of Afghanistan

Afghan IDPs return home

After two decades of conflict and natural disasters, Afghanistan represents the world's largest displaced population. Over 5 million refugees, mainly in Pakistan and Iran, are the most visible expression of this massive human upheaval. But IDPs – estimated at over a million – represent another huge but less transparent humanitarian challenge.

IOM began to work with IDPs in the west and north of Afghanistan in the early summer of 2001. Subsequently its activities expanded from camp management to the voluntary return and reintegration of IDPs into their home communities throughout the country.

In July 2001, at the request of UNOCHA, IOM started to coordinate relief work in the giant Maslakh and Shaidayee IDP camps in the western province of Herat. At about the same time, it assumed responsibility for the Baghe-Sherkat and Amirabad camps in the northern province of Kunduz.

117

5) As quoted by Holtzman (1999).
6) IOM *Press Briefing Notes*, 15 February 2002.

Most IDPs in Maslakh, eight square kilometres of mud huts and tents in the desert between Herat and the Iranian border, came from the western provinces of Badghis, Ghor and Faryab. Poverty-stricken, illiterate and often starving, the majority had been driven off their land and into the camp by four successive years of drought.

As an open camp accepting all bona fide IDPs, Maslakh proved difficult to manage. Seeing the camp as an income-generating source of international aid, the virtually bankrupt Taliban authorities deliberately inflated estimated IDP numbers to increase aid deliveries. Herat's urban poor also swelled the camp in the hope of benefiting from distributions of food and non-food items.

When the events of September 11, 2001, triggered an evacuation of IOM and UN international staff from Afghanistan, IOM local staff continued to work in the Herat and Kunduz camps throughout the coalition bombing campaign.

In October 2001, even before the end of hostilities, IOM began a race to deliver the shelter and non-food supplies needed to help the IDPs survive the bitterly cold Afghan winter. In Herat, it employed IDPs to make 5.4 million mud bricks and commissioned the construction and rehabilitation of nearly 10,000 traditional mud shelters.

Over the next four months, it dispatched some 40 road convoys, including 30 cross border convoys from Iran, Tajikistan and Turkmenistan to destinations in Herat, Faryab, Balkh, Kunduz, and Badakshan provinces, carrying over 270,000 blankets and quilts, 150,000 items of winter clothing, 236,000 pairs of boots and socks, 20,000 tents, plastic tarpaulins and other essential items. Internal convoys from Kabul also carried supplies to the north.

But following the winter, with the defeat of the Taliban and the onset of the spring planting season, the focus of IOM programmes began to shift towards returning the IDPs to their villages from the crowded dependency of the camps.

The management problems of the Herat camps, and in particular identifying genuine IDPs from the urban poor, began to be resolved. In February 2002, IOM conducted a registration in Maslakh showing an IDP population of 112,000, down from previous estimates of over 300,000.

In Mazar-e-Sharif, where 19 camps around the city suggested a similar number of IDPs, IOM launched an initiative with the local authorities and the NGO IRC (International Rescue Committee) to resolve the problem. Food was distributed near the city homes of non-IDPs living in the camps to persuade them to leave. Nearly 250,000 responded, freeing up IOM resources to focus on the remaining 50,000 genuine IDPs.

By April 2002, IOM had established offices in Herat, Qal-e-Naw, Chaghcharan, Maimana, Andkhoi, Mazar, Kunduz, Taloqan, Faizabad, Kabul, and Kandahar, forming the core of a country-wide internal transport network for IDP and refugee returns.

Some of the first IDP families to ask for help to return home came from the Shomali plain north of Kabul. The front line between the warring Taliban and Northern Alliance factions, half the Shomali population had fled north to IDP camps in the Panjsher Valley, while others had fled south, seeking refuge in the squalid former Soviet compound in Kabul.

Between January and April 2002, two joint IOM-UNHCR operations emptied the Panjsher camps and the former Soviet compound to return nearly 23,000 IDPs to their villages in the Shomali.

In March 2002, IOM started to move IDPs from the Herat camps, mainly to Badghis province. By early May, over 40,000 people had left the camps to return home in time for the spring planting season. In the north, a similar picture unfolded with another 48,000 leaving the Mazar camps for their villages with IOM convoys.

Returning IDP families were given reintegration packages usually including wheat, seeds, blankets, soap and other items, such as agricultural tools.

Therefore, development projects addressing root causes need to be implemented in addition to current relief efforts in displacement situations. In this regard, relief agencies and development agencies need to coordinate more. This is also important in order to avoid affected populations becoming dependent on international relief, as well as for the displacement to be concluded sustainably. Capacity-building elements should form part of a comprehensive relief effort in order to prepare populations for return or reintegration. Kent suggests redefining the concept of a "continuum from relief to development". Rather than a sequential "continuum", agencies should be conceptualizing a "parallelism" where development planning is integrated into the relief effort. "In other words, the provision of emergency assistance to the displaced and the planning of development programs should occur simultaneously and in a mutually reinforcing manner" (Deng and Cohen, 1998). Again, there is widespread rhetoric on the need to combine relief with development and some progress has been made. However, it is not yet done in a systematic, managed way. All actors in internal displacement situations are responsible for making sure their projects are sustainable, and for coordinating the developing of a country strategy for the issue. Deng states that "[…] the crisis of displacement should be seen as a wake-up call and an opportunity for addressing the deeper, structural ills of the country to forge a national common ground and a collective vision for nation-building" (E/CN.4/2002/95/Add.3 at 12).

B) Anticipate Movements and Plan for Reducing their Impacts

A key tool in migration management is early warning capability of population movements and information sharing. Research on migration patterns, trends and motives is especially important to the international community in its quest to effectively address migration problems and manage migration flows. One of IOM's functions, for example, is to provide analysis of current migration trends.

Early warning of potential conflict is also a key tool in this prevention phase. Well before population movements have commenced, there will be indicators of potential conflict, and relevant steps should be taken by humanitarian actors to prevent conflict from erupting. More information sharing in this regard between humanitarian actors and research institutions could lead to the development of projects which address root causes in a practical way. For example, UNESCO has an early-warning project on ethnic conflict in the CIS States, aimed at policy makers. Even if they are not expressed in an action-oriented way, its findings should be shared with all international actors in the region so that steps can be taken before the crisis begins.

Undoubtedly, early warning capabilities for internal displacement and population movements are also essential in the search for better management. Early warning systems can be used to predict migration flows and prepare states. Actors such as IOM can play a role in supplying a state with advisory services, rapid analysis of potential and

actual migratory flows, and assistance in preparing for them. For example, in conjunction with WFP and OCHA, IOM is carrying out activities as part of a Migration Tracking Network project in Ethiopia. These include a field survey and the development of a database management software application. The aim is to provide more reliable data on population movements, and an information-sharing and early warning system in order to enhance the ability of the government and the international community to provide timely assistance[7].

Such tools are especially important in cases where displacement can be easily predicted, for example, as a result of a planned development project such as the construction of a dam. Concrete measures can be taken to prevent displacement from occurring, or to mitigate its effects. For example, appropriate planning prior to the construction of a dam means that while some communities may have to be relocated, internal displacement necessitating assistance and protection need not occur. The Copenhagen Programme of Action urges Governments into selecting, wherever possible "development schemes that do not displace local populations, and designing an appropriate policy and legal framework to compensate the displaced for their losses, to help them to re-establish their livelihoods and to promote their recovery from social and cultural disruption" (1995, Section II).

Indeed, the Guiding Principles stipulate that the prohibition of arbitrary displacement includes displacement in cases of large-scale development projects that are not justified by compelling and overriding public interests (Principle 6 (2)(c)). Donor institutions therefore have a particular responsibility to provide support and incentives for creating such a framework, particularly in developing countries. Management in this sense refers to strategic planning, taking into account who will be affected and how, and how to minimize disruption caused.

The same is largely true of environmentally induced population displacements, including natural disasters and human-made disasters such as severe environmental degradation caused by nuclear or hazardous waste contamination. In this regard, useful work has been done by UNHCR, IOM and the Refugee Policy Group at the International Symposium on Environmentally-Induced Population Displacements and Environmental Impacts Resulting from Mass Migrations (Geneva April 1996). The Symposium studied prevention, mitigation and

7) IOM *Press Briefing Notes*, 24 July 2001.

rehabilitation measures for internal displacement caused by environmental disasters. Its recommendations show the importance of recognizing how such disasters link to population displacements, and the role of various actors in managing these situations. Practical and realistic measures were proposed to address this form of displacement. This is an example of migration management tools already being used for internal displacement. Follow-up work is equally important in encouraging similar initiatives so that such outcomes translate into practical action.

C) Implementing the Relevant Framework

Broadly speaking, the concept of a migration management framework includes the institutions and instruments relevant to addressing migration, either at the bilateral, regional or global levels. Coordination among relevant institutions, including national actors, and harmonization of applicable instruments is often the goal of establishing and maintaining a migration framework.

This aspect of migration management can be usefully translated to internal displacement. States should be assisted or encouraged to develop a normative framework to address displacement issues if they arise. As the Representative on Internal Displacement writes: "[P]rimary responsibility for the internally displaced lay with the states concerned, which should seek to strengthen laws, policies and institutions to enhance the national response" (E/CN .4/2002/95 Add.3 at 13). The first and most essential step which can be taken in developing a comprehensive migration strategy addressing displacement is to develop a clear legislative framework to provide national protection.

Importantly, laws affecting or relating to internal displacement should incorporate the norms contained in the Guiding Principles. The international community can and does assist in this area: training modules have been developed by the Norwegian Refugee Council and the Inter-Agency Standing Committee to promote understanding of the principles; workshops have been held in several countries[8] focussing on capacity-building and improving response to the protection and assistance needs of IDPs at local and international level. As stated, the Representative also uses the Guiding Principles in his discussions with governments as a model for legislation. Migration organizations such as IOM also play a role in using the Guiding Principles in technical cooperation work with governments. Part of IOM's technical cooperation activities focus on the drafting of national migration legislation, an appropriate vehicle for incorporating rights and obligations regarding internal displacement.

Only a handful of states which experience displacement have passed specific laws on the topic. Azerbaijan was the first of the former Soviet States to adopt a national law on internally displaced persons in 1992. Persons covered by the law are entitled to a number of guarantees such as temporary accommodation, medical assistance, education, access to food and industrial goods. In 1999, a law on refugees and IDPs was adopted, together with a new law on the social protection of IDPs and people with equivalent status, which also provides certain minimum guarantees. The laws followed a visit of the Representative to Azerbaijan, the first such mission after the completion of the Guiding Principles (see E/CN.4/1999/79 at § 22).

Colombia also passed a law in 1997 regarding forced displacement. The Constitutional Court in Colombia has ruled that the Guiding Principles should be used as the parameters for establishing rules and for interpreting this law[9].

In addition to the existence of relevant norms, coordination among relevant actors is also essential to this notion of a migration framework. At the most basic level, there needs to be coordination, information sharing and cooperation among government bodies. Given the complexity of internal displacement, a variety of different government bodies or ministries may have a role to play in addressing IDP needs. To this end, establishing working groups on internal displacement involving the representatives of different governmental authorities should be encouraged.

To cite one example of moving towards a relevant framework, the Government of Angola has developed minimum operational standards for the return and resettlement of IDPs in collaboration with OCHA. These led to the publishing of a decree on Norms for the Resettlement of Displaced Populations in January 2001. The draft norms had been widely discussed by UN Agencies, NGOs, donors and government representatives. The norms describe preconditions for resettlement as well as targets for post-relocation assistance. Under the leadership of the Ministry

8) In 2001, workshops were held in Burundi, Colombia, India, Sierra Leone. In previous years, they had been held in Burma, Angola, Georgia, Uganda and the Philippines. Workshops have been scheduled in 2002 for Indonesia, Afghanistan and Kenya.

9) Cases T-227/97 and T-186589/T-201615/Z-2459.

for Assistance and Social Resettlement, a technical working group was formed in February 2001 to develop standard operating procedures for implementing these norms. The working group was made up of 11 government ministries and departments, UN agencies and NGOs, and aimed at producing legally binding procedures to guarantee the standardized application of the norms across the country, as well as at identifying benchmarks for monitoring the resettlement process[10]. The Guiding Principles were used as a standard in developing the norms and procedures. This is a concrete example of how a migration management concept, such as the development of a relevant framework is already being applied to internal displacement, whether or not one relates the two.

D) Return, Resettlement and Reintegration

Voluntary return of irregular migrants and failed asylum seekers is considered a cornerstone of sound migration management. It safeguards the integrity of asylum systems and reinforces orderly migration practices. Evidently, such aims are not relevant to internal displacement, where IDPs seek to return to their place of origin and resettle themselves. However, the underlying requirements of successful international returns can be usefully and relevantly transferred to internal displacement: returns should be voluntary and based on an informed decision; returns should only be to a safe environment; and reintegration measures should be implemented to ensure that the return can be sustainable.

Unfortunately, international or national attention focuses elsewhere when immediate needs of IDPs have been met and displacement situations can go on for years with no realistic end in sight. Decades of conflict in some countries means that returns are not sustainable, and waves of displacement may occur whereby a new outbreak of conflict provokes further displacements. Therefore, the sustainability of returns is often a political question, depending primarily on security factors. Where the country involved faces development or reconstruction challenges, sound migration management recognizes that return can only be sustainable when undertaken in harmony with development or reconstruction projects. The integration of relief and development is therefore equally relevant at this phase of displacement, to ensure that the displacement does not reoccur.

Regaining Sight of the Broader Picture

As stated, the international actors involved in responding to IDP situations have their specific mandate, whether it is food, health, children, shelter and so on. Each player assists IDPs within the context of that mandate. Without creating a new IDP agency, it is necessary to consider ways of ensuring that the broader picture is taken into account, not just when an IDP situation occurs, but more generally in order to prevent displacement from occurring at all. This requires recognition of the broader interests which can affect responses to internal displacement. The issue is not only between individual IDPs, their governments and humanitarian agencies; other actors can play an important role, including regional bodies, donors and third countries.

Regional migration fora should incorporate internal displacement as a migration concern in order to assist and advise governments and organizations dealing with assisting displaced populations. Although the issue of state sovereignty may be raised to limit discussion, any humanitarian crises will have broader impacts for the region, for example in the areas of trade, investment and foreign policy irrespective of whether they are limited within the territory of one state. A number of regional consultative processes in operation today (see also **chapter 8**) have emerged in recognition of states' need to address migration in a multilateral way. In other words, recognizing that international migration can no longer be addressed unilaterally or even bilaterally, states increasingly support regional processes to discuss migration issues and determine appropriate strategies.

Of the many regional processes currently underway, the follow-up process to the CIS Conference has specifically incorporated internal displacement within its terms of reference. Its Programme of Action (1996) refers to encouraging safe and voluntary return of IDPs, recognizing that the rebuilding of civil society is of primary importance to facilitate return. Flowing from the Programme of Action, IOM and UNHCR have instituted a number of successful programmes in participating states mainly with the aim of developing the institutional capacity of CIS country governments in achieving durable solutions for population displacement problems. Regional fora may also be the appropriate place to discuss political resolutions to the causes of displacement.

121

10) Report of the Secretary-General on the United Nations Office in Angola
S/2001/351 – § 27, 11 April 2001.

Donors also play an important role in putting humanitarian assistance in a broader policy perspective. Rudge critiques the EU in the adequacy and effectiveness of humanitarian assistance aid, suggesting that "a policy in this area might be expected to take note of the bigger political debate on internally displaced people currently going on in other international for a […] it could be expected to be informed by inputs from other parts of the Commission and the Council of Ministers concerned with wider political and economic relations between the EU as a whole and other states. […] There is little evidence that the actions of the Commission in favour of IDPs either take note of the wider debate or derive from a comprehensive, cross-department rationale" (Rudge, 2002).

In fairness, the EU is not the only donor body against which such critiques can be levelled. It is incontrovertible that humanitarian assistance should not be provided in isolation. To assist the "parallelism" between emergency relief and development, actors including donors should be encouraged to insist on the broader context of their contributions. The place of assistance and relief should be readily identifiable in the broader strategy for a particular country or region, taking into account the range of human rights issues, good governance, conflict prevention and development issues. Useful work in this regard has begun: following the initial findings of the Rudge report (2002), EU officials have agreed to examine more closely whether a distinct policy on IDPs is needed, or whether IDP concerns should be integrated more effectively into policies addressing overall vulnerability. Further, the Government of Norway has appointed a focal point on IDPs and the findings are being examined by the UK Government (Rudge, 2002). Hopefully, the report will contribute to donor recognition of potential ways to address IDP issues comprehensively.

Third countries can also play a role in preventing internal displacement. It is readily apparent that internal displacement can be part of a migration continuum. In other words, it has secondary effects in its ability to spill over borders affecting neighbouring countries. The causes of internal displacement may also be the same causes prompting others to flee into third countries, or to migrate when circumstances allow. The international migration potential arising from internal displacement must be given adequate attention in international debate on migration.

Furthermore, the connection between the national migration laws and policies of third countries and internal displacement is another area where migration management

can ensure that migration regimes do not inadvertently worsen the problem. Without being implemented in conjunction with development assistance, deterrent refugee policies of northern countries will naturally influence the incidence of internal displacement. As Loescher writes (2000): "[…] Given the continuing intra-state violence in many parts of the world, coupled with the growing readiness of states in both North and South to avert or obstruct mass refugee outflows from such situations by closing their doors to asylum seekers and insisting on the early repatriation of refugee populations, the number of people forcibly displaced and trapped within their own country can be expected to increase". Therefore, international migration management requires sufficient recognition of the nexus between migration policies with development, aid and human rights assistance in countries where displacement is occurring or could occur.

Conclusion

The international community has made significant progress in the last few years in addressing internal displacement. Mechanisms for gathering and sharing information between agencies have been established as have mechanisms for coordination between actors in responding to internal displacement crises. The Representative has developed essential guidelines for IDP protection and successfully promoted and disseminated the framework. There is ongoing investigation into new issues and modalities for improving international response.

However, the most readily apparent weakness in the current system is the lack of a managed, comprehensive strategy which takes into account broader policy issues such as development, conflict prevention as well as the interplay between displacement and international migration. Migration management is the term used for the development of such a broad strategy for migration issues. It can therefore be a useful tool in developing ways to ensure that responses are not *ad hoc*, but are carried out within a recognizable framework. Although certain underlying assumptions of migration management cannot easily be translated to internal displacement, some of the tools are relevant, particularly the concepts of coordination, the relation between population flows and development issues, and the need to implement projects with a longer-term vision. These concepts are sometimes lacking or inadequate in the current response to internal displacement. A more strategic approach can hopefully prevent displacement situations where possible. Where displacement persists, it should be minimized and effective, long-term solutions found.

CHAPTER 8

Managing Migration at the Regional Level – Strategies for Regional Consultation

Migration issues play a key role in international relations and diplomacy at bilateral and multilateral levels. Many governments today would not develop policy on migration issues without considering the impact on other domestic policies; and without considering international migration patterns and foreign policy implications more generally.

Given the considerable growth in the number of international migrants over the last four decades - a tendency projected to continue over the next half century (see also **chapter 1**) - the existing international framework to deal with migratory movements is clearly not equipped to cope. As more people leave their homes in search of better economic prospects, and with inadequate access to legal migration channels to meet rising demand, irregular migration is increasing hand in hand with a dramatic rise of the smuggling and trafficking of migrants (see also **chapter 3**).

This chapter examines the move toward regional and multilateral approaches in managing international migration, particularly in the form of Regional Consultative Processes on migration. It considers briefly various issues affecting migration policy and the impact these have on the focus and functioning of Regional Consultative Processes (RCPs) as cooperative mechanisms for managing international migration, and explores the characteristics common to Regional Consultative Processes as well as limitations and obstacles to the most effective use of these processes. The chapter concludes by offering ten key steps towards ensuring the success of RCPs.

Migration Management – a Shift from Bilateral to Regional Approaches

Over the decades, government response to changing migration patterns has been mainly *ad hoc,* primarily through bilateral arrangements including agreements on labour migration, employment and training, readmission, remittance management and border control.
Such arrangements responded to the "issue of the day" and were often undertaken without considering broader impacts at national, regional or global levels.

Increasingly, and primarily in response to the growing incidence of irregular migration, governments acknowledge that solutions to international migration challenges do not lie in unilateral, or even bilateral, actions. Both developed and developing countries are seeking assistance in coordinating migration policies, realizing that greater problems will ensue if they cannot better manage migration internationally. Limited in their application, bilateral approaches are now increasingly being replaced by multilateral and regional approaches. Such approaches bring states together, either by groups of like-minded states, as in the Intergovernmental Consultations on Asylum, Refugees and Migration Policies in Europe, North America and Australia (IGC) and the European Union (EU), or in groups with diverse interests but common geography, as found in the Regional Conference on Migration (or Puebla Process) for Central and North America. The actual impetus for moving towards the creation of a Regional Consultative Process can be as varied as the processes themselves.

By definition, RCPs are informal groups made up of representatives of government, international organizations and, sometimes, civil society, which share information and experiences on migration-related issues of common interest and concern, and often develop non-binding plans for regional action to address these issues.

The Emergence of Regional Approaches[1]

Since the mid-1980s, numerous RCPs have come into existence. The main processes are detailed below:

Intergovernmental Consultations on Asylum, Refugees and Migration Policies in Europe, North America and Australia (IGC)

As one of the first consultative processes to emerge, many consider the IGC as not truly a "regional" process, but a forum for consultation of like-minded countries aimed at influencing the thinking of participating States as well as intergovernmental organizations such as UNHCR and IOM. An informal, non-decision-making forum for information exchange and discussion on policy directions among sixteen participating governments, the IGC grew out of a meeting initiated by UNHCR in 1985 to discuss "The Arrivals of Asylum-Seekers and Refugees in Europe". Since then, the IGC has expanded its areas of

123

1) See **table 8.1.** for the composition and focus of the main regional approaches.

interest. Currently, six working groups look at issues relating to return, smuggling, data, technology, country of origin information and security. Apart from the working groups, workshops are held, which allow participant states to address specific issues in greater depth.

Budapest Process

Originally a consultative forum aimed at preventing illegal migration from Central and Eastern Europe toward Western Europe (Klekowski, 2001), the Budapest Process, initiated in October 1991, gradually widened its scope to include return and readmission, and visa harmonization. In the autumn of 2001, a new working group emerged on asylum and irregular migration. The 1997 Ministerial Conference of the Budapest Group, held in Prague, adopted a 55 point Plan of Action, which has been partially implemented since then. In May 2002, it was decided to monitor progress and produce a report on the implementation of the Prague recommendations over the past five years.

CIS Conference Process[2]

The Commonwealth of Independent States (CIS) Conference was convened in May 1996 in response to concerns about population displacement problems in the region and potentially beyond, following the break-up of the Soviet Union. The objectives of the Conference were to provide a reliable forum for the countries of the region to discuss population displacement problems in a humanitarian and non-political manner. This included reviewing the population movements in the region, and devising an integrated strategy to enable the countries of the CIS to better cope with and prevent population displacement, and regulate other types of migratory movements on their territories. A joint secretariat, consisting of UNHCR, IOM and the Office for Democratic Institutions and Human Rights (ODIHR) of OSCE, was set up to prepare the Conference, which adopted a Programme of Action and a Steering Group mechanism to monitor and review the follow-up for four years. At the meeting of the Steering Group in July 2000, States agreed that the process would be extended through 2004

to promote and monitor progress. The extended process focuses on four broad thematic issues: assuring continued focus on groups of concern as listed in the original Programme of Action; migration management and combat against trafficking in persons; sustaining the achievements of the non-government organization (NGO) sector; and implementing legislation and avoiding implementation gaps. A high-level review meeting is planned for the end of 2002 to take stock, evaluate gaps and define a course of action for the future.

Regional Conference on Migration (RCM)

The Regional Conference on Migration (also known as the Puebla Process) emerged at a time when Mexico and the United States were entering into a new relationship based upon common interests prompted by the implementation of the North America Free Trade Agreement (NAFTA), including the perceived need to promote orderly migration with due consideration for the human rights of migrants. The relationship was expanded to include other Latin American countries interested in pursuing the same relationship, and with similar interests in migrant rights. Hence the creation in 1996 of the RCM. Initially, the RCM was limited to dialogue, exchange of information and expertise. It addressed issues of common interest – such as how to deal with extra-regional migrants transiting through the region to the United States and Canada. With confidence and trust built, the Process was able to move forward, tackling tougher issues of broader interest. In addition to information sharing and dialogue, technical cooperation has been introduced. Modified at periodical intervals, a consensus Plan of Action identifies objectives and a schedule for implementing concrete initiatives within specific timeframes. Two important characteristics of the RCM are that it brings together countries of origin, transit and destination, and that delegations regularly include representatives from both foreign affairs ministries and migration agencies, fostering more widely coordinated government responses and positions (for further details, see **textbox 8.1.**).

2) The Processes' official designation is: "Regional Conference to address the problems of refugees, displaced persons, other forms of involuntary displacement and returnees in the countries of the Commonwealth of Independent States (CIS) and relevant neighbouring States", extended in 2000 as "Follow-up to the 1996 Geneva Conference on the Problems of Refugees, Displaced Persons, Migration and Asylum Issues".

TEXTBOX 8.1.

The Puebla Process - a Case Study of Regional Consultative Process Development

Formally known as the Regional Conference on Migration, the Puebla Process groups the Central and North American countries and the Dominican Republic together and is the most advanced of the RCPs that are quickly developing. It aptly demonstrates the degree to which these processes can yield substantive benefits to governments and migrants.

The Puebla Process includes three countries which are clearly countries of immigration (Canada, Costa Rica and the United States) and a number of net emigration countries such as El Salvador, Guatemala, Honduras, Nicaragua, and Mexico. At the same time, most are also transit countries. There is significant social, cultural and economic disparity between Canada and the United States and Mexico (where per capita GDP is approximately one-sixth of each of the other two), and in Central America, where Nicaragua's GDP is less than one-third that of Costa Rica's.

Migration became a salient issue in the regional and national agendas during the early 1990s, partly as a result of the 1990-91 recession in the US and Canada, which stimulated anti-immigrant feelings. Most governments in the region regarded migration as an issue of national sovereignty, and did not share information with other governments on the situation of their nationals, on legal or criminal processes against them, or on policy changes which could affect migration. Respect for migrants' rights varied substantially.

By 1995, however, bilateral consultation mechanisms were being explored or established between countries linked by strong population flows. The discussions held by bilateral groups revealed that the issues were of a regional character. Based on this finding, the Mexican government proposed a regional conference on migration. However, many obstacles remained. A recent history of animosity, intervention, and the "lost decade" of war and recession in the region had to be overcome.

3) These include: the Inter-American Development Bank, the Central American Bank for Economic Integration, the United Nations High Commissioner for Refugees, the Inter-American Human Rights Commission and the United Nations Population Fund for Population Analysis.

The first meeting of the Puebla Process took place in Puebla, Mexico in March 1996. At that time, participating delegates agreed to further informal, region-wide consultations to achieve 17 specific objectives, including:

objective knowledge and understanding of migration flows; condemnation of violations of the human rights of documented and undocumented migrants; fostering the cooperation of NGOs and governments; implementing mechanisms for intergovernmental consultation and discussion of migration affairs and for the protection of the rights of migrants; "early warning" mechanisms, allowing neighbouring countries to prepare for changes in migration law and border enforcement; exchange of laws and practices, in order to analyse and improve them; alerting society against trafficking, and promoting laws and practices that effectively reduce it; creating mechanisms for the systematic discussion of migration issues among member governments; promoting control of extra-regional migration; developing new and improved mechanisms to reduce forgery and the fraudulent use of migration-related documents.

The Puebla Process is organized as both an intergovernmental and a social regional forum, led by the vice-ministers of immigration and foreign affairs of each country, as well as a parallel body consisting of national and international NGOs dealing with migrants and migration issues. In addition, IOM, the Centre for Latin American Demography (a part of the United Nations Economic Commission for Latin America and the Caribbean/ECLAC), and a number of other organizations joined the process as observers[3].

The participation of interior and foreign affairs ministries fosters a balance of the governments' domestic and international interests. Increasing collaboration and exchange between governments and NGOs helps guarantee transparency in the various proceedings, and incorporates a sounding board within the process itself which might otherwise be lacking. Intergovernmental organizations have provided technical assistance, carried out studies dealing with specific issues (smuggling and trafficking, women and children migrants, migration and health, diagnostic studies on the state of migration management) and have allowed the process to learn from other similar initiatives, especially from the IGC.

Members agreed that this process should not become a new international organization in order to avoid the cumbersome process of arriving at binding resolutions

125

and their adoption by member governments, as well as the expenses associated with a supranational bureaucracy. Instead, there is a *pro-tempore* secretariat[4], chaired by the country hosting a scheduled meeting and co-chaired by the country in charge of the next meeting. A *virtual* secretariat (web site) contains all relevant information on resolutions and statements, divided into two main areas: one public (www.rcmvs.org) and one devoted to queries and exchanges amongst the member governments.

Since its creation in 1995, five ministerial conferences have been held. Each conference is preceded by a technical meeting where officials, NGOs, and experts discuss specific migration issues and prepare the ground for agreements and recommendations scheduled for discussion at the ministerial conferences. The technical meetings have dealt with trafficking, migration and human rights, migration and development, migration, return and reintegration, protection and consular assistance to migrants, and special issues affecting women and children migrants.

To date, the main achievements of the Puebla Process include:

1) overcoming the lack of communication and mistrust which prevailed in the region;
2) providing a forum for the discussion of domestic and foreign policy developments likely to affect travellers and migrants;
3) informing foreign governments of the situation of their nationals in a destination country, thereby improving consular protection activities and ensuring due process;
4) arriving at procedural agreements for the return/deportation of undocumented and irregular migrants;
5) discussing and learning from each other's best practices in migration management. Although these important achievements are not binding agreements or treaties, they are valuable in preparing the ground for future agreements.

During the most recent meeting in San José, Costa Rica in 2001, the Regional Consultation Group agreed to expand its agenda in three main areas: migration policy and migration management, human rights and migration, and development. A growing concern for the member governments and NGOs, migrant health is a salient aspect of the human rights agenda. Border cooperation and migrant return and reintegration became part of the migration and development agenda.

IOM has carried out a detailed diagnostic study of migration systems in Central America that should pave the way for greater procedural homogenization and possible bilateral agreements within the region[5]. A technical support unit will now function as a permanent, budgeted part of the Puebla Process.

In line with the Process non-binding nature, member governments were invited to agree to the standards and procedures for the return of extra-regional migrants recommended by IOM, and to sign and implement the United Nations Convention Against Transnational Organized Crime, and specifically the "Protocol to Prevent, Suppress and Punish Trafficking in Persons, Especially Women and Children", which has been signed by six of eleven Puebla Process participating states.

Existing information exchange on foreign nationals should be developed into mechanisms for governments to protect these foreign nationals, mainly through the expansion of consular networks, which should pay particular attention to border areas with many foreign nationals. Members agreed to share information on trafficking, exchange best practices, and carry out joint operations against trafficking networks. A series of policy and practice-relevant studies will be commissioned, and new funds sought. Finally, members agreed to incorporate the NGO proposal relating to the protection of migrants human rights, and to facilitate inspection of migrant detention centres, to the extent allowed by national legislation.

The Puebla Process has played a key role in the progress of several bi-national migration negotiations, attesting to its value in successful migration management.

In addition to these achievements, the Process is helping governments to learn to trust each other and to share information and know-how, allowing them to agree on better migration management. Progress has undoubtedly slowed down as a result of the security concerns that followed September 11, 2001; however, thanks in no small measure to the existence of this regional forum, these concerns have not resulted in a breakdown of communication or intergovernmental animosity. Future developments should show the extent to which governments in this regional consultative process can further the migration agenda in this new international setting. The flexibility and informality of the Puebla Process are strong indicators of future success.

4) Now termed "presidency".

5) IOM (2002). *The State of Migration Management in Central America – An Applied Research.* IOM Geneva.

Manila Process

The Manila Process grew out of a seminar organized by IOM in 1996, bringing together 16 countries, plus Hong Kong SAR of China, to address migrant trafficking and irregular migration in the region. Participants expressed an interest not only in preventing and controlling trafficking, but also in root causes of migration such as unequal development and ways of managing regular migration along with irregular migration. The Manila Process has met four times, with IOM serving as the organizer and secretariat. The themes developed in the Manila Process have been enshrined in the 1999 Bangkok Declaration on Irregular Migration.

IOM fosters and supports regional consultation processes

Intergovernmental Asia-Pacific Consultations (APC)

A second Asian process was also established in 1996: the Inter-Governmental Asia-Pacific Consultation on Refugees, Displaced Persons and Migrants (APC). Co-sponsored by IOM and UNHCR, the APC represents 31 countries plus Hong Kong SAR (i.e., all of the countries participating in the Manila Process are represented in the APC) and provides an informal forum for discussing issues related to refugees, displaced persons and increasingly, migration in general. The APC is divided into four sub-regional working groups: South-East Asia, South Asia, Pacific and Mekong Region. Each sub-regional group focuses on specific activities and reports back to the annual plenary. At the APC plenary of November 2001, and based on a questionnaire circulated by the Coordinator among members to gauge future work, a five pillar proposal was suggested by the Coordinator: sensitization and motivation; capacity-building; mainstreaming the APC process; consensus building; and coordination.

South American Conference on Migration (Lima Process)

In July, 1999 representatives from South American countries met in Lima, Peru, at what has since become an annual meeting in order to share views and information on migration issues in that region and to open up channels for dialogue and cooperation. Areas of particular interest include migration, development and integration, with the later addition of migrant rights. At the 2002 Conference in Quito, a Plan of Action was drawn up which includes objectives such as harmonizing and coordinating migration information systems, migration administrations and legislation on migration.

Migration Dialogue for Southern Africa (MIDSA)

The Migration Dialogue for Southern Africa emerged from a technical cooperation workshop for senior government officials from all Southern African governments on migration management, hosted by IOM, the United Nations Institute for Training and Research (UNITAR) and the International Migration Policy Programme (IMP). Course participants resolved that there was a need "to develop, in conjunction with the Southern African Development Community (SADC), a forum for further exchange of information, experience and perspective among Governments on migration policy and practice, to facilitate cooperation". This led to the birth of MIDSA in November 2000 as a process to discuss migration issues, with particular emphasis on the regional movement of people[6]. Through technical cooperation training and information sharing, MIDSA has explored common themes such as border control and labour migration (for further details, see **textbox 8.2.**).

127

6) See also: Southern African Migration Project – MIDSA.
   www.queensu.ca/samp/MIDSA.htm

TEXTBOX 8.2.

The Migration Dialogue for Southern Africa

Free movement of people in Southern Africa is a controversial issue, as it is in the rest of the continent.

Regrouping the 14 countries of the sub-region[7], the Southern African Development Community (SADC), through its secretariat in Gaborone, launched a consultation process in 1993 among its members in order to design and adopt a regional protocol on migration. Six years later, the process stalled without concrete results due to disagreement among the member countries. The stronger SADC economies were concerned that a relaxation of migration flows and controls would be followed by largely one-way movements of people in search of jobs and material well-being. In addition, relaxation of border controls would help create opportunities for cross-border crime syndicates.

As in other parts of the world, the free movement of people in Southern Africa questions the sovereignty of all SADC member countries. The fundamental issue is whether migration should be governed by a regional protocol, or whether it should be subject to domestic legislation[8]. Since 1999, the perspectives of seeing the migration protocol revived are dim unless upcoming SADC summits or its Council of Ministers decide to take up renewed action.

However, Southern Africa is critically lacking reliable and comparable migration data, an appropriate legal framework and efficient coordination at both regional and national levels. Furthermore, the region is experiencing more problems from migrant trafficking by criminal networks and the consequent increase in uncontrolled migration. Therefore, there is a greater need than ever for a regional dialogue between SADC Member States on the critical issue of migration.

In 1999, IOM, the Southern African Migration Project (SAMP) and the United States Immigration and Naturalization Service (INS) organized a regional migration policy and law training course for senior migration officials of SADC member states. Follow-up meetings were organized in Zimbabwe and Zambia. In November 2000, a seminar held in Swaziland confirmed the interest of SADC countries in holding regular meetings on migration issues, which would provide officials with opportunities to exchange experiences. At that time, the Migration Dialogue for Southern Africa (MIDSA) was officially established as a viable framework for regional dialogue on migration.

MIDSA's main goal is to facilitate cooperation among regional governments and contribute to regional migration management by fostering understanding of migratory flows and strengthening regional institutional capacities. MIDSA's long-term objective is to enhance SADC's migration management capacities through a solid network of cooperation.

The dialogue was established as an open and on-going process to support officials from SADC Member States, the SADC secretariat, international and regional organizations to network, exchange experiences, share concerns and develop their knowledge, understanding and capacities in the field of migration[9]. The MIDSA Secretariat plans and coordinates the annual cycle of activities and networks between SADC Member States and the Secretariat as well as interested donors.

SADC Member States hope that the MIDSA process will contribute to shaping policy on migration and provide an appropriate framework for future discussion and problem-solving. For the period 2001-2002, the MIDSA process is focussing on migration data collection, processing and assessment, research on legislation harmonization – entailing a review and comparative study of migration policies and law in the region – and a workshop on border management and intra-regional exchanges.

The next challenge for the MIDSA process is to gradually gear those involved towards action-oriented activities to enhance and streamline migration management in Southern Africa. Tentative plans for 2003-2004 include workshops on labour migration, counter trafficking, forced migration and internally displaced persons, technical cooperation on migration, migration and HIV/AIDS, as well as linkages with the New Partnership for Africa's Development (NEPAD).

7) Angola, Botswana, Democratic Republic of Congo, Lesotho, Malawi, Mauritius, Mozambique, Namibia, Seychelles, South Africa, Swaziland, Tanzania, Zambia, Zimbabwe.
8) *Crossings* (2002). vol.4, no.1, Southern African Migration Project (SAMP), Cape Town, South Africa.
9) *Crossings, op.cit.*

MIDSA can fill the gap left by the demise of the SADC movement protocol. As an inter-agency and inter-governmental initiative, MIDSA responds to SADC member states' recognition of the imperative for greater and closer regional cooperation on migration. As the first of its kind on the continent, MIDSA has the potential to serve as an example for similar initiatives in other regions of Africa.

European Union

While not a RCP *sui generis,* the European Union (EU) could be considered the ultimate regional cooperation test case. Consultations and discussions among EU Member States on issues such as the development of a common community policy on immigration and asylum, a common system of border guards and border management and a common migration database could pave the way to developing regional approaches to migration management (for further details, see **chapter 14** and **textbox 14.2.**).

Other fora

Not all cooperative approaches to international migration have occurred at the bilateral or regional level. Some effort has been made to address migration management at global level. Of particular note, the International Conference on Population and Development in Cairo in 1994 set out the comprehensive range of challenges surrounding the management of international migration. An entire chapter of the Programme of Action was devoted to international migration, both documented and undocumented migrants, and numerous recommendations were adopted at the Conference. But follow-up has been limited, and no international conference on migration has followed as was called for in the Plan of Action, largely due to the perception of unbridgeable differences between the interests of countries of origin and destination.

Other fora for consultation on migration issues have been forged from the same acknowledgement that migration cannot be effectively dealt with unilaterally or even bilaterally. The Summit of the Americas (SOA), particularly since SOA II (Santiago, 1998) and continuing with SOA III (Quebec City, 2001), has addressed migration issues from a hemispheric perspective.

An example of an inter-regional forum for consultation on migration issues is IOM's "Cluster" process between countries of origin and transit in the south Caucasus and destination countries in Western Europe (see also **textbox 13.1.**), which was designed to facilitate, on an informal basis, agreed modes of practical cooperation in "co-managing" migration. These informal discussions have laid the groundwork for bilateral and multilateral agreements, and cooperative projects.

NGO Participation

Governments increasingly recognize that managing migration requires the involvement of more than just government officials and international organizations. Therefore, more and more NGOs at local, regional and international levels are becoming involved in different aspects of the migration process, including assistance to trafficked migrants, integration in countries of settlement, promotion and protection of migrants' rights, and local development projects.

Few RCPs invite the active participation of representatives from local or regional NGOs on a regular basis. The RCPs which did invite NGOs to take part have generally found the experience to be a positive one. In particular, in their Plans of Action and achievements, the CIS Conference and the RCM emphasize the contributions of civil society, particularly NGOs, in developing effective migration policies and programmes.

Complicating Interstate Cooperation – Questions Raised by Issues Affecting Migration Policy[10]

The migration process includes a wide variety of social, political and economic relationships that must be considered in any approach to managing migration. These relationships make RCP challenges more complex as they require participation from a variety of partner agencies within and between governments. A few of the more important migration relationships are mentioned below by way of demonstration.

The link between migration and asylum and between migration and security has brought together policy-makers and practitioners in the ministries of the interior, foreign

129

---

10) Concrete responses to the various specific questions raised here are given throughout the chapters of the thematic section of the present volume.

affairs, security agencies and others. They examine the growing challenges posed by mixed flows, the impact of mixed flows as well as secondary migration on asylum systems and state ability to protect refugees and to guarantee general social stability.

These issues lead to questions about the impact of development and demographic trends on migration, which, in turn, add development agencies and others as partners in strategizing on international migration management. As economies in countries of origin develop, will this lessen the impetus to migrate? What impact do remittances have on economic development in the country of origin? Should policy-makers include consideration of these impacts in their policy discussions on development assistance or other bilateral issues? What role does demography play as an impetus to migration in terms of the continuing rapid population growth of developing countries and the population decline and ageing of much of the developed world? Will migration help to mitigate the impact of a rapidly ageing population?

Very much in the current public limelight is the relationship between migration and xenophobia, along with the migration and social cohesion nexus, bringing in additional interlocutors, including from civil society. Are integration practices causing or contributing to xenophobic behaviour in society, or *vice versa*? Should migrants remain distinct from host country citizens, or should they be given the opportunity to participate fully in their host society? Does increased migration damage the cohesiveness of the host society? What steps need to be taken to ensure the cultural richness offered by migrants enhances competitiveness in today's global society?

Similar questions are being posed with regard to migration and human rights, particularly with respect to the 1990 UN Convention on the Protection of the Rights of All Migrant Workers and Members of their Families. Should migrant workers enjoy the same rights as nationals of the host country? Should undocumented migrants be granted the same rights as documented migrants? If migrants are provided the same rights as host country nationals, what would be the impact if they were also provided access to citizenship, and granted the right to dual citizenship?

While each RCP does not purport to tackle each of these issues, RCP participants are more aware of the multidimensional nature of the migration process and the fact that there is no longer a single government agency dealing with all migration issues. Without this recognition, the

fundamental dynamics of the issues explored through the RCPs could be misunderstood, which could lead to misinformed policy-making. In order to treat each issue comprehensively, linkages and relationships must be understood and all relevant policy-makers (and NGOs, where relevant) should be included in the dialogue. The complexity of trying to manage migration multilaterally, regionally or nationally, is over-layered by two specific trends in international migration: globalization and transnationalism (see also **chapter 1**).

Globalization and Transnationalism

Without being an entirely new phenomenon, increasing economic and political globalization is regularly cited as a new determinant of contemporary migration. What is its impact on RCPs? A growing number of multilateral arrangements in the areas of trade, investment and economic reform are putting pressure on governments to "multilateralize" discussions on immigration reform (Rodrik, 2001). As a result, the relationships between such issues as returns and immigration, returns and trade or returns and development assistance are being examined much more closely and increasingly built into migration policy.

Many multilateral and regional economic groupings have been formed to further discussions on freer movement of goods and services. Historically there has been very little contact between economic or trade groups and migration policy-makers; now these processes are moving more and more towards freer movement of labour to complement the economic integration process. NAFTA contains some limited agreements on labour migration. The Mode 4 negotiations under the General Agreement on Trade in Services (GATS) are grappling with the freer movement of "natural persons". There are regular calls for regional migration policies through regional economic groups such as the Association of South-East Asian Nations (ASEAN), the South American Common Market (MERCOSUR), SADC, the Economic Community of West African States (ECOWAS), the African, Caribbean and Pacific Group of States (ACP) and the Gulf Cooperation Council (GCC)[11]. The challenge is to integrate these narrowly focussed discussions into the broader issue of migration management.

11) **Table 8.2.** provides an overview of the world's regions and their country groupings with migration focus or interest.

The acceptance by an increasing number of governments in both countries of origin and countries of destination, of the concept of dual nationality serves to demonstrate how widely accepted the concept of transnationalism is becoming (Guarnizo and Portes, 2001), and how dual citizenship is seen as a means of fostering continued attachment and loyalty to cultures of origin among emigrants.

However, the phenomenon is not without cost: transnationalism might have an impact on social cohesion in the receiving society, complicating the process of social acceptance and integration. The effects or impacts of transnationalism can add an additional dimension to migration policy development and implementation, as well as to the already complex challenge of developing co-operative approaches as both the country of origin and the country of destination seek to maximize benefit from the migration experience. Many of the various issues affecting migration policy need to be treated differently in fora such as RCPs when considered in conjunction with transnational migration. There is a growing recognition of this fact as some RCPs deal with the issue of transnationalism explicitly[12].

The Role RCPs can Play - Obstacles and Solutions

There are two basic characteristics common to all RCPs: the processes are informal, and the results are non-binding, though very often consensual. Although the focus of each regional process depends upon the interests of the participants, threads common to all RCPs can also be found, which seem to be key for the successful functioning of the process. The most significant of these is the basic recognition of a shared interest in migration, despite differing national interests and experiences. A successful process will begin with issues that bring participants together, rather than moving them apart (Taft, 2000).

Most processes have emerged as a result of specific issues of regional concern. Three clusters of issues have received particularly sustained attention: root causes in countries and regions of origin (push factors and pull factors); international refugee protection for those entitled to it; and orderly migration, including management of labour migration and irregular migration (supply and demand).

The most important role RCPs can play is to get governments of different countries to talk to each other and address issues in a cooperative multilateral setting. Talking and sharing experiences serve to develop relationships, enhance knowledge and understanding and build confidence and trust which is essential in the face of the complexity of the issues being addressed. It is in taking a step-by-step approach to building confidence that areas of potential cooperation begin to expand.

RCPs can enhance understanding of the cause and effect of factors leading to migration, and provide a practical vehicle for maintaining and sharing accurate, reliable and up-to-date data on trends, programmes and policies. Regional processes have been used as fora for discussing and implementing innovative approaches to complex issues, including orderly return programmes, harmonized asylum systems, regional mechanisms for temporary protection and burden sharing and cooperatively combating irregular migration. How do RCPs arrive at the stage where dialogue is meaningful and where the process can be considered successful?

The informal and non-binding nature of RCPs limits the legal strength of their recommendations. This characteristic has been maintained in order to encourage participation as it permits an unbridled search for cooperative approaches and solutions. Some observers consider the effectiveness of the process to be thereby limited; however, there seems to be general agreement among RCP participants that the informality and non-binding nature of the process is not actually a limitation, but rather an enhancement of the free flow of information among states.

In some regions, states have decided to go beyond informal, non-binding exchanges to pursue concrete cooperation and even harmonization. For example, the RCM is exploring the development of a regional system for dealing with irregular movements of extra-regional migrants. Moreover, the EU is developing a common asylum system and making progress towards harmonizing migration policies. The success of an institutional framework for regional migration management in the EU may provoke similar efforts in other regions.

131

12) For example, the RCM recognizes explicitly that the challenges of transnational migration cannot be dealt with on a bilateral basis alone (see also Government of Costa Rica, 2001a).

Other obstacles potentially hindering the success of regional dialogue include:

State Sovereignty

In his Report to the Security Council in June 1992, former UN Secretary General Boutros Boutros-Ghali emphasized that "respect for its [the State's] fundamental sovereignty and integrity are crucial to any common international progress. The time of absolute and exclusive sovereignty, however, has passed. It is the task of leaders of States today to understand this and to find a balance between the needs of good internal governance and the requirements of an ever more interdependent world". The right to determine who may or may not enter and remain in its territory remains a defining prerogative of the nation state, and can act as a real impediment to the willingness of a state to share information, let alone to discuss its policy concerns with other states or to enter into cooperative arrangements. Boutros-Ghali went further to state that "globalism and nationalism need not be viewed as opposing trends, doomed to spur each other on to extremes of reaction. The healthy globalization of contemporary life requires, in the first instance, solid identities and fundamental freedoms" (United Nations, 1992).

RCPs generally aim at maintaining respect for state sovereignty, thereby enabling participants to focus attention on the issues that can be dealt with in the context of an informal, non-binding process. However, this may include discussions on the benefits of common approaches or even of harmonizing policies.

Differing Priorities

Most regional processes include countries of origin, transit and destination. Indeed, most countries today are simultaneously origin, transit and destination countries. Each participating state will have different priorities, and come to the table with its own agenda. For countries of origin, the concern may be an unwillingness to accept forced returns of irregular migrants, or the impact on their country of the phenomenon of brain drain caused by regular migration programmes, or enhancing the benefits of remittances by their nationals. For countries of transit, the interest might be the financial, social and environmental impact of the unauthorized movement of

people across their territory; for countries of destination, the interest could be to discourage irregular migration, return excludable migrants to their countries of origin and encourage the orderly movement of people.

RCP success depends on an agreement at the outset of the process on the nature of the problem or issue to be addressed, recognition of the common and diverging views and interests of participants, and a commitment to act cooperatively. Such preparations in advance of a full and frank discussion are well worth the additional effort. In some RCP's, such advance preparation is undertaken by the dedicated secretariat; in other cases, the host or interim chair, or working group chair will conduct consultations and prepare the documentation for discussion.

Comprehensive Approach

The complex and interdisciplinary nature of migration can complicate RCP efforts. A comprehensive approach will consider an issue at stake from all perspectives and with all relevant partners, and recognize interrelationships with other surrounding issues. The elaboration of a comprehensive approach to managing migration necessitates participation from a whole new set of actors.

This is already happening in some regional processes that have expanded areas of interest beyond just the traditional concerns of refugee protection or irregular migration. Increasingly, regional processes are focussing on labour migration, integration, development and other related issues. Processes like the IOM Cluster approach, the Budapest Process and the EU (if we include this as a process) are shifting emphasis to building partnerships with countries of origin. This brings domestic aid and development agencies into closer collaboration with the interior ministries in developing comprehensive migration and development strategies. Similarly, departments of trade and industry, negotiating the GATS, are increasingly seeking cooperation from their migration policy counterparts. Some participating members of RCPs conduct interdepartmental consultations at home, while processes such as MIDSA include Ministry of Labour representatives around the RCP table.

Lack of Data

Another challenge to many regional processes is the lack of reliable data on migration trends, stocks and flows[13], and information on migration programmes and policies.

Meaningful information and documentation are essential to informed exchanges. Thus, many processes begin with information sharing and analysis and seek to develop a common understanding of terminology and definitions. Through a regional process, participating states can work together to understand the definitional differences in the data and agree on a common interpretation of the shared data while working towards a common goal of maintaining and sharing accurate, reliable and up-to-date data on migration. The development of a statistical information system on migrants in Central America is an important priority for the RCM in this regard.

Overly Ambitious Programmes

A potential obstacle more easily managed than some of those cited above can result from the enthusiasm and optimism of participants for the process. RCPs taking on too many activities at once run the risk of not moving forward on many of them, being spread too thinly. While ensuring that the interests of all participating states are considered, an overly-ambitious programme may also be detrimental to building confidence within the process if all items are not dealt with fully and within the planned time frame.

Dealing with one issue at a time can help to create a level playing field amongst participating states, thereby improving relationships. While this may appear inconsistent with a comprehensive approach towards migration management, the comprehensiveness will come through including all of the relevant stakeholders interested in the issue including other government departments, NGOs and inter-governmental organizations. Comprehensiveness in terms of the range of issues being treated can come over time with a well-planned approach. With this in mind, a focussed and realistic plan of action would seem to achieve more effective results.

Lack of Resources

A serious obstacle faced by most regional processes is the lack of regular and stable funding. Only with secure funding can regular meetings be held and continuity of approach maintained.

Funding can be secured from many sources: through other, related regional institutions, such as SADC, ECOWAS or ASEAN; from participating states as an annual assessed contribution; or from donors who may or may not participate in the process.

Secretariat

Linked to the issue of funding, the form and function of a secretariat is another potential obstacle to a successful RCP. A core secretariat is an essential key to ensuring continuity and stability.

The secretariats of regional consultative processes are often managed by an international organization, e.g., IOM, UNHCR, OSCE, ICMPD. In most cases, international organizations facilitate the discussion of sensitive issues in a non-partisan way. In this manner, certain issues may be brought to the table for open discussion which, under leadership of one or another participating state might not be possible.

Some secretariats function in a purely administrative and organizational capacity, organizing meetings and workshops called by the participating state in the chair. Others are much more independent and proactive in their approach, and will maintain statistical databases and web sites, gather documentation on policy and procedures, produce studies and analytical reports, arrange consultative meetings for policy developers and implementers, and facilitate multi-lateral cooperation.

In addition to having a small technical support unit (secretariat), which IOM helped organize, and which the member state in the rotating chair oversees, the RCM also relies on a virtual secretariat – a web-based information exchange mechanism – which serves to simplify the process of information exchange, thus ensuring that relevant information reaches the contact person quickly and easily. The IGC also maintains a sophisticated web site for the use of its members, which includes studies and reports

133

13) See also **chapters 16** and **17.**

prepared by the secretariat, a database of statistical information gathered by the secretariat and a mechanism for virtual information-sharing.

Most secretariats are funded through voluntary contributions of some or all participating states. Other RCPs, such as the IGC, fund their secretariats through annual contributions required of each member and may also receive technical assistance from an intergovernmental organization such as IOM, ICMPD or UNHCR. RCPs without a working secretariat may rotate financial responsibility for meetings and other activities along with the responsibilities of the chair.

Progress to Date in Cooperation on Migration Management

One of the first multilateral approaches set up to manage a specific movement of individuals was the Comprehensive Plan of Action (CPA) for Indochinese Refugees (see also **chapter 5**). Established in 1989, the CPA consisted of a series of agreements adopted by some 70 countries at the UN-sponsored forum, the International Conference on Indochinese Refugees. The conference was prompted by the desire on the part of the international community to end the push-backs and drownings of "boat people" occurring almost daily in the Gulf of Thailand. The purpose of the CPA was "to resolve the outflow of people, primarily from Vietnam, to other countries in South-East Asia and Hong Kong" (INS, 1979). Its focus was on a comprehensive set of interlocking and mutually dependent agreements and actions involving countries of origin, transit and destination.

There were mixed results from this concerted action, which officially ended on 30 June 1996: push-backs and drownings ended, but many people remained in camps for many years. Nonetheless it is an example of an international consultative process resulting in agreement and coordinated action on a multitude of fronts by countries of origin, transit and destination.

While the results of the CPA can be and have been measured and analysed, it is more difficult to measure the progress of RCPs given their informal, non-binding and confidential nature. However, as building networks and relationships within the region is one of the important objectives of RCPs, the results of these links and the cooperation resulting from maintaining these links can be detected in activities not specifically related to the Regional Consultative Process itself. RCPs can serve as a vehicle for response to major local natural or civic events which have an impact on migration flows through the region and demand immediate and cooperative responses. One example is the implementation of temporary protection mechanisms and regional and international burden-sharing in response to the Kosovo outflow. The immediate regional humanitarian assistance provided during the aftermath of Hurricane Mitch is another good example of a concrete result of the cooperation built through the RCM.

Recent progress on cooperation in migration management can be identified in other areas:
- improvements in data collection and dissemination within a number of consultative groups;
- development and endorsement of various inter-governmental regional declarations (Bangkok Declaration, Dakar Declaration[14]);
- development of a common asylum system among EU countries;
- free movement of labour of EU nationals;
- more common approaches to asylum policies and procedures among countries participating in the IGC; and
- endorsement and implementation of Budapest Group recommendations on the management of irregular migration.

Another development is regional convergence. For example, in the Americas, convergence on many important themes is beginning to take place particularly between the RCM, the Summit of the Americas and Plan Puebla-Panama. The 2002 Vice-Ministerial meeting of the RCM tasked the Secretariat with initiating the necessary contacts with the other processes within the region to identify areas of cooperation and coordination, including with respect to the project of "new and harmonized statistical information systems on migration" (Government of Costa Rica, 2001a).

14) The Dakar Declaration has led to the establishment of the Migration Dialogue for West Africa (MIDWA) in 2002.

134

TEXTBOX 8.3.

Emergence of Common Principles in International Migration Management through Regional Consultative Processes

In managing migration through partnership and co-operation, RCPs recognize the need to uphold broad principles on the safe and orderly movement of persons, for example through facilitating regular migration, managing irregular migration, and ensuring effective protection for migrants. Below are four of the most common elements drawn from RCPs "principles", "recommendations" and "declarations" and which reflect states' commitments under international law, as well as good practices in the field of migration management.

These four principles represent common approaches to issues of common concern across each of the RCP's.

1. Promotion of exchange of information toward a common understanding of migration issues
A better understanding of migration is necessary to obtain a balanced approach towards effective migration management, which facilitates regular migration and prevents irregular migration.

2. Protecting the fundamental human rights of migrants including the right to non-discrimination
The protection of human rights and fundamental freedoms are important factors in the regulation of migratory flows and the achievement of durable solutions to the challenges of internal and international population movement.

3. Reinforcing efforts to prevent and combat irregular migration including smuggling and trafficking
Migration and irregular migration should not be considered in isolation from each other; they should be addressed in a comprehensive and balanced manner. In order to combat smuggling and trafficking, states are encouraged to establish mechanisms for cooperation and information exchange to increase public awareness of the harmful consequences of such activity for society as a whole.

4. Assisted voluntary return as a strategy to reduce irregular migration
A co-ordinated migration framework ensuring the protection of regular migrants and refugees granted asylum requires predictable and durable return programmes. Voluntary return is considered as preferred option for irregular migrants, including victims of trafficking, as well as asylum seekers whose claims have been denied and who have exhausted asylum determination procedures.

The emergence of common non-binding principles through RCPs can benefit an efficient migration management framework. Although some RCP principles address other specific concerns, those discussed above are consistent across various RCPs. This consistency indicates a certain degree of convergence and serves to link the management of migration with stability, economic development and combating transnational crimes including smuggling and trafficking, through a comprehensive and cooperative regional approach. In this light, common RCP principles may contribute to an international migration management framework as they reveal shared understanding and coherence for the benefit of countries of origin, transit and destination.

Asia is also beginning to look at the convergence of certain issues, primarily relating to trafficking and smuggling, through the follow-up to the Bali Conference. In a recent meeting of the APC Mekong sub-regional working group, it was agreed that there should be coordination and complementarity between the two regional groups to avoid overlap and duplication.

As the benefits of regional dialogue become more evident, so too does the recognition that inter-regional dialogue on migration management is necessary. While much migration remains intra-regional, a considerable amount of migratory movement flows across regions. The joint IGC/APC consultation held in Bangkok in April, 2001 was a first step in the direction of inter-regional cooperation. This joint meeting was the first of its kind, offering a unique opportunity to strengthen inter-regional dialogue, to develop shared understanding of the variety of challenges states face in relation to asylum, irregular migration and people smuggling, and to act as a confidence-building measure and as a possible stepping stone to future cooperation.

The Cluster process between the Caucasus and Western Europe, and the Western Mediterranean Conference on Migration ("5 + 5") (see also **textbox 13.2.**) involving five northern and five southern Mediterranean countries of origin, of transit and of destination are further demonstrations of the desire to better manage migration across regions. Like the Cluster, the "5 + 5" will share information and best practices, and will explore common principles for cooperation in managing inter-regional flows.

Increasingly evident is the need to feed the results of the constructive work done in the regions into a more global framework – a consolidation of the disparate achievements of regional and other processes into a set of global guidelines.

The Berne Initiative (see also **textbox 15.2.**), launched in 2001 by the Government of Switzerland, involves consultation with governments of all regions to explore whether there should be an international framework of guiding principles to manage migration. Governments have made it clear that they are not ready for a United Nations conference on migration (United Nations, 2001b). However, the growing number of groups and organizations interested in migration, as well as a number of IOM Member States, are interested in developing a framework of guiding principles to facilitate interstate cooperation in managing migration.

Conclusion

RCPs provide important venues for policy-makers, inter-governmental organizations and civic partners to share information, policies, practices, experiences, ideas and trust, which will help move the global community further along the path toward better managed international migration.

Certain obstacles can hamper the success of regional dialogue, but such obstacles can be overcome by following practical steps which have evolved from the experimentation of most Regional Consultative Processes as good practice. These steps can be summarized in a 10-Point Plan.

10-Point-Plan to a Successful Cooperative Approach in Migration Management

1. Participants must take ownership of the process.

2. There should be continuity with regularly scheduled meetings.

3. There should be common agreement on priorities.

4. Meetings should be focussed on specific issues, with clear and comprehensive objectives.

5. Issues should be focussed on enhancing understanding and regional cooperation in migration management.

6. The process should begin with and be continuously upheld by a compilation and sharing of reliable and accurate data.

7. Meetings should take place at defined administrative levels – for instance at strategic policy level or programme implementation level or at the technical expert level.

8. Participation should be comprehensive – from all relevant ministries, as well as from relevant intergovernmental and non-governmental organizations where appropriate.

9. Funding stability should be provided to ensure continuity.

10. A core secretariat is essential to ensuring regularity and continuity.

One of the most useful outcomes of a successful RCP is the opening of effective informal communication channels and networks among participating states. Regional meetings may take place once or twice (or more) per year, but the channels of informal communications are always open, resulting in more frequent consultation than more formal meetings would usually permit.

RCPs continue to grow because of and in response to the need for enhanced global cooperation and a global framework of guiding principles to manage international migration. This global framework should be based on common understandings, recognition of national and regional interests, state sovereignty, respect for the rule of law and internationally recognized principles, shared appreciation of sound practices in migration management, and mutual trust and partnership (IOM, 2002). Informal and non-binding principles for cooperation emanating from RCPs could serve as a foundation for a global framework of guiding principles for migration management – preserving the same informal and non-binding character at the global level.

TABLE 8.1.

Participation in Major Regional Consultative Processes

Process	Government Participants	Main Areas of Interest
Inter-Governmental Consultations on Asylum, Refugee and Migration Policies in Europe, North America and Australia (**IGC**) (1985)	Australia, Austria, Belgium, Canada, Denmark, Finland, Germany, Ireland, Italy, the Netherlands, Norway, Spain, Sweden, Switzerland, the United Kingdom, the United States and the European Commission	Entry, border control, labour migration, refugees, asylum, technology, country of origin information, data, return, irregular migration, smuggling/trafficking
Budapest Group (1991)	Albania, Australia, Austria, Belarus, Belgium, Bosnia and Herzegovina, Bulgaria, Canada, Croatia, Cyprus, Czech Republic, Denmark, Estonia, Finland, France, Georgia, Germany, Greece, Hungary, Iceland, Ireland, Italy, Latvia, Liechtenstein, Lithuania, FYR Macedonia, Malta, Moldova, Netherlands, Norway, Poland, Portugal, Romania, Russian Federation, Slovakia, Slovenia, Spain, Sweden, Switzerland, Turkey, Ukraine, United Kingdom, United States, the European Commission	Irregular migration, trafficking and smuggling, readmission agreements, return, visa harmonization, asylum, refugees, forced migration, financial and technical assistance
CIS Conference and Follow-up Process (1996)	Armenia, Azerbaijan, Belarus, Georgia, Kazakhstan, Kyrgyzstan, Moldova, Russia, Tajikistan, Turkmenistan, Ukraine, Uzbekistan plus "neighbouring and other relevant States"	Refugees, IDPs, persons in refugee-like situations, repatriation, ecological migrants, migration management (combating illegal migration and trafficking, border management), rights of migrants, return, reintegration, population/ demography, promoting participation by international and local NGOs; implementing legislation
Regional Conference on Migration (**RCM** "Puebla Process") (1996)	Belize, Canada, Costa Rica, Dominican Republic, El Salvador, Guatemala, Honduras, Mexico, Nicaragua, Panama and the United States	Migration policies and management (combating migrant trafficking, travel document security and control, harmonized policies in return of irregular migrants, reintegration of repatriated migrants); statistical information system, border cooperation, refugee protection, migrant rights, migration and development
Manila Process (1996)	Australia, Brunei Darussalam, Cambodia, People's Republic of China, Indonesia, Japan, Republic of Korea, Laos, Malaysia, Myanmar, New Zealand, Papua New Guinea, Philippines, Singapore, Thailand, Vietnam and the Hong Kong SAR of China	Combat irregular migration and migrant trafficking, root causes of regular migration and of irregular migration, return, reintegration, entry/border control, remittances, migrant rights
Inter-Governmental Asia-Pacific Consultations on Refugees, Displaced Persons and Migrants (**APC**) (1996)	Australia, Bangladesh, Bhutan, Brunei Darussalam, Cambodia, China, Timor Leste (to join at the 6th APC plenary), Fiji, Hong Kong SAR of China, India, Indonesia, Japan, Kiribati, Republic of Korea, Laos, Malaysia, Micronesia, Mongolia, Myanmar, Nauru, Nepal, New Caledonia, New Zealand, Pakistan, Papua New Guinea, Philippines, Samoa, Singapore, Solomon Islands, Sri Lanka, Thailand, Vietnam	Irregular migration, asylum, information sharing on reintegration of refugees and returnees, best practices on issues relating to cross-border migration management, common migration and asylum challenges
South American Conference on Migration (**Lima Process**) (1999)	Argentina, Bolivia, Brazil, Chile, Colombia, Ecuador, Guyana, Paraguay, Peru, Surinam, Uruguay, Venezuela	Human rights of migrants, integration, trafficking and smuggling, information exchange, migration and development
Migration Dialogue for Southern Africa (**MIDSA**) (2000)	Angola, Botswana, Comoros, Democratic Republic of Congo, Lesotho, Malawi, Mauritius, Mozambique, Namibia, South Africa, Swaziland, Tanzania, Zambia and Zimbabwe	Migration management, border control, migration and development, causes, dimensions and impacts of migration, harmonizing systems of data collection and immigration policy and legislation, labour migration, irregular movements
Migration Dialogue for West Africa (**MIDWA**) (2001)	Burkina Faso, Cape Verde, Côte d'Ivoire, Gambia, Guinea, Guinea-Bissau, Liberia, Mali, Niger, Nigeria, Senegal, Sierra Leone, Togo	Border management, data collection, labour migration, development, remittances, rights of migrants, irregular migration, trafficking and smuggling, return, reintegration Cluster Process (2001)
Cluster Process (2001)	Armenia, Azerbaijan, Georgia, Belgium, Denmark, Germany, the Netherlands, Switzerland, Sweden	Foster mutual understanding, information campaigns, irregular migration, return and readmission
Bali Ministerial Conference on People Smuggling, Trafficking in Persons and Related Transnational Crime (**Bali Conference**) (2002)	Afghanistan, Australia, Bangladesh, Bhutan, Brunei Darussalam, Cambodia, China, Democratic Republic of Korea, Fiji, France (New Caledonia), India, Indonesia, Iran, Japan, Jordan, Kiribati, Laos, Malaysia, Mongolia, Myanmar, Nauru, Nepal, New Zealand, Pakistan, Palau, Papua New Guinea, Philippines, Republic of Korea, Samoa, Singapore, Solomon Islands, Sri Lanka, Syria, Thailand, Turkey, East Timor, Vanuatu and Vietnam	Migrant smuggling and trafficking, information and intelligence sharing, cooperation in fraudulent document detection, cooperation on border and visa systems, return
Conference on Western Mediterranean Cooperation (**5 + 5**) (2002)	Algeria, France, Italy, Libya, Malta, Mauritania, Morocco, Portugal, Spain, Tunisia	Migration and development (the role of diaspora), labour migration, integration

TABLE 8.2.

Major Regional Groupings with a Migration Focus or Interest

Region	Migration Focus	Migration Interest (prime focus often economic)
North/South/Central America	• Regional Conference on Migration (RCM "Puebla Process") • South American Conference on Migration (Lima Process) • Comision Centro-americana de Directores de Migracion	• Summit of the Americas • Plan Puebla-Panama • South American Common Market (MERCOSUR) • North American Free Trade Area (NAFTA) • Organization of American States (OAS)
Europe	• Commonwealth of Independent States (CIS) • Budapest Group • International Centre for Migration Policy Development (ICMPD)	• European Union • Council of Europe • Organization for Security and Cooperation in Europe (OSCE)
Asia/Pacific	• Inter-Governmental Asia-Pacific Consultations (APC) • Manila Process • Bali Follow-up Process	• Association of South-East Asian Nations (ASEAN) • South Asian Association for Regional Cooperation (SAARC) • Asia-Pacific Economic Cooperation (APEC) • Boao Forum for Asia (BFA) • Pacific Island Forum (PIF)
Africa	• Migration Dialogue for Southern Africa (MIDSA) • Migration Dialogue for West Africa (MIDWA)	• Common Market for Eastern and Southern Africa (COMESA) • Southern African Development Community (SADC) • Economic Community of West African States (ECOWAS) • Organization of African Unity (OAU)
Gulf/Middle East		• Gulf Cooperation Council (GCC)
Inter-regional	• Western Mediterranean Conference on Migration (5 + 5) • Intergovernmental Consultations on Asylum, Refugees and Migration (IGC) • Cluster Process	• African, Caribbean and Pacific Group of States (ACP) • Asia-Europe Meeting (ASEM) • Asian-African Legal Consultative Organization (AALCO) • General Agreement on Trade in Services (GATS) • EuroMed

MIGRATION MANAGEMENT AT WORK

SELECTED GEOGRAPHIC REGIONS

CHAPTER 9

Migration Management in the Traditional Countries of Immigration

This chapter focusses on four states that built themselves *through* immigration, the so-called "classic" or "traditional" countries of immigration (TCIs): Australia, Canada, New Zealand and the United States[1]. These TCIs continue to engage the world migration system actively, even aggressively, accounting for between 1.1 and 1.3 million legal permanent immigrant entries per year (see **table 9.1.**). That number increases by about 500,000 entries when longer-term temporary workers are taken into account and by as many as another 500,000 when net illegal entries are considered.

The overwhelming majority of immigrant entries, both legal and unauthorized, are into the United States. When using other measures, however, the rankings change considerably. On a per capita basis, for instance, the US is the least immigrant-dense among the TCIs. Specifically, both Canada and New Zealand have about 1.5 times as many immigrants per resident as the US, while Australia's foreign-born stock is about 2.2 times larger than the United States'. Similarly, when comparing recent annual average intakes *per capita,* New Zealand admits more than three times as many immigrants per year as the US does, with Canada's and Australia's intakes standing at about almost twice and somewhat less than 1.5 times as large, respectively (see **table 9.2.**)[2].

The immigration source countries for the four TCIs vary enormously but certain observations can be made. Over the last few decades, immigration from Europe has declined dramatically in all instances and been replaced by large and strengthening flows from Asia (see **table 9.3.**). In fact, in all cases but that of the US, Asian immigration accounts for most entries. Immigrants from China and/or India have accounted for the largest numbers of Canadian entries in recent years; Australia and New Zealand count each other's nationals as the largest group of long-term settlers. In the US, Mexican nationals account for about one-fifth of total legal entries, making immigration from the Americas the dominant flow at about 45 per cent of the total. Asian immigration accounts for about 35 per cent of all US intakes.

In all four TCIs, immigrants continue to settle overwhelmingly in the largest cities: New York and Los Angeles (US), Toronto (Canada), Sydney (Australia), and Auckland (New Zealand) - which also tend to have the deepest immigration tradition. In the US, however, the 2000 Census has also documented an increasing dispersion of new immigrants to a host of second tier cities[3] - the first significant such dispersion of immigrants since the Second World War.

With the exception of the US[4], TCIs select and admit immigrants as part of their ongoing nation-building process and thus, more or less directly, include a demographic dimension in their overall decisions on annual immigration target levels[5]. All TCIs rely on immigration explicitly to enhance their economic competitiveness, which is addressed most directly in two avenues of legal entry, economic stream immigration and temporary worker admissions. Many analysts go even further and argue that the enormous reliance of certain US economic sectors (such as perishable-crop agriculture) on large-scale illegal immigration can be largely put down to economic competitiveness. In other words, according to these analysts, the demand for unskilled workers far outweighs concerns about the social problems related to these movements (Stelzer, 2002:7).

The magnitude, long-term nature and ongoing socio-economic importance of immigration have led each of the TCIs to develop and maintain large and complex bureaucracies to manage and regulate the migration process. However, some of the TCIs do so more actively – and some might say "effectively" – than others, particularly in manipulating the admissions' formula to reflect lessons both from administrative management and research and evaluation. Of course, most changes are in response to changing politics.

1) This chapter does not include Israel, which is also generally considered as a traditional country of immigration.
2) Included is an estimate of about 400,000 net annual entries for illegal immigration for the US.
3) Among these new cities of immigration are, for example, Atlanta, Georgia; St. Paul, Minnesota; and Nashville, Tennessee.
4) In the US, the demographic dimension plays a neutral role at best. In all four TCIs, active and well-organized environmentalist and population control lobbies use demographics *against* immigration.
5) New Zealand's recent increases in immigration intakes are thought to stem from concerns over increasing rates of emigration from the country, particularly to Australia.

In all cases but the US, intakes are reviewed regularly and the government sets annual numerical targets and "planning ranges" administratively[6]. This is done in the context of an overall strategy to manage population growth, the labour market and economic performance. Most changes in immigration targets in Australia, Canada and New Zealand are regulatory in nature while some require legislation. Regulatory change tends to be easier in Canada and New Zealand, where the law reserves significant power for the minister; this kind of administrative flexibility was narrowed in Australia in the early 1990s and is virtually non-existent in the United States. On the other hand, legislative change is always difficult as powerful pro-and anti-immigration lobbies drown each other out, making fundamental changes to the *status quo* extremely rare. Legislative changes tend to be the most complicated in the US, where its constitutional doctrine of separating executive from legislative (and judicial) powers makes agreement on highly contentious issues even more difficult.

While all four societies place immigrants at the heart of their nation-building rhetoric, they are devoting more and more of their time arguing about immigration's effects on society (see **chapter 4**). In recent years, three aspects have dominated public discourse: (a) how relevant their immigrant past should be in shaping current policies about immigration; (b) how large the immigrant inflow should be; and (c) the composition of that inflow, that is, how visas should be allocated both among entry streams and across countries of origin. Deep disagreements on these issues - and concern about immigration's contribution to the pace of national social, cultural, and racial change – gave rise to fairly intense scepticism of immigration in the 1990s. None of this scepticism has resulted in powerful immigration exclusionist movements as in some European countries; however, in the 1990s, the Buchanan wing of the Republican Party in the US (Mr. Buchanan left the Party in 2000), the Alliance Party in Canada, the One Nation Party in Australia, and the New Zealand First Party, gave both voice and comfort to anti-immigration movements in the TCIs.

A General Overview of Immigration Systems in the TCIs

All immigration systems in the TCIs have three distinct and common routes or "streams"[7] for foreign-born nationals to enter either permanently[8] or for extended periods of time[9]: family immigration, economic immigration, and humanitarian immigration (see **tables 9.4., 9.5., 9.6.** and **9.7.**).

In addition, all TCIs allocate substantial human, financial, and political (including diplomatic) capital resources to the control of a fourth stream, irregular immigration[10]. In recent years, this unauthorized movement has been increasingly perceived by TCIs as an open-ended challenge to their legal order and efforts to maintain orderly migration regimes.

Irregular immigration is most significant in the US. It has been a major component of US immigration flows for about three decades: currently, there are an estimated eight to nine million unauthorized persons in the US, or between 20 and 25 per cent of the total foreign-born population in the US (United States Census Bureau, 2000a).

Irregular immigration is also growing in the other TCIs. Some informal estimates place the total at about 200,000 for Canada. The insular location of the other two countries and a variety of policy idiosyncrasies in their immigration laws make outright illegal entries and terms of entry violations far less common. These policies include: (a) the availability of the Working Holiday Makers visa, which allows some tourists to obtain short-term employment legally; (b) the Trans-Tasman Travel Arrangement, which gives reciprocal entry, work, and establishment rights to citizens of both countries; and (c) the Advanced Passenger Information System, which allows

143

6) In the US, only the number for overseas refugees is set annually; all other components are preset in a formula changeable only through legislation.

7) This is a term used by all TCIs except the US.

8) The "permanent" rubric is primarily an immigration management classification. It does not measure net immigration nor does it imply that permanent immigrants do not move on. The appropriate terminology for permanent admissions is "lawful permanent residents" for the US, "landed immigrants" for Canada, and "settlers" for Australia and New Zealand.

9) Long-term temporary immigration is by far the fastest-rising regulated immigration stream in the world.

10) In view of consistency in using terminology, throughout this text "irregular migration" incorporates the various appellations of this specific type of migration, including "clandestine migration", "illegal migration", "undocumented migration". See also **chapter 1** on migration terminology and **chapter 3**.

the Australian authorities to decide whether a prospective traveller should be issued a ticket or be required to make a visa application (see **tables 9.13.** and **9.14.**).

This chapter is intended to point out the commonalities among the entry components which have enabled TCIs to occupy such an important place in the world migration system[11]. For instance, the United States, Canada, Australia and New Zealand have traditionally privileged family immigration over economic or humanitarian entry in their immigration systems. In the last decade or so, however, family immigration's pre-eminence within each system was contested on grounds ranging from the category's size and rate of growth to its effect on the "quality" of overall immigration and its interference with the government's ability to manage the inflow valve[12]. As a result, TCIs devote considerable political energy to underscoring the importance of families as basic building blocks of their immigration systems, while limiting growth in the family stream, primarily by narrowing the family relationships that have priority in immigrant selection formula.

Similarly, all TCIs have mechanisms for admitting foreign workers for certain types of employment, both permanent and temporary. All four states are rather generous with permanent visas up front for those admitted under the economic stream, and employ similar screening mechanisms for most such admissions. Finally, all four states are signatories to the relevant refugee-protection instruments, including the 1967 Protocol to the United Nations' Refugee Convention. As such, they resettle refugees relatively liberally and have robust and rather generous asylum adjudication systems when compared with other industrial societies (see **chapter 6**).

Family Immigration[13]

Arguably, orderly and large-scale immigration cannot be built without using family migration as a building block. International legal instruments uphold family (re)unification as a fundamental human rights principle. Furthermore, all TCIs recognize that since foreign workers are not just

production factors and, in the case of refugees, the families of the persecuted are also likely to be persecuted themselves, family migration is an essential by-product of any form of immigration.

None of these reasons, however, make family migration less subject to criticism. On the contrary, the family reunification stream may be the most vulnerable to attack often because it approaches the status of an entitlement. To its detractors, most family stream immigrants are also seen as taxing educational institutions and social infrastructures, creating unwelcome competition for jobs, housing, and social goods, and contributing to ethnic and linguistic divisions. To its defenders, on the other hand, family reunification is a response to and promotion of a central principle of a national ethos: family values. In a more practical vein, this school of thought views families as essential to smoothing immigrants' social, economic, and, gradually, political integration by serving, among others, as buffers and mediators between the individual immigrant and the new environment (Fuchs, 1991).

African migrants arrive in the US

Family immigration is either the dominant or among the largest components of entry in all TCIs. The overwhelming majority of immigrants enter the US, for instance, through the family-immigration stream (see **table 9.4.**). While there are heated debates on the definition and influence of the family class on overall US immigration policy, the principle of family reunification is almost universally accepted as an appropriate centrepiece of US immigration policy. American analytical literature finds that families provide an important private social safety net and critical child-care services which have been shown to bolster economic status

11) See **tables 9.4., 9.5., 9.6.** and **9.7.** for country-specific entry categories.
12) This argument has been least contentious in Canada, where the government has increased its overall intake sufficiently. As a result, the family stream has been able to grow but the more selective components of entry have been allowed to grow even faster.
13) **Table 9.8.** offers a comparative description of each TCI's family immigration system.

among immigrant and disadvantaged groups (Gurak, 1988; Perez, 1986; Tienda and Angel, 1982). Perhaps most important, however, may be the labour-market "grapevine" that operates through families and social connections (Wial, 1988a, 1988b). Family and social linkages provide information about access to the labour market that is essential to an immigrant's survival, making these connections among the strongest predictors of successful economic adaptation (Papademetriou and Muller, 1987, Papademetriou *et al.,* 1989). A successful transition for immigrants, finally, prepares the ground for a solid foundation for their children - the US citizen-workers of the next generation.

The United States selects approximately 70 per cent of its Lawful Permanent Residents (LPRs) through family immigration[14]. The actual number of the family intake (approximately 500,000 to 600,000) appears to be fixed legislatively (legislation sets that number at under 500,000, see **table 9.9.**). In reality, however, the number is flexible, since part of the family immigration stream is numerically unrestricted (US citizens' spouses, parents, and unmarried children under 18) while the numerically limited family preference categories have a visa "floor" of 226,000 visas. Since the supply of the latter relative visas trails behind the demand for them, those who qualify but are unable to get a visa go onto a waiting list or "backlog," awaiting their turn. At the end of 2001, there were about 4.5 million persons waiting for a visa to the United States[15].

Canada's family immigration visas are fundamentally unrestricted. However, the definition of family has been narrowed somewhat over the last decade or so – making it narrower than the US's and more expansive than Australia's. Like the other TCIs, Canada endeavours to simultaneously downplay and maintain the family stream's place in its immigration system. This effort has been somewhat more successful in Canada than in the US, Australia or New Zealand since Canada's immigration programme has been growing steadily in recent years.

As a result, the Canadian Government has been able to increase the size of those components of its immigration programme most Canadians support strongly (primarily the "independent" stream) without visibly disadvantaging the other programmes.

There are few direct barriers to the reunification of immediate families in Canada. The most stringent prerequisite is that the sponsoring or "anchor"-relative must meet an income cut-off level specific to the sponsor's area of residence[16] and be willing to be financially responsible for the beneficiary for a period of up to 10 years. While the first requirement is routinely checked, the second is only intermittently enforced. Similar requirements exist in both the US family reunification system - where the sponsor's income must be at 125 per cent of official poverty guidelines - and for most family-related categories in Australia (see **table 9.8.**).

Canada's family stream planning range total is calculated on the basis of two variables: (a) applications already in the system (processing takes an average of six to eight months, but may last up to a year or more); and (b) expected demand. The system's capacity to issue visas thus is a key programme and numbers-management tool[17] under which Canadian immigration officials abroad become a mechanism for shaping not only the overall size of the program but also its source-country composition. For example, increasing immigration staff in certain places (such as Hong Kong SAR of China, Eastern Europe, or the Far East, to use examples from Canadian programme priorities in the last decade or so) translates *de facto* into a "preference" for immigrants from these areas. In fact, merely choosing which class of prospective immigrants is given scheduling priority by an immigration official can influence dramatically the shape of immigration from a specific country.

Canadian programmatic idiosyncrasies make comparisons among family immigration systems across the TCIs difficult. For instance, Canada offers additional points in its largest immigrant stream – the independent one – for family relationships other than those recognized as numerically

145

---

14) Beginning with financial year 1995, 55,000 (reduced to 50,000 since 1998) visas are distributed by lottery annually to *diversity immigrants.* Diversity immigrants are required to have a high school education or the equivalent, or two years of experience in occupations requiring at least two years of training. Visas under this programme are distributed in inverse proportion to a region's and a country's overall use of US immigrant visas over the previous year (see **tables 9.4.** and **9.9.**).

15) There was also an additional backlog of 324,438 asylum cases by the end of 2001 (see Kramer, 2001).

16) The sponsorship income cut-off as of July 28, 2002 is between CN$ 12,361 for rural areas and CN$ 17,886 for areas with populations of 500,000 or more (CIC, 2002).

17) Unlike the US system's numerical limits, the annual Canadian planning ranges are "an order of magnitude to be aimed at" (Howith and Employment and Immigration Canada, 1988:5), rather than a "quota," "level," "target," "cap" or "ceiling". Only one figure is *firm*: government-assisted refugees.

exempt under its family immigration stream[18]. In addition, the subjective "personal suitability" component of the Canadian point system (see **table 9.10.**) further skews the selection system in ways that cannot be quantified. Without publishing data on how many of the points-tested immigrants gained admission because of the extra family relationship points – and what proportion of the discretionary personal suitability component may favour relatives and by how much – a true comparison is not possible.

The Australian family stream's size, relative to that of the overall immigration programme dropped for the first time in 1997-98 to a little less than half of the total. This milestone was reached after a fairly sustained effort by Australian governments since the mid-1990s to restrict the definition of family for immigration purposes and reduce its size relative to other immigration programme components. However, the reported size of Australia's (and New Zealand's) family stream immigration cannot be compared to that of the other TCIs because only immigration programme entries are included in the country's annual admissions figures. New Zealanders have made up between one-fifth and one-third of total annual settler migration in Australia for the past decade or so and yet enter without a visa and so are not taken into account. In 1999-2000, New Zealanders accounted for about 25 per cent of "long-term settlers" in Australia (see **table 9.3.**).

Citizens of New Zealand can visit, work, reunify with their families, or remain in Australia as permanent settlers under the 1973 Trans-Tasman Travel Arrangement, which essentially formalized a bilateral – and reciprocal – immigration practice begun in the 1920s. The Arrangement also entitled New Zealanders to become Australian citizens within two years after settling without having to meet immigration programme formalities (see **table 9.6.**). New Zealanders also had automatic access to social benefits. Since the establishment of new regulations in 2001, this access as well as formal family reunification rights (for the purpose of settling in Australia) require applications for formal immigrant settler status.

New Zealand sets an annual "global immigration target", which has been increasing in recent years, partly in response to two recessions in the 1990s. In the context of the recessions, greater immigration is seen both as a means of attracting educated and skilled immigrants from east Asia, the source region of the lion's share of immigrants to both Australia and New Zealand, and as the antidote to rising emigration (see **table 9.3.**). Demographically, New Zealand's net migration has fallen from about 20,000 in the early-to-mid-1990s to about 10,000 in the most recent years. Thus the target and programmatic emphasis on the skilled stream have increased in recent years: from about 25,000 in the early 1990s, to 35,000 in the mid-to-latter part of the 1990s, and towards 45,000 since then. In 2000, New Zealand admitted only about one-third of its immigrants through the family stream.

TEXTBOX 9.1.

The Migration Agenda between Mexico and the United States[19]

The Mexico-United States migration agenda can be characterized as being interspersed with lights and shadows.

The 3,200 km border between the two countries is one of the most frequently crossed borders worldwide; it is also a dangerous one. Between 1998 and 2001, more than 1,500 persons lost their lives while trying to enter the United States. The most common causes for a fatal migration outcome are heatstroke and dehydratation, occurring when migrants attempt to cross the border deserts in an irregular fashion.

For the first time, at the beginning of 2001, a number of factors and circumstances in the two countries converged to herald a significant political change in favour of large sectors of migrants. The two presidents accepted that migration issues should be part of the bi-national agenda and assured that they would tackle them without delay. Occurring at the beginning of both their mandates, this was heralded as a considerable achievement and suggested there would be results in the near future.

This common determination was then shaken by the terrorist attacks of September 11, 2001. Although terrorism is the most extreme and unusual outcome of migration, national security considerations suddenly loomed large in the United States and acted as a relatively inflexible filter, which now affects international migrants (not only Mexican) awaiting entry to or wanting to remain in the United States. This situation of uncertainty now overshadows the socio-political

---

18) See **table 9.10.** for a complete description of the "Relative in Canada" factor considered under the current Canadian point system.

19) Text adapted from *IOM News,* June 2002.

Irregular migrants cross the Rio Grande to the US by raft

climate in which Presidents Fox and Bush will have to continue dealing with the migration agenda, subject to the time, content and form constraints that have arisen since September 11.

The agenda has not been hemmed in but has actually been broadened either through the incorporation of new issues, the development of specific issues already on the table, or the need to speed up the process of others. In any event, three premises must remain constant:

• migration must be kept at the top of the agenda of bilateral relations, which is feasible since it depends on the two presidents and their administrations;
• any temptation to act unilaterally must be avoided; this is no easy task as regards the support of the legislature and judiciary in the US, who have adopted a hard stance towards migrants and their legal rights under United States jurisdiction; and
• the issue must be kept clear of national security considerations, which are bound to weigh diversely on any aspect connected with foreign entry to or presence on American soil. While the theme has become more complex, new horizons are opening up which demand new solutions.

The restrictive control measures which have been introduced were to be expected, including the increase in Immigration and Naturalization Service (INS) personnel along the borders and the curtailment of tourist permits from 180 to no more than 30 days. These moves tend to pacify the people and institutions of the United States. However, they should not prevent the possibility of speeding up the processing of the million or so pending requests for legal residence already submitted by Mexicans, even under existing rules. Such action lies within the reach of President Bush's Government. Apart from not causing trouble with the United States Congress, it would bring two immediate benefits: at home, it would strengthen his leadership and broaden his electoral base among Hispanic voters; internationally, it would make the migration issue more prominent on the bilateral agenda with Mexico.

Because they are long-term objectives and despite the fact that the specific time schedules, costs and scope of each have shifted, Mexico has maintained the five main lines of its migration policy with the United States since the events of September 11, 2001:

• legalization of the status of millions of Mexicans residing in the United States without the proper migration permit;

- establishment of a programme for temporary workers;
- border security, based on the Plan of Action for Cooperation on Border Security and the agreement to establish "intelligent borders" between the two countries;
- increase in the number and characteristics of visas for temporary workers; and
- development programmes in Mexican regions with high rates of international emigration.

Some of these issues will be handled at a slower and more cautious pace, or could even be postponed for the time being. Because they are so important, they need convincing and creative treatment. At the end of 2001, Mexico set up a specialized bureau for International Migration Affairs and introduced a procedure that has already begun to show results in the form of consular registration papers for Mexican nationals in the United States regardless of their migratory status. If these documents – as is already the case – gain acceptance by the United States banking system, their validation could produce unsuspected benefits within a relatively short period of time.

In effect, the consular registration document does not infringe United States legislation; nor does it constitute an official migration paper. It serves to identify holders as Mexican nationals and specifies some of their personal details, origin and current residence. To the extent that such a document comes to be accepted by more banks in the United States for the purpose of opening accounts and performing financial transactions, it is likely that a greater number of Mexicans living outside the bounds of migration legislation (totaling an estimated 3.5 million) will apply for it and use it for their banking purposes. This would have the effect of swelling bank deposits. Provided that banks lower their charges on remittances to Mexico and offer more favourable exchange rates as is already happening, there will be a considerable multiplier effect for society and institutions on both sides of the border.

It is worth looking at four statistics that provide a fair appreciation of the potential implications of such an initiative:

- 23 million Mexican nationals or persons of Mexican origin send money back home;
- the amounts involved are growing, amounting to close to US$ 9 billion in 2001;
- Mexicans abroad send only 15 per cent of their income back home and spend 85 per cent locally; and
- the Mexican community contributes close to US$ 82.1 billion a year to US gross domestic product.

This means a substantial amount of capital is currently subject to one of three conditions: either it remains outside the banking system; or it circulates through non-banking circuits; or it makes limited use of the local banking network and its international links. Better conditions would undoubtedly stimulate the opening of new accounts and would give rise to greater deposits and to more frequent and larger remittances, while improving the local economies and social sectors involved in both countries. All these effects could be triggered by the introduction of a consular registration document. Presidents Fox and Bush could give the scheme their personal support to ensure that it becomes generally applicable within a short time.

In addition, if the initiative proves successful, it would add a considerable impetus to bilateral negotiations, since it would help the two governments obtain the support of their respective legislatures, while strengthening social backing to deal with the more controversial aspects of the common migration agenda. If so, future prospects would look distinctly brighter.

Rays of light are beginning to pierce the shadows surrounding international migration for migrants and the bilateral dealings of the Mexican and United States Governments.

Economic Immigration[20]

The second basic immigration stream is economic and selects immigrants based on factors such as an employment offer and/or potential for employment, education/skills/experience, and demonstrated business skills, among others. The economic stream is thought by many in all TCIs to match most directly the interests of the immigrant with those of the labour market and broad economic competitiveness in the receiving society. Thus, it has been at the centre of arguments in favour of international migration for more than 100 years.

Economic migration comprises two basic flows: permanent and temporary. Permanent (also referred to here as "immigrant") visas are rather limited. The TCIs admit roughly between 300,000 and 350,000 principal applicants and their families annually. On the other hand, temporary

20) Called *Employment-based Immigration* in the United States, *Independent and Other Class* in Canada, the *Skill Stream under the Migration Programme* in Australia, and the *Skilled/Business Stream* in New Zealand.

admissions of foreigners (also referred to here as "labour migration") explicitly for work or to obtain the right to work, have been growing in leaps and bounds. In fact, more and more temporary labour migration has become the gateway for ever-increasing numbers of permanent immigrants to initially find their way legally into immigration countries, both within and beyond the TCIs.

Most entries in this stream, whether permanent or temporary, are skewed strongly towards better educated and skilled foreigners. However, both origin and destination countries continue to value admissions for jobs requiring few formal skills but which reward relevant experience. These admissions represent a constant and significant presence in most immigration systems. This is acknowledged in the various schemes for agricultural and other seasonal work, as well as for caregivers and other personal (domestic) services in Canada and elsewhere.

While not all TCIs treat foreigners offering their labour and skills in the international migration system identically, all but the US follow common mechanisms for selecting permanent admissions. The differences between the other TCIs and the United States disappear, however, when it comes to temporary admissions since all TCIs employ similar measures for testing their labour markets when an immigrant's entry is predicated on his or her "match" for a specific job.

Accessing the Global Labour Pool through Temporary Admissions

The growing popularity of temporary admissions across TCIs (and other states) has been accompanied by a remarkable convergence in admissions procedures. Reasons for this convergence include the reality of multilateral agreements, such as those relating to trade-in-services which are anchored on the principle of reciprocity, and demands among economic partners to codify reciprocal access for their nationals in the areas of business, trade, investment, or cultural exchanges. Regional reciprocal arrangements have also proliferated, such as the Trans-Tasman Arrangement and the visa free entry and rights to employment between the US and Canada in about seventy professional occupations under the North American Free Trade Agreement[21]. Finally, certain categories of temporary entry allow employment that is in some ways "incidental" to the visa's primary

purpose, including the following: student visas (under certain more or less restrictive circumstances); trainee or cultural exchange visas, under which a visitor is allowed to work as part of the training or exchange; or "holiday maker" visa holders who are allowed to work for a period of time during their stay in the host country (see **tables 9.11., 9.12., 9.13.** and **9.14.**).

However, there is another more consequential reason for such convergence in practices. With "globalization" having advanced to the point where speaking of national firms may in many ways be anachronistic, competitive pressures have put a premium on cutting-edge technical skills and talent – wherever these may be found. With trade barriers falling and with technology, like capital, recognizing neither borders nor nationality, individual initiative and talent are increasingly recognized as the most valuable global resources. The TCIs have long recognized this, designing and redesigning their immigration systems to offer ready access to those with the desired human capital attributes. This has increasingly led to competition among TCIs in what might be called a human capital accretion "sweepstakes".

The TCIs offer permanent immigration status up front to many of these foreign workers but the administratively simpler temporary-to-permanent entry route is gaining in prominence. Two of the most well-travelled routes in this transition to permanence are outlined below. The first route involves temporary work in the information technology and communications sectors; the US has been most aggressive in this regard with its H-1B visa but the other three TCIs have joined the competition with considerable vigour. In fact, since 2000, in a departure from other TCIs, New Zealand has offered a work permit to applicants who do not have enough points to qualify for permanent residence but would meet the pass mark if they had a job offer, effectively creating a visa for job searchers (Delamere, 1999). The second route is through a country's higher education (see **table 9.15.**). The US is again by far the leader in issuing student visas and has been so for decades. The others, however, are also attempting to gain access to the student talent pool by removing administrative barriers to hiring foreign students fresh out of school and converting them to permanent immigrants in due course.

The expansion of the temporary immigration stream is re-fueling two "old" discourses: the first focusses on the receiving countries' failure to adapt their own training and education systems to the requirements of the so-called "new economy" adequately enough to meet employment needs from within their own labour pool; the second

---

21) Mexicans have similar employment rights but require a visa to enter the US.

issue concerns the effect (and propriety) of deeper and more systematic "helpings" by the TCIs (and, increasingly, by other advanced industrial societies) of the human capital pool in the developing world.

Permanent Economic Stream Admissions

The TCIs and/or their corporate citizens choose the foreign workers they are interested in admitting permanently with an eye to serving national interests. But each country emphasizes different facets of that interest. For instance, all four countries possess some system of labour market tests to protect domestic workers; however, while the US filters most of its economic immigrants through this mechanism, the other TCIs apply the tests less stringently. Similarly, although all TCIs show deference and seek to rectify labour market shortages and skill and locational mismatches, the US relies on these as policy priorities *par excellence*. Conversely, the other three countries are most interested in accruing high quality human capital, typically within a band of constantly revised occupations. In reality, of course, all four selection systems use more than one set of criteria simultaneously and each set is more of a hybrid than a pure set.

The primary focus of US immigration law regarding economic immigration is on rectifying labour market shortages and mismatches, with a marked tendency towards simplifying the labour market tests required. Specifically, the US Immigration and Nationality Act (INA) establishes a maximum quota of 140,000 "permanent" visas for "employment"-based immigration. More than 90 per cent of such visas target well-educated and skilled immigrants and their immediate families (see **table 9.9.**).

Canada, Australia, and New Zealand, on the other hand, have moved away from tying skilled immigration to employment per se and focus increasingly on what might be called a "skills' accretion" formula that rewards qualifications and experience in selected occupations[22]. Accordingly, these TCIs eschew most labour market tests.

The principal agent in each selection scheme varies accordingly. In the US, the principal agent is almost always the employer, both for the permanent and the temporary employment-based systems; in the other three countries, the principal agent for the permanent system is the public servant, with the employer playing a limited role, while employers play a principal role in the fast-expanding temporary worker admissions' system.

In all TCIs, private agents are becoming increasingly active in assisting potentially interested migrants in administrative procedures and paperwork in view of their immigration. These agents publicize their services widely in national and international newspapers and magazines through advertisements. This trends hinges towards a tendency to a certain privatization of the migration process.

Protecting Local Workers

There are two principal domestic worker protection schemes in the TCIs: pre- and post-entry controls. The former is the dominant variant throughout the TCIs, while the latter is a rather recent US innovation dating from 1989 (Papademetriou, 1994).

(a) Pre-entry Controls

One method of selecting foreign workers is to test each application against the available pool of eligible[23] workers interested in the job opening. Called "labour certification" in the US, "job validation" in Canada, and a "labour agreement" (LA) in Australia, this process requires the petitioner (typically the prospective employer) to demonstrate two things to the government's satisfaction: first, that no eligible workers are available for the job in question; and second, that the employment of the foreign national will not depress the wages and working conditions of other workers in similar jobs. Both requirements have proved extremely vexing both on methodological and on administrative grounds. As a result, there is a slowly emerging consensus that questions the value and efficacy of processes that rely on case-by-case assessments for choosing labour-market-bound immigrants as increasingly at odds with today's competitive realities. Most specifically, firms today often choose workers (domestic or foreign) because small differences in attributes (both in the quality and in the specificity of skills) can lead to substantial differences in the firm's ability to compete. The US allows employers to make these choices directly. The other three TCIs have moved towards selecting foreign workers on the basis of a mix of skills, experience, education, and other

22) Since Canada's inauguration of the independent category's main element – "selected workers" – in 1967, the relationship of independent immigration to overall economic growth and labour-market considerations has been affirmed repeatedly (See Canada, 1975; Hawkins, 1989; and Economic Council of Canada, 1991).

23) The term "eligible" workers will be used to denote all local workers, as well as other workers who may have the right to work in each country.

characteristics that presumably maximizes the probability both of immediate and long-term labour market, economic and social success.

(b) Post-entry Controls (Attestations)

Post-entry control systems focus on the terms and conditions of the foreign worker's employment. Unlike the pre-entry test, post-entry controls are entirely a US innovation. The main example is the attestation mechanism.

Attestations are a legally-binding set of employer declarations about the terms and conditions under which a foreign worker will be engaged. Designed to reduce up-front barriers to the entry of needed foreign workers while protecting domestic worker interests through post-entry auditing and enforcement of the relevant terms, attestations aim at fulfilling four major policy objectives: to balance the need to safeguard (and even advance) the interests of domestic workers in terms of wages and working conditions while also offering employers willing to play by pre-agreed rules predictable access to needed foreign workers; to meet an important "public process" test by giving potentially affected parties an opportunity to know about and challenge the matters to which an employer attests; to respond most directly to changing conditions in labour markets while requiring the least amount of hands-on engagement by the government in an area where both data and procedures are weakest; to induce more cooperative labour-management relations in instances where workers' representatives and management work together to obtain the best worker available for a job opening. There is much debate over whether attestations are accomplishing these policy goals or not.

The Points Test

The main difference between the United States and the three other TCIs in economic immigrant selection is that the latter rely systematically on points tests for selecting permanent economic immigrants. Accordingly, only those foreign workers whose quantifiable personal attributes add up to a pre-agreed "pass mark" are allowed to settle[24] (see **tables 9.10., 9.16.** and **9.17.**).

24) The pass mark often fluctuates. In the admittedly extreme case of New Zealand, it can fluctuate weekly! The country's most recent change was made in June 2002, when the pass mark was raised from 25 to 28 in an effort to reduce the inflow of applications under the skilled/business category.

The characteristics currently receiving the highest point totals across all three countries include education and specific training, work experience/offers of employment in occupations in demand, age, and language skills – generally in that order. Business skills and the willingness to invest substantial sums in the country of destination are also rewarded throughout the TCIs, sometimes within the points system (in Australia and New Zealand), and at other times independently of it (the US and Canada).

Generally, supporters perceive several advantages in point selection systems over other selection mechanisms:

- First, they are thought to inspire confidence because they seem to apply universal, and ostensibly hard (i.e., quantitative data-based) selection criteria to economic-stream immigrants. Hence, they are less susceptible to the criticisms associated with the case-by-case system's "gamesmanship" between employers and bureaucrats.
- Second, depending on the attributes a point system emphasizes, it is thought to reassure key segments of the receiving society that economic-stream immigrants are selected based on criteria that place the highest priority on the receiving state's economic interests. In an increasingly competitive world, immigration becomes politically more defensible than the alternatives discussed earlier.
- Third, a point system can adopt new characteristics, discard obsolete ones, and "tweak" the process by changing categories' relative weights and/or the overall pass mark. This is thought to be administratively valuable in that regulators can respond quickly to shifting economic priorities and/or perceptions of what is "good" for the receiving economy and society.
- Finally, properly conceived and implemented, and accompanied by opportunities for firms to select key workers on their own, a points-like system is thought to reinforce the government's ability to manage the system by measuring general occupational trends and gauging broad economic trends.

Humanitarian Admissions

The so-called humanitarian or compassionate category admits refugees and asylum seekers. This admissions stream stems from three factors: a legal obligation (resulting from the signing and ratification of the relevant Geneva Convention); in part, an expression of solidarity with victims of persecution in which the state plays some role; and a grant of protection from violence and chaos.

151

All four TCIs have well-developed and orderly systems for refugee resettlement that distinguish them from virtually any other grouping of states. Among them, the four subject countries have been resettling between 100,000 and 150,000 refugees each year since the early 1990s (see **table 9.1.**). In addition, the TCIs have increasingly had to come to terms with a relatively new phenomenon for them: the adjudication of asylum claims made by applicants relying on them as "first asylum" states (see also **chapter 6**). According to UNHCR, in 2001 alone these four countries received more than 118,000 applications for asylum. Not surprisingly, perhaps, some of the TCI's have responded to this rapidly growing phenomenon with tough measures designed to curb it. This has lead to some criticism by the human rights community. This has particularly been the case with the US and Australia.

US law sets flexible annual targets for resettling refugees and has provisions for adjudicating asylum claims. The resettlement target is set by the executive branch after consultations with civil society and the US Congress. Admissions are usually somewhat below the number authorized, often reflecting administrative capabilities and budgetary considerations. In the last few years, the US has been receiving also about 60,000 asylum requests per year and has been adjudicating favourably between 30 and 40 per cent of them. The US uses a pre-screening standard in these cases that is largely in line with those of other industrial societies.

As suggested above, ordinarily, an asylum seeker's application is screened at the port of entry under a "well-founded fear" standard, the US version of the European Union's "manifestly unfounded"[25] standard. If the applicant passes that initial test, (s)he is allowed into the country pending adjudication of the claim and the Government has 180 days to make a decision on her/his status. During this time, the claimant is not eligible either for work authorization or for other public benefits. If asylum applicants are considered potential flight risks or if their applications raise other "red flag" issues, they are typically put in prison. Finally, the US has a rather extensive regime of temporary protection grants for nationals of countries in severe crisis who are in the US at the time of the grant's declaration.

Canada's refugee determination system is similar to that of the US, at least with respect to resettling overseas refugees[26]. It differs sharply, however, in its asylum adjudication process. While Canada also pre-screens asylum claimants upon arrival, the adjudication process sets it apart from the other TCIs. Here, it has created an independent board that adjudicates asylum claims arguably with greater care and against a set of more inclusive criteria than virtually any other country. The outcomes reflect the Refugee Board's priorities and overall orientation. Canada made favourable adjudications in about 48 per cent of the cases last year, compared with 36 per cent for the US and 40 per cent for Australia. Unlike the US, applicants have access to employment and other benefits during the determination process, only rarely does Canada use detention during this process (unlike either the US or Australia in particular). The care with which Canada adjudicates claims is thought to have contributed to delays in issuing decisions, determination backlogs, and growing numbers of unsubstantiated claims. These and associated issues[27], such as financial considerations, have been to the forefront of Canadian Government policy in recent years and are subject to thorough reviews[28].

Australia has been allocating about 12,000 visas annually for humanitarian admissions recently but, typically, more persons are selected than the number allocated formally, accounting for about 14 per cent of total visas in 2000 (see **tables 9.1.** and **9.6.**). That share is larger relative to Australia's overall migration programme than those of the other TCIs[29]. Specifically, Australia has an "offshore" resettlement programme similar to that of the US and Canada and two Special Humanitarian Programmes (SHP): the in-country SHP for those persecuted but who are still in their countries of origin; and the Global SHP for those who have left their country of origin because of discrimination representing a gross violation of human rights. Those seeking protection under the Global SHP may do so offshore. In addition, Australia has a Special Assistance Category (SAC) for groups of "special concern" to Australia

25) There are twelve grounds upon which an application for asylum may be deemed manifestly unfounded. The most common reason is that at face value the application does not show any grounds for the contention that the applicant is a refugee (see: www.amnesty.ie/act/refug/unapp.shtml).

26) Unlike the other TCIs, a substantial number of refugees in Canada are privately assisted (see **table 9.1.**).

27) Concern with increases in unsubstantiated claims led Canada to impose visa requirements to visitors from an additional eight countries this year. The US and Canada exempt roughly similar numbers of foreign nationals from obtaining a visa prior to traveling to each country - 28 for the US versus 40 for Canada.

28) The RB's resources are pegged on a workload of about 25,000 annual determinations but it has been receiving almost twice as many in the last few years. Many of them come from applicants entering Canada *through* the United States (about 40 per cent of total applications). This has contributed to substantial backlogs and has become an irritant in bilateral Canadian-US relations.

29) It should be recalled, however, that the immigration programme does not count entries by New Zealanders.

Three generations of Iraqis on their way to a new life in Australia

153

who may not otherwise fit within the traditional protection categories[30], and especially for those among them who have close family links in Australia (Hugo, 2001:13-14). Finally, since 1999, Australia has also instituted a Temporary Protection Visa (TPV) for up to three years for persons who enter or attempt to enter Australia by irregular means, i.e., without documentation, but who upon adjudication are found to meet international refugee protection standards. At the end of that period, TPV holders can apply for permanent status or leave. These visas do not allow for family reunification (Inglis, 2002). Australia has also introduced two new visa classes: class 447 secondary movement offshore (temporary) and class 451 secondary movement relocation (temporary).

In 2000-2001, Australia received applications from 13,100 individuals (including 2,239 Afghan and 1,252 Iraqis) for onshore asylum. Of the 5,579 persons who received protection that year, nearly three-quarters were Afghans or Iraqis (some of the decisions involved applicants who had entered in previous years). Of those who were unsuccessful and determined not to be in need of international protection, some have been repatriated but others who have to return remain in detention[31].

Recent arrivals by boat have lead to a strong response by the Australian Government in an attempt to disrupt people smuggling activities. Central components of this policy, known as the "Pacific Strategy", have been the diverting of intercepted boats to their last point of embarcation, processing arrivals on Christmas Island outside Australia's migration zone or transferring arrivals to offshore processing centres in Nauru and Manus (Papua New Guinea) for processing. New Zealand agreed to take a number of the arrivals for processing and has also agreed to take a number of those from Manus and Nauru determined to be refugees. Australia has resettled a number of cases with family links to Australia and Sweden, Canada and Denmark have also taken some persons for resettlement. As of December 2002, Australia had not had a new boat arrival since December 2001. While the "Pacific Strategy" has received widepread support in Australia, it has been questioned both domestically and internationally by the human rights community.

30) The SAC is generally for those facing discrimination, displacement or hardship (see **table 9.6.**).

31) Inglis reports (2002) that the government signed an agreement with Afghanistan in May 2002, whereby it funded the return and reinsertion of Afghan refugees not granted asylum in Australia, a strategy similar to the one used with boat people from China in the early 1990s.

Finally, <u>New Zealand</u> reserves 800 spots for resettling convention refugees. Until 2002, the New Zealand Government left the decision about the country of origin of these refugees up to the discretion of UNHCR. However, the recent wave of Afghan refugees, re-routed by the actions of the Australian authorities, has encouraged New Zealand's Government to restructure its refugee resettlement programme, transferring the decision on refugee acceptance from UNHCR to the New Zealand Immigration Service.

Converging Approaches to Immigration in TCIs

The four immigration systems discussed display considerable convergence while maintaining several of their idiosyncratic characteristics. For instance, all four systems generally maintain strong family immigration and humanitarian programmes despite variable but strong scepticism about each of these streams. Furthermore, all have robust and growing economic stream immigration schemes with increasingly pronounced emphases on strong human capital qualifications. More interestingly perhaps, the search for well-educated and talented foreigners – and the implicit competition for such individuals – has moved all four countries toward less traditional routes and recruitment practices. The most notable include the growth in the numbers of long-term temporary visa-holders and the consequent proliferation of temporary-to-permanent transmission belts. Two groups of foreigners have been particularly targeted in these schemes: information and communications technology professionals and foreign students.

This is not meant to imply that convergence has been absolute. Selection formulae continue to differ and diverge somewhat. US commitment to the family stream continues to be near absolute, for instance, while the other three TCIs have been disentangling themselves somewhat from it. The US continues to place employers at the forefront of economic stream immigration decisions and relies more and more on long-term temporary immigration to enhance global competitiveness. The other three TCIs continue to rely on points selection formulae to accomplish largely similar goals. Furthermore, despite deep recognition that the available case-by-case determination systems for testing labour markets for the availability of eligible workers are costly, time-consuming, and ultimately unsatisfactory, the US continues to rely on them far more so than its TCI counterparts. Similarly, the system of employer attestations

has shown some promise but has been largely ignored by the other three countries.

Nor have otherwise proven systems of managing both impressions and expectations from immigration programmes been adopted by the United States. Canadian, Australian and New Zealand authorities keep a sharp eye on – and clearly articulate – the central purposes of their immigration system. In doing so, they maintain an active balance between social (family), compassionate/humanitarian (refugee), and hard-headed economic (independent and business) needs, while giving economic migration increasing priority over the latter two. In contrast, the US system is much less "public". The lack of transparency can hinder the development of accurate impressions of, and realistic expectations from, the system among the community.

Precisely because they are rather fastidious in furthering social and compassionate principles (e.g., incorporating immigration lessons in their elementary school curricula and promoting themselves as fair-minded and tolerant multicultural societies), Canada (see **textbox 4.2.**), Australia and, to a lesser extent, New Zealand can afford to be, and are, quite aggressive and open about their goals for economic immigration. By contrast, the US has often been far less "impartial" in its allocation of refugee visas.

Finally, the four countries diverge somewhat on the attention they pay to the issue of optics, i.e., the elusive goal of reassuring, if not persuading, the public that immigration policy promotes an orderly and balanced approach to enhancing major social values, policy priorities and concerns. Although all TCIs are struggling in this respect, in many ways the US is far behind the other countries. Failure to engage in such an effort runs the risk of surrendering the initiative to influence popular perceptions of immigration to private interests or to demagogues – an experience shared by all TCIs in the last decade.

Clearly, not all ideas are transferable. The extent to which Canada, Australia, New Zealand and the United States can employ each other's experiences will be affected mainly by the manner and context in which decisions are made. Specifically, the following factors will shape the decision parameters in each instance:

• the branch of government which has ultimate authority over immigration[32];

32) In the United States, Congress enjoys - and guards jealously - primacy on immigration matters. The Administration plays primarily a consultative role.

- the degree of involvement by different political jurisdictions such as states and localities, as well as by the private sector in immigration policy;
- the degree of concentration or diffusion of responsibility for immigration among executive agencies[33]; and
- the extent, quality, and effectiveness of efforts to explain and enlist support for immigration policies among a broad spectrum of interests.

Conclusion

Successful immigration systems rely on a continuous balancing act between family, refugee, independent and business interests and needs; the systems also attach considerable weight to practising transparency in administering the immigration programme. In this regard, the immigration policies of all four TCIs are at a crossroads. They are making similar demands on their immigration system and seem to be travelling on parallel paths, always reviewing their selection formulae in search of politically acceptable solutions to crucial immigration questions.

Questions include the following:

- how to keep immigration policy compatible with economic, labour market, and demographic goals?
- how to allow the economy to regulate the independent-immigrant stream without making it hostage to the business cycle?
- how much to fine-tune the independent stream's selection formula without micromanaging it - especially since such formulae are known to be blunt instruments at best?
- to make the system more attentive to local labour market needs and concerns while maintaining the balance between business and worker interests?
- how to safeguard the flexibility which is essential for successful immigration systems? and
- finally, how to "demystify" immigration systems without undermining the broad support they basically enjoy in each country?

Therein lay the various challenges. Failure to maintain national consensus on the broad aims of immigration may result in piecemeal "reforms" without substantial progress towards the clear goals essential to overall success. And failure to meet and resolve head-on the challenges of programme methodology and management, as well as the perceptual challenges inherent in any selection system, may mire immigration policy in endless legal and political problems, with the consequent loss of the benefits immigration can offer to a receiving country.

If today's trends continue, permanent, "temporary," and irregular immigration will remain robust throughout the next two decades. However, nothing in this analysis suggests that policy decisions about greater immigration will become politically any easier. In fact, the inexorability and cold logic of demography will probably put demographic needs into increasingly sharp conflict with the important social and political interests which oppose immigration in all TCIs (see also **chapter 13**).

These demographic facts are clear. Since the baby boom generation has not produced enough children, its passage from the economic scene will create a void among people of working age. At the same time, an unprecedented retirement age bulge will be created with the added "wrinkle" of the aged now living much longer and consuming more public resources than ever before (Papademetriou, 2002). Thus more old age people will depend on the state and taxes from a dwindling labour base will need to support growing numbers of retirees. Therefore, over the next two decades, society will probably depend more heavily on immigrants for many important socio-economic factors including bolstering the TCI economies through their labour and technical skills, helping to keep retirement and public health systems afloat through their taxes, and, in many cases, keeping production and consumption systems ticking along.

Analytical evidence suggests that opting for much higher immigration is complicated in another key respect: unless a state admits only very young immigrants, an ever-increasing foreign-born population would be required to maintain present-day old-age dependency ratios (UN, 2000). This is mainly due to two reasons: in all but a few of the traditional immigration countries, the age profile of legal permanent immigrants has tended to be very similar to that of local people; with some notable and increasing exceptions, immigrants have tended to adopt the reproductive behaviour of host populations relatively quickly.

155

33) Jurisdictional confusion in the United States often interferes with the development of coherent policies. In fact, joint jurisdictions and overlaps in implementation authority frequently lead to agency competition and inconsistencies in the delivery of programmes.

As an alternative option, more temporary workers will probably be recruited in many advanced industrial societies and thus temporary migration will become more important relative to permanent immigration. It may also become tempting to introduce age biases in permanent immigration formulas, as is the case in Australia, Canada, and New Zealand. Tapping temporary workers more systematically may become more attractive for another reason. The TCIs may seek to postpone decisions about much larger permanent immigration intakes (with that option's social and political difficulties) by opening up their systems to the temporary variant much more widely. They are already moving strongly in that direction. In doing so, however, they ignore analytical findings that show that such a decision often just defers growth in permanent intakes as many temporary workers seek and are increasingly expected to convert to permanent status.

TABLE 9.1.

Immigrant Admissions in TCIs, 2000

	United States[1]	Canada[2]	Australia[3]	New Zealand
Family-sponsored	584,159	60,517	33,470	26,701
Employment-based	107,024	132,118	44,730	18,096
Humanitarian	65,941	30,030	13,750	5,212
Refugees	59,083	16,464	7,120	-
Privately Assisted	-	2,905	-	-
Government Assisted	-	10,661	900	-
Asylum Seekers	6,858	-	5,740	-
Total Immigration	823,035	192,178	105,710	50,009

Notes:

1) Immigrants admitted for lawful permanent residence (LPR), the "Humanitarian" category reflects the number of applicants whose status was adjusted to legal residence in 2000.

2) Totals include immigration to Quebec.

3) "Asylum seekers" means "onshore refugees", i.e. persons meeting the Refugee Convention definition. "Refugees" is the offshore component of the Humanitarian Program, which includes refugees and the Special Humanitarian Program (SHP). "Government assisted" is a calculation of Australia's Special Assistance Category (SAC) and Temporary Safe Heaven visas.

Sources:

Bedford (2002); unpublished data provided by Statistics New Zealand; CIC (2000, 2001); DIMIA (2001); New Zealand Refugee Law (www.refugee.org.nz/); US-INS (2002).

TABLE 9.2.

Foreign Born Population in TCIs, 1995 and 2000[1]

	Foreign Born	Immigrant Inflow	Population	% Foreign Born	Foreign Born per Capita
1995					
United States	23,000,000	720,461	262,803,276	8.8	0.09
Canada	4,725,994	212,860	29,354,000	16.1	0.16
Australia	4,164,100	87,428	18,049,000	23.0	0.23
New Zealand	605,019	61,280	3,604,000	17.5	0.18
2000[2]					
United States	31,100,000	849,807	281,421,906	11.1	0.11
Canada	5,148,250	227,209	31,300,000	16.4	0.16
Australia	4,500,000	94,360	19,117,000	23.6	0.24
New Zealand	689,628	44,598	3,737,280	18.5	0.19

Notes:

1) Figures may not add up exactly due to rounding

2) 2000 Canada data are estimates

Sources:

Bedford (2002); CIC (1999, 2000); DIMIA (2000, 2001); US Census Bureau (2000, 1997).

TABLE 9.3.

TCIs - Inflows of Permanent and Long-Term Settlers by Region of Origin, 1998 and 2000

	Migrants' Origin	1998	2000
UNITED STATES	Asia and the Pacific	223,631	265,400
	Mexico	131,575	173,909
	North America*	111,231	154,686
	Europe	90,793	132,480
	South America	45,394	56,074
	China (People's Republic)	36,884	45,652
	Africa and the Middle East	40,660	44,731
	Canada	10,190	16,210
	Other	7,034	1,181
CANADA	Asia and the Pacific	84,100	120,491
	Europe	38,500	42,875
	Africa and the Middle East	32,600	40,779
	China (People's Republic)	19,779	36,718
	Americas (South and Central)	14,040	16,939
	United States	4,773	5,809
	United Kingdom	3,898	4,648
AUSTRALIA	Asia and the Pacific	33,509	57,118
	United Kingdom	-	48,100
	New Zealand	26,921	43,018
	China (People's Republic)	-	36,300
	Europe	24,977	18,800
	Africa and the Middle East	14,815	13,900
	Americas	5,895	2,400
NEW ZEALAND	Asia and the Pacific	13,712	11,781
	United Kingdom	6,254	6,348
	China (People's Republic)	3,310	4,592
	Japan	4,148	3,715
	Africa and the Middle East	4,014	3,651
	Australia	4,306	3,602
	Europe	2,538	2,623
	Americas	2,174	1,964

Note:
* excluding Canada and Mexico, the source US-INS (2002) is however not providing further information regarding migrant's origin.

Sources:
Australian Bureau of Statistics (www.abs.gov.au/ausstats/); Bedford (2002); CIC (2000); CIC (1999) DIMIA (1999); US-INS (2002).

TABLE 9.4.

Immigrant Classes - United States

Class (approximate proportion of admissions)	Description
Family Reunification (68%)	Applications must be made by US citizens or permanent residents on behalf of family members. Immediate relatives (parents, spouses and unmarried children under 21) of US citizens are exempt from the preference selection system and immigrant visa numbers are made available to them without any numerical limit. All other family reunification applicants must wait for a visa to become available under the numerically limited preference system. No country can obtain more than 25,620 visas under that limit.
Employment-based (18%)	There are five employment-based categories: priority workers, professionals with exceptional ability, skilled or professional workers, immigrant investors, entrepreneurs and special immigrants. These applicants are also subject to the preference system. Can obtain more than 25,620 visas under that limit.
Refugees and Asylum Seekers (8%)	The maximum number of refugee admissions is set annually by the President in consultation with the Congress. The ceiling, 70,000 for FY 2002, can be increased during the year to accommodate additional refugees. Asylum seekers may apply for asylum in the United States within one year of arrival or they may apply at a port of entry. After one year, approved refugees and asylees are eligible to apply for lawful permanent residence. Asylum seekers are denied work authorization for the first six months after they file a claim.
Diversity Immigrants (6%)	50,000 diversity visas are granted annually by lottery to applicants from countries with low rates of immigration to the United States (having sent fewer than 50,000 immigrants in the last five years). No more than 3,500 visas (7 percent of the overall 50,000) may go to applicants from a single country. To qualify, applicants must have a high school diploma or an equivalent and two years of training. Australia and New Zealand are among the eligible countries. Canadian citizens are ineligible for the lottery.
Investment	Granted to investors of between US$1 million and US $3 million in urban areas or US$ 500,000 in rural or high-unemployment areas. Each investment must create employment or "save" the jobs of at least 10 US workers. Investors are granted only "conditional" permanent resident status that is removed after two years.

159

Sources:
Kramer (2001); Papademetriou (1994); US-INS, *The Success of Asylum Reform;* US-INS (2002);
www.ins.gov/graphics/services/residency/family.htm;
www.ins.gov/graphics/services/residency/employment.htm;
www.ins.gov/services/asylum/index.htm;

TABLE 9.5.

Immigrant Classes - Canada[1]

Class (approximate proportion of admissions)	Description
Independent and Other Class (60%)	These individuals apply for permanent residence in Canada on their own initiative and are selected through a point system[2] that assesses the match between their specific skills, talents and economic potential and Canada's economic and labour market needs. The independent class includes investors, entrepreneurs, self-employed persons, assisted-relatives and others that apply at Canadian embassies, consulates.
Family Class (27%)	Individuals applying under this class must be sponsored by a close family member already living in Canada as a citizen or permanent resident. No annual limits are set on the number of family stream visas granted.
Refugee and Humanitarian Class (13%)	Canada accepts between 20,000 and 30,000 UN Convention refugees each year. Application can be made at a port of entry or from within Canada. Refugees can also be sponsored by private individuals and organizations.

Notes:

1) The Canada-Quebec accord gives Quebec responsibility for selecting all independent and refugee class immigrants abroad destined for Quebec.

2) Under the new Canadian immigrant selection system to begin implementation on June 28, 2002, language ability will become critical for acceptance, the number of categories for assessment will be reduced from ten to six and the minimum number of points needed to qualify for admission will increase from 70 to 80.

The current system will be phased out by January 1, 2003.

Source:
CIC (2000)

TABLE 9.6.

Immigrant Classes - Australia

Class (approximate proportion of admissions if known)	Description
A: Migration Program (60%)	
Skill Stream (55%)[1]	Includes independent, employer-nominated, business skills, distinguished talent and family-sponsored skilled migrants who are assessed under the point system. In 2001, over 55 percent of successful applicants were independent migrants. The current pass mark is set at 110 points out of a maximum of 165 points for all subcategories; applicants;are awarded extra points if their skills are deemed to be in demand and applicants must have some command of the English language. In addition, under the skilled stream Australian states and territories can sponsor migrants directly. In 2001-2002, a special "contingency reserve" of 8,000 places was made available in the Skill stream.
Family Stream (45%)[2]	Applicants outside Australia must be sponsored by an Australian or eligible New Zealand citizen or by an Australian permanent resident. Applicants already inside Australia must be "nominated" for permanent residence. The Government sets an annual cap for preferential family applications. Family stream applicants are not subject to the point system and are not required to have English language skills.
B: New Zealand Citizens (30%)	The 1973 Trans-Tasman Arrangement allows New Zealand citizens to enter Australia to visit, live and work under a temporary residence visa (SCV). They are eligible for Australian citizenship after two years of continuous residence in Australia and are not subject to the point system.
C: Humanitarian Program (10%)[3]	Includes the Offshore resettlement program, comprised of the refugee and Special Humanitarian (SHP) programs, the On-shore Protection, and the former Special Assistance Category (SAC). Onshore protection visas are given to applicants already in Australia and can be either temporary (for unauthorized entrants) or permanent (for legal entrants). Applicants who do not meet the requirements either of refugee entry or of the SHP but nonetheless are found to face situations of discrimination, displacement or hardship if they were to return to their home countries are designated as part of the Special Assistance Category. Most SACs required sponsors of applicants to be close family members resident in Australia. Settlement assistance is provided to successful applicants. There are also two new visa classes: class 447 secondary movement offshore (temporary) and class 451 secondary movement relocation (temporary).
Special Eligibility Category	Caters to former citizens and residents of Australia and New Zealand and dependents of New Zealand citizens intending to settle permanently in Australia.

161

Notes:

1) In July 2001 two new skilled visa categories Independent Overseas Student and Australian-sponsored Overseas Student were created to allow tertiary qualified students in Australia who wished to remain permanently at the end of their studies to apply onshore.

2) Family stream migrants include both migration (sponsorship) and permanent residence (nomination) applications.

3) Since 1999 Australia has granted only temporary permits to foreigners seeking asylum who arrived by boat and has denied these applicants the right to family reunification for three years. Beginning August 2001, Australia has been refusing those arriving illegally by boat to land.

Source:
DIMIA (2001)

TABLE 9.7.

Immigrant Classes - New Zealand

Class (approximate proportion of admissions if known)	Description
Skilled/Business Stream (60%)	To be granted entry under the "General Skills" category, an applicant must score enough points to meet a "pass mark" that is adjusted quarterly by the New Zealand Minister of Immigration. Applicants possessing a qualification equivalent to a three-year New Zealand certificate or degree and a minimum of 2 years work experience are most likely to be admitted. Work permit holders who qualify for residence on all other grounds except for the English language requirement can qualify for residence under the General Skills category upon pre-purchase of English language lessons. This category includes the new Talent visa that allows foreigners who pay at least NZ$ 45,000 a year to enter outside the points system and to become eligible for permanent residency after two years.
Family Sponsored Stream (32%)	Citizens or permanent residents apply for this visa on behalf of immediate and non-immediate family members. Accompanying partners and dependent children 16 years and over require English language skills. Family members may also be sponsored under the Family Quota category, a lottery from which about 500 applicants are drawn each year.
International/Humanitarian Stream (8%)	Applicants must be sponsored by a New Zealand resident or citizen relative (immediate or distant). The Government sets the quota of refugee admissions yearly (currently 750).
Business Investor Category	Subcategory of General Skills, divided into three groups: entrepreneur, new investor, employee of relocating businesses, and long-term business visas and permits. Business Investors gain points for business experience, funds they can invest in New Zealand (at least NZ$ 750,000), qualifications, age (maximum is 64) and settlement factors. Business Investors must score a minimum of 12 points as opposed to the 25 points needed for other General Skills applicants in order to qualify for admission. Residence in New Zealand is conditional for two years after arrival.
Australian Citizens	Australian citizens and residents are usually entitled to live, study and work in New Zealand without applying for residence.
Special Residence Categories	Up to 1,100 Samoan citizens living in Samoa or American Samoa who are between the ages of 18 and 45 are permitted to live and work in New Zealand per year. They must have in hand an offer of full-time, permanent employment in New Zealand, have some command of English and may be accompanied by their spouses and dependent children. Residents of Pitcairn Island are eligible for the same treatment.

Source:
NZIS (2000)

TABLE 9.8.

TCIs - Family Programme Descriptions

United States	Citizen or permanent resident must have income at or above 125 percent of the official poverty line in order to sponsor a relative.
Canada	Since 1995, the sponsored family members of refugees have been counted in the separate "refugee category" and the sponsored family members of live-in caregivers are included in the "other" category. Thus, comparisons with the size of the family class in past years will be inaccurate unless these changes are taken into consideration.
Australia	Parents are subject to "balance of family" test. Sponsors of applicants determined to be at risk for becoming public charges or who are in the certain migration categories (including skilled Australian sponsored, skilled regional sponsored, parents, aged dependent relatives, careers and unmarried orphan relatives) are required to sign an Assurance of Support (AoS) agreement.
New Zealand	The minimum English language requirement is level 5 (out of 9) of the general module of the International English Language Testing System. Non-principal applicants under General Skills who do not meet the language requirements are required instead to purchase English language lessons at a cost of NZ$ 1,700 (approx.US$ 796) to NZ$ 6,650 (approx.US$ 3,113), depending on competency level.

Source:
consult previous tables

163

TABLE 9.9.

Preference System - United States[1] (first introduced in 1952)

Category	Unadjusted Limit (Immigration Act of 1990)	Actual Admissions (FY 2000)
Family-sponsored Immigrants[2]	**480,000**	**584,159**
Immediate relatives[3] of U.S. citizens	No limit[3]	346,879
Family-sponsored Preferences	226,000	235,280
First: Unmarried adult (over 21) sons and daughters of US citizens and the children of these unmarried adults.	23,400	2 7,707
Second: Spouses, minor children and unmarried daughters and sons (over age 20) of legal permanent residents. Seventy-seven percent of these visas are reserved for spouses and minor children; the remainder is allocated to unmarried daughters and sons.	114,200	124,595
Third: Married sons and daughters of U.S. citizens, their spouses and minor children.	23,400	22,833
Fourth: Brothers and sisters of adult U.S. citizens and their spouses and children.	65,000	60,145
Employment-based Immigration	**140,000**	**107,024**
First (28.6 %):"Priority workers," including persons of "extraordinary ability"; outstanding professors and researchers; and executives and managers of U.S. multinationals. Offer of employment is required for persons in this category, except those regarded to be of "extraordinary ability".	40,000	27,706
Second (28.6%): Professionals with "exceptional ability" in the sciences, the arts or business. Requires both an offer of U.S. employment and a labour certification. The employment requirement can be waived by the Attorney General in special circumstances.	40,000	20,304
Third (28.6%): Skilled workers (in occupations that require at least two years formal training); professionals (must have bachelor's degrees or appropriate licenses); and other workers (unskilled workers). Number of visas issued to "other workers" is limited to 10,000 per year. Requires a labour certification.	40,000	49,736
Fourth (7.1%): Ministers of religion and employees of religious organizations, foreign medical school graduates, employees of the US government abroad and employees of international organizations defined as "special immigrants."	10,000	9,052
Fifth (7.1%): Employment-creation (investor) visas	10,000	226
Diversity visas[4]	**55,000**	**50,945**
Total Family, Employment and Diversity	**675,000**	**742,128**

Notes:

1) Includes both adjustments and new arrivals.

2) Immediate relatives of adult US citizens (spouses, dependent children and parents) and children born abroad to alien spouses are not subject to a numerical limit.

3) The number of immediate relatives of US citizens included in these figures is assumed to be 254,000, but immediate relatives may enter without limitations. The limit for family-sponsored preference immigrants in a fiscal year is equal to 480,000 minus the number of immediate relatives admitted in the preceding year. The limit of family-sponsored preference visas, however, cannot fall below a minimum of 226,000-the worldwide limit minus 254,000. (INS, January 2002). As a result, the 480,000 "cap" is pieceable.

4) Limit was reduced in 1999 to allow for 5,000 entries under the Nicaraguan Adjustment and Central American Relief Act of 1997 (NACARA program).

Sources:

Kramer (2001); Papademetriou (1994); INS-www.ins.gov/graphics/aboutins/statistics/IMM00yrbk/IMM2000list.htm; www.ins.usdoj.gov/graphics/aboutins/history/2.pdf; www.ins.gov/graphics/services/residency/employment.htm; US Department of State-http://travel.state.gov/visa;employ-based.html.

TABLE 9.10.

Canada - Former versus New Point System (Bill C-11[1])

Former Selection System first introduced in 1967		New Selection System	
Independent applicants must have at least 70 points to qualify for admission		Independent applicants must have at least 80 points to qualify for admission	
Factors considered are:	Points	Factors considered are:	Points
1. Age: Applicants 22 to 44 earn maximum points; a 45-year-old gets eight points, while a 48-year-old receives two. People 49 and older or 18 and younger earn no points.	10	**1. Education:** Maximum points are awarded to applicants that have completed a Master's or Ph.D and at least 17 years of full-time or full-time equivalent studies.	25
2. Education: Higher points are awarded to applicants with post-secondary education or training.	16	**2. Language Ability:** Applicants choose the language (English or French) with which they are most comfortable as the first language. The remaining language is counted as the second language. Points are awarded according to the applicant's ability to read, write, listen to and speak English and French.	20
3. Occupation: Computer programmers and systems analysts earn maximum points as do chefs, heavy-duty equipment mechanics and health care workers.	10	**3. Experience:** Emphasis is placed on the applicant's intended occupation. Must currently have work experience in an occupation that has been identified as having capacity to accept new entrants. Applicants earn ten points for one year's experience in the occupation and five points for each additional year.	25
4. Education/Training Factor: Assesses the applicant's level of training with regard to her/his declared occupation. Points allocated to specific occupations are published by Citizenship and Immigration Canada in the General Occupations List.	18	**4. Arranged Employment:** Applicants with a job offer approved by Human Resources Development Canada (HRDC) or who have been working for at least one year as a temporary employee in an HRDC-approved position earn maximum points.	10
5. Arranged Employment: Employment must be approved by Human Resources Development Canada to earn full points.	10	**5. Age:** Applicants 21 to 44 earn maximum points; a 45-year-old earns eight points, while a 48-year-old receives 2 points. 16 and under and 49 and over earn no points in this category.	10
6. Work Experience: Emphasis is placed on the applicant's intended occupation. Must currently have work experience in an occupation that has been identified as having capacity to accept new entrants.	8	**6. Adaptability:** This category assesses the education, work experience, family reunification status and arranged employment factors of the applicant, her spouse or common-law partner. Job offers that have not been approved by HRDC may be awarded points under this category.	10
7. Language Ability: Applicant is assessed for ability to communicate in English or French. Entrepreneurs and investors are not required to have official language skills in order to qualify.	15		
8. Demographic Factor: This "bonus" number is set by the Canadian government. All applicants receive eight points.	8		
9. Relative in Canada: Five bonus points are awarded if the applicant has a brother, sister, mother, father, grandparent, aunt, uncle, niece or nephew living in Canada as a permanent resident or Canadian citizen.	5		
10. Personal Suitability: Applicants who earn at least 60 points on the first nine requirements may be interviewed by a visa officer, who awards personal-suitability points based on characteristics such as adaptability, motivation, initiative and resourcefulness. It is rare to earn more than 5 to 7 points in this category.	10		
Total Points Possible	110	**Total Points Possible**	100

> **Note:**
> 1) The Immigration and Refugee Protection Act, Bill C-11, received royal assent on November 11, 2001.
>
> **Sources:**
> CIC, www.cic.gc.ca/english/press/02/0201-pre.html;
> www.cic.gc.ca/english/immigr/iindepen-e.html;
> www.cic.gc.ca/english/coming/new-regs.html.

TABLE 9.11.

Working Temporarily in the United States - Selected Sectors

Programme Name	Industry Sector(s)	Duration of visa(s)	Skill and Related Requirements	Additional Information/ Other Requirements	Family	Dual Intent[1] Permitted?
B-1	Business	Up to 6 months (under reconsideration).	Employment by a foreign firm or entity.	Visa holder can only conduct business on behalf of an overseas employer.	No	No
E-1 and E-2	Business	Up to 2 years with indefinite extension.	Visa is for business owners, business managers, and employees.	Visa holder must be in the U.S. to oversee or work for an enterprise that is engaged in trade between the U.S. and a foreign country (E-1) or that represents a substantial investment in the United States (E-2).	Yes	No
H-1B	Information and Communication Technology, Research, Specialty Occupations.	Three-year, one-time renewable visa. Maximum 6 years.	As required by the employer.	Workers receive the same wages and benefits as US workers.	Yes, but no derivative work permit	Yes
H-1C	Nursing	Three-year, non-renewable visa.	Applicants must hold a nurse's license in the home country or in the US, have passed the appropriate exam or be a licensed nurse in the state of intended employment and be fully eligible to practice nursing in the state of employment immediately on entry to the U.S.	Hospitals hiring H-1C nurses must file an attestation with the Department of Labor, stating that the employer is a hospital located in a disadvantaged Health Professional Shortage Area and that, since 1994, at least 35 per cent of its patients are entitled to Medicare and at least 28 percent to Medicaid. Nurses receive the same wages and benefits as do US workers and H-1C nurses can never be more than one-third of the registered nursing staff.	Yes	No
H-2A	Perishable agriculture (e.g. fruit, vegetables, tobacco and horticulture).	Valid for up to one year with extensions totaling three years.	Unskilled or low-skilled.	Employers must pay an enhanced minimum wage (Adverse Effect Wage Rate), provide housing, transportation, meals or access to cooking facilities, etc. and offer a written contract guaranteeing work for 3/4 of the stated period.	No	No
H-2B	Non-Agricultural Sectors (e.g.. Hotel, Restaurant, Construction, Landscaping, Health Care, Manufacturing and Transportation).	Valid for up to 1 year with two possible, but rare, extensions.	Variable	Both the job and the stay of the worker must be temporary. Employers must pay the higher of the minimum or prevailing wage.	No	No
H-3	Trainee	Period of training, up to 2 years.	Applicant must be invited by a U.S. individual or organization.	Training received in the U.S. must not be available in the applicant's country. Any work done while in the U.S. must be incidental and necessary to training.	Yes, but no employment allowed	No
J-1	Exchange visitor in culturally specific programs.	Decided by the duration of the programme.	Must be a teacher, trainee, medical student, college professor, or research specialist.	Sponsor must be accredited through the exchange visitor programme designated by the U.S. State Department. May be required to return to the home country for two years after completion of status in order for a change of status to be applied.	Yes, but no derivative work permit	Depends
L-1	Business	Coming to new office- up to 1 year. Coming to an existing office-up to 3 years (renewable). Maximum stay, 5 to 7 years.	Employee must have been employed with the foreign company in an overseas location for at least 1 year out of the past 3 consecutive years.	Under the L-1 "Blanket Petition Program" a company has only to receive one approval from the INS to transfer a certain number of executive, managerial, and professional employees.	Yes	Yes
M-1	Vocational and nonacademic students.	Up to one year or for the period necessary to complete their course of study plus 30 days thereafter to depart, whichever is less.	Visa holder must have been accepted by an approved school in the United States.	Applicants must possess sufficient funds or have made other arrangements to cover expenses and have sufficient scholastic preparation and knowledge of the English language to pursue a full course of study.	Yes	No
Q-1	Exchange visitor in the sciences, art, education, business, athletics, training or cultural exchange, au pair.	Duration of the exchange programme, up to 15 months.	Demonstration that the applicant is at the very top of the relevant field.	The international cultural exchange programme must be accessible to the U.S. public and can have both a cultural and work component.	Yes	No
R-1	Religious Workers	Valid for an initial period of up to three years, and can be extended for two years, for a total of five consecutive years.	Ministers of religion, religious professionals and other religious workers.	The visa holder must be a member of a religious denomination that has bona fide non-profit status in the United States.	Yes	No
TN	Professions on the NAFTA Occupations List.	Valid for 1 year; may be renewed indefinitely in yearly increments.	Must be a Canadian (TN-1) or Mexican (TN-2) citizen.	Mexican citizens must meet the basic H-1B visa requirements in addition to TN requirements to qualify.	Yes, but no derivative work permit	No

TABLE 9.12.

Working Temporarily in Canada[1] - Selected Sectors

Programme Name	Industry Sector(s)	Duration of visa(s)	Skill Requirements	Additional Information/ Other Requirements	Family	Dual Intent Permitted?
Temporary Foreign Worker Programme	Varied (Information and Communications Technology, manufacturing, education, etc.)	Up to 3 years.	Yes, as appropriate.	Applicant must have a temporary job offer in Canada before application for employment authorization (EA). Employers or industrial sectors that need significant numbers of temporary foreign workers can work with Human Resources Development Canada and Citizenship and Immigration Canada to validate a number of foreign workers under a single set of negotiations.	Yes. Spouses can also work legally.	Yes
Seasonal Agricultural Worker Programme with Commonwealth Caribbean	Harvesting fruits, vegetables and tobacco.	3 years maximum (renewable)	Yes	Caribbean workers must pay a 25 percent "tax" (forced savings) each period to cover the cost of administering the programme.	Yes	No
Seasonal Agricultural Worker Programme with Mexico	Harvesting fruits, vegetables and tobacco.	6 weeks to 8 months	Applicant should be a farmer by profession. Credentials are pre-screened.	Employer pays transportation costs up front, provides accommodations, pays minimum wage and takes deductions for unemployment insurance, taxes and pension fund payments. Mexican workers pay a 4 percent "tax" per pay period. Employees' last paycheck is withheld and a tax refund offered to encourage return to Mexico.	No	No
NAFTA Business Visitor	Business visitors, professionals (including university professors), intra-company transferees or traders and investors.	Up to 6 months or length of time required to fulfill service obligation; Investors have no time limit.	Applicants must be Mexican or U.S. citizens; must qualify for one of the four business criteria described in the NAFTA (see NAFTA Industry Sectors column); must be seeking only temporary entry; and must meet the universal requirements covering temporary entry into Canada.	The NAFTA has no effect on a post-secondary institution's policy to "hire Canadians first".	Yes, but spouses must go through the regular job validation process required by all temporary workers to Canada.	No
General Agreement in Trade and Services Business Visitor	Business	Duration of negotiation, service, or meeting	Must be a business person from a GATS member nation with primary income outside of Canada.	Applicant is exempt from the Employment Authorization requirement and cannot receive remuneration from Canada or sell goods or services directly to the public.	No	No
Trainees	Business	Duration of training	As defined by Canadian company.	Training must be with a Canadian parent or subsidiary company.	No	No
Live-In Caregiver Programme	Child care, elder care, care for disabled.	1 year (renewable)	High school diploma or equivalent; 6 months training or 12 months experience; English or French language ability.	None	No	Yes
Foreign Tour Operators	Tourism	Length of tourist activity.	Certified Tour Operator.	Requires an Employment Authorization issued by Human Resources Development Canada (HRDC).	No	No

Note:

1) Temporary applicants to Quebec must have their employment offers approved both by Human Resources Development Canada (HRDC) and the Ministère des Relations avec les Citoyens et de l'Immigration (MRCI) (www.immq.gouv.qc.ca/anglais/how_immigrate/workers/general.html).

Sources:

Center for Immigration Studies (2002); CIC-www.cic.gc.ca/english/visit/index.html; www.cic.gc.ca/english/visit/gats_e.html); IOM, (2000).

TABLE 9.11.

Note:

1) Dual intent means "an intention to immigrate at some time in the future while properly maintaining a non-immigrant status in the present" (Chang, 2001).

Sources:

Bender's Immigration and Nationality Act (2001); Chang and Boos (2001); Congressional Research Service (2001); Farm Worker Justice Fund (2001); Immigration Support Services - www.immigrationsupport.com; US Department of State (2000); Visa Now - www.VisaNow.com); Zhang, Bush, Gao and Associates -www.hooyou.com/nonimmigration/b1.html; www.hooyou.com/L%20visa/Benefit%20of%20L%20visa.html

167

TABLE 9.13.

Working and Training Temporarily in Australia - Selected Sectors

Programme Name	Industry Sector(s)	Duration of visa(s)	Skill Requirements	Additional Information/ Other Requirements	Family	Dual Intent Permitted?
Skilled Temporary Resident Programme (short and long-stay)	Information and Communication Technology Education, Manufacturing, Research, etc.	3 years (renewable once); 4 years (renewable) for the category "Education"; 3 months-4 years for long-stay visa holders.	Yes	Applicants must have health insurance and adequate funds to support themselves for the duration of their stay in Australia.	Yes	Yes
Working Holiday Makers (WHM)	Any sector. WHM visa-holders cannot work for any one employer for more than three months.	Up to 1 year (non-renewable)	No. Programme is for single or married people, aged 18 to 25, unaccompanied by children.	None	Yes (after status change)	Yes
Short-validity Business Visitor/ Long-validity Business Visitor/ Sponsored Business Visitor	Business	Multiple-entry visa, valid for 3 months from date of entry. Short-stay business visa is valid for 12 months, while long-stay visa is valid for the life of the holder's passport. Sponsored business visa is single entry, 3 months only.	Background should be relevant to the nature of the proposed business in Australia.	There should be a need for the applicant's presence, applicant must have funds for their personal support while in Australia and must not engage in remunerative work while in Australia. Visa can be obtained electronically through a number of authorized agents.	Yes	No
Long-stay Business Entry	Business	Multiple entry visa, valid up to 4 years (renewable).	As required by the sponsoring employer.	Labour market test; occupation must be on listed on the DIMIA Occupations List; visa holder may be employed full time in Australia and must be paid at least A$34,075 per year.	Yes	No
Exchange Visitors/ Occupational Trainees	Any sector	Multiple entry, 3 months to 4 years.	As required by the sponsoring employer.	Includes Fulbright Scholars.	Yes	No
Domestic Staff of diplomatic, consular and business executives	Domestic work (e.g., nannies, drivers, cooks, gardeners)	Duration of employer's stay.	As required by the sponsoring employer.	None	No	No

Sources:

Acacia Immigration Australia - www.hwmigration.com/home.htm; DIMIA - www.immi.gov.au/allforms/pdf/456.pdf; http//:evisas.com; Hugo (2001).

TABLE 9.14.

Working Temporarily in New Zealand - Selected Sectors

Programme Name	Industry Sector(s)	Duration of visa(s)	Skill Requirements	Other Requirements	Family	Dual Intent Permitted?
Work-to-Residence Programme (Talent visa and Priority Occupations)	Business, art, sports and cultural work.	2 years. After that, visa-holders with an ongoing offer of employment can become permanent residents.	As required by the recruiting employer.	Employers wishing to use the Talent visa option must become accredited for 12 month intervals. Employers offering work under Priority occupations must prove that the occupation is one in which a critical skills shortage has been certified. Salary must be at least NZ$45,000.	Yes	Yes
Temporary Work Permit	Any sector. Specialty occupations (medical professions included) must be registered with the New Zealand authority governing standards in their field.	Duration of contract or up to 3 years, renewable for 3 years.	Proof of qualifications or experience.	Proof of funds, sponsorship, and intention to repatriate.	Yes	No
Business persons on short-term secondment	Any sector	Duration of contract or up to 12 months.	Proof of qualifications or experience.	Proof of intracompany transfer or offer of New Zealand employment.	Yes	No
Business persons on long-term secondment	Any sector	Up to 3 years.	Proof of qualifications or experience.	Evidence of job appointment and guarantee of repatriation.	Yes	No
South Pacific Temporary Work Program	Any sector	Up to 3 years.	None	None	Yes	Yes
Overseas students wishing to gain practical work experience in New Zealand	Any sector	Up to 6 months.	Evidence of student status and support of educational institution.	An offer of employment in New Zealand.	No	Yes
Medical and Dental Trainees	Medical	Up to 6 months.	Evidence of qualifications.	Letter of acceptance from a New Zealand hospital.	No	No
Domestic staff of diplomatic and consular personnel	Domestic (e.g., housekeepers, nannies, cooks and gardeners)	Up to 3 years (with 12 months extension) or until the employer's tour of duty is complete.	Evidence of suitable training or experience.	Statement of Understanding from the diplomatic or consular officer.	No	No
Domestic staff of seconded business executives	Domestic (e.g., housekeepers, nannies, cooks and gardeners)	Up to date of employment termination or until the end of employer's secondment.	Proof that applicant has been integral to the employer's lifestyle before coming to New Zealand.	Job guarantee and guarantee of repatriation, including a written commitment from the employer.	No	No
Interpreters from Japan	Tourism	Up to 2 years.	Proof that the applicant is qualified to translate Japanese and English.	Job guarantee and guarantee of repatriation.	No	No
Working Holiday Scheme	Any sector. Working Holiday visa-holders can not work for any one employer for more than three months.	Up to 12 months.	No. Programme is for single or married people, aged 18 to 30 unaccompanied by children.	Evidence of sufficient funds to purchase return travel.	No	Yes

Source:
NZIS (2002).

169

TABLE 9.15.

Student Visas, Permits and Admissions in TCIs, 2000

Student Admissions/Authorizations Issued	
United States[1]	699,653
Canada[2]	64,243
Australia	119,103
New Zealand[3]	42,440

Notes:

1) The United States' admissions number includes F-1 (academic students) and M-1 (vocational students) visa holders and their families. When J-1 (exchange visitors) are added, the number of admissions rises to 1,051,396 for FY 2000.

2) Canada's student authorization number does not include applications made by US citizens at Ports of Entry (POEs)

3) New Zealand's student authorization number reflects only accepted off-shore applications

Sources:

CIC - www.cic.gc.ca/english/visit/stats2000/students/all.html; DIMIA (2001); Kramer (2001); New Zealand Ministry of Education - www.minedu.govt.nz/web/document/document_page.cfm?id=4629.

TABLE 9.16.

Australian Points Test in 2002 (first introduced in 1989)

Factors considered	Points
Skilled applicants must score at least 115 points to be granted a visa[1]	
1 - Skill	
• Training specific to the occupation[2]	60
• General occupations	50
• Other general skilled occupations	40
2 - Age (at time of application)	
• 18 to 29 years	30
• 30 to 34 years	25
• 35 to 39 years	20
• 40 to 44 years	15
3 - English language ability	
• Vocational (reasonable command of English)	15
• Competent	20
4 - Specific Work Experience	
• Applicants with 60 points for nominated occupation[3] and 3 years of work (in the 4 years immediately prior to application) in the nominated occupation or closely related occupations receive full points.	10
• Applicants with 40 to 60 points under Skill and experience working in any occupation (despite relevance to the nominated occupation) on the Skilled Occupations List for at least 3 of the 4 years before application.	5
5 - Occupation in Demand[4] / Job offer	
• Occupation in demand, but no job offer	5
• Occupation in demand, with job offer	10
6 - Australian Qualifications	
• Australian qualification: study for at least 12 months full-time in Australia toward the receipt of an Australian post-secondary degree (or higher qualification), diploma, advanced diploma or trade qualification.	5
• Australian Ph.D.	10
7 - Spouse Skills	
• Points are awarded if the applicant's spouse is also able to satisfy the basic requirements of age, English language ability, qualifications, nominated occupation and recent work experience and if s/he obtains a skill assessment.	5
8 - Bonus Points (for any one of the following)	
• Capital investment (minimum AU$100,000) in Australia	5
• Australian work experience: At least 6 months of work experience in one of the occupations on the Skilled Occupations List immediately prior to application.	5
• Fluency in one of Australia's Community Languages (other than English)	5
• Points for Relationship (Applicants with relatives in Australia only)	
• Points are awarded if the applicant or the applicant's spouse is sponsored by a relative who is an Australian citizen or permanent resident.	15

171

Notes:

1) Applicants must gain sufficient points to reach the pass mark. Applications scoring below the pass mark, but above another mark, the "pool mark," are held in reserve for up to two years. If within that time the pass mark is lowered and the reserved score is above the new mark, the application is processed further. As of 2002, the pool mark for the skilled-Australian sponsored category was 105, it stood at 70 for the skilled-independent category. All other pool marks are currently equal to the pass mark of 115.

2) The occupation nominated must be on the Skilled Occupations List published by DIMIA.

3) See Note 2.

4) Published as the Migration Occupations Demand List (MODL).

Sources:

DIMIA - www.immi.gov.au/allforms/skl-pts.htm; Philip Ruddock - www.minister.immi.gov.au/advisory/ptsrev.htm.

TABLE 9.17.

New Zealand Points System - 2002 (first introduced in 1991)

Points System	
Primary applicants must score 28 points to be granted a visa	

1 - Qualifications	Points
Base Qualification:	
• A degree, diploma or trade certificate of minimum 3 years training, study or work experience.	10
Advanced Qualification:	
• Bachelor's degree or equivalent.	11
• Masters degree or higher	12

2 - Employability (Maximum employability points: 25)	
Work Experience	
• 2 years	1
• 10 years	5
• 20 years	10
• Offer of employment (relevant to qualifications and experience)	5
• Offer of employment (not relevant to qualifications and experience)	2

3 - Age (maximum age: 55 years for General Skills, 84 for investors)	
• 18-24 years	8
• 25-29 years	10
• 45-49 years	2

4 - Settlement Factors (Maximum points allowed by law for settlement factors: 7)	
Settlement Funds	
• $100,000	1
• $200,000	2
Partner's Qualifications	
• Base Qualification	1
• Advanced Qualification	2
New Zealand Work Experience	
• 1 year	1
• 2 years	2
Family Sponsorship	3
Non-relevant offer of employment	2

Total Points Possible	44

172

Sources:
New Zealand Embassy in Washington DC, 2002 (public information announcements); New Zealand Immigration Assistance
www.nzimmigration.net.nz/Pages/No8.html; NZIS (1997); The New Zealand Herald (2002).

CHAPTER 10

Mutually Agreed Migration Policies in Latin America

During the 1990s, Latin America experienced various changes in international migration patterns and policies. Added to the difficulties states face in regulating migration through traditional unilateral policies, these changes caused a "governability crisis". This in turn has led to an increase in bilateral and multilateral responses.

Bilateral and multilateral agreements are well rooted within the region and have had varying degrees of success in regulating migratory movements. Certain agreements and understandings are linked to distinctive subregional integration processes (North America Free Trade Agreement, Andean Community, MERCOSUR). In these regional integration zones, both traditional and modern migration flows have continued; causes appear to be linked more to specific factors, such as the development of national markets than to the processes themselves.

Over the past ten years, two regional consultative processes have featured prominently: the Regional Conference on Migration (or Puebla Process), and the South American Forum on International Migration. These bodies have formulated their respective plans of action while retaining a non-binding nature and search for consensus.

The institutional approach to migration in the 1990s revealed policy alternatives. These alternatives were characterized by shared responsibility and consensus between countries of origin and arrival.

Changes in Migration Trends and Policies in Latin America

International migration flows in the region changed during the 1990s. These changes were naturally reflected in new regional migration policies concerning not only the emigration of nationals but also the immigration of foreigners.

Changes in Migratory Flow Trends

An analysis of changes in migration flows in Latin America during the 1990s should take into account traditional flows and the increase in these flows. In this way, the following trends can be highlighted: an increase in inter-Latin American migration to non-bordering countries; a drop in cross-border flows; new Latin American emigration flows to countries outside the region; the disappearance of traditional extra-regional immigration flows into Latin America and, finally, the emergence of new types of immigration.

For traditional emigration flows, the sharp increase in ongoing emigration flows from Mexico, the Caribbean and Central America to the United States in recent decades, should be emphasized (IOM, 2000).

During the 1980s, more than one-third of legal migrants in the United States came from Caribbean countries: currently 80 per cent of legal migrants and 90 per cent of irregular migrants are estimated to originate from this region and Mexico. Thus in the past twenty years, nationals of the Dominican Republic have become the second largest group of immigrants in the United States after Cubans.

Up to 1990, the principal sources of Caribbean migration to the United States were Cuba (736,974 migrants), the Dominican Republic (347,858), and Haiti (225,393). Puerto Rico is considered a special case owing to its political status as a free state associated with the United States, in 1998, its total population was 3.8 million, with a further 2.7 million living in the United States.

Mexican migration to the United States dates back to the first decades of the twentieth century and has been increasing steadily. In 1980, 2,199,221 Mexicans were registered in the United States; this figure increased to 4,298,014 in 1990, and to 7.5 million in 1998, representing 8 per cent of the migrant population. The total may be broken down into 2 million naturalized citizens, 3 million legal migrants, and 2.5 million irregular migrants.

Migration from Central America to the United States has also increased in recent decades. Ninety per cent of the 1.1 million Central Americans who migrated to the United States in the past 175 years, have done so since 1980. Combined with natural disasters such as hurricane Mitch in 1998, the civil wars of the 1980s in El Salvador, Honduras and Nicaragua caused economic crises and substantial population displacement to the north.

173

In Canada, data indicate that migratory flows from the Caribbean, Central America and South America have increased, but less so than to the United States probably because of Canadian migration policies. In 1996, for example, 40,000 Salvadoran migrants were registered in Canada; while according to the United States census 465,433 Salvadorans were registered in the US. Canada receives migrants from the English-speaking Caribbean (Jamaica, Trinidad and Tobago, and Guyana) because it has long-term labour agreements with those countries. These countries are followed by Haiti, which is regarded as a traditional source of immigration. Since the 1980s, Canada has received immigrants from El Salvador and Guatemala. There is minimal immigration from South America (Pellegrino, 2000).

In the past ten years, traditional inter-Latin America migration flows to neighbouring countries have been maintained. Typical flows include those from Nicaragua to Costa Rica; the migration of Haitians to the Dominican Republic (an estimated 500,000 persons) (see also **textbox 10.1.**); in the Southern Cone, Bolivians and Paraguayans to Argentina (approximate totals of 250,000 and 150,000 respectively); and Brazilians to Paraguay (an estimated 150,000 to 250,000 persons) (Palau and Heikel, 1999).

TEXTBOX 10.1.

Migration Realities in Hispaniola

Home to some 16.5 million people, Hispaniola is the most populated island in the Caribbean. Its population is divided equally between the Dominican Republic, which occupies the eastern portion of the island, and Haiti in the west.

Haitian migrant selling flowers in the Dominican Republic

The economic situation varies on each sides of the border. Haiti is the only country of the Americas in the group of the Least Developed Countries; on the other hand, the Dominican Republic has enjoyed steady growth throughout the 1990s at an annual rate of 6 per cent. Relations between both countries improved substantially in 2001 and show signs of greater cooperation. However, the permanent flow of Haitian migrants to the Dominican Republic and the illegal presence of over 500,000 Haitians in the neighbouring country constitute a permanent source of tension.

Haitians in the Dominican Republic

Often smuggled into the country, Haitians form the backbone of important legal and illegal labour networks in the Dominican Republic. They occupy jobs in a wide range of industries including agriculture (sugar cane, coffee, rice and vegetable plantations), construction or services. Haitians are also present in the informal sector, working as small traders, street vendors, gardeners or prostitutes.

Although many Dominican employers benefit directly from the supply of low-wage Haitian labour, the receiving country's economy and society pay a price for the steady inflow of Haitians. The large supply of cheap Haitian migrant workers lowers the wages of unskilled Dominican labourers and reduces incentives for improving productivity. It also places the Dominican Republic's public services under additional pressure, especially education and health.

Although deportees have been treated better since 2001, most Haitian workers in the Dominican Republic still live under constant threat of deportation. In 2000, a total of 14,639 Haitians were deported; estimates for 2001 are in the range of 12,000 deportations.

Apart from poor socio-economic conditions and lack of access to basic services, most Haitian migrants and their families do not possess appropriate identity documentation; many of those born in the Dominican Republic are deprived, *de facto*, of their Haitian citizenship.

Haitian circular migration, including deportation and voluntary return, has an effect on the spread of infectious diseases, especially HIV/AIDS, in both countries. Outbreaks of tuberculosis in the Dominican Republic are often closely linked to migratory flows.

While Haitian migratory flows towards the Dominican Republic remain relatively stable, Haitian emigration across the sea has systematically increased since 2001. This trend is due to the growing importance of people-smuggling groups. In recent years, an average of 250 persons per month have been deported to Haiti from the Bahamas. The Bahamas reports that arrivals are currently increasing by 30 to 40 per cent. Reports of Haitians intercepted in Cuban waters on their way north to Florida or the Bahamas have risen from 389 in 1999, and 648 in 2000, to 1,021 in 2001. In January and February 2002 alone, over 600 Haitians were rescued by the Cuban Navy. The US Coast Guard intercepted 973 Haitians in 1999, 1,131 in 2000, and 1,856 in 2001.

Dominant migration patterns in the Dominican Republic

Trafficking of Dominican women continues to be a significant problem. In the last five years, traditional destinations in Europe and the Dutch Antilles have become less important. Argentina has emerged as a main destination housing an estimated 5,000 Dominican women (see **textbox 3.1.**). Many trafficked Dominican girls and young women are also found in Costa Rica and Haiti. At the same time, Haitian children are trafficked into the Dominican Republic, destined for bonded work on plantations or begging in urban areas.

Smuggling of Dominicans into Puerto Rico continues; however, better coordination between the Dominican Navy and the US Coast Guard, has increased the number of interceptions since last year. This coordination led to the dismantling of thirty smuggling gangs in 2001. Moreover, the Dominican Republic has become an important transit country for migrants from Albania, China, Iran or Russia smuggled to the USA. Over 150 persons of different nationalities in transit to the USA were detained last year before being sent back home.

According to the 2000 census in the United States, 874,000 Dominicans live in the USA, including 407,000 in the State of New York and 109,000 in Puerto Rico. However, some US scholars believe that these figures do not accurately represent the situation. Up to 250,000 additional Dominicans might actually live in the USA in an irregular situation, especially in Puerto Rico.

Remittances from Dominicans abroad continue to be a major source of income for the country. Estimated at US$ 1.9 billion in 2000, remittances equal 70 per cent of tourism revenues, the fastest growing economic sector in the Dominican Republic. In 2000, 1.6 million Dominicans received remittances from family members abroad. Estimated at around US$ 400 to 500 million per year, remittances also represent an important aspect of Haiti's economy.

Existing migration legislation in both countries is outdated. Legislation dates from 1939 in the Dominican Republic and from 1964 in Haiti. The Dominican Government has been waiting for Santo Domingo's Congress approval of a new migration law since mid-2001. Attempts to discuss new legislation in Haiti have so far been unproductive.

In December 2001, the Dominican Government signed a migration agreement with Spain to cover the following: establishment of a legal labour migration scheme between both countries; definitions of migrant categories; and the fixing of quotas. Traditionally, Dominican migrants to Spain have been mainly women. Providers of domestic services will probably continue to form a large part of future legal migration flows, followed by other low-skilled or semi-skilled migrant categories.

The increase in inter-Latin American migration to non-neighbouring countries is by no means as large as the traditional migration mentioned above. However, this migration is increasing both quantitatively and qualitatively.

Firstly, new flows from the Caribbean area to Venezuela (Suárez Sarmiento, 2000) or, more recently, to Argentina should be mentioned. The latter flow is usually associated with the trafficking of women from the Dominican Republic (see **textbox 3.1.**).

Another important process during the past decade has been Peruvian emigration. There is greater Peruvian migration to traditional destinations such as the United States, but also to various Latin American countries. This emigration now affects practically the whole region (Torales, 1993).

The armed conflict in Colombia has also spurred new flows to neighbouring and non-neighbouring countries. Some 600,000 migrants have left the country over the past three years[1].

Generally speaking, a drop in traditional inter-Latin American cross-border flows can be observed over the past twenty years (Pellegrino, 2000). An example is labour migration from Colombia to Ecuador and Venezuela. However, as mentioned above, these flows would appear to be increasing again at present through forced displacement.

Traditional cross-border flows from Chile and Uruguay to Argentina have also visibly declined. In the last months of 2001, the flows appear to have reversed as Chilean, Paraguayan and Bolivian cross-border migrants returned home because of growing unemployment and the devaluation of the Argentine currency, which directly restricts chances of sending money home.

The increase or emergence of migration flows from Latin America to other regions can also be observed in recent decades. Examples include migration from Brazil to Japan, calculated by some sources at about 150,000 persons (Patarra and Baeninger, 1996), and from Brazil to the United States, where the total Brazilian population is currently estimated at 700,000 (Baeninger, 2000).

Another growing trend in recent years has been the increase in Latin American emigrants to Spain and Italy, which are consolidating their position as countries of destination. The Ecuadorian population in Spain constitutes one of the most important sources of labour in the southern agricultural regions. Peruvians, Colombians and Dominicans also now emigrate to these European countries, and have been joined by a growing number of emigrants from Argentina and Uruguay as a result of the economic crisis in these countries during the late 1990s. In percentage terms, Latin American migration to Spain in 1999 increased by about 13.5 per cent over the previous year and in 2000 by about 19.9 per cent, with an increase of 33,255 persons for a total of 199,964 migrants of Latin American origin in 2000. Ecuador represents the highest figure for Latin American migration to Spain in 2000 by nationality, with 30,878 legal residents and a 138 per cent increase over the period 1999-2000; Peru follows Ecuador with

27,888 residents but no increase, and the Dominican Republic, with a total of 26,481 immigrants. The number of Colombians totals 24,702 and increased by 81.2 per cent over the year. The three other prominent nationalities are Cubans, Argentines and Brazilians, with less than 20,000 residents (Government Department for Foreigners and Immigration, Spain, 2000).

Lastly, the disappearance and the emergence of specific extra-regional immigration flows into Latin America should be mentioned.

Immigration from Western Europe ended with the last flows to Venezuela in the 1970s, although a flow from Eastern Europe developed after the fall of the Berlin Wall. Migration from Asia (basically from Korea and China) is continuing but the Latin American countries frequently represent a transitional stage in emigration to the north (Mera, 1997). In addition, there has been a growing flow of highly qualified human resources in recent years linked to the setting up of multinational companies in countries with sustained economic growth.

Changes in Migration Policies

The Latin American governments appear to be at a crossroads in migration policy between national policies and the search for new alternatives.

Policy changes are clearer concerning the **emigration of nationals.** Traditionally, no responsibility was claimed towards emigrants. Now there is growing tendency to institute policies committed to nationals living abroad. Governments in countries of origin are concerned about the effects of emigration both in the countries of arrival and in the home country.

Thus, both the remittance transfer mechanisms and the destination of remittances (in the case of Mexico, 80 per cent goes to direct consumption) are important subjects in government policies. Another important emigration aspect is the possibility of voting abroad in elections held in the country of origin. In South America, this right has already been granted in countries such as Argentina, Brazil, Colombia, Peru and Venezuela; it is being implemented in the Dominican Republic and is being discussed in other countries, such as Chile and Uruguay.

1) According to the entry and departure data for Colombians compiled by the Directorate for Foreigners within the Colombian Administrative Department of Security (DAS).

In addition, the principle of "dual nationality" – traditionally denied by most Latin American governments to their citizens - is granted in countries such as Colombia, Mexico and the Dominican Republic, from which there are substantial emigration flows. This principle is opening the doors to political participation by emigrants in their countries of residence without the risk of losing their own nationality.

Countries of origin have also been intervening more in the defence of emigrants' human rights. Governments have been active at presidential summit level in adopting new "proactive" consular policies or programmes to re-establish links with nationals abroad.

The proactive consular policy aims at linking communities of nationals with the country of origin, protecting social, labour and political rights, maintaining culture, education, etc. In order to do this, the consulates are modifying their activities at the request of their citizens and identifying problems and seeking solutions for the national community abroad through effective and ongoing action.

The case of Mexico is notable in terms of consular protection, with 43 consulates in the United States. These consulates provide legal defence programmes for victims of human rights violations and programmes aimed at migrant minors and international adoption, and also legal assistance to persons under sentence of death. Another country which recently began a proactive consular policy is Brazil, which has considerable migrant communities in New York, Miami and Boston in the United States, and Ciudad del Este in Paraguay.

In recent years several Latin American countries, notably Chile, El Salvador, Mexico, Peru, Venezuela and Colombia have established linkage programmes with nationals abroad and are also undertaking similar activities in Argentina, Uruguay and Brazil (Granes *et al.,* 1998).

The process is more complex for **immigration policies.** As in other parts of the world, governments of the region would appear to be treading a path between maintaining traditional restrictive policies and searching for new areas and alternatives.

Established in the 1930s, the restrictive approach was prompted by the desire to protect labour markets hit by crisis and high unemployment levels. Migration restrictions have grown for a variety of reasons up to the present day (Mármora, 1995).

The so-called "lost decade" of the 1980s coincided with the slow recovery of democratic institutions in several countries of the region. This again moved the basis of migration restriction to the "protection of native labour". This argument remained as a basic substratum in the 1990s, when two new supposed threats from migration emerged: the intensive use of health and education services, and the security problems associated with the increase in drug trafficking and international terrorism. The latter became a new policy priority following the terrorist acts of September 11, 2001. It is difficult to say how much these factors will influence current and future international migration policies.

A "migration crisis" has been provoked in cases such as Europe because of the following factors: the development of restrictive policies to address the widespread economic crisis in most countries of the region; the continuity of the migration processes (some migrants having been resident for over half a century); and the emergence of new small-scale but highly visible flows (Hollifield, 1997; Withol De Wenden, 1999). In the context of Latin America, this chapter describes this situation as a migration "governability" crisis[2].

This crisis can be seen in different situations related to both migration *per se* and broader problems affecting national societies and inter-country relations. The most visible manifestations include the growth in irregular migration; the increase in incidents of xenophobia and discrimination; the increase in "migration business"[3]; the inconsistency between migration policies and the regional economic integration areas; problems in bilateral relations between countries with cross-border migration flows; and outdated migration policies on manpower requirements and population replacement.

---

2) "Migration governability" means the possibility for Governments to reconcile the characteristics, causes and effects of migration movements with the social demands and expectations relating to them, and the actual possibilities of states to respond to them (Calcagno and Mármora, 1993). Like any other form of governability, migration governability is based on two essential conditions which every government must address if it does not wish to be undermined: legitimacy and effectiveness (Arbos and Giner, 1993). In its turn legitimacy is based on at least three requirements: equity, legality and transparency, while effectiveness is based on objective information for decision-making, the continuing adaptation of legal provisions and the modernization of migration administration (Mármora, 1997).

3) "Migration business" means different forms of illegal dealings involving migrants such as trafficking in persons, governmental administrative corruption and overpriced privatization of activities, including compilation of documents, frontier controls, computerization of data, etc.

Government responses to these crises have been problematic owing to their "unilateralist" design and application (Sassen, 1996). Consequently, governments have increasingly adopted bilateral and multilateral approaches.

Intergovernmental Migration Agreements and Understandings

Several reasons account for the increase in efforts to achieve bilateral and multilateral agreement among countries and within the various regions: new and old migration situations, and changes in how migration is perceived and in states' autonomous political capacity when faced with migration movements. The relatively formal understandings reached represent a new kind of contemporary migration governability among nations.

The main examples include bilateral and multilateral agreements and understandings on migration questions *per se* or related matters, such as social security or migrant health and education (Mármora, 1994).

Over the past ten years in particular, bilateral and multilateral migration agreements have generally aimed at managing existing migration flows better, including the following aspects: regularizing the situation of irregular migrants; facilitating the deportation of irregular migrants; facilitating or establishing more controls on cross-border migration movements; and selectively organizing the flow of already-established migrant workers.

Bilateral Agreements

During the past 50 years, bilateral consensus on migration has manifested itself through agreements aimed at restricting migration movements; regularizing the situation of irregular migrants; promoting migration; establishing areas of free movement; facilitating return and protecting migrants' rights.

In an analysis of 168 bilateral agreements identified during the past half century, a distinction may be drawn between those signed among Latin American countries and those between Latin American countries and extra-regional countries. Of the agreements cited, 42 per cent were signed among Latin American countries and 58 per cent with countries in other regions (see also **statistics table 10.1.**).

TABLE 10.1.

Bilateral migration agreements in Latin America (1948-2000)

Policies	Objectives of the agreements	1948-1973 Among Latin American countries		1948-1973 Between Latin American and other countries		1974-1990 Among Latin American countries		1974-1990 Between Latin American and other countries		1991-2000 Among Latin American countries		1991-2000 Between Latin American and other countries		TOTAL	Percentage of TOTAL
		Number	%	Number	%	Number	%	Number	%	Number	%	Number	%		
Restriction	Readmission											9	22.5	9	5.3
	Frontier control														
	Trafficking														
Regularization		2	9.5	1	3.03	1	6.6			5	14.2	1	2.5	10	5.9
Promotion	Labour agreements	6	28.6			3	20	3	20	5	14.2	5	12.5	22	13
	General agreements			10	30.3	1	6.6	1	6.6			2	5	14	8.3
Liberalization	Free movement	11	52.4	14	42.4	7	46.6	6	40	13	37.1	18	45	69	41
Return	Assisted							1	6.6	5	14.2	1	2.5	7	4.1
	Extradition			5	15			3	20	7	20	10	25	25	14.8
Migrant Protection		2	9.5	3	9	3	20	1	6.6			3	7.5	12	7.1
Total		21	12.5	33	19.6	15	8.9	15	8.9	35	20.8	49	29.2	168	100

Source:
IOM Buenos Aires.

If bilateral agreements are analysed over three different periods – from the post-war years to 1973; from 1973 to 1990; and from 1991 to 2000 – some distinctive features can be observed in the third period.

Firstly, half of the agreements have been signed since 1991, which demonstrates a clear increase in this methodology of tackling migration issues among countries of the region.

In addition, promotion and free movement agreements dominated in the post-war years (relating to visa facilitation); however, the last ten years have seen an increase in agreements on the readmission of irregular migrants (47 per cent of agreements signed between Latin American and other countries) and assisted return agreements. Agreements on the regularization of irregular migrants, especially among Latin American countries, have also increased.

The 1990s in South America featured agreements signed between Colombia and Ecuador, and the agreements recently signed by Argentina with Bolivia, Peru and Paraguay. In August and September 2000, various agreements were signed between Colombia and Ecuador, including the Permanent Statute on Migration and the Memorandum of Understanding between the Deputy Ministers for Foreign Affairs of the two countries on the procedure for dealing with displacement in frontier areas. The aim is to combat illegal drug trafficking and to ensure common action on all aspects of this problem.

The most important aspect of the agreements concluded by Argentina with Bolivia, Peru and Paraguay is that the governments undertake to regularize the nationals of the other signatory countries. In this case, migrants are protected *de facto* and *de jure,* with the direct intervention of their government of origin. Furthermore, the agreement contains provisions from the International Convention on the Protection of the Rights of All Migrant Workers and Members of Their Families (see also **textbox 1.4.**) and provisions of the various ILO conventions and recommendations even though these instruments have not been ratified by the governments concerned.

In Central America in January 1993, an agreement was signed between Costa Rica and Nicaragua to regulate cross-border labour migration. The main objective was to curb uncontrolled irregular migration. The agreement establishes mechanisms for regulating the entry and sojourn of Nicaraguan migrant workers through recruitment, migration procedures and labour conditions. During the fourth Bi-National Meeting of Nicaragua and Costa Rica in 1997, specific measures were established to document the migrants covered by this agreement (IOM, 2001).

Progress has been made in the United States in the past decade through a series of agreements with Mexico (see also **textbox 9.1.**): the 1996 memorandum of understanding for the protection of nationals; the 1998 memorandum for internal consultation mechanisms, which enables Mexican consuls to meet United States immigration officials when faced with specific problems involving migrants and gives the consuls access to detention centres; the 1998 memorandum of understanding between the National Population Council and the Immigration and Naturalization Service (INS) for the exchange of information on labour markets; the 1999 memorandum of understanding and cooperation to combat frontier violence; the 2000 memorandum of understanding between the migration services and the INS on the recovery of migrants; and the 2000 review mechanism to deal with frontier violence, under which the consuls review detected cases with prosecutors.

As regards Mexico's bilateral relations with Central American countries, reference should be made to the bi-national commissions established with Guatemala, Honduras, and El Salvador. Migration issues have also been highlighted in more general bilateral agreements, such as the integrated cooperation agreement between Cuba and Venezuela, signed in 2000. Article 6 provides for the signing of a migration agreement in order to facilitate the work of specialist officials on associated working missions.

Significant progress has been made in Haiti and the Dominican Republic in the context of the bilateral joint commission set up by the two countries; agreements include the memorandum of understanding on migration matters, signed in June 1998; the agreement on postal services for migration matters, signed in the same month; the protocol of understanding on repatriation mechanisms, of December 1999; and the declaration on recruitment conditions for their nationals, of February 2000 (State Secretariat for Foreign Affairs, Santo Domingo, 2000).

As regards agreements between Latin American and extra-regional governments, Ecuador and Colombia have recently signed significant agreements with Spain. The agreements cover both regularization and promotion issues by identifying Latin American labour migrants to meet labour shortfalls in Spain.

179

Apart from the formal agreements, significant bilateral progress in the Latin American region has been achieved through such events as the Sao Paulo bilateral meeting between Brazil and Paraguay on migration in June 2000; joint activities by Argentina and Chile aimed at establishing free movement between the two countries; and the bilateral meetings on migration held between Ecuador and Peru and between Venezuela and Colombia, *inter alia*.

Multilateral Agreements

Like bilateral agreements, the multilateral treatment of migration questions is deep-rooted in Latin America. As elsewhere in the world, multilateral agreements and understandings on migration have developed in different ways and with different objectives.

Thus, multilateral agreements on specific aspects include the free movement of persons in a particular regional area or the consular attention paid to Latin Americans abroad[4]; the migration agreements included in regional integration areas; and the *ad hoc* processes known as regional consultative processes.

Starting back in the 1960s, free movement agreements include the following two landmark agreements: the international land agreement signed by Argentina, Brazil and Uruguay, with the accession of Chile, Paraguay and Peru in 1966; and the agreement to facilitate the transit of persons between Argentina, Bolivia and Peru in the inter-oceanic "Liberators' Corridor" in 1988. In addition, migration issues have been included in regional integration areas on three occasions: the case of the Andean Community, formalized in the Andean Instrument on Labour Migration; in Central America, developed through the Central American Organization on Migration (OCAM); and the various MERCOSUR commissions in the Southern Cone.

a) The Andean Instrument on Labour Migration

The longest and most formal experience to link migration to regional integration is the Andean Instrument on Labour Migration, which forms part of the Simon Rodriguez Agreement on Social and Labour Integration, signed by the member countries of the Cartagena Agreement in October 1973. This process exemplifies how a "soft" law may become positive law: the Government of Venezuela adopted legislation on foreigner registration in 1981 which regularized over one-quarter of illegally-resident migrants (Mármora, 1994). The Andean Instrument on Labour Migration was also pivotal in three additional respects: standardizing migration categories; devising procedures for recruiting workers; and establishing implementation mechanisms. It was the first regional agreement in the Americas to lay down migration procedures and categories (Mármora, 1994).

The Andean Instrument's impact on migration policies declined in the 1980s, but its significance and scope were reaffirmed in the labour integration trends which arose within the subregion. Thus, at the Second Conference of Labour Ministers of the Andean Group, held in La Paz in October 1991, agreement was reached on the need to reactivate the Simon Rodriguez Agreement and to prepare a text updating Decision 116 (Andean Instrument on Labour Migration) of the Board of the Cartagena Agreement.

Coming into effect in November 1994, the agreement between Colombia and Ecuador on irregular migrants clearly reflects the spirit of the Instrument. The Instrument is updated, developed and used as a framework in the fifth preambular paragraph of the agreement.

The Andean Instrument on Labour Migration was applied most widely during the 1970s, after which it was used little. It has been revived in recent years in order to re-dynamize the free movement of persons in the Andean region (López Bustillo, 2000). Reference should be made to recent measures taken by the Andean Community, such as: Decision 501 on frontier integration zones of the Andean Community, which in paragraph (e) promotes free transit and proposes harmonization and simplification procedures and the elimination of obstacles impeding migration procedures; Decision 502 on bi-national frontier centres; Decision 503 on the recognition of identity documents; Decision 504 on an Andean passport; and Decision 527 on modification of the Andean Migration Card.

4) This subject was one of the earliest dealt with and was covered in the Caracas Agreement on Consuls of 1915.

b) Central American Organization on Migration

Central America made multilateral progress on migration matters with the setting-up of the Central American Organization on Migration (OCAM). This body was set up at the Meeting of Central American Migration Directors-General at San José (Costa Rica) on 5 October 1990 in the context of the Permanent Secretariat of the General Treaty on Central American Economic Integration (SIECA). SIECA will serve as the Organization's Technical Secretariat and IOM will act in a technical advisory capacity. OCAM subsequently became a body of the Meeting of Central American Migration Directors-General. Progress has been made on migration control, the harmonization of legal provisions, and the facilitation of frontier transit.

Thus, control emerged as a main issue at the meeting of legal advisors from the various migration departments, held in El Salvador in May 1992. The basic objective was the "analysis of the illegal trafficking in persons in Central America". At this point, control will not affect the entry of irregular immigrants, but the transit of these immigrants to developed countries in the north. Problems did not include the potential impact of irregular immigrants on local labour markets but "the financial problems involved in the maintenance costs of foreign detainees", "the corruption of officials", and the "political pressures of the migrants' countries of destination on the Governments of the area" (Directores-Generales de Migraciones, Centroamérica, 1992).

Two control instruments should be mentioned: entry and departure forms, and identity documents (standardization efforts have been made).

In this regard, the proposal to modernize and standardize passports in the subregion deserves mention. This proposal was put forward at the first OCAM meeting and agreed to at the second, while the passport format was established at the third meeting (SIECA, 1990a/b; 1991).

The harmonization of migration procedures and legislation among OCAM countries emerged as one of the goals of the Project on Migration Instruments and Policies for the Integration of Latin America. In addition, the facilitation of frontier transit was taken up at the first OCAM meeting.

Reference was made to "facilitating the transit of nationals between various countries" as one of the organization's underlying principles (SIECA, 1990a). The second OCAM meeting made progress on having standard opening hours at frontier posts (SIECA, 1990b).

Various activities were developed during the 1990s. The most recent agreements attached special importance to the Migration Information System for Central America; multilateral activities for the assisted return of extra-regional migrants; the need for information campaigns on the risks involved in trafficking of migrants; the modernization of migration management in Central America; the training of regional officials, and issues relating to the standardization of migration procedures.

c) MERCOSUR

Following the initiation of the Asunción Treaty in 1991, migration also began to be addressed within MERCOSUR in such areas as the customs and socio-labour sectors (Mármora and Cassarino, 1996).

Within the organic framework of MERCOSUR, migration and labour mobility, and associated development questions were taken up by Subgroup No. 10 on Labour Affairs, Employment and Social Security (SGT10); the MERCOSUR Socio-Labour Commission; the Group on Liberalization of Trade Services; and the Economic and Social Consultative Forum.

In 1995, SGT10 replaced Working Subgroup No. 11, which was the original MERCOSUR body dealing with socio-labour questions. From that time onwards, discussions on the movement of labour shifted focus and the concept of labour migration was substituted for free movement of labour.

Labour migration within the SGT10 was institutionalized in one of its three commissions. In 1997, a tripartite *ad hoc* commission on labour migration was established in the framework of Thematic Commission II.

It was considered important to study the conditions in which work develops in frontier regions as these areas have similar social, cultural, economic and labour practices.

181

A draft study was approved for the tenth meeting of SGT10 in 1999. Argentina, Peru and Uruguay proposed the drafting of a survey on frontier workers as part of the planned diagnostic study. The other phase provides for a structural diagnostic study of frontier areas.

Another significant activity was the signing of the Multilateral Agreement on Social Security within MERCOSUR in December 1997. This agreement shall be applied to workers of any other nationality resident in the territory of any party provided they have worked in that territory.

MERCOSUR's Socio-Labour Commission drafts reports and studies on the status of each of the rights concerned and implementation in each member country. One of the three studies planned for 2002 by the Commission's national sections will concern migrant workers' rights.

This study could constitute a useful starting-point in establishing the situation of labour migrants in the region. It would not only cover the normative frameworks but also the mechanisms for ensuring labour migrants' rights as well as relevant institutional and social practices. In addition, it would be broader in scope since it would not be restricted to the frontier region (Pérez Vichich, 2002).

Furthermore, the structural changes aimed at establishing the free movement of capital and goods have affected all regional economic and labour activity through new labour mobility systems and circuits as well as by the geographical displacement of workers. In this connection, the so-called third freedom – freedom of trade in services – should be incorporated.

In the light of this, the proposal for a MERCOSUR visa was explored at the twelfth meeting of the MERCOSUR Group on Services held in March 2001.

This visa would be limited to persons providing services in a member country other than their own for determined periods, and who are working as: corporate management personnel, senior personnel, highly-qualified technicians or specialists, executives, managers, representatives, scientists, journalists or teachers, inter alia.

Lastly, the Economic and Social Consultative Forum (FCES), which derived from the organic redefinition of MERCOSUR established in the Ouro Preto Protocol of 1994, is responsible for monitoring, analysing and evaluating the social and economic impact of integration policies, whether they be sectoral, national, regional or international. Based on the question received by the Common Market Group[5] in 1999 on migration in frontier areas, the FCES began broad discussions on frontier problems, adopting a comprehensive approach that incorporated economic, commercial and socio-labour aspects. On several occasions, meetings were held with representatives of companies in MERCOSUR frontier areas, with significant participation from civil society. As a result, agreement was reached in December 1999 on local cross-border transit between two member States of MERCOSUR, Bolivia and Chile, and in June 2000 on the regulations for the local cross-border transit regime between the same.

Regional Consultative Processes

Regional consultative processes mean government consultations in a given region to seek general consensus and to exchange information in an informal, open and non-binding atmosphere (Klekowski, 2001) (see also **chapter 8**). The following may be identified in Latin America at the present time: the Regional Conference on Migration (Puebla Process), and the South American Forum on Migration.

Both processes have clear antecedents in terms of procedures and underlying principles. The most important antecedent are the various regional conferences organized in recent decades by IOM, and the regional seminars and South American conference convened by the International Labour Organization (ILO) in the 1970s.

The former Intergovernmental Committee for European Migration (ICEM) (from 1980, the Intergovernmental Committee for Migration (ICM), before becoming IOM in 1989) held a number of regional conferences and seminars which made it possible to coordinate regional government objectives and activities regarding migration priorities.

The seminars on labour migration policies organized by ILO and the Government of Colombia[6] were attended by delegates from Argentina, Bolivia, Brazil, Colombia,

---

5) Highest operational body within MERCOSUR.
6) Held in May 1978 in the city of Medellín and in November 1980 in the city of Cali.

Ecuador, Honduras, Mexico, Peru and Venezuela, and also representatives of various international organizations[7] and non-governmental organizations[8].

The purpose was to discuss and seek common views on the various migration problems in participating countries. Prominent conclusions and recommendations included the following: the treatment of the institutional aspects of labour migration policies in the region, emphasizing the need for a Latin American agreement to cover the various aspects of protecting migrant workers rights; the establishment of official channels for regulating migration flows; the monitoring and evaluation of agreements on the subject; and the coordination of institutional migration systems among the various governments.

In addition, the seminars recommended the coordination of integration policies; the retention of potential migrants and the return of skilled personnel; the collective recruitment of migrant workers; social benefits for migrants; socio-economic assistance for seasonal migrants; the regularization of undocumented migrants; educational policies for migrants; the linkage of migration flows to development and labour markets; and the improvement of migration statistics. The seminars also discussed the need to maintain a system of periodic meetings in order to foster compliance with recommendations.

Four ICEM/ICM seminars should be mentioned, in which all Member Governments participated[9]:

- The regional seminar held in Cartagena in 1983 made specific progress on consolidating an information system through the Centre for Information on Migration for Latin America, and on establishing cooperation for exchanging skilled human resources among countries of the region.

- The regional seminar of 1987 held discussions on the important relationship between migration and development; the need to establish a permanent information process among countries to ascertain the demand for and supply of skilled human resources; and the need for technical cooperation in carrying out migration policies and programmes linked to population and employment policies.

- Known as "Migration for Development", the 1990 regional seminar assembled representatives of the 18 governments. They agreed on the various links between migration and development; the reverse transfer of technology caused by migration; the necessary programming of government migration policies in conjunction with their respective development policies; the coordination of IOM with government multilateral and bilateral efforts; the expansion of migrant return programmes; the intensification of migration with capital programmes; the necessary adaptation of legal instruments and information and administration relating to migration; the need to include non-governmental sectors in migration policies; and the link between regional integration and migration.

- The 1993 seminar concentrated on regional integration and sustained development, recommending that IOM should cooperate with the technical secretariats of the various integration processes under way in the region, including the North America Free Trade Agreement and CARICOM[10], through regional technical meetings. In addition, the seminar recommended that greater efforts should be made to harmonize and/or standardize the legislative provisions on migration in the region; that subregional migration and development projects should be initiated with due consideration for the integration areas established; that the subject of migration should be linked to the United Nations World Conference on Human Rights; and that regional coordination and consultation mechanisms for migration should be intensified.

Given these antecedents, it is clear that the regional consultation processes in Latin America did not only begin in the mid-1990s to address new migration situations. The Puebla Process and the South American Forum are systematically consolidating and implementing measures

183

---

7) United Nations Development Programme (UNDP), Latin American Faculty of Social Sciences (FLACSO), Inter-American Centre for Labour Administration (CIAT), United Nations Population Fund (UNFPA), UNESCO, Simon Rodriguez Agreement, Intergovernmental Committee for European Migration (ICEM), and Employment Programme for Latin America and the Caribbean (PREALC).

8) Regional Population Centre Corporation, Central University of Venezuela, University of Medellín, Columbia University, University of Los Andes, Queens College New York, Cúcuta Refugee Reception Centre and representatives of Colombian employers' and workers' organizations.

9) Latin American Regional Seminar on Migration and Horizontal Technical Cooperation between Latin American Countries with respect to Skilled Human Resources, Cartagena, 1983; Latin American Regional Seminar, Dominican Republic, 1987; Latin American Regional Seminar, La Paz, 1990; and Latin America Regional Seminar, Punta del Este, 1993.

10) Caribbean integration process: "Caribbean Community".

already established in the region several decades ago. These processes emerged because of two sets of factors: factors which are common to this type of process in various parts of the world; and factors specific to each process.

In addition to the efforts already mentioned for better migration management, a direct initiative stemmed from the International Population Conference, held in Cairo in 1994. The Conference discussed the initiative of a group of governments to promote the holding of an international conference on migration[11].

a) The Puebla Process

In relation to the Puebla Process (see also **textbox 8.1.**), the antecedent of the Cairo Conference was fundamental. In conjunction with other governments, the Government of the United States of America proposed a series of gradual regional processes. Once developed, these processes could form the basis of an eventual international conference on the subject. Further to this proposal, the United States Government promoted the holding of the Puebla Conference in conjunction with the Governments of Mexico and Canada, and including the Central American countries.
Subsequently, the North America Free Trade Agreement was initiated as an agreement on free commercial movement, excluding the movement of persons, even though the movement of persons was considered one of the main justifications of the Agreement[12].

With the invitation of Central American countries to attend the conference, this process was initiated as a response to the major regional migration problem, namely, irregular migration[13]. These countries had already developed the OCAM Action Programme, which served as a basis for some of the activities proposed under the Puebla Process Plan of Action.

Started in 1996, the Puebla Process regroups the following countries: Belize, Canada, Costa Rica, El Salvador, Guatemala, Honduras, Mexico, Nicaragua, Panama, the United States, and, joining later, the Dominican Republic.

One of the most immediate precedents for the Puebla Process was the 1990 setting up of the above-mentioned OCAM, a regional organ established by the Migration Directors-General of Costa Rica, El Salvador, Guatemala, Honduras, Nicaragua and Panama. The aim was to develop joint initiatives on immigration issues.

The Tuxtla II Presidential Summit was held in February 1996. This meeting took up the question of migration in the region and endeavoured to provide an integrated response to population movements. This meeting may be regarded as another antecedent giving rise to the First Regional Conference on Migration, held in Puebla (Mexico) in March of the same year, in which the United States and Canada also participated. This first meeting outlined the main subjects of interest of participating countries, the course to be followed with regard to cooperation among governments, and the underlying principles of such cooperation.

The Second Regional Conference of Migration was held in Panama in March 1997. Important decisions included the formal establishment of the Regional Consultation Group; the establishment of the Coordinating Commission; and the adoption of a Plan of Action to be implemented by the regional group.

11) In its chapter on international migration, the programme of action of the Conference established as one of the objectives: to encourage cooperation and dialogue between countries of origin and countries of destination in order to maximize the benefits of migration for the persons concerned and to increase the probability that migration will have a positive impact on the development of the receiving countries and the countries of origin (International Conference on Population and Development, Programme of Action, Cairo, 1994).

12) The announcement, in February 1991, that Canada, Mexico and the United States were to negotiate a free trade agreement generated considerable speculation about its effects on migration movements. President Salinas of Mexico stated that Mexico would prefer "to export tomatoes and not Mexican tomato pickers"; President Bush of the United States said that the North American Free Trade Agreement was "the only way of reducing migration pressure" (Cornelius and Martin, 1993:485), and the United States International Trade Commission concluded that the effects of the North America Free Trade Agreement would make it possible to reduce the flow of undocumented migrants (Acevedo and Espenshade, 1992:735).

13) In this connection, the United States Congress established the "Commission for the Study of International Migration and Cooperative Economic Development" in 1986 through the Immigration Reform Control Act. The Commission was made up of members of the Democratic and Republican Parties with the aim of examining the factors prompting undocumented immigration into the United States from countries of the Western hemisphere. In the recommendations of the final report submitted in July 1990, the Commission emphasized the need for cooperation with the countries of origin of migration in order to reduce the flow of irregular immigrants.

The Third Conference was held in Ottawa (Canada) in February 1998. It agreed to organize a seminar in Tegucigalpa (Honduras) in November of the same year on the return of regional and extra-regional migrants and the reintegration of regional migrants; and a further seminar in Guatemala on consular protection and assistance during the first quarter of 1999.

The Fourth Regional Conference held in San Salvador (El Salvador) in 1999 was one of the first meetings of regional governments following the hurricane Mitch disaster and much of the meeting was devoted to this question.

The Fifth Regional Conference was held in March 2000 in Washington D.C. At this occasion, delegates reaffirmed their governments' political commitment to maintain and consolidate the Forum as an area for dialogue and cooperation.

Lastly, the Sixth Regional Conference was held in San José (Costa Rica) in March 2001. The plan of action adopted revolves around three themes: migration policies and management; human rights; and migration and development.

b) The South American Forum on Migration

The South American Forum on Migration[14] also traced its origin back to governments commitments made at the Cairo International Population Conference, but also from the development of ongoing multilateral and bilateral subregional activities, both in the Andean Community and in MERCOSUR. In this respect, the South American Forum on Migration can be considered an attempt to consolidate existing progress at subregional level rather than the beginning of a consultative process. Based on this progress, the objective is to expand and systematically plan these activities in the region.

The South American Forum started operations in Lima in 1999 through the South American Meeting on Migration, Integration and Development. This work continued in Buenos Aires (2000) and Santiago (Chile) in 2001, with the first and second South American Conferences on International Migration.

Priorities agreed on by governments at the Buenos Aires conference included the establishment of a permanent forum for coordination and consultation on migration questions; the need to unite efforts to ensure the protection, defence and promotion of migrant rights; and the urgent need to modernize migration management and national legislation (South American Conference on Migration, 2000).

At the second conference, governments made progress in consolidating the Forum, concentrating on priority subjects such as free movement within the region; trafficking; protecting migrants' rights; and also the possibility of joint policies for the benefit of South American migrants to other regions.

In December 2001, a technical seminar of the Forum was held in Cartagena de Indies (Colombia), which outlined a plan of action to be submitted at the third conference.

c) Characteristics of the Consultative Processes

Although the processes described have not been formally assessed, some of their objectives, activities and achievements can be outlined.

Common features of both processes include explicit government recognition of: (a) the close link between migration and the degree of development of countries; (b) the need for orderly and legal migration; and (c) the importance of migrants' human rights.

In operational terms, noteworthy activities include measures to combat trafficking in migrants, the exchange of information, the institutional strengthening of migration administration, and the regional harmonization of migration legislation and consular policies.

Specific achievements on the movement or lawful situation of migrants are different in each process. For the Puebla Process, unlawful migration has remained a priority element in the proceedings of the various conferences. This subject has been linked to both migrant trafficking and migrants' human rights. The process continues to be based on a consultative plan of action, the search for a common language among governments and the exchange of information. Concrete measures include programmes for repatriating irregular migrants, combating trafficking in persons and the modernization of frontier control systems.

---

14) Composed of Argentina, Bolivia, Brazil, Chile, Colombia, Ecuador, Guyana, Paraguay, Peru, Surinam, Uruguay and Venezuela.

In the South American Forum, the top priorities emerging include free movement within the region (already dealt with in the Andean Community and MERCOSUR) and the protection of migrants' human rights, with special emphasis on South American emigrants in other regions. In addition, the trafficking in persons to or from the region is considered a priority. Action plans are geared to these objectives and include coordinated proactive consular policies; the formulation of a South American protocol against trafficking; and greater freedom of movement of people within the region.

The Impact of International Agreements on Migration

A recurrent theme in the analysis of migration policies concerns the impact of international agreements on migration. In this respect, it is important to identify linkages between regional economic or commercial integration agreements and migration-specific bilateral or multilateral agreements or consensus processes.

As regards economic or commercial agreements, it is important to distinguish between those which include the movement of persons as a factor in integration (MERCOSUR, Andean Community, Central American Common Market) and those which do not (NAFTA). Notwithstanding this differentiation, generally speaking, Latin American migration would appear to be more closely linked to structural economic and labour market changes than to the commercial integration areas which have developed in recent years.

During the late 1990s, Latin American emigration changed from a visibly growing trend to an explosive exodus. The background to this phenomenon can be found in the socio-economic "pending agenda" facing Latin America at the end of the decade (Ocampo, 2001).

The early 1990s were characterized by widespread optimism. Liberalization of trade and national financial markets and the growing liberalization of capital flows, sometimes accompanied by structural reforms in tax systems and broad privatization processes – these factors made it possible to correct fiscal imbalances, end inflation, increase exports and direct foreign investment flows as well as to strengthen and initiate economic integration processes. Nevertheless, the result has been frustrating in terms of economic growth, productive conversion, greater productivity and reduction of inequalities (ECLAC, 2001).

Regional production in the early 1970s was growing at about 6 per cent annually; towards the end of that decade, it fell to 1.5 per cent and then to zero during the 1980s. During the early 1990s, production recovered to 3 per cent and peaked in 1997 at about 5.3 per cent, dropping sharply in 1998 and sinking into negative growth in 1999 almost throughout Latin America, followed by a weak recovery in 2000 (Franco and Sáinz, 2001).

Against this economic background, labour markets have shown limited capacity to generate productive jobs, with growing unemployment, a concentration of jobs in the informal sector, and a widening income gap between skilled and non-skilled labour (Ocampo, 2000).

When the rate of growth in Latin America declined towards the end of the 1990s, there were increases in overt unemployment, the percentages of non-permanent paid labour, and the number of workers without a work contract and social security (Altenburg et al., 2001).

The North America Free Trade Agreement

The North America Free Trade Agreement (NAFTA) does not explicitly include the question of migration, but discussions on the effects of the Agreement on the movement of persons have been and continue to be of great importance. The possible impact of NAFTA on migration gave rise to a number of analyses and forecasts during its initial stage.

In principle, there was general consensus on the effects of migrant expulsions in rural areas of Mexico (Ortiz Miranda, 1993; Acevedo and Espenshade, 1992). Models such as that applied by Levy and Van Winsbergen established different perspectives over a nine-year time-frame: with immediate NAFTA liberalization, there would be improvements in economic efficiency but also substantial migration – some 700,000 persons – in a single year. In a progressive scenario, the number of emigrants leaving rural areas annually would be around 200,000 (Hinojosa Ojeda and Robinson, 1991). Other studies predicted the emigration of 800,000 workers from rural areas in a scenario of total liberalization (Hinojosa Ojeda and Robinson, 1991). Calva's analyses predicted the displacement of 15 million persons from the Mexican agricultural sector during the 1990s (1992). Luis Tellez, Under-Secretary for Planning in the Mexican Ministry of Agriculture and Hydraulic Resources, considered that some 15 million Mexican farm workers would emigrate over a period of two decades, while about 1.4 million would move by the year 2002 as a result of free trade and agrarian reforms (Martin, 1993; Cornelius, 1992).

Notwithstanding these forecasts, some analysts suggested different reasons for not overestimating the impact of NAFTA on rural emigration from Mexico. Their arguments were based on the fact that many Mexican inhabitants of rural areas had already diversified their income sources and that the free trade area could induce more United States farmers to expand into Mexico (Cornelius and Martin, *op. cit.*).

There were various interpretations of the destination and patterns of this probable migration. Firstly, reference was made to the inevitable rural-urban migration to Mexican cities (Ortiz Miranda, 1993). Nevertheless, urban labour markets only have a limited absorption capacity despite the probable increase in industrial demand generated by NAFTA. Thus, flows would be directed to other destinations. The assembly industry on the northern frontier might attract labour, given the 500,000 jobs created in the 1980s. However, the low wages and hard working conditions offered in this industry could represent possible reasons to emigrate to the United States.

According to the forecasts of various analysts, this emigration flow would increase over the first 15 years and then stabilize (Acevedo and Espenshade, 1992; Hinojosa Ojeda, 1994; Marshall, 1993). Despite these projections, others argued that widespread internal migration in Mexico caused by economic restructuring would not necessarily result in greater international emigration.

This proposition was maintained by Cornelius and Martin, who stated that there were no reasons why Mexican internal migration to areas producing export crops in the north-west and to the assembly plants on the United States frontier should automatically result in international migration. Two reasons are put forward: in the first case, family recruitment strategy in regions of expansion such as Sinaloa was not encouraging emigration to the United States as this usually involved single men; in the second case, evidence suggested that most assembly plant workers came from neighbouring regions, i.e., not from the centre and south of Mexico, where the greatest unemployment from NAFTA was expected. A survey of 1,200 assembly plant workers revealed that only 7.3 per cent hoped to work in the United States (Cornelius and Martin, 1993).

Notwithstanding these analyses, experts agreed that migration to the United States would continue since the wage gap between the two countries might narrow with the development of NAFTA but would never close completely. In any event, it is important to remember that labour migration is not simply a response to differences in wages. In Europe, wage levelling was not necessary to curb migration from Spain, Portugal and Italy to the north. The so-called "hope factor" in the economic recovery and stability of the society of origin may act as a variable key in the retention of potential migrants (Cornelius and Martin, 1993).

Beyond these structural determinants of migration movements, integration processes such as NAFTA need to develop immediate policies or actions in order to prevent the integration process from promoting migration and even to reduce such flows in its application.

Firstly, despite the disruptive effect of NAFTA on small-scale agriculture in Mexico, total emigration to the United States would have been greater in the absence of trade liberalization (Cornelius and Martin, 1993). For the time being, free trade and foreign investment are the main stimuli in generating jobs to keep potential migrants in Mexico. But it is important that the Mexican rural economy is liberalized gradually, thereby preserving some protection for small farmers.

NAFTA and other subregional integration processes also need to consider the linkage between labour legislation and trade. Labour legislation was a vital element in the policies and institutions adopted by industrialized democracies in order to produce the longest period of more or less equitable prosperity between 1945 and 1974 (Marshall, 1993). Some critics maintain that it is difficult to link labour legislation to trade. Nevertheless, the experience of the United States would appear to belie this view, provided meticulous control is exercised in order to ensure effective compliance. Similarly, labour legislation has improved economic efficiency and reduced job-cutting in most developed democratic societies by eliminating subsidies to companies that do not pay acceptable wages or provide minimum working conditions (Marshall, 1993). Harmonization and uniform enforcement of labour legislation in member countries in the integration area can reduce the factors promoting irregular migration based on the exploitation of immigrant labour. Such exploitation both forces migrants out of their countries of origin and attracts irregular migrants in the country of arrival.

More recent analyses of the effects of NAFTA on migration flows between Mexico and the United States maintain that these flows are not caused by the Agreement itself but the subjacent processes of productive conversion. More specifically, labour migration in recent years between these two countries can be explained by the changing dynamics of labour markets in both countries. According to Canales (2000), these changes are characterized by a growing polarization and segmentation of labour markets in the United States, and by greater insecurity and poor employment conditions in Mexico. Both processes seem to be creating a dynamic for the expulsion and attraction of migrants independent of the trade agreement between the two countries.

Economic and Commercial Integration Processes in Central America

Economic and commercial integration processes in Central America have had little impact on migration movements. Whereas total intra-regional and extra-regional migration were at similar levels in the 1970s, currently over 90 per cent of Central America migration concerns persons leaving the region for other countries, primarily the United States (Maguid, 2001).

The Central American Common Market has made some progress towards a free trade zone (with the exception of Honduras) and to setting common external tariffs. This integration process aims at achieving compatibility between inward integration and outward integration. The economic and social effect of eliminating export subsidies in the free zones in 2003 is still not known (ECLAC, 2001).

Notwithstanding the progress and questions raised by this process, it does not appear to be instrumental in the migration flows observed over the past decade nor in the changes in flow. This migration can mainly be attributed to other causes, such as population displacement caused by social and political exclusion processes; establishment of production and consumption patterns that harm the ecosystem; institutional reforms which have modified the state's role as a generator of employment, provider of services and regulator of markets, thereby impacting people's living and working conditions and reproduction patterns; greater labour flexibility and its effects on labour market conditions; and the reduction of geographical distances in cultural terms as a result of globalization (CELADE/ECLAC, 1999).

For labour markets, it is possible to identify both the forces of attraction in the more developed countries and forces of expulsion from most of the Central American countries. Unlike Canada and the United States, wages in Central American countries have declined in real terms. There is growing unemployment and a greater proportion of jobs in sectors of lower average productivity (ECLAC, 1996). The unemployment situation worsened rapidly when recession recurred in 1995 and 1996.

In earlier decades, migration movements were mainly forced movements arising from armed conflicts; modern causes appear to be determined by variables such as macro-economic conditions, the dynamics of labour markets, the imbalance between demographic growth and job-creation capacity, the inequitable distribution of income and the exclusion of broad sectors of the population (Maguid, 2001).

The Case of South America

In South America, the impact of economic integration agreements on migration is essentially determined by the structural economic conditions of the countries concerned, the impact on labour markets and, in some cases, by armed conflicts.

The main migration processes among South American countries have traditionally been made up of flows from Colombia to Venezuela, from Bolivia, Chile, Paraguay and Uruguay to Argentina, and from Brazil to Paraguay.

Of the 1,309,956 intra-regional migrants in the Southern Cone during the 1990s, a total of 818,363 were in Argentina and 203,970 in Brazil. In the same period, 927,992 intra-regional migrants were registered in the Andean Community, 650,011 in Venezuela alone. Of these, 598,893 are from Colombia (IMILA).

The scale of migration between these countries does not seem to have been affected significantly by MERCOSUR migration measures, the implementation of the Andean Instrument on Labour Migration, or even the increase in intra-regional trade.

As regards macro-economic effects, some countries continued to stagnate and face problems achieving significant growth within the partial recovery of the Latin American economy in 2000. Growth rates in Argentina, Ecuador and Colombia were below the regional average (Calcagno *et al.,* 2001).

Argentina is encountering stagnation problems primarily in its external sector. Severe indebtedness and the dena-tionalization of many companies mean that net payments of interest and profits constitute a structural burden on its balance of payments. In 2000, the domestic political situation in Ecuador worsened and sharp devaluation occurred. This in turn had a considerable impact on inflation and the regressive redistribution of income. The continuation and worsening of the internal conflict in Colombia have been preventing an increase in oil production and slowing down the recovery of investment (Calcagno *et al.,* 2001).

The increase in unemployment is a clear factor in Argentina, which traditionally had an average unemployment rate of under 4 per cent up to the 1990s. Unemployment reached 12.9 per cent in 1999 and 14.3 per cent in 2000 (Franco and Sáinz, 2001), and exceeded 20 per cent in January 2002. Growing job insecurity is also apparent in countries such as Ecuador, where non-permanent employment increased by about 45.1 per cent in 1997, and in Colombia, where it rose from 6.6 per cent in 1980 to 20 per cent in 1997 (Franco and Sáinz, 2001). Against this background, the emigration of South Americans has increased rapidly during the past decade despite the development of regional integration processes. This is noticeable throughout the region, with striking examples in countries such as Argentina, Ecuador and Colombia, where the general effect of the economic crisis may be observed. However, they each present different characteristics in terms of the immediate causes of emigration and the composition of migration flows.

As regards emigration flows, and despite the relative reliability of available data[15], the crisis has had an obvious effect on Argentine emigration, even though Argentina continues to receive substantial immigration from other South American countries. The entry and departure balance for Argentines over the past five years has been very irregular, but a clear negative trend is nevertheless apparent. Thus, the balance recorded at the country's main international airport shifted from -19,756 in 1995, to -5,102 in 1996, falling again to -14,436 in 1997, becoming positive in 1998 with a balance of 17,967, only to become negative again in 1999 with -8,110[16]. Over the five-year period, this irregular pattern indicates an average of about 6,000 Argentines emigrating annually, a figure which fell sharply in 2000 to a negative balance of -87,068[17] Argentines who remained abroad; the figure for 2001 was -62,880, and there was a negative balance of -23,198 for the month of January 2002 alone[18] (see also **textbox 10.2.**).

15) Given that census data provide us with a more precise view of the population as a whole, and that this emigration process is occurring at the end of the decade, ongoing entry and departure statistics have been employed in order to establish annual balances, as well as other types of information, such as opinion polls, to establish the motives and wishes expressed by migrants.

16) Data from the Argentine National Department for Migration (monthly reports).

17) In this case, there would appear to be a discrepancy in relation to another information source: that of the computerized system, which provides a negative balance of -79,773 for 2000. Although sub-stantially different, this does not affect the main observable balance.

18) According to estimates by the Argentine National Department for Migration.

TEXTBOX 10.2.

Focus on Argentina - the effects of the economic crisis on migration[19]

The banging of saucepans resounded through the centre of the quiet Galician town of Vigo like an echo of Buenos Aires. Hundreds of Argentines were protesting, not this time against the corralito (monetary restrictions) or the judges, but to officialize their migration status. They are among the stream of Argentine nationals leaving for other countries, just like thousands of erstwhile South American immigrants who came to Argentina and who are increasingly heading back home.

Despite being made up of incoming settlers, Argentina is now more like an exit port. This historic change may have intensified in recent months and reveals special characteristics. Reasons go well beyond simplistic explanations and affect not only the present but also the future.

Migrant children begging from motorists

A first striking observation is the growing number of Chileans, Peruvians, Bolivians and Paraguayans who left Argentina for their respective countries in December 2001. This event usually occurs at the end of practically each year when migrants go back to visit their families, but might well now become an actual return to the home countries. Those involved are generally migrants who arrived relatively recently, attracted by job opportunities in sectors left vacant by Argentines and by the prospect of sending money home to their families from their earnings. They constitute a highly mobile form of labour migration and respond to new labour market opportunities, which is to be expected

given the current economic situation. This indeed pays tribute to the theory of the "silent invasion", put forward by some xenophobic commentators in recent years. What we are currently witnessing are "transmigrations", which are taking place all over the world as people move rapidly to seek better alternatives in work areas that transcend borders.

This also partly explains the exodus of Argentines who are unemployed, disillusioned or simply tired of the prevailing economic and political instability.

Neither of these two types of emigration is casual or spontaneous. As often occurs with economic migration, both types of emigration have been accelerating in recent months as the crisis deepens.

The flow of Argentines leaving the country has increased in the last two years (2000-2002). From 1997 to 1999, the differences between the total number of Argentines leaving and those entering through "Ezeiza" international airport of Buenos Aires show that 5,000 people remained abroad each year. In 2000, the negative balance jumped to 80,000; although the final figures are not yet available, this number seems to have remained constant in 2001. According to a survey carried out in November 2001 by the *Sociedad de Estudios Laborales* (SEL) in the country's main cities (Federal Capital, Greater Buenos Aires, Córdoba, Rosario, Mendoza and Tucumán), 2 per cent of those questioned said that they had made up their minds and taken practical steps to emigrate in the next twelve months. This means that about half a million people were fully engaged in the process of emigrating.

The same survey reported that 37 per cent had chosen Spain as their destination, 18 per cent the United States, and 11 per cent Italy. If these population movements eventually take place, a new equilibrium will be reached between the number of Argentines in Spain and Italy and the number of people from those two countries currently living in Argentina. At present, there are believed to be approximately ten Spaniards and twenty Italians in Argentina for every Argentine residing in Spain or Italy.

The differences lie in the composition of the migratory flows: the Argentines emigrating now are better educated than the European immigrants who arrived in the country in the post-war era.

But those are not the only destinations chosen by the departing Argentines: Poland, Israel, New Zealand, Japan, Canada, Mexico, not to mention neighbouring countries such as Uruguay, Chile and Brazil, are also feeling the presence of these new immigrants, who are upsetting traditional trends. According to available data and estimates, a projected US$ 10 billion will be required to resettle and educate the estimated flow of 500,000 Argentine emigrants over this period (of whom 20 per cent would have completed higher education and 50 per cent secondary education).

But even with the enormous cost implications for Argentina and the input it represents for host countries, the situation is far from rosy for emigrants leaving without obtaining either the nationality or a legal residence permit for the country of destination. Both Spain and Italy have recently passed laws imposing heavy restrictions on irregular migrants. Similarly, the United States have hardened their policy since the attacks of 11 September 2001 and at least 300,000 irregular migrants face the possibility of being detained or deported. Furthermore, the incoming Argentine emigrants do not necessarily match the unmet labour requirements in the host countries and will probably end up doing jobs they would not touch in their own country.

Meanwhile, many Argentines have either not decided to leave or are determined to stay in the country - 98 per cent according to the above-mentioned survey. They also say that they are fed up with the *corralito,* which has robbed them or their savings. Others are tired of looking for work and not finding any; a growing number of other people say they do not know if they will have anything to eat tomorrow. This exasperation is expressed through unusual reactions unrelated to explanations of the current crisis which suggest that the Argentine problem is due to a kind of opportunistic and greedy individualism among people lacking a sense of the common good. What we are in fact seeing these days among vast sectors of the population is exactly the opposite. The spontaneous call for changes has exploded into saucepan banging, roadblocks and pressure on supermarkets, leading to the reappearance of partici-patory movements such as neighbourhood gatherings, groups of demonstrators or virtual networks. These people have no partisan flags or organized structures but have plenty of spirit. More inclined to protest than to propose, these Argentines do not intend to emigrate for the time being and seem to be trying to build a different world, seeking solutions to common problems. When asked why they are mobilized, many of these people cannot voice any practical suggestions and sometimes merely express a wish: "Because I do not want my children to have to leave our country !".

Ecuador is a traditional migration country. Ecuadorians constitute the second largest South American national group registered in the United States after Colombians (ECLAC-IOM, 1998). In the 1970s, emigration to the United States grew at an average rate of 8.5 per cent. During that decade, between 4,000 and 5,000 Ecuadorians entered the United States, and this trend grew in the 1980s. Nevertheless, Ecuador has in its turn attracted Colombians and Peruvians over the past decade (León Albán, 1997).

Ecuadorian emigrants originate primarily from rural areas although the starting point for many is in the cities. Ecuador's migration balance is negative[20]. A total of 531,987 Ecuadorians would appear to have left their country and not returned between January 1992 and April 2001: two-thirds of these emigrants (approximately 350,000) appear to have left during the past three years.

According to the analyses and hypotheses developed on these movements, up to 1997, the emigrants were primarily middle-class and self-employed workers and, to a lesser extent, farmers. This emigration would appear to have been prompted basically by the effects of state transfor-mation and private sector adjustments on wages and unemployment levels (León Albán, 1997). Since 1998, emigration has basically concerned the indigenous peasant sectors. This process (in the case of migration to Spain) is notable in that it is reviving an emigration trend which practically ended in the 1920s: the transatlantic movements of rural workers between Europe and the Americas, although, today the movement is in the opposite direction.

In **Colombia,** the internal armed conflict should be added to the common factors determining migration in Latin America. The conflict has grown over the past ten years in terms of the geographic expansion of fighting fronts[21] (see also **textbox 10.3.**).

191

---

19) Extract from an article published in the Argentine daily *Clarin.*
20) In the case of foreigners, the positive balance for entry into Ecuador is double that of emigrating foreigners, but figures are unreliable since 87 per cent of this balance would appear to be made up of Colombians entering via the frontier where there has been high under-registration on the Colombian side.
21) In 1986, the Armed Revolutionary Forces of Colombia (FARC) had 3,600 fighters and 32 fronts: by 1995, the number of fighters had risen to 7,000 and the fronts to 60. The other significant guerrilla group, the National Liberation Army, grew over the same period from 800 fighters and 11 fronts to 3,000 fighters and 32 fronts (Rangel Suárez, 1998).

TEXTBOX 10.3.

Managing Migration in Colombia

Colombia is a good example of the increasing repercussions and ramifications of migratory flows. Migration is now a central part of everyday life in the country. Unfortunately, some of the current trends highlight a certain pessimism, which seems justified by the growing exodus of Colombian nationals. According to government statistics *(Anuario estadístico de entradas y salidas internacionales)*, some 280,000 Colombians left the country in 2000 and have not returned. Coupled with alarming news of the human rights violations more and more migrants suffer at the hands of criminal networks, this provides a somewhat sombre perspective on the issue of migration. However, there are opportunities in the short, medium and long-term for better migration management.

Although the brain drain of skilled Colombians reflects negative trends, the increase in remittances to families left behind is becoming an important aspect of the country's economy.

Furthermore, the exodus can lead to commercial and cultural opportunities and a closer link between Colombians living in the country and those who have chosen to live abroad. The private sector has already prepared for this. Many Colombian companies are now establishing branch offices abroad in places with large Colombian communities. In addition, the potential political influence of these communities, for example the Colombian community in the United States, is beginning to show its strength. The involvement of the Colombian community in matters such as the Temporary Protection System of the US Government can help reinforce initiatives set up by the Colombian Government.

Labour migration schemes constitute another challenge on the road to orderly and humane migration flows. A recent example is the agreement signed between the Governments of Colombia and Spain. Labour migration not only strengthens relations between countries of origin, transit and destination, but it is an essential tool for protecting the rights of migrants entering a job market in a foreign country in order to provide stable and dignified employment.

The trafficking of human beings demands greater preventive efforts as well as assistance and reintegration for the victims. Recent statistics show that Colombia follows only Brazil and the Dominican Republic as the countries in Latin America with the highest number of trafficking victims. Because there are no measures to fight trafficking, action and policies are urgently needed. IOM is working with the government to provide technical training and assistance to officials. It is also vital to protect the victims and to arrest, prosecute and convict criminals. At the same time, IOM is planning an information campaign to alert potential victims of the risks of being deceived by traffickers and stands ready to assist the government in providing protection and reintegration assistance to the victims.

It is encouraging to see that the Colombian Government and civil society are on the same road to better-managed migration, supported by international cooperation. The ongoing discussions on the trafficking and smuggling of human beings through meetings and seminars, the training of diplomatic staff, the ratification of international instruments, and updating domestic legislation – all these are positive signs of Colombian society's will to tackle migration matters. These steps are an important beginning for the long road that lies ahead.

The recent high-level technical consultations meeting in Cartagena de Indias, as part of the South American Conference on Migration, highlighted the leadership role taken by Colombia in regional efforts to manage migration.

The guerrilla movement has evolved in several respects: from being essentially ideological in character, it is now politically pragmatic and rules over large parts of the country; from having scant resources, it is now highly solvent financially, mainly based on its commercial association with drugs traffic; and from a position of limited military capacity, it now displays its power in various parts of the country.

Thus, the number of paramilitary groups has multiplied, with the result that a police problem has become a political-military problem. The policy of terror imposed by the paramilitary groups has given rise to large-scale forced population displacement. At present, Colombia is characterized by one of the highest levels of internal displacement in the world, involving an approximate total of 2,100,000 persons (Rangel Suárez, 1998) (see also **chapter 7**).

Combined with ordinary criminality, the armed conflict led to an annual homicide rate in 1994 of 78 persons for every 100,000 inhabitants[22]. In 1997, it was estimated that 69 per cent of all murders were perpetrated by paramilitaries, 24 per cent by the guerrillas, and 7 per cent by state forces. In addition, the abduction industry is growing steadily. Abduction is used without discrimination by guerrilla groups and ordinary criminals. In 1996, 45 per cent of all abductions committed throughout the world occurred in Colombia, with an average of four abductions a day. This situation directly impacts on Colombian emigration.

In surveys conducted among Colombian residents in the United States, 76 per cent of interviewees mentioned violence as the reason for their decision to emigrate; only 24 per cent referred to economic reasons. Some 80 per cent of emigrants were ranked as middle-class, 5 per cent as upper class, and 15 per cent as lower class ("Casa" Fundacion, 2001).

The migration balance for Colombians leaving via the country's main airports[23] for the period 1996-2000 showed close to half a million emigrants, most of whom left for the United States (353,055) and Europe (114,292).

The difference between the two destinations is that Colombian emigration to the United States tripled between 1996 and 2000 (from 37,524 to 105,315), while emigration to Europe doubled over the same period (from 18,139 to 41,178). These figures have a special dynamic of their own if we consider Spain, where emigration by Colombians increased tenfold, from 2,576 in 1996 to 29,593 in 2000. The growth in Colombian emigration has been clearly confirmed over the past two years: the balance recorded for the period May 1999-May 2000 (152,700 persons) was three times higher than the balance for the previous year.

Another example illustrating the differences in Latin American migration processes is that of Brazil. Up to 1980, Brazilians would migrate to different regions of Latin America. After 1980, a new trend began with migration to various destinations: Australia, Europe, Asia, the United States and, to a lesser extent, Canada. The reason for the change in the migrants' destination was mainly the socio-economic deterioration affecting the whole of Latin America and the ease with which long-distance displacement can take place. The United States and Japan are the destinations of the new Brazilian migration flows. In Japan, the migrants are in general the so-called *nikkeijin* – the children, grand-children and great grandchildren of Japanese (Katsuco Kawamura, 2000). Brazil is estimated to have received US$ 1.5 billion in remittances from Japan alone in 1999. Like other Latin American migration patterns, Brazilian emigration has been caused by worsening opportunities on national labour markets. However, economic liberalization and the growth in external investment have produced a flow of immigrants into Brazil. Foreign professionals, technicians and executives, generally connected with multinational corporations, increased tenfold over the period from 1993 to 2001, when they totalled 16,297; of these, 19.3 per cent were American, 12.7 per cent British, 7.5 per cent Chinese, 5.7 per cent French, 4.4 per cent Japanese, 4 per cent German. The remainder were from different European and Latin American countries.

Conclusion

During the past decade, Latin America's migration processes and institutional responses resemble those in other regions of the world, but with specific historical reference points and causes.

Migration flows have diversified as they have in other regions. The linkage between these changes and both globalization and regional integration processes is being investigated. In addition, attempts are being made to replace unilateral policies with various consensual institutional responses to tackle migration management problems. As regards the linkages between migration, globalization and regional integration processes, the Latin American experience may be compared with that of other "emerging" countries in other parts of the world.

Economic globalization took place in Latin American countries through structural adjustment programmes, accompanied by privatization policies, trade liberalization and movements of capital. This enabled Latin American countries to recover economically following the "lost decade" of the 1980s. This trend stagnated in the late 1990s but began to recover in some countries as from 2000. In this process, economic growth was not accompanied by positive social benefits since incomes and employment fell in most countries of the region and there was widespread job insecurity. The deterioration of labour markets in turn leads to higher poverty indices, social marginality, public insecurity, and to a social decline among broad sectors of the middle classes. The sharp

22) This rate is much higher than other countries with high levels of violence, such as Jamaica (28) or Russia (20) (Montenegro and Posada, 2001).
23) Data from the Directorate for Foreigners, Administrative Department of Security (DAS).

increase in emigration from Latin America over the past decade may be placed against this background. In other words, the effects of economic globalization have clearly tended to drive people out of countries of the region.

It is still too early to draw valid conclusions on the impact of regional commercial integration processes on the movements of persons. Nevertheless, the movement of capital, technology and goods arising from the integration processes does not seem to have had a noticeable impact on migration to date except in a few sectors involving skilled human resources. The expected retention of potential migrants is not yet apparent.

The growth in Latin American emigration flows to other regions in the 1990s was accompanied by a marked increase in remittances from migrants to their countries of origin. As observed in other parts of the world, these remittances have enabled migrants' families to improve their well-being but yield little impact on development (see also **chapter 12**). Moreover, in the long term, these remittances may set an example and encourage other members of as yet non-migrant families to emigrate (Tapinos, 2000).

In terms of government response, Latin American migration flows have changed considerably over the last decade. These changes have been accompanied by new government perceptions of migration issues and the adoption of new policies. As elsewhere in the world, a "migration governability crisis" has emerged owing to weaker state power over the movement of persons and the advent of new social agents in defining policies in each country. This crisis demonstrates the growing difficulties states face in managing migration alone. This in turn had led to the growth of alternative migration management approaches, such as bilateral and multilateral agreements and understandings.

In Latin America, these practices have been developed over the past 50 years. However, they increased during the 1990s through bilateral agreements and understandings and by including migration in subregional integration processes. Finally migration management was also formally included in consultation processes such as the Puebla Process or the South American Forum on International Migration.

In terms of impact on migration, it is important to distinguish between the effects on flows and on migration governability in the various countries. Neither migration agreements and understandings nor the regional integration economic and trade agreements would appear to have had a significant effect on migration flows for the following

two reasons: agreements and understandings have normally been reached to influence already developed migration patterns; migration flows are more closely influenced by macro-economic dynamics and changes in the labour markets of these countries than by the specific economic effects of regional integration processes.

The gradual move from unilateral policies to intragovernmental understandings and agreements clearly represents a step forward in making policy more legitimate and effective, based on greater common responsibility between countries of origin and destination on migration questions.

It is difficult to predict whether the multilateral approach will substitute for unilateral migration practices and policies or be frozen in what experts have defined as a sort of "diplomatic hypocrisy" (Martin, 1989). Will bilateral progress succeed in overcoming the impediments of legal administration? Even if bilateral or multilateral agreements are complied with, will it be possible to genuinely move from "exhortation" to legislation. What will be the true effect on the migrant? More freedom of movement? More respect for human rights? Or more restrictions? In this regard, Costa Lascoux (1992) stated that "it is easier to formulate an agreement on a coercive control system than a common asylum policy" at government meetings.

As with unilateral approaches, multilateral and bilateral migration management or governability can also encounter obstacles on the path to legislation. Frequently, the agreement is neutralized by regulations which are subsequently limited by national legislation; this legislation may in turn be influenced by political and economic pressures. Moreover, legislation can be applied inadequately through administrative corruption and/or the anti-migrant prejudice of the officials responsible for its enforcement.

These questions may undermine optimism about the development and effective results of these new bilateral and multilateral areas. However, the open dialogue and search for common ground in recent years on a subject traditionally charged with distrust and conflict have been very important. There has been progress towards accepting the diversity of migration in a context of equality and towards comprehensive protection of migrants' human rights. These elements allow "mutually-agreed governability" to be considered a legitimate and effective component of migration management in an increasingly globalized world. Therefore, these agreements and consultation processes represent a crucial step in institutional response, reflecting joint government responsibility vis-à-vis current

CHAPTER 11

Driving Forces of Labour Migration in Asia

In terms of contemporary migration issues, what distinguishes Asia from other regions is the rapid growth of a market-led intra-regional migration system. Except for the long festering ethnic war in Sri Lanka, the region witnessed relatively few refugee-producing violent conflicts in the last decade. Asia featured two prominent events: the opening up to the global economy of two giant economies, China and India; and the financial crisis that put the brakes on the rapid growth of the "tiger" economies in South-East Asia.

With the end of the cold war, regional energies have turned to modernizing productive infrastructures and producing goods for the global market, absorbing huge amounts of foreign capital and generating employment and higher per capita incomes in the process. With the exhaustion of their labour reserves, Hong Kong, Japan, Malaysia, the Republic of Korea, Singapore and Taiwan[1] progressively turned to external sources to meet labour shortages. This led to the rapid emergence of a regional labour migration system which has withstood the financial crisis and seems to be becoming permanent despite of avowed policy of all the states not to allow permanent settlement.

External migration remains insignificant to this day in the huge continental states with their vast reserves of labour. In China and India, growing mobility of migrant labour has thus far been largely contained within their borders. However, elsewhere in the region the uneven pace of industrialization has led to greater and more diversified cross-border movements. Although many Asian workers found their way to the oil-rich region of the Persian Gulf, the 1990s saw more workers moving to better-paying jobs closer to home, notably in South-East Asia. Aside from Japan, the more attractive destinations became Hong Kong, the Republic of Korea, Malaysia, Singapore and Taiwan. Being more remote from the sub-region, workers in the Indian sub-continent largely went to Saudi Arabia, Kuwait, and the other Gulf States, but the number of Bangladeshi plantation workers in Malaysia rose considerably, and there have been increases in Sri Lankan domestic helpers in Singapore, and Nepalese construction workers in the

Republic of Korea. At the same time, the traditional migration front along Thailand's borders with Myanmar and Laos became active as the country's per capita income jumped far ahead of that of its immediate neighbours.

The Big Picture

From 1995 to 1999, some 2 million Asian workers were reported reportedly left their countries every year under contracts to work abroad. Several categories of other migrants should be added to this average: at least another 600,000 people left without registering, because it was not required (as is the case with professionals in India); some people were admitted as "trainees"; people who left for tourism or business but found jobs abroad (based on numbers who overstayed their visas); and people who crossed borders clandestinely but later registered and became documented when the receiving states granted amnesty and a chance to acquire a legal status.

A comparison of outflows from countries of origin and counted foreign populations (stocks) in destination countries shows that the migration system is characterized by high turn-over or relatively short stay of migrant workers. For example, almost 500,000 Filipinos registered employment contracts in Hong Kong over the period 1997-2000, but the Hong Kong authorities reported a Filipino worker population of just over 151,000 in 2001. Many had obviously returned again and again, registering every time their contracts were renewed. This pattern holds true also for other migration destinations of Asian workers within Asia and the Middle East.

Table 11.1. presents estimates of the scale of labour emigration[2]. Over 1.2 million of the 2.6 million migrants originated from southern Asian countries. Many of these

2) The size of the labour migration movements for the entire region is very difficult to establish because of the weakness of the monitoring systems on both sides of the migration chain, unpoliced borders and the prevalence of illegals working among those admitted for other purposes. Important movements such as those across the Nepal-Indian border, across the long Myanmar-Thai border, across the Straits of Malacca between Indonesia and Malaysia, and from the Chinese mainland to Taiwan, have largely gone unrecorded and are seldom reckoned in studies of migration in the region. Even where there is closer monitoring, the reported data are often hard to compare because of differences in concepts and measures used. To draw a rough map of the recent developments one has to rely on assorted administrative reports coming from emigration control bodies in the major Asian countries of origin and attempt to validate them from the immigration statistics of the countries of destination. Especially in the latter countries, national censuses would have been more reliable sources but they are conducted too infrequently to serve our purpose.

1) Throughout this text, "Hong Kong" refers to the Hong Kong Special Administrative Region of China; "Taiwan" refers to the Taiwan Province of China; "the Republic of Korea" and "South Korea" are used indifferently

workers followed earlier compatriots who went to the Persian Gulf region to perform all types of service and maintenance jobs, build houses, serve as store-keepers or security guards. But the period did see a small but significant flow of professionals and technical workers heading for North America and Europe. There were also significant flows to South-East Asia to work in plantations in Malaysia, as domestic workers in Singapore, and in the building industry in the Republic of Korea. Some were too poor to venture far away, such as the many thousands of farmers from Nepal's valleys who migrated regularly during planting and harvesting seasons in north-east India, as well as young women who were trafficked for sexual exploitation and ended up, for instance, in Bombay's brothels.

Another 1.3 million migrant workers came from South-East Asia, notably Filipinos, Indonesians, Thais, Burmese, and Vietnamese. Young Indonesian men easily found their way to Malaysia to take up unskilled and semi-skilled jobs in the building industry, helping to construct its new capital city and the world's tallest building in Kuala Lumpur. Women found their way to Saudi Arabia to work as domestics. While the Philippines and Thailand also sent large numbers of workers to fill unskilled jobs in neighbouring countries and the Gulf States, their migrant workforces also included large numbers of nurses, engineers, computer systems developers, geodetic surveyors, teachers, artists and entertainers.

TABLE 11.1.

Estimated Annual Emigration of Labour from Asian Countries

Country	Data available	Recorded average annual labour emigration[1] (in 000's)	Adjustment[2] Required for Excluded or Undocumented flows (in 000's)	Main destination countries/regions
South Asia				
India[3]	1995-98	400	+200	Gulf, USA, East Asia
Bangladesh	1995-99	263	+53	Gulf, SE Asia, India
Pakistan	1995-98	127	+25	Gulf, USA, Western Europe
Sri Lanka	1996-99	163	+16	Gulf, Singapore, India
Nepal				Honk Kong, South Korea
South-East Asia				
Indonesia	1995-99	288	+14	Malaysia, Gulf
Philippines	1995-99	426[4]	+128	SE Asia, Gulf, USA, Europe
Thailand	1995-99	193		Taiwan, Japan,
Others (Myamar, Vietnam, Malaysia, Laos, etc.)		32[5]	+120	Thailand, Singapore, Australia, Europe
China	2000	102[6]	+100	Japan, South Korea, SE Asia, USA

Notes:

1) From record of workers registering temporary employment contracts with authorities before departure. Does not include those emigrating for permanent settlement in foreign countries; students who work; undocumented workers leaving under the guise of tourism, business or other non-work purposes.

2) Adjustments are based on several sources including destination country data on foreign nationals admitted on temporary work visas like the H1B in the USA, the numbers "overstaying" their visas, registration by undocumented foreign workers (e.g. in Thailand and in Malaysia), and estimates of undocumented foreign workers in other regions.

3) India: data includes only those registered by Protector of Emigrants; graduates of tertiary education are not required to register, nor those with previous experience working abroad.

4) Philippine law requires all departing migrant workers to register with authorities including those who have previously registered and are renewing contracts. The figure showed is based on "new hires" only in order to avoid double counting an average of 136,000 re-hired workers every year.

5) Data only available from Vietnam.

6) As of the end of November 2001 it was reported that Chinese contracting companies had 460,000 employees working abroad. From this stock data, we estimate an annual outflow at 92,000. To this figures can be added annual placements of 10,000 individuals reported by authorized overseas employment service agents.

Source:

Statistics compiled from reports of migration bureaux and author's estimates of undocumented migrant populations.

Practically all these workers found their jobs through private recruitment companies who linked up with job brokers in Taipei, Singapore, Hong Kong, Kuwait or Riyadh. These employment agents were known to have charged exorbitant fees for their services but were instrumental in expanding the opportunities abroad for migrant workers.

The recorded flows for the two periods (1990-1994 and 1995-1999) show that gross emigration rose at an annual rate of 6 per cent in the region as a whole. This means that migration grew twice as fast on average than the labour force in the countries of origin, justifying the claim that mobility has risen significantly in some parts of the region. This growth was initially even higher in South-East Asia, but the financial crisis which hit the region in 1997, and whose effects are still being felt in some places today, put the brakes at least momentarily on further expansion.

An Emerging Asian Migration System

Asia itself absorbed an increasing proportion of the growing mobile labour force. Countries in the region were admitting fewer than 6 per cent of the small numbers migrating for work at the close of the 1970s, but over 40 per cent of those migrating over the second half of the 1990s. This reckoning excludes the movements of labour within China (see also **textbox 11.1.**) and India. Much of the earlier migrant labour flows consisted of unskilled labour, mostly male, recruited for the building industry in Hong Kong and Singapore, and later Kuala Lumpur and Bangkok. Towards the mid 1980s, the demand for foreign labour progressively shifted to female workers, as women in the rapidly industrializing countries left housework to fill vacancies in industry. Legions of Indonesian, Filipino, and Sri Lankan female domestic helpers were brought in to take over child care and house cleaning in Malaysia, Singapore and Hong Kong.

TEXTBOX 11.1.

Changes in Contemporary Chinese Migration

Migration flows in and from China are undergoing fundamental changes. From the end of the 1970s until the early 1990s, spontaneous migration in China was mainly triggered by internal reform policies. The abolition of the commune system in rural areas, the emergence of the private sector in urban areas, and the relaxation of overall control of human mobility led to the internal migration of some 70 to 80 million persons by the late 1990s. These people are known as the "floating population".

There was virtually no spontaneous international emigration from China during most of the "Cultural Revolution", which lasted 1966 to 1976. Emigration from southern China, through overseas family connections, resumed in the early 1970s, but only in very small numbers. Migration flows became significant after the economic reforms of 1978 and the 1985 emigration law, which granted ordinary citizens passports as long as they could provide invitation letters and sponsorships from overseas.

At the turn of the twentieth century, China's migration had become increasingly tied to economic globalization. The dimension of globalization is reflected in the following basic trends in migration in and from China:

- China's integration into the global economy, particularly its accession to the World Trade Organization (WTO) in December 2001, is expected to lead to profound economic restructuring. At the end of 1999, 6.5 million workers had been laid off from state firms and were still without jobs. The entry into WTO may accelerate this trend. An additional 20 million urban workers could be laid off. Furthermore, there is an "idle labour force" of some 128 million in rural areas, and an estimated 40 million additional agricultural jobs that may be lost over the next decade. To bring China in line with international practices following its entry into WTO, by 2005, all Chinese citizens in cities and larger towns will be able to apply for a passport by presenting their identity card and residence documents to the authorities. This will probably increase the volume of migration both inside and from mainland China.

- The profile of emigrants from China is becoming increasingly complex. The most visible emigrants fit into two different categories: students and highly skilled

197

workers, who are sought after by different countries, and irregular migrants, which destination countries are trying to prevent from entering. Since 1978, some 320,000 Chinese students have studied abroad. During the academic year 2000–2001, the numbers of students from mainland China in some European countries doubled or even tripled. Currently, some 40,000 students from mainland China study in the United Kingdom. International companies also target China as a source country for highly skilled professionals. The United Kingdom and Ireland have been trying to recruit nurses from China. Chinese computer engineers form a major group of H-1B visa holders in the USA (a temporary work visa for highly skilled professionals). But on the other hand, irregular migrants from China attract a great deal of attention. Although irregular migration from China to many different parts of the world is a relatively new phenomenon, it is considered a special case owing to the sophistication of the smuggling organizations (so-called "snakehead" gangs), the large amounts of money involved, and the brutality of the means adopted by smugglers. Annually, 25,000 to 50,000 Chinese irregular migrants enter the USA alone. Irregular migrants are reported to pay up to US$ 35,000 to the smugglers in order to enter the US, about US$ 15,000 for Europe and US$ 10,000 for other Asian countries such as Japan[3]. In 2001, Chinese police arrested some 1,400 persons involved in trafficking and smuggling of migrants.

- More locations in China are now involved in emigration. Traditionally, emigrants from China were mainly concentrated in the southern and south-eastern provinces of Zhejiang, Fujian and Guandong. Recently, north-eastern China, particularly the provinces of Liaoning, Shandong and the city of Beijing, has become an important source of emigration. This may be explained by the fact that north-eastern China registers a major concentration of state-owned enterprises and some recent emigrants are laid-off workers from state-owned enterprises. Many of them are trying their luck as traders migrating to Russia and Central and Eastern Europe. There are also sizeable groups of agriculture and construction workers from Shandong Province in Russia. About 73,000 Chinese are estimated to reside in South Korea illegally, many of them from the north-eastern province of Jilin. There is also evidence that human smuggling groups recruit potential irregular emigrants from the north-eastern region.

3) Figures from the author and Salt, J. (2001).
Current Trends in International Migration in Europe, Council of Europe.

- Destination countries for Chinese emigrants have also become increasingly diversified. After 1978, Chinese migrants originally targeted North America and Australia. According to the USA census, some 947,000 migrants from mainland China were living in the USA in March 2001. In recent years, Europe has become a new destination area. In Spain, for example, the number of Chinese migrants has increased dramatically; Chinese now account for an estimated 43 percent of all Asian migrants in Spain. The Dover tragedy in June 2000, in which 58 Chinese nationals lost their lives while being smuggled into the United Kingdom, and the frequent discovery of irregular migrants from China in the Balkans and Eastern and Central Europe, suggests that Europe may be the new frontier area of human smuggling from China; although the growing trends may not be as dramatic as some observers think. Central and Eastern Europe have become a significantly strategic place for migration from China. About 27,000 Chinese moved to Hungary in 1991 after a visa waiver system was instituted in 1989. Serbia hosted more than 50,000 Chinese in 2000. Migrants from China are also increasingly moving to other Asian countries. In 2000, about 340,000 Chinese nationals were registered in Japan, 85,000 in South Korea, 137,000 in the Philippines, and 230,000 in Thailand. Sizeable numbers of Chinese, mainly traders and construction workers, can also be found in Africa and Latin America.

- While emigration from China is increasing, legal and irregular immigration to China is also rising. Legal migrants to China are mainly transferees of multinational corporations, experts hired by Chinese companies and students. For example, Chinese airlines employ foreign flight attendants. A total of 824,000 foreign experts worked in China between 1978 and 1999. In 2001, China was estimated to host over 50,000 irregular migrants. More than 6,000 irregular migrants were discovered by the Chinese police during the first half of 2002. Most of them were from China's neighbouring countries.

Globalization of migration requires closer international cooperation in order to crack down on human smuggling and to maximize the benefits of migration. Since 2000, China has taken significant steps in this direction. Regular meetings on the subject of migration management are being held between China and Australia, Canada and the USA. China became an Observer State of the International Organization for Migration in June 2001. Among other activities, a migration information exchange visit by a Chinese delegation to Switzerland, Hungary and Croatia was organized by IOM in May 2001. In June 2001,

China and IOM jointly organized a workshop in Beijing on Operational Cooperation to Combat Irregular Migration, Trafficking and Smuggling of Migrants. Together with Spain and Germany, China co-initiated the ASEM Ministerial Conference on Cooperation for the Management of Migratory Flows between Europe and Asia, in Spain in April 2002.

While the pace of industrialization and its impact on labour market conditions help to explain some of these movements, factors like ethnicity, geography and state policy have played a more important role in shaping this migration system. The biggest destination countries appeared not to be exclusively the richest countries like Japan, the Republic of Korea or Singapore, but also middle-income countries such as Malaysia and Thailand, and even a low-income country like India. In 1997 alone, some 318,000 Indonesians[4] registered with their manpower department to go and work in Malaysia. It is difficult to say how many more went there clandestinely. In the last amnesty programme in Thailand, the authorities reported over half a million Burmese working in the country. The Thais themselves have been emigrating to work abroad. In 1999, some 115,000 Thai workers were recruited and left for Taiwan and another 18,000 for Malaysia.

The early 1990s saw significant changes in the regional labour market, as several economies became production centres for transnational companies seeking more flexible sources of labour to mass produce semi-conductors and related components. These industries typically required young workers able to work for long hours, performing tedious, repetitive operations. The first economies to host them, such as Taiwan and Malaysia, were not the ones with abundant labour supplies but they attracted the transnational companies because of their well-developed infrastructure, and more open policies to foreign investments. Labour shortages, however, soon emerged as more attractive opportunities were opened to native workers. To find workers to take their place, host countries eventually opened their doors to foreign labour.

4) On the phenomenon of Indonesia as a transit country for irregular migration, see textbox 3.2.
5) A large proportion of this figure (some 1.78 million) comes from the estimated undocumented foreign worker population in Pakistan and India. The rest can probably be treated with more confidence since they come from official sources. For example, Japan, the Republic of Korea and Australia have a reliable count of foreignerswho have overstayed their visas.

TABLE 11.2.

Intra-Asian Labour Migration - estimated number of non-national Asian workers in selected countries, circa 2000

Country of employement	Authorized + (w/o work permit) Stock estimate 000's	Estimated Rate of Growth[1] p.a. %	Main countries/regions of origin
India[2]	(580)		Tibet, Nepal, Bangladesh, Sri Lanka - Afghanistan
Pakistan[3]	(1,200)		Afghanistan, Bangladesh, Myanmar
Malaysia	850 + (200)	1.5[5]	Indonesia, Philippines, Thailand, Bangladesh
Thailand	103 + (562)		Myanmar, Laos, Bangladesh, India
Singapore	590 + (17)	9.1	Indonesia, Malaysia, China, Philippines, Thailand
Brunei	80		Indonesia, Malaysia, Philippines
Hong Kong	310	6.6	Philippines, Thailand
China	60		Hong Kong, Japan,
Taiwan	380 + (3)	9.2	Thailand, Philippines, Indonesia
Japan	710 + (192)	4.5	South Korea, China, Philippines, Thailand
South Korea	123 + (163)	8.0	China, Philippines
Australia[5]	138 + (20)		China, Vietnam, SE Asia, India

Notes:
1) Estimated from most recent 5-year period.
2) It is assumed that half of the estimated 1.2 million refugees have joined the workforce.
3) It is assumed that half of the estimated 2.5 million refugees have joined the workforce.
4) The number of migrant workers actually grew rapidly from 1993 to 1998, but the financial crisis led to a sharp drop.
5) Of the 242,000 permanent residents originating from Asia added between 1993 and 2000 we used the average LFPR (57%) of all overseas-born Australians to derive the estimate. Authorities estimated that some 28,000 non-citizens were unlawfully in Australia in mid-2000. We assumed 70 per cent were engaged in one form of employment or another.

Sources:
Japan Institute of Labour, Workshop on Labour Markets and Migration in Asia, February 2002 – Tokyo, various country reports presented by participants (see bibliographic references for individual authors).

The population of Asian migrant workers employed in the region still represents a rather insignificant proportion of the aggregate regional work force. At the beginning of the new century, it is estimated that they numbered about 6.2 million, probably a million more than the number of Asian workers in the Middle East, and just slightly more than the total number of persons born in Asia living in Western Europe and North America[5]. **Table 11.2.** gathers the available data from official sources in receiving countries (except for India and Pakistan), showing that a large pro-portion (about 42 per cent) of this worker migration has taken place in South-East Asia.

What is more important is the high growth rate of migrant worker populations in each country, even during a period that was marked by an unprecedented financial crisis. The foreign worker population from other Asian countries continued to grow at a brisk pace throughout the second half of the 1990s. In Malaysia, where the financial crisis reversed the rapid economic growth, the numbers of registered foreign workers more than doubled in five years from 532,000 in 1993 to 1.1 million in 1998.

The regional migration system is largely built on temporary foreign worker policies since attitudes to immigration, especially of unskilled workers, remain fairly closed. No country in the region considers itself open to permanent immigration except to the highly qualified. Where official policy allows it, unskilled foreign workers can be employed on one-year renewable work permits. Immigration laws in both Japan and the Republic of Korea do not allow unskilled foreign workers to be employed even for temporary periods. Notwithstanding these limitations, the system has thrived because there is a strong and growing demand for labour in some countries, and there are labour surpluses in others. In these two countries, the legal restriction on the admission and employment of unskilled foreign labour has been ingeniously circumvented through the so-called "foreign trainee" schemes. In addition, Japan encouraged and subsidized the return of nikkeijin or foreign nationals of Japanese descent, mostly the children or grandchildren of those who settled in South America (see **textbox 11.2.**).

TEXTBOX 11.2.

Demography and Migration in Japan

As a country with an ageing population and one of the lowest fertility rates in the world (1.2 children per woman), Japan's population is projected to decline in the coming decades. The population of 126.9 million in 2000 is projected to drop to 100.6 million by 2050. The percentage of the working age population (15 to 64 years) is expected to shrink from 68.1 per cent to 53.6 per cent during the same period. The percentage of elderly people (over 65 years) is expected to rise from 17.4 per cent in 2000 to 35.7 per cent in 2050. At the same time, the percentage of young people (0 to 14 years) is expected to drop from 14.6 per cent to 10.8 per cent.

According to the Replacement Migration Report published by the United Nations in 2000, Japan would need 609,000 immigrants per year until 2050 in order to maintain the size of its working-age population at 1995 levels. If the number of immigrants does not increase, Japan will not be able to maintain its current Potential Support Ratio[6] which was 4.8 in 1995. In the absence of immigration, the ratio will drop to 1.7 by 2050, with dramatic consequences for the country's labour market and social security reserves.

In order to pre-empt these major demographic and labour market changes starting in the 1990s, the government has adopted various measures to facilitate labour migration flows into Japan. One measure has been to revise and expand job categories for hiring foreign workers; ten new job categories, including legal affairs, accounting, research and education have been established. The government has also introduced long-term visas and the provision of resident permits to foreigners of Japanese descent (the so-called *nikkeijin*).

The *Basic Plan for Immigration Control,* a policy paper proposed by the Ministry of Justice in March 2000, also recognizes the need to review current policies in order to allow foreign specialists to work in areas of high demand and short supply on the national labour market[7]. The existing system includes no immigration quota for employment. Employers are required to prove that a prospective foreign worker meets established standards with respect to skill and salary conditions. In past years, the number of foreigners entering Japan for employment has been steadily increasing despite the economic recession.

In 2001, a total of 141,954 immigrants entered Japan for employment (**table 1**) which corresponded to a 9.3 per cent increase (12,086 persons) from the previous year. Among the 14 job categories for which visas are currently delivered, there has been an increase of 14 per cent in the entertainer category (117,839 persons), as compared to the year 2000. This entertainer category includes actors, singers, and professional athletes. However, some of the entertainers are actually recruited to work in the sex industry. A total of 71,678 (60.8 per cent) of foreign entertainers were Filipinos, recruited by employment agencies operating in Japan and the Philippines.

6) The relationship between the segment of the population making up the workforce and that of persons above 65 is referred to as the Potential Support Ratio. This ratio indicates the number of people of employment age for every person above 65.
7) Ministry of Justice (2000). *Basic Plan for Immigration Control (Second edition).*

TABLE 1

Foreigners entering Japan for the purposes of employment, 1997-2001 (flow figures)

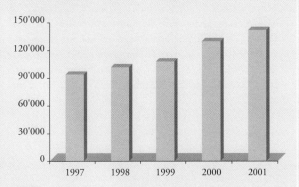

Source:
Ministry of Justice, Japan (2002) - the data exclude diplomatic and other official entries

But at the same time, there was a drop in 2000 in the number of immigrants arriving with visa categories including international service and humanities (such as translators), company transferees, engineers and other skilled workers, compared to the previous year. This reflects a decline in business activities in Japan. Many of these migrants come from neighbouring Asian countries, such as South Korea and China, but others are arriving from Australia, the United Kingdom and the United States.

Besides immigration for employment, some 47,348 students and 49,319 reuniting family members entered Japan in 2001. These persons have direct access to Japan's labour market. Chinese and South Korean students represent the majority of the students, while Brazilians and Chinese are the major beneficiaries of family reunification schemes.

The latest development in Japan's immigration policy is a gradual expansion of its foreign trainee scheme, which operates independently from the immigration stream for employment (**table 2**). Introduced in 1993, the foreign trainee scheme provides training in Japan to persons from developing countries in neighbouring Asia for a maximum of three years. The skills acquired are in the machine-, metal-, textile-, construction, agriculture and agricultural production industries.

During the first year of training, the trainees attend a series of lectures, followed by on-the-job training. Upon completion of the first year, a successful trainee becomes a "technical intern", a status that allows an additional two-year stay and training in Japan. Although "technical interns"

are not recognized as workers, they are fully paid and granted basic worker's rights. At the end of their assignment, "technical interns" are required to return home.

In 2001, Japan received 59,068 trainees, an increase of 5,000 from the previous year. More than 60 per cent of the trainees were Chinese, followed by Indonesians (12.4 per cent), and Filipinos (7.6 per cent). The total number of trainees has increased by 19 per cent over the last five years.

Although the principal aim of Japan's trainee scheme is to increase the capacity of developing countries through skill transfers, trainee schemes are considered to be an indispensable labour-provider for Japan's agriculture and manufacturing industries. The *Basic Plan for Immigration Control* encourages the further expansion of the trainee scheme.

A sharply declining working population and an ageing population cast doubts over whether Japan can sustain its economy and social security system within the bounds of existing immigration schemes. Along with countries such as Germany and the United Kingdom, which have recently taken major steps to revise their respective immigration polices, Japan may undertake a comprehensive review of its immigration policies in the near future.

TABLE 2

Trainee entries to Japan, 1997-2001 (flow figures)

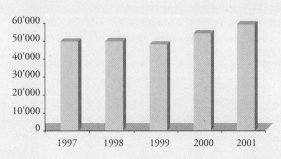

Source:
Ministry of Justice, Japan (2002)

The lack of recognition in official immigration policy of labour market shortages, on the one hand, and government capacity to implement policy on the other, have led to a high incidence of irregular migration and illegal employment in some countries. One of the countries most vulnerable to irregular migration is Thailand, which has long land borders with Myanmar, Laos, and Cambodia. Rapid industrialization during the 1980s and 1990s led to an exodus of labour away from low-wage sectors like fishing, rice milling, garments, construction, and domestic services. Because the country's laws did not allow the admission and employment of unskilled foreign labour, a market for undocumented foreign labour quickly developed. It is hardly surprising that by 2000 there were nearly 5.5 undocumented workers for each registered foreign worker in Thailand.

The Republic of Korea exhausted its labour surpluses in agriculture at least a decade earlier, but its national security concerns ensured its borders would not be penetrated by clandestine migration (see **textbox 11.3.**). What breached the wall was its decision to follow Japan and install a "foreign trainee system" in response to pressures from the Federation of Small Business, whose members were particularly affected by labour shortages. It was not long before the trainee system led to a swelling in the ranks of undocumented foreign workers who earned more as "illegals" than as "trainees".

TEXTBOX 11.3.

Focus on Smuggling and Trafficking in South Korea

Irregular migrants often face imprisonment and deportation in SE Asia

In 2001, 11,584 South Koreans emigrated, mainly to Canada (49 per cent), the United States (39 per cent), New Zealand (7 per cent), and Australia (4 per cent). In the same year, the Ministry of Justice reported an increase of 61,418 foreigners entering the country. However, it may be deceptive to use these figures to make any definite statements about net migration in the Republic of Korea. As there is no permanent residence visa issued by the South Korean government, most foreigners residing in South Korea do so for a finite period of time, defined by their particular visa category. Two important visa categories have been increasingly used by foreigners in recent years: the industrial training visa and the family visit visa.

In 2001, industrial training visas were issued to 28,092 persons from the People's Republic of China and various South-East and southern Asian countries. Family visit visas were granted to 40,027 persons entering the country to stay with their Korean family. This last group is mostly made up of ethnic Koreans from the People's Republic of China. The total from these two visa categories alone exceeds the estimated net number of foreigners staying in South Korea in 2001. There are few other statistical indicators available to clarify who is really staying in Korea on a long-term basis. The Republic of Korea still does not have an immigration law per se, but can nevertheless be considered a *de facto* country of immigration. Since the mid-1980s, immigrants have been entering the country both legally and irregularly.

Smuggling and trafficking may be difficult to distinguish in most real-life cases; however, they frequently appear to be separate and distinct phenomena in South Korea. Smuggling into South Korea utilizing either fraudulent documentation or rough sea travel, tends to involve ethnic Koreans from China; trafficking into the country almost exclusively involves women from the Philippines and more recently Russia and Commonwealth of Independent States (CIS) countries. The women enter South Korea with valid E-6 (entertainer) visas or tourist visas.

Smuggling requires travel papers such as official Chinese documents, Korean invitation letters, and/or a lost or stolen passport from a Chinese or South Korean national. The average fee for the service is about Yuan 700,000 (approximately US$ 85,000 - in July 2002). According to official statistics, the number of people entering South Korea with false documents has been increasing annually, with 1,708 in 1998, 2,383 in 1999, and 5,780 in 2000.

TABLE 1

Number of Persons Smuggled to South Korea, 1994 to 2001

Year	1994	1995	1996	1997	1998	1999	2000	2001*	Total
No. Cases	21	45	71	104	120	59	N/a	n/a	
Ethnic Koreans Involved	72	441	764	864	158	210	1045	427	3981
Total No. Persons Involved	124	488	809	1399	303	288	1172	440	5023

*Note:
2001 values reflect data collected until May 31, 2001

Source:
Korean National Police Agency records

Still others attempt to enter the country by sea paying between 500,000 and 700,000 Yuan (between US$ 60,000 and 85,000 - in July 2002), with about a 50 per cent success rate. Most of those smuggled leave ports in north-eastern Chinese provinces, such as Daren or Dandong, and spend two or three days in international waters. Then they change to South Korean fishing boats and enter various ports on the western side of the Korean peninsula. Of late, some southern Chinese ports and eastern ports of South Korea have also been used, indicating that the smuggling networks are diversifying their routes.

The first smuggling cases of ethnic Koreans from China arriving by sea were discovered in 1994. The number of such cases peaked in 1997, when 1,399 persons were caught, and then dropped during Korea's economic downturn during the Asian financial crisis of 1998. Since 2000, the number of such cases has been increasing again (**table 1**).

TABLE 2

Entertainer Visa Holders in South Korea, 1995 to 2000

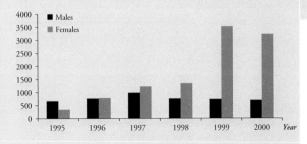

Source:
Ministry of Justice, *Departure and Arrival Control Year Book Series.*

The E-6 visa used for trafficking women into South Korea was created in 1994 in order to supply singers, musicians, and dancers to the Korean entertainment industry. However, the illustration below provides evidence of a lopsided demand for foreign female entertainers (E6 visa holders) even as the number of male entertainers has been declining since the beginning of the Asian financial crisis. In fact, the number of female foreign entertainers doubled in 1999, following Korea's recovery from the crisis (**table 2**).

Estimates from official statistics suggest that up to 5,000 women could have been trafficked into South Korea for the sex industry since the mid-1990s, although the actual number may be much higher. Filipino women have always made up the majority of Asian entertainers coming to South Korea. However, significant numbers of women from central Asian regions such as Uzbekistan, Kazakhstan, and Kyrgyzstan, began entering South Korea as entertainers in 1999. Also noticeable is the recent surge in the numbers of female entertainers from European countries, mainly Russia, Belarus and Ukraine. Since 1999, hundreds of Russian women have reportedly arrived in South Korea with non-working visas such as a B-2 tourist/transit visa or a short-term 90-day C-3 visitors visa, working at bars in Seoul and the southern port city of Pusan.

In summary, migration organization in Asia was left largely in the hands of the private sector. Labour agreements encompassing the supply of migrant labour and migrant protection have been the exception rather than the rule. Efforts by countries of origin to exercise more control over migration processes have been restricted by the reluctance or unwillingness of destination countries to enter into agreements which would reduce their ability to use migration as a flexible labour source in their countries.

The few exceptions include the agreements between Malaysia and a few governments like Bangladesh for the supply of plantation labour. The measures taken by the Philippine Government to unilaterally impose minimum acceptable wages for its nationals being recruited by different countries has led to unskilled Filipino workers being priced out of some markets like Taiwan and Singapore in the face of competition among suppliers.

Determinants of Demand for Migrant Labour

There is no doubt that many factors have contributed to the growth of labour migration in the region, but among them the only ones that lend themselves easily to measurement are the economic and demographic changes in origin and destination countries. These include measures of a country's overall economic performance, the existence of reserves of labour such as underemployed workers in

agriculture and women not participating in the labour force, the relative levels and the growth of wages, a country's openness as indicated by exports, and the size of the foreign workforce relative to the native one.

Table 11.3. gathers data on the growth of the foreign labour force in selected major destination countries, the increase in gross domestic product (GDP) (1990-99), growth of employment vis-à-vis growth of the labour force, the participation of women in the labour force, and the growth of average wages in manufacturing. Since temporary labour migration from Asia went very largely to only two sub-regions – South-East Asia and the Gulf States - a look at representative countries from both regions is instructive.

The growth in output greatly outpaced the growth of the labour force in all countries except Saudi Arabia. Singapore's economy grew four times faster than its work

TABLE 11.3.

Employment of Asian migrant labour in the 1990s and possible "pull" indicators

	S.Arabia	Kuwait	Malaysia	Japan	Singapore	S.Korea
1. GDP growth (1990-99)	1.6	5.0	7.3	1.3	8.0	5.7
2. LF growth (1990-98)	3.5	4.1[1]	3.5	0.9	2.0	2.3
3. Employment growth/ native LF[3] growth	1.16[2]	0.82	1.02	1.0	N/A	0.98
4. LFPR[4] in agriculture %	20	2	21	5	0	11.0
5. LFPR of women (25-54 years)	23.3	56.6	50.2	66.5	64	56.6
6. Wage increase in manufacturing (1999) 1990=100	N/A	72[5]	183	129	201	153
7. Foreign LF/Total LF circa 1999	57	82	18.1	1.1	27.9	1.4
8. Foreign LF change in stock (index)	1992=100 1999=108	1990=100 2000=138	1993=100 2000=150	1990=100 2000=237	1993=100 2000=306	1992=100 2000=707
9. Growth % p.a.	1.1	3.0	6[6]	9	17	27.8

Notes:

1) Based on 1990-99 LF data.

2) Based on change from 1980 to 1992.

3) Labour Force.

4) Labour Force Proportion.

5) The Iraqi invasion of Kuwait in 1990 caused a sudden drop in average wages, therefore we used the 1989 wage level as the base and traced the change to 1997. This shows a decline in average wages over the period. If the lower 1990 wages are used, 125 would be obtained for 1997.

6) The foreign workforce in Malaysia actually rose faster from 532,700 in 1993 to 1.4 million in 1997, but dropped after the financial crisis.

Sources:

World Bank (2001); ILO (2002); Asian Development Bank (2001).

force, suggesting important structural changes that allowed a jump in labour productivity. The Malaysian and South Korean economies grew at more than twice the rate of their workforces. The underlying structural changes in these economies are suggested by row 4. Clearly no more underemployed labour can be drawn from agriculture in Japan and Kuwait, and from the city-state of Singapore. Whether or not agricultural labour surpluses still exist in the Republic of Korea also appears questionable in spite of the higher percentage reported employed in that sector[8]. In Malaysia, large reported shortages of labour in the plantation sector, side by side with the still relatively large proportion of labour (21 per cent) in that sector, suggest a lack of geographical mobility from one rural area to another and the unwillingness of native workers to work in plantations located in remote, sparsely-populated regions. Also, there seems to be greater scope for increasing the participation of women in Malaysia and South Korea, and certainly in Saudi Arabia and Kuwait.

The relative size of foreign worker populations and its growth over time is indicated by different measures in the last three rows. The two Gulf States continued to rely heavily on foreign labour: Kuwait employed some 412,000 foreign workers in 1980 (or 85 per cent of the labour force) and just over 1 million in 1999 (or 82 per cent of the labour force); Saudi Arabia had only 723,000 foreign workers in 1975 at the start of the oil boom. By 1985, this figure had climbed to 3.5 million, the majority being Yemenis and construction workers from Pakistan, India, the Philippines, Thailand, and the Republic of Korea. The worries about the presence of a large foreign population led to the "Saudization policy", which was introduced in 1985. Since then, the number of foreign workers appears to have stabilized. In 1992, the foreign workforce was reported to be lower at 3.03 million, but it grew slowly afterwards at just over 1 per cent a year. Interestingly, the gender composition of the foreign workforce changed as the number of women climbed from 12 per cent in 1992 to 33 per cent in 1999, reflecting the reduction in construction employment and the growth of domestic services (see **textbox 11.4.**).

TEXTBOX 11.4.

Migration Patterns in the Gulf States[9]

In 1981, the countries of the Gulf Region established the Gulf Cooperation Council (GCC). The GCC comprises six countries: Bahrain, Kuwait, Oman, Qatar, Saudi Arabia and the United Arab Emirates.

A unique feature of GCC States is the extremely high percentage of non-nationals in their populations, especially in their labour forces. Expatriates account for more than one-quarter of the labour force in all GCC States, reaching over three-quarters in some. Foreign nationals constitute most of the population in some GCC States. In contrast, non-nationals from countries outside the European Union represent no more than 10 per cent of the population in most EU countries.

The six GCC States share a number of characteristics: they are all young political entities (Saudi Arabia became a Kingdom in 1932, Kuwait attained independence in 1961 and the other emirates followed in 1971 upon Britain's withdrawal from the area); their people share a common Arab identity, and Islam plays a crucial role both in the functioning of the states and in the lives of the individuals themselves; they look back to a common recent history, specifically the link to Britain as a former British protectorate; they share a Bedouin heritage; their economies are based largely on oil and gas production and pursue a similar liberal, free-market orientation. Economic development in all the sates relies considerably on the contribution of large numbers of foreign workers. Finally, their political systems may be referred to as conservative monarchies[10].

The discovery of oil dramatically changed demographic composition in the Gulf States, leading to a sharp increase in the importation of foreign workers. Kuwait was one of the first countries to start operating oil wells, and attracted large numbers of foreign workers. By 1965, foreigners outnumbered the local population.

Migration patterns changed when the GCC States started to recruit workers from Asian countries. The GCC States

---

8) Between 1995 and 2000 the work force employed in agriculture in South Korea actually declined by 47,000.

9) Extracted from a draft IOM report, July 2002, entitled:
   Migrants from the Maghreb and Mashreq countries:
   A comparison of experiences in Western Europe and the Gulf region.
10) Kapiszewski, A. (2001). *Nationals and Expatriates. Population*
   and labour dilemmas of the Gulf Cooperation Council States.
   Ithaca Press, Reading.

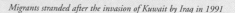

Migrants stranded after the invasion of Kuwait by Iraq in 1991

had become highly dependent on foreign labour, predominantly Arab workers. Once welcoming to Arab immigrants, the conservative GCC monarchies started to realize that large-scale immigration from other Arab countries also implied importing radical social and political ideas, including a pan-Arab ideology, which implicitly favoured the abolition of the conservative Gulf monarchies, and the creation of one "Arab" nation with a freely circulating labour force. Newly found oil wealth began to divide the Arab world: on the one hand, the rich oil states stressed their sovereignty; on the other, the poorer Arab states emphasized their "Arab" identity to justify the sharing of the oil revenues between the whole of the "Arab nation".

This was one reason leading GCC States to recruit increasing numbers of migrant workers from Asia; the second reason was economic: Asian workers were generally considered more productive, their wages were lower and it was easier to employ them in "3D" jobs (dirty, difficult and dangerous). More than in the past, the introduction of Asian workers underlined the temporary character of labour immigration to the GCC States.

Non-nationals are not eligible for either permanent residence status or citizenship in any of the GCC states except for a foreign woman marrying a national. There is a general lack of other methods for integrating immigrant populations into the receiving societies. Immigrants arrive in the GCC countries mainly to work, not to live there permanently or to bring their families. If all immigrants were allowed to stay and family reunification was generally permitted, the national population could well find itself in the minority in a number of GCC States (**table 1**).

Another key difference between the GCC States and Europe is demographic development. The demographic problems confronting Europe's ageing societies do not have the same importance in the GCC States. The national populations of GCC States are young and their governments are more concerned with the availability of suitable employment opportunities for future labour market entrants. Whilst European countries have been considering increasing immigration, particularly skilled migration, GCC States have been trying to reduce their reliance on foreign workers. However, thus far, GCC governments' attempts to reduce their dependence on foreign workers have met with only limited success. The predominance of foreign labour persists since both foreign and GCC employers find it to their advantage to hire expatriate workers who are considered to be more productive and less expensive to employ.

TABLE 1

Expatriate Population as Percentage of Total Population in the GCC States, 1975-1999 (estimates, in thousand)

	1975	1980	1985	1995	1999 (estimate)
Bahrain					
Total Expats	60.0	103.4	158.6	223.9	227.8
% of expats/total	22.9%	30.7%	36.5%	38.2%	36.2%
Kuwait					
Total Expats	687.1	971.3	1,226.8	1,250.7	1,466.0
% of expats/total	61.9%	71.5%	72.3%	63.9%	65.5%
Oman					
Total Expats	100.0	179.0	220.0	586.0	653.1
% of expats/total	13.1%	18.2%	18.4%	27.3%	26.7%
Qatar					
Total Expats	84.0	122.0	126.0	385.0	443.8
% of expats/total	56.9%	59.1%	52.3%	70.4%	70.4%
Saudi Arabia					
Total Expats	937.0	2,382.0	3.878.0	5,475.0	5,321.9
% of expats/total	13.3%	24.6%	30.7%	29.2%	24.7%
United Arab Emirates					
Total Expats	330.8	697.3	713.0	1,781.0	1,576.6
% of expats/total	63.0%	71.3%	63.8%	74.9%	67.2%
Total					
Total Expats	9721.6	4,455.0	6,322.4	9,701.6	9,689.2
% of expats/total	22.6%	32.9%	36.5%	36.8%	32.7%

Source:
Girgis, M. (2000). *National Versus migrant Workers in the GCC: Coping with Change.*

Although GCC States have not been able to reduce their dependence on all foreign workers, they have managed to reduce the relative size of the Arab non-national population including many workers from the Mashreq countries (Egypt, Jordan, Lebanon, Palestine, and Syria). These foreign workers have been most severely affected by GCC countries efforts to reduce the size of the expatriate labour force since many Arab workers hold jobs that can be performed by GCC nationals.

The foreign labour population is still insignificant in Japan and the Republic of Korea, but it is growing rapidly, particularly in Korea. The rapid ageing of the Japanese work force will sooner or later push the issue of opening to immigration to the forefront of public debate. There are already questions regarding the sustainability of its social security system as dependency ratios reach untenable levels (for an instructive comparison with Europe, see **chapter 13**). In Singapore, despite earlier policies aimed at discouraging the employment of foreign labour, the foreign worker share of the overall workforce has actually reached an all time high of 28 per cent.

The eighth row shows an index with different base years due to unavailability of data. The last row shows annual (compound) rates of growth to allow easier comparison of country experiences. The employment of foreign workers seems to be correlated to the decadal average rate of economic growth as measured by GDP, as well as to the growth in exports, which is no doubt related to the latter. Foreign worker populations grew more slowly in countries with slower growth than in Saudi Arabia (compared to Kuwait), and in Japan (compared to South Korea and Singapore). This relationship would also have held for Malaysia, where the growth rate of the foreign workforce was approaching 15 per cent a year before the financial crisis, but the latter made the average for the whole period (1993-2000) lower.

Notably in Saudi Arabia, which relies heavily on imported foreign labour, the total labour force (row 2) grew much faster than the foreign labour force (row 9). This can only be due to the growth of the Saudi workforce. There appears to have been a baby boom much earlier, since the Saudi population aged between 20 and 34 rose at a compound rate of over 8 per cent annually from 1996 to 1999.

The impact of foreign workers on average wages cannot be expected to be significant in Japan or the Republic of Korea, where they still represent a very small part of the workforce; however in Kuwait, where foreign workers represent some 82 per cent of the workforce, the impact is unmistakable. Average wages in manufacturing dropped between 1989 and 1997 by some 28 per cent. It would be interesting to investigate whether this was significant in the case of Malaysia and Singapore. Rough indicators show rapid rises in spite of the high admissions of foreign labour in both countries. For example, in Malaysia, average wages in the private sector rose annually at double digit levels for many occupations, until the financial crisis started to bite in 2000 (Kassim, 2002). However, the question to ask is how much higher wages would have grown without foreign labour.

Emigration and the Push Factors

The four Asian countries shown in **table 11.4.**, namely the Philippines, India, Indonesia and Bangladesh, experienced an estimated yearly outflow of about 1.8 million migrant workers, or just over one-seventh of one per cent of their aggregate population in 1998. There are however significant differences among the countries: in the Philippines,

TABLE 11.4.

Major countries of emigration and possible "push" indicators

		Philippines	India	Indonesia	Bangladesh
1. Labour outflow/additionnal LF[1]	1995-2000	0.29	0.06	0.22	0.13
2. LF growth rate	1980-1999	2.6	2.0	2.8	2.6
3. Growth of industry employment	1990	2.2	6.33	7.7	7
	1999	2.8	6.75	11.5	4.1
4. % Employed in agriculture	1996-1998	47	63 (1980)	41	54
5. *Per capita* income (PPP) US$	-	3,990	2,230	2,660	1,530
6. GDP p.c.average growth p.a.	1965-1999	0.9	2.4	4.8	1.3
	1995-1998	0.4	3.4	-2	2.8
7. Exports of goods+services *per capita* US$	-	492	48.4	269	47
8. Exports as % of GDP	1980	24	6	34	4
	1998	56	12	28	14
9. Telephone mainlines per 1000 pop.	-	37	22	27	30

Note:

1) The cumulative emigration flow over 1995 to 2000 divided by the additional workers who joined the labour force over the same period.

Sources:

World Bank (2001); ILO (2002); Asian Development Bank (2001).

29 workers emigrated every year for every 100 workers who joined the labour force; only one out of every 17 new workers in India left the country for employment. Emigration from Indonesia has also grown significantly over the years, followed far behind by Bangladesh.

Why are Filipinos and Indonesians more likely to work abroad than Indians and Bangladeshis? Income differentials with destination countries seem to be a poor predictor of the rate of labour emigration, as is apparent from a comparison of the countries' *per capita* incomes expressed in purchasing power parity (PPP). The Philippines and Indonesia have higher incomes *per capita* than India or Bangladesh, but both also have higher emigration rates. However, this would be consistent with the general assumption in migration literature that emigration propensities are low at very low levels of income. They rise as incomes rise because migration requires resources, information, and larger economic transactions between the origin and the destination countries (see **chapter 1**). It is of course possible that the highly aggregated data hide more than they reveal about the real relationships. At a lower than national-level of aggregation, an inverse relation between income and emigration rate may still hold, but there are unfortunately no statistics to trace the emigration rate by level of income within each country.

Row 7 shows the growth rates in *per capita* income – first, over the long period from 1965 to 1999, and then for the period 1995 to 1998. A comparison of the latter with the rate of labour emigration suggests that the expectation of an inverse relation is justified. More slowly improving incomes at home were associated with higher rates of labour emigration, while faster growth meant lower rates of emigration. However, the longer history of income improvements presented in the 1965 to 1999 averages does not indicate this. Indeed, in Bangladesh, emigration has been rising continuously over the years, apparently unaffected by income fluctuations. The relationship between population growth and propensity to emigrate in an agricultural country remains unclear.

Industrial employment outpaced the growth of the labour force in the four countries, impressively in the case of India and Indonesia, but only marginally in the Philippines. In India and Indonesia, industrial employment rose two to four times faster than the long-term average growth rate of the labour force. These four countries, however, started out with large labour resources, with many people still employed in agriculture, especially in India and Bangladesh. Real wages had not risen to any significant

degree in agriculture, dampening any wage pressures that might have been generated by greater absorption in industry.

Is the rate of emigration a function of a country's integration through trade with the global economy? This is a big question that we cannot hope to properly address here. However, some rough indicators appear to support this common perception. The last four rows indicate the outward orientation of the countries through exports of goods and services. Exports accounted for a very small share of the output of the two southern Asian economies which also had small emigration rates; the two South-East Asian economies were considerably more outward oriented. From 1980, these countries, except for Indonesia, considerably increased their share of exports. The differences were large nevertheless. The Philippines had the highest emigration rate and exported on a *per capita* basis more than ten times the value of goods and services exported by India or Bangladesh, and slightly less than double that of Indonesia.

Skill Dimension of Asian Migration

Contemporary labour migration in Asia has a bottom-heavy structure dominated by the movement of blue collar workers. Since the mid 1970s, most people who left their countries in southern and South-East Asia for work were recruited to perform jobs in construction, small factories, domestic services and agriculture. Only a thin layer of managers, professionals and technicians, mostly employed by transnational corporations, topped the migration flows within and out of the region. The structure reflected the more rapid expansion of labour-intensive sectors like manufacturing and construction in the rapidly industrializing economies of the region, as well as the social changes taking place. The unmet demand for labour in the early stages of industrialization was for construction workers, assembly-line production workers, and female migrant domestics, who could replace women leaving household work to pursue employment outside the home. The demand for migrant labour progressively began to be more varied in technical composition only in the 1990s, when global competition in the development of computer software and IT equipment intensified.

Unlike the unskilled workers who mainly moved from the less to the more developed countries, highly-skilled moved in all directions – from the less to the more developed countries and vice versa, among the less developed, and of course among the developed countries themselves.

Table 11.5. shows the information available on registered stocks and flows of highly-skilled foreigners in Asia and the Pacific. These flows represent foreign workers admitted for employment, which means that they intended to stay for at least a year[11].

Column 3 shows highly-skilled foreigners from all countries granted a visa or permit entitling them to work. Generally, the highly skilled foreign workers did not have a large presence in any of the other countries, except for Singapore, where they represented about 5 per cent of the work force. One must however be careful in drawing conclusions from these statistics since the numbers may not fully reflect their importance to these economies. The 220,000 reported for China accompanied the direct foreign investments that were crucial to the rapid modernization of its infrastructure and industry, and sterling economic performance over the past two decades. On the other hand, highly skilled workers were mainly engaged in teaching languages and in entertainment (a wide category, which may include prostitution) in the Republic of Korea.

The movement of the highly-skilled into the countries of the region is clearly related to the flows of foreign direct

TABLE 11.5.

Immigration to the Asia Pacific region of the highly-skilled, 2000

Destination country	Flows	Stocks	Principal Countries of Origin
Australia	44,730	N/A	UK (23%),USA (10%), Japan (6%),China (4%)
China	220,000	N/A	No data
Indonesia	N/A	22,800	Japan (15%), Australia (10%), South Korea(8%), Philippines (6%), Thailand (5%)
South Korea	34,700	17,700	US, Canada, Japan, UK
Malaysia	N/A	31,949	Japan (17%), India (17%), Singapore (9%), China (7%), Taiwan (4%), Philippines (4%)
Singapore	N/A	110,500	No data
Thailand	44,100	N/A	OECD (72%) of which Japan (30%) Other sources: Taiwan, China, India, Philippines
Vietnam	N/A	30,000	Hong Kong, Taiwan, South Korea, Singapore, Thailand

Source:
Japan Institute of Labour, Workshop on Labour Markets and Migration in Asia, Tokyo 2002, various country reports.

11) The dimensions and character of the movement of the highly-skilled for purposes of work is extremely difficult to monitor and assess because many countries in the region offer visa-free admission for short-term periods to nationals of developed countries and to nationals of partner-countries in regional economic groupings. For example, among the countries of the Association of South East Asian Nations (ASEAN), there has been a long-standing agreement for visa-free admission if the purpose of entry is short-term stay such as tourism or business. In practice, the recording of foreigners who enter a country for purposes of work usually starts when their stay is expected to go beyond the usual visa-free period of two weeks to one month.

investments (FDI). State policies provide specifically for the liberal admission of managers and technical personnel needed to facilitate the establishment of subsidiaries or branches of transnational corporations. Singapore has a relatively huge share of the population of highly-skilled immigrants in the region, no doubt due to its position as the hub of operations of many transnational companies and as a regional transport and trading centre. The numbers in China and in Vietnam are not very large relative to the size of their respective economies, but are nonetheless impressive when one considers their history.

The emergence of Asia as the dominant source of immigrants to North America and Australia is well documented, and the recent competition for Indian IT workers highlights the importance of Asia as a source of highly trained and educated migrant workers. In Australia in 1999, Asian-born immigrants numbered 868,900 or 19.4 per cent of all foreign-born. In Canada in 1996, some 1,081,000 or 21.8 per cent of all foreign-born were born in Asia. In the European Member States of the OECD, a total of 1,242,000 Asian nationals were reported in 1999 (OECD, 2001). But more significant is the fact that Asians represented a large proportion of the immigration of highly-skilled especially to the United States, Canada, and Australia (see **chapter 9**). In the United States, Martin (2002) reported that in 1998 Asians accounted for one-third of immigrants, but only half of those who received employment-based immigration visas. According to the US State Department, close to 69 per cent of all who were granted the employer-sponsored visa (H-1B) to the USA 1990 to 1997 came from only four Asian countries (see **table 11.6.**). In Britain, some 18,257 foreign IT professionals were admitted in 2000, including 11,474 from India (Khadria,2001).

TABLE 11.6.

United States H-1B visas issued to Asians, 1990 to 1997

Country of Origin	Number	Share %
China	12,367	4.5
India	97,675	35.5
Japan	23,504	8.5
Philippines	55,734	20.2
Sub-total	189,280	68.7
Total all countries	275,278	100.0

Source:
US Department of State

The flows of the highly-skilled can be assessed not only from the numbers passing through this "employment gate", but also those passing through the "academic gate", which today number some half a million foreigners on "student visas" and another 300,000 on cultural "exchange visitors"

visas (J1). During the 1990s, Asians dominated foreign student admissions to USA colleges and universities, with some 55,000 students from China and 46,000 from South Korea reported in 1998.

Many foreign students tend to enter the labour market during their stay, and many eventually become permanent residents. Those who graduate with doctorates are especially likely to stay and teach in the United States. According to the National Science Foundation, there were 23,559 science and engineering faculty members of Asian origin in the United States in 1997, accounting for over half of all foreign and 10.5 per cent of the total number of academics, foreign and native, in these fields (National Science Foundation, 2000).

As mentioned at the beginning of this chapter, the migration flows within Asia and to regions other than the immigration countries of North America and Australia consisted mainly of people recruited to perform blue-collar work. Our knowledge of these migrant workers flows comes from registrations of work contracts required by the countries of origin, mostly for short-periods of employment. Technical and skilled workers represented a tiny proportion of the flows from Bangladesh, Pakistan, Sri Lanka, and Thailand, but much larger in the Philippines. In the case of India, the size of the share of the highly-skilled is difficult to predict since data concern registrations from people with lower education qualifications. In India, the law does not require college graduates (and those who have previously worked abroad) to submit their contracts to the Protector of Emigrants for approval prior to accepting employment abroad[12]. Looking at changes over time, the flow becomes slightly less-skilled in the case of Pakistan, Sri Lanka, and Bangladesh; did not change in Thailand; and improved in the Philippines[13]. **Table 11.7.** presents a sampling of these differences.

12) The offices of the Protector of Emigrants were established during the British period to stop the abuses committed against natives being shipped to the colonies as coolie labour. Under the system, the Protector of Emigrants must approve offers of jobs abroad and must ensure that the workers entering into employment contracts understand the terms of these contracts.
13) One should note that the category "professionals" in the case of the Philippines includes many artists and entertainers.

TABLE 11.7.

Skill mix or occupational classification – flow data for selected labour-sending countries

PHILIPPINES				SRI LANKA		
	1980	1987	1998		1992	1997
Professionals	15.5%	27.6%	25.3%	High level	1%	0.4%
Administrative	0.5	0.4	0.1	Middle level	5	3.4
Clerical	3.4	3.6	1.3	Skilled	18	16.4
Sales	0.3	1.0	1.1	Unskilled	8	13.6
Service	14.9	33.7	27.7	Housemaid	68	66.2
Agriculture	1.0	0.6	0.1			
Production	64.4	33.2	34.3			
Others	-	0.1	0.6			

BANGLADESH			PAKISTAN		
	1977-86	1998		1990	1996
Professionals + Semi Prof	6.5%	3.5%	Professional	9.5%	7.1%
Skilled	34.7	27.9	Service	21.3	19.7
Semi Skilled	7.8	19.2	Production	63.2	60.0
Unskilled	51.0	49.2	Others	6.0	13.2

INDIA	
	1985
Professionals	5.20%
Skilled/semi skilled	47.0
Unskilled	40.1
Service	-
Other	7.7

THAILAND					
	1981	by educational level:*		1999	2000
Professionals	-				
Skilled/semi skilled	40.5%	Below college degree		98%	97.80%
Unskilled	21.50	College degree		1.9	2.1
Service	-	Others		0.1	0.1
Other	38.00				
		by occupation:*			
		Academic/professional		2.0	2.2
		Management/administration		1.3	1.2
		Commerce		6.7	8.5
		Others		90.0	88.1

Sources:

Philippine Overseas Employment Administration; Scalabrini Migration Centre Atlas, Tan (1989); Thailand Department of Employment.

There is little sign that the emigration of the highly-skilled has caused concern over "brain drain" or an impact on development in countries of the region (see **chapter 12** for a comparison with Africa). This may be partly due to the existence of large numbers of unemployed educated youth in many countries. It is also probably because pro-spects of working abroad have increased the expected returns to additional years of education and led many people to invest in more schooling, especially in occupations in high demand overseas. Thus, one observes the pheno-menon of demand creating its own supply. In India, the number of graduates in IT technology has grown considerably over the past five years. According to Khadria (2002), India already produces about 70,000 to 85,000 software engineers, and about 45,000 other IT graduates every year, but the Indian Institutes of technology are still under pressure to increase their intake of students. In the Philippines, a very significant shift in enrolment in favour of engineering and information technologies has also been observed (Alburo and Abella, 2002). It already has a large nursing education infrastructure because of the demand for nurses, clearly stimulated by expected salaries abroad and not at home.

Will Temporary Migration Policies be Maintained?

Both countries of origin and destination view labour migration as a temporary phenomenon that would one day wind down when no longer needed. This presumably would come when economic structures complete their adjustment to conditions in the labour market. Today, no country in Asia considers itself open to permanent settlement by immigrants, a right granted by law or constitution only to immediate family members of their own nationals who marry foreigners or children from these unions.

In Japan and the Republic of Korea, doors are shut not only to permanent immigration, but also to the admission for employment of unskilled foreign labour. Explicit policies allowing the temporary admission and employment of the latter however do exist in Brunei Darussalam, Hong Kong, Malaysia, Singapore and Taiwan. Thailand is currently confronted with the huge problem of undocumented foreign labour and is still debating whether or not to adopt a law providing documentation and employment.

Unskilled foreign labour has been admitted solely to address transitory imbalances in the labour market. Labour immigration policies in Singapore and Malaysia even feature a "foreign workers levy", a head tax charged to the employer of foreign workers to serve as a disincentive by making it more expensive to employ foreigners versus native workers. Although renewable, work permits usually only last one year. A work permit is tied to a specific employer, making it difficult for foreign worker to be mobile on local labour markets. In all Asian states and territories, family reunification is only granted to workers earning over a certain minimum threshold salary, effectively excluding all unskilled labour. The whole panoply of labour immigration regu-

lations has been designed to make the labour market more flexible and to minimize settlement opportunities for foreigners without the right qualifications.

To date, nothing indicates that temporary foreign worker policies will be abandoned as they were, for example, in Western Europe during the recession in the second half of the 1970s. The Asian financial crisis, which turned out to be an economic crisis of major proportions, led to the forced return of thousands of migrant workers particularly from Malaysia, South Korea, and Thailand, but this was merely a temporary adjustment. Policies were not changed; they were merely suspended in some countries. Flows of foreign labour from South-East Asia to Hong Kong, Japan, the Republic of Korea, Singapore, and Taiwan dipped slightly in 1997 and 1998, but they quickly recovered thereafter. The population of migrant workers grew substantially in all countries of the region from the beginning of the 1990s to 2000, when the numbers reached some 6.3 million.

There are several reasons why the temporary policies are likely to stay: one reason is the absence of any political opposition to the presence of foreign workers, probably because they are still perceived as "guest workers", people who are there for a limited period of time, no matter how long they eventually stay. Unlike in Europe, the "revolving door" strategy is widely seen to be working. Secondly, foreign workers are employed in construction, domestic services, plantations, and small-scale manufacturing, doing work that national workers shun. Their entry therefore did not displace native workers. Moreover, policies for temporary foreign workers bar their mobility in the domestic labour market, confining them to certain occupations and sectors, further reducing competition with native workers. Thirdly, labour institutions like trade unions that normally oppose policies to make the market more flexible, have not opposed the admission of foreign labour. They have been largely indifferent to the issue of labour immigration.

Conclusion

The foregoing analysis of recent experiences in Asian labour migration enables the following observations and conclusions to be made:

• Over the last 10 years, labour mobility in the region has increased considerably, as indicated by the fact that the mobile workforce is now growing at twice or more the rate of the labour force.
• This increasing mobility has been largely brought about by demand factors, as economic expansion in some countries has outpaced the growth of their native labour force.

• While the employment of foreign workers is clearly influenced by the rate of economic growth, other factors such as ethnicity, geography, and state policies also clearly influence the development of this migration system.

• Immigration has been used effectively as a short-term measure to increase labour market flexibility, particularly in sectors such as export industries, tourism, agriculture, and construction;

• There are indications that the mobility of a country's workforce is related positively to its integration through trade with the global economy.

• There is some evidence of "path dependence" as foreign worker populations have continued rising in spite of downturns in the economy of receiving countries and policies aimed at discouraging foreign labour employment.

• There is *a prima facie* case for asserting that the movement of the highly-skilled into the countries of the region has largely been the consequence of foreign capital flows, particularly to those countries that did not have a large labour surplus.

• Unlike the movement of the unskilled, which was largely from the less to the more developed countries, highly-skilled have moved in all directions.

The countries in the region have shown different capacities for labour migration management: strong states with a long history of concern over national security have demonstrated the will and the capacity to limit numbers of foreigners living and working within their territories[14]; in other countries, labour migration has been much more responsive to stimulus for movement. Other factors playing an important role include the existence of a large informal economy; previous history of absorption of other ethnic communities like the Bengalis in Malaysia; weak labour institutions; pressures from business groups; and the absence of organized political opposition to immigration. It is clear however, especially after the financial crisis, that migration management is a growing challenge for all, and economic interests alone cannot always be the decisive factor in guiding decisions. As foreign communities expand and economies are configured to the availability of foreign labour, it is necessary to guarantee social progress, communal harmony and economic stability. This is a more relevant parameter for successful migration policy.

14) Recent events in Malaysia demonstrate, however, that the management of irregular labour migration continues to pose challenges to the region. In response to rising levels of criminality, in summer 2002, Malaysia repatriated several hundreds of thousands of irregular labour migrants to Indonesia and the Philippines. Notwithstanding the fact that Malaysia expressed its willingness to accept workers back once their situation regularized, these events show that the management of labour migration, and especially its irregular expressions, remains a work in progress.

CHAPTER 12

Linkages between Brain Drain, Labour Migration and Remittances in Africa

In the foreseeable future, labour-related migration within and from Africa is expected to remain a major social and economic pattern. Brain drain - an important sub-set of labour-related migration - is one of the most serious migration issues of concern to African countries as it has development implications.

According to the World Bank's *World Development Report,* "cross-border migration, combined with the brain drain from developing to industrial countries will be one of the major forces shaping the landscape of the twenty-first century" (World Bank and International Bank for Reconstruction and Development, 2000).

This chapter examines the linkages between brain drain, unskilled and semi-skilled labour migration, and remittances. After describing brain drain and labour migration patterns from a sub-regional perspective, it considers the question whether African countries gain or lose when their workers and brightest talents go abroad. Through an analysis of the impact of remittances on countries of origin, the chapter demonstrates that migration can contribute significantly to the development of African countries. The positive impact of remittances could even be amplified if more appropriate national policies to channel and use them were put in place systematically.

Fathoming the link between migration and development, the chapter concludes that governments in countries of origin and destination ought to invest in partnerships that allow migration to be managed comprehensively and sustainably as positive consequences of labour-related migration can be factored into development policies.

Major Characteristics of Brain Drain and Labour Migration

Definitions

By applying the criteria "level of education" to migrants, one can distinguish between two broad categories of labour-related migration:

• brain drain,
• labour migration.

The term **brain drain** describes the cross-border movement of highly skilled persons who stay abroad for a longer period of time. Highly skilled persons are defined as having studied or currently studying for a university degree or possessing equivalent experience in a given academic field.

In most cases, the loss of highly skilled professionals is critically resented in African countries of origin as they are active in important development fields: agriculture, business, education, engineering, health, science, etc. Most migrants in these professional categories leave their country of origin in order to maximize the return on their investment in education and training by moving in search of the highest paid and/or most rewarding employment (Iredale, 2002). Brain drain also involves African students who move abroad in order to further their education.

The growing number of highly skilled African women leaving their home countries is also noteworthy. The brain drain has been "feminized" in recent years as more and more African women are becoming as qualified and skilled as men (see also **textbox 1.1.**).

The dominant, classical path of brain drain used to be emigration from a former colony to a former metropolitan power: from francophone West and North Africa to France; from anglophone Africa to the United Kingdom as well as the USA and Canada; from the Great Lakes region to Belgium; and from lusophone Africa to Portugal. Later, as these movements became less intense, intra-African migration as well as emigration from Africa to less traditional destination countries in the Middle East, Asia or Latin America emerged and gathered momentum.

Movements of highly skilled persons within Africa are often referred to as brain circulation. African brain circulation began as a way of replacing expatriate manpower that

215

had returned to their countries of origin in Asia, Europe or North America. Research underlines the temporary nature of brain circulation and the fact that most migrants return home for several reasons, including rigid immigration legislation as well as certain xenophobic tendencies in some African countries. However, in reality, the return does not always take place (Weiss, 1998).

Labour migration involves people with fewer qualifications and skills than those considered highly skilled. The major formal difference between labour migrants and brain drain migrants is that the latter possess a university degree. Labour migrants include documented and undocumented, semi-skilled and unskilled workers, active in agriculture, industry, services or the informal sector. Labour migrants may be temporary contract workers or blue collar labourers. Billsborrow (1997) adds the categories of free-moving migrants and frontier workers migrating for the purpose of securing employment or undertaking self-employment.

Similar to brain drain, labour migration occurs either within the African continent or between the continent and overseas.

Geographic Dimensions of Brain Drain

No systematic data are available on brain drain in Africa. Most countries do not take stock of who migrates, the migrants' motives and length of stay abroad. However, available fragmentary information on highly skilled African migrants provides useful insights into the scale of the phenomenon.

Brain drain patterns in **North Africa** are largely shaped by the sub-region's geographic proximity and historic ties with Europe. The dominant brain drain flow is from the three French-speaking countries Algeria, Morocco and Tunisia to France or Belgium, but also increasingly Italy. Some movements to North America also take place. Highly skilled Egyptians favour southern Europe and the UK as well as North American destinations. Brain circulation between North African countries and other countries of the continent is relatively small. Egypt, however, is an important destination for academics from Arabic-speaking countries in Africa.

Over the last thirty years, **West Africa** has been the most important source of brain drain from Africa. As of the 1970s, inflation and recession sparked the emigration of nationals of Gambia, Ghana, Liberia and Sierra Leone –

notably engineers, applied scientists and medical personnel. Within the sub-region, many skilled migrants from Burkina Faso, Guinea, Mali and Senegal went to Côte d'Ivoire. The 1980s and 1990s witnessed substantial brain circulation of West Africans, especially to Libya, South Africa and Zimbabwe. As the economy of Nigeria declined at the end of the 1980s, Nigerians joined the stream of skilled migrants to overseas destinations. Over 20,000 Nigerian doctors are practising in Canada and the United States, a figure that is thought to be underestimated (Tettey, 2002).

In **Central Africa,** the two major countries of origin are the Democratic Republic of Congo (DRC) and Cameroon. In the early 1990s, the Republic of Congo emerged as a major destination for intra-regional migrants. When countries of the Economic Community of the Great Lakes[1] signed a convention on the free movement of labour, which was expected to increase the volume of skilled migrants, political instability in the region prevented this opportunity from developing further. Two small Central African countries have become important destinations of both skilled and unskilled workers in the last couple of years: oil- and mineral-rich Equatorial Guinea and Gabon.

In **East Africa,** the three closely connected countries of Uganda, Kenya and Tanzania used to have figures on population exchange, based on censuses, in addition to data assembled by the statistics department of the East African Community (EAC). For many years, EAC has been facilitating the exchange of highly skilled workers: for example Kenya and Tanzania benefitted from the immigration of highly skilled professionals from Uganda during the oppressive Amin regime. During the same period, a number of skilled Ugandans also emigrated to South Africa's homelands, and later to Zimbabwe and Botswana. For several decades, the war-torn countries in the Horn of Africa – Eritrea, Ethiopia, Somalia and Sudan – did not only produce huge numbers of refugees but also legions of highly skilled emigrants.

The case of Sudan is illustrative. In 1978, Sudan lost 17 per cent of its doctors and dentists, 30 percent of its engineers, 20 per cent of its university lecturers and 45 per cent of its surveyors through emigration overseas (Stalker, 1994; Tettey, 2002). The Ministry of Labour in Khartoum estimated that in that same year, about 180,000 Sudanese worked in the Gulf countries, 135,000 of them in Saudi Arabia alone. By 1995, some 500,000 skilled Sudanese worked abroad. Back home in Sudan, some of these were replaced by Ethiopians.

1) DRC, Burundi and Rwanda.

In **Southern Africa,** Malawi, Mozambique, Zambia and Zimbabwe produce skilled migrants who are leaving to the three economically buoyant countries in the sub-region: Botswana, Namibia and South Africa. These three major immigration countries are well endowed with abundant natural resources and have prospered thanks to sound economic management and governance, but depend heavily on highly skilled human resources from the rest of the Southern African Development Community (SADC) Member States and other African regions. On the other hand, however, skilled nationals of these countries often emigrate overseas. A recent survey of South Africa revealed that one-third of white South-Africans and slightly more than one-fifth of black South-Africans interviewed in 1999 contemplate migrating overseas in order to benefit from better working conditions (Mattes and Richmond, 2000). Skilled workers emigrating from South Africa are estimated to have cost the country some US$ 7.8 billion in lost human capital since 1997, and this trend has retarded economic growth (Selassie and Weiss, 2002).

Geographic Dimensions of Labour Migration

For generations, labour migration in and from Africa has been driven by the agricultural seasons, climatic conditions that influence crop planting or livestock breeding as well as the existence of labour-intensive branches of industry and mining.

The largest numbers of African labour migrants in Europe originate from **North Africa.** Moroccan, Algerians and, to a lesser extent, Egyptians and Tunisians form the bulk of the semi-skilled and unskilled African migrants to the countries of the European Union (EU). The main sectors of employment are industry, agriculture, but also retail commerce and the services. Another dominant flow is that of Egyptian unskilled and semi-skilled workers to countries of the Persian Gulf where they occupy construction industry, service industry and domestic services positions. Traditionally, North African countries feature among the biggest receivers of overseas remittances worldwide.

West Africa presents a mix of political and economic fortunes that determine labour migration patterns. Labour-exporting countries include Burkina Faso, Mali and Ghana (an importer before the Aliens' Compliance Act of 1969, turned exporter since the mid-1970's). For a long time, Côte d'Ivoire was the sub-region's major labour-importing country because of its flourishing plantation industry. Following violence against foreigners in the aftermath of the 2000 election, many migrants from Côte d'Ivoire's northern neighbours have returned home. Once a magnet for foreign labourers, especially during the oil boom of the early 1980s, Nigeria carried out mass deportations of foreigners in 1983 and 1985 as economic conditions deteriorated in the country.

Efforts to organize labour migration at regional level began in 1979 with the enactment of the protocol on free movement of people of the Economic Community of West African States (ECOWAS). Capitalizing on the free movement of labour in the region, the Protocol allows citizens from member countries to travel visa-free for 90 days and grants them the right to residence. Countries in northern Africa are often countries of destination, or transit, for labour migrants from Africa. Well-known migrant routes cross the Sahara from Ghana, Niger or Nigeria to Algeria or Libya. Many of these labour migrants ultimately attempt to reach Europe.

In **Central Africa,** the major labour-exporting countries are Angola, Cameroon, the Central African Republic and Chad. Many of their agricultural workers used to immigrate to Sao Tome and Principe and Equatorial Guinea, to work on cocoa, coffee and sugar plantations during the heyday of these agricultural commodities in the 1970s and the early 1980s. With a growing mining industry, migration streams shifted to the mining areas of Gabon, the Congo, DRC and Angola (Stalker, 1994).

Gabon, the wealthiest country in the sub-region in terms of per capita income, stands out as the principal labour importer owing to its diverse natural resources, including oil, forestry, manganese and uranium. However, in a move to "gabonize" the labour force, the Government of Gabon has restricted foreigners' access to its labour market.

Since 1995, Equatorial Guinea has become a major importer of labour due to its large offshore petrol reserves, discovered in the mid-1990s.

In **East Africa,** a well established labour migration pattern leads from the countries in the Horn of Africa to the Gulf States. Indeed, war-torn and drought-stricken Ethiopia, Eritrea or Somalia, traditionally produce numerous unskilled labourers who migrate to the Gulf States, particularly the United Arab Emirates, Qatar and Saudi Arabia, where they occupy menial jobs in the services and domestic fields.

217

In **Southern Africa,** the Republic of South Africa is the major labour-importing magnet[2]. In fact, as the continent's strongest and most diversified economy, South Africa is Africa's undisputed major country of destination. Most African countries have established regular or irregular labour migratory flows with South Africa. Since the early twentieth century, labour migration to South Africa has been a well-known phenomenon that spurred exploitation of the country's mineral wealth. South Africa relied heavily on its neighbouring countries as suppliers of large numbers of unskilled labourers – Botswana, Lesotho, Malawi, Mozambique and Swaziland. Although labour migration has decreased over the last two decades through the recruitment of domestic workers, it has not ceased completely. Half of all migrants from Lesotho, 40 percent from Mozambique and 35 percent from Zimbabwe, claim that the prospect of finding employment in South Africa's mining industry is the principal pull-factor prompting them to migrate "down south" (McDonald *et al.,* 2000).

Based on latest available statistical data, IOM estimates that some 3.8 million Africans live in Europe, North America and Australia (see **table 12.1.**), including several hundred thousand high level professionals. According to the World Bank, some 80,000 highly qualified people leave the continent annually to work overseas (Weiss, 2001). This figure does not include the many students who leave the continent to study overseas.

Causes

Surveys conducted by IOM among African returnees, carried out in the framework of its Return of Qualified African Nationals Programme in the mid-1990s, revealed as many different reasons explaining why (highly skilled) Africans have left their country of origin as people interviewed. However, apart from migrants' personal preferences and experiences, migration is prompted by a number of common factors in both countries of origin and destination.

Applicable to both highly skilled and unskilled migrants, the hit-list of the most frequently mentioned "push" factors prompting migrants to leave their country of origin, and "pull" factors attracting migrants to enter a specific country of destination includes the following (Fadayomi, 1996):

Push-factors
- poor socio-economic living conditions;
- unemployment, increasing the dependency burden of household wage-earners;
- drops in real income, currency devaluation and rising cost of living;
- rigid government employment systems;
- professional isolation;
- tribal/ethnic discrimination in appointments and personnel policies;
- corruption;
- employer discrimination against the qualifications held (e.g., bias against degrees obtained in former socialist countries);
- competition with expatriates.

Pull-factors
- higher salaries;
- greater job mobility and professional career development;
- fewer bureaucratic controls and higher standards of living;
- acquisition of high-level skills;
- foreign scholarships and educational support;
- active presence of recruitment agents.

The most important driving force behind labour migration is economic disparity among African countries. Countries with plentiful resources attract migrant labour from far and near; countries with large-scale agricultural sectors attract large numbers of farm labourers; countries with industrial infrastructure attract workers. Conversely, countries with scarcer natural resources but abundant skilled and semi-skilled human resources generally export labour.

Both migrant networks and strong links between migrants and relatives back home sustain labour migration in many African countries. These are part of the broader social imperative of the extended family system that has sustained "chain migration" over generations. In any African society of origin, emigrants provide hope for survival, improving socio-economic status and represent an opportunity for younger relatives to join earlier migrants who are well established in their new abode. Once a member of the family (nuclear or extended) emigrates, he/she is expected to create employment opportunities for, and permit visits and subsequent migration of, other relatives back home. The chain process sustains links between migrants and those left behind, and indeed with the wider community from which the migrant originates (see also **textbox 12.1.**).

2) **Chapter 3** provides information on the new South African Immigration Act.

TABLE 12.1.

The African diaspora in selected countries of Europe and North America[1] (stock data)

	France	Italy	UK[2]	Germany	Spain	NL[2]	Belgium	Portugal	CH[2]	Sweden	USA	CAN[3]
Years[4]	1990	2000	2000	2000	2001	2000	2001	2000	2000	2001	1999	1996
Totals	**1652400**	**411492**	**373000**	**300611**	**261385**	**149764**	**143745**	**89516**	**35446**	**25651**	**36700**	**229300**
Algeria	614200	11435	15000	17186	13847	917	7685	91	3023	500	789	
Angola	N/A	1199	5000	7456	801	1184	654	17695	1797	158	57	
Barundi	N/A	N/A	N/A	423	N/A	N/A	N/A	2	262	N/A	16	
Benin	4300	N/A	N/A	1100	N/A	N/A	4	135	N/A	59		
Botswana	N/A	N/A	1000	96	N/A	N/A	N/A	6	8	N/A	5	
Burkina Faso	N/A	N/A	N/A	1417	N/A	N/A	N/A	2	140	N/A	17	
Cameroon	18000	2433	N/A	8397	784	365	1689	17	1535	77	826	
Cape Verde	N/A	4611	N/A	552	2052	1567	N/A	43797	971	61	909	
CAR[5]	4100	N/A	N/A	121	N/A	N/A	N/A	5	23	N/A	3	
Chad	1400	N/A	N/A	343	N/A	N/A	N/A	N/A	56	N/A	24	
Comoros	3000	N/A	N/A	56	N/A	N/A	N/A	N/A	4	N/A	N/A	
Congo	12800	N/A	N/A	1223	N/A	N/A	N/A	40	379	N/A	190	
Côte d'Ivoire	16700	N/A	N/A	2646	N/A	N/A	N/A	83	696	N/A	305	
Djibouti	N/A	N/A	N/A	75	N/A	N/A	N/A	1	5	N/A	6	
DRC[5]	N/A	2710	10000	16090	674	1887	11337	208	2954	679	88	
Egypt	6300	33652	9000	13811	952	2771	696	57	1591	592	4429	
Eritrea	N/A	3118	N/A	3873	N/A	226	N/A	N/A	590	965	326	
Ethiopia	N/A	7229	8000	16470	3	1280	N/A	10	1018	2400	4272	
Gabon	3000	194	N/A	238	96	28	N/A	1	57	N/A	4	
Gambia	N/A	377	3000	2565	25	123	N/A	2	150	1560	183	
Ghana	2800	21807	33000	22602	8840	3887	1540	31	1182	439	3714	
Guinea	5900	N/A	N/A	1953	1837	199	N/A	367	245	N/A	6	
Guinea-Bissau	N/A	N/A	N/A	541	N/A	N/A	N/A	14140	34	N/A	134	
Guinea-Equatorial	N/A	50	N/A	105	4507	N/A	N/A	N/A	13	2	1	
Kenya	N/A	625	15000	4431	245	368	N/A	284	972	623	1412	
Lesotho	N/A	N/A	N/A	108	N/A	N/A	N/A	4	11	N/A	5	
Liberia	N/A	194	N/A	3796	484	569	N/A	38	122	78	1358	
Libya	N/A	1924	12000	2643	164	119	N/A	42	382	146	156	
Madagascar	9800	N/A	N/A	651	N/A	N/A	N/A	5	384	N/A	26	
Malawi	N/A	N/A	3000	125	N/A	N/A	N/A	22	22	N/A	41	
Mali	37700	N/A	N/A	813	N/A	N/A	N/A	63	105	N/A	72	
Mauritania	6600	641	N/A	493	3764	69	N/A	24	49	10	2971	
Mauritius	13000	N/A	9000	859	N/A	N/A	N/A	12	855	N/A	38	
Mozambique	N/A	N/A	N/A	2698	N/A	N/A	N/A	4503	40	N/A	31	
Morocco	572700	170905	8000	81450	199782	119726	106822	330	5349	1234	24	
Namibia	N/A	N/A	N/A	327	N/A	N/A	N/A	N/A	19	N/A	13	
Niger	900	N/A	N/A	882	N/A	N/A	N/A	N/A	34	N/A	12	
Nigeria	N/A	17340	45000	15351	3292	1978	963	72	991	401	6769	
Rwanda	N/A	486	N/A	947	93	145	702	22	364	108	98	
Sao Tome And Principe	N/A	N/A	N/A	48	N/A	N/A	N/A	4795	1	N/A	6	
Senegal	43700	35188	N/A	2621	11051	167	754	382	781	109	370	
Seychelles	N/A	N/A	1000	210	N/A	N/A	N/A	2	90	N/A	10	
Sierra Leone	N/A	575	5000	5575	577	338	N/A	93	83	124	976	
Somalia	N/A	12174	54000	8350	70	5296	N/A	1	1411	11535	1710	
South Africa	N/A	467	57000	4936	360	2512	712	1793	963	311	1580	
Sudan	N/A	583	N/A	4697	121	1113	N/A	15	452	411	1354	
Swaziland	N/A	N/A	N/A	62	N/A	N/A	N/A	10	12	N/A	8	
Tanzania	N/A	505	6000	1015	48	256	N/A	326	221	406	316	
Togo	6000	914	N/A	11513	59	236	N/A	9	308	130	254	
Tunisia	206300	55213	1000	24260	643	1312	3615	27	4054	797	150	
Uganda	N/A	371	15000	1334	13	167	N/A	7	242	803	250	
Western Sahara	N/A	N/A	N/A	N/A	N/A	N/A	N/A	N/A	6	N/A	N/A	
Zambia	N/A	177	3000	382	10	105	N/A	8	73	104	143	
Zimbabwe	N/A	N/A	21000	528	N/A	N/A	N/A	68	182	N/A	184	
Other/ not stated	63200	24395	34000	167	6191	854	6576	N/A	N/A	888	N/A	

Notes:

1) Data provided for Europe and Canada are census population by country of birth. For the United States, the numbers reflect immigrants by country of birth.

2) United Kingdom, the Netherlands, and Switzerland.

3) More detailed information on countries of birth is not available; non-permanent residents are not included in this total number.

4) The most recent official data for each country.

5) Central African Republic and Democratic Republic of Congo.

Sources:

Council of Europe (2001); US Department of Justice and Immigration and Naturalization Service (1999); Statistics Canada, Statistic Reference Center – NCR (1996).

TEXTBOX 12.1.

Migration – a reflection of socio-economic dynamics in Africa

Migration in Africa has always been a major socio-economic issue and is inseparable from African's way of life. Travelling to escape poor conditions in the place of origin as well as to "reach" and move beyond the horizon is a permanent feature of African life. The African migratory context is reflected in many ways: nomads migrating in search of pastureland; young men from the countryside setting off to work in the city; women traders seeking the best bargains; highly qualified and educated professionals who are tempted to work overseas; or refugees fleeing a civil war or a natural disaster.

To the north and south of the Sahara, migration is so highly diversified that a myriad of situations, motivations, desires and constraints determines the migration movements of individuals, families and entire peoples.

Whether movements are voluntary or forced, temporary or definitive, Africa's extraordinary migration dynamics have helped to mould societies, cultures and countries. Contrary to common belief, they do not merely reflect misery and its related constraints. Migration flows are shaped by a highly changeable combination of historical, economic, demographic, political or environmental factors within any one country, region or between the continent and overseas destinations.

African migration is far from being limited merely to the South-North axis and to movements stemming from the growing inequality between a prosperous North and a deprived South. Inter-African migration far outstrips the volume of workers or asylum seekers knocking at the doors of industrialized countries. The mosaic of African migration offers a varied picture. In the African context, it is difficult to distinguish between internal and international migration or regular and irregular migration for a number of reasons: the cultures, languages and colonial experiences common to several countries; existing ties with former European powers; established migration networks, which revolve around seasonal or cyclical economic opportunities.

Family solidarity plays a fundamental role in shaping migration. In Africa, migration is still largely a "family affair": even those family members who do not migrate are still deeply involved in the process. A family will do its best to provide financial assistance to one of its members, generally the eldest son, with a view to placing him in the labour migration circuit. The idea is to recoup the investment in his education, specifically through remittances. This source of revenue is essential to the survival of many families, often providing as much as 80 per cent of their needs. Immigrant wages have grown in importance thanks to the existence of migration networks, which enable older migrants in turn to receive newcomers and help them integrate and find work. Money remittances from migrants are also vital to Africa's economies, contributing considerably to GDP in some African countries.

The origin of migration movements can be attributed as much to migrants' mobility as to survival. Migration for survival is caused by pressures stemming from rapid population growth, poverty, deteriorating economic and employment conditions, or even armed conflict. As a result of crises and insecurity, countries of destination are becoming countries of origin for migrants, and *vice versa*. This transforms many African countries into both host and sending countries of migration flows.

Although each region has its centres of attraction which exert influence far beyond regional boundaries, migration structure is often determined by geographic proximity of the country of destination. South Africa's mining industry, and to a lesser extent that of Zambia, draws labour from the overpopulated bordering countries of Malawi and Mozambique. Commercial agriculture in Côte d'Ivoire cannot operate without labour from Mali and Burkina Faso. Besides, Africa's leading countries of immigration have always demonstrated exemplary solidarity toward immigrants. This social aspect cannot be overshadowed even by the recent outbursts of xenophobia in southern and western Africa.

One of the recent changes to African migration has been a growing feminization, which suggests that traditional social roles have been modified considerably. Whereas men used to leave to search for work, more and more women are now striking out on their own to seek economic independence. Women currently make up half of Africa's migrants. Doctors, domestic workers or businesswomen, they are now migrating not only within borders, but increasingly abroad.

Can we therefore conclude that free movement of people in Africa is about to become a reality? Although the protocols governing some regional cooperation organizations do envision free circulation of people as well as freedom of establishment and residence, these provisions are only rarely applied. For the time being, only ECOWAS is applying a protocol on the free movement of persons, although it is somewhat vague on the right of residence.

More intense regional cooperation could pave the way for even greater labour and skill mobility and be a driver for sustainable development. In the long run, the prospects of economic integration on the continent could encourage this mobility. Regularization of migration flows for the benefit of African economies and the migrants themselves is a vast project. Decision-makers are very slowly getting to grips with this idea, a long time after African people have made it a reality.

Since the late 1980s, structural adjustment programmes (SAP) have caused social and economic upheavals, sparking the exodus of skilled and highly skilled professionals. Entrenchment of civil servants to downsize the civil service "waterhead" has dealt a blow to households that relied on their civil servants as principal breadwinners. Privatization of state corporations forced the public sector to lay off large numbers of employees; cost recovery (user fees) levied on social services has imposed a burden on households, most of which cannot even meet their basic needs. As in many African countries, employees in the affected sectors predicted a bleak future; they tended to emigrate to seek better opportunities elsewhere. Also, the non-agricultural sector has failed to hire labour since the 1980s, when many public sector workers were entrenched in various countries[3], mainly as victims of SAP-driven reforms (Adepoju, 1995).

Salary discrepancies and differences in working conditions between African and developed countries stimulate brain drain. Most African economies have experienced wage freezes, currency devaluation and rampant inflation. These conditions lead skilled people to seek safer countries where remuneration is consistent with qualifications and working experience, and where currencies are less subject to devaluation than in Africa.

The quality of overseas education adds to the weight of brain drain pull factors. Overseas education is considered better than in national institutions, and so students are more likely to emigrate. In migrating overseas for higher education, many Africans have earned similar qualifications

than their western counterparts. Moreover, the growth of transnational corporations has internationalized the market for high-level human resources and increased opportunities for Africans abroad. Overseas employers often prefer professionals educated in reputable institutions.

Another problem is high unemployment among university graduates. Since the end of the 1980s, widespread joblessness has prevailed among university graduates in many countries. While there were only isolated cases of unemployment among degree holders in the 1980s, they have become the norm in the 1990s, putting highly educated and skilled people frequently in desperate situations.

Furthermore, specific circumstances such as political persecution, military coups, repression of educated citizens defying authority and the volatile wave of multi-party politics at the turn of the 1990s precipitated fear and uncertainty, turning emigration into an alternative to domestic problems. Many highly skilled nationals from Burkina Faso, Congo, DRC, Ethiopia, Ghana, Guinea, Kenya, Mali, Nigeria or Uganda emigrated because of traumatic violent circumstances. Many African academics, political activists and other intellectuals whose views were at odds with the political establishment have been long-term immigrants in some developed countries.

Last but not least, emigration has been prompted by population growth, which has resulted in rapid growth of the overall labour force. High fertility rates account for the rapid increase in the number of persons of working age, and the continent's population grows at an annual rate of nearly 3 per cent. Therefore, migratory pressure in search of jobs within and outside the continent will intensify for the millions of Africans entering the labour market every year.

Consequences

Migration has two main effects in countries of destination: additional manpower, skilled or unskilled, contributes to economic growth and development; however, this may also lead to arise in xenophobia in host societies, especially during economic recession. However, there seem to be no linear linkages from cause to effect as both aspects often occur simultaneously in the same country.

221

3) Such as Cameroon, Congo, Gabon, Guinea, Senegal, Sierra Leone, Tanzania, Togo and Uganda.

In many cases, countries of destination hardly acknowledge migrants' contribution to development. Today, highly skilled immigrants often bring along an unusual skill mix due to their specific training backgrounds and experience, which is often absent in countries of destination. In some instances, however, brain migration turned out to be a mere "brain waste", whereby skilled people end up in either irrelevant positions or working for much lower wages than their qualifications merit (Salt, 1993). However, highly skilled migrants from developing countries are becoming a more attractive resource for industrial countries as these countries experience demographic shifts characterized by skilled labour force shortages in certain sectors of their economies (see **textbox 12.2.** and **chapter 13**).

TEXTBOX 12.2.

Filling the Labour Market Gaps in the United Kingdom with Help from Africa[4]

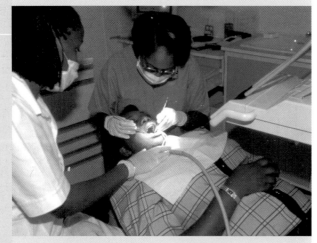

Thousands of skilled Africans have left the continent to work in industrialized countries

With a fast-declining population, Western European countries have become increasingly dependent on migrant workers to fill their labour shortfalls in many of their economic and social services sectors. In the United Kingdom alone, up to 1.2 million migrants, many unskilled, will be needed in the next few years to replace workers entering retirement.

However, educated Africans attracted to countries like the United Kingdom by the prospects of earning higher wages and finding better working conditions are often disappointed and frustrated when they arrive because of red tape and local immigration laws.

Thousands of Africans with PhDs, doctorates, degrees, diplomas and certificates currently in developed countries are being excluded from performing the jobs they are trained or qualified for, and are doing manual low paid work instead. The United Kingdom alone hosts several tens of thousand of qualified professionals from Ghana, Kenya, Nigeria or South Africa.

Acknowledging its need for migrant labour, the United Kingdom is currently considering the idea of introducing a work permit system to help deal with skill shortages.

As concerns xenophobia, migrants have been accused of stealing jobs from nationals, abusing public services and social welfare, fuelling crime and insecurity and carrying and spreading diseases. African migrants become victims of racial discrimination not only overseas[5]. In Southern Africa, results of SAMP research show that growing xenophobia and social exclusion impede brain circulation to the three major destinations in Southern Africa (Oucho, 2001a). Some citizens of these countries are unwelcoming towards other Africans and do not distinguish between skilled and unskilled or documented and undocumented immigrants. The SAMP survey revealed that most of their citizens have never lived in other African countries and hence their xenophobia reflects apprehension of foreigners whom they meet for the first time (Oucho, 2001a).

An analysis of the effects of migration on countries of origin is even more complex. Certainly, the emigration of highly skilled nationals in particular leads to a significant loss of skills available for development. Yet, labour migration and brain circulation lead to a more efficient allocation of manpower within the African continent as well as overseas, and decreases social tensions in the countries of origin. Migrants acquire new skills and experience that are useful for their home countries, and transfer significant parts of their earnings. Migrants stimulate trade between their countries of origin and the host countries (Lowell, 2001). Recent studies explore this nexus between migration

---

4) Adapted in extracts from Selassie and Weiss (2002). "The Brain Drain – Africa's Achilles Heel", *World Markets in Focus 2002,* World Markets Research Centre, London.

5) See intervention of South African Minister Essop Pahad on "Migration, xenophobia and intolerance in Africa", during IOM November 2001 Council session (IOM, 2002a).

and home-country development and inquire about the optimal level of brain drain (Lowell, 2001; Beine *et al.,* 2002; IOM, 2002b). While it is ultimately difficult to determine such an optimal level, a consideration of the risks and potentials makes it possible to formulate general policy challenges.

On the negative side, migration leads to a lack of skilled manpower in key-sectors of national development. In general, the sectors of health, education, and technological development are most severely hit. Consequentially, the development of these sectors lags behind, or is completely suspended. The assumption that other well-qualified nationals can easily replace those lost in brain drain is simplistic because the replacements often lack the necessary experience and exposure to maximize productivity and output. The exodus of skills has forced the most affected African countries to recruit expatriates as replacements. Africa spends an estimated US$ 4 billion annually on recruiting some 100,000 skilled expatriates (Selassie and Weiss, 2002). Yet, these expatriates are no long-term replacements but often an integral part of the foreign aid package for developing countries and thus do not contribute to sustainable development. Most Africans are indignant about this trend, which they view as another form of foreign domination.

On the social front, long-term migration negatively affects the male/female ratio and leads to disrupted family structures, which, in turn, might affect the growing feminization of migration in Africa.

In 1991, for instance, 10,961 (82,7 per cent) of the 13,239 Botswana nationals registered as residents abroad were males. The population's average sex ratio of 91[6] illustrates a strong female dominance. Experience from South African mines shows that migrant workers often tend to create new families in the destination country, while maintaining others back home. By staying abroad for long periods of time, the migrant mine workers might lose touch with their families in their homeland, which may lead spouses back home to create new households or become single parents. Census data from Botswana and Lesotho confirm an alarming increase in single female parent households. However, because of its industrial centres, the Southern Africa sub-region is in a somewhat special situation with respect to the household situations described.

The positive effects of migration mainly depend on the backward linkage of migrants to their home country, naturally including remittances and the transfers of knowledge and technology.

The return of migrants who have acquired new skills and knowledge abroad can be considered a form of knowledge transfer. In as much as the application of knowledge depends on the availability of technology, knowledge transfer is necessarily accompanied by a technology transfer. Even in case the migrants do not return home, however, they can still contribute to the development of their home countries. While staying abroad, they might promote cooperation between universities, technological research centres and business associations of the home and host countries. Internet- and satellite-based information technology greatly enhances this cooperation potential.

In this light, migration can contribute to development in countries of origin. A crucial policy challenge of the future is to involve the skilled members of the African diaspora in innovative forms of cooperation and knowledge transfer to promote the expansion and sustainability of key-sectors for national development.

A special issue of *Africa Insight* on brain drain, asked the pertinent question whether "the outflow of skilled people [will] kill the African renaissance?" While underlining the potential danger of brain drain for the development process on the continent, especially when the lost skills can never be recovered, the authors McDonald and Crush emphasize the importance of brain circulation to propel African development as it involves redistribution of human resources within the continent. If this redistribution is done rationally, it could attract highly skilled emigrants to return back home from overseas in a chain reaction (McDonald and Crush, 2000).

223

6) For every 100 female residents, there are 91 male residents.

TEXTBOX 12.3.

Dealing with Migration Issues in Morocco

In 2001, an estimated 2.5. million Moroccans resided overseas, representing almost 10 per cent of Morocco's total population.

Morocco's international migration patterns continue to be predominantly oriented towards the European Union (EU). But since the late 1980s, final destinations have been diversifying with Moroccan migrants now living in Algeria, Burkina Faso, Canada, Libya, the United States, the Arab Gulf countries and Senegal.

There are two major groups of receiving countries in the EU:

• Belgium, France, Germany, and the Netherlands feature among the long-established destinations. Family reunification, the feminization of migration as well as social mobility and improved integration (such as through naturalization in the host country) have characterized the Moroccan population in these countries since the 1960s.

• Italy and Spain are two of the most recent EU destinations. Since the early 1990s, the number of Moroccan migrants in both countries has increased dramatically. A dominant feature of Moroccan migration to these countries is the increasing number or irregular migrants.

International migration has important repercussions for Morocco's economy. One of its most important aspects is migrant remittances. Today, remittances are having an unprecedented impact on the country's economy. In 2001, there was in increase of 57.5 per cent in the amount received in 2000. In 2001, remittances totalled some 36 billion Moroccan Dirhams (some US$ 3.3 billion). Remittances represent a considerable proportion of GDP and contribute to readjusting Morocco's balance of trade deficit (**table 1**); they also constitute one of the main generators of foreign currencies together with tourism. However, this recent significant growth in remittances can be put down to the devaluation by 5 per cent of the Moroccan Dirham in April 2001. Also, September 11 and the transition to the Euro, may have had a psychological impact on the saving behaviour of Moroccan migrants.

An examination of the origin of migrant remittances reveals growing diversity in the destination countries of Moroccan migrants and the strong links with family and communities back home maintained by the diaspora in these countries (**table 2**).

Despite the growing focus on irregular immigration into Spain and Italy, as well as campaigns to regularize irregular migrants in both these countries, the thorny issue of undocumented migration from Morocco remains largely untackled. Since the mid-1990s, Morocco has increasingly become a transit country for migrants from Sub-Saharan Africa (including Malians, Burkinabés or Ghanaians) *en route* to Europe. Hundreds of people die every year braving the dangerous crossings of the Strait of Gibraltar to Spain's mainland or the Atlantic Ocean to reach the Canary Islands, in unseaworthy vessels. These deaths in *pateras* (small boats) are a subject of concern to Moroccan authorities and are receiving more and more attention in Moroccan and European media.

In August 2001, King Mohammed VI presented a series of new guidelines for his Government, including migration. He announced the establishment of a global, coherent

TABLE 1.

Morocco - migrants' remittances and balance of trade deficit*, 1996 to 2001

	1996	1997	1998	1999	2000	2001
Total remittances	18 873.8	21 033.4	19 310.9	19 001.5	22 961.6	36 162.8
Trade balance deficit	-24 599.5	-23 655.5	-30 068.0	-32 314.0	-43 310.1	-43 420.0
As % of the trade balance deficit	76.7	88.9	64.2	58.8	53	83.3

Note:
* in million Moroccan Dirhams

Source:
Office des changes

and integrated new policy to be responsive to the country's migrant community. It favours the emergence of new dynamic migrant elites in politics, science, technology, culture and sport. New mechanisms are directed towards strengthening the positive impact of migrant remittances in terms of productive investments and national development.

Two public foundations are involved in migration management issues: the Mohammed V Foundation deals with the summer return of Moroccan migrants to the country *(opérations de transit)*; the Hassan II Foundation covers the settlement of legal and administrative disputes involving Moroccan migrants abroad. The ongoing work of both foundations is one of Morocco's top priorities. Furthermore, the Hassan II Foundation plans to work towards enhancing the cultural influence of Morocco in host countries. The

specific objective is to favour the emergence of partnerships between migrant associations and host communities.

Morocco's migrant community is also being encouraged to become more closely involved in the cultural, social, and economic development of Morocco. To help reach this goal, IOM and the Hassan II Foundation created a project titled "Observatory on the Moroccan Community Living Abroad". The Observatory's task is to strengthen Morocco's capacity to document migration trends and to establish an integrated research system to collect and disseminate information on Moroccans abroad.

TABLE 2

Geographical origin of Moroccan migrant's remittances (2000)

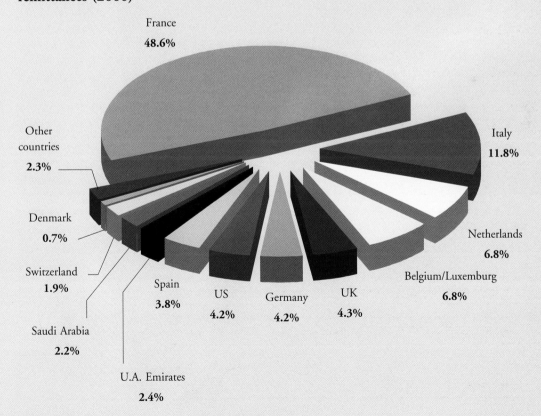

France 48.6%

Italy 11.8%

Other countries 2.3%

Denmark 0.7%

Netherlands 6.8%

Switzerland 1.9%

Belgium/Luxemburg 6.8%

Spain 3.8%

US 4.2%

Germany 4.2%

UK 4.3%

Saudi Arabia 2.2%

U.A. Emirates 2.4%

Source:
Office des changes

Migrant Remittances

One of the most promising outcomes of labour-related migration for countries of origin is migrants' remittances. The term can be defined as the portion of an international migrant's earnings sent back from the host country to the country of origin (Puri and Ritzema, 1999). It is necessary to distinguish official remittances that are transferred via official bank channels and are, therefore, recorded in the country's statistics, from unofficial (often referred to as informal) remittances that are sent back via private money courier systems, friends or relatives or carried home by the migrants themselves.

Throughout the last decade, more and more attention has been paid to the potential of migrants' remittances to contribute to the development of countries of origin. Various studies have been undertaken to estimate the scale and nature of remittances, and investigate their impact on development in countries of origin. Generally, research is confronted with a lack of sufficient and reliable data. African data are especially scarce, which is why most studies focus on other regions, such as the Middle East, Latin America or South-East Asia. Still, given that these studies describe general determinants of remittances and possible ways of enhancing their development efficiency, many findings apply to the African continent.

The Economic Importance of Remittances

The balance of payments statistics of the International Monetary Fund, one of the major data sources of official remittances, reveals a significant global increase of migrants' transfers from US$ 43 billion in 1980 to over US$ 70 billion in 1995. A similar tendency can be observed in most African countries (**table 12.2.**). In the cases of Cape Verde, Cameroon, Ghana, Madagascar, Mali, Morocco, Senegal, Togo and Tunisia, the amount of annual official remittances increased by almost 100 per cent.

At the same time, a country-specific, year-by-year analysis displays the high volatility and subsequent unpredictability of the transfers. The standard deviation from the annual averages of the years 1980 to 1999 spans 17 per cent in the case of Egypt to over 50 per cent in the cases of Cameroon, Cape Verde, Niger, and Togo. In Botswana, Ghana, Lesotho, and Nigeria, it even exceeds 100 per cent. Reasons for this volatility are extremely diverse and generally reflect the structure of the diaspora, the economic developments in the respective countries of destination, and the political environment in the countries of origin. Still, it is safe to say that developing countries' economies cannot currently rely on a steady flow of migrants' financial transfers (**table 12.3.**).

TABLE 12.2.

Annual remittances to selected African countries (in million US$)

Country/Year	1975	1980	1985	1995	1999 (estimate)
Egypt, Arab Rep.	2696.00	3496.20	3742.60	3279.00	3772.40
Morocco	1053.69	967.16	2006.35	1969.50	1938.11
Nigeria	12.80	10.07	10.01	803.55	1301.06
Tunisia	318.55	270.82	551.04	679.88	761.24
Senegal	74.78	55.05	90.83	86.49	92.78
Mali	59.40	67.00	106.92	112.11	83.81
Benin	77.00	38.06	88.77	92.43	72.81
Cape Verde	40.06	20.76	56.03	103.95	68.53
Burkina Faso	150.27	125.88	139.67	88.73	66.74
Cameroon	11.00	46.70	60.60	28.24	..
Ghana	0.50	0.40	6.00	17.30	30.70
Niger	5.88	2.10	13.06	6.34	7.24
Madagascar	0.38	4.57	4.48	8.95	7.19
Lesotho	..	..	..	0.79	0.69
Togo	9.93	15.41	26.87	15.02	0.03
TOTAL	4510.24	5120.18	6903.23	7292.28	8203.33

Source:
World Bank (2001).

TABLE 12.3.

Volatility of annual official remittances from 1980 to 1999 (in million US$)

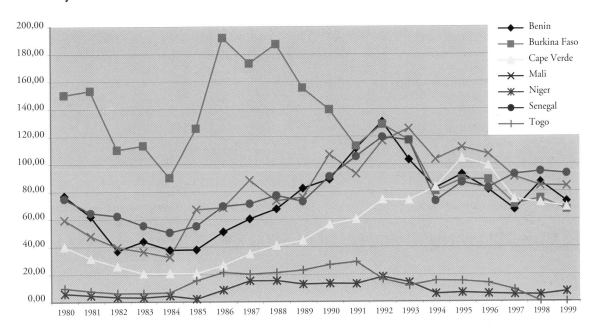

Source:
Calculations on the basis of World Bank (2001)

Nonetheless, official remittances do represent considerable financial inflows in many developing countries, and are, therefore, an economic reality that should not be neglected. In Benin, their average of the years 1980 to 1999 amounts to 4.5 per cent of gross domestic product (GDP), in Burkina Faso to 5.8 per cent, and in Cape Verde to 13.5 per cent. Moreover, a comparison of the annual inflows of official development aid (ODA), foreign direct investment (FDI), and official remittances reveals that with the exception of Nigeria and Cameroon remittances account for considerably more of financial inflows than FDI[7] (**table 12.4.**). Given that the economic environment in most developing countries is not conducive to attracting FDI, remittances could play a major role in further developing the countries' economies.

Remittances are even more important if informal remittances are taken into account. Admittedly, given the current lack of reliable data, it is difficult to draw any far-reaching conclusions. However, studies on Sudan, Egypt, and several South-East Asian countries estimate that the informal remittances double, and in some cases even triple the total amount of migrants' financial transfers (Lowell, 2001; Puri and Ritzema, 1999). A major reason to transfer money through informal channels is the still inadequately developed banking systems in countries of origin. Thus it is safe to assume that informal remittances are very important in Africa.

7) In Nigeria, the oil boom during the 1980s triggered the high inflow of foreign capital. In Tunisia, the relatively big share of foreign direct investment is due to the expansion of the tourism sector.

TABLE 12.4.

Financial inflows - ODA, FDI, and official remittances (average of the years 1980 to 1999)

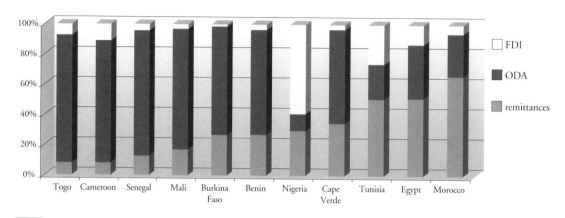

Source:
Calculations on the basis of World Bank (2001)

Determinants

The amount transferred home depends on the migrant's personal and family situation, i.e., the total amount earned, the amount saved, as well as the number of dependants back home. These factors differ in every individual case and hinder easy generalizations.

Nevertheless, two general tendencies can be distinguished: firstly, the better educated migrants will be less likely to remit (Lowell, 2001); secondly, the higher earning migrants tend to transfer a smaller share of their income (Puri and Ritzema, 1999). In other words, highly-educated migrants tend to be more independent from their relatives back home, and migrants with high salaries tend to save or invest significant parts of their financial resources in the respective host countries.

Since better educated migrants often earn better salaries, migrants can be generally divided into two groups for the purpose of studying remittance patterns: highly educated, well-paid migrants who tend to keep most of their savings in the host country; relatively under-educated migrants who earn less but tend to transfer home a larger percentage of their earnings. Therefore, migrants moving within unskilled or semi-skilled labour migration flows play a different role with respect to remittances than those migrating on the account of brain drain.

A study of the remittances patterns among the two groups requires analysis of the factors that would increase the likelihood of money transfers.

Well-educated and well-remunerated migrants tend to factor the political, economic and financial situation in their home country into their decision to remit. Political stability, the macro-economic environment, legal mechanisms to prevent fraud and corruption, and credible investment opportunities – these factors constitute the framework necessary to attract the portion of savings which is not used to support families or relatives. Additionally, if the inflation rate is higher than the interest rate, depositing money on bank accounts results in a loss in real terms. Unless the interest rate is favourable, commercial banks will not manage to attract savings and many of the highly skilled, well-paid migrants will continue to keep their savings in foreign bank accounts or invest in host countries.

Migrants' savings abroad represent enormous potential for additional remittances. Even if the economic environment of the home country cannot compete with that of the host country, and even if the interest rate in the home country is lower than in the host country, remittances can still be attracted provided investments in the home country are not overly risky, and as long as the real interest rate is not negative. Unlike foreign investors who base their decision mainly on rational criteria of a cost-benefit-calculation, migrants usually preserve emotional links to their home country, and so their decision is based not only on objective criteria, but also on subjective factors such as prestige as well as a desire to help development in their home country.

In the case of lower-paid, under-educated migrants, a few factors need to be outlined. In most cases, these migrants do not have the option of keeping their savings in the host countries, mainly because of the dependency of relatives in their country of origin. Instead, they try to find the most favourable way to transfer their earnings back home either through official or informal channels. The choice is determined by exchange rates, bank charges for transfers, the development of the banking system in the country of origin, and the real interest rate, determined by the inflation rate in the home country. While studies show that one factor alone cannot explain the ratio of informally transferred remittances, the interplay of the above-mentioned factors clearly influences the amount of informal transfers.

Athukorola (1993)[8] investigates the relationship between the informal remittance ratio and three macro-economic indicators: the real deposit rate[9], the financial intermediation ratio[10], and the black market premium[11]. He shows that more money is transmitted informally in countries with a comparably high black market premium, an underdeveloped financial sector and a low real interest rate. To put it simply, migrants will tend to use informal channels if they lose considerable sums of money through the use of official channels. Indeed, many officially transferred remittances simply get lost en route owing to bank fees and exchange rates, especially in countries of origin where local currency is overvalued. Many of these countries do

not allow savings deposits on foreign currency accounts and their banks frequently lack provision for this. Also, a migrant will prefer unofficial exchange channels, such as the black market, if he can make a profit. As a consequence, informal channels that circumvent losses and offer earnings are used more frequently, and the share of informally remitted financial resources is growing.

In sum, external as well as internal factors impact on the stability of remittances. A migrant's willingness to remit money is directly influenced by a country's macro-economic management and performance, its banking and investment climate, and the physical reliability of remittances' transfers. Conversely, the frequency of remittances will be directly determined by a migrant's professional situation: job stability, personal situation in the country of destination, number of dependants to sustain abroad, etc.

Impact

Most remittances are sent back to support the migrants' families. Thus, the most obvious impact of remittances is to increase the income of the migrants' households in the countries of origin. Yet, remittances also impact the macro-economic environment, since they increase the total purchasing power of a given economy. As obvious and simple as this relation appears, careful analysis is required in order to obtain the whole picture of possible effects. In particular, remittances do not necessarily have positive effects on socio-economic development in countries of origin.

Let us consider a few negative consequences. Firstly, remittances generate dependency among migrants' households as well as in the economy generally, especially if they represent a main source of foreign currency in the country of origin. As remittances can be highly volatile, countries might suddenly find themselves without financial assets that contributed to national development as well as household income.

229

8) Quoted in Puri and Ritzema (1999). Although Athukorola's study related to South-East Asia, it contains interesting information also applicable to an African context.

9) The real deposit rate is mainly determined by the inflation in a given country, that is the increase of costs of living. The higher the inflation, the lower the real gains of savings (the real interest rate) for a given nominal interest rate.

10) The financial intermediation rate shows the financial development of an economy. Money is "the oil in the motor of the economy", a basis for efficient allocation. The lower the amount of money that circulates in an economy given a fixed inflation rate, the less efficient are the market allocations. The intermediation rate is expressed by the ratio between the available amount of money in an economy (M2) and the total GDP: M2/GDP. Generally, the higher the rate, the higher the economic activities in a country.

11) Indicates the additional earnings if foreign currency is exchanged on the black market: black market exchange rate x 100 / official exchange rate.

The volatility of remittances can be illustrated by the example of Burkina Faso. Here, the total amount of official remittances dropped down by from US$ 187 million in 1988 to US$ 112 million in 1991, and continued to decrease to US$ 67 million in 1999, which is a total decrease of two thirds[12]. In the meantime, the annual average growth rate of the GDP decreased from approximately 5 per cent in the years 1980-1988, to –3 per cent in the years 1989-1994, and only slowly increased again to reach the average of 1.7 per cent until 1999. In 1980, remittances represented 8.8 per cent of GDP, dropping sharply to 2.6 per cent in 1999. While this drop in remittances alone cannot explain this decrease in economic growth, it was an important contributory factor.

Obviously, a drop in remittances does not only affect national economies but also the individuals who depend on money transfers from abroad. Transfers from family members often constitute more than 50 per cent of household income used for consumption; less money means that consumption has to be reduced drastically.

Remittances can also trigger an increase in local income divergences, depending on how migrant families use the received money. Generally, remittances contribute to the subsistence of the respective households. Yet, they are often used to buy import goods such as washing machines or television sets, or more importantly food that is not locally produced (Lowell, 2001). In this case, the demand for local goods drops while the imports increase. Subsequently, local production is hit badly and local income and wages drop. Thus, the poor get even poorer while those who are better off get even better access to imported luxury goods.

However, remittances can aid local development if translated into additional demand for local/national products. In this case, local productivity and consequentially local wages increase, and income differences slowly decrease. If there is a supporting economic framework, multiplier-effects boost economic activities. Moreover, at the macro-economic level, the total amount of money available increases without affecting the inflation rate[13], the balance of payments improves, and the national currency becomes stronger. This mechanism, however, is only activated by greater demand for productive goods. The purchase of real estate and land does not increase local productivity.

Additionally, remittance transfer and savings mechanisms in the home country are equally important. Earnings sent from abroad only influence economic development if they access the national financial system. As long as remittances are informally transmitted and "kept in the kitchen drawer", they will not contribute to local or national development. Savings can only create multiplier effects if they are accessible to other economic actors.

Management

How can the positive effects of remittances be encouraged while preventing or, at least, limiting possible negative consequences? First of all, the ratio of officially transferred financial resources should be enhanced in order to increase the development efficiency of remittances. Additionally, the significant resources of the diaspora that are currently invested or saved abroad should be mobilized. African countries can encourage official transfers and mobilize new resources by providing a favourable exchange rate, the option to use foreign bank accounts in the country of origin, and especially bank accounts that guarantee a positive real interest rate. The most important precondition, however, is to develop efficient official transfer mechanisms that offer services at acceptable rates.

The experiences of three banks in Paris - the *Banque de l'Habitat du Sénégal,* the *Banque de l'Habitat du Mali,* and the lately opened *Banque des Ivoiriens de France* – demonstrate the potential of innovative official transfer mechanisms. By offering a special transfer scheme to Côte d'Ivoire, Mali and Senegal, the banks currently undertake more than 400 transfers a day, with significantly lower fees than private money courier services (Enogo, 2002). In 1999, for instance, more than US$ 24 million were officially transferred to Senegal via this scheme, representing approximately 26 per cent of the total official remittances to Senegal that year.

12) Interestingly enough, the total amount of remittances increased during the political uncertainties of the first part of the 1980s. Especially during the period of the Sankara government 1983-1987, fighting against foreign economic domination, the inflow increased in a major way. After the assassination of former President Thomas Sankara in 1987, however, the remittances decreased sharply, and never reached their previous level although the political situation of the country stabilised during the 1990s.

13) Given the low capital-intensity of production in most African countries, additional financial resources can be expected to trigger an important growth of productivity, and thus the inflation rate will not increase.

Secondly, remittances should be channelled into underdeveloped rural areas as multiplier effects are significantly higher there. This is mainly because the consumption rate there is higher. Hence, additional financial resources translate almost entirely into additional demand.

Thirdly, the production could be enhanced significantly through the pooling of remittances and creation of platforms for economic activities such as local credit cooperatives or special investment schemes. It is neither possible nor desirable to channel remittances transferred for family subsistence in the country of origin into investments; however, incentives could be offered to the migrants and their families to keep the "surplus money", remaining after the daily expenses are covered, on official bank accounts in order to make them accessible to other economic actors. Moreover, it is also possible to create incentives for productive investments. Currently, the residual financial resources of migrants' families are mainly invested in unproductive assets such as real estate, land, and imported luxury goods because these investments appear to be safe. As soon as local credit cooperatives prove that investments in productive activities yield revenues, carry little risk and trigger multiplier effects, general investment behaviour is likely to change. However, local credit cooperatives are not the only productive channel for remittances in Africa. Secure bank deposits in foreign or local currency at favourable rates would certainly represent an attractive alternative to labour migrants and have beneficial effects on the home country economy.

The issue of micro-finance institutions, and especially the ability of credit cooperatives to strengthen development has been discussed in more detail by a number of studies (Krahnen and Schmidt, 1995; ILO, 2000). Such grassroots cooperatives are still rare in African countries. Nonetheless, some research has found evidence of the use of channelled remittances at the community level in Africa. Over the years, migrants' associations, or more correctly migrants-cum-non-migrants network associations, such as "home improvement unions" in Nigeria and "social welfare associations" in Kenya and other countries (Oucho, 1996) generate "pooled" remittances from the community members' contributions.

Experience has shown that cooperatives can successfully contribute to development if fraud and corruption are successfully combated and if the established partnerships are envisioned and designed to be long-lasting. The government needs to provide the necessary legal framework and appropriate economic incentives. Simultaneously,

an efficient system to transfer financial assets is required. In summary, the efficient use of remittances for local development should be based on a partnership involving associations of the African diaspora, local community associations, financial institutions in both countries of origin and countries of destination and, finally, the governments of the respective countries of origin. Such a partnership would facilitate an increase in the ratio of officially remitted financial assets as well as attracting further resources of the African diaspora. This partnership would also make transfers less volatile and countries of origin less dependent.

TEXTBOX 12.4.

The migration context in Tunisia

Tunisia's expatriate community currently represents almost 8 per cent of the country's total population. From a mere 15,000 people in 1954, the figure had reached 689,108 in 2001 and was distributed in the following regions: 589,075 (84.5%) in Europe; 91,347 (13%) in the other Maghreb and Arab States; 16,333 (2.5%) in the United States and Canada. In Europe, Tunisians reside mainly in France (65%), Italy, Germany and Belgium.

Owing to economic, demographic and social factors, Tunisian migration initially took the form of individual and collective labour migration. Since 1973-74, however, it has become more family-oriented (family reunification) and seasonal for a small number of qualified workers who meet labour market requirements in the countries of destination.

The composition of Tunisian emigration has also changed since the 1980s, with the emergence of new migrant generations. Consequently children under the age of 16 and women now make up 25 per cent and 23 per cent of total Tunisian migration, respectively. This is the result of a combination of family reunions, marriages and births in countries of residence. Similarly, the number of Tunisian scientists and researchers abroad has grown markedly, especially in Europe and North America. The recently established register of such persons contains 4,800 names.

Because Tunisians resident abroad are an integral part of the national community, Tunisia, under the leadership of President Ben Ali, has been collaborating closely with host countries to safeguard their rights and enhance living and residence conditions.

Accordingly, Tunisia has adopted a global strategy for Tunisians abroad. There are three basic objectives: to protect and safeguard their interests; to preserve their cultural identity and consolidate links with Tunisia; and to encourage the participation of Tunisian migrants in national development.

The Tunisian Government has enacted laws and taken appropriate steps to respond to the expectations and concerns of its citizens, and to protect their rights. Accordingly, 12 bilateral social security agreements have been concluded, 8 with states of the European Union; other agreements are currently being negotiated.
In addition, special programmes will inform expatriate Tunisians of the country's achievements and existing investment opportunities beyond the incentives and other benefits available to them in various sectors.

Tunisia is also paying special attention to young, second and third-generation Tunisians abroad. The aim is to preserve their identity and consolidate integration in the host countries so that these people may become vehicles for dialogue and cooperation between those countries and Tunisia. Tunisia's migration policy devotes constant attention to Tunisian women and families resident abroad through the following measures: creating socio-cultural entities in many European countries and in North America; and stepping up the presence of social counsellors and social workers in the host countries.

This policy is being implemented principally by the Office for Tunisians Abroad (OTE) under the supervision of the Ministry for Social Affairs. Since its creation in 1988, the OTE has been operating in both Tunisia and host countries through a technical and administrative network made up of 17 regional delegations located in high-immigration areas; 58 social counsellors; 10 social workers operating out of the various consulates and diplomatic missions abroad; and 16 *"Espaces Femme et Deuxième Génération"* (Women and Second- Generation Forums) in the main European and North American cities with large numbers of resident Tunisian families. A programme is underway in host countries to bolster the structures of Tunisian community associations abroad, which currently include 383 associations and 428 welfare societies.

Furthermore, the Ministry of Vocational Training and Employment and the Tunisian Agency for Technical Cooperation are playing a pivotal role in managing migration flows of skilled and unskilled Tunisian workers.

A new migration management policy has been implemented to select and orient candidates for emigration in order to ease the admission and social and professional integration of Tunisian workers in host countries. In this regard, Tunisia signed a bilateral cooperation agreement with Italy in 2000. A networked database covering the sectors and profiles of the 5,000 Tunisian candidates for emigration provides an interesting example of how to facilitate the recruitment process as well as how to match and jointly manage employment supply and demand between country of origin and host contrary.

Moreover, Tunisia was the first country on the southern Mediterranean shore to conclude an association agreement with the European Union in 1995 as part of its strategy. Although the main purpose is to establish a free trade area by 2008, the agreement also includes a social section, which is in itself a significant achievement for Tunisia. This section is a key frame of reference for protecting and strengthening the rights of Tunisians resident in European Union states. The agreement also established a working party, which met for the first time in Brussels in April 2001. The working party is also responsible for following up the social cooperation part of the agreement, which aims at establishing a social dialogue between Tunisia and the European Union with a view to making progress on the movement of workers, equal treatment, and the social integration of nationals of both parties.

The Migration and Development Nexus

Migration can contribute significantly to the development of African countries. According to some authors and based on evidence and political interests, migrants urgently need to be viewed and understood as a development resource.

The authors of a recent IOM study on the migration-development nexus provide a series of reasons as to why this reinforcement is necessary (IOM, 2002b):

• remittances by migrants are likely to be double the size of aid and may be at least as effective in targeting the poor in both conflict-ridden and stable developing countries;

• migrant diasporas are engaged in a variety of transnational practices, such as relief, investment, cultural exchange, political advocacy, with direct effects on international development cooperation;

- both private and public sectors in developed countries recognize their immediate and long-term dependence on immigrant labour with an ever more complex skills mixture[14];

- policies for development cooperation, humanitarian relief, migration and refugee protection are internally inconsistent and occasionally mutually contradictory.

Some of these trends and concerns could be addressed by viewing migrant diasporas, composed by unskilled, semi-skilled and highly skilled migrants, as a development resource and by seeking links between aid and migrants' transnational practices.

In order to fully unfold migration-development potential, two main challenges need to be addressed by African countries: the establishment of orderly migration flows to facilitate efficient management; and the implementation of viable strategies linking migration and development.

Migration Management in Africa

In the past, migration management was not a priority on the policy agenda of many African countries. However, most of the continent's sub-regional groupings now contain treaties and protocols facilitating economic integration and cooperation in a variety of areas. These instruments range from education and training to trade, transport, communications and also migration. Conversely, the prominence of migration issues on regional groupings' agendas is also beginning to have a positive impact on legislation and policy in individual countries[15].

With respect to the free movement of people, many economic groupings (ECOWAS, EAC, COMESA and SADC) have attained the first stage but are reluctant to proceed to the next controversial stage of the "right of residence and establishment". In the SADC, major immigration countries strongly oppose this stage, arguing, among other things, that economic disparity among the member states is likely to generate floods of immigrants. The COMESA treaty underlines "free movement of skilled labour and services", yet this is far from being implemented. Even

ECOWAS with a much longer experience in regional integration has found it difficult to convince its Member States to transcend the visa-free entry stage to the right of residence and establishment before finally eliminating national boundaries (Adepoju, 2002).

Still, SADC countries, for example, recently initiated a process aimed at carefully developing a regional migration regime while circumventing gridlock situations. The "Migration Dialogue for Southern Africa" (MIDSA) involves all SADC Member States and was set up after previous SADC efforts failed to develop and establish a regional protocol on the movement of people (see also **textbox 8.2.**).

A pan-African approach to migration management would ensure greater orderliness and predictability in movements of people, serving and balancing the interests of the sending and receiving countries and migrants alike (Ghosh, 2000). The establishment of the African Economic Community (AEC) is heading into this direction; article 43 addresses "free movement of persons, rights of residence and establishment". Yet, if sub-regional institutions cannot agree on free movement and its implications, how can a pan-African organization be expected to succeed? Regional arrangements should probably be established before a common African solution can be envisioned.

Strategies to Link Migration and Development

Building on efficient migration management, regional and international strategies linking migration and development should be introduced.

In as much as the causes and effects of migration are complex, the linkages between migration and development are not as simple as they may appear. Large cross-border movements can be a response to the ever-increasing gaps in living standards and income between countries; this often means a loss of human capital where it is most needed for development. At the same time, emigration from Africa can help to alleviate imbalances, including population pressures; furthermore, the mobilization of human and financial resources abroad can become an additional force of origin country development (IOM, 2000).

Cooperation between countries of destination, transit and origin is required to fully appreciate and develop the positive benefits of migration and reduce potential divergences of interest from all countries involved. Recognizing

233

14) See also **chapter 13.**
15) An assessment of national legislative and policy frameworks covering migration and related management, and their linkages with actions undertaken at regional level, would appear to be an interesting area for policy-oriented research in Africa.

common migration interests, governments are increasingly negotiating strategies supporting both the sustainable development of sending countries and the labour needs of receiving countries – while giving due regard to migrants' rights. These kinds of negotiated arrangements are based on integrated policy approaches that link migration to development cooperation, trade and investment, as well as demographic and social development at the regional, national and international levels (IOM, 2000). For instance, the Cotonou Agreement between the EU and the group of Africa-Caribbean-Pacific countries (ACP) covers some of these elements and represents a promising basis for common migration management (see **textbox 14.1.**).

Meaningful management of labour-related migration and remittances to harness their targeted contribution to development efforts could have a potentially enormous positive impact on African countries at national, community and family levels. The present problem, however, is that the linkages between brain drain, labour migration and remittances and their impact on development are only fragmentarily understood and favoured by governments in many of the continent's countries.

Undoubtedly, brain drain has deprived African countries of many of the well-educated and skilled nationals they invested in for years. Brain drain problems cannot simply be solved by replacing emigrants with younger generations. Instead, it is necessary to develop innovative forms of emigrant return and contribution as well as strategies for better sharing of knowledge, skills and experience with non-migrants in view of national development priorities. Definitive return of skilled migrants does not appear to be viable as long as socio-economic and political conditions in African countries continue to deteriorate.

In its 2001 programme of action, the New Partnership for African Development (NEPAD) plans to reverse the brain drain by "building critical human resources for Africa's development" and to "develop strategies for utilising the (…) know-how and skills of Africans in the diaspora for the development of Africa". It shows that African leaders have started to acknowledge the importance of this issue.

IOM's programme "Migration for Development in Africa" (MIDA) represents a dynamic response to the migration-related objectives of NEPAD. It aims at building part-nerships between host countries and countries of origin that foster positive effects of migration for both while limiting the negative effects of the brain drain (see also **textboxes 12.5.** and **15.1.**).

TEXTBOX 12.5.

A Migrant's Story – Happy to be back in the Democratic Republic of the Congo

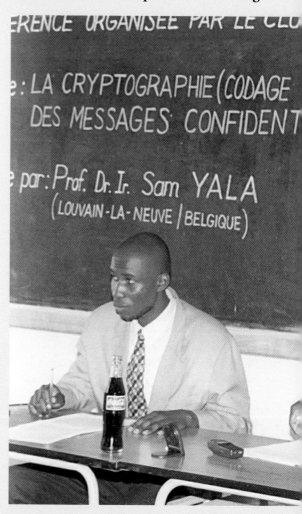

In the summer of 2002, 33 academics and professionals from the Democratic Republic of the Congo and from Burundi who were living and working in Belgium, decided to join the IOM Migration for Development in Africa Programme (MIDA). The programme aims at transferring the skills and resources from the diaspora to support development on the African continent.

One participant in the programme was Professor Edouard Malambu, who lectures physics at the University of Brussels. Professor Malambu returned to Kinshasa for two months where he lectured at Kinshasa University. "The university currently houses between 20,000 and

Seven Congolese academics returned over the summer of 2002: some to teach mechanical and electrical engineering, and others to teach environmental sciences. One returnee, a medical doctor, taught physiotherapy at Kinshasa's Institut Supérieur des Techniques Médicales.

According to MIDA programme coordinator Margaret Kabamba, many Congolese professionals currently living and working in Belgium have expressed a strong interest in joining the programme: "They feel that after having spent many years abroad, they should share some of their knowledge and time with students and other colleagues who, up to now, have felt somewhat forgotten".

MIDA participants who return to the DRC to teach on temporary assignments receive a Euro 1,200 grant, payable in two instalments.

The Congolese Minister of Labour and Social Affairs, Marie-Ange Lukiana Mufwankolo met the first returnees. She praised their dedication and said more African professionals should follow their example. "MIDA can help revert the devastating effects of the brain drain, which each year deprives Africa of thousands of its best and brightest. Our country desperately needs those competencies. We are fully prepared to receive more MIDA candidates, even for shorter periods of time", she said.

MIDA is also addressing the need for qualified human resources in neighbouring Burundi and Rwanda. The programme seeks to build synergies and partnerships between governments, civil society, universities and the private sector.

As a first step, MIDA identifies skills and resources in the diaspora before matching those skills and resources with requirements in African countries. Then, the programme organizes the temporary return of qualified professionals. Another approach to containing the brain drain is to organize the "virtual" return of skills by employing modern information technology. IOM will work with the *Agence Universitaire de la Francophonie* and with the African Virtual University (AVU), a "university without walls", which uses modern information and communication technologies to provide direct access to some of the best learning resources abroad.

235

A DRC academic working in Belgium returns home on a teaching visit

30,000 students. But it suffers from a chronic lack of qualified staff and resources. This establishment had a reputation for excellence, but so many things have gone wrong. But still, when I heard that IOM offered the possibility for Congolese academics to complete temporary assignments at Kinshasa University, I jumped on it ! This programme works because there are many Congolese in the diaspora who are committed to the development of their country. Not all are ready to leave the country where they have studied and built their lives, but most are ready to give some of their time to try and plug the brain drain".

Set up by the World Bank and launched in 1997, AVU has provided students and professionals in 17 African countries with over 3,000 hours of interactive instruction in English and French. More than 24,000 students have completed semester-long courses in technology, engineering, business and the sciences. Over 3,500 professionals have attended executive and professional management seminars on topics such as strategy and innovation, entrepreneurship and e-commerce.

MIDA builds on and expands IOM's Return and Reintegration of Qualified African Nationals Programme (RQAN), which was launched in 1993. RQAN helped more than 2,000 experienced nationals return home to contribute to national development.

Conclusions

Over the next decades, Africa will continue to experience large-scale population movements, especially outwards. Labour-related migration will continue to provide a way to escape poverty or other forms of hardship at home; however, it also provides a way for educated, skilled and qualified persons to expand their career potential in today's increasingly globalized world. Nonetheless, migration and its linkage to development should not be considered solely from the economic point of view. Migration cannot be reduced to an economic act and migrants viewed only as labourers. Other social, cultural and political aspects also have to be taken into account – conflict and human rights abuse associated with poor governance have become key factors in compelling much current migration in Africa. It is no coincidence that conflict-ridden countries often experience severe economic difficulties (IOM, 2002b).

This chapter has demonstrated that migration can be both costly and beneficial for African countries. The main cost is the significant loss of human capital and subsequent manpower gaps in key-sectors for national development. However, migration contributes to balancing economic growth within Africa, and enhances knowledge and technology transfers from developed countries. In particular, remittances from the African diaspora contribute in major ways to the cumulative national purchasing power as well as to individual household income. However, remittances are poorly managed and unpredictable at present. Migration management approaches in Africa should include viable schemes for converting remittances into productive assets, including the following: better remittance services in order to reduce leakages and waste in the transfer process; the guarantee that migrant workers have the right to choose the preferred channels for remittance transfer; and, ultimately, the provision of market conforming investment opportunities aimed at increasing the development potential of remittances.

Linking migration and development means building a partnership between countries of origin and host countries, and between the associations of the diaspora and local private sector initiatives. Governments of both sending and receiving countries should formulate and implement migration policies that enable different categories of African migrants to improve their professional options while contributing to development back home. There is growing international consensus on the usefulness of constructive migration policy cooperation to address the demographic requirements of certain developed countries and the imperfect functioning of their complex labour markets, as well as the development imperatives of countries in Africa (IOM, 2002a).

TEXTBOX 12.6.

A Migrant's Story – "You're a Big Girl Now", from Sudan to the United States

Resettlement in the US brought a new life for one of the "Lost Girls" of the Sudan

236

"Now you are a big girl, don't forget to take care of yourself and learn how to pray." These were the last words spoken by her mother when she was six years old. Her family had fled Sudan three years earlier and was living in Ethiopia. It was the first day of school and her mother had dropped her off at kindergarten. She remembers the moment well. Three hours later, the town was in flames and Aduei was on the run - without her family - part of a mass exodus of refugee children who had fled Sudan's civil war, and were now fleeing Ethiopia for the very same reasons.

"I did not realize until I was 14 that my mother had said something important to me," Aduei says.

She had left Sudan with her family intact: her mother, two brothers and a sister. She would have three peaceful years in exile. The war in Sudan restarted in 1983, the year before she was born. By 1987, it had intensified and the mass exodus began, mostly to Ethiopia. Aduei's father was on the front line when her family decided they should leave. That same year, some 25,000 - 30,000 refugees, mostly young unaccompanied boys and thousands of girls, straggled into Ethiopia, starving and traumatized. Their parents and siblings were killed and their homes destroyed. The boys were put in camps, and lived communally; the girls were dispersed into foster families. Three years later, a rebel group overthrew the Ethiopian government and rebel soldiers attacked the refugees. Separated from her family, Aduei fled. Staying one step ahead of the bullets, she reached the Gilo River, which had swollen with rain. She had to make a choice - jump into the crocodile-infested river or be shot. For those who crossed back into Sudan there would be no peace. The twice-exiled group was soon attacked again. They continued to flee south to Kenya.

In Kenya, the were the same living conditions for unaccompanied minors as in Ethiopia: most boys lived in groups, and the youngest boys and unaccompanied girls went into foster families. Aduei managed some semblance of family and was registered on the ration card of a male cousin. Again, she was lucky. The ration card would change her life. Because of their age and number, and their communal living arrangements, the boys remained a cohesive identifiable unit. They were compelling cases for resettlement. Dubbed the "Lost Boys", the US Government soon felt obliged to act. A few lucky girls, 89 to be exact, went with them to Kakuma to be resettled to the United States, because of some family bond to a brother, a cousin, or a male relative in that group.

The girls without relatives were required to live with foster families in the camps. Girls are assets as they can work and later marry, bringing a "bride price" to their guardians. According to researchers, forced marriage was high on the list of "Lost Girl" concerns. Out of the 33 girls between the ages of 14 and 17, research showed that 28 were living "moderately to severely abusive" situations; 17 were prevented from attending school; 12 had experienced some form of sexual abuse.

Aduei was one of the lucky ones

Today, she is a young 18-year old woman, whose experiences set her apart from the American teenagers around her. Her classmates did not know much about the war in Sudan when she first arrived in her adopted hometown of Boston. "If you have never been in war, you will never know the smell or the taste of it", she says. "Most of my friends here are innocent."

Innocence aside, they share many of the same anxieties such as what will they do in life. Aduei sobers quickly when envisioning her future. "I want to do something with people like me", she says. "When I look back and see young girls like me in Sudan, it bothers me. It bothers me all the time." Her desire to work with refugee girls is well within her reach. She speaks five languages: Dinka, Swahili, Arabic, Spanish and English, and has great wisdom for someone her age.

Her message to the other 88 Sudanese girls: "Take this opportunity to do something good in life. Don't waste it."

She relates her experience to her Second World War studies in school. "I am everything. I am Jewish, Muslim, and Christian. Religion is being used as a tool for hate. Two million are dead in Sudan. Two hundred years from now people will think, 'why did they do it?'. There is no point in killing people for religion."

Aduei also confides, "Like Dr. Martin Luther King, Jr., I have a dream". Her dream is not only for peace in Sudan, but for the creation of a Sudanese girls' school. She even has a more modest dream, in case the former proves too ambitious, to give at least two or three girls a chance at a better life through scholarship. "I don't care where they come from. We never had educated women in Sudan". In every statement, education is emphasized and tolerance is her message.

237

Like the American teenagers around her, college weighs heavily on her mind. She is preparing for entrance exams and would like to go to school in Boston, Washington, DC or North Carolina - Boston, to remain near her foster parents, former Peace Corps volunteers; Washington, DC, "because that is where important things happen"; and North Carolina, because her adopted US grandmother lives there. But she is not sure she will be able to enroll in the fall. She works after school at a local pharmacy and is worried about the money she will need for her education.

Recently, Aduei received two great surprises. She found out that one of her brothers is alive and living in a refugee camp near Dadaab, Kenya. And a few months ago, Aduei's uncle called with more good news and a telephone number. Aduei's mother was located in Uganda. "I called her, but I didn't think it was her. We spoke in Dinka, and it was hard because I don't ever speak in Dinka anymore. I was like, is this my mom? I didn't think so, until she said those words to me. They were the last words she said to me, and they are the only thing I remember. Then, I knew it was my mom."

238

"Now you are a big girl, don't forget to take care of yourself and learn how to pray".

CHAPTER 13

International Labour Migration and Demographic Change in Europe

After nearly 30 years of pursuing restrictive immigration and asylum policies, many European Union (EU) countries have begun to reassess their migration policies and to call for a different approach. For the first time in many years, several governments are considering the benefits of labour migration and the possibilities and merits of increasing immigration for demographic and other reasons.

For example, in 2001 Germany's Independent Commission on Migration[1] concluded: "We need immigration to Germany because the population here is getting older: life expectancy is increasing while the number of children born per family remains low and the number of births is decreasing" (Independent Commission on Migration to Germany, 2001:11).

The European Commission (EC) has also argued strongly in favour of a new approach. In November 2000, the EC published a Communication on a Community Immigration Policy, in which it stated that: "It is clear from an analysis of the economic and demographic context of the (European) Union and of the countries of origin, that the 'zero' immigration policies of the past 30 years are no longer appropriate" (EC, 2000:3).

This is an important statement as the EU committed itself in 1999, according to the Amsterdam Treaty and the Tampere summit decisions, to developing a common immigration and asylum policy by 2004. However, many governments remain cautious regarding such proposals. Anti-immigration parties' electoral successes in several European countries during 2000-2002 indicate that immigration in Europe is still seen by many as a "problem" to be solved through tight control, rather than by management (see also **chapter 14**).

The new debate about the future direction of migration in Europe has been prompted by several factors: economic concerns about skill shortages in certain employment sectors; growing awareness of the global competition for the highly skilled; a desire to provide alternatives to irregular migration, and concerns over demographic trends in Europe.

The chapter focusses on the last of these concerns – the likely impact of ageing and population decline on European labour markets and the implications for future international migration policy. The chapter begins with a historical overview of migration trends in Europe during the second half of the twentieth century, and then examines the likely demographic changes expected to affect Europe over the next 50 years. Potential strategies to offset population decline and ageing are discussed.

This is followed by an examination of current labour-migration policies in Europe; the extent to which demographic considerations are influencing the development of new labour-migration initiatives in Western Europe; and the likely impact of such policies on demographic change.

Migration Trends in the Second Half of the Twentieth Century

Western Europe[2]

During the 1950s, most Western Europe countries still registered a negative migration balance[3]. Some countries – in relative terms most notably Portugal and Ireland, in absolute terms also Italy, Spain and Greece – lost a substantial number of their citizens emigrating for economic reasons overseas as well as to other European countries: in particular to Belgium, France, West Germany, Sweden and Switzerland. Large-scale recruitment of foreign labour had already started or, as in the case of France and Switzerland, had resumed after an interruption during the Second World War. In West Germany, ethnic German immigration from Central and Eastern Europe and the inflow of citizens from the German Democratic Republic also played a significant role.

Since the 1960s, immigration started to outweigh emigration also in other Western European countries, namely Austria, Denmark, the Netherlands, and Norway. For economic

239

1) The so-called Süssmuth Commission, named after its President Rita Süssmuth.

2) Included here are the current 15 EU countries, Liechtenstein, Norway and Switzerland.

3) I.e., the balance between emigration and immigration, see also **textbox 1.2.**

and demographic reasons, the inflow of labour to these countries had started five to ten years later. All these countries stopped recruiting foreign labour in 1973-74. Although many labour migrants returned to their countries of origin, others remained and were joined by their dependent family members (i.e. spouses and minor children).

In the 1980s and 1990s, migration balances also turned positive for the first time in Finland, Ireland, the United Kingdom and later also in Greece, Italy, Portugal and Spain. Apart from the United Kingdom, all these countries had been traditional sending countries of economic migrants. Initially, their migration patterns changed as former labour migrants returned home from the Benelux, France, Germany, Sweden, Switzerland and the UK. But during the 1990s, all countries of Southern Europe experienced an inflow of foreign labour and other foreign immigrants (see **table 13.1.**).

In the forty years between 1960 and 2000, Western Europe's population increased by 4.3 per cent through a net inflow of some 16.7 million people. In absolute terms, the main receiving countries were Germany (net migration balance 1960-2000: +8.5 million[4]), France (+3.9 million), the Netherlands (+1.0 million), the UK (+0.9 million) and Switzerland (+0.8 million). Relative to population size, the largest net gain through international migration was registered in

---

4) Germany is analyzed in its present borders, migration flows between East and West Germany are therefore not included in this figure.

TABLE 13.1.

Net migration flows in Western Europe, 1960-2000

	Average Annual Net Migration Balance			Cumulative Net Flow					
	1960-1990	1990-2000	1960-2000	1960-1990		1990-2000		1960-2000	
				In 000s	As % of population	In 000s	As % of population	In 000s	As % of population
Austria	1.3	3.6	1.9	308	4.0	294	3.6	602	7.5
Belgium	0.9	1.5	1.0	247	2.5	153	1.5	400	3.9
Denmark	0.6	2.5	1.1	97	1.9	129	2.4	226	4.2
Finland	-1.0	1.3	-0.5	-140	-2.8	64	1.2	-76	-1.5
France	2.1	1.0	1.8	3,270	5.8	585	1.0	3,855	6.5
Germany	2.1	4.4	2.6	4,857	6.1	3,638	4.4	8,495	10.4
Greece	-0.1	4.2	1.0	27	0.3	442	4.2	469	4.4
Iceland	-1.4	-0.4	-1.1	-9	-3.5	-1	-0.4	-10	-3.5
Ireland	-3.0	2.4	-1.6	-285	-8.1	91	2.4	-194	-5.1
Italy	-0.6	2.0	0.0	-904	-1.6	1,177	2	273	0.5
Luxembourg	5.4	10.0	6.5	58	15.2	42	9.7	100	22.8
Netherlands	1.5	2.3	1.7	644	4.3	360	2.3	1,004	6.3
Norway	0.8	2.0	1.1	98	2.3	88	2	186	4.2
Portugal	-4.6	0.3	-3.4	-1,197	-12.1	35	0.4	-1,162	-11.6
Spain	-0.3	0.9	0.0	-286	-0.7	358	0.9	72	0.2
Sweden	1.9	2.2	2.0	476	5.6	194	2.2	670	7.6
Switzerland	3.0	3.3	3.1	569	8.3	235	3.3	804	11.2
U. Kingdom	0.1	1.5	0.4	114	0.2	827	1.4	941	1.6

Sources:
UN. *World Population Prospects - The 2000 Revision;* Brücker (2002); Calculations: Brücker and Demography at Humboldt University Berlin

Luxembourg (1960-2000: +22.8 per cent of total population), Switzerland (+11.2 per cent), Germany (+10.4 per cent), Sweden (+7.6 per cent) and Austria (+7.5 per cent). Slightly more than half of Western Europe's demographic net gain through legal migration took place during the last decade. Between 1990 and 2000, this net gain amounted to an additional 8.7 million people. In absolute terms during this period, Germany (net migration balance 1990-2000: +3.6 million), Italy (+1.2 million) and the UK (+0.8 million) had the largest net inflow. Relative to population size, the net migration balance was again the largest in Luxembourg (1990-2000: +9.7 per cent), followed by Germany (+4.4 per cent), Greece (+4.2 per cent) and Austria (+3.6 per cent of total population).

In 1950, Western Europe was home to only 3.8 million foreign citizens. By 1970-71, this number had risen to almost 11 million and to 20,5 million by the beginning of the twenty-first century. Another 8 million people are foreign-born but not foreign nationals as they either already immigrated as citizens of a European country or had obtained citizenship in this country in the meantime (Council of Europe, 2001; Münz, 2002).

Central and Eastern Europe[5]

In Central and Eastern Europe, the "iron curtain" and various national administrative measures restricted the number of emigrants as they prevented people from travelling to western countries. Emigration was high only in years of political crisis: e.g., 1956 from Hungary; 1968 from Czechoslovakia; 1980-81 from Poland and 1989 from the German Democratic Republic.

In "normal" years only members of ethnic or ethno-religious minorities with strong support from a western nation were able to leave, namely ethnic Germans (*Aussiedler*), Jews, ethnic Turks, slavophone Muslims and ethnic Greeks. The main exception was former Yugoslavia, where citizens were allowed to work as foreign labourers in various western countries already during the 1960s. Later, Poland followed this example. The situation changed in 1989-90, when the "iron curtain" fell and travel restrictions ended. Immediately following these momentous events, there was a short but intensive wave of emigration from Central and Eastern Europe. More importantly,

5) Included here are Albania, Bosnia-Herzegovina, Bulgaria, Croatia, the Czech Republic, Estonia, Hungary, Latvia, Lithuania, FYR of Macedonia, Poland, Romania, Slovakia, Slovenia and the Federal Republic of Yugoslavia.

civil wars and ethnic cleansing in Croatia, Bosnia and later in Serbia/Kosovo led to massive emigration and expulsion to neighbouring countries and Western Europe.

As a result of economically, politically and ethnically motivated emigration, most countries of Central and Eastern Europe recorded a negative migration balance. Between 1960 and 2000, the whole region lost at least 4.7 million people (almost 3 per cent of its total population) through migration. In absolute terms, the main sending countries were former Yugoslavia (net migration balance 1960-2000: -1.2 million), Poland (-1.1 million), Romania (-1.0 million) and Albania (-0.7 million). Relative to population size the net loss through international migration was by far the largest in Albania (-21.3 per cent) and Bulgaria (-10.6 per cent), followed by former Yugoslavia (-5.5 per cent) and Romania (-4.6 per cent). More than half of the net outflow from this region occurred during the last decade (from 1990 to 2000).

Thus, immigration has played an important part in boosting population growth in Western Europe over the last decade in some countries, while balancing the excess of deaths over births in others. In contrast, emigration from Central and Eastern Europe has been high, with only relatively little immigration or return migration balancing the net loss.

241

TEXTBOX 13.1.

Migration Dynamics in the South Caucasus

Elderly migrants return to Russia from the former Soviet Republics

Situated at the intersection of key trade routes between Europe and Asia, between Russia and the Middle East, the three countries of the South Caucasus have historically been an area of migration. With the break-up of the Soviet Union, Armenia, Azerbaijan and Georgia, like other former Soviet Republics, had to establish national migration management systems for the first time along with all the other responsibilities of independent sovereign governments.

Unlike many other parts of the former Soviet Union, the South Caucasus countries were fortunate in that their populations were relatively homogeneous: Azeris and Armenians comprise over 90 per cent of the population of their respective countries; Georgia is more diversified. But all three countries have suffered from inter-ethnic conflict. Existing economic difficulties have been made worse by these still unresolved conflicts with the following results: large numbers of displaced persons and refugees, poor relations with neighbours, and donor and corporate reluctance to invest. The main push factors prompting people to leave to seek better opportunities elsewhere include lack of economic opportunity (high unemployment and low salaries), and prolonged displacement. Furthermore, proximity to other conflict-affected areas have made the countries vulnerable to inflows and use as transit countries for conflict-affected people from e.g. Afghanistan, Chechnya and Iraq.

IOM has been working with all three countries since the mid 1990s to help build governments capacity to establish and make functional a unified system for managing migration processes. The programmes have focussed on upgrading the equipment and management systems at airports and other border crossing points, training officials in issues such as migration legislation and administration, document inspection, computer usage and English language. Border Guard training centres have recently been opened with IOM assistance in all three countries. Capacity-building assistance has also been provided to local NGOs operating in the migration area.

In Armenia and Azerbaijan, IOM has been providing business training and small loans to refugees, displaced persons and people with no or low income who are vulnerable to displacement in order to enhance their self sufficiency and integration or sustainability in local communities.

In addition to the push factor of poor economic circumstances in all three countries, Armenia's history has led to the existence of a very substantial diaspora, which acts also as a pull factor, drawing others from Armenia to seek opportunities and find ready assistance from friends and relatives in the outside world. Since independence in 1991, an estimated 800,000 to 1 million Armenians have emigrated out of a total population of less than four million people.

Although the pace of emigration has slowed from its peak in the late 1990s, net emigration still persists. Much of the flow is directed towards the Russian Federation, and consists of both seasonal and longer-term flows.

Similarly, many Georgians and Azeris seek to leave their countries in substantial numbers in search of better opportunities. Although access to labour markets in the Russian Federation is more difficult than during the Soviet period, historical ties, habit, language and proximity, mean that migrants from the Southern Caucasus find it easier to work in Russia than anywhere else outside their own countries. However, many try their luck in EU countries lured by higher wages and perceived better opportunities in Western Europe, with the added possibility of using it as a jumping off point to go to North America.

In the case of Azerbaijan, many migrants lodged asylum claims on arrival in European countries in the early years. But recent statistics show a sharp drop in the number of such applications, with potential migrants now apparently turning to middlemen and travel agencies to arrange their travel and work in the underground economies of destination countries, which makes them more vulnerable to exploitation by smugglers and traffickers. By contrast, the number of Georgian asylum seekers in Europe has risen sharply in the last two years. This flow is continuing in 2002, particularly in Germany, Belgium, the Netherlands, France, and Switzerland. Many Georgians continue to arrive in Europe with the help of smugglers, or overstay visas and remain illegally.

In the last two years, IOM research in the region has helped define details and demonstrated the extent of the three countries as places of origin and transit of irregular migrants, and the vulnerability of people to exploitation due to lack of information. Trafficking in persons, especially of young women to the United Arab Emirates, Turkey and Europe is rising.

As part of the strategy to counter false information about migration opportunities and raise awareness of the dangers of irregular migration, smuggling and trafficking, IOM, in close coordination with the governments and local NGOs, is implementing information campaigns in all three countries, targeting particular groups and, where relevant, regions revealed in research as being particularly vulnerable. In addition, other measures to ensure ongoing access to accurate and unbiased information, such as the establishment of hotlines, migrant advice, information, service or consultation centres, have been planned or put in place.

But it is not easy to halt the outflow while the economic situation in the region is so depressed. A recent IOM study on the return and reintegration of failed asylum seekers and irregular migrants returning from Western Europe to their countries of origin in the South Caucasus showed that the lack of opportunity and difficulty of reintegrating at home make it more likely that even people who had unpleasant experiences abroad will try to go abroad again, and to do so irregularly with all the known risks this entails.

Looking at the future, Azerbaijan's carbon reserves make its economy likely to pick up more quickly than the other two countries. It will need to create migration structures to cope with immigration as it becomes a significant country of destination.

An innovative multilateral process in migration management, called the Cluster Process and facilitated by IOM, was launched in 2001. In this process, initially five and latterly six Western European countries and the three countries of the South Caucasus have been meeting to foster greater mutual understanding of the circumstances and constraints of countries of origin and transit on the one side, and countries of destination on the other, and to identify practical ways in which each can contribute towards

finding acceptable solutions to migration challenges. Real progress for greater cooperation has been made on a range of issues, with some collaboration being implemented through IOM programmes such as the information campaigns referred to above, and other activities being arranged bilaterally through the nurturing of direct communication channels.

Demographic Perspectives for the Twenty-First Century

Most Europeans share the same demographic destiny, characterized by an ageing society. One reason is a pervasive low fertility rate; the other unrelated reason is high and ever-increasing life expectancy in most parts of Europe. As a result, in most countries the number of people above 65 years of age is projected to increase until the year 2025 by 10 to 100 per cent and, until the year 2050 by 30 to 150 per cent. The increase will be particularly marked in countries with relatively young populations and higher fertility rates; the increase will be less significant in countries with very low fertility rates, as smaller birth cohorts will be reaching retirement over the next decades (see **graph 13.3.**).

243

GRAPH 13.3.

Relative population decline in selected European countries, 2000-2050, age group 65+, as % of population

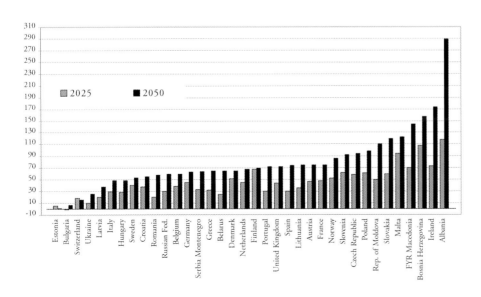

Sources:
United Nations.
World Population Prospects - The 2000 Revision;
OECD Online-Database, www.oecd.org, May 2002;
Calculation:
Humboldt-University Berlin.

In Western Europe, the number of people aged 65 or more will increase from 63.4 million (2002) to 92.0 million by 2025 (+37.2 per cent) and then gradually decline to 84.3 million (2050). In Central and Eastern Europe, the respective numbers are 16.6 million (2002), rising to 23.6 million in 2025 (+41 per cent) and to 29.2 million in 2050.

Low fertility rates in Europe will clearly bring about a drop in the number of young local and foreign residents from EU countries entering European labour markets, which will probably entail an overall contraction of the working-age population (aged 15-65). In the absence of significant immigration, this group would decline in most European countries by 2 to 22 per cent up to the year 2025 and by a further 10 to 55 per cent by 2050. The sole exceptions are countries that still have a relatively young population and high fertility rates, such as Albania or Ireland (see **graph 13.4.**).

Moreover, over the next decades in countries such as the United Kingdom, France and the Netherlands, the population aged between 15 and 65 will register only a moderate decline. Thus, in France the projected decline is only -0.2 million (-0.5 per cent) up to 2025, but is expected to reach -4.3 million (-8.4 per cent) by 2050; similarly, the United Kingdom will register almost no decline up to 2025 (-0.2 million or -0.6 per cent), but this decline is projected to reach -4.8 million (-12.3 per cent) by 2050.

GRAPH 13.4.

Relative population decline in selected European countries, 2000-2050, age group 15-64 years, as % of population

On the other hand (and in the absence of mass immigration) countries with very low fertility rates would experience the largest contraction of their active populations. Thus, Germany's working-age population is projected to decline sharply by -6.0 million or -10.7 per cent up to 2025, and by a further -15.7 million or -28.2 per cent until 2050. In neighbouring Poland, the decline is projected to reach -2.3 million (-8.6 per cent) and -7.7 million (-29.1 per cent) by 2025 and 2050, respectively. Italy's working-age population will also drop sharply by –5.7 million (-14.8 per cent) and of a further -16.3 million (-41.9 per cent) up to 2025 and 2050, respectively; Spain's population at working age is projected to shrink by -3.9 million (-14.8 per cent) up to 2025 and by a further -11.4 million (-41.5 per cent) by 2050. The situation is similar for most other Central and Eastern European countries.

Thus, without mass immigration, the Western European population between the ages of 15 and 65 is projected to decrease from 259.4 million (2000) to 237.3 million (-8.5 per cent) by 2025 and to 162.8 million (-37.2 per cent) by 2050. The working-age population in Central and Eastern Europe is expected to decline from 88 million (2000) to 80 million (-9.2 per cent) by 2025 and to 61 million (-30.9 per cent) by 2050[6]. However, the relative decline in the economically active population would be less as only 60 to 80 per cent of this age group are currently either employed or self-employed.

6) All these projections published by UN Population Division (2000) are based on optimistic assumptions of stable or slightly increasing fertility rates and further increases in life expectancy. The UN projections analyze population dynamics in the absence of mass immigration or emigration.

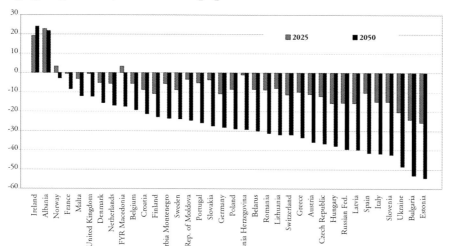

Source:
United Nations.
World Population Prospects - The 2000 Revision;
OECD Online-Database, www.oecd.org, May 2002;
Calculation:
Humboldt-University Berlin.

244

Three possible strategies could offset or at least mitigate the foreseeable absolute decline in the population aged between 15 and 65[7].

- The first and most obvious strategy is to discourage early retirement. In most EU countries today, over half of the persons between the ages of 55 and 65 are retired or economically inactive. The main exceptions are Sweden and Denmark. Higher participation rates among those aged 55+ would keep more people in the work force. The main prerequisite to ensuring their continued active involvement is the creation and/or maintenance of employment opportunities (most importantly a functioning labour market) for members of this age group.

- Another strategy is to increase the participation rate of women. This would be particularly promising in southern Europe, Belgium and Ireland, where female participation is still very low. However, this approach can only be successful if women's attitudes to working outside the home change, especially in the cases of housewives and mothers. Employers should also increase employment opportunities for women. At institutional level, better childcare facilities should be planned and school attendance expanded to cover most of the working day.

- A third strategy would aim at compensating future gaps in the labour market through recourse to immigrants. To be successful, such an approach presupposes the capacity to determine the nature and extent of likely labour gaps and the possibility to recruit expatriates with the requisite skills to meet these unmet demands in European labour markets. Moreover, the target immigrant population should be mobile and willing to move to a particular European country or region.

In the short term, the recruitment of foreign labour does appear to be the simplest way to fill vacancies. In the medium term (until 2020-25), countries which either experience no or only a modest decline in the number of people of working age (less than -5 per cent), for example France, Ireland, the Netherlands and the UK are unlikely to face demographically-induced labour shortages. However, future potential mismatches between the demand for particular qualifications and the skills provided by the national education systems, may still render the recruitment of foreign workers necessary.

In the absence of immigration, countries which register only a relatively modest decline in their active populations (-5 to -10 per cent) together with low or medium labour-force participation rates (less than 75 per cent: e.g. Belgium, Portugal, Greece) could either encourage labour immigration or expand participation from their domestic labour base. Countries characterized by a considerable drop in their active population (more than -10 per cent) together with low or moderate labour-force participation rates may find it necessary to both recruit foreign labour and expand domestic labour forces. Germany, Italy and Spain fall into this category.

In the absence of immigration, countries experiencing significant decline in their working populations together with high employment rates (Switzerland) will have to rely more and more on the recruitment of foreign workers (see **table 13.2.**).

In the longer term (up to 2050), without mass immigration nearly all European countries will experience a decline of between 10 and 50 per cent in their active populations aged 15 to 65. This will almost inevitably lead to the systematic recruitment of both skilled and semi-skilled or unqualified foreign labour on a larger scale than at present.

However, as demonstrated by the United Nations (2000), mass migration will not be able to reverse the process of population ageing in Europe, but can be useful in mitigating the impact of ageing on the work force. In order to stabilize the size of the working population in the European Union (current EU-15), an annual net gain of some 550,000 foreign workers and professionals would be necessary up to 2010 and of a further 1.6 million *per annum* between 2010 and 2050, totalling a net inflow of 68 million people between 2003 and 2050[8]. This would be equal to 16.8 per cent of the total population of the EU-15, or an annual net immigration of +3.8 per 1000 inhabitants (as against an annual average of +2.2 per 1000 during the 1990s and of +0.7 per 1000 between 1960 and 1989). Given that only around two-thirds of the current population of working age are gainfully employed, the current

245

---

7) These measures include: raising fertility rates, increasing labour supply, improving the training and education levels of the existing workforce, reducing unemployment and reforming the financing of health care and pension systems (see OECD, 1998 and 1991; Coleman, 1992, 995; Feld, 2000; Tapinos, 2000).

8) In the light of current reluctance in Europe to accept the permanent inflow of high numbers of foreigners, one can question whether these perspectives are realistic.

TABLE 13.2.

**Labour force participation and projected population decline 2000-2050
in selected European countries, age group 15-64 years**

Labour Force Participation Rate 2000, Age Group 15-64 years			
(Persons aged 15-64 years employed or searching employment as percentage of total population aged 15-64 years)			
	>75%	**66-75%**	**<66%**
PROJECTED POPULATION DECLINE 2000 – 2025 — **>10%**	**Switzerland** (81.8; 15.7)	**Austria** (70.3; 11.1) **Finland** (74.2; 10.8) **Germany** (72.2; 10.7) **Czech Republic** (71.6; 12.1)	**Italy** (60.3; 14.8) **Spain** (65.3; 10.4) **Hungary** (60.2; 15.6)
5-10%	**Denmark** (80.0; 5.2) **Sweden** (78.9; 8.7)	**Portugal** (71.1; 5.1)	**Belgium** (65.2; 5.6) **Greece** (63.0; 9.7) **Poland** (65.8; 8.6)
<5% (or increase)	**United Kingdom** (76.6; 0.6)	**France** (68.0; 0.5) **Netherlands** (74.6; 2.1) **Ireland** (67.4; -19.2) **Slovak Republic** (70.1; 3.6)	

Sources:

UN. *World Population Prospects - The 2000 Revision;* OECD Online-Database, www.oecd.org, update April 2002; Calculation: Humboldt-University Berlin.

EU Member States would need an additional 46 million labour migrants up to 2050 to keep the work force constant[9].

Countries in Central and Eastern Europe are facing similar problems. Until 2025, they will require a net inflow of 8 million people to stabilize their working-age population. At present, these figures would appear to underestimate the size of the necessary inflow as many studies predict that some 3 to 5 million citizens of Central and Eastern Europe would move to Western Europe for economic reasons during the first 15 years following EU enlargement (Fassmann and Münz, 2002). However, the Central and Eastern European countries are themselves becoming a target for labour migrants, while demographically-induced labour shortages will reduce their emigration potential. Future demographic trends appear to be clear. Europe faces an ageing and declining population. Western Europe

9) As many of them would be followed by dependent family members, the probable size of total immigration would be higher.

can look back on its experience of labour recruitment as a practical solution to labour shortages. However, one main question still remains unanswered: are Europeans willing to accept large-scale immigration, not as a temporary phenomenon, but as a planned and permanent process? A review of current European initiatives to attract more foreign workers suggests that the emphasis is very much on recruiting limited numbers of skilled workers on a temporary or permanent basis.

TEXTBOX 13.2.

Migration Dynamics in the Western Mediterranean

Migration dynamics in the Western Mediterranean[10] are both homogenous and complex. Down through the ages, migration flows in this region have remained close-knit owing to geographical proximity and economic and cultural similarities. The region may be regarded as one of the main international migration interfaces between the South and the North.

Generally speaking, Maghrebi citizens make up the largest foreign communities in southern Europe. Mostly from Algeria, Morocco and Tunisia, over one and a half million migrants from these countries are concentrated in the countries of the "Latin arc". While emigrants of Algerian origin are located almost exclusively in France, Moroccan and Tunisian communities are spread over several host countries. Throughout the whole of Europe, Maghrebi migrants are outnumbered only by migrants of Turkish origin.

Trans-Mediterranean migration patterns show that departure restrictions for the traditional countries of destination are not necessarily curbing new arrivals, which are continuing through family reunions and irregular entries. Instead, such restrictions often cause changes in the geographical distribution of these flows, redirecting them towards relatively more accessible destinations such as Italy and Spain.

Around the middle of the twentieth century, the number of migrants from the Maghreb increased because of special

programmes set up by countries in Western Europe to attract foreign workers in order to cover labour shortages generated by economic prosperity. When economic growth slowed in the mid-1970s, Maghrebi migration diminished considerably. It recovered somewhat in the 1980s, and again during the 1990s, but this increase was partly due to flows of irregular migrants.

Emigrant remittances play a critical role in the Maghrebi economies. They represent a substantial injection of hard currencies into these countries of origin, especially at a time when export earnings are being whittled away by falling international commodity prices.

Although irregular migration is nothing new, its scale and impact now affect a growing number of sending, transit and destination countries all across the Western Mediterranean region. Requiring a global and balanced response, this complex problem is a matter of serious concern for two major reasons: the welfare and individual rights of irregular migrants and the welfare of Maghrebi communities legally established in Europe; and the impact on migration management policies in all the countries concerned. Regularization attempts by individual European countries to solve irregular migration have had limited success.

Mindful of the complexity of migration dynamics in the Western Mediterranean, IOM, in close collaboration with the five countries of the Arab Maghreb Union (Algeria, Libya, Morocco, Mauritania, Tunisia) and the five countries of the "Latin arc" (France, Italy, Malta, Portugal, Spain), is pressing ahead with an informal process of regional dialogue (officially called the Western Mediterranean Cooperation Process, or "5+5") on migration issues of common interest. The initiative aims at encouraging region-wide concerted action on migration and cooperation mechanisms between the countries on both shores of the Western Mediterranean in order to devise appropriate and coordinated responses to the various migration issues facing the region. More specifically, the IOM initiative aims at creating opportunities for migration-related dialogue, exchanges and experiments and at studying current trends in this field. It also aims at combating irregular migration. In the long run, the "5+5" process is striving to optimize the economic and social benefits of regular migration for the countries of origin, transit and destination.

---

10) The Western Mediterranean comprises the five countries on the south shore making up the Arab Maghreb Union (Algeria, Libya, Morocco, Mauritania and Tunisia) and the five countries of the north shore, the so-called "Latin arc" (Spain, France, Italy, Malta and Portugal).

Recent Measures to Recruit Foreign Workers in Western Europe

Faced with skill shortages, population decline and ageing, European countries have begun to take new, but cautious, initiatives to admit more labour migrants. Many European governments are aware that public opinion polls suggest there is little public support for further immigration. For example, a poll published in the German newspaper *Die Woche* in July 2000 showed that 63 per cent of those interviewed thought that Germany did not need any more immigrants[11]. However, employers who are experiencing skilled-labour shortages have been calling on governments to open up new labour migration channels for foreign workers. Hence, many countries experience tensions between public and private policies on labour market interventions.

The limited measures introduced to attract foreign workers can be broadly divided into two categories: a relaxation of the entry requirements under existing schemes, and the creation of new labour migration channels. But, most of the new initiatives are relatively modest and aim to attract the highly skilled (see **table 13.5.**). For some countries, this represents an attractive alternative to other entry routes for less skilled migrants, such as family reunification and asylum channels that allow states little opportunity to influence the skill levels and mix of new entrants, or the duration of their stay. However, even here labour migration schemes have been restricted to certain categories of workers such as those employed in the IT sector and health-related sectors (OECD, 2002).

In EU countries, work permit systems represent the main way for foreign workers from non-EU countries to enter for employment. However, conditions governing the granting of work permits as well as the types of permits, vary enormously among European countries (see **table 13.5.**). This diversity is highlighted in a comparative study on the admission of third-country nationals for either employment or self-employed economic activities prepared for the EC (ECOTEC, 2001). The study shows that both third-country nationals wishing to be admitted to work in the EU, and EU employers in need of third-country workers, are confronted with "sometimes highly complex administrative procedures" with "only a few common rules and principles applicable in all Member States" (ECOTEC, 2001).

The European work-permit systems are essentially employer-led: an employer is granted a permit for a foreign worker if there is a proper match for the necessary skills and a labour-market test is conducted in which the employer demonstrates that no suitable local workers are available and that the pay and working conditions are no less favourable than those offered to local workers[12].

New Regular Labour Migration Initiatives

Several European countries have recently introduced measures to facilitate the entry and labour market access for skilled labour migrants, including providing easier access to labour markets for dependants and exempting a broader range of occupations from labour-market tests, i.e., not having to demonstrate that no suitable local worker is available to fill a vacancy. Other types of measures make it easier for migrants to change employers and to switch their status from a student to a work-permit holder.

In the United Kingdom, a series of measures were implemented in 2000 to make it easier and quicker for employers to obtain a work permit for a wider range of jobs. Thus, the qualifications required to obtain a work permit were significantly reduced (i.e., to graduates with no previous working experience) and the residence validity increased from four to five years. A new pilot scheme was launched to enable multinational companies to certify work permits themselves for their intra-company transferees – a practice that was, however, discontinued subsequently. Work permits can now be applied for electronically. Labour-market testing requirements were also eased to enable foreign workers to change employers without needing a new work permit, provided the new activity is in the same field as that covered by the existing work permit.

A second approach has been to introduce new labour migration programmes. One of the best known examples of a new labour migration scheme for skilled workers is the German "Green Card" programme. In August 2000, Germany introduced the so-called "Green Card" initiative to facilitate the recruitment of computer engineers, IT-experts and software developers. Between August 2000 and March 2002, 11,984 "Green Cards" were issued. These provide access to the German labour market for a period of five years. Most of the recruited computer and IT-experts came from India, Russia, the Ukraine and Central Europe.

---

11) Cited in Laczko (2002).

12) For a comparison of work permit systems in traditional countries of immigration, see **chapter 9.**

TABLE 13.5.

Labour Migration Schemes in Selected Countries

A) Skilled Labour

Country	Type of permit		Application filed by:		Skills targeted	Quota	Labour-market testing	Change of status for foreign student on completion of studies	Priority processing
	Permanent	Temporary	Employer	Migrant					
Australia*	For special qualifications	✓	✓	✓	Business skills, medicine, education	---		✓	
Belgium**		✓	✓	✓		n.a	✓	n.a	✓
Canada*	✓	✓		Migrants apply once they have a job offer	General skills, IT specialists, construction, engineering	✓		One year	Facilitated processing for IT specialists
Czech Republic		✓	✓				A point system for temporary skilled workers is under consideration	✓	n.a
Denmark		✓	✓		IT, medicine, biotechnology				Fast track
France		✓	✓		Science, research and IT			Facilitated for IT student	Fast track
Germany Green Card Programme		✓			IT; specialists can contact the Federal Employment Service which coordinates between employers and applicants	✓	✓	IT students	For IT students: one week
Italy		✓	✓		IT	✓		n.a	
Ireland		✓	✓		IT construction, engineering			✓	Fast tack
New Zealand* Talent visa***	✓	✓ ✓		✓		n.a. re talent visa	n.a. re talent visa	✓	
Netherlands		✓	✓		IT		National but no regional test for skilled workers	✓	2 weeks
Japan		✓	✓					✓	
Singapore Technopreneur Pass		✓		✓	IT specialists	n.a		✓	4-6 weeks
Spain****		✓							
UK		✓	For general work permits	By innovators and highly-skilled workers			For general work permits	Visa switching currently under consideration	Fast Track
USA Green card for skilled	For skilled workers			✓		✓	✓	Special reserve for IT students 20,000	
H1B programme		✓	✓		✓		✓		

*   an existing job offer increases the points granted.
**   allows free-lance workers with combined commercial/technical skills.
***   introduced in March 2002 temporary/permanent?
****   no permit requirement for foreign specialists, researchers and university professors

249

B) Unskilled Labour

Country	Entry schemes for unskilled foreign labour migrants			Other admission channels			
	Work permit scheme based on unskilled work* Numbers	Special seasonal work scheme Numbers	Other labour migration programmes Numbers	Family reunion	Asylum seekers (2001)	Mass regularization programmes since 1990	Working holiday-makers (WHM)
Australia				64,000 (2000)	11,570		76,570 (2000)
Austria		Quota of 8,000 person p.a., 6-month limit	Harvest helpers, Quota of 7,000	12,200 (2000)	30,135		
Belgium	1 year No quota			4,871 (2000)	24,549	In process: Of 50,680 applications 2,226 are regularised	✓
Canada		Approx 15,000 p.a. , for several years		60,515 (2000)	42,746		✓
Denmark			Trainee and contract workers 1,074 (1998)	9,500 (1999)	12,403		✓
France		7,929 (2000) 6 months		65,000 (1999)	47,263	75,600 (1997-1999)	
Greece	✓	6 month		n.a.	3,083 (2000)	369,629 (1998-1999)	
Germany		223,400 (1999) 3 months	Contract workers 40,000 (1999) trainees		88,363		
Italy	12,000 (2001)			308,200 (1999)	9,620	130,745 (1999)	
Ireland	✓				10,324		✓
Japan			Trainee scheme	n.a			✓
Netherlands		✓			32,579		✓
Spain	✓	Details to be set	Favourable treatment for certain Latin American nationals	n.a	9,219	150,000 (1991-1996)	
UK		Quota 15,200, 7 months		65,200 (1999)	71,700 without dependants		approx. 40,000
USA	✓	quota 66,000 max. 1 year		584,159 (2000)	86,394		

*an existing job offer increases the number of points granted.

IOM; OECD 2000 and 2001, Home Office 2002, Ecotec 2001.

The granting of a "Green Card" is subject to procedures similar to those governing the award of work permits in other countries. Thus, the award must be preceded by a labour-market test and the employment office must demonstrate the need for a skilled employee that cannot be met by a domestic or an EU specialist. Both the qualifications of the candidate and the working conditions offered are checked to ensure that they meet the job requirements and comply with national standards, respectively. However, the spouse of a "Green Card" holder may take up employment only after a waiting period of one year.

Since late 2001, Germany also issues "Green Cards" to nurses and other qualified para-medical professionals.

In <u>France</u>, new directives concerning the recruitment of highly skilled workers have been in force since January 2002. Even before this, companies were able to employ IT-specialists once the French Labour Ministry had accepted their application. In contrast to the German Green Card regulation, France did not impose any quota for highly-skilled immigrants. Since 2002, employers have the opportunity to fill job openings in all sectors of the economy with qualified international labour migrants from non-EU countries by applying to the Labour Ministry for work and residence permits. This ministry is responsible for examining whether the international migrant would be employed and remunerated in accordance with his or her qualifications. If affirmative, the Labour Ministry, together with the Ministry of the Interior, approves the employer's application without further bureaucratic delay.

A different type of scheme called the "Highly Skilled Migrants Programme" was launched in the United Kingdom in January 2002. This scheme is particularly notable as it enables highly skilled workers to seek work in the United Kingdom in the absence of a specific job offer, subject to certain conditions. Thus, applicants able to satisfy certain preconditions in terms of qualifications and independent financial means may engage in an independent economic activity.

This new UK pilot scheme is based on a points assessment scheme[13]. Although such schemes have been widely used for many years in countries such as Canada and Australia, they have rarely been adopted in Europe. The aim is to attract highly skilled and qualified persons, able to support themselves and their family without recourse to public funds. During the first year of this scheme, a limit on the number of admissions is not planned.

Management of Labour Migration of Unskilled Workers

Given current high levels of unemployment, most EU countries are reluctant to re-open new labour migration channels for unskilled workers which have been largely closed since the early 1970s. However, some policy-makers believe that the introduction of schemes to attract unskilled workers might help to reduce irregular migration.

In Germany, for example, the report by the Süssmuth Commission recommended that priority be given to recruiting skilled migrants, with the primary objective of creating additional employment opportunities for the domestic workforce. The Commission advised that the immigration of poorly qualified workers is not a viable

option at present, with the exception of seasonal and temporary employment.

Germany recruits significant numbers of temporary contract and guest-workers under bilateral quota agreements with some 13 countries in Central, Eastern and south-eastern Europe. Quotas have been reduced in recent years as unemployment has risen in Germany. In 1997, Germany recruited more than 226,000 seasonal workers (IOM, 2000). Several other EU countries also have agreements to recruit seasonal labour. France, for example, has concluded labour agreements with Morocco, Poland, Senegal and Tunisia. Italy has concluded a labour migration agreement with Albania (see **textbox 13.3.**).

TEXTBOX 13.3.

A Migrant's Story – A New Start through Regular Labour Migration from Albania to Italy

Albanian migrants cook pizzas in Italy

"I believe the reason I am in Rome and have this job is because I am an avid reader of newspapers. One day I read an advertisement from IOM about the selection of individuals for employment in Italy. I applied immediately because I knew IOM was an international organization that I could trust; unlike private organizations that advertise employment abroad but after charging a high fee disappear into thin air."

Klodian Grozhdani is one of the more than 1,500 successful Albanian job seekers that have travelled to Italy

13) In Australia, Canada and New Zealand, points systems test the education, skills, language ability, and other characteristics that these countries regard as important for facilitating the integration of immigrants. The points systems are aimed primarily at testing likely economic success (see also **chapter 9**).

under an agreement signed in May 2000 between IOM and the Italian Ministry of Labour and Social Policies.

This labour migration programme is addressing the needs of the Italian labour market and managing labour migration flows from Albania and the Balkans. It will allow 5,000 Albanians the chance to work for one year at a time in Italy. So far it has attracted 24,580 applicants.

Of the 9,496 applicants interviewed by the IOM office in Tirana, 4,404 successfully passed professional and linguistic tests. Most applicants are men aged between 18 and 39, with secondary education and experience in the construction, agriculture, hospitality and para-medical sectors.

Klodian fits the profile of most applicants. "I am 22 years old. I graduated from secondary school in 1997, but unfortunately there are very few jobs available in my country so I thought of migrating to find a job. But because there was no organized migration for Albanians, I decided, like many others, to cross illegally into Macedonia. Macedonia is near my hometown. I looked for work for a couple of weeks but found nothing. Since I didn't find a job and had spent all of my money, I decided to go to Greece where there are more opportunities and the pay is better. And in fact I found a job, in a farm, a job I never thought I would do".

"I worked for a few months and saved my money. But luck was not on my side. One day the police stopped me and found that I had no documents. I was taken to the station and physically mistreated. At that moment, I decided never to cross another border illegally. The next day the police escorted me back to Albania. Back home I had many odd jobs – in a tapestry shop, a caramel factory, and in a metal factory."

After being interviewed, successful applicants are registered in the IOM database, which is periodically sent to the Italian authorities and is available on the Internet for Italian employers to search for potential employees. By matching skills to existing vacancies, the database allows applicants to travel to Italy with a contract in hand and to start work immediately.

Before leaving Albania, participants receive counselling and participate in an orientation course given by IOM Tirana. Once in Italy, IOM Rome provides orientation and vocational training courses to some of the newly arrived.

Klodian was accepted for the programme and flew to Rome. "When I arrived I went to the IOM office in Rome.

They offered the chance to participate in a training programme. I chose upholstery. At the end of the course I found a job immediately in the 'De Santis' upholstery firm. Now I have a skill that I can use anywhere in the world. What is my future? I don't know. Of course, I want to be close to my family in Albania and for sure one day I will go back, but for now it is too early to start think about this. I live in Italy and am very happy with my work."

This regular labour migration programme is also open to people from the Balkans already residing in Italy.

Flurije Lekaj was born in Prizren, Kosovo but was living in Rome when she decided to apply for the IOM programme. "My father is a lawyer, he lost his job because of his political views and was forced to leave the family behind and travel to Italy in 1994. In 1998 he decided to take all his family out of Kosovo because the crisis was reaching an irreversible point. And that is exactly what occurred. In 1999, we finally joined our father in Rome. I began school and two years later I decided to start working. It was very difficult for me to find a job. Finally, one day I got a job in a bar, working illegally three hours per day. Unfortunately, the job lasted only one month and I was left feeling depressed because I knew that finding another job would be extremely hard for me. One day I read in the newspaper about the IOM programme offering training and eventual employment. I applied immediately and began training as a pizza assistant. A teacher needed someone to assist the pizza maker in his restaurant and so, one month later, I began to work in the restaurant *Il Sorriso*. I am very happy that I have a job I like and I earn a relatively good salary. But this job has given me something even more important than money – peace of mind – and that is a very valuable thing for a migrant."

She is young but is already thinking of the future. "My future, for sure I will return to Kosovo. My father and mother have already returned. My father is practising law again and is busy rebuilding our home that was destroyed during the war. But with his income alone, he cannot finance the reconstruction and restore our family's financial situation. My brothers and I are contributing from our incomes here in Italy. For this reason I will remain in Rome for another three years or so and then perhaps I will return to Kosovo. I am not sure whether I will work as pizza maker in Kosovo or go back to school. But in Italy, pizza is made very well and people all over the world love pizza, so I think there will always be a need for a pizza maker !".

In the absence of legal labour migration channels, hundreds of thousands of workers have found illegal work in Europe (see also **textbox 13.4.**). By definition, estimates of the number of illegally employed workers in Europe should be treated with caution, but it is likely that in 1998 there were as many as 3 million undocumented migrants in Europe, compared to fewer than 2 million in 1991 (IOM, 2000). Many of these workers are engaged in low-skilled and low-paid work which many EU nationals are no longer interested in, or at least not at the levels of pay offered. As mentioned earlier, some countries, especially those in southern Europe, have introduced programmes to offer these workers a regular status. During the 1990s, Belgium, France, Greece, Italy, Portugal and Spain all enacted amnesty programmes for undocumented migrants. More than one million workers were included in these programmes between 1991 and 2001 (OECD, 2000; *Migration und Bevölkerung*, 2002).

TEXTBOX 13.4.

Irregular Migration into Europe[14]

IOM estimates that currently there is a stock of at least three million irregular migrants in the European Union, up from two million a decade ago, despite moves to legalize half of them. However, this figure can be regarded as an educated guess in the absence of any official count, which would be hard to establish anyway because of the clandestine nature of irregular migration flows.

The World Migration Report 2000 reported a maximum of three million irregular migrants in Europe in 1998. "The figure of three million is still valid, but it's undoubtedly a basic minimum now. The real figure is probably much higher", IOM spokesman Jean-Philippe Chauzy said at a recent Geneva press conference. "Nobody really has accurate data on irregular migrants. We only have estimates of those without identity documents in the Schengen area, but nobody has a very clear view of the matter," he added, referring to the Schengen agreement on free cross-border travel within certain EU countries.

Already in 2000, IOM pointed out that stricter controls appeared to have benefited organized crime since it had become increasingly difficult to enter Western Europe without the help of trafficking networks and/or smugglers.

Most irregular migrants arrive through the Mediterranean region and Eastern Europe. It is estimated that annually, hundreds of thousands of irregular migrants from Africa, Eastern Europe, the Middle East, Central Asia and China attempt to enter the European Union.

A few examples of estimates of flows and stocks of irregular migrants[15]:

• in 2001 alone, close to 10,000 irregular migrants were intercepted near or along the coast of Tarifa (Cadiz) in Spain;

• the German Police Trade Union believes that some 100,000 irregulars are smuggled into Germany each year;

• some 95,000 Albanians, Romanians and Iraqis are illegally entering Greece each year;

• according to the United Kingdom Immigration Service Union, there are up to one million irregular migrants in the United Kingdom;

• Belgium's anti-racism centre estimates the number of irregular migrants at around 90,000;

• Irish Police estimates that some 10,000 irregular immigrants are working in the country;

• it is estimated that there are some 500,000 irregular migrants in France and some 60,000 in Portugal.

The Spanish authorities have identified a trafficking network that runs north from Mali, Senegal and other sub-Saharan countries, through Morocco and into Spain, often passing through the Canary Islands.

Chauzy pointed out that gangs in Albania are well-established, and there is a thriving illicit trade based on smuggling migrants on all sides of the Mediterranean Sea. "In the Strait of Otranto, there is a constant flow of powerful small craft ferrying people between the Albanian coast and Puglia in southern Italy, the same around Gibraltar". Thousands of irregular migrants arrive ashore in Italy and Spain, ready to move on to France, Germany, Switzerland, the United Kingdom or other wealthy northern European states. The human toll of irregular immigration is high as hundreds of people die every year in Europe while trying

253

14) Part of the information provided in this textbox is from an article by Catherine Rama, 27 May 2002, *Agence France Press*, Geneva.

15) Figures quoted from "EU Immigration Factbox", 25 April 2002, *Reuters*, London.

to cross borders illegally, driven by fear of persecution in their own country or the desire for better economic opportunities.

Five countries in the EU set up schemes to legalize the status of those illegal arrivals. IOM and the Organization for Economic Cooperation and Development (OECD) estimate that these schemes affected about 1.5 million people during the 1990s: Italy regularized 716,000 irregular migrants in three waves; Greece accepted 370,000 people in 1997-1998, mainly from the Balkans and Eastern Europe; Spain effectively regularized 260,000 immigrants mainly from Africa and Latin America; Portugal legalized 61,000 migrants.

In many cases, the legalization of the immigrants' status is not matched by pan-European measures to tackle the market for clandestine workers in Western Europe, where there is a demand for cheap and easily exploited labour. Ultimately this means that the flow of irregular migrants is not stemmed. "When there's a desire to manage migration, one has to fight against clandestine labour in a uniform manner", Chauzy commented.

At a spring 2002 meeting in Geneva, European countries examined steps to set up a temporary resident permit for migrants victims of traffickers, similar to a system currently implemented in Italy and Belgium. In return, the migrants would testify in order to help authorities track down and dismantle smuggling rings.

Despite the scale of irregular migration, there are few examples of new labour migration schemes targeting unskilled foreign workers, although in some countries the introduction of such measures has been discussed.

In the United Kingdom, for example, there has been a recent debate on establishing such a scheme. On 3 October 2001, the Home Secretary announced his intention under the headline "a concerted drive against illegal immigration" to begin talks with employers and trade unions on creating more opportunities for unskilled workers to find employment in the country. He argued for a "sensible and managed basis" for those seeking legal employment in the UK, emphasizing that "a properly managed system of legal migration would be a body-blow to the gangmasters and traffickers who bring people to the country illegally"[16] (see also **chapter 3**).

16) Cited by Spencer (2001).

Re-opening a channel for unskilled workers in the UK is likely to give rise to difficult political and policy questions. Despite the clear demand for such labour, some argue that the government should consider the potential impact of admitting unskilled migrants on public services and on public opinion, and the support they will need to integrate successfully during their stay. In February 2002, the government announced its intention to expand opportunities for seasonal employment in the UK. By proposing to expand the "working holidaymakers" scheme, which offers temporary work for young people, the government specifically expressed the hope that the demand for labour currently supplied by illegal workers might thereby be undercut (Home Office, 2002).

Even where governments are creating opportunities for less skilled workers, the emphasis is on short-term employment to meet specific labour demands, and the conditions differ considerably from those offered to skilled workers. Austria, for example, has decided to extend seasonal employment possibilities beyond the traditional tourism, agriculture and construction sectors and introduced an annual quota of 15,000 persons. However, such seasonal workers will not be permitted to bring their families to Austria, nor will they be able to upgrade their residence status or work permit.

Since 1994, the proportion of international labour migrants from non-EU countries has been limited to 8 per cent of the entire Austrian work force. Thus, some legal immigrants admitted under applicable immigration provisions do not have access to the Austrian labour market and, despite having lived legally in Austria for an extended period of time, did not receive work permits until the Integration Decree was introduced in June 2000. Women were most affected by the decree (König *et al.*, 2001).

In summary, although current efforts to open new labour migration channels in Europe remain fairly modest (Apap, 2001), they represent a significant policy change and signal greater acknowledgement of the merits of opening new migration channels. In Germany, in particular, there has been a much wider debate about the future of immigration and the contribution of immigrants to German society (see **textbox 13.5.**).

TEXTBOX 13.5.

Dispositions of a Planned German Immigration Law

In its final report published in July 2001, the Süssmuth Commission argued that Germany would need immigrants throughout the twenty-first century and should officially acknowledge itself as an immigration country. It recommended opening both permanent and temporary labour-migration channels, applying the Australian/Canadian points-based models.

Germany, Berlin "Bundestag"

However, in mid-December 2002, just two weeks before it was due to come into force, the German constitutional court blocked the landmark immigration law that was based on the recommendations of the Süssmuth Commission by invalidating a controversial vote on that law in the upper house of the German Parliament (*Bundesrat*). The legislation would have allowed a controlled stream of skilled non-European Union foreigners into Germany for the first time since the 1970s, when it ended a programme to attract "guest workers", mainly from Turkey. *Inter alia,* the bill proposed to include dispositions on the following:

International Labour Migration

• The admission of highly qualified persons and of new business entrepreneurs based on an individual evaluation and without a set quota on the number of persons admitted under this category. Such persons would be granted permanent residence in Germany from the time of their admission.

• The admission of economically active immigrants based on a points system. In addition to appropriate qualifi-

cations and independent means for self and family support, the admission of international labour migrants would be determined by age (preference for younger adults), level of education, linguistic abilities and whether or not a position in Germany has already been offered.

• Priority given in the selection process to candidates from future EU Member States. The planned seven-year transition period preceding the free movement of people from future EU Member States into German and Western European labour markets could thereby be structured on a more gradual basis.

• The recruitment of labour migrants for an initially limited period of up to five years. Accordingly, local branches of the Federal Employment Offices would decide whether vacancies should be filled through the international recruitment of workers. On expiration of initial work and residence permits, international labour migrants would have the possibility to apply for an extension of their permits.

• On completion of studies in Germany, foreign students would be able to work in Germany subject to the approval of the labour-market administration. In addition, foreign students who have completed their studies in Germany would be granted the right to continue residing in Germany for the purpose of finding a job.

• New means for international labour migrants to enter the German labour market, resulting from the planned integration of work and residence permits. Two types of residence permits were proposed: a limited (with the possibility of extension) and permanent residence permit. Generally, persons legally admitted into Germany who do not apply for asylum would receive access to the German labour market. This would particularly benefit migrants who arrived under family reunification programmes, certain groups of refugees and many of the foreigners who had previously only been given leave to stay (*Duldung*, i.e., tolerated persons). Tolerated persons cannot be legally repatriated despite the rejection of their asylum application due to the principle of "non-refoulement" under the Geneva Convention.

255

New Institutions

- Transformation of the Federal Office for the Recognition of Foreign Refugees into the Federal Office for Migration and Asylum. The new Federal Office would be charged with co-ordinating the work of the Foreign Office and the Labour Administration and of organizations representing migrant interests; the administration of the migrant selection process in accordance with the point-based system; the running of the central migrant database; the recognition/rejection of asylum applications; the facilitation of voluntary returns of rejected asylum applicants and irregular migrants.

Asylum

- Temporary status for asylum seekers persecuted for gender-specific reasons and for persons persecuted by individuals in their home countries. Refugees as defined by the Geneva Convention (*kleines Asyl* or minimum asylum), would be given complete access to the labour market. Refugee status would be re-evaluated three years after being granted.

Compulsory Departure from Germany

- No freedom of movement in Germany for persons facing compulsory future departure. These persons would be housed in detention centres. Furthermore, the misleading of immigration authorities regarding one's personal identity or citizenship would be considered a crime.

Family Reunion

- Standard age for children (non EU-citizens) admitted to Germany within the framework of family reunions: 12 years. However, the maximum age would be set at 18 for children immigrating together with their parents (i.e., without intentional delay by the parents concerning family reunion), as well as for children who have an adequate knowledge of the German language and for those of highly qualified international labour migrants.

Integration

- Target group: new and earlier migrants (with up to 6 years of residence in Germany), with a poor knowledge of the German language, would be entitled to participate in language and general orientation courses. The legislator would reserve the possibility of sanctioning non-participation in integration courses and rewarding successful participation with more rapid naturalization procedures.

According to Germany's Interior Minister Otto Schily, the law would have given Germany the most modern immigration legislation in Europe. The bill might be revived in 2003 after a new vote and subsequent negotiations between representatives of both houses of the German Parliament.

Conclusion

Demographic change presents European societies with a broad range of economic and social challenges. This chapter has shown that in the long run (up to 2050) and in the absence of substantial immigration, nearly all European countries will experience a 10 and 50 per cent decline in the size of their active populations between the ages of 15 and 65. According to current demographic projections, an annual net gain of just over half a million foreign workers might be necessary up to 2010 in order to stabilize the size of the working population in the European Union.

However, on its own, an increase in labour migration to Western Europe is unlikely to be a solution to declining and ageing populations; however, combined with other measures, it could represent an important instrument for governments to respond better to such demographic challenges. As the Report of the Independent Commission on Migration to Germany concluded: "managed immigration of qualified workers should increase the supply of labour and gainful employment, thus helping to stabilize social security systems" (p.80).

At present, countries in Western Europe are probably not ready to promote a substantial increase in permanent immigration. Greater emphasis on selective and temporary labour migration into Western Europe, aimed specifically at meeting skill shortages in certain occupations and industries, is more likely.

However, even modest steps to increase temporary and skilled labour migration may not be popular in Europe. Given the wide-spread migration-related security concerns in European countries, for selective labour-migration schemes will only be successful if governments step up their efforts to inform and convince public opinion of the potential benefits of migration.

Governments also face a related policy challenge from irregular labour immigration. Despite restrictive immigration policies, large irregular migration movements into Western Europe continued over the last decade – even during times of high unemployment. If more countries began to accept that their economies needed these workers, demographic pressures would ease since these mainly young workers would contribute to social insurance and social security systems.

257

CHAPTER 14

Towards a Common Immigration Policy for the European Union

Asylum and migration have been on the agenda of the European Union (EU), and before that of the European Community, since the 1980s. With the signing of the Single European Act in 1986, there was recognition of the need to develop new forms of intergovernmental cooperation in order to manage the frontier-free area which was to be established. A first concrete step was the signature in 1990 of the Dublin Convention, designed to determine the Member State responsible for examining an asylum application lodged in one of them.

The coming into force in 1993 of the Maastricht Treaty introduced the obligation of cooperation within a single institutional structure, the so-called third pillar, in which immigration and asylum were recognized as matters of "common interest". This was at a time when the number of asylum seekers and immigrants to the European Union was increasing rapidly, peaking at 1.3 million in 1992. The main reasons included dissolution of the Soviet Union and the subsequent reunification of Germany, as well as the war in the Balkans and the break-up of the former Yugoslavia.

The Maastricht Treaty provided new opportunities for developing a comprehensive approach to immigration and asylum policies. Although the recommendations were not binding, the Member States identified many of the issues between 1993 and 1999, which were subsequently incorporated into the Amsterdam Treaty. Also during this period, the Commission produced a communication on immigration and asylum policies, which was adopted by the Council in 1994[1]. The aim was to stimulate a wide-ranging debate on the challenges which migration pressures and the integration of legal immigrants posed for the Union as a whole.

However, only when the Amsterdam Treaty came into force in May 1999 were European institutions given the necessary treaty-based competence to develop asylum and migration policies. Within the context of establishing an area of freedom, security and justice, a new Title IV was drafted to cover visas, asylum, immigration and other policies related to the free movement of persons. A new article 63 set out the measures which were to be adopted and fixed a deadline of 2004 for asylum measures, which were described in some detail. The development of asylum measures was to be based on full respect for the Geneva Convention of 1951 and its 1967 Protocol and on other relevant international treaties and obligations of Member States.

Two main areas for Community action on migration were identified: conditions of entry and residence for third country nationals and illegal immigration and residence. Furthermore, measures were to be based on two important principles: the establishment of minimum standards for safeguarding the rights of third country nationals, and the inclusion of conditions for legal residents in one Member State to settle in another.

The application of this Title of the Amsterdam Treaty is limited with respect to three Member States (Denmark, Ireland and the United Kingdom) by special protocols. Denmark does not participate in decisions affecting the area of freedom, security and justice, apart from certain aspects of visa policy; and Ireland and the United Kingdom decide whether to opt-in on a case-by-case basis but with the possibility of signing up to a particular measure once adopted by the other 13 Member States. A further particularity of Title IV is the decision-making arrangements which are in force for a transitional period of five years. These require a unanimous decision of the Council (with the exception of certain measures related to visas and border control) on any proposal from the Commission or arising from an initiative of a Member State for the transitional period of five years. The European Parliament must be consulted on all such proposals but there is no co-decision procedure.

A special meeting of the European Council to discuss the development of a Union of freedom, security and justice was held in Tampere (Finland) in October 1999. Heads of State and Government agreed on a detailed programme of action including the development of a common EU policy on asylum and migration. Since then, the Commission has put forward a wide range of measures needed to meet the targets set by the Treaty as further

1) COM(94)23 of 23.02.1994: *Communication from the Commission to the Council and the European Parliament on Immigration and Asylum Policies.*

defined by the European Council in Tampere, within the 5-year period set. A scoreboard[2] set up to chart progress is regularly up-dated by the Commission.

The Tampere Milestones

The Tampere Council agreed on a number of policy orientations and priorities to make the European Union an area of freedom, security and justice and a reality for both EU citizens and third country nationals granted access to Member States. At the meeting, heads of State and Government called for the development of "a common EU asylum and migration policy", which should include the following elements:

- **Partnership with countries of origin** in managing migration including more comprehensive co-development policies. This would involve coordinating the Union's internal and external policies and taking the causes of migration into account when developing these policies. The objective is to minimize the negative effects and maximize the positive effects of migration to both sending and receiving countries as well as promoting voluntary return and re-admission agreements (see also **textbox 14.1.**).

- The development of **a common European asylum system** based on a fully inclusive interpretation of the Geneva Convention. In a first phase, the Council called for the adoption of common minimum standards in the areas identified in Article 63 of the Amsterdam Treaty: criteria and mechanisms for determining which Member State is responsible for considering an application for asylum submitted by a third country national in one of the Member States (communitarization of the Dublin Convention); the establishment of EURODAC (a European system for exchanging finger-prints); minimum standards for reception conditions for asylum seekers; minimum standards for giving temporary protection in the event of mass influx based on solidarity between the Member States; and minimum standards on procedures for granting or withdrawing refugee status and for the qualification and status of third country nationals and stateless persons as refugees or as persons in need of international protection. In a second phase, the development of a common procedure and a uniform status in these areas should be developed.

- **Fair treatment of third country nationals** aiming as far as possible at the granting of comparable rights and obligations to those of nationals of the Member State concerned. This acknowledges the necessity to pay greater attention in the future to settling and integrating the refugees and migrants admitted.

- **A comprehensive approach to the management of migratory flows** to achieve orderly migration. The Commission has proposed that this must involve clarifying the legal channels for immigration and coordinating and reinforcing efforts to combat illegal immigration, smuggling and trafficking and control of the EU's external borders, including developing further the common policy on visas.

While undertaking the preparation of the legal instruments called for by this ambitious programme, the Commission began to work immediately following the Council on two communications on asylum and immigration – a reflection of the view that each needs its own specific approach but that they are "closely related", to use the expression in the Tampere conclusions. This approach recognizes that persons seeking asylum have rights which are governed by international obligations and that these must be safeguarded. Issued on 22 November 2000[3], these communications set out for wide debate within the EU the Commission's ideas on how the common policy called for by the European Council could be developed and implemented.

TEXTBOX 14.1.

Migration Dispositions in the Cotonou Agreement

Signed on 23 June 2000, the Cotonou Agreement aims at building a partnership between the EU and 77 countries situated in Africa, the Caribbean and the Pacific (ACPs), in order to reduce and eventually eradicate poverty by promoting sustainable development, capacity building, and integration into the world economy (art. 1).

Based on the principle of equality between all the countries involved and stressing the ACP's ownership of development

---

2) COM(2002)261 final of 30.5.2002: *Biannual update of the Scoreboard to review progress on the creation of an area of 'Freedom, Security and Justice' in the European Union.*

3) COM(2000)755: *Communication on a common asylum procedure and a uniform statute valid throughout the Union for persons who are granted asylum, and (COM(2000)757): Communication on a Community Immigration Policy,* both dated 22 November 2000.

strategies, the concluding parties agreed to emphasize political dialogue, development cooperation and trade relations as specific areas of concern.

Migration is an important element of the political dialogue which seeks to explore different dimensions of cooperation (art. 8, 13). Moreover, management of migration is one of the priorities in the field of technical cooperation, which should assist ACPs in developing national and regional manpower resources (art. 79, 80).

Given the significant scale of labour migration between the ACPs and the EU, article 13 sets forth a framework for migration management which should include:

- Respect of the rights of migrants shall be guaranteed. Rooted in international law and human rights dispositions, an important component of this is the commitment to fair treatment (absence of discriminatory practices) of migrants who reside legally on the territories of the concluding parties.

- Strategies to tackle root-causes of massive migration flows – This should aim at "supporting the economic and social development of the regions from which migrants originate". The training of ACP nationals and the access to education in the EU for ACP students are two explicitly mentioned elements of such strategies.

- Regulations to counter irregular migration – The parties are committed to return and re-admit all nationals who are in an irregular situation. To this end, bilateral readmission and return agreements shall be concluded.

Based on principles of cost-efficiency and ownership, technical cooperation should enhance the transfer of knowledge, develop national and regional human capacities and promote the exchange between EU and ACP professionals (art. 79, 80). As an integral element of technical cooperation, the EU is committed to support the ACP's efforts to reverse the brain drain (art. 80).

Developing the Common Policy

In line with the strategy set out in the conclusions of the Tampere Council, the common policy is being developed in two phases: the establishment of minimum standards and harmonization of legislation in a number of key areas; progressively followed by the development of a more uniform status and common procedures.

These two phases, including a timetable, were very clearly spelled out with respect to asylum in the Amsterdam Treaty as further elaborated by the European Council in Tampere, and then at the mid-term review in Laeken (Belgium) in December 2001. The first phase must be completed by 2004 and provides for the Union to adopt, on the basis of Commission proposals, a number of legal instruments to establish minimum standards on the admission, reception and status of asylum seekers, refugees and displaced persons. The Commission has moved rapidly to put forward proposals for the necessary legislation to the Council, some of which have already been adopted.

The Member States have reached agreement on two pieces of legislation. In December 2000, a Council regulation was adopted establishing the EURODAC system[4] for the comparison of fingerprints of applicants for asylum in order to enhance the efficiency of the Dublin Convention, which defines criteria and mechanisms on Member States' responsibility to review asylum claims in the EU. Then, in July 2001, the Directive on temporary protection in case of mass influx of displaced persons[5] was adopted. Agreement on the Commission's proposals for a directive on reception conditions for asylum seekers was reached in the Council in April 2002[6].

261

Legislation, which is still under discussion in the Council, concerns the granting and withdrawing of refugee status based on proposals adopted by the Commission in September 2000; the updating of the Dublin Convention on the basis of proposals adopted by the Commission in July 2001[7]; and a proposal for a directive on the refugee

---

4) Council Decision of 11 December 2000 concerning the establishment of "Eurodac" for the comparison of fingerprints for the effective application of the Dublin Convention on the state responsible for examining applications for asylum lodged in one of the European Union Member States (Council Regulation 2000/2725/EC).

5) Council Decision of 20 July 2001 on minimum standards for giving temporary protection in the event of a mass influx of displaced persons and on measures promoting a balance of efforts among Member States in receiving such persons and bearing the consequences there of (Council Directive 2001/55/EC).

6) COM(2001)181 of 3.04.01: *Proposal for a Council Directive laying down minimum standards on the reception of applicants for asylum in Member States.*

7) COM(2001)447 of 26.07.01: *Proposal for a Council regulation establishing the criteria and mechanisms for determining the Member State responsible for examining an asylum application lodged in one of the Member States by a third country national ('Dublin II').*

qualification and status and on subsidiary forms of protection, adopted by the Commission in September 2001[8]. These last instruments and proposals were put on the Council table during the fiftieth anniversary of the 1951 Geneva Convention. The Commission believes that they make an important contribution to strengthening the international protection regime.

At the same time, a European Refugee Fund, endowed with Euro 216 million for the period 2000 to 2004, has been established to support Member States' efforts to deal with asylum seekers, refugees and displaced persons as far as reception, integration and voluntary returns are concerned[9] (see also **chapter 6**).

Several difficult issues remain to be solved, such as access to work for asylum seekers, the extent and speed with which harmonization should take place, reflecting different views and practices among Member States. The solutions will require strong political commitment and willingness to compromise. In this context great care was taken in drafting the proposals on both asylum and immigration to take into account the existing differences in national policies and to discuss these informally with Member States during the drafting process. However, the objective is also to put forward solutions to problems which reflect best practice and will provide added value for the EU.

The communication on asylum of November 2000 put forward for debate a number of different options for the second phase, i.e., how to move from the present flexible approach based on the adoption of minimum standards, to a truly European asylum system with common procedures and full application of the Dublin system. These ideas were developed in the first annual report on the application of the communication of November 2000, issued in November 2001[10]. They include proposals for adopting an open coordination procedure in the asylum area, which could in the long term involve agreeing on European

guidelines and gearing national policy to meeting these objectives. This should make it much easier to develop convergence and strengthen moves towards a European approach. The length of the first phase will depend on the rhythm of the work done.

The rationale for a common asylum policy is perhaps more readily accepted than is the case with immigration policy. However, in view of the interactions between the two areas, the Commission believes that migration management requires the implementation of a total package. Such a package must include policy coordination on legal migration and on admission and residency conditions for migrants and so the Commission has also put forward a two-phased approach to develop a common policy in this area.

A Community Immigration Policy

The principal concern here, as with asylum, is to find better ways – through European-wide cooperation – to manage migration more effectively. In its communication on a Community Immigration Policy (COM(2000)757) of November 2000 the Commission described the method it intended to follow to develop a common policy in this area and in particular suggested a more transparent approach to labour migration. This was based on an analysis of the situation with respect to migration flows and on the changing demographic and economic context of the EU (see also **chapter 13**) and of countries of origin of migrants seeking entry to Member States of the Union.

The Economic and Demographic Context

In the 1990s, migratory movements in Europe were greater than at any time since the Second World War. The flows increased dramatically as the EU became a major destination for people from third countries. The 1990s were also a decade which saw new migration trends and patterns emerge with new sources, such as the countries of Eastern Europe and the Balkans, and greater diversification of people on the move: refugees, asylum seekers, displaced persons, family members of migrants already established in the Union, migrant workers and growing numbers of business migrants. The flows have become more flexible and dynamic – short-term and cross-border movements in particular have increased. There have also been large numbers of illegal migrants, often smuggled in by traffickers, sometimes with tragic results, and then subject to exploitation in new forms of

8) COM (2001)510 of 12.09.01: *Proposal for a Council Directive laying down minimum standards for the qualification and status of third country nationals and stateless persons as refugees, in accordance with the 1951 Convention relating to the status of refugees and the 1967 protocol, or as persons who otherwise need international protection.*

9) Council Decision of 28 September 2000 establishing a European Refugee Fund (2000/596/EC).

10) COM(2001)710 of 28.11.01: *Communication from the Commission to the Council and the European Parliament on the common asylum policy, introducing an open coordination method* (First report by the Commission on the application of communication COM(755)final of 22.11.01).

modern slavery (see **chapters 1** and **2**). The growth of regularization, or "amnesty", programmes in several Member States in recent years bears witness to the difficulty of preventing illegal migration (see also **textbox 13.4.**).

The growing number of labour migrants who make up an important part of these flows is a reflection of significant sectoral and regional shortages of manpower which are now apparent in the EU. In certain countries, these are in highly qualified areas such as the new technologies and the health sector. But there are also recruitment difficulties in lower skilled sectors, such as agriculture, construction industry, tourism and domestic services. The Union is developing new European-wide strategies to deal with these changes, particularly in the economic and social field, but it also recognizes that a measured and controlled immigration policy will make these strategies successful.

One explanation of this demand for manpower lies in the demographic situation of the Union, and two tendencies in particular: a decline in growth, and a marked ageing of the population. The age structure of the population of the 15 Member States will change dramatically in the next decades and the share of older people (64 years and over) is expected to reach an average of 27 per cent of total population in 2020. This will be accompanied by a gradual reduction in the working age population which can already be seen in some Member States. The general tendency in all the Central and Eastern European candidate countries is similar[11]. There are clearly national and regional differences in the extent of the likely changes and in the time-scale; however, migratory balance has become the principal component of demographic growth throughout the Union (see also **chapter 13**).

The primary instrument for tackling labour market shortages is, and remains, the full implementation of the European employment strategy and the new policies being developed at European level to deal with these changes: bringing more women into the labour force; encouraging older people to work until retirement age; and making training and education more responsive to labour market needs. The EU is also reviewing the consequences of an ageing population on social security and pensions systems and proposing new measures to deal with its impact. However, analysis suggests that, in spite of these measures,

existing and future labour supplies within the EU will not be sufficient to meet labour market needs, at least in the short-term. For this reason, a number of Member States are already recruiting from third countries.

Therefore, in its November 2000 communication on immigration, the Commission proposed abandoning the so-called "zero immigration" policies of the last decades of the twentieth century and formulating a controlled and coordinated migration policy for the EU. Such a policy would include transparent migration procedures to respond to both labour market needs and new patterns and pressures of migration flows on the Union. These proposals reflect the Commission's view that existing national policies have proven inadequate in managing migration effectively, especially in an EU without, or with greatly diminished, internal borders, and secondly that economic migration has generally played a positive role in economic development. A Community immigration policy should aim at ensuring orderly migration flows and, consequently, provide impetus to the fight against irregular migration and the associated problems of smuggling and trafficking.

As reaffirmed by the European Council in Tampere, the Commission's proposals are based on the premise that the right to seek asylum must continue to be guaranteed as the cornerstone of EU policy and that the EU will continue to play its part in receiving asylum seekers in accordance with its international obligations. Economic migration is not a substitute for asylum and will not prevent illegal migration but it is hoped that, by providing a legal alternative, illegal flows will be reduced as will pressure on asylum systems (see also **chapter 6**).

Other elements of the common policy called for by the Council include the following: admission and conditions of residence of third country nationals; strengthening integration policies; stepping up measures to combat irregular migration and the phenomena associated with it; and involving third countries more closely in managing migration flows and addressing root causes of migration.

Policy on Admission and Residence

With respect to entry and residence conditions for third country nationals, the first phase of the two-step approach put forward is the establishment of a normative framework laying down minimum standards. The proposals for the initial package of legislative measures for implementing this common legal framework will shortly be completed

---

11) The following countries are candidates for EU accession in 2004: Cyprus, Czech Republic, Estonia, Hungary, Latvia, Lithuania, Malta, Poland, Slovakia, Slovenia.

by the Commission. Those concerning family reunification were originally put forth for discussion in the Council in December 1999. A second, amended version was adopted by the Commission on 2 May 2002[12]. This takes a new approach to the points on which agreement has not yet been reached, concerning the definition of family members, and incorporates the compromises already reached in the Council on other aspects of the text. The provision of greater flexibility in certain areas is based on two factors: the use of a stand-still clause to ensure that the derogations made available are not applicable if such clauses did not already exist in national legislation when the European directive was adopted; and secondly, the setting of a deadline for the next stage of harmonization for family reunification.

Meanwhile, proposals on the status of long-term resident third country nationals[13] were put forward in March 2001, and a draft directive on admission for the purposes of employment[14] was adopted by the Commission in July 2001. These draft directives are currently under discussion in the Council. The Commission's proposals on long-term resident status provide for a certain flexibility concerning movement between Member States and set out the conditions under which migrants granted this status in one country could take up residence in another. The proposals also include a set of uniform rights which they should enjoy, and which are as near as possible to those of EU citizens, e.g., the right to reside, to receive education and to work, as well as the principle of non-discrimination with respect to nationals. The package of legislation will be completed by the summer of 2002 with a draft directive concerning the admission of students, and a further directive dealing with admission for non-remunerated activities.

To date, it has been extremely difficult to reach agreement in the Council on immigration legislation. Family reunion is perhaps the most contentious issue to be dealt with and is also the only directive that will directly affect the number of migrants eligible to enter the EU. While most family members are or will be workers, too, and given that family reunion is one of the key factors in successful integration, there are wide differences among Member States in a number of key areas. However, this is a crucial component of the total package of legislation, and the resolution of these difficulties will clearly indicate the political commitment of Member States to establish the instruments required for successful migration management.

Promoting Integration and Fighting Racism, Xenophobia and Social Exclusion

In Tampere, the European Council insisted on the importance of accompanying the common policy on the admission and residence of third-country nationals with the development of more vigorous integration policies. It is becoming increasingly evident that lack of investment in adequate integration strategies results, in the longer term, in higher unemployment of second and third generation migrants and social problems which can be exacerbated by racism and xenophobia (see also **chapter 4**).

It is perhaps a paradox that while migration movements are becoming more fluid and some categories of migrant, such as the highly skilled, are becoming more mobile as integral part of their career patterns, the need to invest from the beginning in specific integration programmes for migrants is now widely recognized. This is a national responsibility which often falls on local and regional authorities and non-governmental organizations which require adequate resources to carry it out. Furthermore exchanges of experience and good practice at European level should be especially useful.

For a number of years, the EU Commission has taken action to support Member States' efforts in this area. Immigrants have benefited from a large number of Community programmes, notably those financed through the European Structural Funds, particularly for education and training to facilitate access to the labour market. Measures to ensure the integration of migrants in the workplace are also included in the European Employment Guidelines. Over the period 1996-1999 the Commission financed over 700 transnational projects specifically aimed at promoting the integration of immigrants and ethnic minority communities, multicultural integration and the integration of refugees. From 2000, projects to support refugee integration were incorporated within the European Refugee Fund. Subject to the allocation of the necessary budgetary

12) COM(1999)638 of 1.12.1999: *Proposal for a Council Directive on the right to family reunification,*
COM(2000)624 of 10.10.2000: *Amended proposal for a Council Directive on the right to family reunification,*
COM(2002)225 of 02.05.02: *Amended proposal for a Council Directive on the right to family reunification.*
13) COM(2001)127 of 13.03.01: *Proposal for a Council Directive concerning the status of third country nationals who are long term residents.*
14) COM(2001)386 of 11.07.01: *Proposal for a Council Directive on the conditions of entry and residence of third-country nationals for the purpose of paid employment and self-employed economic activities.*

resources, the Commission proposes to introduce a new programme of preparatory actions to promote the integration of migrants over the period 2003-2005. This will enable the Commission to favour the exchange of information and good practice among Member States particularly among local and regional authorities, non-governmental organizations and others involved in developing and implementing integration policies, including migrants themselves.

Integration also implies the acquisition of both rights and responsibilities; thus the Commissions' proposals for the admission of third-country nationals are based on the principle of equal treatment with nationals with respect to working conditions and on defining the rights and responsibilities to be accorded to migrants depending on length of stay. The Charter of Fundamental Rights is the starting point; it stipulates all the fundamental rights respected in the Union.

The Tampere Council also called for stronger measures to enhance non-discrimination in all aspects of life. Implementing Article 13 of the EC Treaty, a package of anti-discrimination measures was successfully adopted in record time by the Council in 2000. It consists of directives on racial discrimination and on discrimination in employment together with a Community Action Programme:

- the directive on racial discrimination (2000/43/EC) will provide a minimum level of protection against racial discrimination common to all Member States;

- the employment discrimination directive (2000/78/EC) prohibits discrimination on grounds of religion and belief, disability, age and sexual orientation. It does so only in the field of employment and does not require the establishment of an equality body;

- the action programme to combat discrimination came into force on 1 January 2001. It will run for six years with a budget of just under Euros 100 million;

- the Commission has also established the European Monitoring Centre on Racism and Xenophobia in Vienna, which carries out research on racism, xenophobia and anti-Semitism in Europe, analysing the causes and effects and identifying examples of good practice;

- in November 2001, the Commission also adopted a proposal for a Council framework decision on combating racism and xenophobia (COM(2001)664), which aims at approximating the laws and regulations of Member States concerning racist and xenophobic offices in order to ensure that racism and xenophobia are effectively and dissuasively punishable in all Member States and to improve judicial cooperation in this area.

Combating Illegal Immigration

In its communication on immigration of November 2000, the Commission underlines that developing effective measures to prevent and combat illegal immigration must be an essential component of the Community immigration policy. This issue became a priority for the Commission when it adopted a Communication on this issue in November 2001[15]. In order to make EU action more effective, a comprehensive "actors-in-the-chain" approach has been proposed which focusses on a number of priorities. The most sensitive points of the long chain range from "recruitment" by the smugglers in the country of origin, via passage through a number of transit countries and often to illegal work or other forms of exploitation in the country of destination. The communication identified six action areas for help prevent and combat illegal immigration by adding a European dimension to Member States efforts: proposals on visa policy; developing arrangements for information exchange; border management; reinforcing police cooperation; improving cooperation and coordination of aliens law and criminal law; and return and readmission policy. Based on these proposals, on 28 February 2002, the Council adopted a new action plan to combat illegal immigration, smuggling and trafficking, which is now being implemented. The plan contains a number of measures to reinforce cooperation and develop a more effective policy.

The Commission adopted an additional proposal in February 2002 to tackle the smuggling and trafficking of human beings. The draft directive provides for the issue of short-term residence permits to trafficking victims who cooperate with the competent authorities in destination countries.

265

---

15) COM(2001)672 of 15.11.01: *Communication on a common policy on illegal immigration.*

As a first follow-up action, the Commission published a Green Paper on return of illegal residents in the EU in April 2002[16]. This paper seeks to structure discussions on better cooperation among Member States by developing a European approach to provide more effective measures for forced returns where necessary. This was followed in May by a Communication on integrated management of the Union's external borders[17], which proposes new measures for better cooperation and stronger border controls.

Undeclared work also has an impact on irregular migration. The availability of such jobs in the EU acts as a pull factor for irregular migrants, although the problem is not restricted to migrants alone. The Commission has recently published a report which in follow-up to its Communication of 1998 on undeclared work. The report reviews existing policies to combat undeclared work, and evaluates their effectiveness, individually and in combination, in different Member States[18]. Its findings were incorporated into the Commission's 2002 evaluation of the European Employment Strategy.

Developing Partnerships with Third Countries

For countries of origin, emigration often results in brain drain, which may damage development prospects (see **chapter 12**). A sustainable and well-managed migration policy depends, therefore, upon an effective partnership with countries of origin designed to create "win-win" situations, that is, to maximize the benefits and minimize the negative impact of migration on countries of origin and destination, and the migrants themselves. The Commission has proposed that migration issues be placed higher on the political agenda and that dialogue with third countries be developed within contexts such as trade and development as well as with respect to the impact of emigration and orderly migration management.

The six action plans prepared by the High Level Working Group an Asylum and Immigration illustrate this new approach. A new budget line for migration cooperation with third countries has been created with a total amount of Euro 10 million in 2001 and Euro 12.5 million in 2002

(B7-667). It is being used to support operations with third countries to enhance Community capacity for migration management.

With respect to re-admission, an agreement has been concluded with the Hong Kong Special Administrative region of China, and negotiations continue with Morocco, Pakistan, Russia and Sri Lanka. However, since the Tampere Council, a much wider range of migration issues, going beyond border controls and re-admission, are now in discussion and the number of third countries involved is steadily growing. New attention is also being paid to the phenomena within trade and association agreements. This new dialogue is just beginning, but it has made a very promising start. A framework programme for developing cooperation in the fields of justice and home affairs has recently been agreed with the Mediterranean countries. An important element of this programme concerns cooperation on the management of migration flows between the EU and the Mediterranean partners and the integration of migrants from North Africa in the Member States (see also **textbox 13.2.**). In addition, a first meeting at ministerial level between the ASEM[19] countries and the EU on cooperation for the management of migratory flows was held in Lanzarote (Canary Islands - Spain) on 4 and 5 April 2002 within the context of the Asia-Europe dialogue. Discussions with China on preventing illegal migration have developed well in recent months. Initiatives such as these will continue to be developed in the years ahead.

Open Coordination through Exchange of Information and Best Practices

A further element in the development of the common policy proposed by the Commission as a complement to the legislative framework is an open coordination mechanism designed to encourage the progressive convergence of the policies of the Member States over time. In July 2001, the Commission adopted a communication setting out its proposals for such a method[20] for the Community immigration policy and proposed a similar procedure for asylum in its first report of November 2001[21] on developing of the common asylum policy.

16) COM(2002)175 of 10.04.02: *Communication on a Community return policy on illegal residents.*
17) COM(2002)233 of 07.05.02: *Communication on the integrated management of the external borders of the Member States of the European Union.*
18) Regioplan (2001). *Undeclared labour in Europe. Towards an integrated approach of combating undeclared labour,* October, Regioplan Publications no.424, Regioplan Research Advice and Information.
19) The Asia-Europe Meeting (ASEM) groups heads of government of 25 countries and the European Commission. Participants to ASEM include 10 Asian states (Brunei Darussalam, China, Indonesia, Japan, Republic of Korea, Malaysia, the Philippines, Singapore, Thailand and Vietnam) and the 15 EU Member States.
20) COM(2001)386 of 11.07.01: *op.cit.*
21) COM(2001)710 of 28.11.01: *op.cit.*

The principal elements of this method, which is used in other areas of the Community policy-making, are the adoption by the Council of European guidelines or objectives and the preparation of national action plans designed to realize them. The Commission believes that such a procedure would be helpful since, although Title IV of the Treaty establishes Community competence in the area of migration and asylum, a complementary process would be useful in promoting convergence. This is particularly the case with respect to immigration as there are a number of areas where responsibility for migration policy remains with the Member States: notably the magnitude of economic migration and the elements of integration of migrants; and other areas where a coordinated approach is necessary to realize the strategic goals agreed on in Tampere, e.g., fighting irregular migration, trafficking and smuggling effectively

TEXTBOX 14.2.

Immigration at the 2002 European Union Summit in Seville

Immigration was a major topic of discussion at the Seville Summit held on 21 and 22 June 2002 to mark the end of the Spanish Presidency of the European Union. The Heads of State and of Government of the Fifteen concluded by adopting a common agreement on ways to combat irregular immigration and set themselves a timetable for implementing a common immigration and asylum policy.

The agreement calls for better cooperation with countries of origin and transit of irregular migrants and envisages better border management and control, as well as readmission agreements. Readmission agreements should not only apply to nationals of these countries detained in the Union, but also to irregular migrants from third countries. However, there was no provision for the Union to implement systematic sanctions against third countries that fail to cooperate adequately in curbing illegal emigration.

The option of sanctions is included in the European plan as a last resort provided development cooperation is not negatively affected in any way. Any such decision would have to be taken unanimously by member countries.

Indeed, supported by Germany and Italy, the United Kingdom and Spain attempted to set out a policy for economic sanctions against third countries that neglect

to stem irregular migration flows in the weeks leading up to the summit. In the face of opposition from France and Sweden, the Fifteen finally settled for a call to dialogue and coordination among all the countries concerned.

The Heads of State and of Government also approved a plan for the progressive implementation of joint management of the Union's external borders, together with a precise timetable. Among other things, the plan envisages joint operations at external borders and a network of immigration liaison officers by the end of 2002. However, no timetable was set for creating a European border police force, even though this is viewed as the most emblematic project.

Fences are not the solution to Europe's migration challenges

267

The Fifteen put paid to current discussions about "Fortress Europe". According to the outgoing President of the Union, José Maria Aznar[22], "We want Europe to remain a land of hospitality, we need immigrants". Europe therefore needs an immigration and asylum policy, which Heads of State and Government undertook to implement as soon as possible. A timetable was set, *inter alia*, for adopting common provisions on family reunification (before June 2003) and harmonizing asylum procedures (end 2003). In Mr. Aznar's words, the measures must "strike a fair balance between, on the one hand, a policy for the integration of lawfully resident immigrants and an asylum policy complying with international conventions [...], and, on the other, resolute action to combat illegal immigration and trafficking in human beings".

In its July 2001 communication on this issue, the Commission makes proposals for immigration guidelines in four broad areas: management of migration flows; admission of economic migrants; partnership with third countries and integration of third-country nationals. Such a procedure will facilitate coordination and consistency among national policies, provide for a review of the operation of Community legislation, and the exchange of information and of good practice, which will be especially important in the area of integration. It will also assist the Commission in evaluating the impact of each of the legal instruments and the interaction between different policies, e.g., how far a more open policy of legal immigration reduces the pressure on illegal movements.

As a first step, following the request from the Laeken European Council to reinforce the exchange of information at European level on asylum and migration, the Commission has established a mechanism for regular expert meetings to consider issues of immigration and asylum policy in a cooperative fashion.

Future Perspectives

The programme set by the heads of State and Government is very ambitious. It represents a unique attempt to create a regional approach to migration and asylum. Irrespective of the position of the three "opt-out" countries – Denmark, Ireland and the UK – it will be a common system which applies in one of the largest regions in the world affected by migration movements, all the more so since the EU is set to enlarge over the next few years. As Member States move steadily towards closer union, with the abolition of most internal border controls and greater convergence in economic and employment policy, a common approach to asylum and immigration becomes more and more necessary.

TEXTBOX 14.3.

Free Movement in Europe – the Schengen Agreement

The Schengen Agreement is an intergovernmental agreement creating a European free-movement zone without controls at internal land, water and airport frontiers – the so-called "Schengen Area".

Initially signed in June 1985 by Belgium, France, Germany, Luxembourg and the Netherlands, the Schengen Agreement has been extended to currently include almost every EU Member State, with the exception of Ireland and the United Kingdom. Italy signed the agreement in 1990, Portugal and Spain in 1991, Greece in 1992, Austria in 1995 and Denmark, Finland and Sweden in 1996. Iceland and Norway signed an agreement with the EU in 1999 to extend the Schengen area. These two countries are also signatories of the Nordic Passport Union, which abolished border checks between the five Nordic countries.

When the Schengen Agreement came into effect in 1995, it abolished the internal borders of the signatory states and created a single external border where immigration checks are carried out in accordance with a single set of rules. Common rules regarding visas, asylum rights and checks at external borders were adopted to allow the free movement of persons within the Schengen Area.

In order to reconcile freedom and security, freedom of movement was accompanied by a range of compensatory measures, including coordination between the police,

22) *La Libre Belgique*, Brussels, 23 June 2002.

customs and the judiciary; and initiatives to combat terrorism and organized crime. Designed to improve police and judicial cooperation and policies on visas, immigration and the free movement of people, the Schengen Information System (SIS) was set up to pool data on the movement of people and goods.

Although the Schengen agreement was concluded outside the context of the European Union, it has been brought into the realm of the Union under the Amsterdam Treaty. States seeking accession to the EU must have border regimes which meet Schengen standards.

In Laeken, the Heads of State and of Government recognized that progress had been slow. However, they did renew their commitment to establishing the common policy as soon as possible and asked for a new approach to be developed. This is particularly necessary given the time required for adopting European legislation and developing new migration legislation in several Member States. Laeken also stressed the importance of decisions taken being transposed into national law and/or implemented rapidly once agreed upon. Since the Laeken summit, progress has been made towards establishing a common immigration policy, notably with the adoption of the action plan on illegal immigration. Efforts are being made to speed up the decision-making process and, together with the adoption by the Commission of a principle of greater flexibility within the context of a phased approach to convergence, it is expected that agreement will be reached very soon on the proposals for family reunion.

Meanwhile, the Commission will be paying greater attention to the issue of integration, to setting priorities and identifying the resources required to develop a comprehensive approach. An important component should be a framework ensuring participation from all groups involved: local and regional actors, social partners, civil society and migrants themselves in developing and implementing national strategy. A number of Member States are now taking a fresh look at developing of settlement programmes for new migrants and their families, including the provision of appropriate language training and information on the cultural, political and social characteristics of the country concerned. More discussion is required and more information should be exchanged on such policies and the best ways to implement them.

In this context, it is also useful to reflect further on the nature of citizenship and to reaffirm the fundamental European values enshrined in the Charter of Fundamental Rights. The European Convention[23] on the future of the Union, which will be completing its work in 2003, will be discussing whether the Charter should be incorporated into the revised Treaty. The rights enshrined in it reflect EU Member State moral and political values: respect for the dignity of the human being, freedom, equality and solidarity, citizenship and justice. It is certainly important to reaffirm Europe's commitment to tolerance and the respect of diversity which implies a strong condemnation of intolerance and fundamentalism. The Convention will also be considering whether or not to recommend that the EU adhere to the European Convention on Human Rights.

Considerable efforts for compromise and goodwill will be required to achieve the objectives agreed on in Tampere. However, migration pressures on the EU will continue and only coordination and cooperation can establish the policies and practices necessary to manage these flows effectively.

23) The purpose of the European Convention is to propose new EU framework and structures which are geared to global changes, the needs of European citizens and the future development of the EU. Created following the Laeken European Council in December 2001, the Convention brings together representatives of governments, national parliaments, the European Parliament and the European Commission. See also: www.european-convention.eu.int.

CHAPTER 15

Elements of a more Global Approach to Migration Management

In the ever-widening debate on migration, the question about how far migration can and needs to be regulated globally is a recurring one. There is growing awareness that national policies are inadequate for the more global challenges of migration, and that new or revised approaches to migration are needed (European Commission, 2000a; Salt, 2000; Koser, 2001). Some people believe that national immigration policies should be embedded in a multilateral framework, like trade and investment (Ghosh, 2000).

Contemporary population movements are highly complex, diverse and inter-connected with other global processes. They involve ever increasing numbers of countries, as origin, transit and destination points, often all three in one. These movements interact dynamically with development, trade, security, health and stability trends; and increasingly demand the attention of all these policy areas in government.

While governments are mainly responsible for regulating migration, there is a growing view that migration policies are being driven by migrants themselves, or private agents either brokering labour exchanges or preying on the needs of vulnerable persons. The flows are mixed with humanitarian and non-humanitarian cases within the same asylum systems; faced with this situation, states need to balance their international obligations with national responsibilities.

Irregular movements create their own global dynamics, particularly where cross-border criminal networks are involved. Governments can pay a high political price if communities feel borders are not being managed credibly; the stakes are much higher since September 11, 2001. Such perceptions can fuel extreme political and community reactions (Martin and Martin, 2002b), with more expensive consequences in the longer term than the costs of border management.

At the same time, more is known today about the huge benefits migrants can bring both countries of origin and destination alike (Nyberg-Sorensen *et al.,* 2002). While governments still pursue unilateral policies, there is a greater awareness of the transnational character of migration and how to manage it better. This awareness is starting to shape new partnerships among states at trade, cultural and political levels. Traditional approaches to border management have often tended not to keep pace with these changes, and have not offered lasting solutions; so governments are looking to diversified and joint approaches.

Convergent approaches are already evolving among states in many areas, particularly where there are issues of mutual concern, for example along common borders. Partnerships and more similar approaches are being developed, which could pave the way for a more global agenda on migration. But this is still a far cry from a global migration management system, which pre-supposes a high degree of policy coherence within and among governments.

This chapter looks at a selection of contemporary migration issues that illustrate a critical need for more consistent and coherent approaches across states: labour migration; smuggling and trafficking; women and migration, assisted voluntary returns; integration; migrant health and international cooperation[1]. It examines why and how migration could be regulated more systematically and globally. Some shifts in policy and practice are already occurring towards a more common approach; however, serious obstacles remain within and among states. The chapter points to the need for a central cohering mechanism to support and guide states' efforts in considering more commonality of migration rules and practices.

Labour Migration

Labour migration poses one of the biggest challenges to migration policy makers in the twenty-first century[2]. People are moving to seek work on a scale beyond the scope of current regulatory mechanisms, and the clandestine, often criminally-based flows elude the capacities of national and international enforcement authorities[3]. This type of migration is permanently at risk of slipping out of government control, yet the patterns of movement lend themselves well to systematization, e.g., along trade and commerce lines.

1) The different chapters of the thematic section analyse these issues from a thematic as well as a geographical point of view.
2) According to the International Labour Organization (ILO), an estimated 60 to 65 million persons are economically active in a country other than their own (GB/283/2/1, two hundred eighty third session, Geneva – March 2002). Including family members and irregular labour migrants, this figure rises to 120 million, according to Juan Somavia, ILO director general (2002).
3) For example, it is estimated that 300,000 undocumented workers enter the USA every year (World Bank, 2001).

271

Given demographic dynamics in most western states (UN, 2000a), labour migration is experiencing some of the most rapid changes in trends and policy responses. In 2000, for example, a study opined that Western European states are less inclined to facilitate skilled entry than the traditional countries of immigration (Christian, 2000). However, this is no longer the case in 2002, as demonstrated by efforts in Germany and the United Kingdom to compete for highly skilled personnel on the global market.

ILO points to three contemporary features of labour migration not adequately provided for in the ILO Labour Conventions or national immigration laws, which challenge traditional efforts to regulate migration: feminization, privatization and regionalization (ILO, 1999). National policy and legislation do not address the growing feminization of migrant labour and rise in exploitation of women and children by traffickers or unscrupulous employers. The privatization of migration means that migration policy is driven more and more by employers and even further removed from government through sub-contracting arrangements. Finally, regional agreements tend to be inward-directed, and need, *inter alia,* to be examined against the standards of the ILO Conventions and General Agreement on Trade in Services (GATS).

Many government policies have not been able to keep pace with labour market developments, and the need for legislative frameworks to permit rapid responses to labour shortages. Current labour migration regimes are highly varied and complicated, particularly in Europe, where employers in need of third country nationals are often confronted with complex administrative procedures and very few common rules and principles across Member States (ECOTEC, 2001).

To be competitive in a world of globalized economies and communications, governments and industry in advanced societies need increasingly flexible, expeditious visa policies, while being mindful of the imperative to regulate more strictly on protecting rights and conditions. Opening up legal immigration routes for surplus labour can have the secondary benefit of reducing demand for smugglers and traffickers. Diversified policies being pursued by some forward-looking recruiting countries include:

- choices about temporary or permanent residence;
- less restrictive visa conditions[4];
- immigrant integration support[5];
- removal of work permit/labour market testing for high skill/demand jobs[6];
- no employer/job offer requirement for high skill/demand sectors[7];
- greater investor possibilities;
- tapping into foreign student/apprentice populations[8].

A number of EU states are already taking tentative steps towards opening up new labour migration channels in their region[9], but under the supra-national competency of the EU, which aims at establishing a common legal framework on admission of economic migrants. This would combine more flexible provisions for mobility of third country nationals with an EU Residence Permit[10], clearer standards and principles on migrants' rights, simpler immigration procedures, and regard for domestic labour markets.

Regarding the shadow labour market, the ILO recently commissioned a study of how to curb irregular labour immigration through employer sanctions, which yields some interesting lessons learned in France, Germany and the US (Doomernik, 1998). The study shows how a mixture of innovative approaches can help check irregular immigration in highly industrialized receiving countries. These include the combination of sanctions with effective

---

4) I.e., longer visa validity, change of employer/visa status, work rights for spouse and other family members.

5) I.e., access to mainstream services; language training; anti-discrimination and xenophobia campaigns in the host community.

6) As already exists for ICT workers in France, Germany, the Netherlands and the UK (reduced labour market testing to enable change of employer), and Ireland for immigrants with a job offer.

7) Some countries (UK and Germany) are considering to adopt the mathematically-based "Skills Assessment Scheme" tried over many decades by Australia and Canada, to select qualified/skilled migrants on the basis of language, qualifications, connection with the country and employability.

8) For many governments, their overseas student programmes are ready pools of qualified/skilled persons who a) have adjusted to their new temporary homes, and b) bring local qualifications to the job (e.g., France, Germany, Italy, and Norway).

9) Germany's "Green Card" programme for IT specialists begun in 2001; Denmark is introducing a Green Card-like programme in needy labour sectors; the Netherlands is loosening its Regulations to admit highly qualified migrants in the Science, Management and ICT sectors, without labour market testing; Norway is aiming to recruit 5,000 highly skilled migrants in 2002, and is looking at the possibility of non-skilled immigration.

10) Member States are generally adopting the EC's recommendation for a one-stop-shop "Workers Residence Permit".

border control; better coordination of labour and immigration enforcement; higher penalties against employers and contractors, or sub-contractors; and innovative use of law, technology and research.

But measures to combat irregular migration will lack any serious impact if there is no public support and understanding for them. This is often the case among communities, employers and civil society in Europe and the US, who oppose sanctions against employers because they harm those small scale businesses that most need illegal labour to remain competitive. The ILO report thus recommends improving public relations with the community; ensuring strong industrial relations among the social partners; and providing incentives for employer groups to cooperate with the authorities.

These are new tactics and procedures intended to ensure the workability and legitimacy of labour migration. In countries like Australia and Canada, they have been combined in various ways with policies to ensure social stability between migrants and their host communities – an approach increasingly adopted by other countries (United Kingdom Home Office, 2002). New integration paradigms are essential, since migrants will become more and more "permanent" the longer they reside in a foreign land, despite the increasingly temporary nature of labour migration.

A US report predicts that western governments are unlikely to open their borders to people from lower income countries in the coming years (National Intelligence Council, 2000). This certainly tallies with EU members' caution about opening up unskilled migration programmes for non-EU nationals. Nevertheless, a number of western governments are doing exactly this out of labour planning necessity (e.g., Austria and the United Kingdom). This is partly in the expectation that "managed" labour migration would avert further smuggling and trafficking.

Labour-exporting countries face the often conflicting goals of maximizing labour exports while guaranteeing protection and fair treatment for their workers. This is increasingly difficult at a time when new supply sources are driving up competition and lowering employment standards to the detriment of migrants' welfare against the background of attractive new markets opening up in recruiting countries.

Labour migration is also not exclusively a South-North or East-West phenomenon, but South-South and East-East as well. South Africa receives a large number of regular and irregular labour migrants from its neighbours as do the Russian Federation or India. The management of such flows is important for regional stability. Skilled migration tends to be the most mobile and multi-directional form of labour migration, also among developing countries.

GATS potentially provides the multilateral framework for regulating (and protecting) the movement of migrant workers; however, for some observers, it is the "least developed policy making forum" to achieve that (Christian, 2000). They believe that a mixture of regulatory frameworks are more likely to meet the needs of the various complex scenarios - bilateral, regional and multilateral and indeed, that regional frameworks will ultimately be more liberalizing in movements of the highly skilled than GATS (Christian, *op.cit.*).

Ratification of the International Convention on the Protection of the Rights of all Migrant Workers and members of their Families" will be the key to effective management of the interests of labour migrants and labour exporting countries (United Nations Economic Commission for Latin America, 2002). The challenge will be how to implement and enforce it globally.

Diaspora and Development

Recruiting countries increasingly understand that labour migration is more than an "ephemeral manpower policy adjustment" for countries of origin, but that it can also be an indirect form of development support, e.g., through remittances from abroad (Ghosh, 2000). It can also strengthen foreign relations between origin and destination countries. Furthermore, migrant remittances could be twice the size of aid and just as targeted in poverty eradication (Nyberg-Sorensen *et al.,* 2002).

The way that this form of migration is managed can contribute to other, larger efforts at development and growth for both countries. This is as true for the upper end of the labour market as for the lower (including e.g., IT specialists propelled towards the needy information/communication industries in Europe, North America and Japan; and Mexican agricultural workers in the USA, or Maghrebi agricultural workers in Spain)[11].

11) The USA has in recent years steadily increased its visa ceiling for foreign professionals, and Indian computer specialists in Silicon Valley are now reaping the benefits by remitting funds to their home communities and opening up further market access at both ends of the migration spectrum (OECD, 2001b). Tunisia offers another good example in this respect.

273

Countries of destination need to plan and invest more in human capacity-building in regular source countries. By opening up legal migration channels, they help relieve emigration pressures and maintain irregular immigration at manageable levels.

Interestingly, initiatives to ensure such a balanced approach to labour migration are being carried out at the sectoral level. For example, the Commonwealth is seeking to establish a code of practice for the international recruitment of health workers, particularly from developing countries. This would take account of the combined interests of the countries of origin, recruiting countries and the migrants, and include measures like: the facilitated return of recruitees, training programmes to enable returnees to be integrated again into the home labour market, protection of pay and work conditions.

In this way also, migrant diasporas can play a key role as development resources for their country or region of origin. The IOM programme Migration for Development in Africa (MIDA) seeks to galvanize the proactive "investment" of African emigrants in the development of their continent through physical or virtual capacity building actions (see **textbox 15.1**). Countries of origin like Armenia, Bangladesh, India, Morocco, Tunisia and Yemen have established institutional mechanisms to manage this phenomenon. Armenia has set up a diaspora desk in the Ministry of Foreign Affairs, and India has a high level parliamentary committee on diaspora.

TEXTBOX 15.1.

Migration for Development in Africa – an IOM programme

The programme on "Migration for Development in Africa" (MIDA) was launched by IOM in 2001 in response to the growing need of African countries to harness contributions from their diaspora for development.

Some twenty countries met in Libreville in April 2001 to outline requirements in sectors lacking qualified human resources. They requested IOM cooperation in formulating and identifying a programme based on the lessons learned from the different phases of the Return and Reintegration of Qualified African Nationals Programme (RQAN), which ran between 1983 and 1999.

At the OAU Lusaka Summit in July 2001, decision 614 – which was supported by many countries while being prepared – commissioned IOM to initiate activities that would enable Member Countries to match the skills and resources available in host countries with shortcomings in human resource supply identified by governments in countries of origin.

Reversing the brain drain holds the key to Africa's development

Over the past year, this institutional recognition has paved the way for an enhanced implementation of Articles 13, 79 and 80 of the Cotonou Agreements between countries of the European Union and ACP countries (see **textbox 14.1.**).

A truly novel approach to the brain drain issue, the underlying principle of MIDA is that regular migrants do not wish to give up the employment and social protection rights acquired in their host country even if they are obviously keen to help development in their own country, albeit by means other than permanent return.

Technically, the project is based on a precise identification of needs by sector and employment level in African countries using a real-time relational database, which is completed in the host countries by adding the curricula vitae of qualified migrants interested in participating.

Managed by IOM together with all parties concerned, this matching of data makes it possible to identify the best profile for each post or mission.

Possible forms of participation range from repeated short stays to complete a project in conjunction with locally available human resources; skill transfers through consultation or distance teaching using electronic media or video; to fund-raising for a micro-enterprise, a local development project or support for private sector development.

The use of information technologies yields considerable economies of scale when compared with programmes that entail the definitive return of the migrant and his family.

To implement MIDA programmes, authorities in the beneficiary country must appoint a national correspondent to liaise with the various local entities concerned (ministries, universities, enterprises, associations), with authorities in the partner country or institution, and with IOM.

In the host country or countries, a coordinator is also appointed to work with the administrations concerned (Ministries of Foreign Affairs, the Interior, Labour), with diaspora associations, and the embassies of the beneficiary country or countries which have detailed information on their nationals. As part of this, an intensive information campaign will be held among diaspora associations.

An initial programme is being funded by Belgium to target the Great Lakes region. The MIDA concept has two main focuses:

* geographical programmes by country (Burkina Faso, Cape Verde, Ghana, Sudan) or by region (Mano River, ECOWAS, SADC);

* sectoral programmes, depending on shared regional or continental priorities (technical capacity building in the health sector, private sector development through joint ventures between countries in the North and South).

Several African countries have decided to make MIDA a national priority, proving that the programme is being "appropriated" and that it fills a need. These countries currently include Benin, Cape Verde, Ghana, Kenya, Sudan and Yemen, though several others have already announced their intention to follow suit.

This national approach (inclusion in the National Indicative Programme or in poverty reduction programmes) makes it possible to approach development partners that are genuinely interested in supporting programmes in line with the expectations of African countries. This covers both bilateral cooperation (the United States, Belgium, the Netherlands, and France) and development banks (African

Development Bank, World Bank, Islamic Development Bank), as well as foundations or private companies.

The essential prerequisites to MIDA's success and sustainability include greater recognition of migrants' potential contributions to development in their home countries and the creation of a legal and regulatory framework to enable persons to be effectively mobile (attractive investment code, single window, laws on the entry and stay of foreigners).

It is also vital that the international community be encouraged to pay more attention to the close link between migration and development. This should have two objectives: foster the integration of migrants into the civil societies of host countries; and to enable them to contribute to development in their countries of origin through expertise and economic resources.

Migrants' skills and remittances can drive development in their countries of origin substantially, provided they are allocated to sectors and projects essential to the country's economic takeoff and its people's social well-being.

This is the central issue of MIDA. Its originality is paving the way for IOM to work with many partners in both African and developed countries.

275

While the World Bank, the Inter-American Development Bank and others have recently begun to understand the development potential of diasporas, there is as yet little institutional planning and utilization of this force by countries of destination. Many countries of origin also do not yet have the regulatory frameworks in place to enable returning migrants to re-insert themselves or re-invest in their communities of origin. These would include such fundamental facilities as the transferability of retirement pensions.

As a first step, governments and international organizations like ILO and IOM need to examine and discuss some concrete, workable models for diaspora-strengthening; and subsequently, how to incorporate these models into national and international law.

Smuggling and Trafficking of Migrants

There is a considerable body of international law, declarations and plans of action concerning smuggling and trafficking problems. However, only three legal instruments put forward concrete ways to manage these illicit phenomena: the two protocols to the UN Convention on Transnational Organized Crime, and the US Victims of Trafficking and Violence Protection Act of 2000. Once ratified, the respective protocols relating to smuggling and trafficking are likely to be the guiding documents for all governments on how to manage these forms of irregular migration.

The protocols are particularly significant by drawing a definitional distinction between the willing compliance of a smuggled person and the victimization of a trafficked person, thereby giving clearer direction for targeted policy responses. In reality, practitioners know that there is often little distinction between the two - e.g., trafficking more often than not starts with willing compliance - and the human rights violations on both counts can be the same. This opens the way for protection of victims, which is a new facet of migration policy, traditionally focussed more on control. Most governments still do not sufficiently distinguish between "facilitating" irregular migration and trafficking persons. Other states are forging ahead with new protection laws[12].

This protection focusses particularly on persons whose status as victims continues to be ignored in detention, during deportation and upon return by many – if not most – countries of origin, transit and destination. Regarding prosecution, the instruments specifically call on nations to concertedly criminalize both smuggling and trafficking. The trafficking protocol and the US Act oblige states to extend support and protection to the victims, especially when they act as witnesses during criminal proceedings against the traffickers.

The victims should also be assisted in returning safely to their countries of origin. The repatriation clause of the trafficking protocol includes specifically the obligation of countries of origin to accept the return of nationals who were victims of trafficking. The protocol also calls for training of appropriate authorities in prevention,

protection and prosecution; and for more research and information sharing on the subject, i.e., closer transnational cooperation.

To ensure adherence to this, the US Government has taken the initiative to establish minimum standards for eliminating trafficking, applicable both to the USA and to other governments around the world. These standards provide a basis for the State Department's annual report on global progress in combating trafficking, and eventually for adjusting assistance to other countries in accordance with their respective rate of progress. The USA describes this form of global invigilation over counter trafficking policies as "bolstering international political will to combat the issue" (US Department of State, 2002).

This unilateral action by the US Government in many ways fills a vacuum that exists around the international Protocol, which lacks the necessary institutional follow-up mechanism to enforce and monitor adherence to its principles.

Women and Migration

Although almost half the 175 million migrants in the world today are women, state laws are still ill equipped to reflect this reality. Pundits agree this situation warrants special treatment in migration policies, but there is still insufficient provision in state laws to cover this.

In a number of labour-exporting countries, women account for the majority of labour emigrants (Henshall Momsen, 1999). In countries like the Philippines and Bangladesh, they are increasingly the main source of family support, contributing substantially to economic growth through their earnings and remittances.

Yet in many receiving countries, women migrants continue to be subjected to gross human rights abuse, and labour and sexual exploitation. Women often suffer multiple victimization because of gender, migrant/asylum status, ethnicity, religion, social class, or caste. They are also compelled or coerced into becoming migrants or refugees on these grounds[13].

12) Italy recently introduced into its law on immigration (*decreto legislativo no.286*, 25 July 1998) provisions to grant a special residence permit to victims of trafficking. This would give them access to social assistance, education and employment, and possible change of status to permanent residence.

13) See the report of the UN Special Rapporteur on Violence against Women (E/CN.4/2001/73/Add 2, § 20) regarding women from Myanmar in Thailand, India and Bangladesh. See also the Report of the Latin America and Caribbean Regional Seminar of Experts on Economic, Social and Legal Measures to Combat Racism, with particular reference to vulnerable groups (Santiago, Chile, 25-27 Oct. 2000, A/CONF.189/PC.2/5, § 62).

The basic international principles of protection of women are covered in the 1979 Convention on the Elimination of all Forms of Discrimination against Women (CEDAW), the various human rights conventions and labour treaties, and in countless recommendations and guidelines provided by the international agencies and special bodies reporting to the UN[14]. Yet little of this is reflected in national legislation relating to migration, despite good intentions at the regional level[15].

Some countries of origin have taken the lead in changing their laws to empower women migrants and protect them abroad. *Inter alia,* the Philippines has introduced a Migrant Workers Act (1995) to promote and protect the welfare of migrant workers and their families, and punish offenders. Protective measures have been instituted in the areas of recruitment, employment conditions and repatriation.

In countries of destination, policies relating to admission, residence permits, access to the labour market and integration can play an important role in supporting the position of women in the host society. Yet surprisingly few governments have included gender-specific provisions in their immigration policy or law, and still register women primarily as dependants of male migrants. Many have stringent entry policies with unintended adverse consequences for women. The UN warns that overly strict immigration policies can increase the vulnerability of women to violence, abuse and control, particularly in the work place[16].

The Canadian Government has an extensive track record of supporting overseas aid programmes to combat violence against women, and factoring gender concerns into its national immigration programme. Notably, Canada Immigration and Citizenship (CIC) has devised a useful model of gender-directed immigration policy making. Following a "gender based analysis" matrix, every new immigration policy and legislative issue is subjected to the test of potential gender impacts, and an assessment is made regarding the need for further research, data collection and monitoring.

This facet of migration is clearly drawing new responses from governments, but still requires more regulatory action at both ends of the migration spectrum. States should review existing laws and practices in this area and integrate the gender perspective better into migration policy and legislation.

The Special Challenge of Unaccompanied Minors

The prevalence of unaccompanied minors (UAMs) in the asylum and migration pipelines of some western states is reaching alarming proportions[17] (UNHCR, 2000). The minors are mostly categorized as victims of trafficking; however, the phenomenon is more complex, since many of these adolescents are knowingly complicit in irregular migration and other illicit practices. Many host governments have inadequate policies and/or laws to cope with the issue.

Repatriation programme from FYR of Macedonia to Kosovo

14) See the Commission on Human Rights Resolution 1997/43, § 5, and 1998/51, § 8; recommendations on the gender dimensions of Racial Discrimination by the Committee on the Elimination of Racial Discrimination; and various Human Rights Watch reports on human rights abuse against women migrants in Asia, Middle East and Africa.

15) The EU has devised a Community Framework Strategy on Gender Equality, 2001-2005, and some "Best Practices Guidelines" on measures to combat domestic, sexual and workplace violence are under finalization. But there is nothing specific to women migrants, although they are broadly covered under the Treaty of Amsterdam's anti-discrimination provisions. This lack of focus on the issue is reflected in most of the Member States' immigration policy and legislation.

16) UNGA, "Review of Reports, Studies and other Documentation for the Preparatory Committee and the World Conference (against Racism, Racial Discrimination, Xenophobia and related Intolerance), A/CONF.189/PC.3.5, 27 July 2001. This is a report to the Preparatory Committee by the Special Rapporteur of the Commission on Human Rights on violence against women.

17) At the Intergovernmental Conference (IGC) Full Round in Oxford in June 2002, the Netherlands, Switzerland, Norway, Belgium, Canada and Denmark reported notable increases in unaccompanied minors seeking asylum (45 per cent in the last year for the Netherlands most originating from Angola, Sierra Leone, Guinea and Iraq). The EU STOP programme in 2001 reported some 10,000 cases in Germany in 2000, 4,835 cases in the Netherlands in 2000 and 2,016 minor asylum seekers in Belgium in 1999 (IOM, 2001).

Since many of the children never enter the asylum systems, there are not enough data for fully informed policy decisions; indeed there is a dearth of research on migrant children in general.

Nevertheless, there is a clear increase in recent trafficking mainly affecting girls, mostly for labour exploitation (including sexual services and begging). Many are dispatched by their family as advance guard for remaining family members. Most are rejected for asylum or not adjudicated because of lack of verifiable identity. The most common problems are:

- identification and family tracing (if traced, families often deny their links with the child);

- legal guardianship of the child during its sojourn in the country of destination (some countries of origin have insufficient or non-existent laws on this);

- care and maintenance (detention is difficult; and open shelters are often not enough to protect the mainly adolescent children from drug or sex traffickers);

- human rights/protection (the rights of the child relate mostly to care/maintenance, education and family unification, not to protection);

- return and reintegration (linked to difficulties related to identification and family tracing).

National legislation in host countries will probably not cover all five areas satisfactorily. Practical measures, such as care and maintenance are often frustrated by the unscrupulous activities of traffickers, who pursue migrant adolescents even after they have entered a safe shelter. Many children have been subject to abuse and exploitation, and require special psycho-social counselling. Many disappear, which makes it a serious law enforcement issue (IOM, 2001). These problems are frequently compounded by the lack of cooperation of the family and/or country of origin.

This type of irregular migration is attracted by the combination of generous asylum protection systems and difficulty in returning the children. The Netherlands found that its generous residence policy for such cases indirectly attracted more unaccompanied minors; since 2001, the country has pursued a more restrictive policy of reception and return. The government has a longstanding special policy on unaccompanied minors, which requires the appointment of a guardian and availability of proper

care facilities in the country of origin before return. Other countries are pursuing similar approaches.

Some of the best work in establishing good practices and operating procedures has been done by the United Nations High Commissioner for Refugees (UNHCR, 2000) and the Save the Children Fund jointly through the "Separated Children in Europe" programme, and by International Social Services (ISS), UNICEF, International Committee of the Red Cross (ICRC), IOM[18] and non-governmental organizations around the world.

Research and experience demonstrate that this area of migration management urgently requires more international regulation, more information, training and awareness raising of affected governments and agencies; and some agreed standard practices. Common legal definitions are needed, as are common approaches to care, maintenance, return and reintegration.

Assisted Voluntary Return (AVR)

Return migration is an emerging area of migration policy concern. Given the multi-directional nature of migration, large numbers of migrants return home spontaneously at any time[19]. However, returns of persons unable to stay in the host countries should be regulated in ways that protect the migrants' integrity while dissuading them from future irregular migration. This is vital to the proper functioning of the asylum and immigration systems, and for migrants' protection.

While most persons unable to remain in their host countries are still returned forcibly by governments, AVR has emerged as a more effective counter strategy over

18) With the restoration of peace in Rwanda in 1995, IOM worked with ICRC and the Governments of Italy and Rwanda to return thousands of separated or orphaned Rwandan children, many seriously injured, to their home country. The programme included counselling, tracing, medical escorting, reception, reintegration and monitoring, particularly of follow-up surgical interventions and physiotherapy. There have been similar safe returns of trafficked and other children to Cambodia, Vietnam and Mali; and the Netherlands will soon commence the assisted return of unaccompanied minors to Angola. IOM has also trained police, border guards, judiciary and government officials in the Balkans, South-East Asia, South Asia and Central and Eastern European Countries, and conducted information campaigns in schools and communities against trafficking of women and children.

19) Ghosh (2000) estimates that some 30 per cent of the migrants who came to the USA from 1908 to 1957 returned to their home countries again.

the past two decades. It is an integral part of a comprehensive approach that includes efficient asylum systems, effective border control and forced expulsions where necessary. Mostly tested and proven in Europe[20], it offers governments a more humane and cost effective alternative to the classic enforcement action following asylum rejections. Even when conducted on a small scale, AVR can help counter public perceptions that state sovereignty and security are being undermined by irregular migration; its persuasion is based on greater dignity for the migrant/rejected asylum seeker, less cost for the government, and political face-saving between countries of origin and destination.

Return migration is likely to be most sustainable and cost effective when it is voluntary, protective of migrant rights and linked to development opportunities in the country of origin. When it is quick, and complemented by some opportunities for legal immigration, it could even help deter further irregular immigration[21]. At the microeconomic level, its sustainability through longer term reintegration support can help redress the conditions that caused the migrant to leave in the first place. Countries of destination have increasingly understood the critical role voluntary returnees can play in rehabilitating and developing countries of origin and have invested in the selective return and job placement of qualified nationals, also from among asylum caseloads[22] (Nyberg-Sorensen *et al.,* 2002).

Voluntary return is one area of migration management where bi- and multi-lateral actions are already quite advanced – although not always in a formalized way. In its recent Green Paper on Return, the EC considers return to be an area where there could be one solution for many countries (European Commission, 2002). In practice, this has already occurred, with the mass return of more than 380,000 Bosnians and Kosovars from 40 different

countries of destination in 1996–2002 under IOM's AVR programme for Kosovo. A similar multilateral programme is now under way for Afghanistan.

The Bosnia and Kosovo programmes offer blueprints for other similar scenarios around the world, and can apply to the full range of persons seeking or needing to return home, but without the means to do so, including stranded students and migrants, victims of trafficking and other vulnerable groups (ethnic minorities, unaccompanied minors, aged and sick persons).

But policies in countries of destination continue to vary widely on AVR application, particularly in regard to eligibility and size/nature of re-installation or reintegration assistance for the same return "caseload", this figure may range from modest pocket money through several thousand dollars per family, and finally to employment generation schemes such as micro-enterprise projects[23]. This is not practically and politically efficient and can lead to "shopping around" by the returnees, and discrepancies in their treatment by countries of destination.

Synchronized approaches to this issue are essential. The return programmes run by governments and IOM over decades have yielded some well-tried good practices[24]. However, most states still lack the regulatory basis for such voluntary return programmes, in part because of the dearth of international precepts covering either the origin or destination ends of the return spectrum[25]. This is slowly

20) AVR began with the German REAG (Reintegration and Emigration of Asylum Seekers from Germany) programme in 1979, and was expanded to other parts of Europe and neighbouring CEE, Baltic and Balkan countries. Today, IOM operates more than 30 AVR programmes for returns to more than 100 countries. In the past 10 years, IOM has assisted some 1.6 million migrants in their voluntary return.
21) There is a need to research whether regular immigration programmes induce people to stay home and wait their turn.
22) For example, through IOM's Return of Qualified Nationals programmes for Rwanda, Bosnia and Herzegovina, Kosovo and Afghanistan.
23) When 37 countries began returning the displaced and temporarily protected Kosovars, there were almost as many different financial incentives available as returning countries.
24) IOM prescribes in its Policy and Guidelines on AVR the following elements for a comprehensive approach to voluntary return: information/counselling (based on country-of-origin information); pre-departure education and vocational training (also proven to be most cost efficient and conducive to reintegration if undertaken in the home country after arrival) ; "look and see" visits to the home country; special support for vulnerable groups (e.g., psycho-social counselling/medical attention for victims of trafficking); travel assistance (documents, tickets, transit assistance, escorts if necessary); reception in the country of origin; modest financial assistance package (baggage allowance, pocket money, reinstallation grant); post-arrival referrals to NGOs; support groups; medical support; post-arrival reintegration support programmes (micro-enterprise, salary supplementation, other job placement and employment generation schemes).
25) Similarly, operational principles relating to voluntary return agreed among governments are lacking, although such principles do exist in relation to involuntary return.

changing, with the efforts of, e.g., the UK, Germany, Italy and Belgium to enshrine AVRs in their immigration laws[26].

Incentives to Voluntariness

In the absence of international precepts on voluntary return, it still seems to be best negotiated at the bilateral level, and with the use of incentives to secure cooperation from both the migrant and the country of origin. Both players are essential in identifying and documenting the returnee – and ultimately to the returnee reaching and staying home. The biggest incentives for the migrant are linked to living and working conditions in the home country and increasingly also the selective possibility of working legally in the host country for a certain period of time. For countries of origin, the biggest incentive invariably relates to trade and legal immigration opportunities for their surplus labour.

Since many returnee cases are rejected asylum seekers, a number of destination countries are experimenting with multi-pronged initiatives that can prepare the asylum seeker for either integration into the host country or return to the country of origin, depending on the outcome of his/her application[27].

Regarding the conditions for return and reintegration in the country of origin, little guidance is offered under international law. While the migrant's right to return is clear in international human rights law[28], there is insufficient obligation on the country of origin to accept back the returnee. Overall, there is a lack of international coherence on the best approach to be adopted in dealing with return and reintegration. Notwithstanding the framework pro-

vided by the Cairo Plan and the Protocols supplementing the UN Convention Against Transnational Organized Crime, the implementation of the provisions of such international documents has thus far not helped create a conducive environment for the reintegration of former migrants, even in regions of high return such as Latin America.

Some countries of destination are trying to redress this in very practical ways, e.g., by investing in reintegration strategies at the returning end to ensure greater sustainability of return. This is the case in Finland, Germany, the Netherlands or Switzerland.

Since development ministries are still largely reluctant to mix migration and development solutions, more and more immigration ministries in countries of destination are diversifying their budgets to fund such micro-economic solutions. In developing countries, these can help bridge the gap between immediate return support and longer term development. More and more governments are establishing linkages between migration and development, and challenging relevant international funding agencies to support combined solutions.

Readmission Agreements

Readmission agreements can offer a useful vehicle for negotiating mutually satisfactory return arrangements, and include development-related incentives for the country of origin. But, as they are not commonly binding under international law, they are largely negotiated bilaterally and are restricted to the modalities and timeframes for processing forced return. Some broader agreements allow for both forced and voluntary return, and return of third country nationals and stateless persons to transit countries.

The incentives to cooperate, including more generous aid deals, are often negotiated by countries of destination outside, or on the margins of, the actual agreement. They can include development aid and labour migration opportunities as a carrot, but can also withhold the same as a stick to ensure cooperation from the country of origin.

Readmission agreements tend to be less effective with countries of transit, as these often do not have the necessary experience and resources to return the persons to their countries of origin (IOM, 1999). Transit countries can thus be skeptical of the agreements, arguing that they only make sense if they in turn have agreements with the

26) The new UK bill devotes an entire section to resettlement of both voluntary and involuntary returnees, with a funding base for motivational strategies for reintegration.

27) The Netherlands offers asylum seekers vocational training to facilitate either smooth integration into the Dutch labour market or eventual reintegration in the country of origin depending on the asylum decision. The new UK Bill also allows for "explore and prepare" visits by potential returnees, as well as the monitoring of success of returns.

28) The obligation of states to readmit their own nationals is enshrined under international conventional law as a right to return. It is specified under several human rights instruments, including: Article 13(2) of the Universal Declaration of Human Rights; Article 12(4) of the International Covenant on Civil and Political Rights; Article 5(d)(ii) of the International Convention on the Elimination of All Forms of Racial Discrimination; and in regional human rights conventions as well as in the national legislation of various countries.

countries of origin. Countries of destination need to consider providing the technical support to make this possible.

To some extent, readmission agreements are an immediate remedy for the lack of international law on return migration; and would become superfluous where such precepts existed (and were enforced). To avoid "shopping around" for the best deal, the EU has devised a standardized model agreement for its Member States, which has been unevenly adopted. Such agreements can provide a reassuring framework for transparent cooperation; but countries of origin and transit need stronger capacity to manage the returns and onward movements.

While some governments are slowly changing their approach to meet the new realities of return migration, many areas are still inadequately covered, such as the need to assist and protect vulnerable groups, such as unaccompanied minors, who account for an ever increasing proportion of asylum seekers and irregular migrants in Europe. There is also an urgent need for statistical information on the scale and profile of potential return populations and in some cases, the legislative frameworks to deal with information. A number of destination countries need to address the issue of privacy laws, which currently hamper efforts to survey potential returnees or monitor their progress after return. Yet, this information would be vital for future policy development.

Practice is far ahead of the law in the area of voluntary return migration. But slowly and surely, the ground is being laid for more global approaches.

Integration

Migrant integration is a relatively new focus for many governments, and an increasingly important element of any comprehensive approach to migration management. A key indicator to successful immigration is the extent to which migrants and their new host societies have adjusted to each other over time. Well planned integration policies can both complement, and ensure the integrity of, regular immigration programmes; they also contribute to general social stability through strategies of cohesion in diversity.

There is no uniform concept of integration or any international legal provisions obliging states to adopt a particular approach. In the absence of such international norms, international human rights law is particularly relevant to policy makers. Legal instruments providing for "the principle of non-discrimination, enjoyment of economic, social and cultural rights and freedom" are enshrined in various conventions. Although such instruments are binding only for those states that have ratified them, they inspire, influence and reinforce national policies[29].

The way states address integration depends on how they view nationhood and society, and the status of immigrants in that equation. Thus the practices can vary widely, ranging from the French assimilationist model to the more multicultural models of Australia and Canada.

In Australia and Canada, multiculturalism has been a state-supported programme respecting the rights of migrants to preserve their cultural heritage and ensure community understanding of cultural difference "learning to see through borders" (Hughes, 1993). Integration is an integral part of the permanent migration regimes of those countries, and citizenship is both the final outcome and reward for integration. In Europe, on the other hand, where most immigration has been for temporary labour, integration policies have evolved quite recently. European integration strategies have been largely reactive and focussed on specific problems of resettlement after arrival, rather than forming part of a broad-based integration policy. Often, they have been honed by political attitudes of the moment.

These variances largely reflect historically different approaches to permanent and temporary migration, but also the fact that the many elements linked to integration (e.g., housing, education, employment, welfare) are usually scattered across ministries. In a move to consolidate these elements and link them with other aspects of migration management, in 1969, Sweden created the Swedish Immigration Board to cover residence permits, citizenship and integration in one ministry; Denmark recently created a central Ministry for Refugee, Immigration and Integration Affairs. The planned German immigration law included integration in its approach to migration management.

Initiatives may differ from one EU Member State to another, but the principle of equality of rights and duties is nevertheless a common denominator upon which successful integration, including citizenship, could be built.

29) Examples are the Convention on the Protection of the Rights of All Migrant Workers and Members of their Families (MWC), the European Convention on Human Rights (ECHR), the European Social Charter (ESC) and others. See also UNESCO intervention at IOM's fiftieth anniversary Council Session in November 2001 (IOM, 2002a).

281

The Charter of Fundamental Rights of the European Union protects the fundamental rights of all persons regardless of their nationality or place of residence, fostering equality of treatment between migrants and citizens of the Union.

Citizenship or Nationality

Citizenship or nationality forms an integral part of the integration process in many countries, the achievement of full participation in the social, political, economic and cultural life of the host country. For traditional countries of immigration, where migrants have had an active role in nation-building, it is an important step in a lifetime (or generations beyond) of integration effort by permanent immigrants and is located within multicultural policies that embrace the diversity of culture, ethnicity and faith of the migrants (IOM, 2002b). Some European states are now moving in a similar direction (UK Home Office, 2002).

While fundamentally an issue of state sovereignty, the challenges posed by citizenship and nationality can be very similar across states. These begin with the question of legal right to acquisition (principle of *jus soli* or *jus sanguinis*), which may already be determined by the national constitution or charter[30]. A number of states have actively narrowed eligibility, on grounds of abuse of the system *inter alia*[31]. The transnational nature of migration today also directly challenges governments to consider dual or multiple nationality in order to facilitate global mobility, particularly between countries of origin and destination. This can be contentious, both at political or bilateral levels and because of the administrative complexities it raises.

Little in international law would override state sovereignty on the issue of citizenship or nationality[32]; but there may well be sufficient grounds in international law for some soft rights for migrants to warrant promoting some baseline principles in this area.

Governments are increasingly considering policies that approach the general issue of integration in a harmonized way, at least at the regional level. The EU, for example, has "acknowledged the need to approximate national legislation on the conditions for admission and residence of third country nationals" and calls for a vigorous integration policy granting third country nationals rights and obligations comparable to those of EU citizens[33].

But the September 11 events brought changes in the priority setting of immigration policy makers, with many governments focussing first on their own border security. In a rapidly changing world, growing insecurity can result in migrants becoming the scapegoats for all social ills. The events of September 11 have highlighted an important fact about the resettlement of migrants, namely that social alienation and disaffection can increase their susceptibility to recruitment into anti-social, possibly violent activities against their own host society. Clearly, this is only one facet of a larger, more complex issue relating to global intercultural relations and conflict resolution; but there is a clear need for policies to prevent racism, xenophobia and discrimination.

Partnerships with countries of origin can help promote understanding of the issues that either create or dissipate such tensions. Migration is a continuum, and host authorities increasingly understand that, e.g., educational programmes for migrant children should take account of the curricula (or lack thereof) they were exposed to prior to leaving their countries of origin; or that educational qualifications need proper recognition, or adjustment to facilitate employment. Countries of origin can also benefit from a successful integration process of their nationals in the host country through remittances and other commercial and cultural ties, and from the experience, knowledge, know-how and training they bring back with them if they return.

Given that integration can help promote social stability, there is a common interest in ensuring some clear international principles on integration. There is a plethora of tried practices in a number of countries, which need to be

30) E.g., the Irish Constitution gives every person born on Irish territory the right to nationality.

31) E.g., Australia and the UK, which require that one parent is a citizen (or a permanent resident in Australia).

32) See the 1997 European Convention on Nationality, the 1948 Universal Declaration of Human Rights, the 1966 International Covenant on Civil and Political Rights, and the Hague Convention of 1930.

33) See the Presidency Conclusions, Tampere 1999. The EU is working towards a common European approach to social integration of third-country nationals, based on equal rights, free movement and some measures to enhance immigrants' economic and socio-cultural position against xenophobia and racial discrimination.

collated and reviewed for potential baseline standards[34]. These principles require consolidation before governments seriously consider a global approach to migrant integration.

Migration and Health

This is one of the most critical aspects of migration management today, yet is rarely discussed outside the informed circles of a few international and national entities directly dealing with it (e.g., WHO, IOM, UNAIDS and some immigrant-receiving states). It has been neglected in much government research and policy-making on migration. With the exception of traditional countries of immigration, migrant health is generally inadequately covered in immigration law, indeed in international law in the broader sense.

There are serious social, economic, ethical, legal and security-related reasons why migration health warrants early and consistent attention. When pathologies move with people, they can affect communities at all points on the migration spectrum – in countries of origin, transit and destination. Population mobility contributes to the rise and/or re-introduction of certain transmissible diseases; given that AIDS, TB and malaria now cost some five and a half million lives every year, the future is likely to challenge policy makers more seriously in this area (WHO, 2002).

Migrant health has been an important element of securing borders. Health controls were the first form of immigration control for some countries, and this clearly remains a cogent argument for managing irregular migration, but without singling out the migrants *per se* as the cause. It is a cross-cutting issue affecting other policy areas, such as labour migration. HIV/AIDS, for example, is a major new concern for both labour recruiting and exporting states, particularly in Africa and parts of Asia. It can be both a major human tragedy and a financial disaster for exporting countries trying to attract the interest of labour-recruiting countries.

Although it is a transnational issue, cross-border references are limited, like much of international migration law. The Committee of the International Convention on Economic, Social and Cultural Rights has provided a general comment on the right to health; however, an individual's universal right to health in a country other than his/her own does not automatically oblige a foreign government to assist him/her. Similarly, the right to leave a country is not automatically complemented by the right to enter another one (see **chapter 1**).

Where rule of law prevails, states are most likely to accept responsibility for the health of migrants regardless of their status. To act otherwise could violate principles relating to inhumane and degrading treatment (Convention Against Torture and the European Convention on Human Rights - ECHR). This can affect a range of government policies and practices, such as migrant return. Where governments are committed to return irregular migrants, serious health conditions may well modify such actions, based on an assessment of "real risk" under article 3 of the Convention against Torture.

There is a growing body of jurisprudence on the forced return of persons with ailments, particularly in the European Court of Human Rights, based in Strasbourg. Health issues will increasingly impinge on policies relating to labour migration, return, trafficking and cross-border movements generally. In the future, governments, and private and corporate sponsors of migration will need to ensure adequate medical cover for migrants.

Are international standards required? Some observers note that health falls into the category of social and economic rights, which by international law does not warrant the same inalienable status of "absolute norm" as civil and political rights (Van Krieken, 2001a). Thus both inter-national treaties and jurisprudence are unlikely to go much further than to propose "good practice" in this area.

34) Integration policies can be targeted, e.g., provide newcomers with language and vocational training, counselling on social and labour issues or general, aimed at improving the conditions of all persons marginalized or at risk of becoming so, through training for long-term unemployed, employment creation measures, vocational training and apprenticeships for unemployed youth, etc. Integration strategies also take account of the self-perceptions of migrants: how they view their presence in a foreign country. Is it temporary? Do they want their children to integrate? Ideally, successful integration is achieved when immigrants hold a position similar to their native counterparts. There are also interesting models of government policies on "ethnic affairs" (e.g., Australia) aimed at ensuring social stability among diverse communities.

283

Governments need to address several important issues before seriously considering a global approach to health in the migration field:

- the non-binding nature of current international law, which in any case is limited in its application to cross-border situations;

- poor, often non-existing, primary public health care in countries of origin;

- the multi-disciplinary nature of the issue (ethics, public health, finances, etc);

- lack of research and data; a lack of clarity about human rights aspects, and individual state responsibility, particularly in the migration context.

Inter-State Cooperation Frameworks

With the increasing global interdependence of trade and economics, governments are compelled to look for more collective solutions to migration, firstly as a matter of operational expedience, and secondly to ensure that the integration of countries of origin into the globalization process is not jeopardized by unmanaged migration (OECD, 2001a+b). The question is how much of this rhetoric is actually being translated into practice.

A US report shows that international cooperation mechanisms more than tripled between 1970 and 1997 with globalization; many of the agreements on standards and practices were initiated by self-selected private networks. The report predicts that in the next years such cooperation is likely to increase most in the areas of law enforcement; environment, health; counter-terrorism and humanitarian assistance to persons displaced by conflicts, natural disasters, etc. (NIC, 2000). Migration touches all these areas.

While incomplete, there is a body of international precepts to support global cooperation, mostly relating to human rights, development, transnational crime and the need for inter-state cooperation. For example, the International Conference on Population and Development (ICPD) held in Cairo in 1994 pointed the way to comprehensive forms of migration management, including the obligation for countries of origin to accept back their returning emigrants.

But the Cairo Plan of Action is not binding on states; and even where an international treaty espousing similar principles may be binding, the often cumbersome ratification processes can prevent it from becoming fully effective. There is very little to point to in the follow-up to Cairo besides some more concerted global training efforts among governments.

GATS also aims at managing global migration; however, it has a limited definition of migrating service providers and does not intervene in national entry control legislation.

Other more recent international instruments directly bearing on migration cooperation are the UN Protocols against smuggling and trafficking. As stated above, these are seminal for a more global approach to managing irregular migration, and innovative in criminalizing smuggling and trafficking, and (in the case of the trafficking protocol) protecting the victims. Like the Cairo Plan of Action, the protocols also make countries of origin accept responsibility for their citizens returned by host countries.

Regional Consultative Processes

Regional consultative processes also clearly offer a more realistic context for common approaches to migration management. Common borders tend to call for common approaches, even if only for efficiency and economies of scale – the overriding incentive being the economic/trade advantages of integration[35]. Allowing for variations in their organization, political agendas and timeframes, the regional fora discussed in earlier chapters mostly pursue the same objectives, namely: border integrity, regulated labour migration, national/regional security and human rights. The easiest element to agree on still seems to be border control.

The EU experiment, combining a plan of action, timelines, checks and balances and incentives offers an interesting blueprint for multilateral migration management. What could make it work is the built-in flexibility for Member States to pursue their own implementation strategies. But this flexibility can also seriously undermine harmonization as EU guidelines are generally not binding; the principle of subsidiarity does not oblige Member States

35) This also provides timelines on the achievement of harmonization: in the case of the EU, 1 May, 2004. Similar incentives are at work in the EU enlargement process, where EU candidate countries are encouraged to commit to the "acquis" through systematic training, instruction, expert exchanges, twinning and other capacity-building incentives.

to implement them. EU directives may oblige the state to aim for the prescribed results but have little power to influence the means.

The recent EU Ministerial Summit in Seville again confirmed the lack of progress in coordinating and harmonizing migration and asylum policies among EU countries (see **textbox 14.2.**). At the Tampere Summit in 1999, the 15 EU Member States gave an undertaking to harmonize legislation; but in reality, each member is pursuing its own national solutions[36].

In the Americas, there is a gradual adoption of more flexible common principles, and a progressively more interactive approach particularly on border management. In Africa, several economic cooperation treaties provide for the elimination of obstacles to cross-border movements among regional states[37]. In Asia, in addition to existing fora such as the APC, Manila and Bangkok processes, the regional Conference on People Smuggling, Trafficking in Persons and related Transnational Crime, held in Bali in February 2002, brought together the largest gathering of Asia and Oceania governments to explore ways of managing irregular migration in the region. Two expert working groups will present concrete joint initiatives to a follow-up ministerial meeting in 2003.

But while these processes have clearly laid solid foundations for dialogue, and increased mutual understanding among states sharing borders and migration challenges, many concrete measures still need to be carried out. Some important steps have been taken to open borders and agree on visa (or non-visa) regimes, but the next steps, e.g., towards guaranteeing migrants' rights to resettle and integrate, or the portability of their qualifications and rights, have still not been legislated for.

Inter-Regional Approaches

At inter-regional levels too, more activity is currently underway to broaden dialogue and cooperation on the full, global spectrum of population movement. The 2002 ASEM conference in Lanzarote - Spain, involving 10 Asian and 15 European states, marked a step forward in managing migration cooperatively between Asia and Europe[38]. Importantly, agreement was reached on joint initiatives to identify/document migrants for return and establish a global network of Immigration and Consular Liaison Officers. This network directly complements EU efforts to develop a global immigration liaison officer structure to address international security issues; it also mirrors longstanding national initiatives of countries like Australia, Canada and the USA to shift the locus of border management further abroad. Other efforts covering similar policy issues include the IGC/APC meeting in 2001, the "Cluster" process between South Caucasus and select Western European states (see also **textbox 13.1.**); the Bern Initiative (see also **textbox 15.2.**); and the Cotonou Agreement (see also **textbox 14.1.**)[39].

285

---

36) Efforts to ensure that common terms of references balance regional commonality with national individuality have not progressed far (notably on the proposal for a Directive on Family Reunification). One way of moving this forward could be to replace the "unanimity rule" with a "qualified majority voting" arrangement as provided for in the EU treaties.

37) For example, the 1975 Treaty establishing the West African Economic Community paved the way for visa-free movement and residence, including for work and commercial activities, within the region (Sohn and Burgenthal, 1992). ECOWAS has also adopted various protocols (pursuant to the Treaty of Lagos) for the cross-border economic movement of persons. These protocols contain provisions for both the protection of migrant human rights, and the obligations of migrants in host countries.

38) The resulting Ministerial Declaration of ASEM (Asia-Europe Meeting) provides a platform for future joint actions in managing migration, particularly illegal immigration into countries of destination, to the mutual benefit of all parties.

39) The IGC and APC fora last year joined forces in Bangkok to discuss cross-regional issues relating largely to the management of irregular and secondary asylum flows. The "Cluster" initiative, brokered by IOM in 2001, in response to the EC call for partnerships between countries of origin and destination, has resulted in concrete projects to manage irregular migration between regions and facilitate their return and reintegration. The Bern Initiative, brokered in 2001 by the Swiss Government has the potential for transnational negotiation of migration management, albeit at the doctrinal and principles level rather than a more practical one. Its biggest challenge will be to reach agreement on parameters of commonality among countries of origin and destination – particularly in view of the uneven capacities of engaged countries to manage migration. The Cotonou Agreement establishes a broad framework for cooperation between the EU and African, Caribbean and Pacific countries, on sustainable development, capacity building and integration into the global economy. It includes a cooperation agreement on returns of migrants from Europe.

TEXTBOX 15.2.

The Berne Initiative – A Global Consultative Process for Inter-State Cooperation on Migration Management

Governments in all regions of the world are acutely aware of the growing importance of international migration and the fact that global population mobility is unlikely to diminish in the near future. International migration policies largely remain a matter of sovereign prerogative, and there are natural differences in migration interests between origin, transit and destination countries in developing and industrialized regions. Nevertheless, the ever-growing number of migrants and complexity of migratory movements within and across regions high-light the need to develop a cooperative inter-state approach. The time has come to explore the basic parameters of a possible international framework aimed at facilitating co-operation among states in planning and managing the humane and orderly movement of people.

Switzerland, Bern "Bundeshaus"

The fundamental premise for such a possible framework is that inter-state collaboration should be based on the following aspects: common understandings; recognition of national and regional interests; state sovereignty; respect for the rule of law and internationally recognized principles; shared appreciation of sound practices in migration mana-gement; mutual trust and partnership; and transparency, predictability and coherence.

With this in mind, in 2001 the Government of Switzerland took the initiative to launch a consultative process with governments of migrant source, transit and destination countries, inter-governmental agencies, non-governmental agencies and academics, to analyse and define common policy interests in migration management and cooperation. The process aims at assessing the feasibility of elaborating a framework of guiding principles that could in the future serve to facilitate co-operation among states in managing international migration. As a first step, a symposium was convened to launch the debate on this crucial issue.

Government Interests and Perspectives

The symposium identified interests common to all states, as well as mutual benefits that can be derived from enhanced inter-state cooperation. Concurrently, it considered the diverging interests and perspectives of origin, transit and destination countries, recognizing that these differences should be bridged.

Interests common to all countries were recognized as follows:

• Maintaining good inter-state relations; fostering national and international security and stability; strengthening joint management of borders; encouraging economic growth and maintaining financial stability; combating migrant trafficking and smuggling; ensuring protection and equal and fair treatment of migrants; managing migration on the basis of state sovereignty and the rule of law; and encouraging cultural enrichment through migration.

Mutual benefits from enhanced inter-state cooperation were identified as follows:

• Meeting labour market needs in receiving countries and labour demands in source countries; responding to demographic developments; developing mutually beneficial return and reintegration policies; maximizing the effective use of remittances; increasing and facilitating development cooperation, direct foreign investment and reducing barriers to trade in services; combating irregular migration more effectively, including migrant smuggling and human trafficking.

Principal migration interests of origin, destination and transit countries respectively, were identified as follows:

- Countries of origin: Relieving pressure on national labour markets through out-migration; promoting skills of national work forces; avoiding negative effects of brain drain while taking advantage of positive effects of skilled workers' out-migration; ensuring protection of migrants abroad; fostering economic development through migrant training, planned and regular flows of remittances, reducing trade obstacles and promoting of foreign direct investment, and benefits from increased development cooperation.

- Countries of destination: Encouraging legal migration and discouraging irregular migration, including migrant smuggling and human trafficking; effective integration of immigrants; return of non-authorized migrants; planned immigration to compensate for labour shortages and population decline; and protection of refugees and other vulnerable groups.

- Countries of transit: Effective combating of human trafficking by criminal organizations; minimizing the negative financial, social and economic effects of unauthorized movement of migrants across national territory; maintaining good relations and strengthening common actions with neighbouring countries.

A Balanced Approach to Migration

The symposium recognized the need for a balanced approach in facilitating regular migration and preventing irregular migration, and emphasized that the root causes of migration are related to broader economic, social and development issues. *Inter alia,* regulated migration contributes to fostering economic growth, good neighbourly relations, security, the rule of law and cultural diversity. However, there is growing dissatisfaction concerning current trends in irregular migration, especially the greater involvement of international criminal organizations in smuggling and trafficking. The undermining of state sovereignty and security by uncontrolled and irregular migration was recognized as a major concern for many countries, both in developing and industrialized regions, with important financial, economic, social and legal implications. Greater understanding and cooperation on these issues were considered essential.

While participants recognized that states should not unduly restrict cross-border movements, they have an obligation to ensure the security, social stability and economic and general well-being of their own nationals. Concurrently, they are bound under international law to protect refugees and migrant rights. All states thus face the common challenge of developing migration policies that reconcile these objectives, while contributing towards sustainable development, promoting global economic growth, fostering democracy and preventing conflicts. Symposium participants decided to pursue the idea of developing a framework of guiding principles for migration management, through an on-going and broader process of consultations.

The basis of understanding for such a framework could include the following general considerations:

- active involvement and participation of interested states in all regions, acting in a spirit of partnership, trust, transparency, good neighbourly relations, and in respect of the sovereignty and interests of all states;

- recognition that migration must be addressed in a balanced manner, considering that its root causes are related to a broader economic, social, developmental and environmental context, including lack of employment, inadequate access to education and health, and international trade and financial policies:

- recognition that migration generally benefits societies and migrants, that regular migration and integration of migrants should be encouraged, and that irregular migration should not constitute an alternative to regular migration;

- respect for the human rights of all migrants;

- respect for the principle of *non-refoulement* of refugees and providing protection to other vulnerable persons;

- recognition of the importance of systematic exchange of timely and accurate information and data on all forms of migration, including irregular migration and illegal employment; and further analysis of existing procedures, laws and "best practices" for migration management;

- combating all forms of terrorism and criminality linked to migration.

287

Given the slow pace of action from these processes, policy makers need to be cautious about, and check the risks and costs of, international cooperation (NIC, 2000). In addition to the many political obstacles to inter-state cooperation, an important lesson learned from the above-mentioned multilateral endeavours is that migration management techniques cannot easily be transposed from one country to another – or be tailored uniformly to everyone. In all the regional processes – in Europe, Latin America, Asia or Africa – there continue to be major institutional barriers to cross-border mobility, often compounded by lack of resources and capacity in the countries of origin and transit.

Some experts believe that a global framework of common principles, and clearer mandates and cooperation are needed to overcome the shortcomings of regional approaches (Ghosh, 2000). The concept is compelling: enhance the predictability of international migration policies and practices; lessen costs/administrative strain; remove arbitrariness in managing movements; improve transparency; protect human rights better; boost the confidence of the general public in the whole migration system. But it seems hardly possible to institutionalize the concept at this point, given the many obstacles that still exist within and among governments.

Conclusion

This chapter has illustrated how transparency and consistency among government policies and practices is becoming essential with growing global awareness and discussion of migration and its inter-connectedness. The reasons are born equally out of the necessity to balance the interests of developed and developing countries, protect migrant rights, and ensure the integrity of migration.

The areas examined above are not exhaustive, but illustrate how migration policy and management are slowly shifting from individual to more joint, common approaches, and how much still needs to be consolidated in government policy-making, administration and practice before states find themselves on an equal footing for global dialogue and cooperation. Relationships between countries of origin, transit and destination are changing, and the mutual benefits of migration are being explored; however, both national and international mechanisms are still inadequate for ensuring such global coherence.

Practical convergences may eventually provide the foundation for harmonized policies at national and international levels. But this will be a long process, involving complex legal and territorial resolutions. Currently, the differences in policy and practice are too great and each has some impact on other areas of migration policy. At the most basic level of definitions and terminology, for example, if there is no agreement on age of "majority" for children then there will be little agreement on the definition of an "unaccompanied minor", or the concomitant policy responses.

Globally, there may be sufficient legal provisions to begin framing a more multilateral approach to migration[40]. But the most urgent problems seem to be the scattered and disparate nature of international precepts, and the lack of institutional follow-up and enforcement of any relevant treaties.

For example, on the issue of human rights, a key interface of individual and state interests, there is a proliferation of international treaties, mechanisms and vigilant bodies to define and protect migrants in specific circumstances (refugees, labour migrants, children, victims of trafficking), but there is no consolidated repository or reference point for all aspects of migrants' rights. Such a repository would extend beyond the reach of fundamental human rights and protection concerns to embrace the full range of political and social rights (citizenship, right to vote, access to services, health) applicable to migrants, regardless of their status.

Given this situation, governments themselves have had to resort to unilateral and bilateral actions to ensure that international standards are incorporated into national law and duly adhered to at least among states linked by agreements[41]. This is clearly one of the major achievements of the US Government's annual global report on trafficking, which uses a public accountability approach to increase dialogue and action among countries. Notable

40) For example, the ILO Conventions, GATS, Multilateral Agreement on Investments, Charter of the United Nations (art.71 creates the possibility for ECOSOC to collaborate with NGOs, and this could be adapted to suit a global migration framework) (Ghosh, 2000).

41) The notable example being the attempt by Commonwealth States to establish a common code of practice for the international recruitment of health workers, particularly from developing countries. To all appearances a minor migration issue, this actually touches on some major global policy themes: development, brain drain, public health, human resource management, financial management etc.; and it cuts across a number of regions: Africa, Asia, Caribbean, Pacific.

is the preparedness on the part of the US Government to supplement its "good behaviour" review with actions to build the capacities of those states unable to cope with their migrant trafficking problem. An interesting catalyst for cooperation, this unique, unilateral initiative fills a vacuum, not of principles and instruction, but of action.

This brings to light another major obstacle to global migration cooperation: the lack of capacity and/or resources in some states to be an equal partner in global or bilateral cooperation. Increasingly, countries of origin and transit use this issue to resist one-sided cooperation proposals by countries of destination, particularly on the case of return migration. Countries of destination are therefore beginning to invest in migration management capacity-building at source in order to ensure equal partnership.

Current regional processes have also demonstrated that there may be value at this stage in considering flexible global approaches to migration management, which allow for national autonomy and difference in policy design and implementation (United Nations Commission for Latin America, 2002). Governments could adopt policies governed by some principles of commonality, without establishing a formal global "management" regime[42]. A start could be made at purely functional levels by identifying existing operational approximations and commonalities, and the extent to which these form a sufficient platform on which to build further, more solid global cooperation.

Several practical steps could be taken to strengthen the basis for globally coherent migration management, including the following:

- surveying and collating the disparate laws and practices in all areas of migration management; preparing a compendium of comprehensive "good practices" based on indicators of success agreed by governments representing all points on the migration spectrum; ensuring a comprehensive policy approach;

- taking stock of the convergences and commonalities that already exist, and the extent to which there is a ready platform for further global consolidation;

- establishing more consistent definitions and mechanisms to collect and share migration statistics, which has been problematic even in regional cooperation[43] (see also **chapter 16**); defining legislative frameworks to deal with information sharing - e.g., national privacy laws. (Governments may wish to strengthen the practical mechanism of migration "observatories"[44], such as the ones already supported by the EU and IOM);

- establishing global partnership fora to regularly involve all countries of origin, transit and destination in discussion on how to regulate labour migration and curb irregular migration;
- creating a conducive atmosphere in the host country to welcome and maximize migrant contributions to social diversity, through integration.

To plan and oversee these steps, governments may need a central global mechanism to tackle migration in its many and complex manifestations. In the same way that WHO deals with health, WTO with trade, UNHCR with refugees, ILO with labour, a global migration organization, such as IOM, could monitor, record, bring to light, comment on current practices against international precepts; and help develop global standards and norms to regulate migration to the mutual benefit of countries of origin, transit and destination (Martin and Martin, 2001a).

IOM is well positioned to assume such a role, owing to its broad migration mandate, membership and representation in countries of origin, transit and destination. In line with its mandate, and responding to some governments' requests, IOM has already embarked on a process of global stock-taking of migration policies and practices[45]. Importantly, it can draw on its own stockpile of well-tried migration management practices, particularly in some "niche" areas like AVR, counter trafficking and technical cooperation on migration, to ensure that any policies proposed for global applicability have been proven on the ground.

42) This is likely to be the direction that the EU will take with its common policy on "Return of Illegal Immigrants", expected to be presented by the end of 2002.

43) The Süssmuth report calls for a "largely uniform European standard" for immigration statistics gathering and recording, and an extensive pan-European harmonization of statistical surveys.
44) The EU is supporting the establishment of a migration observatory in Morocco, with the Government of Morocco and IOM. IOM is also seeking to establish such facilities in South Africa and South Asia, to provide governments current data on movements in the regions, and their motives and aims. Such observatories can serve as information platforms for on-the-ground and political cooperation; and be linked to form global networks of information/communication on migration.
45) IOM launched its own global policy dialogue forum in the context of the IOM Council session in November 2001.

STATISTICS SECTION

CHAPTER 16

Statistics and the Management of International Migration – A Perspective from the United Nations

Modern management requires information: information to control operations, assess efficiency, monitor trends and plan future action. The management of international migration is no exception. Yet, in most countries, even those receiving significant numbers of international migrants annually, the information available to manage international migration and its consequences fails to meet the needs of managers[1].

Information can take many forms but statistics on the flows and stocks of international migrants are crucial. This chapter will examine the reasons for the inadequacy of international migration statistics. The discussion will focus on general conceptualization problems affecting international migration and the effects on the collection and processing of international migration statistics. It will argue that the generation of statistics on international migration is closely linked to existing processes for managing or controlling the flows or stocks of international migrants. Consequently, any information gathered during those processes will naturally reflect the legal and regulatory framework established to define and manage international migration. Without an understanding of that framework, it will be difficult or misleading to interpret the statistics: wider availability of the statistics would yield few benefits and there would be fewer incentives to improve data and their dissemination.

---

1) Although this chapter will focus mostly on the needs of those directly involved in the management of international migration, international migration statistics are also relevant for policy-makers and trade negotiators. Indeed, international migration statistics have an important bearing on the measurement of service transactions involving the international movement of natural persons. Relevant guidelines on that measurement can be found in United Nations (2000).

If the quality, timeliness and transparency of international migration statistics are to be improved, analysts need to understand available data better and devise ways of using them meaningfully, especially at national level. To do this, analysts and international migration managers need to work closely together.

The Institutional Setting for Gathering International Migration Statistics

International migration statistics are produced at the national level. Hence, to understand why international migration statistics continue to be inadequate and why progress in improving them has been slow, it is useful to consider the national institutional context for compiling statistics on international migration. This context should then be compared with the institutional context in which recommendations for better international migration statistics have been developed.

Since the late 1940s, when the United Nations began to work on the international coordination of statistical activities, international migration statistics have been considered a part of demographic statistics, i.e., part of the full set of data and indicators allowing the dynamics of population change to be understood at country level. Consequently, the Demographic and Social Statistics Branch of the United Nations Statistics Division is in charge of compiling and improving international migration statistics. At country level, the natural counterparts to the United Nations Statistics Division are Member State's national statistical offices. Therefore, the United Nations Statistics Division usually coordinates work on demographic and social statistics in collaboration with national statistical offices, which are generally in charge both of gathering statistics outright (as, for example, by carrying out censuses and sample surveys) or of coordinating the processing and dissemination of statistics generated by other government entities.

However, national statistical offices are often not responsible for gathering statistics on international migration. The government institutions charged with managing international migration are usually those gathering the basic statistical information related to the control of entry, stay or exercise of economic activity of international migrants. Because those institutions accord priority to the operational aspects of international migration management, little attention and few resources are generally devoted to the processing, analysis or dissemination of the statistical information obtained. Even when the institutions in charge of managing international migration produce and disseminate consolidated statistics on a periodic basis, the latter are often presented in ways that do not permit detailed analysis of international migration trends or the construction of indicators useful for management purposes. Furthermore, national statistical offices are generally not involved in processing or disseminating the data generated by these institutions. As a result, the information routinely gathered in relation to the admission, stay or economic activity of international migrants is often not used to inform managers and decision-makers about characteristics of the process.

Although there is long-standing recognition that better international migration statistics are required, there has been slow progress in improving the statistics available. International efforts to standardize international migration statistics date from the 1920s. Thus, at its fourth session in 1922, the International Labour Conference recommended that agreements be reached on a uniform definition of the term "emigrant" and on a uniform method of recording information regarding emigration and immigration (United Nations, 1949). In 1932, the International Labour Organization convened an International Conference of Migration Statisticians that adopted the first set of international recommendations for improving international migration statistics (United Nations, 1949). The establishment of the United Nations after the Second World War provided a new forum for the discussion of such issues. In 1953 the United Nations adopted a set of recommendations for improving international migration statistics, which built upon those made by the International Conference of Migration Statisticians (United Nations, 1953). Since then, the United Nations has revised the recommendations twice, first in 1976 and most recently in 1997 (United Nations, 1980 and 1998a). Revisions have been necessary both to take account of the changing context of international migration and because the recommendations have generally not been implemented.

To understand why the long-standing recommendations on international migration statistics have failed to make much headway, several issues need to be considered. The first is the lack of a direct relationship between the United Nations Statistics Division and the government institutions in charge of managing international migration. As a consequence, the recommendations made by the United Nations have not necessarily reached those actually in charge of compiling and processing information on international migrants and have therefore had a low chance of influencing the approaches and procedures followed by the government offices in charge of managing international migration. A second and related issue is that the United Nations recommendations on international migration statistics have generally been developed by population experts rather than by persons engaged in managing international migration. Hence, they reflect the goals and concerns of persons who view international migration primarily as a component of population change and who have traditionally given low priority to management considerations. The third issue is that migration managers conceive their main task as being the implementation of international migration laws and regulations accord low priority to the processing, analysis or dissemination of statistics generated by migration management. Furthermore, the very sensitivity of international migration issues may sometimes dissuade managers from making accessible the detailed statistics necessary to assess the dynamics of international migration and its management.

This chapter maintains that tangible improvements in the availability and quality of international migration statistics can only be achieved by bridging the gap between the work of demographers and statisticians on the one hand and migration managers on the other. A first step would be to ensure that people involved in managing migration or in providing guidance to managers understand the contribution that demographers and statisticians have already made in establishing a framework for improving international migration statistics. The next step entails fostering a dialogue between analysts and managers at country level, in order to permit analysts to obtain a better understanding of the needs and challenges faced by managers and to allow managers to assess the advantages inherent in timely access to relevant information and analysis. Timely and relevant statistics can only be disseminated more widely when analysts learn to address the issues of concern to managers and managers become convinced that data and their interpretation matter.

Who is an International Migrant?

All the groups that address the problem of improving global statistics on international migration have realized that any improvement needs to be based on a clear and measurable concept of who is an international migrant. Therefore, a common thread in the successive sets of recommendations on international migration statistics has been to refine the concept of international migrant (see also **chapter 1**).

In its purest definition, migration involves a definitive physical move from one location to another. For international migration, the locations involved are clearly two distinct countries. However, it is less obvious how to establish whether international migration is definitive. The search for a universal definition of the international migrant has therefore centred on providing explicit criteria to decide if a person's move from one country to another is definitive.

Already in the 1920s, it was clear that not all international travellers were migrants. That point is even more patent today when international mobility has reached unprecedented levels. Persons moving from one country to another for tourism should clearly not be considered international migrants and need not be included in international migration statistics. But there are many travellers whose cases are less clear cut. Should persons moving to study abroad, for instance, be considered international migrants? What about persons moving to work temporarily abroad? Should opera singers or tennis players engaged in international tours be considered migrants? What about international civil servants? Or armed forces stationed abroad? From a migration manager's point of view, these examples would be addressed by granting different types of visas or permits to persons applying to enter the country for different purposes. For a demographer wishing to account for population changes over time, a person's purpose for entering a country is essentially irrelevant. What matters is whether the person remains in the country for a sufficiently long time. Since population changes are normally measured one year at a time, persons who stay for at least a year would need to be accounted for together with their logical counterparts, i.e., persons who remain abroad for more than a year.

International recommendations on international migration statistics have evolved around the concept of international migrant developed by demographers. In the *United Nations Recommendations on International Migration Statistics*

adopted in 1976 (United Nations, 1980), for instance, international migrants are characterized as "persons who, having been continuously present in the country of origin for more than a year, leave it to remain in the country of destination for more than a year"[2]. This definition makes no mention of the citizenship or nationality of the migrants involved. Nor does it make any reference to visas or permits to enter or stay in the country of destination, or to legal or other constraints involved in leaving the country of origin. Thus, by capturing only the essence of migration and separating it from the concrete processes through which international migration is managed, this definition is completely generic and applies both to migrants who are subject to control and those who are exempt. Furthermore, by steering away from considerations regarding the regulatory and legal facets of international migration management, this definition has the potential to produce perfectly comparable international migration data were it to be used by all countries. The fact that the definition makes no distinction among migrants in terms of legal status or citizenship, ensures complete coverage. Therefore, it can serve as a model for assessing the coverage of actual international migration statistics. Lastly, the symmetry with which the definition treats the country of origin and the country of destination is also worthy of emulation: ideally, information obtained in the country of destination on migrants originating in a given country should be identical to similar information obtained in the country of origin about emigrants to that country of destination.

However, it is not straightforward to obtain accurate migration data in conformity with this definition. Its drawbacks become apparent when actual data collection systems are considered. The 1976 United Nations Recommendations on Statistics of International Migration refer to three types of data collection systems: border collection, registration and field inquiries (United Nations, 1980). For present purposes, it suffices to consider border collection, namely, the process whereby information on international migrants is obtained at the point of arrival or departure of a country. Thus, persons entering the country would be asked whether they had been present in the country during the past 12 months. Those who had not would then be asked whether they intended to remain in the country for more than 12 months. Those

2) Actually, the full set of United Nations recommendations on international migration statistics are more complex than suggested in this section. However, for the purpose of this discussion, only the most essential elements of the definitions proposed by the United Nations will be highlighted.

answering in the affirmative would be considered immigrants. Similarly, persons leaving the country would be asked whether they had been continuously present in the country for the past 12 months. Those who had would be asked whether they were intending to remain abroad for more than 12 months. Those answering in the affirmative would be considered emigrants. As the report on the United Nations Recommendations itself notes, a "drawback of border collection for identifying migrants is that it depends to a considerable extent on declarations of intent, some of which may be more in the nature of hopes than of reasonable expectations" (United Nations, 1980:9). Perhaps more pertinently, if questions about intentions regarding length of stay are posed or reviewed by officials in charge of border control, it is unlikely that they will reflect true intentions, especially in the case of foreigners whose admission to the country depends on fulfilling certain requirements. Thus, foreign persons holding visas or permits allowing only short stays in the country are unlikely to jeopardize their chances of admission by declaring that their intention is to stay for more than a year. That is, the stated intention of persons subject to control will probably reflect the constraints on length of stay imposed by the receiving state rather than their actual intentions.

Different reporting biases may be common in the case of departing persons. Residents departing with the aim of staying abroad for lengthy periods may avoid reporting that fact if their prolonged absence might render them ineligible for certain benefits. Furthermore, as formulated in the 1976 Recommendations, the definition of international migrant requires that a person leave a country and remain abroad continuously for more than one year. Given the modern ease of transportation, many persons who would otherwise be considered migrants might not meet the definition criteria if they make annual visits to the country of origin.

To avoid excluding those persons from the emigrant group, the 1997 Revision of the *United Nations Recommendations* adopted a modified formulation for the definition of international migrant, namely, "a person who moves to a country other than that of his or her usual residence for a period of at least a year (12 months), so that the country of destination effectively becomes his or her new country of usual residence"(United Nations, 1998a:10). This definition is complemented by an explicit definition of country of usual residence as "the country in which a person lives, where he or she spends the daily period of rest". It is further stated that "temporary travel abroad for purposes of recreation, holiday, visits to friends and relatives,

business, medical treatment or religious pilgrimage does not change a person's country of usual residence" (United Nations, 1998a:10). Although this formulation is somewhat better suited as a basis for measuring international migration than the 1976 Recommendations, it still mainly embodies the demographic perspective. To bridge the gap between demography and international migration management, the 1997 Revision of the *United Nations Recommendations* provides a framework for the compilation of statistics on inflows and outflows of international migrants that merges the demographic approach with the statistical concepts most commonly found in statistics reflecting the management process. The merits of this approach are discussed below.

The State's Perspective in the Measurement of International Migration

An analysis of definitions and concepts underlying national sources of international migration statistics indicates that, whether explicitly or implicitly, legal or regulatory considerations influence the characterization of international migrants (Bilsborrow *et al.,* 1997). That is, the collection of information on international migrants is so closely linked to state prerogative to decide who can enter its territory and under what conditions that legal aspects cannot be removed from the measurement of international migration. Furthermore, if successful, such a detachment would limit the policy relevance of the statistics obtained. For that reason, a more useful approach is to take explicit account of government views and practices in devising a framework for the categorization and analysis of international migration statistics. Such an approach was adopted in preparing the 1997 Revision of the *United Nations Recommendations on Statistics of International Migration* (United Nations, 1998a). To understand its relevance, this section discusses the legal or "quasi-legal" nature of the concepts underlying national sources of statistics on international migration.

Before proceeding, let us consider again the basic question: "Who is an international migrant?" and try to answer it from the state's perspective. Given that today's world is partitioned into sovereign states, each of which has the right to determine who enters its territory and under what conditions, international travel is only possible if one country allows the admission of the citizens of another. Although countries generally allow the entry and short-term stay of foreigners, the long-term stay of foreigners or their exercise of particular activities, such as training, education or employment, may be permitted only under certain circumstances. It is this prerogative of governments to control the length of stay and type of activity of foreigners in their territories that sets international migration apart from other types of geographical mobility. Citizenship, therefore, is a crucial criterion in identifying and classifying international migrants. According to the set of definitions of international migrants compiled in 1977 by the United Nations, 45 of 90 countries that distinguished international migrants from general international travellers for statistical purposes, used citizenship as the identifying criterion (Zlotnik, 1987).

It is normal practice that persons entering or departing from a given state be subject to differential treatment according to their citizenship. Differentiation of citizens and foreigners at the time of border control is justified by international law. Thus, the Universal Declaration of Human Rights establishes that every person has the right to leave any country, including his or her own, and that every person has the right to return to his or her own country (see also **chapter 1**). Consequently, states tend to exercise minimal control over persons leaving their respective territories, whether those persons are their own citizens or not, and over the entry of their own citizens into their respective territories. In contrast, foreigners entering the state's territory are more likely to be controlled. This asymmetrical treatment of international migrants according to citizenship is reflected in how national statistical offices cover international migration. Statistical information tends to be more commonly available on inflows of international migrants than outflows, and on the inflow of foreign international migrants than the migration of citizens.

One advantage of using citizenship to identify or classify international migrants is its potential "objectivity" since, if data are gathered at the point of entry into or departure from a country or through another type of administrative procedure, it is almost certain that proof of citizenship will be required to complete the administrative formalities involved. Thus, unlike other possible identifiers, citizenship is established by tangible evidence (e.g., by a passport). Changes of citizenship are possible and persons with double or multiple nationality can cause inconsistencies in international statistical comparisons. However, the crucial role of citizenship in determining the relationship between the international migrant and the state makes it mandatory to capture this aspect in all statistical information on international migrants.

Citizenship is also relevant in considering the consequences of international migration, since persons who are allowed to stay in a country other than their own on a conditional basis may be subject to constraints in terms of employment, access to services or freedom of movement. Furthermore, foreign residents with limited rights cannot always count on the government of the host country to protect their interests or uphold their rights. However, one drawback of citizenship is that the rules to acquire it vary significantly from one country to another. Furthermore, in countries where the acquisition of citizenship is based on the principle of *jus sanguinis,* foreign residents need not be international migrants in the sense that they may have never lived outside the country where they reside. This distinction is relevant when dealing with data sources that refer to the stock rather than the flow of foreigners but it does not invalidate the need for information on the number and characteristics of foreigners residing within the territory of a given state.

The use of citizenship as a key criterion to classify international migrants should not be exclusive to foreigners. There are many reasons for requiring statistical information also on persons migrating to and from their countries of citizenship. From a demographic perspective, the addition of a person to a population through international migration has the same effect whether the person is a foreigner or not. From an economic perspective as well, an additional worker represents one more economically active person irrespective of legal nationality. Consequently, persons returning to their countries of origin or persons moving to countries where they have a right to citizenship should not be excluded from international migration statistics, since their economic, social and demographic impact in the countries receiving them is likely to be relevant. This point has become more critical in recent times when large numbers of persons have "returned" to the countries of their forebears where they have been granted almost an automatic right to citizenship. In many such instances, the statistical systems in place to account for the inflow of international migrants have not covered such "returnees" because they have not been considered foreigners.

In summary, the policy relevance of citizenship should be considered when establishing guidelines for the collection, processing, dissemination and analysis of international migration statistics; however, it does not constitute a sufficient criterion to identify international migrants. To distinguish between international migration and international travel, states employ two other criteria, either implicitly or explicitly: a minimum length of stay in the

297

country of destination; or a particular purpose for moving to that country or for leaving the country of origin.

Time is often used to determine international migrant status, but it can mean different things. Compare, for instance, the definition of immigrants adopted by the United States: "aliens lawfully accorded the privilege of residing permanently in the United States" with that used by the Netherlands: "nationals intending to stay in the Netherlands for more than 30 days and aliens intending to stay for more than 180 days" (United States Immigration and Naturalization Service, 1993; United Nations, 1978). Although time is used in both definitions, its concrete application is different. In the definition used by the Netherlands, durations are not only expressed in terms of definite numbers, they are also meant to represent actual durations of stay since it is expected that intended durations will become actual ones. In contrast, in the United States, the term "permanently" cannot be interpreted to represent an actual duration of stay. The time criterion, in this instance, refers to the length of validity of the privilege granted by the United States. It is a potential time accorded to the immigrant, who may or may not realize that potential. The term "legal time" has been used to denote a time criterion expressed in terms of the limitations (or lack of them) set by the receiving state on the potential period of stay of an international migrant (Zlotnik, 1987). It is contrasted with "actual time", a term that refers to the intended or actual stay of the migrant concerned.

Legal time is closely associated with legal residence. It represents the time constraints (or lack thereof) set by laws or regulations of the receiving state on the right to legal residence granted to a foreign person. Legal time does not necessarily represent either actual or intended length of stay. Consequently, the actual stay of an international migrant in the receiving country may differ considerably from that specified by legal time. Temporary migrant workers, for instance, may stay in the country of employment for lengthy periods although, at any given time, their permit of stay may be restricted to a year or less. Thus, although at any given time the expected *de jure* length of stay is limited, the potential for *de facto* permanence exists. However, since it is not possible to know *a priori* what the actual length of stay will end up being, statistics are likely to reflect only the limited, *de jure* period of stay granted to the temporary migrant worker at any given time.

Although few statistical systems explicitly acknowledge that their definitions of migrant categories are based on the concept of legal time, it often underlies them. Legal time also probably influences the declaration of intended length of stay made by international migrants subject to border control. Indeed, when a foreigner entering a country is asked by immigration authorities to state his or her expected duration of stay, it is unlikely that the person will report a duration that contravenes the one allowed by law or by the specific visa or entry permit that the person holds.

The second criterion, purpose of stay, is particularly important in determining international migrant status when linked to the exercise of an economic activity. Thus, 21 of the 90 countries or areas that provided specific definitions of immigrants and emigrants to the United Nations in 1977 considered the exercise of an economic activity in a country other than their own as a factor distinguishing international migrants from other travellers (Zlotnik, 1987). Yet, working abroad is not the only purpose of stay relevant for the characterization of international migrants. Studying abroad, training in another country, moving to join family members living abroad, fleeing persecution or seeking a safe haven from conflict in the country of origin – all these factors have been recognized by states as purposes of stay warranting special treatment.

As with the time criterion, purpose of stay can be interpreted in two ways: a reflection of an international migrants' subjective intentions, or as the reason for admission validated by the receiving state. Although there is probably a high correlation between the two, it is important not to assume that the purpose of stay validated by the state accurately mirrors migrant's intentions. Furthermore, statistical accounting should not be based on people's intentions, which are complex and subject to change. In contrast, the state's view is relevant not only from a policy perspective but also because it determines the conditions under which a person can legally be admitted into its territory. Note, however, that the state has limited capacity to impose admission conditions on its own returning citizens.

The state's control over the international migration of foreigners usually starts in the country of origin through the issuance of visas or other permits allowing entry, stay or the exercise of economic activity in the state's territory. Therefore, the type of visa granted can be used to establish purpose of stay. Generally, the restrictions imposed by visas or permits refer not only to the type of activities that a foreign person can legally engage in but also to the duration of stay.

Thus, the duration and purpose of stay allowed by the state are often closely linked criteria from the regulatory perspective. Combined with citizenship, these criteria provide the necessary basis for classifying international migrants into policy-relevant categories. The general framework proposed in the 1997 Revision of the *United Nations Recommendations on Statistics of International Migration* presents the key categories for classifying international migrants and suggests how statistics for those categories can be used to derive measures of international migration that conform better with the general definition of international migrant proposed in the Recommendations.

The Sources of International Migration Statistics

In order to appreciate the strategy adopted by the 1997 Revision of the *United Nations Recommendations on Statistics of International Migration* to work towards improving international migration statistics, it is useful to review briefly the types of data sources generating international migration statistics today. A detailed analysis of those sources can be found in Bilsborrow *et al.* (1997) as well as in the 1997 Recommendations (United Nations, 1998a).

Four types of data collection systems are distinguished in the 1997 Recommendations: (a) administrative registers; (b) other administrative sources; (c) border collection; and (d) field inquiries. The greater focus on administrative registers and other administrative sources of international migration statistics represents an important change in perspective in relation to previous Recommendations. Indeed, because of the emphasis on the general definition of international migration prevailing in the past, the use of border collection data appeared to be preferred over administrative sources (United Nations, 1980 and 1985). For administrative sources, the emphasis was on utilizing population registers, which were more likely to produce statistics in line with the general definition. Obviously not enough attention was given to utilizing data produced by administrative sources operating in regulatory aspects of international migration management. Recognizing the utility of such data, the 1997 Recommendations contain a more systematic treatment of the different sources available and suggest ways to employ them as building blocs in assembling a more comprehensive data reporting system on international migration.

Administrative registers include population registers, registers of foreigners and other special types of registers covering particular groups of persons, such as asylum-seekers. A register is a data collection system providing for the continuous recording of selected information pertaining to each member of the target population. A register must be operated and organized along legal lines. While the main purpose of registration is administrative, a register can be used to compile up-to-date statistical information on the size and characteristics of the target population. Depending on the purpose of the register, different types of changes in the status of members of the target population are subject to registration. The registers of interest for the generation of statistics of international migration are those recording changes in country of residence of target population. Typically, the target population of an administrative register is a subset of the population present in a country. Population registers generally cover only the *de jure* population of a country (i.e., persons having the right to legal residence in that country and normally living in it). Consequently, the rules establishing who is a legal and usual resident determine who should be inscribed in and who should be deregistered from the register. Those rules are set by law or administrative regulation and are unlikely to be altered to ensure better international comparability. The quality of the statistics derived from any register depends on the degree of compliance with the rules determining its operation and such compliance in turn depends on the incentives and disincentives that individuals have to abide by the rules of registration.

Relatively few countries maintain national population registers that allow international migration statistics to be derived. They are mostly located in Europe. Because the rules governing inscription in or deregistration from the population register vary from country to country and depend on the citizenship of the person being registered or deregistered, population registers do not necessarily produce internally consistent or internationally comparable statistics on international migration. However, the possibility of longitudinal follow-up of the population can be used to derive more internationally consistent statistics, provided special processing of the data at the individual level is carried out[3]. Because national statistical offices are

---

3) Issues of confidentiality and privacy can restrict the use of data for the purposes outlined here. Furthermore, unless individuals trust that the confidentiality of statistical information will be protected, compliance with statistical reporting and the accuracy of such reporting may be compromised.

usually in charge of processing and analysing the data generated by population registers, improvements of this type can be coordinated by the United Nations Statistics Division.

Registers of foreigners operate similarly to population registers but cover only foreigners who are legal residents of the country concerned. As with national population registers, the conditions under which foreigners are inscribed in or deregistered from the register of foreigners characterize persons who can be considered international migrants. Registers of foreigners usually accord priority to recording the migration status of each person registered, including the type of residence permit and its duration of validity, and consequently can provide information on specific categories of international migrants. One drawback of these registers is that, although they normally achieve a relatively complete coverage of the inflow of foreigners granted permission to reside in the country, there is less coverage of persons leaving the country for lengthy periods, mainly because the loss of acquired rights dissuades departing foreigners from deregistering.

300 Other administrative sources of international migration statistics derive from the variety of administrative procedures designed to control international migration. Such administrative sources usually only concern specific subsets of international migrants: thus, statistics on residence permits refer only to foreigners; work permits refer only to economically active foreigners; statistics on exit permits refer only to citizens; and those obtained from the official clearance of departing migrant workers cover only those economically active citizens whose contracts to work abroad must be scrutinized before departure. Certain administrative sources refer to even more specific groups: the number of asylum applications filed over a period, for instance, is an indicator of the inflow of asylum-seekers. Similarly, the number of deportations during a year is only indicative of a segment of the migrant population with an irregular status, as is the case with data derived from regularization drives. Reports from recruitment and placement agencies can yield statistics indicating the number of citizens leaving to work abroad. These statistics sources share a common trait: they reflect administrative procedures rather than people. Thus the number of residence permits issued during a year may not be equivalent to the number of persons admitted that year if a person can receive several residence permits in a year or if a permit covers several individuals (main migrant and dependants, for instance).

In order to ensure that statistics derived from administrative sources are adequately used and interpreted, it is necessary to describe in some detail the procedures that they reflect. Furthermore, appropriate coding and processing of administrative data can permit the extraction of useful indicators about the migration process and its management. However, administrative data are rarely used this way, mainly because the primary sources are seldom accessible to analysts. In addition, the government agencies in charge of gathering and processing the information have no institutional links with national statistical offices and therefore are unlikely to be informed about the potential uses of the data at hand and of improvements suggested to foster international comparability. Much remains to be done with respect to these sources of information. As the 1997 Recommendations state: "Although none of the administrative sources reviewed is capable of producing information on all international migrants, the information they yield is nevertheless valuable and should not be discarded because it is partial. It is therefore important to provide a means of compiling and disseminating the various types of data available in ways that make clear their meaning and coverage" (United Nations, 1998a:22).

The third type of source of international migration statistics involves the collection of information at ports of entry into and departure from a country. Border collection has provided the data collection model underlying the formulation of previous recommendations on international migration statistics (United Nations, 1985). Statistic collection at borders can be based on administrative or statistical criteria. According to the former, the status of persons arriving and departing is established by documentary evidence (passports, visas, residence permits etc.); on the other hand, statistical criteria require information to be recorded that cannot necessarily be inferred from documentary evidence and that is gathered using standardized forms filled in by arriving and departing passengers. Statistics obtained from border collection have the advantage of reflecting actual moves with a high degree of accuracy in terms of timing, mode of transport and place. However, it is very costly to obtain information from all persons arriving to and departing from a country and small errors in the coverage of arrivals or departures can result in sizeable errors in the difference between the two, which is a measure of net international migration. Hence it is important to devise criteria that enable international migrants to be identified from among the general travelling public so that data collection efforts can be better targeted. In practice, statistics derived from border collection rarely provide the best measures of international migration flows because of the difficulties involved in gathering reliable information from a large volume of people subject to different degrees of control depending on their citizenship, mode of transport and port of entry.

A number of strategies have been used to reduce data collection loads at borders. Some countries gather detailed information only from a representative sample of all arriving and departing passengers; other countries gather information only on foreigners or only on foreigners admitted under certain types of visas. Yet other countries focus only on citizens. A common problem of statistics collected at borders is that they tend to be more comprehensive on arrivals than departures, since greater control is exercised upon entry than upon exit.

About a third of all countries reported statistics based on border collection to the United Nations in the early 1990s, but only 29 of them distinguished immigrants and emigrants from general travellers (United Nations, 1991). Furthermore, the criteria used to identify international migrants did not always comply with the recommendations made by the United Nations. Given the widespread use of this method of data collection, a more concerted effort could be made to improve the statistics gathered. An important first step would be to document clearly the criteria actually used to distinguish international migrants from general travellers. To the extent that national statistical offices are involved in processing border statistics, the United Nations Statistics Division is well placed to begin this fact-finding process.

Household-based field inquiries include censuses and household surveys of different types. In general, household-based field inquiries do not yield reliable statistics on international migration flows since, by their very nature, they cannot cover the movements of persons who have left the country by the time the inquiry is carried out. Nevertheless, some censuses have gathered information on place of residence one or five years before enumeration from all persons canvassed, thus obtaining the number of international migrants who arrived over the period considered and were present in the country at the time of enumeration. Some censuses have also attempted to measure emigration by asking respondents to report household members who have left to live abroad. Such information tends to be unreliable and usually underestimates emigration levels because it excludes households who have emigrated in their entirety. Censuses are best used to measure the international migrant stock by recording the place of birth, the previous country of residence and the citizenship of persons canvassed. Recommendations

on the use of censuses to measure the stock of international migrants have been included in both the 1997 *Recommendations on Statistics of International Migration* and in the *Principles and Recommendations for Population and Housing Censuses* (United Nations, 1998a, b). In this area, the United Nations Statistics Division is very well placed to collaborate with national statistical offices in improving statistics on the international migrant stock.

In summary, the major sources of statistical information on international migration are quite diverse and many of them reflect the intrinsic logic of the regulatory machinery used to control international migration. Furthermore, the growing complexity of international migration flows and existing systems to manage these flows have given rise to new data collection systems that remain under-utilized for analytical purposes. Both their existence and evolution has opened up new opportunities for coordinating efforts to improve the availability and transparency of statistics on international migration.

The International Organization for Migration has already collaborated with the United Nations in disseminating the 1997 *Recommendations on Statistics of International Migration* among persons involved in managing international migration. Because of its institutional links with the national agencies managing migration, the International Organization for Migration is well placed to foster collaboration between migration managers and statisticians in an effort to devise concrete mechanisms for disseminating available data within the comparative framework suggested by the United Nations Recommendations.

A Framework for the Organization of International Migration Statistics

A key innovation of the 1997 *Recommendations on Statistics of International Migration* is the recognition that a tool was required in order to advance the improvement and international comparability of international migration statistics. This tool would assess the limitations of existing data with respect to ideal expectations from a consistent application of the general definition of international migrants. Given that data collection systems often cover only a subset of all relevant events, it is usually necessary to piece together the data produced by different data sources in order to obtain a comprehensive picture of the full spectrum of international movements that qualify as international migration. Therefore, the tool devised took the form of a framework for integrating the varied information available.

The framework was based on a taxonomy of inflows and outflows of international travellers that included the types of migrants most often subject to differential control under the legal and regulatory systems states commonly employ to manage international migration. Therefore the framework not only provides a standard way of organizing the statistical information produced by different sources but also explicitly allows policy-relevant concepts and definitions to be taken into account. The framework is "maximal" because it includes all major categories of persons crossing international borders; but for all the categories relevant to international migration measurement, data are presented and classified by duration of stay (or absence) and so it is easier to identify persons satisfying the general international migrant definition (i.e., "long-term migrant" as defined in the Recommendations). To add maximum flexibility to the framework, and recognizing that different data sources determine duration of stay according to different criteria, codes are used to indicate the type of criterion used (legal time vs. actual time, for instance). Such a strategy facilitates the appropriate interpretation and use of available data and raises awareness about the causes of the lack of comparability of the data derived from different sources or referring to different countries. This is the first necessary step to devise ways of improving comparability in the future.

Although the United Nations Recommendations were issued in 1998 and have been widely distributed, the framework has only just started to be applied to the compilation and analysis of available statistics on international migration. An understanding of the framework and its objectives requires commitment, and its use requires access to all the sources of information on international migration available in a country. Therefore, one important obstacle to using the framework is the lack of coordination that often exists among national agencies in charge of gathering different types of information on international migration. In addition, although the framework was developed to accommodate most of the types of international migrants commonly distinguished in state regulations, the nomenclature used probably does not match national usage exactly; moreover, the task of finding conceptual equivalents might dissuade potential users from exploring its applicability to their specific case.

To promote the use of the framework and better understanding of the shortcomings and gaps in existing migration statistics, annotated examples of its application should be produced and national workshops held with participation from both statisticians and managers in discussions and framework application. Such activities would enable the suitability of the framework's contents and structure to be assessed. Modifications could be introduced based on those experiences and the process of questioning the relevance and meaning of available statistics can be started. As suggested in the introduction, available data can only be utilized meaningfully if they are fully understood. Even if progress towards better international comparability continues to be slow, use of the United Nations Recommendations as a basis for integrating and improving the use of national sources of international migration statistics should be achievable over the short term.

CHAPTER 17

A Selection of Statistics on International Migration

The availability of reliable international migration statistics is a crucial obstacle faced by policy makers, managers, academics and all others dealing with migration issues. As international migration has moved to the forefront of the international agenda, the need for timely, accurate and comparable information has increased enormously.

Appropriate formulation and successful implementation of migration policies, and strategies for management, can only reflect the needs and requirements of all parties involved in international migration management if they are supported by a range of tools that facilitate the regular monitoring of trends and changes.

Chapter 16 critically analyses the relationship between international migration and statistics, outlining the specific limitations and opportunities inherent to this area. This chapter presents a cross-cutting synthesis of quantitative data available on international migration. It draws from a variety of sources and introduces material on a few selected patterns of international migration. These are paramount in understanding the international migration phenomenon and, subsequently, the formulation and implementation of migration management policies.

While many different sources (countries, IGOs, NGOs) have been consulted to establish this chapter, its short-comings are obvious and some of the material is outdated.

One problem lies in the timeliness, accuracy and comparability of data. Often, different sources contain different data on the same subjects.

The relative scarcity of flow data is noticeable, as compared to stock data. Presenting precise and comprehensive data on irregular migration is virtually impossible because of the nature of irregular migration itself (see **chapter 3**). Ultimately, translating the complexity of the migration world in all its facets through a selection of essentially incomplete statistical snapshots remains a challenge.

The various migration patterns illustrated in this chapter cover the following areas:
1. Countries providing data on international migration
2. Stocks of foreign-born population
3. Major immigration and emigration countries
4. Female migration
5. Labour migration
6. Migration of students and highly-skilled persons
7. Migrant remittances
8. Humanitarian migration
9. Irregular migration

1. Countries providing data on international migration

Many countries provide statistics on migration; however, only a few do this in a systematic way. **Table 17.1.** shows the number of countries which collected and published statistics on long-term emigrants and immigrants (migrating for at least 12 months) over the last 3 decades (from 1971 to 2000).

303

TABLE 17.1.

Number of Countries Providing Statistics on Long-Term Emigrants and Immigrants, 1971-2000

	1971-1980		1981-1990		1991-2000	
	Emigrants	Immigrants	Emigrants	Immigrants	Emigrants	Immigrants
Africa (55)	7	7	3	4	6	4
Americas (51)	8	14	4	7	9	12
Asia (50)	3	5	3	3	8	9
Europe (47)	20	21	23	23	27	28
Oceania (26)	3	5	3	4	2	3
Total (229)*	41	52	36	41	52	56

Note:
* Figures are for the total number of countries/territories in 2002.

Source:
United Nations (2002a)

Most of the data-producing countries are in Europe; on an intra-continental comparison, the percentage of African countries is the weakest. Interestingly, the number of data-producing countries has not evolved substantially over the past 30 years, indicating a certain immobility in this specific field of statistics.

2. Stocks of Foreign-Born Population

According to the United Nations, there were some 175 million international migrants in 2000, well over double the 84 million in 1975. The number of international migrants has steadily increased over the last 4 decades (**table 17.2.**).

Today, the migrant population represents some 2.9 per cent of the total world population; put differently, 1 out of every 35 persons is an international migrant. If all international migrants lived in one place, it would be the world's fifth biggest country.

TABLE 17.2.

The World's Foreign-Born Population from 1965 to 2000

Year	World Foreign-Born Population (in thousands)
1965	75,214
1975	84,494
1985	105,194
1990	119,761
2000	175,000

Sources:
United Nations (2002b); Population Reference Bureau (2002), Zlotnik, H. (1998)

Table 17.3. shows the geographical distribution of the world's international migrants. Although Europe and Asia shelter the largest number of migrants, the percentage of migrants vis-à-vis total population is much higher in Oceania-Pacific and North America. These two continents include four traditional countries of immigration (see **chapter 9**).

TABLE 17.3.

World Population and Migrant Stocks by Continent, 2000

	Total Population (in millions)	Migrant Stocks (in millions)	Per cent of population (%)
Asia	3672,3	49,7	1,4
Africa	793,6	16,2	2,1
Europe	727,3	56,1	7,7
Latin America / Caribbean	518,8	5,9	2,1
North America	313,1	40,8	13,0
Oceania-Pacific	30,5	5,8	1,1
Global*	**6056,7**	**174,7**	**2,9**

Note:
* does not add up due to rounding

Source:
United Nations (2002b)

3. Major Immigration and Emigration Countries

A view of the top immigration and emigration countries over the last 30 years reveals interesting information. Between 1970 and 1995, some of the top 10 countries of immigration were developing countries, while all of the top 15 countries of emigration were to be found in the developing world (**tables 17.4.** and **17.5.**). This underlines the existence of strong migration flows between countries in the developing world (see **chapter 1**).

The leading net immigration country was the United States, while Mexico topped the list of emigration countries. In some cases, there is a direct link between countries listed in both tables. Most immigrants to the United States come from Mexico; many immigrants to the Russian Federation migrate from Kazakhstan; countries in the Persian Gulf (Saudi Arabia or United Arab Emirates) employ large numbers of migrants from South and South-East Asia (Bangladesh, Philippines, Sri Lanka).

TABLE 17.4.

Top 10 Countries of Immigration, 1970-1995

Country	Net Number of Immigrants (in millions)
United States	16.7
Russian Federation	4.1
Saudi Arabia	3.4
India	3.3
Canada	3.3
Germany	2.7
France	1.4
Australia	1.4
Turkey	1.3
United Arab Emirates	1.3

Source:
United Nations (1999)

TABLE 17.5.

Top 10 Countries of Emigration, 1970-1995

Country	Net Number of Emigrants (in millions)
Mexico	-6.0
Bangladesh	-4.1
Afghanistan	-4.1
Philippines	-2.9
Kazakhstan	-2.6
Vietnam	-2.0
Rwanda	-1.7
Sri Lanka	-1.5
Colombia	-1.3
Bosnia and Herzegovina	-1.2

Source:
United Nations (1999)

Table 17.6. presents the latest available data on international migration stocks. The United States and the Russian Federation continue to top the list of countries with the largest numbers of international migrants. Some of the countries listed are "permanent migration" countries (e.g., Australia, Canada and United States), others are "temporary migration" countries attracting migrants mainly for limited-duration employment purposes (Saudi Arabia, India, Côte d'Ivoire).

TABLE 17.6.

Top 15 Countries with the Largest International Migrant Stock, 2000

Country	Net Number of Migrants (in millions)
USA	35.0
Russian Federation	13.3
Germany	7.3
Ukraine	6.9
France	6.3
India	6.3
Canada	5.8
Saudi Arabia	5.3
Australia	4.7
Pakistan	4.2
United Kingdom	4.0
Kazakhstan	3.0
Côte d'Ivoire	2.3
Iran	2.3
Israel	2.3

Source:
United Nations (2002)

The list of countries with the highest proportion of migrants in their total population is very diversified (**table 17.7.**). Six out of the top 8 countries are in the Middle East. Four of the traditional countries of immigration are also in the list. Three former Soviet Republics registered large numbers of Russian migrants within their borders upon attaining independence in the early 1990s. In Africa, the Gabonese petrol industry has attracted massive flows of immigrants.

TABLE 17.7.

Top 15 Countries with Highest Percentage of Migrants in Total Population, 2000

Country	Percentage of Migrants in Total Population
United Arab Emirates	73.8
Kuwait	57.9
Jordan	39.6
Israel	37.4
Singapore	33.6
Oman	26.9
Estonia	26.2
Saudi Arabia	25.8
Latvia	25.3
Switzerland	25.1
Australia	24.6
New Zealand	22.5
Gabon	20.3
Canada	18.9
Kazakhstan	18.7

Source:
United Nations (2002)

4. Female Migration

Recent global data on female migration patterns are difficult to find. Although published in 2000, the UN publication *The World's Women 2000: Trends and Statistics* uses data drawn from censuses conducted in 1990. The United Nations estimates that women make up around 48 percent of all international migrants (see **textbox 1.1.**).

Tables 17.8. and 17.9. show countries with high and low ratios of female to male migrants. In some cases, figures for countries with a high ratio of female migrants may reflect a high incidence of irregular migration, i.e., trafficking. Research suggests that the three countries topping **table 17.9.** are among the major countries of origin of women and girls trafficked into forced labour or prostitution. With respect to countries with low ratios of female migrants, it is interesting to note that 8 out of the top 10 countries are in the Middle East.

TABLE 17.8.

Top 10 Emigration Countries with High Ratios of Female to Male Migrants, 1990

Country	Females per 100 Male International Migrants
Nepal	251
Mozambique	133
Yugoslavia*	132
Comoros	131
Haiti	131
Romania	131
Albania	131
Italy	130
Aruba	126
Iceland	125

Note:
* Refers to the former Federal Republic of Yugoslavia, now Serbia-Montenegro

Source:
United Nations (2000)

TABLE 17.9.

Top 10 Emigration Countries with Low Ratios of Female to Male Migrants, 1990

Country	Females per 100 Male International Migrants
Yemen	15
Sierra Leone	32
Qatar	35
Bahrain	39
Lebanon	39
Cuba	40
Libya	44
United Arab Emirates	50
Saudi Arabia	50
Oman	50

Source:
United Nations (2000)

5. Labour Migration

According to the International Labour Organization, an estimated 60 to 65 million people are economically active in a country other than their own (McClure-ILO, 2002). If family members and estimated numbers of irregular labour migrants are included, this figure rises to some 120 million (Somavia, 2002).

Data on stocks of foreign labour (**graph 17.10.**) may include foreigners already in the country, but entering the labour force for the very first time. For OECD countries, the increase in the foreign labour force for the five-year period between 1995 and 1999 is highest in Italy (125 per cent), the Republic of Korea (78.2 per cent) and Denmark (49.6 per cent). This increase is lowest in Sweden (0.9 per cent) and France (1.3 per cent). Germany and Switzerland experienced a decrease in their foreign labour force over the period in question (-0.8 per cent and –3.8 per cent). Countries with the lowest foreign labour stocks in 1999 generally had the highest percentage increases in their stocks between 1995 and 1999.

GRAPH 17.10.

Foreign Labour Force in Selected OECD countries, 1999

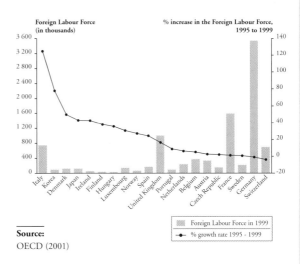

Source:
OECD (2001)

Asia has large numbers of international labour migrants (see **chapter 11**). Malaysia and Singapore can be singled out for the high percentage of migrants among their labour force (**table 17.11.**). In both countries, the number of legally residing foreign workers is particularly high compared to those without legal stay. On the other end of the scale, countries such as Japan and the Republic of Korea have some of the most indigenous workforces in the region. There, migrant workers only represent 1 per cent of the total labour force.

307

TABLE 17.11.

Migrants in Labour Importing Countries in Asia, 2000

Country	National Labour Force (in thousands)	Total Migrant Population (in thousands)	Legal Migrant Workers (in thousands)	Migrant Workers Illegal Status (in thousands)	Migrant Percentage of Labour Force (in thousands)
Hong Kong SAR	3,380	300	235	78	9
Japan	68,000	670	420	63	1
Rep. Korea	22,000	310	95	31	1
Malaysia	9,600	1,239	789	64	13
Taiwan (China)	10,000	345	329	96	3
Thailand	34,000	1,000	700	70	3
Singapore	2,190	960	940	98	44
Total	**149,170**	**4,824**	**3,508**	**73**	**3**

Source:
Population Reference Bureau (2002)

6. Migration of Students and Highly-Skilled Persons

Geographic proximity and historic linkages dominate migratory patterns of students (**table 17.12.**). Worldwide, the biggest foreign students contingents can be found in the United States, the United Kingdom, Germany and France. In Asia and Africa, Japan and South Africa are other important host countries for foreign students.

To a large extent, foreign students originate from a country in the same continent they study in: i.e., most Asians study in Asia, Europeans in Europe, and Africans in Africa. This suggests that geographic proximity plays an important role in determining the place of study abroad. However, there are exceptions to this pattern: most foreign students in Cuba originate from Africa; in the United States, students from Asia make up the majority of the foreign student population. Former colonial powers Belgium, France and Portugal count large numbers of African students; one in every three students in the United Kingdom is from Asia.

TABLE 17.12.

Foreign Students in Higher Education in Selected Countries by Continent of Origin, various years

Host Country	Year	Total	% Foreign Students	% Distribution of Foreign Students by Continent of Origin						
				AFRICA	NORTH AMERICA	SOUTH AMERICA	ASIA	EUROPE	OCEANIA	N/A
AFRICA										
Egypt	1995/96	6,726	0.8	23.3	0.1	-	75.1	1.5	-	-
Morocco	1994/95	3,617	1.5	73.2	-	-	12.1	1.2	-	13.5
South Africa	1994	12,625	2	61	2.8	1.2	5.2	28.6	1.3	-
Togo	1996/97	480	3.7	97.1	1	-	-	1.3	-	0.6
AMERICAS										
Argentina	1994	12,678	-	-	-	75	-	4.4	-	20.7
Cuba	1996/97	4,243	3.8	76.4	10	8.3	4.8	.5		
Guyana	1994/95	38	0.5	-	-	-	-	-	-	-
United States	1995/96	453,785	3.2	4.6	10.7	4.9	64.1	14.8	0.9	-
ASIA										
Japan	1994/95	53,511	1.4	0.8	2.7	1.2	92.1	2.5	0.6	-
Rep. of Korea	1996/97	2,143	0.1	0.7	16.8	4.7	72.8	3.7	1.3	-
Qatar	1996/97	1,360	16	13.6	0.3	-	86	0.1	-	-
Turkey	1994/95	14,719	1.3	4.4	0.2	0	55	20.6	0.1	19.6
U.Arab Emirate	1996/97	1,584	9.8	16.5	0.3	-	80.3	0.6	-	2.4
EUROPE										
Belgium	1994/95	34,966	9.9	31.3	1.3	2.2	8.3	55	0	1.9
France	1995/96	138,191	-	51.7	3.6	2.7	13.4	27.6	0.1	0.9
Germany	1996/97	165,977	7.8	9.1	3.3	2.3	36.2	47.2	0.2	1.6
Ireland	1996/97	5,975	4.4	4.3	19.3	0.1	21.1	52.8	1.2	1.2
Italy	1996/97	24,858	1.3	12.2	2.7	3.6	12.1	65.9	0.2	3.3
Portugal	1994/95	6,140	2	49.8	6.2	22	0.6	19.1	0.3	2
Russian Fed.	1994/95	73,172	1.6	5.1	0.4	0.7	53.6	40.2	-	-
Spain	1994/95	21,403	1.4	10.3	7.2	15.3	4.1	62.7	0.2	0.2
Sweden	1996/97	12,189	4.4	3.5	5.3	3.2	19.1	67.7	0.5	0.7
UK	1996/97	198,839	10.5	7.1	7.8	1.2	34.2	46.2	0.9	2.6
OCEANIA										
Australia	1997	102,284	9.8	-	-	-	-	-	-	-
New Zealand	1997	6,415	3.9	0.8	0.7	4.2	70.8	5.5	16.6	1.4

Source:
UNESCO (1999). Reproduced by permission of UNESCO

Table 17.13. shows the top 5 countries of origin of foreign students in selected OECD countries in 1998. Data here also illustrate the role of geographic proximity. Italy and Japan are the two countries with the most homogenous group of foreign students with 49 per cent of Greek students and 45 per cent of Chinese, respectively.

TABLE 17.13.

Top 5 Countries of Origin of Foreign Students in Selected OECD Countries, 1998

Host country	1st	%*	2nd	%	3rd	%	4th	%	5th	%
Australia	Malaysia	14.7	Singapore	13.4	Hong Kong SAR	12.2	Indonesia	7.2	UK	4.9
Austria	Italy	23.3	Germany	19.1	Turkey	4.0	Bulgaria	3.7	Iran	3.3
Canada	France	10.7	USA	10.0	Hong Kong SAR	8.2	China	7.2	Japan	4.0
Denmark	Norway	10.5	Iceland	5.7	Germany	5.3	Sweden	3.9	Iran	3.9
France	Morocco	11.8	Algeria	10.9	Germany	3.5	Tunisia	3.4	-	-
Germany	Turkey	15.2	Iran	5.2	Greece	5.0	Austria	4.0	Italy	4.0
Italy	Greece	49.1	Germany	4.4	-	-	-	-	-	-
Japan	China	45.6	Rep. of Korea	33.0	Malaysia	3.7	-	-	-	-
New Zealand	Malaysia	32.0	Japan	6.1	Hong Kong	4.9	USA	4.9	Thailand	4.8
Spain	France	13.4	Germany	11.0	Italy	10.0	UK	8.1	Morocco	6.8
Switzerland	Germany	22.4	Italy	15.6	France	10.6	Spain	6.0	-	-
UK	Greece	12.1	Malaysia	8.2	Ireland	7.8	Germany	6.2	France	6.0
USA	China	9.8	Japan	9.8	Rep. of Korea	8.9	India	7.0	Canada	4.6

Note:
* % of total stock of foreign students enrolled

Source:
OECD (2001)

7. Migrant Remittances

Remittances are a greater source of foreign exchange in developing countries than all forms of foreign aid combined. The volume of migrant remittances to countries in the developing world has increased rapidly in recent years.

Many migrant remittances are sent through unofficial channels and are therefore not captured by official statistical sources on migrant remittances. For example, the IMF estimates that remittances to all countries in 1999 amounted to US$ 63 billion, however, other experts believe that total remittances in the same year amounted to more than US$ 100 billion if unofficial channels are taken into account (Gammeltoft, 2002).

Illustrating the close linkages between diaspora and the countries of origin, remittances represent a very positive outcomes of migration patterns. While many of the major destination countries for remittances are in the developing world, developed countries with traditionally strong emigration flows are also recipients, such as Spain, Portugal or Greece (**table 17.14.**). In recent years, these countries have in their turn become major countries of immigration: some of the money remitted back home to Turkey or Morocco for example is earned in Greece or Spain.

TABLE 17.14.

Top 20 Receiving Countries of Migrants Remittances, 2000

Country	Remittances (US$ in thousands)
India	11,585,699
Mexico	6,572,599
Turkey	4,560,000
Egypt	3,747,000
Spain	3,414,414
Portugal	3,131,162
Morocco	2,160,999
Bangladesh	1,948,999
Jordan	1,845,133
El Salvador	1,750,770
Dominican Republic	1,688,999
Greece	1,613,100
Colombia	1,553,900
Ecuador	1,316,700
Yemen	1,255,206
Indonesia	1,190,000
Sri Lanka	1,142,329
Brazil	1,112,999
Pakistan	982,899
Jamaica	789,299

Source:
World Bank (2002)

Table 17.15. shows fluctuations in migrant remittances over the last fifteen years. Europe was the most important source region for migrant remittances to developing countries at the end of the 1980s; however, by 1991, it had been replaced by Asia. Since then, Asia has continued to be the most important region from which remittances are sent. Generally, the amount of remittances virtually doubled from 1988 to 1999.

TABLE 17.15.

Migrant Remittances from Various World Regions, 1988 to 1999

Year	Region of Origin					Destination	
	Africa	Americas	Middle East	Asia	Europe	Developing Total	World Total
1988	2,998*	3,194	5,644	6,365	6,396	24,597	34,568
1989	3,119	3,737	4,828	6,921	9,370	27,975	37,847
1990	3,589	4,751	6,320	6,777	12,722	34,159	45,933
1991	3,423	5,793	5,539	7,317	4,924	26,996	38,998
1992	4,838	7,252	8,005	7,254	3,280	30,629	43,573
1993	4,946	7,470	7,782	7,807	3,534	31,539	43,727
1994	4,884	9,653	5,864	11,097	3,938	35,436	47,598
1995	5,383	11,499	5,590	11,786	5,113	39,371	51,761
1996	5,464	11,239	5,825	15,380	5,609	43,517	55,896
1997	6,389	12,036	6,560	21,066	6,130	52,181	63,153
1998	6,492	13,235	6,154	15,566	7,650	49,097	60,409
1999	5,993	14,589	6,203	17,906	6,520	51,211	62,976

Note: * in US$ millions   **Source:** IMF

8. Humanitarian migration

a) Refugees

TABLE 17.16.

The World's Refugees by Region of Asylum, 1999-2001 (in thousands)

Region	1999	2000	2001
Africa	3,523.4	3,627.4	3,283.9
Asia	4,782.0	5,383.4	5,770.3
Europe	2,543.6	2,310.1	2,227.9
Latin America & the Caribbean	61.5	37.9	37.4
North America	644.5	635.2	645.1
Oceania-Pacific	70.7	68.4	65.4
Total	11,625.7	12,062.5	12,029.9

Source:
UNHCR (2002b)

According to UNHCR, there were some 12,029,900 refugees worldwide in 2001, representing a slight decrease from the previous year but an increase of some 400.000 as compared to 1999 (**table 17.16.**). Asia remains the major host region for refugees worldwide, followed by Africa and Europe.

Tables 17.17. and **17.18.** show the top 10 sending and host countries of refugees from 1999 to 2001. The composition of both lists has largely remained unaltered over the last three years. Most refugee host countries are safe neighbouring countries of countries in conflict (i.e., Iran and Pakistan bordering Afghanistan, Guinea bordering Sierra Leone, Tanzania bordering the DR Congo, etc.), other countries, such as the United States, have well established refugee resettlement programmes or a tradition of hosting refugees such as Germany.

TABLE 17.17.

Top 10 Refugee Sending Countries, 1999-2001 (in thousands)

	1999		2000		2001
Afghanistan	2,601	Afghanistan	3,586	Afghanistan	3,809
Iraq	641	Burundi	568	Burundi	554
Bosnia-Herzegovina	600	Iraq	525	Iraq	530
Burundi	527	Bosnia-Herzegovina	509	Sudan	489
Somalia	524	Sudan	493	Angola	471
Sierra Leone	490	Somalia	475	Bosnia-Herzegovina	450
Sudan	485	Angola	433	Somalia	439
Vietnam	406	Sierra Leone	402	DR Congo	392
Angola	353	Eritrea	376	Vietnam	370
Croatia	351	DR Congo	371	Occup. Palest. Territ.	349

Source:
UNHCR (2002b)

TABLE 17.18.

Top 10 Refugee Host Countries, 1999-2001 (in thousands)

1999		2000		2001	
Iran	1,835	Pakistan	2,001	Pakistan	2,198
Pakistan	1,202	Iran	1,868	Iran	1,868
Germany	975	Germany	906	Germany	903
Tanzania	622	Tanzania	680	Tanzania	646
United States	521	United States	508	United States	515
FR Yugoslavia	501	FR Yugoslavia	484	FR Yugoslavia	400
Guinea	501	Guinea	427	DR Congo	362
Sudan	391	Sudan	414	Sudan	349
Armenia	296	DR Congo	332	China	295
China	293	China	294	Zambia	284

Source:
UNHCR (2002b)

b) Internally Displaced Persons (IDPs)

According to the Global IDP project, there were some 25 million IDPs worldwide in 2001-2002, distributed in 47 countries. Africa is home to the largest IDP contingent, with Angola and Sudan and the Democratic Republic of Congo as the leading IDP countries. More than one out of every three countries with an IDP population is African.

In the Middle East, Turkey and Iraq are the worst affected countries. Europe's largest IDP populations are found in the Russian Federation and in former Yugoslavia. Myanmar has the largest IDP population in Asia. Colombia is host to most IDPs in South America.

TABLE 17.19.

IDP Estimates by Country

Countries	Number of IDPs	Date
Afghanistan	900,000-1,200,000	April 2002
Algeria	200,000	June 2001
Angola	4,100,000	Nov. 2001
Armenia	40,000	2001
Azerbaijan	570,000	2001
Bangladesh	500,000	2000
Bosnia-Herzegovina	440,000	Jan. 2002
Burundi	475,000	Feb. 2002
Colombia	2,100,000	2001
Croatia	22,000	April 2002
Cyprus	210,000	2000
Democratic Republic of Congo	2,200,000	Feb. 2002
Eritrea	57,000	March 2002
Ethiopia	12,500	Feb. 2002
FR Yugoslavia	330,000	Jan. 2002
Georgia	270,000	2002
Guatemala	100,000-250,000	2001
Guinea	250,000	end-2001
Guinea-Bissau	2,000	Feb. 2001
India	500,000	March 2001
Indonesia	1,300,000	April 2002
Iraq	700,000	2001
Israel	200,000	2001
Kenya	200,000	March 2001
Lebanon	300,000	2002
Liberia	80,000	March 2002
Macedonia	17,000	April 2002
Mexico	10,000	Dec. 2000
Myanmar	600,000-1,000,000	Jan. 2002
Nigeria	500,000	Nov. 2001
Pakistan	3,000	Aug. 2001
Palestinian Territories	9,000-20,000	2001
Peru	60,000	2001
Philippines	140,000	Dec. 2001
Rep. of Congo	150,000	Oct. 2001
Russian Federation	460,000	End-2001
Rwanda	150,000	2001
Senegal	6,000	Aug. 2001
Sierra Leone	247,000	Nov. 2001
Solomon Islands	30,000	April 2001
Somalia	400,000	Nov. 2001
Sri Lanka	800,000	April 2002
Sudan	4,000,000	Nov. 2001
Syrian Arab Republic	300,000	2001
Turkey	1,000,000	March 2002
Uganda	550,000	March 2002
Uzbekistan	3,500	2001

Source: Global IDP Project (2002)

9. Irregular Migration

Irregular migration continues to be a complex phenomenon on which accurate and reliable data are not readily available. Most data problems concerning the subject of irregular migration stem from technical and institutional difficulties encountered in data collection.

Table 17.20. presents some estimates of annual flows of irregular migrants from various sources. Disparities are large and it often remains unclear how the sources calculate the figures provided.

According to the US State Department (2001), some 700,000 to 2 million women and children are trafficked across international borders each year. D. Papademetriou from the Migration Policy Institute estimates that some 500,0000 persons enter four traditional countries of immigration illegally every year. The Swedish NGO Kvinnaforum estimates that 500,000 women are trafficked each year into countries of Western Europe. Reported by *The Economist,* the International Centre for Migration Policy Development estimates that 500,000 illegal migrants enter the EU each year. According to a recent UNICEF report, an estimated 120,000 women and children are being trafficked into the EU each year, mostly through the Balkans.

TABLE 17.20.

Overview of Estimated Annual Flows of Irregular Migrants

Region of Destination	Estimates
Worldwide*	700,000-2,000,000
Australia, Canada, New Zealand, USA**	500,000
Western Europe***	500,000
European Union****	500,000
European Union*****	120,000

Notes:

* United States Department of State (2001); ** Papademetriou (2003); *** Kvinnaforum (1999); **** The Economist (2002); ***** UNICEF et al. (2002)

People smuggling is a very lucrative business generating billions of US dollars in revenues every year. As with commercial transportation costs, the fees paid to migrant smugglers increase proportionally to the distance covered between country of origin and destination.

Table 17.21. shows that the most expensive fees paid to smugglers for travel to the United States were for journeys originating from China. The least expensive fees were acquitted for "simple" border crossing assistance from Mexico. Transatlantic travel from countries in Asia and Europe to the United States, Canada and Argentina are among the most expensive.

Smuggling fees may also be determined by the level of auxiliary services provided by the trafficker, such as fake identification documents, job brokering, visas etc. (Salt, 2001). As data in this field are difficult to collect, it is important to note that information on smuggling fees is based on individual cases.

TABLE 17.21.

Fees Paid to Smugglers for Travel Assistance to Selected Destinations

Origin	Destination	Price (US$ per person)
EUROPE		
Bulgaria	Europe	4,000
Greece	France, Italy, Germany	800 - 1,200
Turkey	Greece	1,400
Hungary	Slovenia	1,500
Kurdistan	Germany	3,000
North Africa	Spain	2000 - 3,500
Sri Lanka	Turkey	4,000
Pakistan	Turkey	4,000
Dominican Republic	Europe	4,000 - 10,000
Dominican Republic	Austria	5,000
China	Europe	10,000 - 15,000
Afghanistan / Lebanon	Germany	5,000 - 10,000
Iraq	Europe	4,100 - 5,000
Iran	Europe	5,000
Palestine	Europe	5,000
NORTH AMERICA		
China	New York	35,000
China	USA	30,000
Middle-East	USA	1,000 - 15,000
Pakistan / India	USA	25,000
Mexico	Los Angeles	200 - 400
Iran / Iraq	Canada	10,000
Venezuela	Canada	1,000 - 2,500

Source:
Salt, J. (2001)

315

ANNEXES

General Bibliography

Chapter 1

Arango, J. (2000). "Expliquer les migrations: un regard critique", *Revue internationale des sciences sociales,* no.165, UNESCO, Paris.

Badie, B. and M.C. Smouts (1999). *Le retournement du monde. Sociologie de la scène internationale,* 3ʳᵈ edition, Presses de Science Po and Dalloz, Paris.

Bernard, P. (2002). *Immigration: le défi mondial*, Collection Folio/Actuel, Gallimard, Paris.

Castles, S. and M.J. Miller (1996). *The Age of Migration: International Population Movements in the Modern World*, Macmillan, London.

Castles, S. (2000). "Les migrations internationales au début du XXIᵉ siècle: tendances et problèmes mondiaux", *Revue internationale des sciences sociales*, no.165, UNESCO, Paris.

Davis, K. (1988). "Social Science Approaches to International Migration", in: M.S. Teitelbaum and J.M. Winter (Ed.), *Population and Resources in Western Intellectual Traditions*, The Population Council, New York.

Dumont, G.F. (1995). *Les migrations internationales. Les nouvelles logiques migratoires*, Sedes, Paris.

-------- (2001). "Les sophismes migratoires de la République", *Panoramiques*, no.55, 4ᵗʰ quarter, Paris.

Farine, P. (2002). "L'avenir des migrations: vers une société de la mobilité ?", *Migrations Société*, 14(79), January-February, Paris.

Garson, J.P. and C. Thoreau (1999). "Typologie des migrations et analyse de l'intégration", in: Dewitte, P., *Immigration et intégration, l'état des savoirs*, La Découverte, Paris.

Held, D. *et al.* (1999). *Global Transformations: Politics, Economics and Culture*, Polity, Cambridge.

Kastoryano, R. (2000). " Immigration, communautés transnationales et citoyenneté", *Revue internationale des sciences sociales*, no. 165, UNESCO, Paris.

Le Monde (2002). "Le grand dossier: L'immigration en Europe", 9 and 10 June, Paris.

Martin, P. and J. Widgren (2002). " International Migration: Facing the Challenge", *Population Bulletin*, 57(1), Population Reference Bureau, Washington D.C.

McKinley, B., A. Klekowski von Koppenfels and F. Laczko (2001). " Challenges for the 21ˢᵗ Century", *Forum for Applied Research and Public Policy*, 16(2), Summer, University of Tennessee, Tennessee Valley Authority.

IOM (International Organization for Migration). (2000). *Etat de la migration dans le monde en 2000*, IOM and United Nations, Geneva.

-------- (2001). "Les nouveaux chiffres de l'OIM sur l'ampleur mondiale de la traite", *Traite des Migrants – Bulletin Trimestriel*, no.23, April, Geneva.

-------- (2002). *Dialogue international sur la migration – la 82ᵉ session du Conseil de l'OIM*, IOM Migration Policy and Research Programme Programme, Geneva.

Perruchoud, R. (1992). "Persons falling under the mandate of the International Organization for Migration (IOM) and to whom the Organization may provide migration services", *International Journal of Refugee Law*, 4(2), Oxford University Press, Oxford.

-------- (2002). *Intervention de l'OIM devant la Commission des Droits de l'Homme des Nations Unies*, 14 April, Geneva.

Petit, V. (2000). "Les migrations internationales", in: Charbit, Yves, *La population des pays en développement*, Les études de la Documentation Française, Paris.

Sassen, S. (2002). "Les migrations ne surgissent pas du néant", *Le Monde diplomatique, Histoire(s) d'immigration, Manière de voir*, no.62, March-April, Paris.

Simon, G. (2001). "Les nouvelles mobilités internationales", *Le Journal du CNRS*, no.134, February, Meudon and Paris.

Tacoli, C. and D. Okali (2001). *The Links between Migration, Globalisation and Sustainable Development*, Opinion, World Summit on Sustainable Development, International Institute for Environment and Development, London.

Teitelbaum, M.S. (2002). "The Role of the State in International Migration", *The Brown Journal of World Affairs*, Winter, 8(2).

Weiss, T.L. (1998). *Migrants nigérians - La diaspora dans le Sud-Ouest du Cameroun,* Editions L'Harmattan, Série Culture et Politique, Collection Géographie et Cultures, Paris.

-------- (2001a). "L'Afrique à la poursuite de ses cerveaux", *Jeune Afrique / L'intelligent*, no.2104, 8 - 14 May, Paris.

-------- (2001b). "Migration und Terrorismus. Vernünftige Massnahmen in einer mobilen Welt", *Neue Zürcher Zeitung*, no.254, 222ⁿᵈ year, 1ˢᵗ November, Zürich.

Withol de Wenden, C. (2001). "Un essai de typologie des nouvelles mobilités", *Hommes et Migrations*, no.1233, September-October, Paris.

World Bank (2002). *Globalization, Growth, and Poverty. Building an Inclusive World Economy*. World Bank Policy Research Report, World Bank and Oxford University Press, Washington D.C. and Oxford.

UNHCR (United Nations High Commissioner for Refugees), (2000). *Les Réfugiés dans le Monde. Cinquante ans d'action humanitaire*, UNHCR, Geneva.

-------- (2001a). *Asylum Applications in Industrialized Countries: 1980 – 1999. Trends in Asylum Application Lodged in 37, Mostly Industrialized, Countries*, UNHCR, Unité des données démographiques, Section des données démographiques et géographiques, Geneva.

-------- (2001b). 2001 UNHCR *Population Statistics (Provisional)*, UNHCR, Unité des données démographiques, Section des données démographiques et géographiques, Geneva.

-------- (2002). *Statistical Yearbook 2001*, UNHCR Population Data Unit, Population and Geographic Data Section, Geneva.

United Nations (1998). *Recommendations on Statistics of International Migration: Revision 1*, Statistical Papers, no.58, rev.1, New York.

-------- (2002). *International Migration 2002 – Wallchart*, Population Division, New York.

Zlotnik, H. (1998). "International Migration 1965-1996: An Overview", *Population and Development Review*, no.3.

Chapter 2

Battistella, G. (2002). "Les tendances migratoires en Asie et en Australie", *Migrations Société*, 14(79), January-February.

Canales, A. (2000). "Migration internationale et flexibilité du travail dans le contexte de l'ALENA", no.165, September, UNESCO, Paris.

Castles, S. and M. Miller (1998). *The Age of Migration,* 2nd edition, MacMillan, London.

CEPAL (Comisión Económica para América Latina y el Caribe) - CELADE (Centro Latinoamericano y Caribeño de Demografía), (2000). "Migration internationale en Amérique latine", *Boletin Demografico*, no.65.

De Lobkovicz, W. (2002). *L'Europe et la sécurité intérieure*, La Documentation Française, Paris.

The Economist (2002). "Migration statistics. Cross-frontier chaos", 15 June, London.

Eurostat (2000). *European Social Statistics – Migration – 2000*, European Commission, Eurostat, Luxembourg.

Guerassimov, C. (2002). "L'impact de la nouvelle migration chinoise sur les relations de la Grande-Bretagne avec la République populaire de Chine", *Bulletin du CAP*, Ministère des Affaires Etrangères, no.75, February, Paris.

ILO (International Labour Organization), (2002a). *Un avenir sans travail des enfants*. Rapport global en vertu du suivi de la Déclaration de l'OIT (ILO) relative aux principes et droits fondamentaux eu travail, Geneva.

-------- (2002b). *Le travail des enfants en Afrique*, Feuillet d'informations additionnel à la Déclaration de l'OIT (ILO) relative aux principes et droits fondamentaux du travail, Geneva.

IOM (International Organization for Migration), (2002a). *Dialogue international sur la migration – 82e session du Conseil, 27-29 novembre 2001*, Geneva.

-------- (2002b). *Trafficking for Sexual Exploitation: The Case of the Russian Federation*, IOM Migration Research Series, no.7, Geneva.

-------- (2002c). *Migration Trends in Eastern Europe and Central Asia / 2001-2002 Review*, Geneva.

Martin, P. and J. Widgren (2002). "International Migration: Facing the Challenge", *Population Bulletin*, 57(1), Population Reference Bureau, Washington D.C.

Miller, M. (2002). "Les tendances des migrations internationales vers et en Amérique du Nord à la suite du 11 septembre : un premier aperçu", *Migrations Société*, 14(79), January-February.

OECD (Organization for Economic Cooperation and Development), (2000). *SOPEMI - Tendances des migrations internationales*, Système d'observation permanente des migrations, Annual Report, OECD, Paris.

-------- (2002). *Résumé des principales tendances migratoires à l'issue de la réunion des correspondants du SOPEMI*, Système d'observation permanente des migrations, Groupe de travail sur les migrations, Paris.

Piore, M. (1979). *Birds of passage: Migrant Labor and Industrial Societies*, Harvard University Press, Cambridge.

Santillo, M. (2002). "Les mouvements migratoires en Amérique Latine: bilan et perspectives", *Migrations Société*, 14(79), January-February.

UNHCR (United Nations High Commissioner for Refugees), (2001a). *Les réfugiés dans le monde. Cinquante ans d'action humanitaire*, UNHCR, Geneva.

-------- (2001b). *Asylum Applications in Industrialized Countries: 1980 – 1999. Trends in Asylum Application Lodged in 37, Mostly Industrialized, Countries*. UNHCR, Unité des données démographiques, Section des données démographiques et géographiques, Geneva.

-------- (2001c). *2000 Global Refugee Trends*, UNHCR, Geneva.

United Nations (2000). *Replacement Migration: Is It a Solution to Declining and Ageing Populations* ?, UN Population Division, New York.

-------- (2002). *International Migration 2002 – Wallchart*, UN Population Division, New York.

Van Krieken, P. (Ed.), (2001). *The Migration Acquis Handbook*, T.M.C. Asser Press, The Hague.

Weil, P. (2001). "Populations en mouvements, Etat inerte ?", in: Fauroux, R. and B. Spitz (Eds.), *Notre Etat. Le livre vérité de la fonction publique,* Robert Laffont, Paris.

Weiss, T.L. (1999). "Géographie des migrations de travail en Afrique australe", in: J.R. Pitte and A.L. Sanguin (Eds.), *Géographie et Liberté – mélanges en hommage à Paul Claval*, Editions L'Harmattan, Paris, L'Harmattan Incorporated, Montréal, Collection Géographie et Cultures.

-------- (2001a). "Combattre l'amalgame entre migration et terrorisme", *La Quinzaine européenne,* 15 October - 4 November, Brussels and Strasbourg.

-------- (2001b). "Esquisse d'une géographie des migrations en Afrique", *Acta Géographica / La Géographie – Revue de la Société de Géographie de France,* 1503(01)IV, Paris.

Withol de Wenden, C. (2001). *Le point sur l'Europe des migrations*, La Documentation Française, Paris.

Zolberg, A. (1992). "Reforming the back door : perspectives historiques sur la réforme de la politique américaine d'immigration", in: J. Costa-Lascoux et P. Weil (Eds.), *Logiques d'Etats et immigration,* Kimé, Paris.

Chapter 3

European Commission (2001). *Communication on a Common Policy on Illegal Immigration*, COM(2001)672, Brussels.

Ghosh, B. (1998). *Huddled Masses and Uncertain Shores: Insights into Irregular Migration*, Marinus Nijhoff Publishers, London.

IOM (International Organization for Migration), (2002). *International Dialogue on Migration –
82ᵈ session of the Council, 27-29 November 2001*, IOM, Geneva.

Kvinnaforum (1999). *Crossing Borders against Trafficking in Women and Girls. A Resource Book for Working against
Trafficking in the Baltic Sea*. Stockholm – quoted by UNICEF et al. (2002).

Migration News (2002). 9(6), (www.migration.ucdavis.edu).

National Foreign Intelligence Board (2001). *Growing Global Migration and its Implications for the United States*, March,
NIE 2001-02D.

OECD (Organization for Economic Cooperation and Development), (2000). *Combating the Illegal Employment
of Foreign Workers*,. OECD, Paris.

United Kingdom Home Department (2002). *Secure Borders, Safe Haven: Integration with Diversity in Modern Britain.*
Document presented to Parliament by the Secretary of State for the Home Department by Command of Her Majesty,
February, CM 5387, London, (www.official-documents.co.uk/documents/cm53/387/cm5387.pdf)

UNICEF (United Nations Children Fund), UNHCHR (United Nations Office of the High Commissioner
for Human Rights), OSCE-ODIHR (Organisation for Security and Cooperation in Europe - Office for Democratic
Institutions and Human Rights), (2002). *Trafficking in Human Beings in Southeastern Europe*. UNICEF, UNHCHR,
OSCE-ODIHR, Warsaw.

United States Department of Justice (2002). News Conference - Administrative Change to Board of Immigration
Appeals, Attorney General Transcript, Department Conference Centre, Washington D.C.,
(www.usdoj.gov/ag/speeches/2002/020602transcriptadministrativechangetobia.htm)

Unites States Department of State (2001). *Victims of Trafficking and Violence Protection Act of 2000, Trafficking
in Persons Report*, Washington D.C.

United States Immigration and Naturalization Service. *US Immigration and Naturalization Service Fact Sheets*,
Washington D.C., (www.ins.usdoj.gov/graphics/faqs.htm)

Chapter 4

Bommes, M., S. Castles and C. Wihtol de Wenden (Eds.), (1999). *Migration and Social Change in Australia, France
and Germany*, Institut für Migrationsforschung und Interkulturelle Studien (IMIS), Universität Osnabrück.

Deutsches PISA-Konsortium (Ed.), (2001). PISA 2000 – *Basiskompetenzen von Schülerinnen und Schülern
im internationalen Vergleich*, Opladen, Leske and Budrich.

Huntington, S. (1993). "The Clash of Civilisations ?", *Foreign Affairs*, 72(3):24.

IOM (International Organization for Migration), (2002). *International Dialogue on Migration –
82ᵈ Session of the Council 27-29 November 2001*, IOM Migration Policy and Research Programme, Geneva.

John, B. (1997). "Anmerkungen zum Thema Zuwanderung und Innere Sicherheit", in: Angenendt, S. (Ed.), *Migration
und Flucht. Aufgaben und Strategien für Deutschland, Europa und die internationale Gemeinschaft*, Bundeszentrale für
politische Bildung, Schriftenreihe no.342, Bonn.

Levine, R.A. (2002). "Europe needs to rethink its reluctant welcome", *International Herald Tribune*, 25 April.

Ministry of the Interior and Kingdom Relations (2000). *Integration Monitor 2000,* Minorities Integration Policy Department, The Hague, The Netherlands.

Pfaff, W. (2002). "And then face the immigration challenge", *International Herald Tribune*, 3 May.

UNESCO (United Nations Educational, Scientific and Cultural Organization), (2001). *Multicultural Policies and Modes of Citizenship in Europe*, United Kingdom, Ashgate.

Wortham, A. (2001). "The Melting Pot", *The World, September,* 16(10):261-291.

Chapter 5

CDC (Centers for Disease Control and Prevention), (2001). *TB Elimination: Now Is the Time,* (www.cdc.gov/nchstp/tb/pubs/nowisthetime/ pdfs/nowisthetime.pdf).

Global Drug Facility (2001). *Stop TB Partnership – Fact Sheet.*

Heath, T.C. *et al.* (1998). *The International Journal of Tuberculosis and Lung Diseases*, 2(8): 647-654.

Hersi, A. *et al.* (1998). *Canadian Respiratory Journal,* 6(2): 155-160.

IOM (International Organization for Migration), (1992). *International Migration, Quarterly Review.* Special Issue: Migration and Health in the 1990s, vol.XXX.

-------- (2001). *Medical Manual,* IOM Medical Health Services Division, Geneva.

-------- (2002a). *Migration Health Services - 2001 Annual Report,* IOM Medical Health Services Division, Geneva.

-------- (2002b). *Migration and Health Newsletter*, no.1, IOM Medical Health Services Division, Geneva.

Javate de Dios, A. (1999). "Macro-economic policies and their impact on sexual exploitation and trafficking of women and girls: issues, responses and challenges", UNAIDS conference, satellite symposium, 22-28 October, Kuala Lumpur, Malaysia.

Lambregts-van Weezenbeek, C.S. (1998). *The International Journal for Tuberculosis and Lung Diseases*, 2(4):288-295.

Lohrmann, R. (1994). "International migration: trends and prospects", in: International Social Security Association (Ed.), *Migration: a Worldwide Challenge for Social Security,* Studies and Research, no.35.

OSCE and ODIHR (Organisation for Security and Cooperation in Europe, Office for Democratic Institutions and Human Rights), (1999). *Trafficking in Human Beings : Implications for the OSCE*, Review Conference, September, ODIHR background paper 99/3.

Peroff, N. (in draft, March 2001). *HIV and Reproductive Health Risks to Trafficked Women in the Sex Industry*, IOM medical programme for Bosnia and Herzegovina.

Sahly, H.M. *et al.* (2001). *Journal of Infectious Diseases,* 183(3):461-468.

Satar, S., J. Tetro and V. Springthorpe (1999). "Impact of changing societal trends on the spread of infections in American and Canadian homes", *American Journal of Infection Control*, 27: 4-21.

Sbabaro, J.A. (2001). "Lest the tide return", *Chest*, 120:328-330, American College of Chest Physicians.

Steel, Z. and D.M. Silove (2001). "The mental health implications of detaining asylum seekers", *Medical Journal of Australia*, 175: 596-599.

UNHCR (United Nations High Commissioner for Refugees), (1996). *The Indo-Chinese exodus and the CPA*, *Special* Report, June, Geneva.

Weiss, *et al.* (2001). *American Journal of Respiratory and Critical Care Medicine*, 164(6): 914-915.

WHO (World Health Organization), (2001). *World Health Report 2001. Mental Health: New Understanding – New Hope.*

Yuen, L.K. *et al.* (1999). *Journal for Clinical Microbiology*, 37(12): 3844-3850.

Chapter 6

Harns, C. (2001). *Capacity Building at the Migration-Asylum Crossroads: Issues and Examples from IOM Experience*, IOM - for the UNHCR Global Consultations Regional Meeting in Cairo, 3 – 5 July.

IOM (International Organization for Migration), (2002). *International Dialogue on Migration – 82nd Session of the Council, 27-29 November 2001*, IOM – Migration Policy and Research Programme, Geneva.

Martin, S. (2001). "Global migration trends and asylum", *UNHCR Working Paper no. 41*, April, Geneva.

Miko, F.T. (2000). *Trafficking in Women and Children: The US and International Response*, Congressional Research Service Report 98-649 C, (www.qweb.kvinnoforum.se/trafficking/onlinearticles.html).

United Nations (2000). *Replacement Migration: Is it a Solution to Declining and Ageing Populations?*, UN Population Division, New York.

-------- (2001). *World Population ageing: 1950-2050*, Department of Economic and Social Affairs, Population Division, New York, (www.un.org/esa/population/publications/worldageing19502050/pdf).

UNHCR (United Nations High Commissioner for Refugees), (1989). *Executive Committee Conclusions: Problem of Refugees and Asylum Seekers Who Move in an Irregular Manner from a Country in Which They Had Already Found Protection*, no.58 (XL), 13 October, Geneva.

-------- (2001a). *Asylum Applications in Industrialized Countries: 1980–1999, Trends in Asylum Applications Lodged in 37, Mostly Industrialized, Countries*, Population Data Unit, Population and Geographic Data Section, Geneva.

-------- (2001b). *Trends in Asylum Decisions in 38 Countries, 1999-2000, A Comparative Analysis of Asylum Statistics and Indicators in 38, Mostly Industrialized, Countries*, UNHCR Population Data Unit, Population and Geographical Data Section, Geneva.

-------- (2002). Agenda for Protection, *Standing Committee of the Executive Committee of the High Commissioner's Programme*, 26 June, Geneva.

UNHCR (United Nations High Commissioner for Refugees) and IOM (International Organization for Migration), (2001). *Refugee Protection and Migration Control: Perspectives from UNHCR and IOM*, "Joint Paper", UNHCR's Global Consultations on International Protection, 31 May, Geneva.

United States Government (1999). Briefing on *Global Trafficking in Women and Children: Assessing the Magnitude, Washington* D.C.

Chapter 7

Copenhagen Programme of Action (1995). Adopted by the World Summit for Social Development, Copenhagen, 6-12 March, Section II.

Deng, F.M. (2000). Foreword to: *War Brought Us Here*, Save the Children, London.

Deng, F.M. and R. Cohen (1998). *Masses in Flight*, The Brookings Institution, Washington D.C .

Ghosh, B. (2000). "New international regime for orderly movement of people: what will it look like ?", in: B. Ghosh (Ed.), *Managing Migration – Time for a New International Regime* ?, Oxford University Press, Oxford.

Holtzman, S. (1999). "Rethinking relief and development", in: *Transitions from Conflict*, The Brookings Institution Project on Internal Displacement, Occasional Paper, Washington D.C.

IASC (Inter-Agency Standing Committee), (1999). *Manual on Field Practice in Internal Displacement*, Policy Paper Series, no.1, New York.

-------- (2000). *Protection of Internally Displaced Persons*. Policy Paper Series, no.2, New York.

ICRC (International Committee of the Red Cross), (2000). "The Mandate and Role of the International Committee of the Red Cross", *International Review of the Red Cross*, 838:491-500, 30 June.

Kent, R.C. (1998). *Building Bridges*, quoted in Deng and Cohen (1998).

IOM (International Organization for Migration), (2001). *The Link between Migration and Development in the Least Developed Countries*, Geneva.

Loescher, G. (2000). "Forced migration in the post-Cold War era: the need for a comprehensive approach", in: B. Ghosh (Ed.), *Managing Migration – Time for a New International Regime* ?, Oxford University Press, Oxford.

McDowell, C. (Ed.), (1996). *Understanding Impoverishment the Consequences of Development Induced Displacement*. Berghahn, Providence.

UNOCHA (United Nations Office for the Coordination of Humanitarian Affairs), (1996). *Guiding Principles on Internal Displacement.*

Report of the Representative of the Secretary General on Internally Displaced Persons, Mr. Francis M. Deng, submitted pursuant to Commission on Human Rights Resolution 1998/50, E/CN.4/1999/79, 25 January 1999.

Report of the Representative of the Secretary-General on Internally Displaced Persons, Mr. Francis Deng, submitted pursuant to Commission on Human Rights resolution 2001/54, E/CN.4/2002/95 Add.3 10 December 2001.

Report of the Representative of the Secretary General on Internally Displaced Persons, Mr. Francis M. Deng, submitted pursuant to Commission on Human Rights Resolution 2001/54, E/CN.4/2002/95, 16 January 2002.

Rudge, P. (2002). *The Need for a More Focused Response: European Donor Policies Toward Internally Displaced Persons*, Brookings-CUNY Project on Internal Displacement, Norwegian Refugee Council and the US Committee for Refugees.

Salt, J. (2000). *Towards a Migration Management Strategy. Report of the Restricted Working Group on a Migration Management Strategy and Summary of the Proceedings of the Seminar on Managing Migration in the Wider Europe.* Council of Europe, Strasbourg.

Special Coordinator for the Network on Internal Displacement (2001). *Interim Report* (unpublished), 9 April.

Tarschys, D. (1998). *Opening Address of the Seminar on Managing Migration in the Wider Europe*, Secretary General of Council of Europe, Strasbourg, 12-13 October.

World Bank (1994). *Resettlement and Development: The Bankwide Review of Projects Involving Involuntary Displacement 1986-1993*, The Environment Department, Washington D.C.

Zartman, W. (1989). *Ripe for Resolution : Conflict and Intervention in Africa*, Oxford University Press, Oxford.

Chapter 8

Duschinsky, P. (2000). *The Role of Non-Governmental Organizations: the Puebla Process Experience*, Symposium on International Migration in the Americas, San José, September 4 – 6.

Ghosh, B. (2000). "Towards a new international regime for orderly movements of people", in: B. Ghosh (Ed.), *Managing Migration : Time for a New International Regime* ?, Oxford University Press, Oxford.

-------- (2000). "New international regime for orderly movements of people: What ill t look like?, in: B. Ghosh (Ed.). *Managing Migration: Time for a New International Regime* ?, Oxford University Press, Oxford.

Government of Costa Rica (2001a). *Convergence of Regional Processes in the Americas in Addressing Migration Issues*, RCM President *pro-tempore* with the cooperation of IOM San José, Heredia, Costa Rica, 14 – 16 November.

-------- (2001b). *Report on Establishment of the Technical Support Unit (TSU) of the Regional Conference on Migration (RCM)*, RCM President *pro-tempore* with the cooperation of IOM San José, Heredia, Costa Rica, 14 – 16 November.

Guarnizo, L.E and A. Portes (2001). *From Assimilation to Transnationalism: Determinants of Transnational Political Action among Contemporary Migrants*, Princeton University.

Guiraudon, V. and C. Joppke (Eds.), (2001). *Controlling a New Migration World*, Routledge, London.

Heisler, B. (2000). "The sociology of immigration", in: C.B. Brettell and J.F. Hollified (Eds.), *Migration Theory: Talking Across Disciplines*, Routledge, New York.

Hollifield, J. F. (2000). "The politics of international migration: How can We bring the State back in ?", in: C.B. Brettell and J.F. Hollified (Eds.), *Migration Theory: Talking Across Disciplines*, Routledge, New York.

-------- (2000). "Migration and the 'new' international order: the missing regime", in: B. Ghosh (Ed.), *Managing Migration: Time for a New International Regime?*, Oxford University Press, Oxford.

INS (Immigration and Naturalization Service), (1979). "This month in immigration history", (www.ins.usdoj.gov/graphics/aboutins/history/july79.htm).

IOM (International Organization for Migration), (2001). *Special Issue: International Migration Policies,* Quarterly Review, 39(6) Special Issue 2/2001.

-------- (2002a). *A Global Consultative Process for Inter-State Co-operation on Migration Management,* Information Note no.1, May, The Berne Initiative.

-------- (2002b). *The State of Migration Management in Central America – An Applied Research*, IOM, Geneva.

Keely, C. (2000). "Demography and international migration", in: C.B. Brettell J.F. and Hollified (Eds.), *Migration Theory: Talking Across Disciplines.* Routledge, New York.

Klekowski von Koppenfels, A. (2001). *The Role of Regional Consultative Processes in Managing International Migration*, IOM Migration Research Series, no.3, Geneva.

Kritz, M.M. (2001). "Population growth and international migration: Is there a link", in: A. Zolberg and P. Benda (Eds.), Global Migrants *Global Refugees Problems and Solutions*, Berghahn Books, New York.

Loescher, G. (2000). "Forced migration in the post-Cold War era: the need for a comprehensive approach", in B. Ghosh (Ed.), *Managing Migration Time for a New International Regime* ?, Oxford University Press, Oxford.

Mahler S.J. (2000). *Migration and Transnational Issues. Recent Trends and Prospects for 2020, CA 2020,* Working Paper no.4, Hamburg, Institut für Iberoamerika-Kunde.

Martin, P. and J.E., Taylor (2001). "Managing migration: the role of economic policies", in: A. Zolberg and P. Benda (Eds.), *Global Migrants Global Refugees Problems and Solutions*, Berghahn Books, New York.

Martin, S. (2002). "Toward a global migration regime", *Georgetown Journal of International Affairs*, vol.1.

-------- (2001). "Heavy traffic: international migration in an era of globalization", *Brookings Review*,19(4): 41-44, Washington D.C.

Miller, M.J. (2000). "International migration in post-Cold War international relations", in: B. Ghosh (Ed.), *Managing Migration Time for a New International Regime* ?, Oxford University Press, Oxford.

Overbeek, H. (2000). "Globalization, sovereignty, and transnational regulation: reshaping the governance of international migration", in: B. Ghosh (Ed.), *Managing Migration. Time for a New International Regime* ?, Oxford University Press, Oxford.

Rodrik D. (2001). "Mobilising the world's labour assets", Financial Times, 17 December.

Taft, J. (2000). *Inaugural Remarks*, Fifth Regional Conference on Migration, (www.state.gov/policy_remarks/2000).

The 5th International Metropolis Conference (2000). Managing Migration Through Partnership : The Role of Consultative Processes, Workshop 5, (www.international.metropolis.net/events/vancouver/papers/Summary5E.html).

United Nations (1992). Report of the Secretary-General Pursuant to the Statement Adopted by the Summit Meeting of the Security Council on 31 Jan. 1992, A/47/277-S/24111 17 June.

-------- (2000). "Follow-Up to the 1996 Geneva Conference on the Problems of Refugees, Displaced Persons, Migration and Asylum Issues". *Bi-monthly Newsletter on Refugee and IDP Related Issues,* Refuge no.5, 13. (www.una.org.ge/refuge/052000/4.html).

-------- (2001a). *Population, Environment and Development - The Concise Report, Table 1,* United Nations Population Division, New York, (www.un.org/esa/population/unpop.htm).

-------- (2001b). *International migration and development,* including the question of the convening of a United Nations conference on international migration and development to address migration issues", Report of the Secretary-General Pursuant to General Assembly. UN Doc. A/56/167, 3 July 2001.

-------- (2002). *International Migration and Development.* Resolution adopted by the General Assembly A/56/563, 21 February 2002.

Zolberg, A and P. Benda (Eds.), (2001). *Global Migrants Global Refugees: Problems and Solutions.* Berghahn Books, London.

Chapter 9

Acacia Immigration Australia. *Australian Visa Categories,* (www.hwmigration.com/home.htm).

Australian Bureau of Statistics, (www.abs.gov.au/ausstats).

Bedford, R. (2002). Unpublished data provided by Statistics New Zealand. Hamilton: Migration Research Group, University of Waikato, New Zealand.

Bender's Immigration and Nationality Act Pamphlet (2001). Editor's Publishing Staff, Lexis Publishing, New York.

Camarota, S. and J. Keeley (2001). *The New Ellis Islands: Examining Non-Traditional Areas of Immigrant Settlement in the 1990s,* Center for Immigration Studies, (www.cis.org/articles/2001/back1101.html).

Canada (1975). *Report of Special Joint Committee of the Senate and the House of Commins on Immigration Policy,* Ottawa.

Chang and Boos (2002). *Immigrant Intent and the Dual Intent Doctrine,* (www.americanlaw.com/dintent.html).

Citizenship and Immigration Canada (2002). *Immigrating to Canada,* (www.cic.gc.ca/english/immigrate/index.html).

-------- (2001). Facts and Figures 2000 : *Immigration Overview,* Ottawa, Minister of Public Works and Government Services Canada.

-------- (1999). *Annual Immigration Plan for the Year 2000,* (http://www.cic.gc.ca/english/pub/anrep00.html).

-------- (1997). *Sponsorship,* (www.cic.gc.ca/english/newcomer/fact_07e.html).

Delamere, Hon. Tuariki - Minister of Immigration (1999). "Immigration changes to enhance New Zealand's attractions", Media Statement, 29 October, Wellington.

Department of Immigration and Multicultural and Indigenous Affairs (2002). *Population Flows: Immigration Aspects - 2001 Edition*, Belconnen, Commonwealth of Australia, February.

Department of Immigration and Multicultural and Indigenous Affairs. "Visiting Australia", (www.immi.gov.au/level2/02_visit.htm).

Economic Council of Canada (1991). *Economic and Social Impacts of Immigration*, Ottawa.

Edwards, J.R.jr. (2001). *Homosexuals and Immigration: Developments in the United States and Beyond*, Center for Immigration Studies, (www.cis.org/articles/1999/Backgrounder599/back599.html).

Employment and Immigration Canada (1988). *Demographic Considerations in Determining Future Levels of Immigration to Canada*, Report prepared for the Experts' meeting on Demography and Migration, OECD, Paris 3-4 October.

Evisas.com. "Frequently Asked Questions", (www.evisas.com).

Farmworker Justice Fund, Inc. (2001). *The Basics About Guestworker Programs*, (www.fwjustice.org).

Foreignborn.com (2002). "Family Immigration", (http://foreignborn.com/visas_imm/immigrant_visas/3family_immigration.htm).

Fuchs, L. (1991). *The American Kaleidoscope: Race, Ethnicity and the Civic Culture*, Wesleyan University Press.

Gurak, D. (1988). *Labor Force Status and Transitions of Dominican and Colombian Immigrants*, Paper presented at the US Department of Labor Conference on Immigration, Washington D.C., September.

Hawkins, F. (1989). *Canada and Immigration: Public Policy and Public Concern*, Montreal, McGill-Queen's University Press.

Howith, H.G. and Employment and Immigration Canada (1988). *Immigration Levels Planning: The First Decade*, Population Working Paper no.7, Policy and Programme Development Immigration.

Hugo, G. (2001). *International Migration and Agricultural Labour in Australia*, Paper prepared for Changing Face Workshop, Imperial Valley, California, 16-18 January.

Human Resources Development Canada (2002). *Tour Operators,* (http://www.hrdc-drhc.gc.ca/).

Immigration Support Services (2002). *Visa Overview*, (www.immigrationsupport.com).

Inglis, C. (2002). "Australia's Transformation." *Migration Information Source*, (www.migrationinformation.org).

IOM (International Organization for Migration), (2000). *World Migration Report 2000*, IOM and United Nations, Geneva.

Kramer, R. G. (2001). *Developments in International Migration to the United States: 2001*, Paper prepared for the Continuous Reporting System on Migration (SOPEMI) of the Organization for Economic Cooperation and Development (OECD), Paris.

Lieken, R. S. (2002). *Enchilada Lite: A Post-9/11 Mexican Migration Agreement*, Washington D.C., Centerfor Immigration Studies, March.

Ministère des Relations avec les Citoyens et de l'Immigration. *How to Immigrate,* (www.immq.gouv.qc.ca/anglais/index.html).

New Zealand Embassy in Washington D.C. (2002). Public information announcements.

New Zealand Herald (2002). "Stiffer residence rules to limit number of applicants", June 12.

New Zealand Immigration Assistance. "New Zealand Immigration Assistance Newsletter 8", (www.nzimmigration.net.nz/Pages/No8.html).

New Zealand Immigration Service (1997). *New Zealand Immigration Policy and Trends,* Paper prepared for the Population Conference, Wellington, November 13-14.

-------- *Information Facts,* (www.immigration.govt.nz/research_and_information/).

-------- *Migrating to New Zealand,* (www.immigration.govt.nz/).

-------- *Operations Manual,* (www.immigration.govt.nz/operations_manual/).

New Zealand Ministry of Education. *Education Statistics News Sheet,* (www.minedu.govt.nz/web/document/document_page.cfm?id=4629).

New Zealand Press Association (2002). *Orchardist Says Shortage of Pickers due to Waning Work-Ethic*, March 4.

New Zealand Refugee Law (2002). (www.refugee.org.nz).

Papademetriou, D. (2002). *Reflections on International Migration and its Future,* The J. Douglas Gibson Lecture, Queen's University School of Policy Studies, Kingston, Ontario.

-------- (1994). "International migration in North America: issues, policies, implications", in: *International Migration: Regional Processes and Responses.* M. Macura and D. Coleman (Eds.), New York, United Nations.

Papademetriou, D. and T. Muller (1987). *Recent Immigration to New York: Labor Market and Social Policy Issues,* Report prepared for the National Commission for Employment Policy, Washington D.C., February.

Papademetriou, D. *et al.* (1989) *The Effects of Immigration on the US Economy and Labor Market*, Division of Immigration Policy and Research, Report 1, Washington D.C., US Department of Labor.

Perez, L. (1986). "Immigrant economic adjustment and family organization: the Cuban success story reexamined", *International Migration Review,* 20(1):420.

"President Signs Nursing Relief Bill", *76 Interpreter Releases 1688,* November 22, 1999.

Ruddock, P. – Minister for Immigration. *Review of Migration Points Test,* (www.minister.immi.gov.au/advisory/ptsrev.htm).

Stelzer, I. M. (2001). *Immigration Policy for an Age of Mass Movement*, London: Institute of Economic Affairs.

331

The Globe and Mail (1999). "Could you get into Canada?", Saturday, November 13, p.A16.

Tienda, M. and R. Angel (1982). "Headship and household composition among Blacks, Hispanics, and other Whites", *Social Forces* 61(2): 508-529.

United Nations (2000). *Replacement Migration: Is It a Solution to Declining and Ageing Populations?* UN Population Division, New York.

United States Census Bureau (2000a). *Current Population Survey*, US Census Bureau, Bureau of Labour Statistics, Washington D.C.

-------- (2000b). "The foreign born population in the United States", Current Population Reports: Population Characteristics, by L. Lollock, March, (www.census.gov/prod/2000pubs/p20-534.pdf).

-------- (1996). "The foreign-born population: 1996", *Current Population Reports: Population Characteristics*, K.. Hansen and C. Faber, March, (www.census.gov/prod/2/pop/p20/p20-494.pdf).

United States Department of State (2000). *Report of the Visa Office 1998, Washington* D.C., Department of State, Bureau of Consular Affairs, December.

-------- (2001). Unpublished 2000 statistics from the Visa Office.

United States Department of State. *Tips for US visas: Employment-based visas*, (www.travel.state.gov/visa;employ-based.html).

United States Immigration and Naturalization Service (2002). *Annual Report, Legal Immigration Fiscal Year 2000,* January.

United States Immigration and Naturalization Service. *The Success of Asylum Reform and the Evolving and Expanding Role of INS Asylum Officers*, J. Langolis, (www.ins.gov/graphics/services/asylum/langlois.htm).

-------- INS *Statistical Yearbook Fiscal Year 2000,* (www.ins.gov/graphics/aboutins/statistics/IMM00yrbk/IMM2000list.htm).

-------- *Immigration Services and Benefits,* (www.ins.gov/graphics/services/index.htm)

Wial, H. (1988a). *Job Mobility Paths in Recent Immigrants in the US Labor Market,* Paper presented at the US Department of Labor Conference on Immigration, Washington D.C., September.

-------- (1988b). *The Transition from Secondary to Primary Employment: Jobs and Workers in Ethnic Neighborhood Labor Markets,* Boston, Massachusetts, Massachusetts Institute of Technology.

Zhang and Associates, P.C. (2002). *Immigration Library,* (http://www.hooyou.com/immigration_lib/index.asp).

Chapter 10

Acevedo, D. and T. Espenshade (1992). "Implications of a North American Free Trade Agreement for Mexican Migration into the United States", *Population and Development Review*, 18(4).

Altenburg, T., R. Qualmann. and J. Weller (2001). *Modernización económica y empleo en América Latina. Propuestas para un desarrollo incluyente*, CEPAL, Serie Macroeconómica del Desarrollo, División de Desarrollo Económico, Santiago de Chile.

Arbos, X. and S. Giner (1993). *La gobernabilidad: ciudadanía y democracia en la encrucijada mundial*, Siglo XXI, España Ed., Madrid.

Baeninger, R. (2000). "Brasileiros na América Latina: o que revela o Projeto IMILA-CELADE", Seminário Internacional Migrações Internacionais-Contribuições para Políticas, CNPD, Brasilia.

Calcagno, A. and L. Mármora (1993). *Migración Internacional y Desarrollo Sostenible y Compartido*, Taller de Migración y Desarrollo Humano Sostenible, PNUD-OIM, BUE/93/001.

Calcagno, A., S. Manuelito and G. Ryd (2001). "Proyecciones latinoamericanas 2000-2001", *CEPAL, Serie Estudios estadísticos y perspectivas, División de Estadísticas y Proyecciones Económicas*, Santiago de Chile.

Calva, J. (1992). *Probables efectos de un tratado de libre comercio en el Campo,* México DF, México, Fontamara.

Canales, A. (2000). "Migración y flexibilidad laboral en el contexto de NAFTA", Las migraciones internacionales 2000, *Revista Internacional de Ciencias Sociales*, no.165.

CEPAL (Comisión Económica para América Latina y el Caribe) - CELADE (Centro Latinoamericano y Caribeño de Demografía), (1999). *Migración y desarrollo en América del Norte y Centroamérica: una visión sintética,* Santiago de Chile.

CEPAL (Comisión Económica para América Latina), (2001a). *Una década de luces y sombras : América Latina y el Caribe en los años noventa,* Santiago de Chile.

-------- (2001b). *Pasado, presente y futuro del proceso de integración centroamericano,* LC/MEX/L.500.

-------- (1996). *América Latina y el Caribe, 1980-1995. 15 años de desempeño económico* (LC/G.1925), Santiago de Chile.

CEPAL-OIM (1998). *Ecuador - un examen de la migración internacional en la Comunidad Andina usando datos censales,* Proyecto SIMICA, Fascículo 5, Santiago de Chile.

Conferencia Sudamericana sobre Migraciones (2000). *Declaración*, Mayo de 2000, Buenos Aires.

Cornelius, W. (1992). "The politics and economics of reforming the ejido sector in Mexico: an overview and research agenda", *LASA Forum*, 23(3).

Cornelius, W. y P. Martin (1993). "The uncertain connection: free trade and rural Mexican migration to the United States", *International Migration Review,* vol.XXVII.

Costa-Lascoux, J. (1992). "Vers une Europe des citoyens ? ", in: J. Costa-Lascoux and P. Weil (Eds.), *Logiques d'Etats et Immigrations*, Editions Kimé, Paris.

Delegación del Gobierno para la Extranjería y la Inmigración (2000). *Anuario Estadístico de Extranjería,* Ministerio del Interior de España, Spain.

Directores Generales de Migraciones, Centroamérica (1992). "Políticas de control sobre las corrientes migratorias en Centroamérica", in: *Seminario La migración internacional: su impacto en Centroamérica*, San José de Costa Rica.

Franco, R. and P. Sáinz (2001). "La agenda social latinoamericana del año 2000", *Revista de la CEPAL*, no. 73, April 2001.

Fundación "Casa" (2001). *Encuesta a colombianos residentes en Estados Unidos*, Miami.

Granes, J., A. Morales and J.B. Meyer (1998). "Las potencialidades y limitaciones de la red Celdas de investigadores colombianos en el exterior: los proyectos internacionales conjuntos, un estudio de casos", in: J. Charum and J.B. Meyer (Eds.), *El nuevo nomadismo científico, la perspectiva latinoamericana,* Escuela Superior de Administración Pública, Bogotá.

Hinojosa Ojeda, R. (1994). "L'accord de libre-échange nord-américain et les migrations", *Migration et Developpement,* OECD, Paris.

Hinojosa Ojeda, R. and S. Robinson (1991). *Alternative Scenarios of US-Mexico Integration: A computable general equilibrium approach,* Working Paper no.609, Department of Agricultural and Resource Economics, University of California, Berkeley.

Hollifield, J. (1997). *L'immigration et l'état-nation à la recherche d'un modèle national,* L'Harmattan, Paris and Montreal.

IMILA (Investigación de la Migración Internacional en Latinoamérica.), (www.eclac.cl/celade/proyectos/migracion/IMILA00e.html).

IOM (International Organization for Migration), (1991). *Aspectos jurídicos e institucionales de las migraciones en Venezuela*, Colombia.

-------- (2000). *Informe sobre las Migraciones en el Mundo en 2000*, IOM and United Nations, Geneva.

-------- (2001). *Estudio binacional: Situación migratoria entre Costa Rica y Nicaragua*, Geneva.

Katsuco Kawamura, L. (2000). "A questão cultural e a discriminação social na migração de brasileiros ao Japão", Seminário Internacional Migrações Internacionais-Contribuições para Políticas, CNPD, Brasilia.

Klekowski von Koppenfels, A. (2001). "The Role of Regional Consultative Processes in Managing International Migration", *IOM Migration Research Series,* IOM, no.3.

León Albán, J. (1997). *Las migraciones en el Ecuador,* Quito, Ecuador.

López Bustillo, A. (2000). "Perspectivas en el ámbito de las migraciones, derivadas del objetivo adoptado por el Consejo Presidencial Andino relativo a la conformación del Mercado Común Andino para el año 2005", *Seminario Internacional de Políticas Migratorias,* Bogotá.

Maguid, A. (2001), (unpublished). *Gente en movimiento: Dinámica y movimiento de las migraciones internacionales en Centroamérica,* IOM, San José.

Mármora, L. (1994). "Desarrollo sostenido y políticas migratorias: su tratamiento en los espacios latinoamericanos de integración", *Revista de la OIM sobre Migraciones en América Latina,* 12(1/3), CIMAL (Centro de Información sobre Migraciones en América Latina) – IOM (OIM).

-------- (1995). "Logiques politiques et intégration régionale", in: *Revue Européenne des Migrations Internationales " Amérique Latine ",* 11(2), Université de Poitiers, France.

-------- (1997). *Políticas y administración para la gobernabilidad migratoria,* documento presentado por la OIM en la II Conferencia Regional de Migraciones del Proceso Puebla, Panama.

Mármora, L. and Cassarino, M. (1996). "La variable migratoria en el MERCOSUR (Su tratamiento y propuestas para la armonización de políticas)", in: *Migraciones y MERCOSUR,* Comisión Episcopal para la Pastoral de Migraciones, Fundación Comisión Católica Argentina de Migraciones, November 1996.

Marshall, R. (1993). "The implication of the North American Free Trade Agreement for workers", Backgrounder, *Center for Immigration Studies,* no.2-93.

Martin, P. (1993). "Trade and migration: the case of NAFTA", *Asian and Pacific Migration Journal,* 2(3).

Mera, C. (1997). *La emigración coreana en Buenos Aires: Multiculturalismo en el espacio urbano,* Eudeba, Buenos Aires.

Montenegro, A. and C. Posada (2001). *La violencia en Colombia,* Alfaomega-Cambio, Bogotá.

Ocampo, J.A. (2001). "La agenda pendiente", *en Notas de la CEPAL,* no.15, March.

Ortiz Miranda, C. (1993). "The North American Free Trade Agreement, Potential Migration Consequences", *Migration World,* vol.XXI, no.1.

Palau, T. and M.V. Heikel (1999). *Los campesinos, el Estado y la frontera agrícola,* Base-Pispal, Asuncion.

Patarra, N. and R. Baeninger (1996). "Migrações internacionais recentes: o caso do Brasil", in: N. Patarra, *Emigração e imigração internacionais no Brasil contemporaneo,* Programa Interinstitucional e avaliação e acompanhamento das migrações internacionais no Brasil, Campinas.

Pellegrino, A. (2000). *Migrantes latinoamericanos y caribeños: síntesis histórica y tendencias recientes,* Documento de referencia, Versión Preliminar, CEPAL-CELADE, Información sobre la migración internacional en América Latina y el Caribe (1960-1990) en base a la información censal reunida en el Proyecto IMILA, Santiago de Chile.

Pérez Vichich, N. (2002), (unpublished). *La movilidad de los trabajadores en la agenda del MERCOSUR,* Buenos Aires.

Rangel Suárez, A. (1998). *Colombia: Guerra en el fin de siglo,* Universidad de los Andes, Bogotá.

Sassen, S. (1996). *Losing control ?,* Columbia University Press, New York.

Secretaría de Estado de Relaciones Exteriores (2000). *Convenios bilaterales entre la República Dominicana y Haití,* Santo Domingo.

SIECA (Secretariat for Central American Economic Integration), (1990a). *I Reunión de la Organización Centroamericana de Migración,* San José de Costa Rica.

-------- (1990b). *II Reunión de la Organización Centroamericana de Migración,* Managua.

-------- (1991). *III Reunión de la Organización Centroamericana de Migración,* Managua.

335

Suárez Sarmiento, N. (2000). *Diagnóstico sobre las migraciones caribeñas hacia Venezuela,* PLACMI (Programa Latinoamericano de Cooperación Técnica en Materia Migratoria) - IOM.

Tapinos, G. (2000). "Mundialización, integración regional, migraciones internacionales", Las migraciones internacionales 2000, *Revista Internacional de Ciencias Sociales,* no.165, Paris.

Torales, P. (1993). *Migraciones e integración en el Cono Sur (la experiencia del MERCOSUR),* IOM, Buenos Aires.

Wihtol De Wenden, C. (1999). *Faut-il ouvrir les frontières?* Presse de Sciences Po, Paris.

Chapter 11

Alburo, F. and D. Abella (2002). *Skilled Labour Migration from Developing Countries: Case Study on the Philippines,* ILO International Migration Papers 51, ILO, Geneva.

Asian Development Bank (2001). *Key Indicators 2001,* Asian Development Bank, Manila.

Girgis, M. (2000). *National Versus Migrant Workers in the GCC: Coping with Change.* Submitted to the Mediterranean Development Forum Labour Workshop, Cairo Egypt, March 5 - 8.

ILO (International Labour Organization), (2002). *Key Indicators of the Labour Market 2001-2002,* ILO, Geneva.

IOM (International Organization for Migration), (draft report July 2002). *Migrants from the Maghreb and Mashreq countries: A Comparison of experiences in Western Europe and the Gulf region,* IOM, Geneva.

Japan Ministry of Justice (2000). *Basic Plan for Immigration Control, 2nd* edition, Tokyo.

Kapiszewski, A. (2001). *Nationals and Expatriates. Population and Labour Dilemmas of the Gulf Cooperation Council States,* Ithaca Press, Reading.

Khadria, B. (2002). *Skilled Labour Migration from Developing Countries: Study on India,* ILO International Migration Papers 50, ILO, Geneva.

Korea Ministry of Justice. *Departure and Arrival Control Year Book Series,* Seoul.

Ministry of Justice of Japan (2000). *Basic Plan for Immigration Control* (2nd edition).

Ministry of Justice of South Korea. *Departure and Arrival Control Year Book Series.*

National Bank of Kuwait (1999). *Economic and Financial Quarterly, 2*(99).

National Science Foundation (2000). *Science and Engineering Indicators 2000,* vols.1 and 2, Washington D.C.

OECD (Organization for Economic Cooperation and Development), (2001a). *SOPEMI - Trends in International Migration: Continuous Reporting System on Migration,* Annual Report, OECD, Paris.

Salt, J. (2001). *Current Trends in International Migration in Europe, Council of Europe,* Strasbourg.

Scalabrini Migration Centre, Manila, (www.scalabrini.asn.au/atlas.)

Shah, N. (1995). "Emigration dynamics from and within South Asia", *International Migration Quarterly Review,* vol.XXXIII.

Tan, E. and D. Canlas (1989). "Migrants, saving remittances and labor supply: The Philippine case", in: Rashid, A. (Ed.), *To the Gulf and Back,* International Labour Organization, Asian Regional Team on Emplyment (ARTEP), New Delhi.

United Nations (2000). *Replacement Migration: Is It a Solution to Declining and Ageing Populations* ?, UN Population Division, New York.

World Bank (2001). *World Development Indicators 2001*, Oxford University Press, New York.

-------- (2000). *Entering the 21st century World Development Report 1999-2000,* Oxford University Press, New York.

* Unpublished papers and country reports presented at the Workshop on International Migration and Labour Markets in Asia, February 2002 in Tokyo, sponsored by the Japan Institute of Labour and the Ministry of Labour of Japan, in cooperation with OECD and ILO:

Chiu, S.W.K. "Hong Kong"

Go, S. "Philippines"

Hugo, G. "Australia"

Iguchi, Y. "The Movement of the Highly-Skilled in Asia – Present Situation and Future Prospect"

Iguchi, Y. "Japan"

Kassim, A. "Malaysia"

Lee, J.S. "Chinese Taipei"

Martin, P. "Highly Skilled Asian Workers in the US"

Nguyen, X.N. "Vietnam"

OECD. "Trends in Migration Movements with a Special Focus on Asian Migration to OECD Countries"

Soeprobo, T.B. "Indonesia"

Yoo, K. "Republic of Korea"

Yap, M. "Singapore"

Yongyuth, C. "Thailand"

Zhang, F. "People's Republic of China"

Chapter 12

Adepoju, A. (1995). "Migration in Africa: an overview", in: J. Baker and T.A. Aina (Eds.), *The Migration Experience in Africa.* Nordiska Afrikainstitutet, Uppsala.

Adepoju, A. (2002). "Fostering free movement of persons in West Africa: achievements, constraints and prospects for intraregional migration", *International Migration,* 40(2), International Organization for Migration, Geneva.

Athukorala, P. (1993). *Enhancing Development Impact of Migrant Remittances: A Review of Asian Experiences,* International Labour Organization, New Dehli.

Beine, M., F. Docquier and H. Rapoport (2002). *Brain Drain and LDC's Growth – Winners and Losers,* (www.univ-lille1.fr/medee/siute/docs_fevrier_2002/2002_09_ab.pdf).

Bilsborrow, R., G. Hugo, A. Obera and H. Zlotnik (Eds.), (1997). *International Migration Statistics: Guidelines for Improving Data Collection Systems,* International Labour Organization, Geneva.

Canada Statistics, Statistics Reference Center – NCR (1996). *1996 Census,* (www.statcan.ca/english/census96/nov4/immig.htm).

Council of Europe (2001). *Demographic Yearbook,* Strasbourg, (www.coe.int/T/e/social_cohesion/population/demographic_year_book/2001_edition/).

Dodson, B. (2002). *Gender and the Brain Drain from South Africa,* Migration Policy Series no.23, South African Migration Project (SAMP), Cape Town : Institute for Democracy in South Africa (IDASA) and Kingston, Ontario, Queen's University.

Enogo, O. (2002). "Transferts d'argent bon marché", *Jeune Afrique / L'Intelligent,* no.2164, 1–7 July, Paris.

Fadayomi, T. (1996). "Brain drain and brain gain in Africa: causes, dimensions and consequences", in: T. Hammar and A. Adepoju (Eds.), *International Migration in and from Africa.* Dakar and Stockholm.

Ghosh, B. (Ed.), (2000). *Managing Migration: Time for a New International Regime ?*, Oxford University Press, Oxford.

ILO (International Labour Organization), (2000). *Making the Best of Globalisation: Migrant Worker Remittances and Micro-Finance*, Workshop Report, ILO, Geneva.

IOM (International Organization for Migration), (2000). *The Link between Migration and Development in the Least Developed Countries – IOM's Vision and Problematic Approach.* IOM, Geneva.

-------- (2002a). *International Dialogue on Migration – 82nd Session of the Council 27-29 November 2001,* IOM Migration Policy and Research Programme, Geneva.

-------- (2002b). *The Migration-Development Nexus – Evidence and Policy Options,* IOM Migration Research Series, no.8, Geneva.

Iredale, R. (2001). "The migration of professionals: theories and typologies", *International Migration,* 39(5), SI 1/2001.

Krahnen, J. and R. Schmidt (1995). *On the Theory of Credit Cooperatives: Equity and Onlending in a Multi-Tier System,* ILO working paper, no.11, Geneva.

Lowell, L. (2001). *Some Developmental Effects of the International Migration of Highly Skilled Persons,* ILO International Migration Papers, no.46, Geneva.

Mattes, R. and W. Richmond (2000). "The brain drain: What do skilled South Africans think ?", in J. Crush (Ed.), *Losing Our Minds: Skills Migration and the South African Brain Drain.* Migration Policy Series, no.18. Institute for Democracy in South Africa (IDASA), Cape Town and Queen's University, Kingston, Ontario.

McDonald, D. and J. Crush (2000). "Understanding skilled migration in Southern Africa", *Africa Insight 30(2)3-9. The Brain Drain: Will the outflow of skilled people kill the African Renaissance?*

Oucho, J. (1996). *Urban Migrants and Rural Development in Kenya.* Nairobi University Press, Nairobi.

-------- (2001a). "International migration, xenophobia and social exclusion in Southern Africa", presented at the *Southern African Research Institute for Policy Analysis (SARIPS) Annual Colloquium 2001*, Harare, Zimbabwe, October 23-26.

-------- (2001b). *Does Migration Foster or Stifle Development ?*, Professorial Inaugural Lecture delivered at the University of Botswana, 10 October.

Puri, S. and T. Ritzema (1999). *Migrant Worker Remittances, Micro-finance and the Informal Economy: Prospects and Issues,* ILO working paper, no.21. Geneva.

Salt, J. (1993). "External international migration", in: D. Noin and R. Woods (Eds.), *The changing population of Europe.* Oxford, Blackwell.

Selassie, G. and T.L. Weiss (2002). "The brain drain – Africa's Achilles heel", *World Markets in Focus 2002,* World Markets Research Centre, London.

Stalker, P. (1994). *The Work of Strangers: A Survey of International Migration.* International Labour Organization, Geneva.

Tettey, W. (2002). "Africa's brain drain: exploring possibilities for its positive utilization through the networked communities", *Mots Pluriels*, no.20, February.

US Department of Justice and Immigration and Naturalization Service (1999). *Statistical Yearbook*, Washington D.C., (www.ins.usdoj.gov/graphics/aboutins/statistics/index.htm).

Weiss, T.L. (1998). *Migrants nigérians - La diaspora dans le Sud-Ouest du Cameroun,* Editions L'Harmattan, Culture et Politique, Collection Géographie et Cultures, Paris.

-------- (2001). "L'Afrique à la poursuite de ses cerveaux", *Jeune Afrique / L'intelligent*, no.2104, 8-14 May, Paris.

World Bank (1998). *Workers in an Integrating World - World Development Report*, Oxford University Press, New York.

-------- (2001). *World Development Indicators 2001,* World Bank Group – Development Data, (www.worldbank.org/data/wdi2001/).

World Bank and International Bank for Reconstruction and Development (2000). *Entering the 21st century - World Development Report*, Oxford University Press, New York.

339

Chapter 13

Apap, J. (2001). *Shaping Europe's Migration Policy, New Regimes for the Employment of Third Country Nationals: A Comparison of Strategies in Germany, Sweden, the Netherlands and the UK*, Centre for European Policy Studies, Working Documents, no.179, Brussels.

Brücker, H. (2002). *Can International Migration Solve the Problems of European Labour Markets?*, United Nations Commission for Europe, Economic Survey of Europe, no.2.

Coleman, D. (1992). "Does Europe need immigrants ? Population and work force projections", *International Migration Review*, 26(2):413-461, Summer, New York.

-------- (1995). "International migration: demographic and socio economic consequences in the United Kingdom and Europe", *International Migration Review*, 29(1):155-206, Spring, New York.

-------- (2002). *The European Demographic Future: its History and Challenges,* Paper presented at the conference The Political Economy of Global Change 1950-2050, Bellagio, Italy, April, 8-12.

ECOTEC (2001). *Admission of Third Country Nationals for Paid Employment or Self Employed Activity*, ECOTEC, Brussels.

European Commission (2000). Communication from the Commission to the Council and the European Parliament on a community immigration policy, COM(2000)757 final.

Feld, S. (2000). "Active Population Growth and Immigration Hypotheses in Western Europe", *European Journal of Population,* 16(1):3-40, Kluwer, the Netherlands.

Home Office (2002). Secure Borders, Safe Haven: Integration with Diversity in Modern Britain, CM 5387, Home Office, London.

Independent Commission on Migration to Germany (2001). Structuring Immigration, Fostering Integration, Berlin.

IOM (International Organization for Migration), (2000). *World Migration Report 2000.* IOM and United Nations, Geneva.

König, K., D. Schwab and P. Zuser (2001). *Migrantinnen in Wien 2000,* Wiener Integrationsfonds, Wien.

Münz, R. and H. Fassmann (2002). "EU enlargement and future East-West migration", in: *New Challenges for Migration Policy in Central and Eastern Europe,* IOM/UN, Geneva.

Laczko, F. (2002). "New directions for migration policy in Europe", *Philosophical Transactions of the Royal Society of London*, Series B, 29 April 2002, 357(1420), London.

OECD (Organization for Economic Cooperation & Development), (1991). *Migration: The Demographic Aspects,* OECD, Paris.

-------- (1998). *Ageing Populations: The Social Policy Implications*, OECD, Paris.

-------- (2000). *SOPEMI - Trends in International Migration: Continuous Reporting System on Migration,* Annual Report 2000, OECD, Paris.

----- (2002). *SOPEMI - Trends in International Migration: Continuous Reporting System on Migration,* Annual Report 2002, OECD, Paris.

Reuters (2002). "EU Immigration Factbox", 25 April, London.

Salt, J. (2000). Current Trends in International Migration in Europe, *Council of Europe*, Strasbourg.

Spencer, S. (2001). "UK migration policy 2001", in: Policy Recommendations for EU Migration Policies, King Baudouin Foundation, Brussels, Belgium.

Stalker, P. (1994). The Work of Strangers, International Labour Organization, Geneva.

Tapinos, G. (2000). Le rôle des migrations dans l'attenuation des effets du vieillissement démographique, OCDE, Groupe de travail sur les migrations, Paris.

United Nations (2000). *Replacement Migration: Is It a Solution to Declining and Ageing Populations?, UN Population* Division, New York.

Chapter 14

Official EU Documents/Communications

European Commision (1994). *Communication from the Commission to the Council and the European Parliament on Immigration and Asylum Policies.* COM(1994)23.

-------- (1999). *Proposal for a Council Directive on the Right to Family Reunification.* (1999)638.

-------- (2000). *Amended Proposal for a Council Directive on the Right to Family Reunification.* COM(2000)624.

-------- (2000). *Communication on a Common Asylum Procedure and a Uniform Statute Valid throughout the Union for Persons who are Granted Asylum.* COM(2000)755.

-------- (2000). *Communication on a Community Immigration Policy.* COM(2000)755.

-------- (2001). *Proposal for a Council Directive Concerning the Status of Third Country Nationals who are Long Term Residents.* COM(2001)127.

-------- (2001). *Proposal for a Council Directive Laying down Minimum Standards on the Reception of Applicants for Asylum in Member States.* COM(2001)181.

-------- (2001). *Proposal for a Council Directive on the Conditions of Entry and Residence of Third-Country Nationals for the Purpose of Paid eEmployment and Self-Employed Economic Activities.* COM(2001)386.

-------- (2001). *Proposal for a Council Regulation Establishing the Criteria and Mechanisms for Determining the Member State Responsible for Examining an Asylum Application Lodged in One of the Member States by a Third Country National*(Dublin II). COM(2001)447.

-------- (2001). *Proposal for a Council Directive Laying Down Minimum Standards for the Qualification and Status of Third Country Nationals and Stateless Persons as Refugees, in Accordance with the 1951 Convention Relating to the Status of Refugees and the 1967 Protocol, or as Persons who otherwise Need International Protection.* COM(2001)510.

-------- (2001). *Communication on a Common Policy on Illegal Immigration.* COM(2001)672.

-------- (2001). *Communication from the Commission to the Council and the European Parliament on the Common Asylum Policy, Introducing an Open Coordination Method (First report by the Commission on the application of communication* COM (755) final of 22.11.01). COM(2001)710.

-------- (2002). *Amended Proposal for a Council Directive on the Right to Family Reunification.* COM(2002)225.

-------- (2002). *Communication on a Community Return Policy on Illegal Residents.* COM(2002)175.

-------- (2002). *Communication Towards Integrated Management of the External Borders of the Member States of the European Union.* COM(2002)233.

-------- (2002). *Biannual Update of the Scoreboard to Review Progress on the Creation of an Area of "Freedom, Security and Justice" in the European Union.* COM(2002)261.

Council Decision of 28 September 2000: Council Decision 2000/596/EC.

Council Decision of 11 December 2000: Council Regulation 2000/2725/EC.

Council Decision of 20 July 2001: Council Directive 2001/55/EC.

Cholewinski, R. (2002). *Borders and Discrimination in the European Union*, Immigration Law Practitioners' Association, London, Migration Policy Group, Brussels.

Council of Europe (2002). *Collection of Treaties - Migration,* Council of Europe Publishing, Strasbourg.

Guild, E. (2001). *Immigration Law in the European Community*, Kluwer Law International, The Hague, Immigration and Asylum Law and Policy in Europe, vol.2.

Guild, E. and C. Harlow (2001), (Eds.). *Implementing Amsterdam: Immigration and Asylum rights in EC Law*, Hart Publishing, Oxford and Portland, Oregon.

Guild, E. and P. Minderhoud (2001), (Eds.). *Security of Residence and Expulsion: Protection of Aliens in Europe*, Kluwer Law International, The Hague, Immigration and Asylum Law and Policy in Europe, vol.1.

Magnusson, L. and J. Ottosson (2002), (Eds.). *Europe - One Labour Market ?*, P.I.E. - Peter Lang, Brussels, Work and Society, no.30.

McLaughlin, G. and J. Salt (2002). *Migration Policies towards Highly-Skilled Workers: Report to the Home Office,* London.

Melis, B. (2001). *Negotiating Europe's Immigration Frontiers*, Kluwer Law International, The Hague, Immigration and Asylum Law and Policy in Europe, vol. 3.

Nascimbene, B. (2001), (Ed.). *Expulsion and Detention of Aliens in the European Union Countries - L'éloignement et la détention des étrangers dans les Etats membres de l'Union Européenne,* Giuffrè Editore, Milan.

Regioplan (2001). *Undeclared Labour in Europe. Towards an Integrated Approach of Combating Undeclared Labour,* October, Regioplan Publications no.424, Regioplan Research Advice and Information.

Van Krieken, P.J. (2001), (Ed.). *The Migration Acquis Handbook,* T.M.C.Asser Press, The Hague, The Netherlands.

Chapter 15

Christian, B. P. (2000). *Facilitating High Skilled Migration to Advanced Industrial Countries:* Comparative Policies, Georgetown University.

Council of Europe (1997). *The Convention on the Protection of the Rights of all Migrant Workers and Members of their Families,* European Court of Human Rights, Strasbourg.

Doomernik, J. (1998). *The Effectiveness of Integration Policies Towards Immigrants and Their Descendants in France, Germany and the Netherlands,* International Migration Papers, no.27, ILO, Geneva.

ECOTEC (2001). *Admission of Third Country Nationals for Paid Employment or Self-Employed Activity,* ECOTEC, Brussels.

European Commission (2000a). *Communication from the Commission to the Council and the European Parliament on a Community Immigration Policy,* COM (2000)757 final.

-------- (2000b). *Communication from the Commission to the Council and the European Parliament – "Towards a Common Asylum Procedure and a Uniform Status, Valid throughout the Union, for Persons Granted Asylum".* COM (2000)755 final.

-------- (2000c). *Amended Proposal for a Council Directive on the Right to Family Reunification.* COM (2000)624 final.

-------- (2001a). *Communication from the Commission to the Council and the European Parliament on a Common Policy on Illegal Immigration.* COM (2001)672 final.

-------- (2001b). *Proposal for a Council Directive on the Conditions of Entry and Residence of Third-Country Nationals for the Purpose of Paid Employment and Self-Employed Economic Activities.* COM (2001)386 final.

-------- (2001c). *Communication from the Commission to the Council and the European Parliament on an Open Method of Coordination for the Community Immigration Policy.* COM(2001)387.

-------- (2002). *Green Paper on a Community Return Policy on Illegal Residents.* COM (2002)175 final.

Ghosh, B. (Ed.), (2000). *Managing Migration – Time for a New International Regime?,* Oxford University Press, Oxford.

Glover, S. et al. (2001). *Migration: An Economic and Social Analysis,* RDS Occasional Paper no.67, Home Office, London.

Hammar, T. and G. Brodmann (Eds.), (1999). *Mechanisms of Immigration Control: A Comparative Analysis of European Regulation Policies,* Oxford, Berghahn.

343

Henshall Momsen, J. (1999). *Gender, Migration and Domestic Service*, Routledge International Studies of Women and Place, Routledge, London.

Hughes, R. (1993). *Culture of Complaint: The Fraying of America,* Oxford University Press, Oxford.

ICMPD (International Center for Migration Policy Development), (1999). *Return of Illegal Migrants,* draft report by the Secretariat of the Budapest Group for the meeting on return and readmission in Paris, ICMPD, Vienna.

Independent Commission on Migration to Germany (2001). *Structuring Immigration, Fostering Integration,* Ministry of the Interior, Berlin.

ILO (International Labour Organization), (1999). *Migrant Workers*, International Labour Conference, eighty-seventh session, report III (part 1b), Geneva.

IOM (International Organization for Migration), (1997a). *IOM Return Policy and Programmes: A Contribution to Combating Irregular Migration*, Document presented at the 74th Session of the Council. MC/INF/236.

-------- (1997b). *The Return of Irregular Migrants: The Challenge for Central and Eastern Europe.* Report prepared for the Odysseus Programme of the European Commission by the Technical Cooperation Centre for Europe and Central Asia, IOM, Vienna.

-------- (1999). *Trafficking in Persons: Update and Perspectives,* Document prepared for the 80th Session of the Council. MC/INF/245.

-------- (2000). *World Migration Report 2000.* IOM and United Nations, Geneva.

-------- (2001). *Trafficking in Unaccompanied Minors for Sexual Exploitation in the European Union,* Pilot Project on the Fight against Trafficking in Human Beings, Research and Networking on Unaccompanied Minors in the European Union, STOP programme, Brussels.

-------- (2002a). *International Dialogue on Migration – 82nd Session of the Council 27-29 November 2001,* IOM Migration Policy and Research Programme, Geneva.

-------- (2002b), (in draft). *Principles and Operational Guidelines for Assisted Voluntary Return and Reintegration of Migrants,* IOM, Geneva.

Koser, K. (2001). *The Return and Reintegration of Rejected Asylum Seekers and Irregular Migrants,* IOM Migration Research Series, no.4, IOM, Geneva.

Lowell, B.L. and A.M. Findlay (2001). *Migration of Highly Skilled Persons from Developing Countries: Impact and Policy Responses,* Final Draft Synthesis Report, ILO Geneva.

Martin, P. and M. Miller (2000). *Employer Sanctions: French, German and US Experiences*, International Migration Papers, no.36, ILO, Geneva.

Martin, P. and S. Martin (2001a). "Heavy traffic: International migration in an era of globalization", *Brookings Review,* 19(4):41-44, The Brookings Institute, Washington D.C.

-------- (2001b). "Immigration and terrorism policy reform challenges", in: *Policy Recommendations for EU Migration Policies,* German Marshall Fund of the United States, Washington D.C. and King Baudouin Foundation, Brussels.

National Intelligence Council (2000). *Global Trends 2015. A Dialogue About the Future with Nongovernment Experts*, Government Printing Office, Washington D.C.

Nyberg-Sorensen, N., N. Van Hear and P. Engberg-Pedersen (2002). *The Migration-Development Nexus. Evidence and Policy Options*, Centre for Development Research, Copenhagen.

OECD (Organization for Economic Cooperation and Development), (2001a). SOPEMI - *Trends in International Migration: Continuous Reporting System on Migration,* Annual Report 2001, OECD, Paris.

-------- (2001b). *Principal Conclusions and Follow-Up Of the Seminar on "International Mobility of Highly Skilled Workers: From Statistical Analysis to the Formulation of Policies"*, OECD, Paris.

Salt, J. (2000). *Towards a Migration Management Strategy*, Report of the restricted working group on a migration management strategy and summary of the proceedings of the seminar on managing migration in the wider Europe, CDMG (2000)11rev., Council of Europe, Strasbourg.

Sohn, L.B. and T. Buergenthal (Eds.), (1992). *The Movement of Persons Across Borders*, Studies in Transnational Legal Policy no.23, American Society of International Law, Washington D.C.

Somavia, J. (2002). "The world's people need decent jobs", *International Herald Tribune*, 27 August.

United Kingdom Home Office (2002). *Secure Borders, Safe Haven: Integration with Diversity in Modern Britain*, London.

United Nations (2000a). *Replacement Migration: Is it a Solution to Declining and Ageing Populations ?*, UN Population Division, New York.

-------- (2000b). *United Nations Convention against Transnational Organized Crime*, signed in Palermo on 15 December.

-------- (2000c). *Protocol to Prevent, Suppress and Punish Trafficking in Persons, especially Women and Children, Supplementing the United Nations Convention against Transnational Organized Crime.*

-------- (2000d). *Protocol against the Smuggling of Migrants by Land, Air and Sea, Supplementing the United Nations Convention against Transnational Organized Crime.*

-------- (2001). *Review of Reports, Studies and Other Documentation for the Preparatory Committee and the World Conference against Racism, Racial Discrimination, Xenophobia and Related Intolerance. A/CONF.189/PC.3/5.*

UNECLAC (United Nations Economic Commissions for Latin America and the Caribbean), (2002). *Globalization and Development,* UN/ECLAC, Santiago de Chile.

UNHCR (United Nations High Commissioner for Refugees), (2000). *Reconciling Migration Control and Refugee Protection in the European Union: A UNHCR perspective,* UNHCR discussion paper, Geneva.

US Department of State (2001). *Trafficking in Persons Report June 2001: Victims of Trafficking and Violence Protection Act 2000,* Washington D.C.

-------- (2002). *Trafficking in Persons Report June 2002: Victims of Trafficking and Violence Protection Act 2000,* Washington D.C.

345

Van Krieken, P. (Ed.), (2001a). *Health, Migration and Return: A Handbook for a Multidisciplinary Approach.* T.M.C. Asser Press, The Hague.

-------- (Ed.), (2001b). *The Migration Acquis Handbook: The Foundation for a Common European Migration Policy,* T.M.C. Asser Press, The Hague.

Van Krieken, P. and O. Ungureanu (2002). *The Migration Acquis 2002 Update*, International Organization for Migration, Vienna.

World Bank (2000). *Engendering Development: Through Gender Equality in Rights, Resources, and Voice,* Oxford University Press, New York.

-------- (2001). *Globalization, Growth and Poverty: Building an Inclusive World Economy,* World Bank Research Report, Washington D.C. and Oxford University Press, New York.

Chapter 16

Bilsborrow, R.E., H. Graeme, A. S. Oberai and H. Zlotnik (1997). *International Migration Statistics : Guidelines for Improving Data Collection Systems,* International Labour Organization, Geneva.

United Nations (1949). *Problems of Migration Statistics,* Population Studies, no.5, New York.

-------- (1953). *International Migration Statistics,* Statistical Papers, no.20.

-------- (1978). *Demographic Yearbook 1977.*

-------- (1980). *Recommendations on Statistics of International Migration,* Statistical Papers, no.58.

-------- (1985). *Consolidated Statistics on All International Arrivals and Departures: A Technical Report,* Studies in Methods, Series F, no.36.

-------- (1991). *Demographic Yearbook 1989.*

-------- (1998a). *Recommendations on Statistics of International Migration: Revision 1*, Statistical Papers, no.58, rev.1.

-------- (1998b). *Principles and Recommendations for Population and Housing Censuses: Revision 1.*, Statistical Papers, series M, no.7/rev.1.

-------- (2000). *Draft Manual on Statistics on International Trade in Services*, United Nations Publications.

United States Immigration and Naturalization Service (1993). *1993 Statistical Yearbook of the Immigration and Naturalization Service,* Government Printing Office, Washington D.C.

Zlotnik, H. (1987). "The concept of international migration as reflected in data collection systems", *International Migration Review*, 21(4):925-946, Winter, New York.

Chapter 17

Caritas (2002). *Immigrazione – Dossier Statistico 2002 – XII Rapporto Sull'Immigrazione Caritas-Migrantes,* Nuovo Anterem, Rome.

Council of Europe (2002). *Recent Demographic Developments in Europe 2001*, Council of Europe Publishing, Strasbourg.

The Economist / Francis Cairncross (2002). "A Survey of Migration", *The Economist,* 365(8297), 2-8 November, London

EUROSTAT and the Directorate General for Employment and Social Affairs (2002). *The Social Situation in the European Union 2002,* Brussels.

Gammeltoft, P. (2002). *Remittances and other financial flows to developing countries*, expert working paper prepared for the Centre for Development Research Study: Migration-Development Links - Evidence and Policy Options, March.

Global IDP Project (2002). *A global overview of internal displacement.* (www.db.idpproject.org).

McClure, I. (2000). "Migrant workers – give them their due", in : ILO. *Gender! Partnerships of Equals: Migrant workers, give them their due,* ILO, Geneva.

ILO (International Labour Organization), (2002). *Document GB/283/2/1 of the 283rd session of the Governing Body,* March, Geneva.

IMF (International Monetary Fund). *Balance of Payments Statistics - Yearbooks,* Washington D.C.

Kvinnaforum (1999). *Crossing Borders against Trafficking in Women and Girls. A Resource Book for Working against Trafficking in the Baltic Sea.* Stockholm – quoted by UNICEF *et al.* (2002).

Martin, S. (2001). *Remittance Flows and Impact*, paper prepared for the Regional Conference on Remittances as a Development Tool, organized by the Multilateral Investment Fund of the Inter-American Development Bank.

OECD (Organization for Economic Cooperation and Development), (2001). SOPEMI - *Trends in International Migration: Continuous Reporting System on Migration*, Annual Report 2001, OECD, Paris.

Papademetriou, D. (2003). *Traditional Countries of Immigration,* World Migration 2003 – Challenges and Responses for People on the Move, International Organization for Migration, World Migration Report Series, vol.2, chapter 9, Geneva.

Population Reference Bureau (2002). *International Migration: Facing the Challenge,* 57(1), Washington D.C.

Salt, J. (2001). *Current Trends in International Migration in Europe,* Council of Europe, Strasbourg.

Somavia, J. (2002). "The world's people need decent jobs", *International Herald Tribune,* 27 August.

UNESCO (United Nations Educational, Scientific and Cultural Organization), (1999). *UNESCO Statistical Yearbook 1999,* UNESCO Publishing, Paris.

UNHCR (United Nations High Commissioner for Refugees), (2002a). *Trends in Asylum Applications in Europe, North America, Australia, New Zealand and Japan,* January – June, UNHCR, Geneva.

-------- (2002b). *Statistical Yearbook 2001*, UNHCR Population Data Unit, Population and Geographic Data Section, Geneva.

UNICEF (United Nations Children Fund), UNHCHR (United Nations Office of the High Commissioner for Human Rights), OSCE-ODIHR (Organisation for Security and Cooperation in Europe - Office for Democratic Institutions and Human Rights), (2002). *Trafficking in Human Beings in Southeastern Europe.* UNICEF, UNOHCHR, OSCE-ODIHR, Warsaw.

United Nations (1999). *The World at 6 Billion*, United Nations Population Division, New York.

-------- (2000). *The World's Women 2000: Trends and Statistics,* United Nations Statistics Division, New York.

-------- (2002). *Activities of the United Nations Statistics Division on International Migration,* United Nations Statistics Division, New York.

-------- (2002). *International Migration 2002 – Wallchart,* United Nations Population Division, New York.

Unites States Department of State (2001). *Victims of Trafficking and Violence Protection Act of 2000, Trafficking in Persons Report,* Washington D.C.

World Bank (2002). *2002 World Development Indicators,* World Bank, Washington D.C.

Zlotnik, H. (1998). *The Dimensions of International Migration: International Migration Levels, Trends and What Existing Data Systems Reveal*, paper prepared for the Technical Symposium on International Migration and Development, The Hague, 29 June – 3 July.

Acronyms and Abbreviations

"5 + 5"	Western Mediterranean Conference on Migration
AALCO	Asian-African Legal Consultative Organization
ACP	African, Caribbean and Pacific countries
AEC	African Economic Community
AGAMI	Action Group on Asylum and Migration Issues
AMUCIB	*Asociación de Mujeres Campesinas e Indígenas de Buenaventura* (NGO)
APC	Intergovernmental Asia-Pacific Consultations
APEC	Asia-Pacific Economic Cooperation
ASEAN	Association of South-East Asian Nations
ASEM	Asia-Europe Meeting
AVR	Assisted Voluntary Return
AVU	African Virtual University
BFA	Boao Forum for Asia
CARICOM	Caribbean Community
CAR	Central African Republic
CDC	Center for Disease Control and Prevention (United States)
CEDAW	Convention on the Elimination of all Forms of Discrimination Against Women
CEE	Central and Eastern Europe
CELADE	*Centro Latinoamericano y Caribeño de Demografía Centroamericana*
CEPAL	*Comisión Económica para América Latina y el Caribe*
CIAT	*Centro Interamericano de Administración del Trabajo*
CIC	Citizenship and Immigration Canada
CIDA	Canadian International Development Agency
CIPROM	*Comité Interinstitucional de Protección de la Mujer Migrante*
CIS	Commonwealth of Independent States
CODHES	*Consultoría para los Derechos Humanos y el Desplazamiento* (NGO)
COIN	*Centro de Orientación e Investigación Integral* (NGO)
COMESA	Common Market for Eastern and Southern Africa
CPA	Comprehensive Plan of Action
DAS	*Datos de la Dirección de Extranjería, Departamento Administrativo de Seguridad* (Colombia)
DIMIA	Department of Immigration and Multicultural and Indigenous Affairs (Australia)
DRC	Democratic Republic of the Congo
EAC	East African Community
ECHR	European Convention on Human Rights
ECOSOC	Economic and Social Council (United Nations)
ECOWAS	Economic Community of West African States
ELN	*Ejército de Liberación Nacional* (Colombia)
ERC	Emergency Relief Coordinator
ESC	European Social Charter
EU	European Union
EXCOM	Executive Committee (IOM)
FAO	Food and Agriculture Organization (United Nations)
FARC	*Fuerzas Armadas Revolucionarias de Colombia*
FCES	*Foro Consultivo Económico y Social*
FDI	Foreign Direct Investment
FLACSO	*Facultad Latinoamericana de Ciencias Sociales*
FRY	Federal Republic of Yugoslavia

FYROM	Former Yugoslav Republic of Macedonia
GATS	General Agreement on Trade in Services
GATT	General Agreement on Tariffs and Trade
GCC	Gulf Cooperation Council
GDP	Gross Domestic Product
GNP	Gross National Product
HIV/AIDS	Human Immunodeficiency Virus/ Acquired Immune Deficiency Syndrome
HRD	Human Resources Development
IASC	Inter-Agency Standing Committee
ICEM	Intergovernmental Committee for European Migration
ICM	Intergovernmental Committee for Migration
ICMPD	International Centre for Migration Policy Development
ICPD	International Conference on Population and Development ("Cairo Conference")
ICRC	International Committee of the Red Cross
ICT	Information and Communication Technology
ICVA	International Council of Voluntary Agencies
IDASA	Institute for Democracy in South Africa
IDPs	Internally Displaced Persons
IFRC	International Federation of Red Cross and Red Crescent Societies
IGC	Intergovernmental Consultations on Asylum, Refugees and Migration Policies in Europe, North America and Australia
ILO	International Labour Organization
IMILA	International Migration in Latin America
IMP	International Migration Policy Programme
INA	Immigration and Nationality Act (United States)
INS	Immigration and Naturalization Service (United States)
IOM	International Organization for Migration
IRC	International Rescue Committee
IRSS	Immigration Research and Statistics Service
ISS	International Social Services
IT	Information Technology
LA	Labour Agreement
LFPR	Labour Force Proportion Rate
LPR	Lawful Permanent Residence
MDR-TB	Multi-Drug Resistant Tuberculosis
MERCOSUR	South American Common Market
MHS	Migration Health Services (IOM)
MIDA	Migration for Development in Africa
MIDSA	Migration Dialogue for Southern Africa
MIDWA	Migration Dialogue for West Africa
MODL	Migration Occupations Demand List
MPMC	Multicultural Policies and Modes of Citizenship in European Cities
MPRP	Migration Policy and Research Programme (IOM)
MRCI	*Ministère des Relations avec les Citoyens et de l'Immigration* (Quebec, Canada)
NACARA	Nicaraguan Adjustment and Central American Relief Act of 1997
NAFTA	North America Free Trade Agreement
NBK	National Bank of Kuwait
NEPAD	New Partnership for Africa's Development
NGO	Non-Governmental Organization
NIC	National Intelligence Council
NZIS	New Zealand Immigration Service

OAS	Organization of American States
OAU	Organization of African Unity
OCAM	*Organización Centroamericana de Migraciones*
OCHA	Office for Coordination of Humanitarian Affairs (United Nations)
ODA	Official Development Aid
ODIHR	Office for Democratic Institutions and Human Rights
OECD	Organization for Economic Cooperation and Development
OSCE	Organization for Security and Cooperation in Europe
OTE	*Office des Tunisiens à l'Étranger* (Tunisia)
OTI	Office of Transition Initiatives (United States)
PIF	Pacific Island Forum
PISA	Programme for International Student Assessment
POEs	Ports of Entry
PPP	Purchasing Power Parity
PREALC	*Programa de Empleo para América Latina y el Caribe*
PRM	Bureau of Population, Refugees and Migration (United States)
RB	Refugee Board (Canada)
RCM	Regional Conference on Migration ("Puebla Process")
RCM	Regional Cooperation Model (Australia – Indonesia)
RCP	Regional Consultative Process
REAG	Reintegration and Emigration of Asylum Seekers from Germany
RQAN	Return and Reintegration of Qualified African Nationals Programme (IOM)
SAARC	South Asian Association for Regional Cooperation
SAC	Special Assistance Category
SADC	Southern African Development Community
SAMP	Southern African Migration Project
SAP	Structural Adjustment Programme
SARIPS	Southern African Research Institute for Policy Analysis
SEL	*Sociedad de Estudios Laborales* (Argentina)
SHP	Special Humanitarian Programmes
SIECA	*Secretaría Permanente del Tratado General de Integración Económica*
SOA	Summit of the Americas
STI	Sexually Transmitted Infections
TB	Tuberculosis
TCIs	Traditional Countries of Immigration
TPV	Temporary Protection Visa
TSU	Technical Support Unit
UAMs	Unaccompanied Minors
UK	United Kingdom
UNAIDS	Joint United Nations Programme on HIV/AIDS
UNDP	United Nations Development Programme
UNECLAC	United Nations Economic Commission for Latin America and the Caribbean
UNESCO	United Nations Educational, Scientific and Cultural Organization
UNFPA	United Nations Population Fund (formerly United Nations Fund for Population Activities)
UNHCHR	United Nations Office of the High Commissioner for Human Rights
UNHCR	United Nations High Commissioner for Refugees
UNICEF	United Nations Children Fund
UNITAR	United Nations Institute for Training and Research
UNPD	United Nations Population Division
USA	United States of America

351

USAID	United States Agency for International Development (AID)
USRP	United States Refugees Programme
USSR	Union of Soviet Socialist Republics
WFP	World Food Program (United Nations)
WHM	Working Holidaymakers
WHO	World Health Organization (United Nations)
WIN	*Wet Inburgering Nieuwkomer* (the Netherlands)
WTO	World Trade Organization

Alphabetical Index

3D - jobs (dirty,
difficult and dangerous)   p. 206
Action Group on Asylum
and Migration Issues (AGAMI)   – international refugee protection
Afghanistan   p. 14, 29, 35, 104, 137, 242, 279, 312-313, 315
    Assisted voluntary return p. 279
    IDPs p. 117-118
    Migration trends p. 35
Africa   p. 16, 25, 29, 89, 138, 215-238, 303-304, 306, 308-309, 312
    Diaspora p. 37, 219-232
    IDPs p. 112
    Irregular employment p. 67
    Migration trends p. 37-40
    Migration management p. 233

African, Caribbean
and Pacific countries (ACPs)   p. 138 ,260-261
Agenda for protection   -international refugee protection
Albania   p. 44, 68, 137, 175, 241, 306
    labour migration p. 51-52
Algeria   p. 37, 45, 94, 137, 216-217, 219, 224, 247, 310, 314
Andean Pact   p. 33
Angola   p. 102, 104, 137, 217, 219, 278, 312-314
Argentina   p. 17, 32-33, 62-63, 137, 174, 176, 182, 185, 188-189, 309-315
    Corralito (monetary restrictions) p. 190-191
    Effects of economic crisis on migration p. 190-191
    Emigration flow p. 188-189
Armenia   p. 43, 137, 242, 313-314
Asia   p. 16, 25, 29-30, 127, 138, 195-14, 216, 303-304, 308-309, 311-312
    Chinese irregular migrants p. 198
    Feminization of migration p. 7, 276-277
    Financial crisis p. 203-213
    Highly skilled migration p. 200
    Human trafficking p. 35
    Labour migration p. 17
    Labour-sending countries p. 212
    Migration trends p. 34-36
    Regional Consultative Process (Bali Process) p. 137-138
    United States H-1B visas p. 211
Asia-Europe Meeting (ASEM)   p. 138, 199, 266, 285
Assimilation   -integration
Assisted voluntary return   p. 42, 278-281
    Kosovo p. 279
    Afghanistan p. 279
Association of South-East Asian Nations
(ASEAN)   p. 130, 133, 138, 210
Asylum management approaches   *United States* p. 105
    Australia p. 105
Asylum seekers   Traditional countries of immigration p. 156

	-international refugee protection
Australia	p. 27-29, 68, 86, 138, 142-172, 193, 198-199, 201, 210, 249-250, 281, 305-306, 309-310, 314
	Asylum management approaches p. 103, 105
	Economic immigration p. 161
	Family immigration p. 161
	Humanitarian immigration p. 161
	Immigration policy p. 36
	Migration trends p. 35-36
	Point system p. 36, 171
	Special Assistance Category (SAC) p. 152
	Special Humanitarian Programs (SHP) p. 152
	Temporary Protection Visa (TPV) p. 152
	Trans-Tasman Travel Agreement p. 36
	Working temporarily p. 168
Austria	p. 28, 44, 137, 240, 243-244, 246, 249-250, 273, 307
AVR	-Assisted voluntary return
Azerbaijan	p. 43, 137, 242, 314
Bahamas	p. 175
Bali Process	p. 137-138
Balkans	p. 44, 61, 198, 252
Bangladesh	p. 28, 34, 63, 137, 204, 208-209, 231-232, 304-305, 311, 314
Belarus	p. 137, 203, 243-244
Belize	p. 137, 184
Belgium	p. 28, 42, 44, 58, 82, 137, 215-216, 224, 231, 239, 245-246, 249-250, 253, 261, 268, 308-309
Benin	p. 219, 275
Berne Initiative	p. 109, 136, 285-287
boat people	p. 134
bona fide refugees	-international refugee protection
Bolivia	p. 17, 32-33, 137, 174, 176, 179-180, 188
Bosnia-Herzegovina	p. 35, 44, 81, 91, 103, 137, 279, 305, 312, 314
Botswana	p. 39-40, 137, 217-219, 223
Brain circulation	p. 215
Brain drain	p. 11, 29, 192, 212, 215-238
Brazil	p. 28, 32-33, 176-177, 188, 192-193, 311
	Brasiguays p. 33
	Emigration p. 193
	Nikkeijin p. 33
Brunei	p. 35, 137, 199, 213
Budapest Process	p. 124, 137-138
Bulgaria	p. 44, 137, 241, 243-244, 310, 315
Burkina Faso	p. 38, 137, 216-217, 219-221, 224, 226-228, 230, 275
Burundi	p. 39, 219, 312, 314
Cambodia	p. 35, 63, 137, 202
Cameroon	p. 38, 216, 219, 226-228
Canada	p. 7, 27-29, 82, 86, 105, 125, 137, 142-172, 174, 184-185, 190, 193, 198, 202, 211, 215, 224, 231, 249-250, 305-306, 310, 314
	Migration policy p. 31-32
	Immigration p. 31-32
	Puebla Process p. 124-126

Economic immigration p. 160
Family immigration p. 160
Humanitarian immigration p. 160
Point system (bill C-11) p. 32, 165
Working temporarily p. 167

Canadian International
Development Agency   p. 277
Caribbean Community (CARICOM)   p. 183
Caribbean   p. 29, 33-34, 173, 175, 183
Cape Verde   p. 137, 219, 226, 228, 275
Central Africa   Migration trends p. 38-39
                                                 Labour migration p. 38-39
                                                 Brain drain p. 215
Central African Republic   p. 217
Central America   p. 138, 173, 181, 188
                                                 Migration trends p. 31
                                                 Economic integration p. 188
Central American Common Market   p. 32, 188
Central American Organization
on Migration (OCAM)   p. 181
Central and Eastern Europe   p. 42, 44, 124, 198, 241, 246
Chad   p. 38, 217, 219
Charter of Fundamental Rights
of the EU   p. 265, 269, 282
Chile   p. 137, 176-177, 182, 185-186, 188
                                                 Migration trends p. 32-33
China   p. 17, 29, 36, 137, 175, 195, 201-202, 210, 313, 315, 310
                                                 Migration trends p. 35-36, 197-198
                                                 Diaspora p. 35-36
Commonwealth (of Nations)   p. 43, 122
CIS Conference Process   p. 124, 137-138
Citizenship   Concepts p. 282
                                                 Jus sanguinis p. 282
                                                 Jus solis p. 282
                                                 Naturalization p. 20
Cluster Process   p. 37-138, 243
Colombia   p. 29, 32-33, 137, 176, 179, 180, 185, 188-189, 305, 311, 314
                                                 IDPs p. 113-114
                                                 Emigration p. 192
                                                 Migration management p. 192
Commission on Human Rights   p. 113
Common European migration
and asylum policy   -EU (European Union)
Common Market for Eastern
and Southern Africa (COMESA)   p. 39
                                                 Treaty p. 233
*Commonwealth
of Independent States (CIS)*   p. 122
                                                 Migration trends p. 43
Community immigration policy   p. 259-263 (-EU European Union)
                                                 Best practices p. 266-267

355

356

Conventions, covenants, protocols

Exchange of information p. 267
Migration management p. 266
Partnerships p. 261-262
1967 Protocol to the United Nations' 1951 Refugee Convention p. 21, 100, 144
Convention on the Elimination of all Forms of Discrimination against Women p. 277
Council of Europe Convention on the Legal Status of Migrant Workers p. 85
Geneva Convention relating to the Status of Refugees p. 10, 16, 21, 64, 98-99, 100-101
International Covenant on Economic Social and Cultural Rights p. 85, 283
International Convention against Torture p. 283
International Convention on the Protection of the Right of all Migrant Workers and Members of Their Families p. 10, 21, 98, 101, 130, 179, 273
Protocols to the United Nations Convention against Transnational Organized Crime p. 21, 104, 280
Protocols to Prevent, suppress, and Punish Trafficking in Persons p. 21, 104, 126
Protocol against the Smuggling of Migrants by land, Sea and Air p. 21, 66, 104, 285

Copenhagen Programme of Action   p. 119
Costa Rica   p. 17, 32-33, 125, 137, 174-175, 179, 182, 184-185
                                        Puebla process p. 124, 137-138
Côte d'Ivoire   p. 17, 25, 137, 217, 219-220
Cotonou Agreement   p. 234, 260-261, 285, 305
Countries of destination   p. 8, 17, 25, 27-29, 33, 35-36
                                        Australia p. 36
                                        Canada p. 31-32
                                        Israel p. 35
                                        Migration policies p. 4
                                        New Zealand p. 36
                                        USA p. 31-32
Countries of origin   Labour migration p. 17
                                        Involvement in integration of immigrants p. 81
Croatia   p. 137, 198, 312, 314
Cuba   p. 33, 173, 176, 307-309
                                        Diaspora in the USA p. 43
Cyprus   p. 137, 314
Czechoslovakia   p. 8, 241
Czech Republic   p. 28, 137, 249-250, 307
Democratic Republic of the Congo   p. 17, 35, 39, 137, 219, 221, 235, 312-313
Demographic trends   -population trends
Denmark   p. 28, 44, 137, 239-240, 244-246, 249-250, 281, 307
Development   Migration – development link p. 231-233
                                        Remittances and development p. 224-231
Diaspora   p. 20, 52, 215-232, 273-274
                                        India p. 35
                                        China p. 35

Displaced persons

Africa p. 219
Definition p. 10
EU common policy p. 261-262
Afghanistan p. 117-118
Colombia p. 113-114

Dominican Republic   p. 62-63, 125, 137, 173-175, 177, 192, 311, 315
Dublin Convention   -European Union
Durban Conference on Racism   p. 22
East Africa   Migration trends p. 37
                              Refugees p. 39, 216
                              Brain drain p. 216
East African Community (EAC) p. 216, 233
East Asia   -Southern, South-East and East Asia
Economic and Social Consultative
Forum (FCES)   p. 180
Economic Community
of West African States (ECOWAS)   p. 133, 137-138, 233, 221, 217
Ecuador   Emigration p. 137, 191
Egypt   p. 21, 34-35, 37, 137, 207, 216-217, 219, 226-228, 309, 311
El Salvador   p. 17, 125, 137, 173-174, 177, 179, 181, 184-185, 311
                              Puebla Process p. 125-126
Equatorial Guinea   p. 38, 137, 216-217
Entertainment visa holders   Korea p. 203
Eritrea   p. 17, 39, 216-217, 219, 312, 314
Estonia   p. 8, 44, 137, 241, 243-244, 263, 306
Ethiopia   Migration tracking network project p. 119
EU (European Union)   p. 17, 19, 32, 44-46, 60-61, 63, 71, 75, 81-82, 86, 102, 109, 123,
                              129, 205, 217, 224, 232, 245, 253, 255-256, 274, 314
                              Amsterdam Treaty p. 68, 239, 259-260, 269
                              Asylum seekers p. 25, 42-43, 45-46, 60, 65, 106, 263, 281
                              Common asylum and migration policy p. 131, 134
                              Common programme of action with Turkey p. 35
                              Communication on immigration and asylum policies
                              p. 259-260, 262
                              Dublin Convention p. 65, 106
                              EURODAC p. 260-261
                              European Commission p. 239, 266, 269
                              European Convention p. 27, 269, 281-283
                              European Council p. 259-264, 268-269
                              European Parliamant p. 259, 262, 269
                              European refugee fund p. 262, 281
                              Green paper on return of illegal residents p. 266
                              Humanitarian assistance aid p. 134
                              Immigration health assessment p. 86-90
                              Irregular migration p. 68, 261, 263, 266-267
                              Laeken Council / Summit p. 269
                              Maastricht Treaty p. 259
                              Migration policy p. 46
                              Migration trends p. 43, 46
                              Privacy directive p. 27

357

	Regional Consultative Process on migration
	p. 123-124, 129, 134, 137-138
	Residence permit p. 265
	Schengen Agreement p. 268-269
	Seville Council / Summit 55, p. 46, 267
	Single European Act p. 259
	Tampere Council / Summit p. 260-261, 265
Europe	p. 6-7, 10-11, 15-17, 19, 23, 25, 27, 29-30, 32, 34-38, 42-46, 60-61, 64, 66, 68, 71, 77, 83-89, 94, 100, 102-103, 106, 123-124, 129, 135, 137-138, 158, 142, 145, 175-177, 187, 191, 193, 196, 198-199, 203, 205-207, 213, 216-218, 224, 231, 239-248, 251, 253-257, 262, 265-266, 268-269, 279, 281, 285, 288, 299, 303-304, 308-309, 311-315
	Migration trends p. 43, 46
	Migration business p. 177
	Migration crisis p. 177
	Chinese irregular migrants p. 197-198
	Irregular migration p. 253-254
European Commission	-European Union
European Convention on Human Rights	p. 269
European employment guidelines	p. 264
European Monitoring Centre on Racism and Xenophobia	p. 265
European Refugee Fund	p. 262
European Structural Funds	p. 264
Family immigration/reunion	p. 144-145, 163
	United States p. 144-145, 159
	Canada p. 145, 160
	Australia p. 146, 161
	New Zealand p. 146, 162
Feminization of migration	p. 7-8
	Asia p. 7
	Human rights abuses p. 7
	Health hazards related to trafficking in women p. 91
	Bangladesh p. 277
	Philippines p. 276-277
Fertility rates	p. 243
Finland	p. 28, 44, 137, 240, 243-246, 259, 280, 307
Forced migration	Definition p. 9, 15
	IDPs p. 111-112
Foreign-born population	Traditional countries of immigration p. 157
Foreign trainee scheme	p. 200
France	p. 8, 28-29, 46, 137, 193, 215, 224, 230-231, 239, 243-246, 249-250, 305, 307-310
Gabon	p. 219, 306
	Gabonization of labour force p. 217
Gambia	p. 137, 219
General Agreement on Trade in Services (GATS)	p. 19, 107, 130, 138, 273, 284, 288
Georgia	p. 137, 314

Germany   p. 27-28, 42, 71-82, 137, 193, 199, 201, 224, 231, 239, 243-246,
                                           249-250, 254-255, 259, 267-268, 280, 305, 307, 309-310, 312-313
                                           Migration trends p. 25
                                           "Green Card" programme p. 27, 248-250
                                           Labour migration p. 248-250
                                           Süssmuth commission p. 239, 251, 255
                                           Immigration law p. 25, 255-256
Ghana   p. 35, 216, 219, 221, 224, 226, 275
Global Consultations
on International Refugee Protection   -international refugee protection
Globalization   p. 4, 12, 20, 27, 29, 30-31, 35, 39, 132, 193, 198
                                           The paradox of p. 14, 18
Good governance   p. 8
Greece   p. 28, 44, 137, 239, 243-246, 253, 310-311, 315
Guatemala   p. 32-33, 125, 137, 179, 314
                                           Puebla Process p. 124-126, 137-138
Guinea   p. 137, 216, 219, 221, 314
Guinea-Bissau   p. 38, 137, 219, 314
Gulf Cooperation Council (GCC)   p. 130, 138
                                           Expatriate population p. 207
                                           Migration pattern p. 205
Gulf States   p. 33-34, 105, 173-174, 179, 306
Haiti   Diaspora in the *United States* p. 34
                                           Emigration to the *Dominican Republic* p. 174-175
Health and migration   p. 283-284
                                           Dimensions of regular migration flows p. 89
                                           Health hazards related to trafficking in women p. 91
                                           HIV/Aids p. 40, 42, 91, 93-95
                                           International Conference on Population and Development p. 85
                                           Mental health p. 85, 91-93
                                           Migration health assessment p. 86-90
                                           Policy priorities p. 94, 96
                                           Right to health care p. 85-86
                                           Tuberculosis p. 86-88, 90, 94-95
                                           WHO, international health regulations p. 87
Hispaniola   p. 33-34, 174-175
HIV/Aids   p. 40, 42, 91, 93-95
                                           Irregular migration flows p. 90
                                           Southern Africa p. 40
                                           IOM activities p. 94
Honduras   Puebla Process p. 125-126, 137
Hong Kong (SAR of China)   Filipino workers p. 195
Human rights of migrants   -rights of migrants
Human smuggling   p. 104
                                           South Korea p. 198, 202-203
                                           United States p. 276
                                           Dominican Republic p. 175
Human trafficking   p. 36, 61-63, 66, 104
                                           Asia p. 34-35
                                           United States p. 276
                                           Dominican Republic p. 33, 175

359

	South Korea p. 202-203
	2000 US Victims of Trafficking and Violence Protection Act p. 276
	Convention on Transnational Organized Crime p. 276
	Russian Federation p. 43-44
	Health hazards related to trafficking in women p. 91
Humanitarian admission	p. 151-152
	Canada p. 152-154, 156
	Australia p. 152-153, 156
	New Zealand p. 152-154
	United States p. 137, 152
Hungary	p. 28, 42, 44, 137, 198, 241, 243-244, 246, 263, 307, 315
Iceland	p. 137, 240, 268, 306, 310
Illegal employment	p. 66-68
	South Africa p. 67
	United Kingdom p. 66-67
Immigrant admissions in TRCs	p. 137, 159, 170
Immigration	Control measures p. 25-26
	Seville summit p. 267-268
Immigration and Naturalization Service (INS)	p. 147, 179
Immigration health assessment	p. 86, 88-90
	European Union p. 86
	Regulations p. 86
Immigration law	p. 265
	Germany p. 25, 255
	Traditional countries of immigration p. 143, 150
India	Diaspora p. 137, 35-36
Indonesia	Irregular migration p. 137, 65-66
Integration	Assimilation p. 72
	Berlin case study p. 72-73
	Commissioner for Migration and Integration, Berlin p. 76-77
	Definition p. 72
	Elements p. 74
	EU Commission p. 259, 264-265, 269
	Involvement of sending countries p. 81
	Migration management p. 261-262, 264, 266, 268
	New German immigration law p. 255
	Netherlands p. 74-75
	United States p. 71
Intergovernmental Consultations on Asylum, Refugees and Migration Policies in Europe, North America and Australia (IGC)	p. 123, 125, 133-135, 137-138
Internally displaced persons (IDPs)	p. 11-113, 116, 120
	Afghanistan p. 120, 117-118
	Colombia p. 113-114, 120
	Definition p. 111
	Guiding principles p. 112-113
	IDPs worldwide p. 111
	Management strategies p. 115-116
	Phases of displacement p. 113

Representative of the United Nations Secretary General on Internally
   Displaced Persons p. 113, 115, 120, 122
Special Coordinator of the Network on Internal Displacement p. 112
United Nations Emergency Relief Coordinator p. 112
Voluntary return p. 117, 121

International asylum regime   -international refugee protection
International Centre for Migration
Policy Development (ICMPD)   p. 133-134, 138
International Conferenceof Migration
Statistics   p. 294
International Conference
on Population and Development (ICPD)   p. 109
                                                                Migrants health p. 85

International Federation
of the Red Cross (IFRC)   p. 112-113
International Labour Office (ILO)   Health standards for migrants p. 85
                                                                Labour conventions p. 271-273, 289
International migrant   Citizenship p. 295, 297, 299
                                                                Criteria for definition p. 296-297
                                                                Definition p. 295
International migration statistics   p. 289, 293-297, 299-303
                                                                Border collection p. 299-301
                                                                Data collection systems p. 295, 299, 301
                                                                Field inquiries p. 192, 295, 299
                                                                Framework for organizations p. 294, 296, 301-302
                                                                International setting p. 293-294
                                                                Sources p. 293, 296, 299-301
International mobility   p. 13, 15, 25-47
International refugee protection   p. 131-132, 137
                                                                Abuse of asylum systems p. 64, 103
                                                                AGAMI (Action Group on Asylum and Migration Issues) p. 109
                                                                Agenda on protection p. 109
                                                                Asylum management approaches p. 102, 106-107
                                                                EU common policy p. 262, 266-268
                                                                Asylum requests worldwide p. 97
                                                                Bona fide refugees p. 104, 107
                                                                Border control measures p. 104-105, 107
                                                                Definition of asylum seeker p. 10
                                                                Development of the asylum regime p. 98-100
                                                                Dublin Convention p. 259-261
                                                                Global Consultations on International Refugee Protection p. 108
                                                                IDPs p. 97
                                                                Manifestly unfounded claims p. 106
                                                                Non-refoulement p. 98
                                                                Norwegian Refugee Council p. 111, 120
                                                                Protection without admission p. 106
                                                                Refugee Policy Group p. 119
                                                                Refugee status claims p. 105
                                                                Refugee status determination p. 106
                                                                Safe country of transit p. 106
                                                                Secondary movements p. 106, 109

International Symposium on Environmentally-Induced Population Displacements IOM (International Organization for Migration)

Temporary protection p. 101, 103, 106

p. 119

p. 5-8, 10, 14, 21, 22-24, 26-27, 62-63, 65-66, 81, 98, 101, 105-106, 108, 125-129, 133, 167, 181-183, 192, 198-199, 218, 222, 225, 232, 234-236, 242-243, 247, 251-254, 274-275, 289
Activities and service areas p. 40
AVR programmes p. 42, 279
Berne Initiative p. 27
Compensation programmes for victims of Nazi persecution p. 42-43
Green card programme, *Germany* p. 27
HIV/Aids p. 94
IDPs p. 114, 117-120
International migration policy dialogue p. 109
Mental health of migrants p. 91-93
Migration and health p. 42, 87-90
Migration Policy and Research Programme p. 42
Migration tracking network project, *Ethiopia* p. 119
Regional Consultative Processes p. 43

Iran
p. 17, 27, 29, 34-35, 44-45, 117-118, 137, 175, 186, 305, 310, 312-313, 315

Iraq
p. 17, 29, 35-36, 45, 65, 93, 137, 153, 204, 206, 242, 253, 277, 312-315

Ireland
p. 17, 28, 45, 137, 198, 239-240, 243-246, 249-250, 259, 268, 272, 307, 309-310

Irregular migration
Definition p. 58
Abuses of human rights p. 61
Characteristics p. 58
Europe p. 60-61, 64-66, 68, 239, 242, 247, 251, 253-254
European Union p. 65, 68, 60-61, 63, 261, 263, 266-267
HIV/Aids p. 90-91
Human trafficking p. 58, 61-63, 66, 68
Illegal employment p. 66-67
Indonesia p. 65-66
Management approaches p. 64
Migrant smuggling p. 60-61, 66-68
Scale p. 58
United Kingdom p. 58, 60, 64, 66-68
United States p. 58, 60-61, 63-64, 66, 68

Israel
Migration trends p. 34-35, 43

Italy
p. 7, 17, 27-29, 33, 37, 44-45, 58, 63, 68, 71, 137, 176, 187, 190-191, 216, 219, 224-225, 231-232, 244, 267-268, 272, 276, 278-280, 306-307, 309-310, 315
Labour migration p. 239-241, 243-247, 249-254

Jamaica
p. 17, 33, 137, 174, 193, 311
Migration to the US p. 33

Japan
p. 25, 28-30, 33, 63, 68, 137, 158, 169, 176, 190, 193, 195-196, 198-202, 204-205, 207-208, 210-211, 213, 249-250, 266, 273, 307-310

362

Nikkeijin p. 200
Migration trends p. 34-36
Basic plan for immigration control p. 200
Demography and migration p. 200
Foreigners p. 201
Trainees p. 201

Jordan   p. 17, 137, 207, 306, 311
Kazakhstan   p. 43, 203, 304-306
Kenya   p. 39, 89, 120, 216, 219, 221-222, 231, 237-238, 275, 314
Kosovo (Province of Yugoslavia)   p. 206
                                                Assisted voluntary return p. 279
Kyrgyzstan   p. 137
Labour migration   p. 12, 15-17, 24, 239, 248-249, 256
                                                Albania p. 241, 251
                                                Andean instrument p. 180
                                                Central Africa p. 216-217
                                                Countries of destination p. 220-222
                                                Countries of origin p. 234, 236, 215-216, 220
                                                East Africa p. 216-217
                                                France p. 240, 249-251
                                                Germany p. 248, 255
                                                Italy p. 239-241, 243-247, 249-254
                                                North Africa p. 215-217
                                                schemes p. 249-251, 254, 257
                                                South Asia p. 196
                                                South-East Asia p. 196
                                                Southern Africa p. 217-218
                                                United Kingdom p. 240, 248, 251, 254
                                                Western Africa p. 217, 220
Laos   p. 35, 137, 195, 196, 199, 202
Latin America   p. 7, 10, 17, 29, 31, 32-33, 45, 89, 101, 124, 125, 173-194
                                                Bilateral agreements p. 178
                                                Dual nationality p. 177
                                                Emigration of nationals p. 176
                                                Governability crisis p. 177
                                                Immigration policies p. 177
                                                Migration flows p. 32, 173
                                                Migration policies p. 176
                                                Multilateral agreements p. 180
Latvia   p. 44, 137, 241, 243, 244, 263, 306
Lawful permanent residence   Traditional countries of immigration p. 156
                                                United States p. 145
Lesotho   p. 39, 128, 137, 218, 219, 223, 226
Liberia   p. 37, 38, 97, 137, 216, 219, 314
Libya   p. 37, 137, 216, 217, 219, 314
Lithuania   p. 44, 137, 241, 243, 244
Luxembourg   p. 28, 45, 240, 241, 268, 307
Macedonia (FYR)   p. 40, 97, 137, 241, 243, 244, 252, 277, 314
Malaysia   p. 17, 34, 35, 66, 91, 137, 195, 197, 199, 200, 204, 208, 210, 213, 214, 266, 307, 308, 310
                                                Migration trends p. 35-37, 195-197

363

Malawi	p. 39, 40, 128, 137, 217, 218, 219, 220
Mali	p. 17, 38, 137, 217, 219, 220, 221, 224, 226, 227, 228, 230, 253, 278
Malta	p. 44, 137, 243, 244, 247, 263
Manila Process	p. 127, 137, 138
Mexico	p. 17, 21, 25, 31, 32, 33, 60, 62, 66, 124, 125, 137, 146-148, 158, 167, 183-184, 186-187, 190, 304, 305, 311, 314, 315
	Maquiladoras p. 32
	Migration agenda p. 146
	Migration to the USA p. 31-32, 173
	Puebla Process p. 123, 124, 125-126, 137, 138
Middle East	p. 7, 17, 34-35, 138, 158, 195, 199
Migrant worker	Definition p. 10
Migration	Causes p. 15-16
	Definitions p. 9-10
	Definition, the geographical criterion p. 8
	Definition, the human criterion p. 9
	Forced migration p. 97, 111-121
	Health p. 95-96
	International cooperation p. 53, 54, 123-140, 284-288
	Migration management p. 52-55, 271-289
	Migration process p. 52-53
	Networks of migration p. 14, 15-16, 25, 27, 28, 30
	Push and pull-factors p. 4, 13, 14, 30, 66, 68, 218
	Security p. 26-27 ,64, 66
	Temporary migration policies p. 213
	Trends p. 25-46
	Typologies p. 11-12
Migration and development	p. 221, 226-236
Migration Dialogue for Southern Africa (MIDSA)	p. 127, 128-129, 233
Migration Dialogie for West Africa (MIDWA)	p. 134, 137, 138
Migration for Development in Africa (MIDA)	p. 234, 274-275
	Lusaka summit p. 274
	National approach p. 275
	Return and Reintegration of Qualified African Nationals (RQAN) p. 275
Migration management	Definition p. 54
Migration management schemes	Foreign trainee scheme p. 200, 201
	Scheme of legalized status (OECD) p. 254
	Working holidaymaker scheme p. 254
Migration theories	Dependency theory p. 13
	Dual labour market theory p. 13
	Migration network theory p. 14
	Neo-classical theory p. 12
	Theory of development in a dual economy p. 12
	Theory of the new economy of professional migration p. 14
	World-system theory p. 13

Moldova	p. 43, 63, 137, 243, 244
Morocco	p. 21, 35, 37, 45, 60, 137, 216, 219, 224-225, 226, 228
	Hassan II Foundation p. 225
	Migration trends p. 37, 224-225
	Migration management approaches p. 224-225
	Remittances p. 224-225
Mozambique	p. 25, 39, 40, 128, 137, 217, 218, 219, 220, 306
Myanmar	p. 35, 63, 137, 195, 199, 202, 276, 313, 314
Namibia	p. 39, 40, 128, 137, 217, 219
Nauru	p. 36, 93, 103, 137, 153, 202
Netherlands	p. 28, 37, 42, 45, 58, 94, 103, 137, 219, 224, 239, 243, 244, 245, 246, 250, 268, 277, 280, 298, 307
	Integration of migrants p. 74-75, 79, 80
Netherlands Antilles	p. 34, 175
New Partnership for African Development (NEPAD)	p. 128, 234
New Zealand	p. 17, 28, 55, 66, 86, 89, 105, 137, 153, 156, 190, 202, 249, 251, 306, 309, 310, 314
	Family immigration p. 145
	Migration trends p. 36
	Trans-Tasman Travel Agreement p. 36
	Working temporarily p. 149
	Economic Immigration p. 149, 150
	Humanitarian immigration p. 153, 154
	Point system p. 151
Nicaragua	p. 17, 32, 125, 137, 164, 173, 174, 179
	Puebla Process p. 125-126, 184-185
Niger	p. 38, 137, 217, 219, 226, 227
Nigeria	p. 16, 37, 38, 137, 216, 217, 219, 221, 222, 226, 227, 228, 231, 314
North Africa	Migration trends p. 37
	Brain drain p. 216
North America	Migration policy trends p. 30, 31-32
North American Free Trade Association (NAFTA)	p. 19, 31, 32, 124, 130, 138, 166, 167, 186-188
Norway	p. 28, 122, 137, 239, 240, 244, 268, 272, 277, 307, 310
Norwegian Refugee Council	p. 111, 120
Oceania – Pacific	p. 25, 29, 45, 285, 303, 304, 309, 312
	Migration trends p. 36-37
Office for the Coordination of Humanitarian Affairs (OCHA)	p. 111, 113, 117, 119, 120
Office of Tunisians Abroad (OTE)	p. 232
Organization for Economic Cooperation and Development (OECD)	p. 28, 79, 307, 310
	scheme of legalized status p. 254
Organized crime	-security and migration
Pacific islands	-Oceania – Pacific
Pacific strategy	p. 153
Pakistan	p. 117, 137, 211, 212, 266, 305, 311, 312, 313, 315
	Migration trends p. 34

Paraguay   p. 32, 33, 137, 174, 176, 179, 180, 185, 188
                                              Brasiguays p. 33

Persecution   p. 15, 29, 61, 73, 85, 97-100, 103, 110
Peru   p. 17, 32, 33, 63, 127, 137, 175-178, 190, 191, 314
Philippines   p. 21, 120, 137, 196-199
                                              Female mobility p. 7
                                              Migration trends p. 34, 35
Point systems   p. 151
                                              Canada p. 152
                                              Australia p. 152
                                              New Zealand p. 154
                                              Germany p. 255

Poland   p. 17, 29, 44, 66, 76, 137, 141, 143, 144, 146, 151, 190
Portugal   p. 28, 42, 45, 137, 187, 215, 219, 243, 244-247, 253, 268, 307,
                                              308, 309, 310, 311

Population trends   Ageing p. 25
                                              Demographic pressure p. 15
                                              Demographic transition in Asia p. 35
                                              Europe p. 239
                                              Growth p. 15

Protocols to international conventions   -Conventions, Covenants and Protocols
Puebla Process, Regional Conference
on Migration (RCM)   p. 125-126, 184-185
Push and pull-factors   -migration
Rwanda   p. 38, 39, 97, 216, 219, 235, 305, 314
Qatar   p. 34, 205, 207, 217, 307, 309
Racism   EU Commission p. 264-265
Readmission agreements   p. 280-281
Receiving countries   -countries of destination
Refoulement, non-refoulement   p. 10, 14, 98, 107
Refugee Policy Group   p. 119
Refugee status determination   p. 101
Refugees   p. 10, 34, 35, 38, 39, 40, 43, 45, 97-110
                                              (-international refugee protection)
                                              Asylum request worldwide p. 29
                                              Definition p. 10
                                              East Africa p. 39
                                              Geneva Convention relating to the Status of Refugees (-conventions)
                                              Traditional countries of immigration p. 151-154
                                              EU common policy p. 260-262
Regional Consultative Processes (RCPs)   p. 27, 33, 43, 70, 121, 123-139
                                              Bali Conference p. 137
                                              Budapest Process p. 124
                                              CIS Conference Process p. 124
                                              Cluster Process p. 137
                                              European Union p. 129
                                              Intergovernmental Asia-Pacific Consultations (ACP) p. 127
                                              Intergovernmental Consultations on Asylum, Refugees and
                                                  Migration Policies in Europe, North America and Australia (IGC)
                                                  p. 123
                                              Manila Process p. 127

Migration Dialogue in Southern Africa (MIDSA) p. 127, 128-129
Puebla Process, Regional Conference on Migration (RCM) p. 124, 125-126
South American Conference on Migration (Lima Process) p. 127

Remittances   p. 14, 17, 18, 20, 35, 217, 226-231, 310-311
     Africa p. 226-231
     Dominican Republic p. 175
     Maghreb p. 247
     Morocco p. 224-225
     Impact p. 229-230
     Management p. 230-231
     Sri Lanka p. 7

Representative of the United
Nations Secretary General
on Internally Displaced Persons   p. 111-112, 113, 115, 120
Republic of the Congo   p. 39, 40, 216, 217, 219, 221, 314
Return migration   Definition p. 9, 17
Right to entry, right to exit   p. 18
Right to health care   - health
Rights of migrants   p. 21-22
     Abuses p. 7, 22, 60-65
     International human rights law p. 99
     International Convention on -Conventions
     United Nations Special Rapporteur on Human Rights of Migrants
     p. 22, 23
Romania   p. 27, 30, 44, 61, 63, 137, 241, 243, 244, 253, 306
Rural-urban migration   p. 29, 34
     West Africa p. 38
Russian Federation   p. 8, 11, 43, 44, 137, 241, 242, 248, 273, 304, 306, 309, 313, 314
Saudi Arabia   p. 34, 195, 196, 204, 207, 208, 217, 304, 305, 306
     Saudization policy p. 205
Seasonal worker   Definition p. 8, 10
Secretariat of the General Treaty
on Central American
Economic Integration (SIECA)   p. 181
Sao Tome and Principe   p. 217, 219
Schengen Agreement   -EU (European Union)
Security and migration   p. 26-27
     Organized crime p. 27, 43
     Terrorism p. 27, 31, 32
Sending countries   countries of origin
Senegal   p. 17, 21, 23, 25, 27, 38, 45, 97, 137, 216, 219, 221, 224, 226-228, 230, 251, 253, 314
Sierra Leone   p. 120, 137, 216, 219, 221, 253, 277, 307, 312, 314
Singapore   p. 137, 195-197, 199, 204-205, 207-208, 210, 213, 249, 266, 306-307, 308, 310
Single European Act   -European Union
Slovakia   p. 44, 137-241, 243-244, 263
Slovenia   p. 44, 137, 241, 243-244, 263
Smuggling   -human smuggling
Social exclusion   EU Commission p. 264

Somalia	p. 17, 29, 39, 78, 97, 137, 216-217, 219, 312, 314
South America	p. 29, 31, 32-33, 127, 130, 137-138, 173-174, 179, 182-188, 185-186, 191-192, 194, 200, 313
	Economic integration p. 188-189
South American Common Market (MERCOSUR)	p. 173, 180-182, 185-186, 189
	Subgroup No. 10 on Labour Affairs, Employment and Social Security (SGT10) p. 181-182
South American Conference on Migration (Lima Process)	p. 127, 137-138
South American Forum	p. 183, 185, 186, 194
South Caucasus	Migration dynamics p. 241-243
South-East Asia	-Southern, South-East and East Asia
Southern Africa	HIV/Aids p. 40
	Migration trends p. 39
	Brain drain p. 215
Southern African Development Community (SADC)	p. 39, 127, 128, 129, 130, 133, 138, 217, 233
Southern African Migration Project (SAMP)	p. 128, 222
Southern, South-East and East Asia	Migration trends p. 35-36
South-Korea	p. 35, 36, 195, 196, 198, 199, 201, 210
	Entertainment visa holders p. 203, 210
	Migration trends p. 35, 36
	Smuggling and trafficking p. 202-203
Spain	p. 17, 29, 33, 44, 45, 60, 63, 71, 137, 175, 176, 179, 187, 190-191, 192, 193, 198, 219, 224, 239, 240, 243, 245, 247, 249, 250, 253, 254, 266, 267, 268, 273, 285, 307, 309, 310, 311, 315
Special Assistance Category (SAC)	p. 152, 153, 161
Special Coordinator of the Network on Internal Displacement	p. 112
Special Humanitarian Programs (SHP)	p. 152, 161
Sri Lanka	p. 17, 21, 29, 34, 35, 45, 65, 113, 137, 195, 196, 197, 199, 211, 212, 266, 304, 311, 314, 315
	Female mobility p. 7
	Remittances p. 7
Sudan	p. 34, 37, 39, 97, 102, 216, 219, 227, 236-238
Süssmuth Commission	p. 239, 251, 255
Swaziland	p. 39, 128, 137, 218, 219
Sweden	p. 27, 28, 29, 45, 46, 71, 105, 137, 153, 219, 239, 240, 241, 243, 244, 245, 246, 267, 268, 281, 307, 309, 310
Swedish Immigration Board	p. 281
Switzerland	p. 28, 29, 42, 43, 45, 63, 136, 137, 198, 225, 239, 240, 241, 242, 243, 244, 245, 246, 248, 253, 277, 280, 285, 306, 307, 310
Taiwan (Province of China)	p. 195, 199, 204, 210, 213, 308
Tajikistan	p. 8, 21, 43, 118, 137
Tanzania	p. 39, 40, 128, 137, 216, 219, 221, 312, 313
Temporary migration policies	-migration
Temporary protection	-international refugee protection
Temporary Protection Visa (TPV)	p. 153, 161
Terrorism	p. 22, 26-27, 31, 32, 104, 146, 177, 269, 287

Thailand   p. 16, 17, 25, 63, 134, 137, 195-196, 198, 199, 202, 210, 211,
                                    212, 166, 276, 308, 310
                                    Migration trends p. 34-35, 195-196

Theories of migration   -migration
Timor Leste   p. 21, 40, 65, 137
Togo   p. 38, 219, 221, 226, 227, 228, 309
Trade liberalization   p. 107
Traditional Countries
of Immigration (TCIs)   p. 142-156
                                    Immigrant admissions p. 156
                                    Foreign-born population p. 142-143, 155
                                    Refugees p. 144, 151, 153, 156, 159
                                    Asylum seekers p. 151-153, 156, 159
                                    Immigration systems p. 143-146

Trafficking   -human trafficking
Trans-Tasman Travel Agreement   -Australia or New Zealand
Tunisia   p. 37, 45, 137, 219, 226-228, 231-232, 310
Turkey   p. 17, 34-35, 44, 45, 72, 75, 76, 81, 137, 242, 255, 305, 309, 310,
                                    311, 313, 315

Uganda   p. 21, 39, 93, 120, 216, 219, 221, 238
Ukraine   p. 29, 43, 44, 89, 137, 203, 243, 244, 248, 305
Unaccompanied minors   p. 93, 277-278
                                    Common problems p. 277
                                    Good practices p. 278

Undocumented persons   p. 6, 10, 16
UNHCR (United Nations High
Commissioner for Refugees)   p. 24, 65, 66, 88, 98, 101-110
United Arab Emirates   p. 34, 205, 207, 217, 225, 242, 304, 305, 306
United Kingdom   p. 8, 17, 25, 28, 29, 75, 137, 215, 222, 259, 267, 272, 305, 307,
                                    308
                                    Irregular employment p. 66-67
                                    Migration trends p. 45
                                    Irregular migration p. 66
                                    Labour migration p. 222, 248-251
                                    Highly skilled migrants programme p. 251

United Nations Economic, Social,
and Cultural Organization (UNESCO) p. 83, 119, 183, 281
United Nations Emergency
Relief Coordinator   p. 112
United Nations recommendations
on international migration statistics p. 294-295
United States   p. 6, 7, 16, 17, 26, 27, 28, 58, 60, 63, 64, 66, 68, 71, 86, 93, 100,
                                    105, 124, 137, 142-146, 157, 158, 159, 163, 173-179, 184, 187,
                                    201, 211, 224, 236, 275, 298, 304, 305, 309, 312, 313, 314, 315
                                    Asylum management approaches p. 105
                                    Freedom of Information Act p. 27
                                    Immigration p. 31-32
                                    INS (Immigration and Naturalization service) p. 31, 64
                                    Integration of migrants p. 71
                                    Immigration and nationality Act p. 150
                                    Irregular migration p. 64

Migration from Mexico p.32, 146-148
Migration policy p. 31-32, 142-156
Puebla Process p. 124-125
Family immigration p.144-145
Working temporarily p.149
Preference system p. 145, 164
Economic immigration p. 148-151
Humanitarian immigration p. 151-154
Migration agenda with Mexico p.146-148
Chinese irregular migrants p. 198
H-1B visas (employment-based visa) p. 211

Universal Declaration of Human Rights   p. 18, 297
Uruguay   p. 19, 21, 32, 137, 185, 188, 191
Venezuela   p. 32, 33, 137, 175, 176, 177, 179, 180, 183, 185, 188
Vietnam   p. 27, 35, 45, 63, 78, 89, 134, 137, 196, 199, 210, 266, 278, 305, 312

West Africa   Migration trends p. 37, 38
                                             Brain drain p. 216
Western Europe   Measures to recruit foreign workers p. 248-256
                                             Migration trends p. 44-46, 239-241

Western Mediterranean
Cooperation Process "5+5"   p. 135, 137, 138, 247
Women and migration   -feminization of migration
Working holidaymaker scheme   p. 254
World Food Programme (WFP)   p. 113, 119
World Health Organization (WHO)   p. 24, 88, 91, 96
                                             Health standards for migrants p. 85
                                             International health regulations p. 87
World Trade Organization (WTO)   p. 19, 197
Xenophobia   p. 19, 22, 220, 221, 222
                                             EU Commission p. 264-265
Yemen   p. 17, 205, 274, 275, 307, 311
Yugoslav Federation
(Serbia and Montenegro)   p. 8, 29, 40, 44, 45, 76, 81, 97, 102, 241, 259, 306, 313, 314
Zambia   p. 39, 40, 128, 137, 217, 219, 220, 313
Zero immigration policies   p. 263
Zimbabwe   p. 17, 39, 40, 128, 137, 216, 217, 218, 219

Photo Credits

More women are migrating independently to be employed abroad   *p. 6*
© Jacques Maillard / ILO

IOM programmes and policies promote regular migration   *p. 19*
© Giuseppe Diffidenti / 1999

Stranded Cambodian migrant fishermen awaiting IOM return assistance   *p. 21*
© Chris Lowenstein Lom / IOM 2001

Azeri border official checks a passport   *p. 26*
© IOM Azerbaijan / 2002

Migration Health   *p. 41*
© All rights reserved

Assisted voluntary returns   *p. 41*
© Nekrawesh / IOM

Movements   *p. 41*
© Claude Salhani / Reuters

Counter-trafficking   *p. 41*
© Nenette Motus / IOM

Mass information   *p. 41*
© H. Davies / Exileimages

Technical cooperation   *p. 41*
© IOM

Labour migration   *p. 41*
© Andrej Gjonej / IOM 2001

German Forced Labour Compensation programme   *p. 41*
© IOM

IOM headquarters in Geneva   *p.53*
© IOM

East Timorese refugees return to the remote Oecussi enclave   *p. 66*
© Chris Lowenstein-Lom / IOM 2000

Education is important for integration   *p. 79*
© Sebastiao Salgado / 1994

Returning Kosovars receiving IOM health screening   *p. 87*
© Giuseppe Diffidenti

IOM psycho-social counselling programme in Kosovo   *p. 92*
© Andrea Balossi / IOM 2000

Asylum seekers and migrants arrive on the Pacific Island of Nauru   *p. 103*
© IOM / 2001

Colombian IDPs   *p. 114*
© All rights reserved

Afghan IDPs return home   *p. 117*
© Jeff Labovitz / IOM

371

IOM fosters and supports regional consultation processes
© IOM
p. 127

African migrants arrive in the US
© Wendy Stone / 1994
p. 144

Irregular migrants cross the Rio Grande to the US by raft
© D. De Cesare / 2002
p. 147

Three generations of Iraqis on their way to a new life in Australia
© Rocio Sanz / IOM 2002
p. 153

Haitian migrant selling flowers in the Dominican Republic
© Niurka Pineiro / IOM 2002
p. 174

Migrant children begging from motorists
© Cemil Alyanak / IOM
p. 181

Irregular migrants often face imprisonment and deportation in SE Asia
© William Barriga / IOM 1999
p. 190

Migrants stranded after the invasion of Kuwait by Iraq in 1991
© Robert Benet / 1990
p. 206

Thousands of skilled Africans have left the continent to work in industrialized countries
© Wendy Stone / 1991
p. 222

A DRC academic working in Belgium returns home on a teaching visit
© All rights reserved
p. 234/235

Resettlement in the US brought a new life for one of the "Lost Girls" of the Sudan
© Lauren Engle / IOM 2002
p. 236

Elderly migrants return to Russia from the former Soviet Republics
© All rights reserved
p. 241

Albanian migrants cook pizzas in Italy
© Andrej Gjonej / IOM 2001
p. 251

Germany, Berlin "Bundestag"
© Presse- und Informationsamt der Bundesregierung/Bundesbildstelle
p. 255

Fences are not the solution to Europe's migration challenges
© Keith Dannemiller / JABA 1997
p. 267

Reversing the brain drain holds the key to Africa's development
© Wendy Stone / 1991
p. 274

Repatriation programme from FYR of Macedonia to Kosovo
© V. Brandjolica / 1999
p. 277

Switzerland, Bern "Bundeshaus"
© Schweizerische Eidgenossenschaft
p. 286

372

MAPS

Map 1
IOM Member and Observer States, December 2002

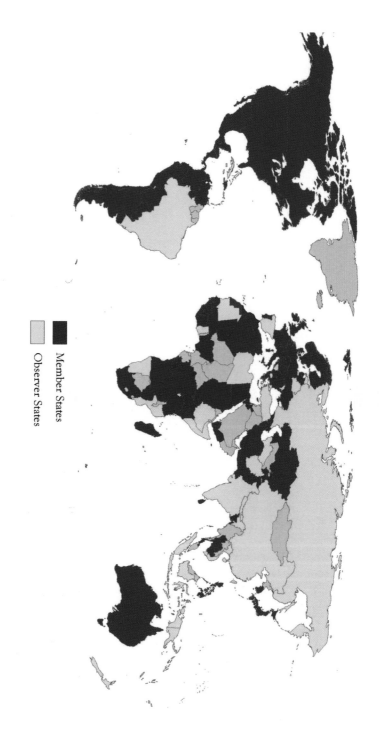

Member States

Observer States

374

Source: IOM

Map 2
Net Migration: Total Numbers, 1995-2000

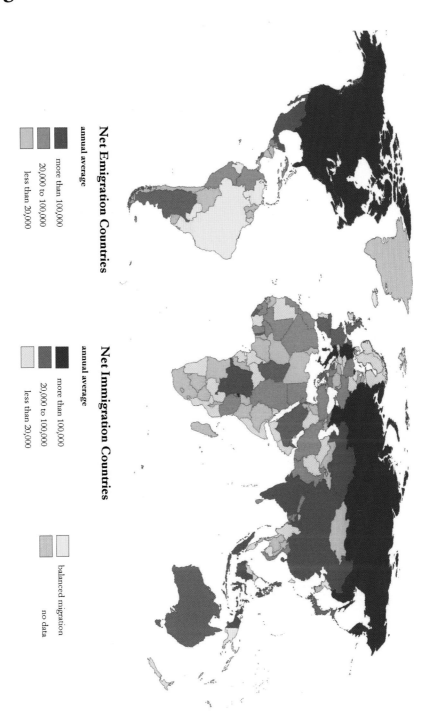

Net Emigration Countries
annual average

more than 100,000

20,000 to 100,000

less than 20,000

Net Immigration Countries
annual average

more than 100,000

20,000 to 100,000

less than 20,000

balanced migration

no data

375

Source:
United Nations (2002). International Migration Wallchart 2002

Map 3
Net Migration: Migration Ratios, 1995-2000

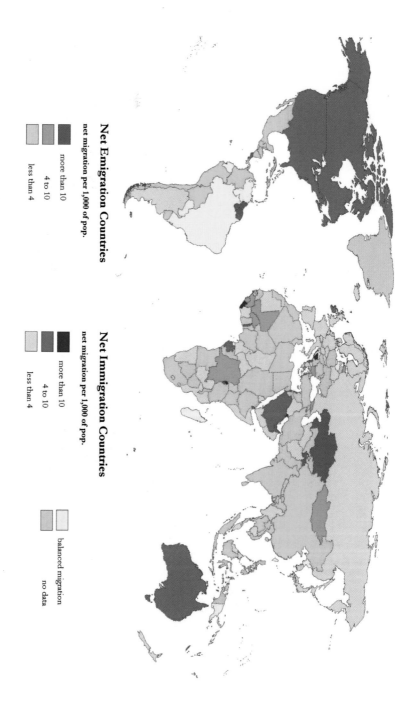

Net Emigration Countries
net migration per 1,000 of pop.

more than 10

4 to 10

less than 4

Net Immigration Countries
net migration per 1,000 of pop.

more than 10

4 to 10

less than 4

balanced migration

no data

Source:
United Nations (2002). International Migration Wallchart 2002

Map 4
Migrant Stocks: Per Cent of Total Population, 2000

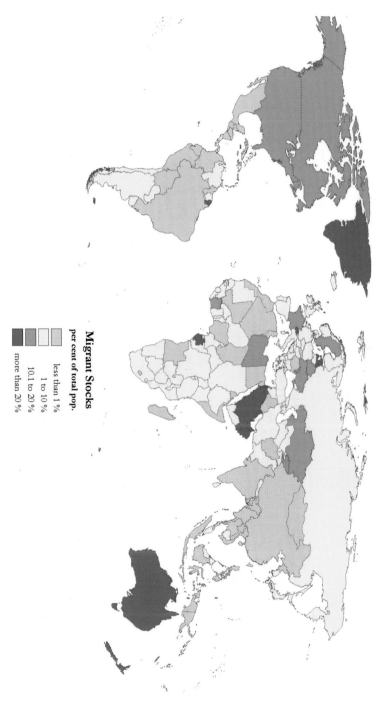

Migrant Stocks
per cent of total pop.

less than 1 %
1 to 10 %
10.1 to 20 %
more than 20 %

Source:
United Nations (2002). International Migration Wallchart 2002

Map 5
Origin of Asylum Seekers in Industrialized Countries, 1997-2001

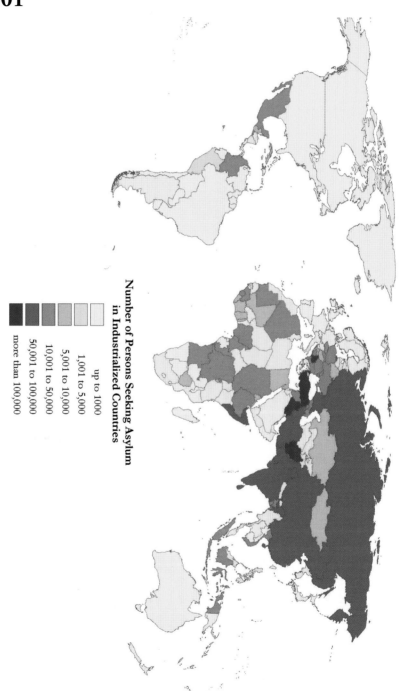

Number of Persons Seeking Asylum
in Industrialized Countries

up to 1000
1,001 to 5,000
5,001 to 10,000
10,001 to 50,000
50,001 to 100,000
more than 100,000

Source:
UNHCR (2002). Statistical Yearbook 2001. http://www.unhcr.ch/statistics

Map 6
Refugee Population by Country or Territory of Asylum, 2001

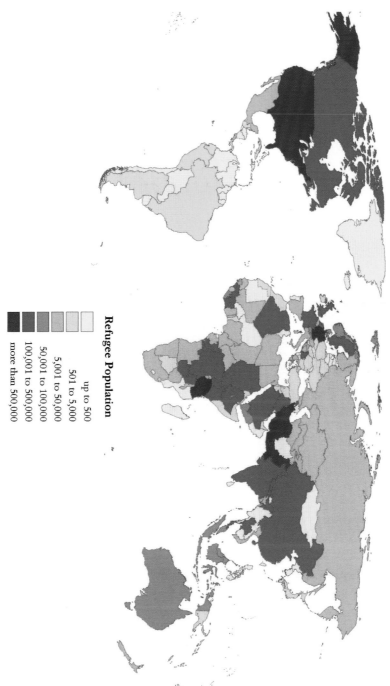

Refugee Population

- up to 500
- 501 to 5,000
- 5,001 to 50,000
- 50,001 to 100,000
- 100,001 to 500,000
- more than 500,000

379

Source:
UNHCR (2002). Statistical Yearbook 2001. http://www.unhcr.ch/statistics

Map 7
Refugee Outflows by Country or Territory of Origin, 1997-2001

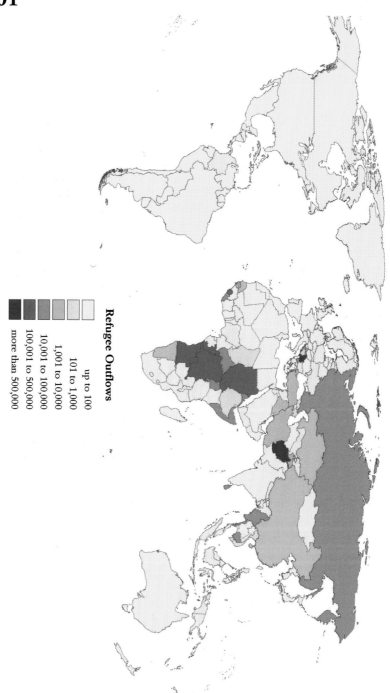

Refugee Outflows

up to 100
101 to 1,000
1,001 to 10,000
10,001 to 100,000
100,001 to 500,000
more than 500,000

Source:
UNHCR (2002). Statistical Yearbook 2001. http://www.unhcr.ch/statistics

Map 8
Internally Displaced Persons

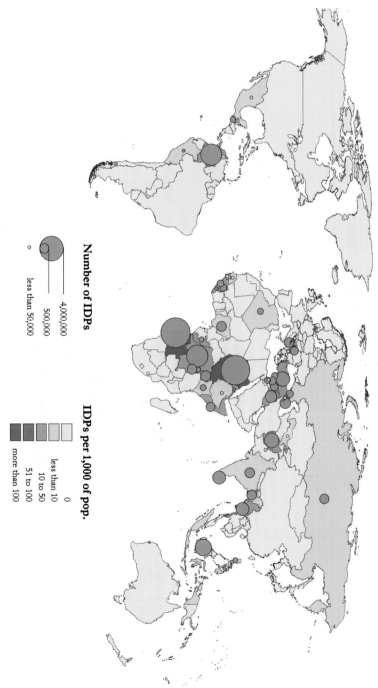

Number of IDPs

4,000,000

500,000

less than 50,000

IDPs per 1,000 of pop.

0

less than 10

10 to 50

51 to 100

more than 100

381

Source:
Global IDP Project (2002)

Map 9
Regional Consultative Processes on Migration (RCPs) 1/2

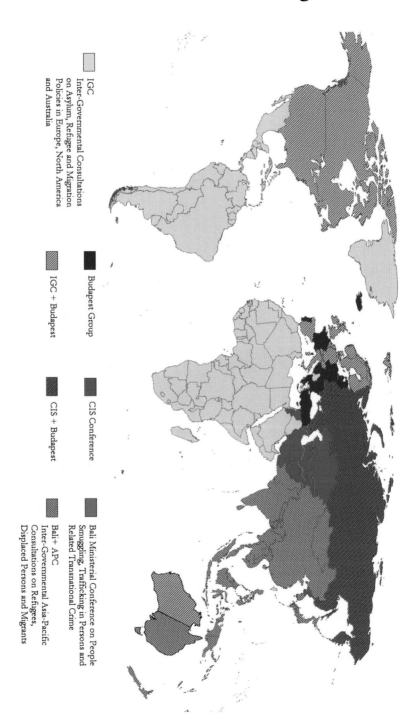

IGC
Inter-Governmental Consultations on Asylum, Refugee and Migration Policies in Europe, North America and Australia

Budapest Group

IGC + Budapest

CIS Conference

CIS + Budapest

Bali Ministerial Conference on People Smuggling, Trafficking in Persons and Related Transnational Crime

Bali+ APC
Inter-Governmental Asia-Pacific Consultations on Refugees, Displaced Persons and Migrants

Source: IOM

Map 10
Regional Consultative Processes on Migration (RCPs) 2/2

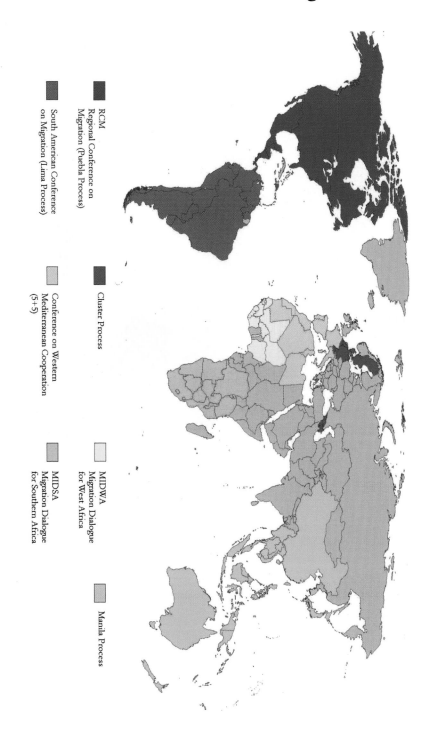

RCM
Regional Conference on
Migration (Puebla Process)

South American Conference
on Migration (Lima Process)

Cluster Process

Conference on Western
Mediterranean Cooperation
(5+5)

MIDWA
Migration Dialogue
for West Africa

MIDSA
Migration Dialogue
for Southern Africa

Manila Process

383

Source: IOM

Map 11
Regional Economic Groupings in Africa

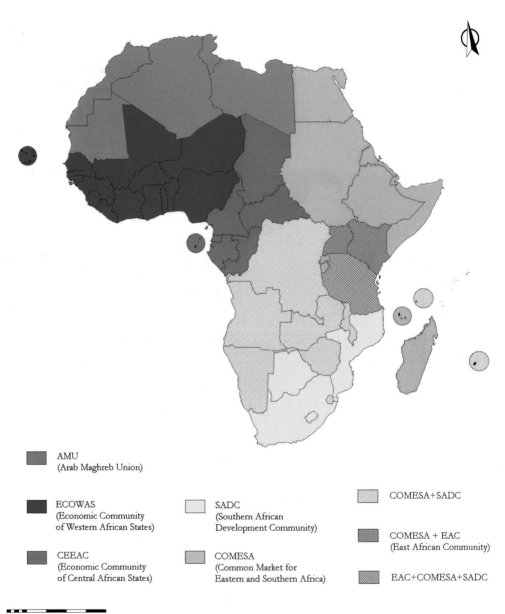

AMU
(Arab Maghreb Union)

ECOWAS
(Economic Community
of Western African States)

CEEAC
(Economic Community
of Central African States)

SADC
(Southern African
Development Community)

COMESA
(Common Market for
Eastern and Southern Africa)

COMESA+SADC

COMESA + EAC
(East African Community)

EAC+COMESA+SADC

2,000 km

Map 12
Remittances to Selected African Countries

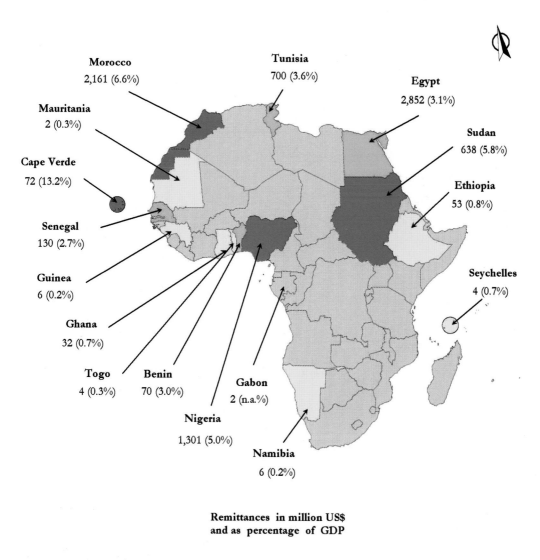

Morocco
2,161 (6.6%)

Tunisia
700 (3.6%)

Egypt
2,852 (3.1%)

Mauritania
2 (0.3%)

Sudan
638 (5.8%)

Cape Verde
72 (13.2%)

Ethiopia
53 (0.8%)

Senegal
130 (2.7%)

Seychelles
4 (0.7%)

Guinea
6 (0.2%)

Ghana
32 (0.7%)

Togo
4 (0.3%)

Benin
70 (3.0%)

Gabon
2 (n.a.%)

Nigeria
1,301 (5.0%)

Namibia
6 (0.2%)

Remittances in million US$
and as percentage of GDP

no data
less than 1%
1% to 5%
more than 5%

2,000 km

385

Source:
United Nations (2002). International Migration Wallchart 2002

Map 13
Africa: Highly Qualified Citizens with Overseas Education

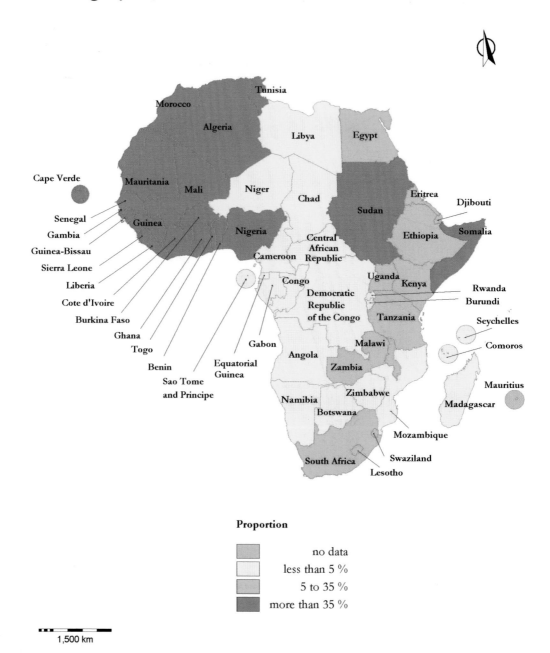

Proportion

- no data
- less than 5 %
- 5 to 35 %
- more than 35 %

1,500 km

Source:

IOM (1999). Feuillet d'information "Programme de Retour et de Réinsertion de Professionnels Africains Hautement Qualifiés" (RQAN)

Map 14
Political Map: Traditional Countries of Immigration

Canada

Ottawa

United States

Washington

2,000 km

387

Jerusalem

Israel

100 km

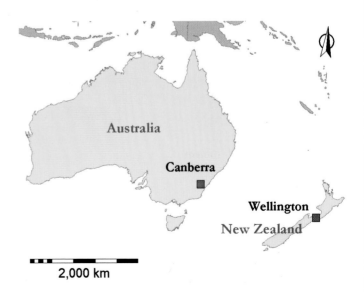

Australia

Canberra

Wellington

New Zealand

2,000 km

Map 15

Latin America: Regional Integration Areas that include Migration Issues

Mexico

Belize

Guatemala Honduras

El Salvador

Nicaragua

Costa Rica Panama

Venezuela

Guyana

Surinam

French Guyana

Colombia

Ecuador

Peru

Brazil

Bolivia

Paraguay

Chile

OCAM
(Central American Commission
of Directors of Migration)

Andean Pact /
Andean Instrument
on Labour Migration

Mercosur
(South American
Common Market)

Argentina

Uruguay

1,000 km

Map 16
Political Map: Islands of the Caribbean

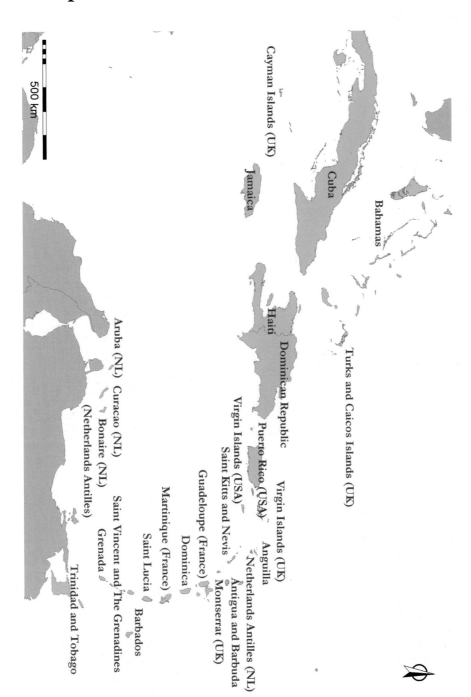

500 km

Cayman Islands (UK)

Jamaica

Cuba

Bahamas

Turks and Caicos Islands (UK)

Haiti

Dominican Republic

Aruba (NL)

Curacao (NL)

Bonaire (NL)
(Netherlands Antilles)

Virgin Islands (USA)

Saint Kitts and Nevis

Puerto Rico (USA)

Virgin Islands (UK)

Anguilla

Netherlands Antilles (NL)

Antigua and Barbuda

Montserrat (UK)

Guadeloupe (France)

Dominica

Martinique (France)

Saint Lucia

Saint Vincent and The Grenadines

Grenada

Barbados

Trinidad and Tobago

389

Map 17
Colombia: Locations of IOM Operations

Source: IOM

Map 18
Afghanistan: Locations of IOM Operations

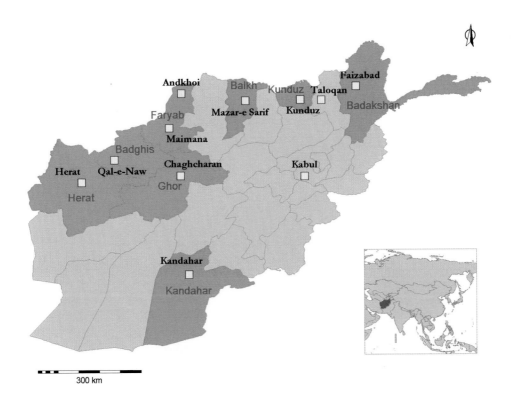

300 km

391

Map 19
Political Map: Asia

392

Map 20

Gulf Cooperation Council: Total Population and Proportions of National and Non-National Population, 2000

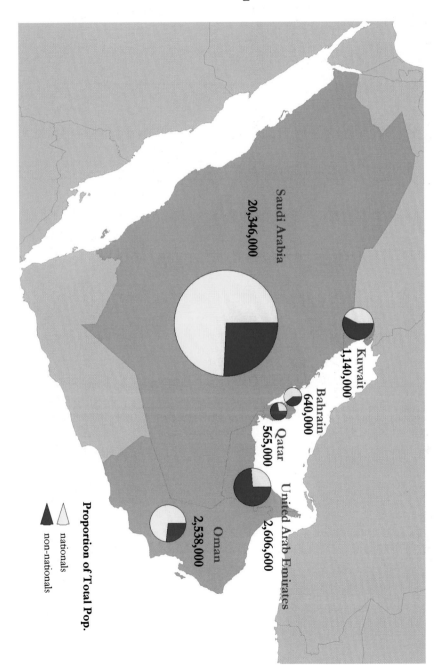

Source:
United Nations (2002). International Migration Wallchart 2002

Map 21
Political Map: Europe

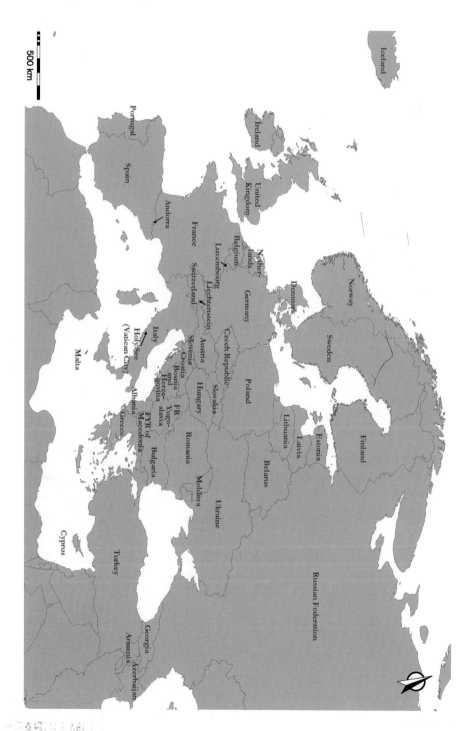

Map 22
European Union: Asylum Seekers, 2001

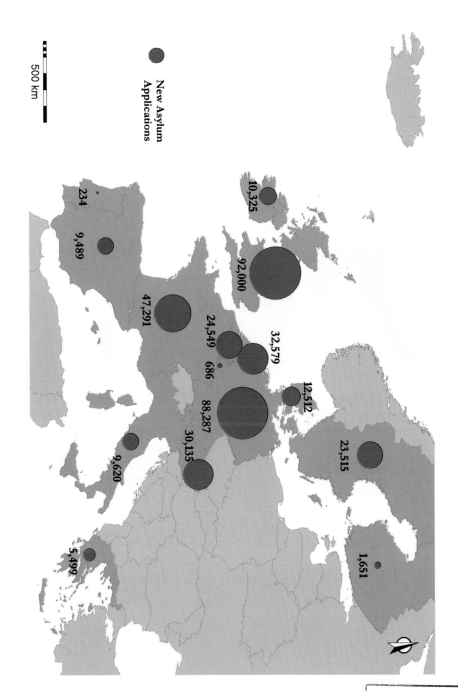

500 km

New Asylum
Applications

234

9,489

10,325

92,000

47,291

24,549

32,579

686

12,512

88,287

23,515

30,135

9,620

5,499

1,651

395

Source:
UNHCR Statistical Yearbook 2001

Map 23

European Union: Migrant Stocks (totals and percentages), 2000

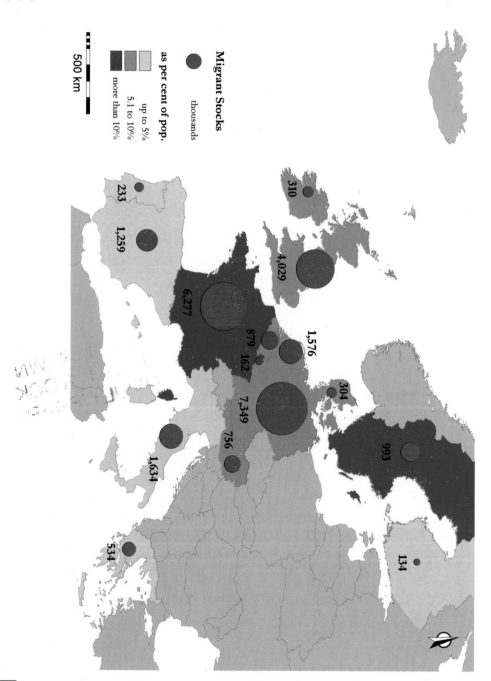

Source:
United Nations (2002). International Migration Wallchart 2002